GW00357406

GW00357405

THE NEUROPSYCHIATRIC GUIDE
TO
MODERN EVERYDAY PSYCHIATRY

The Neuropsychiatric Guide to Modern Everyday Psychiatry

Michael Alan Taylor, M.D.

THE FREE PRESS
A Division of Macmillan, Inc.
NEW YORK

Maxwell Macmillan Canada
TORONTO

Maxwell Macmillan International
NEW YORK OXFORD SINGAPORE SYDNEY

The Free Press
A Division of Macmillan, Inc.
866 Third Avenue, New York, N.Y. 10022

Maxwell Macmillan Canada, Inc.
1200 Eglinton Avenue East
Suite 200
Don Mills, Ontario M3C 3N1

Macmillan, Inc. is part of the Maxwell Communication Group of Companies.

Printed in the United States of America

printing number
1 2 3 4 5 6 7 8 9 10

Library of Congress Cataloging-in-Publication Data

Taylor, Michael Alan
The neuropsychiatric guide to modern everyday psychiatry / Michael Alan Taylor.
p. cm.
Includes bibliographical references and index.
ISBN 0–02–932455–6
1. Psychiatry. 2. Neuropsychiatry. I. Title.
[DNLM: 1. Mental Disorders—diagnosis. 2. Mental Disorders—physiopathology. 3. Mental Disorders—therapy. WM 100 T2443n]
RC454.4.T37 1993
616.89—dc20
DNLM/DLC
for Library of Congress

92–49025
CIP

For
Christopher and Andrew,
Ellen, Classie, and Eddie

Contents

Preface

After homeostasis, the brain's main raison d'être is to drive behavior. All behavior and mental activity reflect brain function. The brain is the organ of the mind. Experience, from uterus to deathbed, affects behavior, but it does so through alterations in brain structure and function. Nowhere is this better illustrated than in studies of synaptic change during learning paradigms, in which stimuli activate a cascade of biochemical events leading to rapid and relatively permanent protein change (933).*

The notion of the mind within a neuroscience framework is paradoxical to some. This need not be the case if one conceptualizes the mind as having meaning only in the context of brain, just as the concept "city" has meaning only in the context of an organized collection of buildings, streets, and groups of people engaged in various functions. The term "city" is shorthand for these structures and functions, just as the term "mind" can be shorthand for what the human brain primarily does.

Psychopathology, as a category of behavior, also reflects brain functioning. It is not surprising, then, that many psychopathologic phenomena were originally described in the neurologic literature and that the traditional study of psychopathology derives from nineteenth- and pre–nineteenth-century neurologists and neurologically trained psychiatrists, or alienists (for example, Freud was trained as a neuropathologist). This traditional understanding of psychopathology as expression of deviant brain structure or function is the essence of neuropsychiatry as conceptualized in this book. More limited definitions circumscribe neuropsychiatry to the study and treatment of patients with neurologic disease (e.g., dementia, epilepsy, stroke), the symptoms of which often include striking psychopathologic phenomena. But in its broadest sense, neuropsychiatry *is* modern psychiatry: the application of insights from basic and clinical neuroscience research to the study of psychopathology and to the treatment of patients experiencing these phenom-

*Numbers in parentheses refer to the end-of-book reference list.

ena. Neuropsychopharmacology, neurophysiology, and neuropsychology are the foundations for this modern psychiatry; biologic psychiatry and behavioral neurology are themes within it.

Thus, the more circumscribed view of neuropsychiatry focuses on patients with traditional neurologic disease and what were previously called the "organic mental disorders." Neuropsychiatry, as envisioned in this book, incorporates all the clinical issues faced by the general psychiatrist with a busy hospital practice. From this perspective, melancholia and obsessive compulsive disorder, for example, are as much neuropsychiatric disorders as are dementia and epileptic psychoses; emotional blunting can be understood as a form of dysprosody and formal thought disorder as speech and language deficit; and neuropsychiatry becomes the principles and skills of clinical neuroscience within the everyday challenges of psychiatric practice. In this framework, the psychiatrist becomes the neuropsychiatrist, not because of subspecialization training but because of a fundamental approach to the understanding and treatment of people with mental disorder. Thus, neuropsychiatry no longer needs to be limited to a few subspecialists caring for a select group of patients. A neuropsychiatric understanding of mental disorder and its treatments can be applied by all psychiatrists to all of their patients.

The humanism of neuropsychiatry, so illusively sought in much of modern medical practice, is found in the manner in which neuropsychiatry is applied: how one interacts with and cares for the person with the illness. Humanism in neuropsychiatry is also found in its nonjudgmental conceptualization of psychiatric disorder. The patient is mentally ill, not because of bad parenting (although bad parenting does not help) or repressed, forbidden sexual urges toward relatives but because he has brain dysfunction.*

What a modern neuropsychiatrist does in practice is analogous to the practice of a neurologist or a cardiologist. Neuropsychiatrists have the luxury of spending more time with each patient and with the patient's family; indeed, they are paid for their time and not the procedure. The basic clinician-patient interactions, however, are similar, as well as the implicit and explicit expectations that society demands (but does not always receive) from these interactions. The patient, experiencing a condition that adversely affects his quality of life and functioning, seeks a remedy for the condition. The clinician is expected to be well trained and knowledgeable. He is supposed to know what he is doing. The patient assumes that he is capable of accurately diagnosing the condition and of prescribing treatment and patient care of demonstrable efficacy.

The neuropsychiatrist, as do all practitioners, assumes great responsibility when he begins these interactions with the patient. Over the years, I, my colleagues, and our students have found that this joint venture best starts with a neuropsychiatric

*Throughout this book, human beings in general are referred to with masculine pronouns simply for ease of expression.

evaluation: a detailed history; a systemic, neurologic, and mental status examination; and the rational and judicious use of laboratory tests. All, hopefully, converge so that a reliable, valid diagnosis is made and the most specific, efficacious treatments prescribed. This book describes these processes. It also illustrates how to identify and organize abnormal behaviors as reflections of brain dysfunction and offers the principles of patient management from this viewpoint within hospital and clinic settings.

Mentally ill patients are also treated by other physicians, nurses, social workers, and psychologists. Their behavioral, social, and psychologic interventions can be compatible with a neuropsychiatric understanding of psychopathology and the application of biologic treatments as the primary agents to alleviate psychopathology. Just as the expertise of these professionals is essential in the care of other sick people, it is essential in the care of the mentally ill as well. They also need a starting point to begin their interactions with patients. Their understanding of the neuropsychiatric evaluation and their competence in parts of it provide a foundation helpful in their initial assessments of mentally ill patients.

Finally, this is not meant to be a heavy-weight textbook taking up space on a shelf. Rather, it is a clinically practical book that can be used to teach the neophyte how to practice psychiatry as neuropsychiatry and to refresh and reinforce more experienced practitioners in their care of patients. The purpose of the book is to synthesize the ideas and skills of basic psychiatric assessment with the principles of clinical neurobiology (behavioral neurology, neuropsychology). Common, classic psychiatric syndromes, along with less well-known regional brain syndromes, are presented from the neurobiologic viewpoint. This spectrum of conditions forms the bulk of everyday psychiatric practice. Discussion of treatment and management issues also provides a reasoned and practical neurobiologic and behavioral approach to the care of the mentally ill. For the neophyte, the basics of assessment, syndrome description, and management can be used as a foundation to patient care. For the more experienced practitioner, the neuropsychiatric framework perhaps offers a fresh view of long-standing clinical challenges.

Although a new book, this text incorporates sections from *General Hospital Psychiatry*, coauthored by Frederick S. Sierles and Richard Abrams (Free Press, 1985). Those sections represent their efforts as much as they do mine.

Acknowledgments

I am indebted to Frederick Sierles, M.D. for his critical and careful review of this manuscript. Drs. Nutan Atre-Vaidya, Lori Moss, and Martin Cohen also made helpful suggestions. Georgette Pfeiffer painstakingly prepared the many drafts of this manuscript and helped with the references. Max Fink taught me how to write and nurtured my career from its beginning.

PART I

Assessment

Chapter

1

Neuropsychiatric Examination: Overview

EXAMINATION GOALS

The neuropsychiatric examination is the traditional mental status examination and psychiatric diagnostic interview carried out and understood from a neuropsychiatric perspective. Much of this examination is conducted without touching the patient. Examination skills, with notable exceptions, primarily depend on how the examiner interacts with the patient. These skills are discussed in depth. The neuropsychiatric examination is complete, however, only in the context of an assessment of the central nervous system (CNS) (the traditional neurologic examination) and other organ systems (the systemic examination). (These procedures are not discussed here, but readers can refer to the textbooks cited as references 80, 256, 258, 790, and 1019 for details of these aspects of patient evaluation.)

The examiner has two primary goals in conducting the neuropsychiatric examination: (1) to establish a reasonable clinician-patient relationship, and (2) to determine a probable diagnosis. The first goal develops when the examiner initially meets the patient. It is necessary for the successful completion of the evaluation and later for the subsequent execution and monitoring of a treatment plan. The second goal is essential for the development of the treatment plan.

Historical information is integral to patient evaluation, but it must be separated from information about the patient's present behavior and experiences. Past and present information is needed for diagnosis; however, present behavior and experiences will change as the illness process changes and as treatments affect that process. The examiner must be clear when referring to past or present behavior. This separation is critical when treating a patient whose condition fluctuates, as is often the case in patients who are suicidal or whose moods shift rapidly. Some affectively ill patients, for example, can shift from stupor to excitement to depression within hours or minutes, and the pattern of shifts needs to be documented. Multiple daily examinations may be necessary, and confusion can result unless each examination is limited to the patient's behavior and experiences at the time of each examination.

A secondary goal of the neuropsychiatric examination is to obtain additional information to begin planning for further evaluation (e.g., neuropsychological testing, brain imaging, electrophysiological measures) and treatment. For example, knowing a patient's hobbies and interests may not be helpful in deciding whether or not he is affectively ill, but it may provide clues to his cognitive strengths and weaknesses that could affect treatment outcome. In such a situation, neuropsychological testing might help in vocational planning following the patient's recovery. Additional personal information, such as the names and interests of the patient's children, may have no diagnostic importance. In cases of long-term treatment, however, this type of information helps the neuropsychiatrist maintain an interest in the patient's life, reinforce the clinician-patient relationship, and increase compliance with treatment.

EXAMINATION STYLE AND STRUCTURE

The style and structure of the examination ultimately is shaped by the examiner's personality. Five basic strategies, however, can facilitate the examination process: (1) establishing a conversational manner and interactive relationship with the patient (i.e., the tone and style of the examination), (2) reinforcing the interactive relationship with personal and supportive comments, (3) using a semistructured format with screening questions to get a sense of the illness pattern and follow-up questions to establish the details, (4) developing a script for each section of the examination, and (5) modifying questions and comments based on the patient's present behavior and statements. Some examiners also find it helpful to develop an interview personality, which they wear, like a suit of clothes, to facilitate the examination. A warm and supportive, yet firm, manner, representing a stereotype of the avuncular country doctor or of the unconventional, but caring, young television doctor, can facilitate the evaluation process.

The evaluation begins when the examiner first sees the patient. By greeting the patient outside the office and chatting with him as he walks to the office and sits down, the examiner sets the tone for the remainder of the examination. Using such phrases as "I'm Dr. so-and-so, I'd like to chat with you for a bit," and commenting about the weather, a recent inpatient activity, or the trip to the clinic or office, as if one were engaging an acquaintance in a conversation, can initially achieve patient trust and cooperation far more than addressing clinical openings to the patient while flipping through his chart. Specific words and phrases one chooses are important. "Hi" is less formal than "hello"; "chat" is more relaxing than "examine" or "talk."

Inpatients often are interviewed by several staff members. Going through it all again is often irritating. Comments by the examiner, such as "I hope I didn't interrupt something," "I'm sorry I had to drag you away from that. . . . This won't take too long, I'll try to get you back as soon as I can," "I know you've seen so-and-so already, but I just want to chat with you awhile about what happened to you just before you came in here" or ". . . what's been happening to you since you've come into the hospital," often placate patients as they recognize that the examiner understands how they feel and is trying to be helpful. Patient uncooperativeness usually results from anxiety, suspicion, or irritability. The examiner who consciously puts the patient at ease and minimizes suspicions and patient irritability is likely to obtain the most useful information from the patient.

A conversational tone increases the examiner's likelihood of getting sufficient and reliable information. He can reinforce by (1) not having a desk between him and the patient, but rather setting chairs kitty-corner to each other (face to face is too aggressive and anxiety provoking for many patients); (2) assuming a relaxed posture and not sitting stiffly like a "judge"; (3) avoiding jargon and using colloquialisms and idioms whenever possible so that terms, such as "episode," "hospitalization," and "diagnosis," become phrases, such as "when you were sick before," "when you last stayed overnight in a hospital," "what your doctors thought was the problem (did they give it a name?)"; and (4) using humor in an appropriate way. Patients also often say and do things that are humorous, and the examiner should not be afraid to laugh or reply in kind. Even the awkwardness of having to complete clinical forms while examining the patient can be minimized by such comments as "I'll be taking a few notes to keep things straight in my mind" or ". . . to be thorough and make sure I don't forget to check on things that may be important."

The examiner can further reinforce the conversational tone through personal and supportive statements to put the patient at ease and give him the sense that the examiner is interested in him as a person and not just as a clinical entity. Manic patients often become cooperative following positive comments about their colorful dress, and dysphoric, depressed patients are more willing to relate their experiences following comments about their obvious distress. Helpful openers might be: "That's a nice hat you have—where did you get it? I like your buttons, what does that one say?" "You really seem to be upset (or very sad or nervous)." If a patient relates a distressing event, it is appropriate to respond with "that's awful" or "that's upsetting." Even if the event is part of a delusion, the patient likely has feelings about it and will appreciate an empathic examiner. It is equally appropriate to respond to positive things the patient may say by making such remarks as "I hope they appreciated what you did," "You must have been pleased by that," You seem better now than the last time you were ill," "The medicine seems to have helped," or "Despite your setback, this past year seems better than the year before."

The conversational tone of the examination relates to its style. Despite the seeming informality, the examination should not be haphazard in content or format. Structure is important; questions and testing procedures should proceed in a logical sequence while remaining responsive to the patient's behavior. Every area of the examination should be covered in a standardized manner. It is rarely useful to rely primarily on open-ended questioning during which the examiner is passive and nondirective. Although the sequence of questions can vary and lead-ins and screening questions must be individualized, a basic sequence of topics and approach for each symptom area should be maintained throughout the examination.

Some typical lead-ins are:

"Sometimes when people feel the way you do now, they also have (or experience) . . ."

"I knew someone who had the same thing happen to him, and he also had . . ."

"You said you've had some difficulties with your memory. Is it the kind of difficulty that . . ."

Typical screening questions are:

"Has there ever been a time when for weeks, or even longer, you were feeling down, sad, depressed, or without energy or interest in things?"

"Have you ever felt the opposite of being depressed, where you were full of energy, excited, or really hyper for more than a few minutes or hours?"

Just as procedures for examining the heart or lungs must be overlearned, procedures for examining specific behavioral areas can, and should, be overlearned. A flexible script or pattern of inquiry for each area of psychopathology or historical topic is essential. Groping for the right words or wondering what to ask next does not build rapport. Specific lead-ins, screening questions, and scripts for evaluating psychopathology are discussed in chapters 3 and 4.

The neuropsychiatric examination is clearly a diagnostic process. Although it is not designed to be therapeutic, patients are often comforted by an examiner who is skillful at his job, knowledgeable about the patient's condition, and empathic to the patient's needs. Nevertheless, the goals of the examination are explicit. Without this evaluation, treatment usually flounders and the patient ultimately suffers. (See Table 1.1 for an outline of the neuropsychiatric examination.)

TABLE 1.1
The Neuropsychiatric Evaluation

Area	*Important Subsections*
I. Historical	
1. Chief complaint	Specific complaint in the patient's own words; age; gender; ethnicity; marital, living, and legal status; referral source; reason for referral
2. History of present episode	Duration, type of onset, precipitating events, predominant signs and symptoms, sequence and patterns of symptom development, treatments, social and interpersonal context of episode, specific references to important screening questions, inclusion and exclusion diagnostic criteria, any life-threatening or dangerous behaviors
3. Past psychiatric history	Age and illness onset, pattern of course, number of episodes, characteristics of episodes, interepisode functioning, co-occurrence or comorbid conditions, treatments and their effects
4. Alcohol	Age of onset of use, degree of use, consequences of use, treatments and their effects
5. Street drugs	Age of onset of use, degree of use, types of drugs, consequences of use, treatments and their effects
6. Antecedents of psychiatric morbidity	Seizure disorder; head injury; gestational, birth and postnatal difficulties; prolonged high fevers; abnormal childhood development; severe bouts with childhood diseases
7. Family	Identification of ages of first-degree relatives, major illnesses of relatives, treatments and their effects

(*continued*)

TABLE 1.1 (*Cont.*)
The Neuropsychiatric Evaluation

Area	*Important Subsections*
8. Personal	Relationships with friends and family, sexual activity and deviation, marriage or companion, children, employment, interests and hobbies, temperament, general cognitive abilities (e.g., math, languages), academic ability, characteristic modes of interacting with people and dealing with problems of living, deviant personality traits
9. Systematic review of symptoms	Particular attention to endocrine, central nervous system, and cardiovascular disorders
II. Behavioral	
1. Appearance	Age, gender, ethnicity, body type, hygiene, dress, level of consciousness, interpersonal manner
2. Motor	Activity; speed and rhythm; extrapyramidal, frontal, and cerebellar features; catatonic features; minor neurologic signs
3. Affect	Range, intensity and quality of mood; lability; relatedness; emotional expression; volition
4. Speech and language	Rate, rhythm, pressure, language (speech processes and formal thought disorder), thought content
5. Delusions	Delusional mood, delusional ideas
6. Perceptual	Other hallucinations, dysmegalopsia and other psychosensory phenomena, illusions
7. First-rank symptoms	Thought broadcasting, experiences of alienation and control, complete voices, delusional perceptions

TABLE 1.1 (*Cont.*)
The Neuropsychiatric Evaluation

Area	
III. Cognitive and behavioral neurologic examination	
1. Level of consciousness, attention, and concentration	Letter cancellation, behavioral changes associated with altered consciousness and orientation (see chapter 5)
2. Screening for diffuse impairment	The Mini-Mental State
3. Specific functions	
A. Motor functions	Overflow, persistence, echopraxia, Gegenhalten, idiokinetic praxis, kinesthetic praxis, constructional praxis, dressing praxis, handedness
B. Language functions	Speech, nonfluent aphasias, fluent aphasias, naming, repetition, writing, reading, prosody
C. Thinking	Problem solving and judgment, comprehension and concept formation, reasoning
D. Memory	Digit span and numbers forward and backward, immediate and delayed recall of words and objects, autobiographic information
E. Visual spatial and higher perceptual function	Constructional tasks, facial recognition, topographic orientation, awareness of illness, spatial recognition
F. Integrating functions	Graphesthesia, stereognosis, novel bimanual tasks
IV. Traditional neurologic examination	See References 258, 790, 1019
V. Systemic examination	See References 80, 256
VI. Laboratory studies	See Chapter 6

TABLE 1.2

Difficult Examination Situations and Techniques to Resolve

Situation	*Techniques for Resolution*
	Mania
A. Overtalkative with press of speech; circumstantial speech or flight of ideas	1. Increase interview structure, use more closed-ended questions, speed up rhythm of questions. 2. Continuously come back to a topic in order to gather all information that can be gathered before letting the interview content "get away." 3. If the patient is interruptible without producing unacceptable irritability, stop the flow of speech and say such things as "I'd like to know more about that later, but right now . . . 4. If flight of ideas is uncontrollable, use the patient's distractibility by switching, with great show, to questions related to specific diagnostic criteria, or have a third party in the room to which you address your questions (e.g., "How old did you say he was?") so that the patient is perhaps stimulated to interrupt you with the answer (e.g., "48"). 5. Begin to ask questions in so soft a voice that the patient becomes distracted by it and asks you what you said. The examiner raising his voice rarely helps.
B. Irritable, tendency to dismiss the question as stupid, to tell examiner to read the information in the chart	1. Switch to the least emotionally laden topics first. 2. If the patient has a constant theme, use it to introduce questions on other topics that must be assessed, even if the sequence strains logic. 3. Do not get insulted. 4. Remain firm but nonjudgmental and matter of fact.
C. Agitated, pacing patient	1. Walk with the patient and have an examination "conversation on the go."

	Depression
A. Psychomotor retardation	1. Slow down rhythm of questions; reduce number of questions; ask more closed-ended, concrete questions. 2. Interview in several 10-15-minute segments, rather than conduct one long interview; 3. Interview in late afternoon when retardation may be less because of diurnal pattern of symptoms.
B. Continuous ruminations	1. Same as for **mania** A, but at a much reduced rate.
	Schizophrenia
A. Avolitional patient with paucity of speech and content	1. Same as for depression. 2. Patient may be willing to do paper-and-pencil cognitive tests and cooperate with systemic examination. 3. The latter can be used as a structure for asking mental status questions.
B. Patient with severe formal thought disorder	1. Same as for avolitional patient. 2. Some information also may be obtained by focusing on visual and pictorial tasks, rather than on verbal tasks and questions.
C. Persecutory delusions and extreme suspiciousness	1. Start with the least emotionally laden topics. 2. Orient the wording of all questions about present episode and psychopathology to the patient's viewpoint. 3. Avoid all phrases that sound judgmental.

Occasionally, patients remain uncooperative or difficult to examine, despite the style and techniques described above. Uncooperativeness often results from irritability. Other examination difficulties can arise from manic or depressive behaviors, the patient's persecutory delusions, frontal lobe dysfunction, and cognitive impairment. Table 1.2 lists the more common examination problems and techniques to help resolve them.

Chapter 2

Principles of Diagnosis and Psychiatric Nosology

Incorporating the principles and skills of the traditional psychiatric evaluation, the neuropsychiatric evaluation is a process to diagnose patients that is based on shared descriptive clinical features (behavioral, historical, laboratory). Because an understanding of the etiology and specific pathophysiology of psychiatric disorders remains elusive, the present-day classification system is a "best guess" approximation. Many patients do not clearly fit into the system's categories. Even among those patients who do and who seem clinically homogeneous, pathophysiologic heterogeneity is likely. Nevertheless, the evaluation process based on our modern knowledge of mental illness permits the clinician to make educated guesses so that treatments can be prescribed with some degree of specificity.

Prior to 1970, psychiatric diagnosis, particularly in the United States, was arbitrary and idiosyncratic. Diagnostic reliability (precision and consistency) was poor (865, 925). During the 1970s, several sets of reliable research diagnostic criteria were developed. This work resulted in publication of the *Diagnostic and Statistical Manual of Mental Disorders,* Third Edition, (DSM-III), the first official diagnostic system in the United States with known reliability and specified criteria for each disorder (60). DSM-III and its revision, DSM-III-R, are not perfect, however, and surveys of practicing U.S. psychiatrists and psychiatric residents (473) revealed that most clinicians do not properly use the criteria based system. The system is perceived as too complex, and the introduction of multiple revisions further complicates its use (1096). No matter how carefully crafted future DSM systems become, they (as the present version) will be limited in use unless properly implemented. Experience and skill are required to match real patients and their symptoms to the criteria. The examiner also must know the relevant data and understand the principles of diagnosis.

THE DIAGNOSTIC PROCESS

Selection of the Probability from the Possibilities

Most clinicians diagnose by pattern recognition. Interpretations of electroencephalograms (EEGs) and most x-rays are done this way. As long as the patient is typical, or a "classic" example (and the clinician had been able to observe many such examples during training), pattern recognition is a reasonable method for classifying patients. Unfortunately, many patients are atypical and do not fit the classic pattern. The DSM system was developed precisely because training programs had, and still have, their different and often idiosyncratic versions of what is classic. Pattern recognition diagnosis can be quite accurate, but it has low reliability, is difficult to teach, and is suitable for a limited number of patients. (See Table 2.1 for a description of some patterns seen by neuropsychiatrists. Until reliable, specific, and sensitive diagnostic laboratory tests for psychiatric illnesses are developed, however, diagnosis will require a reliable, learnable system that can be applied to all patients. This system, the basis for all medical diagnoses, is the probabilistic process of exclusion and inclusion.

A patient's most likely diagnosis is selected from many possibilities; without any information, all diagnoses are equally probable. As the examiner collects information, the probability of any one diagnosis changes. For example, Patient A arrives for evaluation and treatment. Without additional information about age, gender, chief complaint, and other factors, every diagnosis is equally probable. As the examiner collects information, however, the probability that Patient A is suffering from certain conditions diminishes and eventually reaches zero, while the probability favoring other diagnoses increases. Eventually, this continuing process of exclusion and inclusion leaves the examiner with the most likely diagnosis. To illustrate again, if Patient A is male, the possibility of obstetric/gynecologic conditions is zero. If he staggers, slurs his speech, and smells of alcohol, the probability of the diagnosis being acute alcohol intoxication increases, while the probability of most other conditions decreases, many to virtually zero. More information is obviously needed for furthering the exclusion/inclusion process. If, however, the examiner obtains this information properly, the most likely diagnosis will be reached.

The process of exclusion/inclusion by probability has four requirements: The examiner must (1) know the possibilities (i.e., the available diagnostic choices), (2) know the information that is helpful in discriminating patient groups (i.e., which clinical data affect the probabilities and which do not), (3) be able to elicit signs and symptoms (in psychiatry, the psychopathology which affects the probabilities), and (4) be able to identify and properly classify signs and symptoms.

TABLE 2.1

Examples of Diagnostic Patterns Seen by the Neuropsychiatrist

Pattern	*Most Likely Diagnosis*
Hallucinations, delusions, fluctuating language disturbance, loss of emotional expression, loss of drive and ambition, no history indicating coarse brain disease	Schizophrenia
Altered mood (irritability or euphoria), rapid/pressured speech, hyperactivity	
A. Broad affect, no coarse brain	Bipolar affective disorder, mania
B. Shallow mood, avolitional, chronic course	Frontal lobe orbital-medial syndrome
Typical depressive features (e.g., insomnia, anorexia, psychomotor retardation), but without profound unremitting sadness or dysphoria (the words, but not the "music" of depression)	Secondary depression A. With increased muscle tone and bradykinesia–parkinsonism B. With renal stones—parathyroid disease C. With paresis—stroke
Altered or fluctuating level of arousal, agitation, diffuse cognitive impairment, rambling speech	Delirium
Clear consciousness; diffuse cognitive impairment, particularly affecting memory; organizational and problem-solving difficulties	Dementia
Transient and episodic perceptual disturbances and delusions, but no affective blunting	Seizure disorder
Typical and constant anxiety or obsessive compulsive features beginning after age 35 in a male patient	Systemic illness (e.g., endocrinopathy, hypertension), coarse brain disease (e.g., stroke, tumor)
Dementia with ataxia and urinary incontinence	Normal-pressure hydrocephaly

The examiner needs to know the possible diagnostic choices in order to reach the most likely diagnosis. In adult neuropsychiatry, the choices are limited and fall into seven categories (see Table 2.2 for the diagnostic possibilities in each category). Knowing the information that discriminates the possibilities is also essential. For example, early morning awakening and a diurnal change in a sad mood are highly discriminating for the diagnosis of melancholia, whereas loss of insight and inability to answer proverbs have little diagnostic significance. Diagnostically discriminating data are described in detail in Chapters 3 and 4 and in Part II.

Diagnostic success also derives from the examiner's ability to elicit, identify, and properly classify psychopathology and other data that relate to specific conditions. In the example of Patient A, the successful examiner must be able to detect slurred speech and the odor of alcohol and know that these signs correlate with acute alcohol intoxication. This process is enhanced if, when clinically possible, the examiner observes the patient before starting treatment. Observing the patient's behavior (on the hospital unit, in the clinic, during the examination) and obtaining laboratory tests uncontaminated by psychotropic medication are important for accurate diagnosis. Except for certain emergencies, such as the possibility of violence, or when the patient is well known to the clinician and the patient's present state is typical for him, the rule of observation before treatment should be maintained. A rush to institute treatment often results in a stormy course and hit-or-miss management, whereas a few days taken to evaluate the patient properly may save years of suffering and mistreatment and minimize risks of iatrogenic morbidity (i.e., tardive dyskinesia). The following vignettes illustrate the point:

> A 42-year-old woman was hospitalized for worsening depression despite receiving an adequate dose of amitriptyline. During the week prior to admission, she became increasingly agitated and indicated she was experiencing auditory hallucinations. Upon admission, a neuroleptic was immediately added to the antidepressant, but the patient's condition worsened over the next 2 days. Her agitation became severe and her speech unintelligible. A consultant observed that she was flushed, her skin dry, and her pulse high. Anticholinergic delirium was diagnosed, all psychotropic medication was discontinued, subcutaneous physostigmine was administered, and she became essentially symptom-free within 48 hours. After recovery she related ingesting, during the week prior to her admission, significant amounts of an over-the-counter sleep aid with anticholinergic properties. The rush to treat with a neuroleptic, another anticholinergic drug, exacerbated the developing delirium.

> A 62-year-old woman suddenly barred her daughter from the house and accused her of being an impostor. She also said aliens had moved into her neighborhood and switched the houses and neighbors so that her real

TABLE 2.2

Adult Neuropsychiatric Diagnostic Possibilities

1. *Mood Disorders*
   Affective disorder: bipolar, unipolar, mixed, dysthymia, cyclothymia, borderline, bulimia

2. *Schizophrenia*
   Various putative subtypes

3. *Other Psychoses*
   Brief reactive psychosis, schizoaffective, simple delusional disorder, atypical, not otherwise specified

4. *Personality Disorders*
   Extremes of trait:
   Schizoid, schizotypal, paranoid (A)
   Borderline, histrionic, narcissistic (B)
   Passive aggressive/dependent, avoidant (C)
   Antisocial (D)

5. *Personality "Illness"*
   States related to extremes of trait:
   Anxiety disorder: panic disorder, agoraphobia, other phobias, generalized anxiety disorder, obsessive compulsive disorder, Gilles de la Tourette syndrome, post-traumatic stress disorder
   Somatoform disorders (somatization disorder, conversion, hypochondriasis), sexual dysfunctions, adjustment disorder, dissociative disorders

6. *Coarse Brain Disease*
   Syndromes resulting from central nervous system dysfunction or lesions:
   Delirium, intoxications, dementia
   Focal syndromes: frontal, temporoparietal
   Seizure-related syndromes
   Other: postconcussion, amnestic syndromes
   Chronic or intermittent drug- and alcohol-induced disorders; alcohol and drug intoxications and withdrawal
   Symptomatic (1–5)

7. *Problems of Living*
   For example, divorce, bereavement, parent-child difficulties

neighborhood was somewhere else. Her daughter had seen her 2 days earlier and said her mother was well at that time and had no previous psychiatric illness. On admission, the woman was agitated and had difficulty finding her way about the unit. She had no symptoms of depression or mania. The attending physician immediately concluded that the patient had a "late-onset schizophrenia" and planned to prescribe a neuroleptic. A consultant, however, suggested that the acute and late onset in an otherwise psychiatrically well person, the delusions of impostors (Capgras syndrome) and real and false neighborhoods (reduplicative paramnesia), and her difficulties finding her way about the unit (spatial disorientation) possibly indicated a nondominant parietal lobe stroke. This was confirmed with a computed tomography (CT) scan. Rest and support were recommended as the only treatment, and the patient was fully recovered within a week. In addition to illustrating the merits of observation and diagnosis before treatment, this case is an example of the therapeutic benefit of hospitalization and supportive care, without psychotropic medication, for some patients.

Phenomenologic Clinical Method

The phenomenologic clinical method (983) is best suited to the neuropsychiatric examination. It incorporates three principles: (1) objective observation of signs and symptoms independent of immediate interpretation, (2) description using precise terminology, and (3) the assessment of the form of behavior separately from its content.

Objective observation of signs and symptoms is essential for accurate diagnosis. For example: A 36-year-old man was hospitalized, and the admitting psychiatrist felt him to be suicidal. The patient had an 8-year history of progressive deterioration in function, punctuated by recurrent episodes that were characterized by auditory and visual hallucinations and occasional irritability. He was recently fired from the last of many short-lived jobs, and his wife was about to leave him. In each of six previous hospitalizations, he had been diagnosed as a paranoid schizophrenic and treated with neuroleptics. His present hospitalization resulted from his attempt to shoot himself in the chest. When examined by a consultant, he related experiences of seeing a small, shadowy male figure that gradually seemed to approach him, as it became larger, until it was standing next to him on his right. These appearances (occurring many times daily) were always accompanied by fearfulness. Recently, the figure was experienced as beginning to push its way into the patient's body and trying to take it over. The patient felt this. The patient stated he was going to shoot himself in the chest, not to commit suicide but rather to kill the shadowy figure. He was convinced he would not harm himself. The consultant neither elicited nor observed any features of depression or of emotional blunting. Although the above features are consistent with DSM criteria for schizophrenia, the consultant, in objectively summarizing the features as frequent visual and tactile hallucinations associated with fearfulness in the absence of other features of schizophrenia, pursued the evaluation further. He ultimately determined that the patient had a left temporoparietal contusion and a seizure disorder. Treatment with anticonvulsant medication resolved all symptoms and permitted the patient to return home and obtain employment. He remained asymptomatic and functioning well for the next 2 years.

For objective observation to be useful, however, the clinician must be able to characterize in *precise terminology* what he observes. For example, the term "confusion" could refer to an altered state of consciousness (as in delirium), disorientation in clear consciousness (as in dementia), or unintelligible speech (as with a dominant hemisphere stroke), or it could describe a patient who gets easily lost or who cannot find his way about the hospital unit (as with a nondominant hemisphere stroke). Each condition has a different diagnostic implication, which goes unrecognized when each is subsumed under the vague term "confusion." Clinicians also often use imprecise terms, such as incoherent or irrelevant speech or looseness of associations, to describe the speech of patients. The speech of some aphasic stroke patients is incoherent and at times irrelevant to the topic, as is the speech of some schizophrenics and some manics. If the clinician uses the imprecise term, he will not discriminate aphasia from schizophrenic formal thought disorder or manic flight of ideas, and misdiagnosis may occur. Precise terms of greatest diagnostic discrimination should be used in characterizing psychopathology.

The separate assessment of behavioral *form from content* is perhaps the most critical process of the phenomenologic clinical method. This is true because the form of the psychopathology generally reflects the illness process (what the clinician is trying to identify), whereas the content of psychopathology generally reflects the person and his experience. What a patient is talking about, the words spoken by a hallucinated voice, and the specifics of a delusional idea are content. The linkage of speech and word usage, the clarity and duration of a hallucination, and whether the delusional idea derives from other psychopathology or appears suddenly and fully formed are form. Cross-cultural studies (295, 467, 725) have shown that the content of psychopathology varies dramatically, but the form of psychiatric illness is similar across cultures. For example, films of Chinese psychiatrists making rounds in regional mental hospitals clearly reveal the manics (mugging for the camera, saluting, insisting on speaking) from the depressed patients (sad face, motor retardation, agitation) despite all interchanges being conducted in Mandarin. Melancholic patients from rural African villages share with melancholics from industrialized western cities the typical form of depression with its characteristic profound sadness, insomnia, anorexia, psychomotor retardation, and feelings of guilt. What varies is the content of their guilty ideas and ruminations.

Decision-Making Steps

The diagnostic process is a series of decision-making steps. Initially, the clinician obtains a general impression of the patient. If the pattern is clearly recognizable, this initial impression is unlikely to change despite elaborate examination and laboratory assessment (865). The clinician must recognize this tendency and consciously employ the process of selecting the probabilities from the possibilities by using the phenomenologic clinical method to elicit and identify the psychopathology that effects those probabilities. This process proceeds by a series of decisions, each of which increases the likelihood of the final diagnostic choice.

The most fundamental decision is whether the patient has deviant behavior and whether that deviance reflects illness. This decision is critical because it will determine if the patient is to receive any treatment and if the primary treatment will be biologic (e.g., medications, electroconvulsive treatment [ECT]), or psychosocial (e.g., counseling, behavior therapy).

Deciding whether behavior is deviant is not always easy. Almost 50% of individuals without mental disorders have hallucinated at some time in their lives (417), and most people will experience some features of depression (190) following the death of a spouse or other close relative. One shortcoming of the DSM system is that diagnoses are, in part, determined by the number of symptoms experienced, rather than their form and how different symptoms relate to each other. For example, in her studies of bereavement, Clayton found that more than 50% of widows met research criteria for major depression, but neither the widows nor the investigators considered the widows who met these criteria to be ill (190). Simply counting symptoms obviously misses important information. Other investigators have also commented on the limitations of the DSM format and its application in the considertion of symptom interaction (301, 706). Thus, experience, common sense, and the use of time-honored and partially validated processes, such as the phenomenologic clinical method, remain the best guidelines for identifying the truly deviant.

When a decision has been made that the patient has deviant behavior, the examiner must next decide if this deviance is the result of a pathologic process. For example, professional basketball players are deviant (or abnormal) in height. They are more than 1.5 standard deviations above the mean height for American males of their generation. This deviance, however, is not the result of disease. Acromegalics, on the other hand, are deviant in height because of pituitary pathology. Among professional basketball players, the outward character (height) and the internal constitutional determinants of height are on a continuum with the norm. Among acromegalics, the outward character (height) is also on a continuum with the norm, but the internal determinants are not. The patterns of the two height deviations also differ (acromegalics have a typical facial and head bony structure) and illustrate how the interactions of features into patterns can be helpful in diagnosis.

Psychiatric patients with affective disorder and schizophrenia, for example, are clearly deviant in their outward character (behavior). Also, significant evidence exists that these patients are deviant because of brain pathology (50, 140, 165). Within the diagnostic possibilities displayed in Table 2.2, evidence indicates that some pathologic processes underlie all categories except personality disorder and problems of living. Among the personality disorders, Group A patients and some individuals in Groups B and D may have subtle forms of illness, and future data may show them to have pathology. For the rest, the presence of pathology is unknown. Using the analogy of deviant height, individuals in personality disorder Groups A, B, and D might respond to biologic intervention, just as acromegalics can be partially treated. Individuals in Group C, however, if indeed they do not have underlying pathology, are unlikely to respond to biologic treatments.

The logical steps inherent in the diagnostic process begin with the patient's chief complaint. Once the chief complaint is characterized (see Table 1.1), the examiner immediately formulates a dynamic (i.e., working) differential diagnostic list of probabilities, which then guides the gathering of information related to the present illness (see Table 1.1). For example, if the patient is a 45-year-old, married, working, Euro-American man, whose chief complaint is "I'm nervous," the examiner should immediately consider the probable conditions likely to generate such a chief complaint. These would undoubtedly include depression, anxiety disorder, problems of living, adjustment disorder, and thyroid disease. These probabilities then suggest questions and stimulate observational sensitivity to specific signs and symptoms related to these disorders. The first question to be asked, however, is by the examiner of himself: "What are the probabilities that could result in this patient's chief complaint?"

As the examiner collects information related to the present illness, the working differential diagnostic list may change several times, with some initially considered probabilities being eliminated and new ones added. Progressing through the different sections of the evaluation (see Table 1.1), the examiner continuously revises the working list as data affecting the probabilities are collected. Even laboratory studies (see Chapter 6) must be guided by the working differential diagnosis list, with each specific test related to one or more of the choices on the list. When all relevant information has been gathered, the examiner should be left with a single disorder or a small number of choices ranked by their probabilities.

The clinician, therefore, has three conceptual structures that provide the means to reach a diagnostic conclusion: (1) the template of the evaluation (see Table 1.1), (2) the interaction of the working diagnoses list with that template, and (3) both of these as they relate to the basic diagnostic process of eliminating most possibilities and identifying the most likely choices. The skills of data acquisition, identification, and organization are required to use these interacting structures. Specifically, the examiner must be skillful in (1) the techniques and style of the superficially conversational, but semistructured, mental status examination, and (2) the principles of phenomenology—objective observation, precise terminology, and the separation of psychopathologic form from content To be successful in these efforts, the clinician must have a data base: What are the possibilities (i.e., the nosology)? What are the probabilities in the circumstances of his practice (i.e., what conditions are more prevalent and what conditions are almost never seen in his practice setting)? What bits of clinical information affect the probabilities of the possible choices? As this information is gathered, the process of elimination proceeds to its conclusion—the diagnosis. Figure 2.1 illustrates this process of integrating the conceptual structures needed to reach a diagnosis. Part of the dilemma of modern psychiatric clinical practice revolves around continually changing nosology, diagnostic criteria, and data bases that seem to predict diagnoses.

NOSOLOGY

The DSM nosology (i.e., the American Psychiatric Association's classification of mental disorders) and its, or other, sets of diagnostic criteria are used at the beginning and at the end of the diagnostic process. To begin the diagnostic process, the

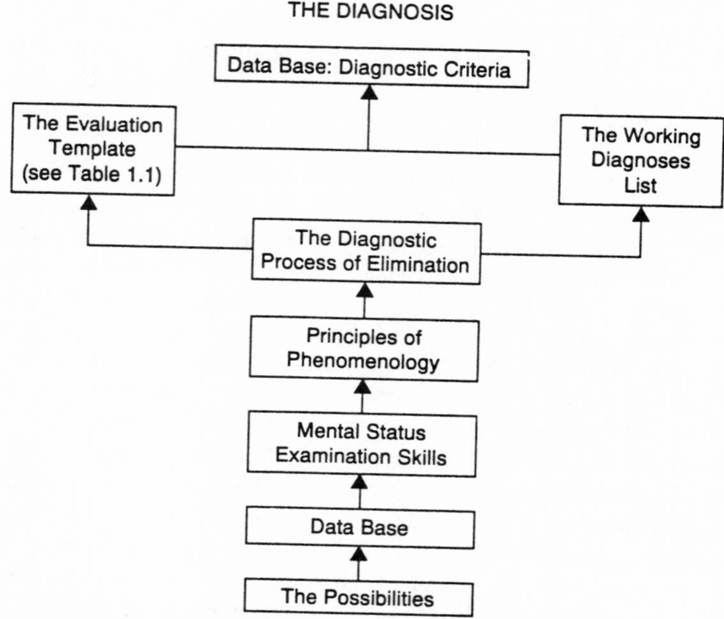

Figure 2.1. Integrated Process Used in Reaching a Diagnosis

clinician must have a reasonable notion of the possibilities to know what to select or eliminate. DSM provides the latest official list of these possibilities. Every psychiatric clinician must know the major DSM categories (e.g., affective disorders, anxiety disorders) and some of the subcategories (e.g., bipolar or unipolar, agoraphobia or obsessive compulsive disorder). The International Classification of Diseases (ICD) provides the remainder of the possibilities, including other diseases of the central nervous system and of other organ systems. Because some of these diseases result in psychiatric disorders, the clinician must have a working knowledge of them. Studies indicate that from 25 to 40% of acutely ill psychiatric inpatients have systemic conditions that either directly cause behavioral changes leading to psychiatric hospitalization or lead to complications that confuse the diagnostic picture or make treatment and management more difficult (1060).

In addition, skilled clinicians know, and the application of DSM criteria demonstrates, that no matter how vigorously criteria are applied some patients will not meet all the required criteria for any diagnosis. DSM provides the "not otherwise specified" (NOS) category for these patients. Experienced and knowledgeable clinicians, however, can further refine this and other amorphous categories (e.g., hallucinosis secondary to coarse brain disease) by their awareness of the scientific literature, which always runs ahead of the official nosology and offers unofficial, but clinically useful, choices (e.g., catatonia as a treatment-responsive syndrome separate from schizophrenia; various frontal and parietal lobe syndromes).

A working knowledge of specific sets of diagnostic criteria is used at the beginning of the evaluation to relate the list of diagnoses to the evaluation template (see Table 1.2). From the chief complaint, for example, the clinician suspects the patient is depressed and so asks a screening question for depression. If the patient endorses this, the clinician must know diagnostic criteria for depression to ask further questions (e.g., about sleep, appetite, changes in libido) and elicit information to confirm or eliminate this possibility. Criteria, therefore, help to shape the structure of the evaluation from its beginning. Once the data collection portion of the evaluation is complete, knowledge of diagnostic criteria is again used to take stock of what has been collected. This is necessary to determine whether the patient's signs and symptoms and historical information meet criteria. If not, does that failure eliminate the possibility, or are enough criteria met to conclude that possibility still is the most probable?

A difficulty in using the DSM system is the misunderstanding that complexity of criteria ensures specificity. Although DSM lists specific criteria, many are not operationally defined and, thus, their use is left to the imagination (i.e., bias, idiosyncrasies) of the examiner. For some diagnostic criteria to be met, for example a patient must have poor concentration or poor memory or must have insomnia. But what does "poor" precisely mean in this context, and where is the point in time in bed when insomnia begins? Among the criteria for dysthymia, no specific operational definition exists for the criteria of "low energy" or "fatigue," "poor concentration," and "difficulty making decisions"; the criteria for generalized anxiety disorders include "feeling keyed-up or on edge" and "difficulty concentrating." There are specific tests of concentration and precise ways of defining various other criteria, but these procedures cannot all be incorporated into the DSM system. Thus, significant latitude remains for idiosyncratic decision making (565). In the hands of researchers using structured interviews and their own operational definitions, reliability for DSM is improved (822).

To illustrate this problem, at the University of Iowa (1074) researchers were asked to use the DSM criteria, the Feighner criteria (299), and the Research Diagnostic Criteria (RDC) (927) research criteria to diagnose independently of each other the same group of patients. These researchers had to interpret, or self-operationalize, what the specific criteria implied but did not specify. As expected, they had some serious diagnostic disagreements. In fact, for 62 of the 98 patients, disagreements on diagnosis occurred in *at least* one of the three diagnostic systems, with a disagreement rate of more than 34%. As the authors conclude, "The Bible may tell us so, but the criteria don't. They are better than what we had, but they are still a long way from perfect."

Clinicians need to be aware that many of the criteria in DSM are not operationally defined and that they must provide these definitions if they are to become more precise diagnosticians. Some help in this regard can be obtained from the scientific literature, in which data are available that suggest what constitutes an abnormal "this" or a deviant "that" and how to go about measuring them. Chapters 3, 4, and 5 focus on these suggested operational definitions.

Finally, trying to maximize diagnostic reliability has led researchers to rely on several structured (the Structured Clinical Interview for DSM-III-R [SCID] [929]) and semistructured (the Scale of the Assessment of Negative Symptoms [SANS] [46] and the Scale for the Assessment of Positive Symptoms [SAPS] [47]) rating scales and clinical interviews for assessing patients. Many researchers who have used these clinical instruments often find that, despite their helpfulness in acquiring specific information from a patient, a complete picture of the patient and his illness is still not available at the end of the process. Several researchers (205) have pointed out this problem and demonstrated why a descriptive narrative that considers the interactions among symptoms is necessary when using structured interviews to ensure that the patient is not lost in the complexity of rigid questions. Regardless of this and other shortcomings (e.g., disrupting the process for establishing a good doctor-patient relationship), some rating scales are of practical help to the clinician in operationalizing criteria or in characterizing syndromes. They are discussed in Chapters 3 and 4.

Chapter 3

Operational Definitions of Major Psychopathology

I. Appearance, Motor Behavior, and Mood and Affect

That operational definitions are necessary for diagnostic criteria to have reliability is an example of the phenomenologic principle that precise terminology and description of form are essential for diagnosis. Precise description of the form of psychopathology makes objective observation possible. For example, a clinician could not discriminate the various forms of formal thought disorder unless he knows the characteristics of each form. The neuropsychiatric evaluation (see Table 1.1) displays the major behavioral areas and their associated psychopathology, which must be assessed to accurately diagnose patients. Each of these areas relates to one or more diagnostic criteria, and their precise description is needed to determine if the observed phenomena meet the operational definitions of those criteria. Rating scales can be helpful in some areas; in many, however, there is no aid other than the continual study of psychopathology.

Appearance

Obvious patient behavior and aspects of general appearance that are helpful in diagnosis (e.g., age, gender, the patient using a walker) are often overlooked by the examiner. Women have greater risks than men for affective and some anxiety disorders. It is rare for an anxiety disorder to develop for the first time after age 35, whereas bipolar affective disorder commonly develops during the third decade of life. Simple observations about gender and age have a big effect on the diagnostic probabilities.

The patient's appearance is always evaluated first. Interviewing or testing the patient is not necessary for this part of the evaluation. When possible, the examiner should greet the patient outside the examining room and walk with him to the place chosen for the interview. This initial, outwardly informal introductory period permits the examiner to observe the patient's motor coordination, gait, and manner. Observation of the patient's behavior on the inpatient unit is also extremely helpful. The examiner should deliberately review the patient's apparent age, gender, race/ethnicity, body type, nutrition, personal hygiene, and level of consciousness. Each of these may affect the diagnostic probabilities, and the examiner should pay attention to these details. Thus, a heavily tattooed young male suggests antisocial personality, whereas a dazed, ataxic woman with urine-stained clothes suggestes normal-pressure hydrocephalus. Physical constitution also should be noted. Small-framed, lanky people with low fat and muscle mass (ectomorphs) are overrepresented among individuals with schizophrenia. Large-framed, heavy-set people with a high fat/muscle ratio (endomorphs) are overrepresented among individuals with affective disorder. Although by no means absolute, the presence of one of these body types alters the clinical probabilities and is thus potentially helpful in the diagnostic process (737). Table 3.1 illustrates correlations between some psychiatric conditions and observations of general appearance.

Motor Behavior

Observations of motor behavior also begin upon meeting the patient. When recorded, these observations should include a description of gait, abnormal movements, frequency of movement, rhythm, coordination, and speed. The wide-based or ataxic gait of the alcoholic, the hesitant gait of the Huntington's chorea patient, the stooped shuffle of the patient with frontal lobe disease, and the manneristic hopping and tiptoe gaits of catatonia are some of the unusual motor behaviors that the examiner can observe while walking with the patient to the examining room.

One of the more common motor disturbances seen in seriously ill patients is *agitation.* An increase in the frequency of non–goal-directed motor behavior, agitation is the motor expression of increased arousal or of an intense mood. It can reflect anxiety, sadness, anger, or euphoria. Pacing, handwringing (suggesting depression), head-rubbing (suggesting schizophrenia), constant shifting of body positions and playing with one's fingers (suggesting anxiety), and picking at one's bed sheets (suggesting delirium) are examples of agitation.

TABLE 3.1

Sample of Correlations of General Appearance with Psychiatric Condition

Feature	*Example*	*Condition at Risk*
Age and gender	Male under age 20	Character and behavior disorder, drug-related conditions
	Female over age 40	Unipolar affective disorder
	Female	Affective disease, somatization disorder
	Male	Sociopathy, schizophrenia
Body type	Endomorph	Affective disorder
	Ectomorph	Schizophrenia
Level of consciousness	Clouded	Acute coarse brain syndrome (delirium)
Personal hygiene	Dirty/unkept	Coarse brain syndrome (acute or chronic), schizophrenia
	Unilateral poor hygiene	Hemispatial neglect
Nutrition	Recent weight loss	Depression
	Chronic malnutrition	Dementia
Manner	Hostile and suspicious	Delusional psychosis, coarse brain disease
Dress	Head decorations, bright colors, scant clothing	Mania
	Multiple layers of clothes	Dementia, mania
	Unilateral abnormalities	Hemispatial neglect

Because of chronic ingestion of neuroleptics, many psychiatric patients exhibit constant jerky finger movements, foot tapping, pelvic thrusts, or repetitive oral movements, such as lip smacking or moving the tongue in and out of the mouth. These movements are manifestations of a coarse brain disorder and characterize the condition termed *tardive dyskinesia* (61). Although tardive dyskinesia typically exacerbates with stress, it is also frequently observed in patients who are calm and should not be confused with agitation.

Psychotic patients often appear odd. Neighbors and total strangers can easily identify these patients by their socially deviant behaviors: talking to themselves, gesticulating, or shouting to the air. Global, usually goal-oriented activities also can be disturbed. The extremes of these changes in levels of activity are termed *hyperactivity* and *hypoactivity*. A patient who is doing too many things at the same time; engages in many conversations, one after the other; and goes from one place to another in quick succession is hyperactive. The patient who sits for long periods and rarely moves or responds to surrounding events is hypoactive. In its extreme form, hyperactivity appears as frantic, constant, impulsive, and incomplete multiple activities, which may appear non-goal-directed. It is invariably associated with an intense excitement state in which the patient is constantly talking and often shouting. Extreme importunate and intrusive behavior and intense irritability or euphoria are usually present (376; also see Chapter 2.) Prior to the availability of biologic treatments, particularly electroconvulsive treatment, patients experiencing extreme excitement occasionally suffered cardiovascular collapse and even death (259). Extreme hyperactivity or excitement is most frequently observed in individuals who satisfy modern diagnostic criteria for mania (376, Chapter 2; 972).

Extreme hypoactivity is termed *stupor*. A stuporous patient may stay motionless for hours, stare fixedly, or follow the examiner about the room with his eyes, yet remain mute and unresponsive to spoken comments and even to painful stimuli (general analgesia) (494). When associated with coarse disease, particularly of the brain stem, the syndrome is termed *akinetic mutism* (969). When coarse disease cannot be demonstrated, such stuporous patients most frequently satisfy diagnostic criteria for affective disorder (376, Chapter 2; 969). Stupor is also a feature of the catatonic syndrome.

Catatonia

The syndrome of catatonia is characterized by specific motor behaviors and by periods of extreme hyperactivity and hypoactivity. The specific motor behaviors, however, can occur independently of the full syndrome. Studies show that 25 to 50% of individuals who exhibit catatonic features have an affective disorder and that about 15 to 20% of patients with bipolar affective disorder exhibit one or more catatonic features: *To scratch a catatonic is, often, to tickle a manic*. Patients who have catatonia as part of their affective disease are indistinguishable from affectively ill patients without catatonia in their demographic characteristics, psychopathology, and treatment response and in the prevalence and pattern of psychiatric illness in their first-degree relatives. Although 5 to 10% of catatonics satisfy diagnostic criteria for schizophrenia, catatonia generally has a favorable treatment response (969). About 10% of acutely ill psychotic inpatients have two or more catatonic features (842).

Catatonic features are described in Table 3.2. Mutism and stupor, although characteristic of catatonia, are not pathognomonic. Other motor behaviors should be present, and most patients have three or more features. There appears to be no relationship among any one feature or number of features and any one diagnosis or response to treatment. Thus, the presence of one or two features has as much diagnostic and treatment significance as the presence of seven or eight features. Three features—mutism, negativism, and stupor—occur together more frequently than by chance (14) and correspond to the clinical syndrome of negativistic stupor (i.e., akinetic mutism or coma vigil secondary to frontal lobe damage, third ventricle tumors, or lesions of the reticular activating system and caudal hypothalamus; 969). Mutism, stereotypy, catalepsy, and automatic obedience also occur together more frequently than by chance (14), correspond to the classic description of catatonia (494), and are associated with the diagnosis of mania. Luria (611) described several patients with catatonia-like symptoms after frontal lobe injury. Dogs with ablated frontal lobes also demonstrate many catatonic features. This relationship between frontal lobe lesions and catatonia-like behaviors is not surprising, as the frontal lobe is intimately involved in the regulation of motor activity (611). The frontal lobe signs of pathologic inertia (difficulty initiating motor acts or stopping them once started) and stimulus bound behavior (motor response to stimuli despite instructions to the contrary) may underlie catatonic features.

Specific procedures to elicit catatonic features are seldom part of the routine mental status examination. The examiner, however, should always test for catatonia when the following behaviors are observed: odd gaits inconsistent with known neurologic disease (e.g., tiptoe walking, hopping), standing in one place for prolonged periods, holding the arms up as if carrying something, shifting position when the examiner shifts position, repeating most of the examiner's questions before answering, responding to most of the examiner's questions with the same question (e.g., Examiner: How old are you? Patient: How old are you?), making odd hand or finger movements that are not typically dyskinetic, performing inconspicuous repetitive actions (e.g., making a series of clicking sounds before or after speaking, tapping or automatically touching objects while walking about), mutism, psychomotor retardation, or speech that becomes progressively less voluble until it becomes a nonunderstandable mumble (prosectic speech). The pattern of psychosis and what appear to be obsessive compulsive behaviors should alert the clinician to the possibility of catatonia.

Patients displaying one or more of the above features while conversing with the examiner may allow themselves to be placed in odd postures; may be unable to resist the examiner moving their arms, despite instructions to the contrary; or may be unable to resist shaking the examiner's proffered hand, despite instructions to the contrary (automatic obedience).

TABLE 3.2
Catatonic Features

Feature	*Description*
Mutism	A state of verbal unresponsiveness, not always associated with immobility
Stupor	Extreme hypoactivity, in which the patient is mute, immobile, and unresponsive to painful stimuli
Catalepsy	Maintenance of postures for long periods. Includes facial postures, such as grimacing, and Schnauzkrampf (lips in an exaggerated pucker); and body postures, such as psychologic pillow (patient lying in bed with his head elevated as if on a pillow), lying in a jackknifed position, sitting with upper and lower portions of body twisted at right angles, holding arms above the head or raised in prayerlike manner, and holding fingers and hands in odd positions
Waxy flexibility	Examiner's experience of the patient offering initial resistance before allowing himself to be postured, similar to that of a bending candle
Mannerisms	Odd purposeful movements, such as hopping instead of walking, walking on tiptoe, or saluting passersby, or exaggerations or stilted caricatures of mundane movements
Stereotypy	Often striking, non–goal-directed, repetitive motor behavior; repetition of phrases and sentences in an automatic fashion, similar to a scratched record, termed *verbigeration* (verbal stereotypy)
Gegenhalten (negativism)	Patient resisting examiner's manipulations, whether light or vigorous, with strength equal to that applied, as if bound to the stimulus of the examiner's actions
Echophenomena	Includes echolalia, in which the patient constantly repeats the examiner's utterances, and echopraxia, in which the patient spontaneously copies the examiner's movements or is unable to refrain from copying the examiner's test movements despite instruction to the contrary

TABLE 3.2 (*Cont.*)
Catatonic Features

Feature	*Description*
Automatic obedience	Despite instructions to the contrary, the patient permitting examiner's light pressure to move his limbs into a new position (posture), which is then maintained by the patient despite instructions to the contrary
Ambitendency	The patient appearing motorically "stuck" in an indecisive, hesitant movement, which results from examiner verbally contradicting his own strong nonverbal signal, such as offering his hand as if to shake hands, while stating, "Don't shake my hand, I don't want you to shake it."

Patients with classic catatonic features are often misdiagnosed because of the false expectation that they must be mute and immobile. In fact, most patients with catatonic features speak and move about. Because motor behavior is regulated by frontal lobe systems, motor abnormalities, (including the catatonic syndrome), severe hyperactivity, and stupor may reflect coarse frontal lobe disease.

There are no official diagnostic criteria for catatonia. Based on their literature review, Fink and Taylor (310) suggested the set of criteria displayed in Table 3.3. Additional frontal lobe and parietal lobe motor behaviors are discussed in Chapters 5 and 13.

Other Spontaneous Abnormal Movements

Abnormal movements long have been recognized as a feature of mental disorder. Nineteenth- and early twentieth-century writers (116, 418, 554) richly described patients with such hyperkinetic phenomena as rocking; twisting truncal movements; ballistic arm movements; athetoid finger and hand movements; forehead wrinkling; grimacing and pouting movements; stereotyped biting and chewing; flicking and licking of the tongue; and rubbing, picking, kneading, tapping, grasping, and pulling behaviors. Patients were said to be uncoordinated, stiff, and fragmented in their movements with a loss of normal smooth-transition movements. Continuous grimacing and twisting of facial features and making snorting, guttural, and clicking sounds were also thought to be common. Kraepelin believed that choreiform movements of the face and fingers were common in dementia praecox, and he (554) and Bleuler (116) each described dementia praecox patients

TABLE 3.3

Proposed Diagnostic Criteria for Catatonia

I. Immobility, mutism, *or* stupor of at least 1 hour's duration, if associated with at least one of the following that can be observed or elicited on two or more occasions: catalepsy, automatic obedience, posturing

OR

II. In the absence of immobility, mutism or stupor, at least two of the following that can be observed or elicited on two or more occasions: stereotypy, echophenomena, catalepsy, automatic obedience, posturing, Gegenhalten (negativism), ambitendency

NOTE: See Table 3.2 for operational definitions.
SOURCE: Adapted from reference 310.

to exhibit tremor, adiadochokinesia, and ataxia ("the cerebellar form of dementia praecox"), grand mal seizures (thought to be an early sign of dementia praecox), transient paralysis after apoplectiform seizures, and wavering movements. The prevalence of these behaviors then and now is unknown but is probably highest among schizophrenics and the chronically ill (116, 554). In a given patient, these behaviors do not appear to change in character or frequency over time, although they occur more often during stress (491). Their apparent high frequency among psychiatric patients in the prepsychotropic drug era probably reflects the inclusion of patients with coarse brain disease, whereas the prevalence of these behaviors today probably reflects drug-induced dysfunction, as well as diagnostic heterogeneity. Drug-induced abnormal movements are strikingly similar to the spontaneous abnormal movements reported in patients during the prepsychotropic drug era. Other than by history, there is no reliable way of discriminating the two phenomena.

Consistent with the prevalence of these abnormal movements in psychotic patients are other data (neuroimaging, neurodevelopmental, neuroanatomic, clinicopathologic) indicating that cerebellar dysfunction may play a role in the pathogenesis of some schizophrenias (970). Table 3.4 displays some of the more typical cerebellarlike features observed in psychotic patients and how to assess these features.

Drug-Induced Abnormal Movements

All psychotropic agents affect motor function. Cyclic antidepressants and lithium have been associated with extrapyramidal syndromes (73, 477). In therapeutic doses, they can produce persistent, fine, and rapid tremors and coordination diffi-

TABLE 3.4
Cerebellarlike Motor Features

Feature	*Description*
Ataxia	Head- or body-weaving movements. Can be observed or tested by asking the patient to heel/toe walk with eyes open for 12 feet. *Dystaxia* is observed when the patient, standing erect with feet together and eyes open, sways or staggers in reaction to slight push to his back.
Dysdiadochokinesia	Inability to perform rapid, alternating movements (20 trials), such as pronation and supination of hands (placed on thighs). Mistakes in placement, breaks in movement, and jerky irregular movements can occur. Having the patient rapidly touch the tip of his thumb with the tip of each finger in sequence (both hands palms up, fingers fully extended on thighs—15 trials) is another test.
Asynergy, dysmetria, intention tremor	Inability to perform smoothly simple motor tasks. The patient is asked to put his arms and hands at his sides and with eyes open, then touch his nose with one and then the other hand, five times with each hand. Loss of speed and fluidity, jerky movement, and performance in stages as if a robot are abnormal responses. Pastpointing (dysmetria) or intention tremor may also be observed at this time.

culties that can impair fine motor performance. Coarse tremors, ataxia, and myoclonus can occur after ingestion of toxic amounts of these compounds. Monoamine oxidase inhibitors may induce agitation. Anxiolytics, in large doses, can also induce ataxia, tremors, and myoclonus (207). Neuroleptics have the most profound effect on motor behavior (61, 261), although they differ widely in potency and capacity to affect motor function. For example, the piperazine phenothiazines are 10 to 30 times as potent in inducing extrapyramidal signs as are other classes of phenothiazines (109).

Parkinsonism is a common manifestation of this potency. Bradykinesia (i.e., decreased frequency of movement) is the earliest and most common feature of drug-induced parkinsonism. It is characterized by an expressionless face, slow initiation of motor activity, loss of secondary movements (such as arm swing, which gives the patient a stiff, frozen appearance), and micrographia (handwriting becomes small and choppy). Bradykinesia is associated with muscle weakness and fatigue; muscle rigidity of the neck, trunk, and extremities; and cogwheeling (a delayed sign in which the examiner, as he flexes and extends the patient's arm at the elbow, feels the arm move in short, stop-and-go arcs, as if periodically stopped by the gears of a wheel). Postural difficulties are also observed, including a flexed posture and deficits in righting responses, as well as a shuffling, propulsive gait. Tremor at rest and during voluntary actions; pill rolling at rest (uncommon in drug-induced states), and a fine perioral tremor (the rabbit syndrome) have been reported. Drug-induced parkinsonism usually begins within a few days of drug administration and seldom occurs for the first time after 3 months of treatment. Symptoms often first appear in the preferred hand. Depending on the neuroleptic and the dose administered, upward of 50% of patients may be affected. The very young, the very old, and women may be most susceptible (61, 261).

Dystonias, sudden muscle spasms, usually begin within the first few days of neuroleptic treatment. They are dramatic, frightening to the patient, and often painful and may recur over several days before they are controlled. Young patients are most vulnerable to these reactions, which commonly include cramps and spasms of the muscles of the face, jaw, neck, throat, and tongue. Oculogyric crisis, blepharospasm, respiratory stridor with cyanosis, torticollis, and opisthotonos can occur, as well as slow, writhing movements of the extremities. Acute dyskinesias without severe muscle spasm also can occur early in treatment. These include tongue protrusion; lip smacking; chewing movements; blinking; athetosis of the fingers and toes; shoulder shrugging; and myoclonic movements of the head, neck, and extremities. The incidence of dystonias rises with the increased usage of high-potency neuroleptics (589).

Akathisia is a state of motor restlessness in which the patient is unable to sit or be still. It is usually associated with a subjective feeling of jitteriness and may be mistaken for a spontaneous panic attack or an exacerbation of psychoses, although patients will often state they are not anxious, just restless. Akathisia usually begins after several days of drug administration and continues to increase in incidence during the first several months of treatment. Severity and duration are variable. Its medical relationship to other drug-induced movements is unknown. Risk factors are unknown. The incidence is about 20%.

Tardive dyskinesia, characterized by an extraordinary variety of abnormal movements, results from prolonged exposure to neuroleptics. Its onset is usually after many months or years of treatment, is often first observed in the preferred hand, and may appear only after dose reduction or discontinuation of neuroleptics; 30 to 50% of patients exposed to prolonged neuroleptic treatment may be affected. Elderly patients and those with preexisting coarse brain conditions may be most vulnerable. Features of tardive dyskinesia include the buccolinguomasticatory syndrome (vermicular movements of the tongue on the floor of the mouth; protruding, twisting, and curling tongue movements combined with sucking, pouting, and bulging of the cheeks), choreiform movements of the extremities, particularly the fingers; ballistic arm movements, gait and postural movements, (shifting of weight, lordosis, rocking and swaying, pelvic thrusting, and rotary movements), grunting vocalizations, respiratory dyskinesias and chest heaving resulting in stridor and cyanosis, and dysphagias. Symptoms exacerbate with stress. Many patients seem unaware of their abnormal movements and some appear to have associated cognitive impairment. Tardive dyskinesia appears to be irreversible (61, 261).

Extrapyramidal side-effect motor features and tardive dyskinesia are so prevalent among psychiatric patients receiving psychotropic medication that the clinician must be able systematically and reliably to determine their presence and extent. These features are disturbing to patients and can interfere with interpersonal and job functioning. In the case of tardive dyskinesia, they may be associated with cognitive deficits further impairing function (1038, 1044).

One of the most widely used rating scales of motor abnormality is the Abnormal Involuntary Movement Scale (AIMS) (404), a 12-item scale that assesses the severity (quality, frequency, amplitude) of abnormal movements of the face and mouth, extremities, and trunk. Table 3.5 displays the AIMS, as modified by Munetz and Benjamin (693), with additional scoring suggestions by Lane et al. (567). Once mastered, the AIMS can be used as a standardized, easily and rapidly administered assessment form as part of the patient's record or as a guideline for the clinician to learn the procedure, so that he can assess abnormal movements without the need of a scale.

Mood and Affect

Most psychiatric conditions are associated with some disturbance in mood. "I'm upset," "I'm nervous," and "I'm sad" are among patients' chief complaints that express an altered mood state. Mood refers to the emotion of the moment. Its qualities include sadness, happiness, anger, anxiety, and disgust. Studies of human emotional expression (155, 858, 859, 1006) suggest that emotion has cognitive and arousal components. Although normal emotional expression requires an integration of brain structure and function bilaterally, there is some evidence that this bilateral association is asymmetric, with brain structures related to nonverbal function (usually right-sided) being more intimately involved. An unresolved debate continues as to whether positive (e.g., happiness) and negative (e.g., sadness) emotions are both bilaterally represented, or whether each is primarily subserved by one hemisphere (544, Chapter 23).

The greater the intensity of the mood (its amplitude), the more likely it is to affect behavior. Physiologically, mood intensity and arousal correlate to the extent

TABLE 3.5

Modified Abnormal Involuntary Movement Scale (AIMS)

Instructions	1. Complete examination procedure before making ratings. 2. For movement ratings, rate highest severity observed. 3. After completion, record results on AIMS flow sheet.	Code: 0 = None 1 = Minimal, may be extreme normal 2 = Mild 3 = Moderate 4 = Severe

		(Circle one)
Facial and oral movements	1. Muscles of facial expression (e.g., movements of forehead, eyebrows, periorbital area.) Include frowning, blinking, grimacing of upper face.	0 1 2 3 4
	2. Lips and perioral area (e.g., puckering, pouting, smacking.)	0 1 2 3 4
	3. Jaw (e.g., biting, clenching, chewing, mouth opening, lateral movement)	0 1 2 3 4
	4. Tongue Rate only increase in movement both in and out of mouth, NOT inability to sustain movement.	0 1 2 3 4
Extremity movements	5. Upper (arms, wrists, hands, fingers) Include choreic movements (rapid, objectively purposeless, irregular, spontaneous) and athetoid movements (slow, irregular, complex, serpentine). DO NOT include tremor (repetitive, regular, rhythmic).	0 1 2 3 4
	6. Lower (legs, knees, ankles, toes) (e.g., lateral knee movement, foot tapping, heel dropping, foot squirming, inversion and eversion of foot.	0 1 2 3 4

TABLE 3.5 (*Cont.*)

Modified Abnormal Involuntary Movement Scale (AIMS)

Trunk movements	7. Neck, shoulders, hips (e.g., rocking, twisting, squirming pelvic gyrations.) Include diaphragmatic movements.	0 1 2 3 4	
Global judgments	8. Severity of abnormal movements Score based on highest single score on items 1–7 above.	None, normal Minimal Mild Moderate Severe	0 1 2 3 4
	9. Incapacitation due to abnormal movements	None, normal Minimal Mild Moderate Severe	0 1 2 3 4
	10. Patient's awareness of abnormal movements	No awareness Aware, no distress Aware, mild distress Aware, moderate distress Aware, severe distress	0 1 2 3 4
Dental	11. Current problems with teeth and/or dentures	No Yes	0 1
	12. Does patient usually wear dentures?	No Yes	0 1

AIMS CONVENTIONS

General Scoring Criteria for Rating Severity of Movement in All Anatomic Areas	*Quality*	*Frequency*	*Amplitude*
0 None; no movements, or quality of movement is not choreic or athetoid, and is consistent with TD.	–		

(*continued*)

TABLE 3.5 (*Cont.*)

Modified Abnormal Involuntary Movement Scale (AIMS)

General Scoring Criteria for Rating Severity of Movement in All Anatomic Areas	*Quality*	*Frequency*	*Amplitude*
1 Minimal, may be extreme normal; movements present are of marginal quality with average frequency, or marginal quality with marginal frequency.	? + ?	+ ? ?	?/+ + ?/+
2 Mild; definitely consistent with TD. Quality, frequency, and amplitude are average.	+	+	+
3 Moderate; above average, TD movement, with either frequency or amplitude above average.	+ +	++ +	+ ++
4 Severe; among the most severe TD movements with either frequency and amplitude both above average or extreme amplitude.	+ +	++ +/++	++ +++

Specific Scoring Criteria

1. Movements are rated only if they possibly might be TD movements (e.g., movement due to other disorders, such as Huntington's chorea, tics, and tremor, would not be noted).
2. Except for upper extremities, movements that occur with elicitation are rated the same as spontaneous movements.
3. Finger movements that occur in the passive hand in parallel with elicitation are scored one lower than finger movements not in parallel with elicitation.
4. Tongue movements can be rated with mouth closed by observing movement of larynx.
5. Assuming adequate quality and frequency, a sufficient condition for giving tongue movement a score of 3 is if the tongue breaks the imaginary plane connecting upper and lower teeth. Thus, the "bon bon" sign would be given a score of 3.
6. Lateral jaw movement clearly distinguishes jaw from lip movement.
7. When lip movement is passive due to tongue or jaw movement, it is not rated.
8. Lip movement is not considered passive in the presence of jaw movement if both upper and lower lips move.

KEY: –, absent; ?, marginal; +, average; ++, above average; +++, extreme.

TD, tardive dyskinesia.

SOURCE: From *Hospital and Community Psychiatry, 39,* no. 11 (p. 1175, Table 1), 1988. "AIMS Conventions" section of this table is from *Journal of Nervous & Mental Disease, 173* (p. 355, Table 2), 1985. Reprinted with permission.

that observations regarding mood intensity can predict pulse, heart rate, blood pressure, and pupillary dilation. Arousal mechanisms, however, are not clearly understood and are complex, as the above physiologic measures often do not correlate with each other, but a reasonable clinical rule is that the more intense the mood, the greater the arousal (672, pp. 134–130).

The association between mood and motor behavior is described above in the section on motor behavior. Mood also affects facial expression, manner, speech, thought processes, thought content, and, when extreme, the development of delusions and perceptual disturbances. These effects are discussed in Chapter 4.

The behavioral area in which mood is expressed is termed affect. Affect can be understood quantitatively as having a range, intensity, and stability. Qualitatively it can be understood as having appropriateness of mood, quality of mood, and relatedness. Mood is the content of affect. They are not synonymous terms.

In mental illness, the quality of mood may become constant despite changes in the patient's immediate surroundings. Many patients with affective disorder express a constant mood of sadness, elation, or irritability. Patients with anxiety states may be in a constant state of apprehension, and patients with schizophrenia may have no expression of mood and appear emotionally blunted and apathetic. Variability of emotional expression over time is the range of affect and can be compared with the variations and modulation in music. In each of the above examples of constant mood, the range of affect is constricted. A person with a constricted affect essentially expresses only one mood over a prolonged period of time, regardless of surrounding events. Thus, either a depressed patient who expresses only sadness or a manic patient who expresses only euphoria has a constricted affect.

In contrast, some patients have rapid mood shifts. For example, they move quickly from tearfulness to laughter or then to angry outbursts. These outbursts often occur with minimal or no provoking stimuli. This instability of emotional expression is termed lability of affect. Constricted affect and lability of affect are opposite extremes in the variability of emotional expression. Regardless of the underlying pathophysiology, many mentally ill individuals have some disturbance in affective variability.

Moods can vary in intensity as well as quality. Intensity of mood refers to the degree or amplitude of emotional expression (i.e., the degree of arousal). Rage is more intense than anger, and euphoria more intense than happiness. In many patients, affectivity can be constricted in range (restricted to a single quality of mood) but with great intensity. The manic, for example, can shout, joke/pun, make grandiose pronouncements, and laugh with great force. He never varies his mood until overcome by exhaustion. His range of affect is severely constricted, but the amplitude of his affect is great.

Mood appropriateness has been overvalued for its diagnostic importance in past official nosologies. Its definition and meaning also have been generally misconstrued. Mood appropriateness refers only to the patient's moods expressed during the examination and is determined, in part, by the examiner's own mental state and empathic understanding of the patient's behavior ("What's appropriate for me is appropriate for the patient"). Inappropriateness of mood quality (laughing in a sad situation) is not a pathognomonic sign and may reflect normal anxiety (e.g., gallows humor), as well as serious illness. Thus, a patient who is angry at being hospitalized against his will has an appropriate mood by the standard of empathic understanding. The examiner would be angry, too, in the same situation. A patient who shows no sadness in stating that a parent died ten years ago has an appropriate lack of mood, because normally intense grief does not last that long. A patient who laughs uproariously when exhibiting a significant injury has an inappropriate mood; by the standard of empathic understanding, the examiner would not think such a situation humorous.

Using the above scheme, it becomes possible to categorize patients' emotional behavior more precisely. A manic who emits prolonged bellylaughs at only mildly humorous situations has an appropriate mood but an inappropriately increased amplitude of mood and constriction of affect (decreased range). A schizophrenic who is apathetic and shows no emotion when seeing his family for the first time in months has an inappropriate mood, constriction of affect, and decreased mood intensity. The patterns of emotional behaviors (Table 3.6) have diagnostic correlation. They are discussed in more detail in Chapters 8 through 18, which deal with specific syndromes.

The most difficult facet of affect to evaluate is relatedness, or the ability of an individual to express warmth, to interact emotionally and empathically, and to establish rapport. Loss of relatedness, often associated with personality deterioration, is observed in patients with dementia and in schizophrenia (formerly called dementia praecox). It is extremely difficult, however, to measure what is missing and to characterize the deterioration in a patient's personality without some sense of his personality before the morbid process began.

In response to this difficulty in evaluating relatedness, several investigators (7, 46, 99) have developed clinical instruments that reliably assess observable behaviors and expressions of interests and feelings and that take into account what clinicians have traditionally meant by loss of relatedness and personality deterioration. Present-day terminology employs the rubric negative symptoms (51, 232), but traditionally these behaviors have been termed *emotional blunting* (116, 552).

The construct of emotional blunting can be divided into (1) loss of emotional expression and (2) avolition (99). Although both deficits often co-occur in the same patients, particularly in schizophrenics, these behavioral divisions of emotional blunting may derive from independent brain systems (avolition: dominant frontal; loss of expression: nondominant frontal) and can be observed separately. Thus, many patients have both deficits, but some have avolition with a sparing of emotional expression or vice versa (also see Chapter 5).

Table 3.7 displays a scale for rating emotional blunting that has good reliability,

TABLE 3.6

Patterns of Affect

Syndrome	*Range*	*Mood Intensity*	*Mood Appropriateness*	*Relatedness*	*Quality of Mood*
Depression	Decreased (constricted)	Increased	Inappropriate	Related	Apprehension, sadness, dysphoria (sadness plus irritability)*
Mania	Decreased or labile	Increased	Inappropriate or appropriate	Related	Euphoria, irritability, sadness
Schizophrenia	Decreased	Decreased	Inappropriate or appropriate	Unrelated	Apathy

*See reference 105.

TABLE 3.7

Emotional Blunting Scale

Item	*Rating*
Loss of Emotional Expression:	
1. Absent, shallow, incongruous mood	0 1 2
2. Constricted affect (narrow range)	0 1 2
3. Unchanging affect (lacks modulation)	0 1 2
4. Expressionless face	0 1 2
5. Unvarying, monotonous voice	0 1 2
6. Difficult to excite emotions/unresponsive	0 1 2
Loss of Volition:	
7. Indifference/unconcern for own present situation	0 1 2
8. Indifference/unconcern for own future (lacks plans, ambition, desires, drive)	0 1 2

KEY: 0, absent; 1, mild (or questionable); 2, severe.

is internally consistent within subscales, and is easily used in a clinical setting (7, 99). Learning to use the scale also provides the clinician with the experience to assess emotional blunting without the direct use of the scale.

Emotional expression is assessed first by observint the patient's facial expressions, tone of voice, and gestures and evaluating the emotional content of the patient's speech. The quality and intensity of mood and the range of affect are all related to emotional expression. The examiner must also elicit emotional responses from the patient by asking questions or by making comments about the usual emotion-related aspects of life: family, friends, good and bad life events, and personal interests. Emotional expression is referred to as prosody. Ross (847) has suggested a functional-anatomic organization of prosody, specifically the affective components of language, and has related these to the nonverbal hemisphere. Ross considers loss of emotional expression as a motor aprosodia that is analogous to motor aphasia. In motor aphasias there is an impairment in the fluent and clear articulation of language, whereas in motor aprosodia there is an impairment in the emotional expression of language. The analogy also incorporates anatomic localization. Thus, as motor aphasia involves the dominant frontal regions, motor aprosodia involves the nondominant frontal regions. Psychiatric patients with loss of emotional expression and neurologic patients with motor aprosodia share similar features: expressionless face, monotonous voice, loss of speech rhythm and musicality, loss of emotional gesturing, and apparent absence of mood. Psychiatric patients with emotional blunting have been shown to have decreased cerebral flood flow and metabolism bifrontally (140) and bilateral frontal cortical atrophy (50). It is unclear, however, whether there is a specific association between the loss of the emotional expression part of emotional blunting and functional and structural abnormalities in the nondominant frontal regions.

In assessing emotional expression, the examiner needs to determine whether the patient has and can express feelings. Inquiring about relationships and feelings toward mates, spouses, children, parents, and siblings and about activities the patient likes to do for fun is usually sufficient in providing the observational information necessary to rate this aspect of emotional blunting.

Volition refers to that aspect of personality and cognition related to planning, drive, ambition, and desires. Patients with frontal lobe lesions, particularly in the dorsolateral parts of the dominant hemisphere (see the above section on motor behavior) are described as avolitional. In its severest form, this loss of volition extends to grooming and hygiene, and avolitional patients often appear slovenly.

In assessing volition, the examiner needs to determine what the patient thinks about his present situation and what are his future plans. Inquiring about past, present, and future work, willingness to stay in the hospital for a prolonged period, plans for having a family, and leisure pursuits is usually sufficient in providing the information necessary to rate this aspect of emotional blunting.

Emotional blunting has been considered a core feature of schizophrenia since the earliest descriptions of the syndrome (116, 552). Patients with emotional blunting have a paucity of emotional response. Thus, their characteristic pattern of affective response is a constricted affect, a decreased intensity of mood, apathy, inappropriateness of mood, and unrelatedness. They are expressionless in facial movements, tone of voice, and social behaviors. These patients are seclusive and avoid social contact, and they are indifferent to hospital staff, visitors, relatives, and their physical environs. They express little affection for their families and acquaintances and are unconcerned about the present situation. They are devoid of libido. They have no plans or desires for the future. When asked how they feel about being in the hospital or how they would feel if they had to remain hospitalized for many months, emotionally blunted patients rarely protest or will blandly state: "Well, I don't want to, but it's okay." If they want to leave the hospital, it is to go to a nursing home or halfway house that lets them watch television all day. In the hospital, they lie on the floor, stand in a corner, or sit alone and interact with no one. They have little interest in hospital activities and prefer to smoke and drink soda pop. Outside the hospital, they have no friends, rarely see their family, do not work, and have no hobbies or interests. When asked, "What would you do if you won ten million dollars in the lottery?" they are at a loss and, beyond saying, "I'd put it in a bank or give it to charity," can think of nothing they would like to do. Occasionally, patients with emotional blunting make silly jokes and express a fatuous, but shallow, mood incongruous to the situation. This is *Witzelsucht* (a German term meaning "searching for wit") and is associated with coarse brain disease.

Clinicians sometimes find it difficult to distinguish the emotional blunting of schizophrenics from the changes in affect resulting from depression. A review of Table 3.6, however, will show that the patterns of affective disturbances are usually different between these two groups of patients. Thus, although depressed patients have a decreased affective range, their mood is often profound and intense, with the quality being sadness, dysphoria, or apprehension. Looked at another way, their emotional expression is not lost. Their facial expression is one of sadness or apprehension; their tone of voice suggests sadness or worry. Further, they are often highly concerned about their predicament. Those who are not psychotic want to get better and resume their lives. Those who are psychotic may be convinced that they are bad, are going to die, or should kill themselves, but these are not the thoughts of someone who is indifferent to his situation or surroundings.

Chapter 4

Operational Definitions of Major Psychopathology

II. Speech and Language, Delusions, Perceptual Phenomena, and First-Rank Symptoms

Speech and Language

Odd communication is a common feature of psychiatric disorders, particularly psychosis. Unfortunately, the organization of language and language disorder has received insufficient attention in most discussions of the mental status examination. The Feighner criteria (299) widely used in schizophrenia research, for example, uses as an all-encompassing thought (language) disorder phrase "verbal production that makes communication difficult because of a lack of logical or understandable organization." DSM-III refers to "illogical" and "incomprehensible" speech, DSM-III-R uses the criterion "incoherence or marked loosening of associations," and a proposal for DSM-IV suggests "disorganized speech." Each of these ignores the different processes of language that are helpful in differential diagnosis. In contrast, the neuropsychiatrist, as does the aphasiologist, considers the form of language fundamental for diagnosis. This is necessary because different disorders of communication are associated with different conditions and with dysfunction in different brain regions.

Bleuler (116) coined the term *thought disorder* to indicate his belief that the abnormal speech of schizophrenics resulted from abnormal thinking. Although several investigators have demonstrated thinking problems in schizophrenics, there are no data indicating a direct causal relationship between thinking problems in schizophrenics and their abnormal utterances. Further, the term *thought disorder* is used by different investigators to refer to different phenomena: the form of utterances (formal thought disorder or aphasialike speech), the content of speech (odd or "bizarre" content putatively reflecting odd or bizarre thought), or odd communication (inappropriate interactions) (569). In this book, the term *formal thought disorder* is used to refer to the aphasialike utterances of patients.

A definitive classification of thought disorders does not exist, but many definitions have moderate reliability (43) and are valid to the extent that they tend to discriminate patient groups (44), predict outcome, and relate to differences on electrophysiological measures (10).

The presence of certain thought disorders suggests particular syndromes. For example, rambling speech is characteristic of acute coarse brain disorders (e.g., deliria, intoxications); driveling speech, perseveration, non sequiturs, derailment, paraphasias, and tangential speech are more often associated with chronic coarse brain disorders (e.g., dementia) and schizophrenia; and flight of ideas is the classic speech pattern in mania. Table 4.1 displays the various types of thought disorders, their definitions, associated conditions, and an example of each.

The form of speech and language differs from thought content. The form of speech is characterized by its rate, pressure, rhythm, idiosyncrasy of word usage, grammar (i.e., the rules of language), syntax (i.e., the organization of words into sentences), and associational linkage. The way a patient speaks is *form*; what he is talking about is *content*. Content primarily reflects cultural and personal life experiences, rather than a disease process. Thought content is rarely of diagnostic importance. Exceptions to this rule are the thoughts of suicide, guilt, and hopelessness often expressed by depressed patients or the grandiose ideas of great wealth, power, or high birth expressed by manics. These thoughts, however, also can be conceptualized as either the content of a profound unremitting sadness, which is the essential psychopathologic form of major depressive illness, or the content of an intense euphoric mood, a cardinal feature of mania. Strange or bizarre ideas are never diagnostic and can occur in many conditions (117, 122, 159, 972).

The evaluation of speech and language is the most difficult aspect of the neuropsychiatric examination to master. It demands considerable concentration and practice. The speech of psychiatric patients is often filled with unusual and fascinating content upon which unwary clinicians can focus to the exclusion of form recognition. Skill in determining speech and language dysfunction can be developed only by consciously asking oneself questions about how the patient is using language. For example:

"What are the rate and rhythm of this patient's speech?"

"Is his speech fluent or halting and dysarthric?"

TABLE 4.1

Thought Disorder

Disorder	*Associated Condition*	*Definition*	*Example*
		Formal Disorders	
	Schizophrenia, chronic coarse brain disease		
Driveling speech		Associations are tightly linked and syntax appears preserved, but the meaning (content) of speech is lost (as if patient were speaking an unfamiliar language). It is similar to double talk. Word salad is its most severe form.	"I'm not rejected by the mechanistic frame, but backhoe or not, who needs that done if he couldn't."
Perseveration		Repetition of stock words and phrases is automatically placed into the flow of speech.	"I've been intellectually involved for years. The intellectual flow of thoughts is manifest. My intelligence, your intelligence are all part of the academic intellectual community."
Non sequiturs		In the absence of flight of ideas, the patient's responses are totally unrelated to the examiner's comments or questions.	Q. "How old are you?" A. "I'm a very practical person."
Derailment		A sudden, disrupted switch from one line of thought to a new parallel line of thought occurs.	"I started in the lumber business what the environmentalists don't understand trees mean jobs."

TABLE 4.1 (*Cont.*)

Thought Disorder

Disorder	*Associated Condition*	*Definition*	*Example*
Tangential speech		Tightly linked associations bypass the goal. Responses are vague, allusive, and beside the point, although the general subject matter is related to the question.	Q. "What type of work do you do?" A. "I work in Chicago." Q. "Yes, but what do you do in Chicago?" A. "I've been there a year." Q. "And what have you been working at for that year?" A. "It's hard work."
Neologism		New words are formed by the improper use of the sound of words or the meaningless combination of two or more words.	Sound: globe for glove Combination: combining parallel and circumstantial into parastantial
Private word usage		Words or phrases are used in an idiosyncratic way, which makes their meaning obscure.	"I can't be responsible for the protoplasmic reticulum of his actions."
Word approximations		Words without precise meaning are used.	Using the word "writer" for pen, the phrase "water coffee heater maker" for percolator.
		Other non–aphasia like speech disorders	
Rambling speech	Acute coarse brain disease, intoxications, deliria	Non–goal-directed speech is used. Meaningful connections between phrases or sentences are lost, but the syntax and meaning of the fragments remains generaly intact. It is almost always associated with a decreased level of consciousness.	"It's too hot, turn it off, turn it off. . . Who's that person? . . . I'm not a plumber. . .. Did it rain?"

Flight of ideas	Mania	Jumping from topic to topic, the speaker often responds to external stimuli. Multiple lines of thought can occur. A line of thought often fails to reach its goal.	"I've been working in Chicago for 15 years. The city is too crowded and what is planned parenthood doing about it? Being a parent is not easy and college is expensive. How do we live within our means? I have the answer and the government budget deficit will be solved."
Clang associations	Mania	Associations are made by the sounds rather than the meaning, of words.	"I started in the lumber, tumbler, number business a while back."
Verbigeration	Catatonia (associated with bipolar affective disorder, coarse brain disease, or schizophrenia)	This is verbal stereotype, in which the patient repeats associations, particularly at the end of a thought, in an automatic manner.	"I've been working in Chicago for 15 years, 15 years, 15 years, years, years."
Circumstantial speech	Mania; chronic alcoholism; interictal temporal lobe epilepsy; aging; some personality disorders	Associations are tightly linked, but extra, nonessential associations are interspersed. The speech takes a circuitous route before reaching the goal.	"How long have I been working in Chicago? Let me tell you it hasn't been easy. All that political stuff, then the recessions. My own health problems added to that, you know, but after all this time things have finally turned out OK. It took 15 years, however."

"Is he using precise words?"

"Does his speech make sense; if not, how are his associations linked?"

It is also helpful at some point in the examination to allow the patient to talk for a bit while the examiner listens, not to the content but solely to the patient's use of language.

Although the rate of speech can reflect cultural patterns, severe deviations are commonly observed in mentally ill patients. Slow or hesitant speech is characteristic of depression, altered states of consciousness, and several coarse brain disorders (91; 135; 555, pp. 77–80; 588). Rapid and pressured speech is characteristic of anxiety and mania. The rhythm or cadence of speech can also be disturbed in mentally ill patients. Hesitant speech is often heard in patients with Huntington's chorea (653); scanning speech (where word sounds are stretched, producing a slow, sliding cadence) is characteristic of multiple sclerosis (588); staccato (abrupt and clipped) speech is often a sign of partial epilepsy (122); adult onset stuttering and palilalia (repetition of one's own verbal output) are observed in patients with extrapyramidal lesions (124); and coprolalia (involuntary utterances of profanity) is associated with Gilles de la Tourette's syndrome (202, 766).

Studies of psychiatric patients and patients with coarse brain disease demonstrate striking similarity of speech and word usage (569). This is not surprising because many of the descriptions of the speech of aphasic patients (particularly those with temporoparietal or thalamic lesions) are identical to descriptions of thought disorder (see Table 4.1). The neurologic and psychiatric terms may differ, but the phenomena described are similar, thus suggesting some overlap in the neurologies of formal thought disorder and of some forms of aphasia (764). Table 4.2 displays a comparison of neurologic and psychiatric terms for these elements of speech disorder. The psychiatric terms are defined, and the neurologic term generally is associated with the same speech abnormality. In-class and out-of-class semantic paraphasias need some explanation. An in-class semantic (referring to the meaning of words) or verbal paraphasia is a word usage that, although imprecise, remains understandable because the approximate word or phrase relates to some characteristic of the precise word (e.g., its basic function or class). Thus, pen, pencil, crayon, and chalk are all writing implements, and the in-class word approximation "writer," although imprecise, conveys the meaning. In contrast, an out-of-class semantic or verbal paraphasia is so far removed from the actual thing that the utterance seems idiosyncratic and the meaning is obscure: private word usage. Circumlocutory speech means that the patient refers to an object, event, or person by using phrases related to function or physical characteristic, rather than calling it by its name. For example, a pen becomes "the thing you write with." It is similar to tangential speech in that the patient appears to have understood the subject being discussed and what information he is being asked to communicate, but he cannot precisely communicate that information. What is uttered is vague and allu-

TABLE 4.2

Aphasia and Formal Thought Disorders

Language Disorder	*Neurologic Term*	*Psychiatric Term*
Semantic disorders	Jargon agrammatism	Driveling
	Paragrammatism	Derailment
	Non sequitur	Non sequitur
	Semantic paraphasia (out of class)	Private word usage
	Portmanteau (combination) word	Neologism
Nominal disorders	Verbal paraphasias (in class)	Word approximation
	Anomia	(No equivalent)
	Circumlocutory speech	Tangentiality
Phonemic disorders	Phonemic paraphasias (literal)	Clanging
	Neologism	Neologism

sive (as in tangential speech), or around the point (circumlocutory speech). Aphasia is discussed further in Chapter 5.

Despite the fact that schizophrenics with formal thought disorder and patients with fluent aphasia have similar abnormalities of speech, the two speech patterns differ. Faber et al. (292) demonstrated this difference by blindly rating transcripts of conversations with schizophrenic and aphasic subjects. Although there was significant overlap in individual forms of speech abnormalities, the investigators could establish who was schizophrenic and who was aphasic, even though the speech content was altered to mask any evidence of psychotic features or odd thought content. Table 4.3 displays the observed differences in speech patterns between the two patient groups.

Delusional Phenomena

No single, totally satisfactory definition of a delusion exists. Most definitions, however, include the concept that a delusion is a false or arbitrary idea developed without adequate proof. This false idea can be fixed or fleeting, but it is always

TABLE 4.3

Schizophrenic and Aphasic Language

Feature	*Schizophrenics*	*Wernicke's Aphasics*
Fluency	Adequate	Adequate
Repetition	Adequate	Poor
Auditory comprehension	Adequate	Poor
Use of complex words	Adequate	Very poor
Word-finding problems	Poor	Very poor
Reduced nouns	Poor	Very poor
Private words	Yes	No
Aphasic elements	Yes	Yes

characterized as "not in keeping with the patient's culture" (417) and as involving some thinking problem resulting in "the making of a relationship without adequate proof." The development of delusional ideas can derive from an altered mood (e.g., euphoria, sadness) that distorts the patient's thinking and leads to false conclusions (e.g., euphoric mood leading to feelings of great power and then to the conclusion of being divine) or result from hallucinations and other psychopathologic experiences (e.g., first-rank symptoms) that are felt by the patient to be real, thus providing the "evidence" to support the delusion (e.g., the hallucinated voices warn against danger, and the patient accepts these voices as real; therefore, there is a plot against him). When a delusional idea develops from other psychopathology (e.g., altered mood, hallucinations) as described above, it is termed a *secondary delusional idea* because it is second in sequence of occurrence and (although never proved) appears to result from the initial psychopathology. Secondary delusional ideas seeming to derive from an altered mood state are termed *mood-congruent.* Secondary delusional ideas seemingly derived from other, non-mood-related psychopathology and all primary delusional ideas are termed *mood- incongruent.* The significance of mood-congruent and mood-incongruent delusions is controversial (see Chapter 11).

Primary delusional ideas appear to evolve without obvious development from other psychopathology. An *autochthonous delusional idea* is a particular type of primary delusional idea that develops suddenly and fully formed, rather than insidiously and in stages. Except for the fact that an autochthonous delusional conclusion is fixed, false, and arbitrarily determined, it is similar in form to the "eureka" phenomenon (417).

Although primary and secondary delusional ideas are arbitrary conclusions reached without adequate proof, the patient can often identify "evidence" to support his notion. For example, a patient who repeatedly received recruitment material from the Army concluded that there existed a dangerous, secret government organization and a plot was afoot to silence him. He cited real problems with electrical blackouts in his neighborhood as confirmatory evidence of the plot. This patient's sequence of thought from recruitment material and electrical blackouts to a plot, although arbitrary, has an understandable connection. His conclusion is delusional, but most observers can follow how he reached it. *Delusional perceptions,* on the other hand, are ideas for which no meaningful connection can be found between the "evidence" and the conclusion. Delusional perceptions are based on real perceptions that are then given great significance and personalized by the patient. For example, a patient concluded that a neighbor was going to kill him because a clothing store put a floral display in its window. Delusional perceptions are primary because they do not develop from any other obvious psychopathology.

The simplest delusional experience is termed a *delusional mood.* This phenomenon is characterized by the intense and persistent feeling that "something is wrong" or that "things are not right" and perhaps sinister. It is akin to, but more severe than, the feeling of being watched or the self-consciousness commonly felt by a sensitive person as he encounters a roomful of noisy people who momentarily, become quiet to observe him. When a patient describes his belief that something "bad" is taking place that will adversely affect him and the examiner asks how he knows this, the patient suffering from a delusional mood responds, "Well, I don't know, I'm not sure. I just feel it." Delusional moods can be observed in many serious psychiatric conditions, following viral illnesses, and in association with coarse brain disorders. The term *ideas of reference* refers to the more specific conclusions reached by some patients with a delusional mood. Apparently developing from their general unease and suspiciousness, these patients begin to feel that people (even strangers in the street) are looking at them, watching them, or talking about them. Delusional mood and ideas of reference do not have diagnostic specificity (417).

Perhaps 30 to 40% of severely ill psychiatric patients are delusional. Delusions, however, are not pathognomonic of schizophrenia and occur with equal frequency in patients with affective disorder and coarse brain disease (13; 159; 555, pp. 18–22, pp. 84–85; 972).

When delusional ideas are accepted as real by patients, they may readily reveal these ideas because they feel them to be obvious to everyone. Some patients, aware that other people might think them crazy, are reluctant to reveal strange but—to them—true ideas. When they do describe plots against their lives, special relationships with God, or national and international intrigues, the examiner should express an immediate interest in "these happenings," acquire more specific information about the situation as would any concerned person about a friend's problems, and ultimately determine the form of the delusion by asking the patient for proof (i.e., "How do you know?").

When examining a patient for delusions, the patient is asked about trouble with neighbors, coworkers, or relatives that might reveal his delusional ideas. If he has already described other psychopathologic experiences, questions about delusions can be related to these experiences. For example, the patient who describes hearing voices can be asked if the voices or the sources of the voices try to harm him in any way. Occasionally, despite more subtle techniques, whether the patient is delusional or not remains unclear and the examiner must be more direct with such questions as: "Did you ever have the experience that people were plotting against you (or trying to hurt you, poison you, spy on you? Did you ever have the experience that you saw or heard something that other people felt was unimportant, but you knew that it was a message or signal just for you?"

Overvalued Ideas

All definitions of primary delusions incorporate the notion that the delusional idea evolves from arbitrary or illogical thinking. Patients with severe obsessive compulsive disorder or hypochondriasis, however, also can express ideas that are fixed, clearly false, and derived from what appears to be arbitrary or illogical thinking (464). An overvalued idea is another example of a thought, usually associated with an intense mood, that takes precedence over all other ideas.

Obsessions, hypochondriacal notions, and overvalued ideas may be difficult to distinguish from some primary delusions (other than autochthonous or delusional perception). Three distinguishing features of overvalued ideas are: (1) their expression is usually isolated, without other features of psychosis; (2) their content is typically mundane (e.g., contamination, health), rather than odd or sinister as in many delusions (e.g., poison plots, aliens from Mars); and (3) the patient, though committed to them, is aware that the ideas, at least when first experienced, are unfounded or exaggerated.

Perceptual Phenomena

Perceptual disturbances are quite common among psychiatric patients. Perceptions without any stimuli (hallucinations) and misperceptions of real external stimuli (illusions) are most frequently observed (417). Hallucinations can occur in all sensory modalities—visual, auditory, olfactory, gustatory, tactile, and visceral—and in a variety of nonpathologic conditions, such as fatigue, distractibility, and falling asleep and awakening. Nearly 50% of people without any mental disorder have hallucinated at some time in their lives (417). Anyone who has heard his name paged when no sound came from the loudspeakers has hallucinated. Table 4.4 displays the different forms of perceptual disturbances, their

TABLE 4.4
Perceptual Disturbances

Form	*Definition*	*Correlations*
Illusion	Misinterpretation of a real stimulus (e.g., a bush swaying in the wind seen as a large, threatening animal)	Can occur in the non-ill, in intense mood states, and with fatigue
Pseudo-hallucination	Any vague, poorly formed hallucination	Can occur in the non-ill, drug intoxications, withdrawal states, and in depression
Hypnagogic/ hypnopompic hallucination	Pseudohallucinations occurring respectively upon falling asleep and awakening	Can occur in the non-ill and in narcolepsy
Incomplete auditory hallucination	Most common perceptual disturbance; a muffled or whispered voice limited to a few words	Nonspecific
Complete auditory hallucination	Most common first-rank symptom; a clear, sustained voice perceived as originating from outside the patient's subjective inner space	Schizophrenia, affective disorder, and psychoses secondary to coarse brain disease
Elementary hallucination	Unformed hallucinations, such as flashes of light, unidentified sounds, smells, and tastes	Toxic and epileptic states
Functional hallucination	A hallucination that occurs only immediately after ordinary stimulation in that particular sensory modality (e.g., hearing voices only when the water faucet is turned on)	Toxic and epileptic states, schizophrenia, and affective disorder, particularly depression

(*continued*)

TABLE 4.4 (*Cont.*)
Perceptual Disturbances

Form	*Definition*	*Correlations*
Extracampine hallucination	A hallucination outside the normal sensory field (e.g., seeing people behind you, hearing people talking in another country)	Toxic and epileptic states and schizophrenia
Metamorphopsia	Dysmegalopsia: perceiving objects as becoming larger (macropsia) or smaller (micropsia); dysmorphopsia: perceiving objects as distorted in shape	Epileptic states, schizophrenia, and bipolar affective disorder
	Dysacousia: Hearing sounds as louder (macrocusia) or softer (microcusia) than they are	Epilepsy and affective disorder
Panoramic visual hallucination	Hallucinating entire scenes of action, as if watching a movie	Epilepsy

definitions, and the disorders to which they best correlate. None is pathognomonic.

Hallucinatory experiences are elicited in a manner similar to that used with delusions. The examiner might ask such questions as: "Have people been bothering you or trying to harm you in any way? Have you seen them following you or plotting against you? Do you overhear their conversations about you? Do they say things to you through electronic devices, such as the TV or radio? Can they touch you even when they are not in the room? Can you feel them? Do they do anything to your food? Do they try to harm you with gas that smells bad?" More general questions take the following form:

> "Have you ever had the experience of hearing someone talking to you or about you, but no one was there with you? Have you ever heard voices in the air, but no one was around?"
>
> "Have you ever had the experience of feeling someone touching or poking you, but no one was there?"

"Have you ever had the experience of smelling something odd or illogical, but there was no usual explanation for it?"

"Have you ever had the experience of seeing something odd, unusual, or frightening that other people didn't see?"

The development of rapport with the patient is vital if adequate information is to be obtained about delusions and perceptual disturbances. A frequently helpful statement is "I have spoken with other people who had experiences [feelings, situations] similar to yours, and they also experienced. . . ." The examiner then offers examples of delusions and hallucinations. Many patients respond with, "Yes, I've had that happen to me, too." Details usually follow. On rare occasions, a fruitful question might be: "Have you recently had any frightening experiences or experiences you couldn't explain?" Examples of "voices" and "visions" can be given. Some chronic patients respond to the direct: "You've heard many patients here complain about being bothered by voices. Has that ever happened to you?"

Occasionally, during a discussion of his delusional ideas or hallucinatory experiences, a patient will ask, "Do you think I'm right?" The best response is, "I understand what you're saying and I know you feel these experiences are true, but I think there is another explanation." When the patient says, "No, there isn't," go on to the next logical topic. If the patient insists on an opinion, the examiner should offer the explanation that the experiences are signs and symptoms of an illness (i.e., the mind playing tricks). After going "on the record," the examiner should not argue. Many patients trust a truthful examiner far more than one who appeases them, treats them as if they were crazy, or disregards their feelings and debates the validity of their experiences.

Psychosensory Symptoms

Psychosensory symptoms, typical of partial epilepsy, also occur in schizophrenia and mood disorders (see Chapter 11). These features overlap in form with some of the perceptual disturbances (hallucinations) previously described. In addition, they include visceral hallucinations, dysmegalopsia and dysacousia, depersonalization and derealization, déjà vu and jamais vu experiences, paroxysmal autonomic and emotional states, and emotional incontinence. Questions to elicit these phenomena include:

"Have you ever experienced the feeling as if there was a foreign object inside your body, or a cold, empty feeling inside your belly that pushes up into your chest?" (visceral hallucination)

"Have you ever experienced hearing sounds as unnaturally too loud or too soft even though other people didn't notice?" (dysacousia)

"Have you ever had the experience, when awake and going about your business, that suddenly things around you don't seem real, as if you were in a dream?" (derealization)

"Have you ever had the experience, when awake and going about your business, that suddenly you feel detached from yourself, as if you were floating above yourself and watching yourself going through the motions?" (depersonalization)

"Have you ever had the experience of going to a new place and having the strong feeling you had been there before and had said and done before the things you were really doing for the first time?" (déjà vu)

"Have you ever had the experience of going to a place where you had been many times, but it all seemed unfamiliar and you didn't recognize the place or the people?" (jamais vu)

"Have you ever had the experience of suddenly feeling very cold or very hot for just a few minutes, but it wasn't because of the temperature in the room or outside? Or suddenly feeling your heart beating very fast or heavily, even though you weren't scared or doing any exercise?" (autonomic paroxysms)

"Have you ever had the experience of being in your usual health when suddenly, for no reason you felt intensely sad (or happy), and, after lasting for a few seconds or minutes, this feeling went away?" (emotional paroxysm)

"Have you ever had the experience where you weren't feeling sad (or happy), but you suddenly found yourself crying (or laughing) for no reason or thought and were embarrassed or frightened by it? (emotional incontinence)

Positive answers to several of the above questions suggest that the patient has a disorder involving temporolimbic dysfunction. If epilepsy can be ruled out, the patient, particularly if he has a mood disorder, may respond to valproic acid or carbamazepine.

First-Rank Symptoms of Schneider

Kurt Schneider, a German psychiatrist, was the first to describe systematically certain clinical phenomena that he termed first-rank symptoms (878). Based solely on his clinical experience, Schneider concluded: "When any of these modes of experiences is undeniably present, and no basic somatic illness can be found, we may make the decisive clinical diagnosis of schizophrenia." Schneider regarded these symptoms as "first-rank" only in the diagnostic sense and offered no theoretical framework to explain them. Schneider's first-rank symptoms generated great interest in the phenomenologic study of schizophrenia, but investigations have demonstrated that, although first-rank symptoms occur in 60 to 75% of rigorously defined schizophrenics, they are also experienced by individuals with affective disorder, particularly during manic episodes. Complete auditory hallucinations are most common, but the precise frequency of each phenomenon is unclear (159, 162, 555, 972). Despite this research, first-rank symptoms have been adopted into the DSM system and form the core features of the inclusion criteria for schizophrenia.

Schneider listed 11 first-rank symptoms, which can be conveniently categorized under five headings: (1) thought broadcasting, (2) experiences of influence, (3) experiences of alienation, (4) complete auditory hallucinations, and (5) delusional perceptions (described above in the subsection on delusional phenomena). Neither Schneider nor the framers of DSM-III and DSM-III-R provide specific operational definitions for each phenomenon. Clinical and research experience, however, suggest that the operationalized definitions given below for categories 1 through 4 are useful.

Thought broadcasting refers to the relatively uncommon phenomenon of a patient literally experiencing his thoughts escaping from his head. The patient "feels" his thoughts diffusing out of him and then hears them in the external world. Patients often have secondary delusional ideas involving telepathy, electronic surveillance, or metaphysical intervention to explain the phenomenon. The examination for thought broadcasting often begins with questions about associated secondary delusional ideas. Once the form of these ideas has been established, the examiner can proceed to such questions as: "Do you feel people know what you're thinking?" "Can others really hear your thoughts?" "You mean, if I were standing next to you, I could hear your thoughts coming out of your head, as loud as my voice?" "Come on, you mean to say it's as if your head were a radio and everyone around you can hear what you're thinking?" When a patient expresses the feeling that others can read his mind or says he believes that people know what he's thinking by the expression on their faces, he most probably has delusional ideas. Only affirmative responses to the above questions, however, satisfy a strict definition of thought broadcasting.

Some patients describe the experience that their body sensations, feelings, impulses, thoughts, and actions are controlled and manipulated by an external agency. They believe that they must passively submit to the experience, which is literally felt on or within their bodies. Schneider termed this passivity phenomenon *experiences of influence*. Patients often develop secondary delusional ideas as explanations of the nature of these experiences. In examining for this phenomenon, the clinician needs to be specific. Productive questions include: "Have people been trying to hypnotize you, turn you into a puppet or a robot?" "Do they use electronics or other energy to make you do things against your will?" "Do you actually feel them moving you . . . forcing you to think those thoughts?" Patients often (and at times correctly) feel that others (family, doctors, nurses) are trying to control them or influence their thinking. To be a first-rank symptom, however, the influence must be (1) physically experienced; (2) be perceived as irresistible; and (3) attributed to a controlling mechanism that is delusional, either fantastic (e.g., ozone rays from the stratosphere) or manifestly improbable (e.g., neighbors beaming microwaves through the cable television box).

In contrast to experiences of influence, *experiences of alienation* are the subjective disowning of one's feelings, thoughts, or movements. The patient experiences (feels) his mental activity or actions literally belonging to someone else. Some patients with large parietal lobe lesions also deny any relationship to certain of their body parts (usually those contralateral to the lesion) (229, 544, Chapter 17). Although this phenomenon is similar to the Schneiderian experience of alienation, cerebral localization has never been demonstrated for any first-rank symptom. The presence of experiences of alienation also can be assessed by first asking about secondary delusional ideas that often accompany them. Specific questions are: "Have you ever had the experience where you were literally forced to think someone else's thoughts?" ". . . where the thoughts in your head belonged to another person?" ". . . where your arms or your legs were not yours, but belonged to someone else?"

Schneider also described hallucinated voices, occurring in clear consciousness, that are clearly audible, experienced as coming from outside the patient's subjective space, and sustained in duration. Using the term *complete auditory hallucinations*, he included in this category voices continually commenting on the patient's actions, multiple voices discussing the patient among themselves, or a voice repeating the patient's thoughts (thought echo). Complete auditory hallucination is the most common first-rank symptom.

Chapter

5

The Cognitive and Behavioral Neurologic Examination

Routine evaluations of neurologic function focus on such areas as the brain stem, cerebellum, basal ganglia, motor and sensory strips, and the long tracts. In contrast, the associational areas of the cortex and their related subcortical structures (areas primarily associated with complex and cognitive behavior) can be overlooked during these evaluations. Modern procedures and tests of higher cortical functions (i.e., language, thinking, memory, visuospatial ability), however, are reliable, valid, and sensitive (431, 544, 595, 672, 1000). They are combined into the cognitive and behavioral neurologic examination for one of two reasons: (1) to confirm previously obtained clinical information or (2) to elicit new information that identifies the many psychiatric patients who have substantial impairment in their higher cognitive functioning. For example, 50 to 75% of schizophrenics and 25 to 50% of bipolar patients have mild to severe cognitive impairment (978). The pattern of impairment among schizophrenics is diffuse and associated with chronicity and emotional blunting. The pattern among bipolar patients is bifrontal and visuospatial (979). Patients with obsessive compulsive disorder exhibit visuospatial and visual memory impairment (125, 1094). Patients with coarse brain disease often present with psychiatric syndromes; the cognitive and behavioral neurologic examination also helps to identify these patients and to determine whether the coarse disease is diffuse or localized.

The clinical cognitive examination section of the neuropsychiatric evaluation can be conceptually divided into three phases: (1) determination of level of consciousness and screening for diffuse impairment, (2) testing of specific cognitive functions, and (3) interpretation of the findings.

Level of Consciousness and Screening for Diffuse Impairment

Determining level of consciousness begins upon meeting the patient. Usually, the neuropsychiatrist is not asked to examine comatose patients (other than from drug overdose); in this uncommon circumstance, the assessment of level of consciousness is straightforward. Most often, the neuropsychiatrist sees patients whose levels of consciousness fall into three broad categories: (1) stupor, (2) mild to moderate decrease in consciousness, and (3) full alertness.

Stupor is associated with catatonia, depression, mania, epilepsy, severe intoxication, and delirium. In profound stupor, the patient is mute and immobile and has generalized analgesia. When stupor is associated with catatonia, the patient appears to be awake and may follow the examiner about the room with his eyes, as do patients with akinetic mutism. Specific catatonic features (e.g., catalepsy, automatic obedience) also are present. Intravenous (IV) sodium amobarbital or a short-acting benzodiazepine in doses titrated to the patient's behavioral response (usually 1–2 mg/kg of sodium amobarbital over 60–120 seconds) transiently resolves the stupor and permits the patient to speak, move about, and take nourishment and fluids. Profound stupor associated with depression also responds to IV sodium amobarbital, thus permitting conversation between the patient and examiner, which often reveals depressive symptoms. The "sodium Amytal interview" is a helpful adjunct to the neuropsychiatric evaluation (969).

The stupor associated with mania is rarely profound. When this is the case, it occurs periodically, alternating with excited states. Kraepelin termed this fluctuation of excited and stuporous states periodic catatonia. More commonly, however, manic patients experience milder and briefer periods of alteration in consciousness, during which they appear perplexed and dazed (i.e., expressionless face, unfocused visual tracking) despite their continued hyperactivity and pressured speech. Their responses to the examiner or staff are perfunctory and vague, and they may appear to be in an excited delirium, which Kraepelin termed delirious mania.

The altered states of consciousness associated with epilepsy, severe intoxication, and delirium differ. In epilepsy, the patient appears awake and may move about and speak, but his actions seem disconnected from external stimuli, as if he is in a trance (not responding when spoken to). The altered state of severe intoxications associated with CNS depressants is usually more profound and constant, whereas the altered state of delirium is more fluctuating (771). Delirium and epilepsy are discussed in detail in Chapters 12 and 13, respectively.

Typically, patients in an altered state of consciousness are unable to perform cognitive tests. Those who can do the tests almost always exhibit diffuse performance deficits. Although the examiner may try to obtain cognitive information from such patients, this effort is best reserved for patients who are alert. An alteration in consciousness indiscriminantly depresses performance on all tests.

In addition to not being perplexed and not looking dazed or as if in a trance, alert individuals are able to attend to a simple continuous task. This can be easily assessed by a letter cancellation test (Figure 5.1). The examiner instructs the patient as follows: "I am going to read a series of letters to you. Every time you hear the letter A, I want you to tap this desk with this pencil." The examiner in a clear, sufficiently loud voice then reads the series of letters at the rate of one letter per second. He records all errors of omission (the patient not responding when the letter A is read, usually associated with distractibility) and comission (the patient responding to letters other than A, usually a sign of perseveration). Two or more errors of either type are clinically significant, and two or more errors of both types suggest either extreme distractibility (as seen in some manic patients) or an altered state of consciousness. If more than five errors occur, further cognitive testing probably will be invalid. Any letter can be substituted for the letter A, so that, if necessary, the test can be given to the same patient many times.

Finally, level of consciousness is also assessed when patients are asked the usual questions of orientation: time, place, person. Of these, the most sensitive to level of consciousness is the time of day, with more than a half-hour error being suspicious.

After the examiner determines that the patient is alert, not overly distracted, and reasonably motivated to cooperate, he screens for diffuse cognitive impairment. A number of screening tests are available. Table 5.1 displays the Mini-Mental State (316). This pencil-and-paper screening test takes about 15 to 20 minutes to administer and provides a numerical score. Scores of 24 or less are suggestive of coarse brain disease, and scores of 20 or less indicate diffuse impairment and correlate reasonably well with diffuse abnormalities on brain imaging studies (1000). However, the Mini-Mental State is not sensitive to localized or small to moderate circumscribed lesions, so that even a score of 30 (while eliminating the possibility of diffuse impairment) does not rule out coarse brain disease. The examiner, therefore, must supplement such screening tests with further tests of specific functions.

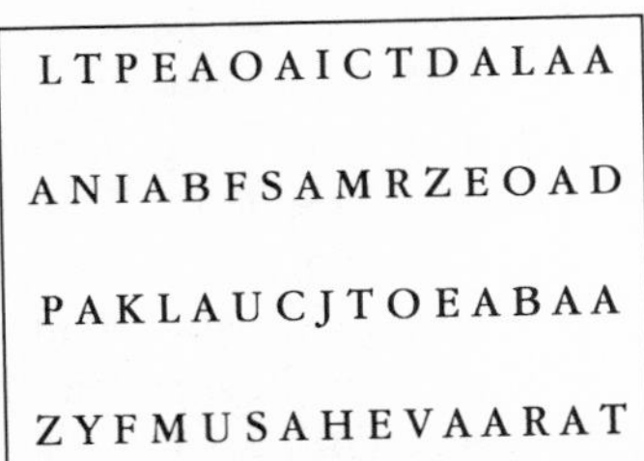
L T P E A O A I C T D A L A A

A N I A B F S A M R Z E O A D

P A K L A U C J T O E A B A A

Z Y F M U S A H E V A A R A T

Figure 5.1. Letter Cancellation Test: The "A" Test

SOURCE: From *Neurobehavioral Disorders: A Clinical Approach* by R. L. Strub and F. N. Black, 1988, Philadelphia: F. A. Davis Company, p. 58. Reprinted with permission.

TABLE 5.1

The Mini-Mental State Examination

Specific Test	*Function*	*Points*	*Score*
1. What is the year/ season/day/date/month?	Orientation	5	
2. What is the state/county/ town/hospital floor?	Orientation	5	
3. Repeat three items.	Registration	3	
4. Serial subtraction of sevens or spell "world" backwards	Concentration	5	
5. Name wristwatch and pen.	Naming	2	
6. Say "No ifs, ands, or buts."	Expressive speech	1	
7. Take this paper in your right hand, fold it in half, and put it on the table.	Three-state command	3	
8. Read "close your eyes" and do it.	Reading	1	
9. Remember the three items from Part 3.	Short-term memory	3	
10. Write a sentence.	Writing	1	
11. Copy intersecting pentagons.	Construction	1	

SOURCE: From "Mini-Mental State" by M. F. Folstein, S. W. Folstein, and P. R. McHugh, 1975, *Journal of Psychiatric Research, 12*. Reprinted with permission.

Testing of Specific Cognitive Functions

Table 5.2 lists the major cognitive functions and the tests used to assess them. As the Mini-Mental State is a screening test, many of its items relate to several functions in Table 5.2. The Mini-Mental State does best in coverage of language function (five items) but does not assess thinking, visual memory, and interhemisphere transfer. When it does assess some functions (e.g., constructional ability), the assessment is incomplete; the examiner must do further testing before he can reach a reasoned conclusion as to the presence of a deficit and its meaning.

In assessing cognitive function, several general rules apply. The examining room should be well lighted and quiet, and the patient should be in a reasonably comfortable position for writing. A hard surface (e.g., desk, dining cart) should be used for testing of writing and drawing. Instructions should be given with the utmost clarity.

Findings should be reported objectively; any error should be recorded as such.

TABLE 5.2

Cognitive Function Assessment

Function	*Tests Used*
Attention and concentration	Serial sevens and spelling "world" backwards (Item 4 on Mini-Mental State), letter cancellation
Motor	Handedness questions, extrapyramidal/cerebellar/frontal motor tasks (see Chapter 3), praxis (constructional [Item 11 on Mini-Mental State], ideomotor, kinesthetic, dressing)
Language	Spontaneous speech, repetition (Item 3 on Mini-Mental State), auditory comprehension (Item 7 on Mini-Mental State), writing (Item 10 on Mini-Mental State), naming (Item 5 on Mini-Mental State), reading (Item 8 on Mini-mental State), reading comprehension
Thinking	Judgment, problem solving, calculations, similarities, verbal and pictorial absurdities
Memory	Verbal immediate recall (Item 3 on Mini-Mental State), visual immediate recall working memory, verbal (Item 9 on Mini-Mental State) and visual delayed recall; biographical memory
Visuospatial	Facial recognition, topographic orientation, spatial neglect, construction (Item 11 on Mini-Mental State)
Integrating functions	Stereognosia, graphesthesia, tests of interhemisphere information transfer and coordination

If an examiner thinks, "Well, he got that wrong only because he was tired, so I won't report it," that is an interpretation, not an observation. The examiner must be prepared to "judge" the normal speed and correctness of the patient's responses against a normal standard, usually his own performance. For example, when the examiner instructs the patient, "Touch your left hand to your right ear," after one trial, the patient should be able to respond to similar commands immediately. The patient may require supportive comments from the examiner (e.g., "Try your best; there's no penalty if you make an error"). The examiner should be patient with individuals whose brain dysfunction makes them slow to reply. The goal of testing is to determine the best, not the worst, performance.

The testing outlined below takes about 45 minutes. If evidence from the history, the mental status, or the Mini-Mental State is suggestive of coarse brain disease, these 45 minutes are well worth the effort. At best, they reveal specific deficits and lesion loci; at worst, they permit the examiner to ask intelligent questions of the neuroradiologist, electroencephalographer or neuropsychologist, so that a specific anatomic or pathophysiologic diagnosis can be made.

If information from the history, mental status examination, and Mini-Mental State converge to indicate no coarse brain disease, it may not be practical to do all of the testing described below. Rather than shortening the examination by reducing the number of trials per test (this strategy reduces reliability) or the number of tests per cognitive function (this strategy reduces validity), the examiner can either defer this part of the examination or, based on the clinical and cognitive screening information available, test those functions likely to give the highest yield for that patient. For example, although the patient's history and mental status examination do not suggest coarse brain disease, some of his comments and responses seem vague or odd, and the examiner decides to test thinking and language; or the patient's description of past events seems a bit disjointed, and the examiner decides to test memory. The risk in deferring this part of the examination is the possibility of increasing false-negative conclusions by omission. Under some circumstances (e.g., overwhelming clinical load, no likely practical effect on treatment), this omission may be justified.

Motor Functions

The assessment of motor behavior is a prominent part of the mental status examination (see Chapter 3). The behavioral neurologic examination requires further testing of motor functions. Chapter 3 describes extrapyramidal and cerebellar motor tests. This chapter describes frontal and parietal lobe motor tests. Table 5.3 and 5.4 display frontal and parietal lobe motor signs and tests. Some of these tests determine the presence of *soft neurologic signs* (e.g., adventitious motor overflow, motor impersistence, Gegenhalten). Although these signs are clear evidence of brain dysfunction, they are less localizing than paralysis or cranial nerve signs; therefore, they are termed "soft." These signs occur in 70% or more of psychotic patients (224, 792).

Adventitious Motor Overflow

Adventitious motor overflow is tested by asking the patient to hold both arms straight out in front of him for 20 seconds; choreiform jerks may appear. Patients with chorea often exhibit sudden involuntary hand movements, which they convert into socially accepted actions (e.g., smoothing hair, fixing tie), and these movements can be readily observed. Adventitious motor overflow, however, must be distinguished from agitation. Unlike agitation, adventitious overflow is not an expression of an intense mood (although anxiety can make it worse) and can be observed in calm individuals (225, 792).

TABLE 5.3
Frontal Lobe Motor Signs

Motor Sign	*Description*
Impersistence	Inability to sustain simple motor tasks (e.g., making a fist, holding out an arm) each for 20 seconds despite adequate sensory function and motor strength. If present only when eyes closed, it may reflect parietal lobe dysfunction.
Perseveration	Unnecessary repetitions or maintenance of a simple movement. When drawing or writing, the same shapes or letters may be repeated.
Inertia	Inability or difficulty in starting or stopping movement. Catalepsy is a striking form of motor inertia.
Adventitious overflow	Choreiform movements and extraneous movements in body parts not involved in a specific movement (e.g., protruding the tongue while writing).
Poor sequencing	Inability to carry out smoothly and rapidly a sequence of actions, such as touching a tabletop alternatively with the side of fist, edge of hand, and palm and breaking contact with the table surface between position changes.

Motor Persistence

The examiner should note whether the patient is able to sustain a motor action. He should ask the patient to perform the following four tasks and note whether the patient is able to continue each task for at least 20 seconds:

1. "Hold out your arms."
2. "Make a fist with both of your hands."
3. "Stick out your tongue."
4. "Close your eyes tightly."

Inability to persist with both extremities with eyes open may be due to the frontal lobe dysfunction called motor impersistence or to motor weakness of one or both upper extremities (544, Chapter 13; 980). To distinguish between the two, motor strength is tested as in the general neurologic examination. Patients with normal motor persistence and strength then should be asked to close their eyes and again hold out their arms for 20 seconds. If one or both arms drift downward before 20 seconds, the parietal lobe contralateral to the drifting hand may be affected (229; 544, Chapter 17).

TABLE 5.4

Parietal Lobe Motor Features: Dyspraxias

Feature	*Description*
Ideomotor	Inability to perform simple motor tasks on command (e.g., demonstrate the use of a key, a hammer, and scissors), despite understanding the task and having adequate motor strength and sensory function. Patient's attempts can range from awkwardness and lack of coordination to grossly nonfunctional movements and using body part as object (e.g., extending index finger as the key rather than using the index finger and thumb to turn the imaginary key). Ideomotor dyspraxia generally suggests dominant parietal lobe dysfunction. When it occurs in the nonpreferred hand only, it may indicate a disconnection syndrome.
Kinesthetic	Inability to position one's hands, arms, and legs on command or inability to copy the examiner's movements despite adequate understanding of the tasks, motor strength, and sensory function. Patient's attempts may be inaccurate or simply aborted, as he seems unable to know what to do with his body to achieve the required positioning. Suggests dysfunction in the parietal lobe contralateral to the affected side.
Constructional	Inability to copy the outline of simple shapes despite adequate understanding of the task, motor strength, and sensory function. Patient's attempts may range from some distortion and rotation of the copy to total loss of its gestalt. Constructional difficulties generally suggest nondominant hemisphere dysfunction. When the performance with the nonpreferred hand is better than that of the preferred hand, the dysfunction may be in the dominant hemisphere or corpus callosum.
Dressing	Inability to dress oneself, despite adequate understanding of the task, motor strength, and sensory function. Patient's attempts may range from putting on clothing (e.g., robe) backwards or upside down to being totally unable to maneuver the garment and his body into the proper positions for dressing. Suggests nondominant hemisphere dysfunction.

Termination of Motor Actions—Perseveration

The frontal lobe is associated with the ability to start and stop motor actions (611). One abnormality of this function is called perseveration, which is the unnecessary repetition or maintenance of action. It can spontaneously occur or be elicited by one of the following four methods:

1. The patient is asked to copy a design or shape that "lends itself" to unnecessary repetition (Figure 5.2).
2. The patient is asked to perform a three-stage command, such as "Take this piece of paper in your right hand, fold it in half, and return it to me." A common perseverated response is for the patient to fold the paper in fourths or eighths.
3. The patient is asked to perform a task, such as "Place your left hand to your right ear" (a test of right-left orientation); despite precise instructions to lower his hand once the task is completed, he maintains the posture on subsequent tasks.
4. Occasionally, a patient is asked to perform a sequence of tasks. If, following a request to do a new task, he continues to perform the earlier requested action, he has perseverated.

Because of such dysfunctions as perseveration, frontal lobe abnormalities often produce false-positive findings on testing of functions of other regions of the brain. For example, a patient is asked to draw the outline of a Greek cross (constructional praxis) after having been asked to draw a square. He again draws a square, which to the untrained examiner could be mistaken for a severely dyspraxic response (544, Chapter 19). In this case, the patient is asked to do a number of drawings to clarify his ability to perform the task. A behavior related to motor perseveration is difficulty in initiating motor tasks. Some patients are virtually

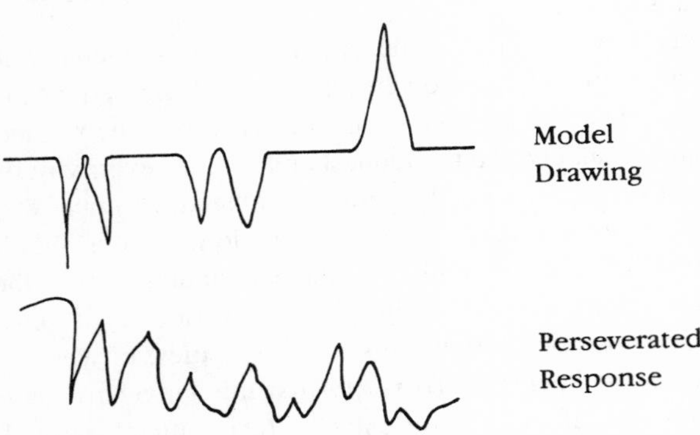

Figure 5.2. A Drawing that Lends Itself to Perseveration

immobile, moving extremely slowly and hesitantly. The combination of difficulty initiating motor tasks and difficulty stopping the task once started (perseveration) is termed *motor inertia* (611).

Motor Sequencing

Motor sequencing can be tested by asking the patient to touch a table surface alternatively with the side of his fist, the edge of his hand, and then his palm. He is to break contact with the table surface between position changes. Thus, the sequence is: side of fist, off the table, edge of hand, off the table, palm, off the table. Each hand is separately tested and about 15 position changes with each hand should be done. After an initial trial or two, a continued hesitancy in position transitions, confusion among positions, or a major disruption of motion indicates problems with sequencing.

Stimulus-Bound Motor Behavior

Normally, one's motor actions can be controlled despite the presence of conflicting or distracting stimuli. In some individuals with cerebral dysfunction (particularly, frontal lobe), this ability is lost. Their motor behaviors become disrupted and then locked to the distracting stimuli. These abnormalities are termed stimulus-bound behavior; they include echopraxia and Gegenhalten (969).

Echopraxia refers to the patient's copying the actions of the examiner, even after receiving specific instructions not to do so. In its severest form, which is rare, the patient spontaneously mimics an action of the examiner. To test the severity, the examiner elevates his hands above his head and maintains this position for several seconds while he has the patient's attention. If the patient elevates his hands, he has echopraxia. At this point, the examiner should say, "You don't have to do that; you don't have to raise your arms." If the patient keeps his arms elevated or if the patient again elevates his arms when the examiner next raises his, the echopraxia is severe.

The examiner may also instruct the patient, "When I touch my nose, you touch your chin." The examiner then touches his nose. If the patient touches his own nose, he has manifested echopraxia. Several trials may be needed to assess (1) whether the patient understood the request and (2) the severity of the echopraxia.

The examiner might also ask the patient to extend his upper extremities in an anterior direction and then state, "I'd like you to do with your right hand what I do with my right hand." Once he thinks that the patient understands the task, he then places the fingers and palm of his right hand in various positions. If the patient copies these hand positions with his left hand (regardless of what he does with his right hand), he has echopraxia. To verify that this latter error is the product of echopraxia, and not left-right disorientation (a dominant parietal dysfunction) (229), the patient is also tested for right-left orientation.

To determine the presence of *Gegenhalten,* the examiner instructs the patient to relax his arms and then attempts to flex and extend the patient's hand, forearm, or arm. If the patient's muscles give equal and opposite resistance to the examiner's maneuvers (despite instructions not to offer any resistance), the patient has manifested Gegenhalten. Gegenhalten can occur with the patient offering equal and opposite resistance to gentle pressure exerted against any part of his body. Although Gegenhalten often localizes to the frontal lobe, it is considered a neurologic "soft sign" (743).

Handedness

Handedness is a crude, but reasonable, clinical measure for predicting which hemisphere is dominant for language; this is helpful in determining the lesion site. Generally speaking, the more right-handed the person, the more likely he is to be dominant for language in the left hemisphere. By definition, the term "dominant hemisphere" refers to the cerebral hemisphere that is organized functionally to process symbolic, usually language-related information. In 97% of people, the dominant hemisphere is the left or dominance is mixed; in 3%, the dominant hemisphere is the right. Ninety percent of people are right-handed (dextral); in all but 1% of right-handers, the left hemisphere is dominant for language. The remaining 10% of people are left-handed (sinistral). Of these, 60% have language organized in the left hemisphere (it is "dominant"), and 40% have mixed dominance for language or language organized in the right hemisphere. Thus, the clinician should be more alert to the possibility of mixed or right hemispheric dominance for language in sinistrals (86, 356).

The assessment of a patient's handedness should be done during the testing of motor function. First, hand preference for writing is determined. The examiner must confirm that the patient's hand preference for writing is a natural tendency and not the product of having been required as a child to write with the nonpreferred hand. To do this, the examiner should ask the patient to state his hand preference and then demonstrate with which hand he pours liquids, holds his knife to cut food, holds scissors, throws a ball, and holds a thread when threading a needle. Most individuals who write with the right hand also use the right hand for these purposes. Left-handers often give mixed responses.

Idiokinetic Praxis

Idiokinetic (ideomotor) praxis (355) is the ability to perform an action from memory on request without props or pantomimed cues. Primary motor and sensory function must be intact, and the patient must understand the tasks asked of him. To rule out the effect of interhemispheric dysconnection, the nonpreferred hand is tested first. For the same reason, the patient should not be allowed to cue himself by restating the instruction. The patient is asked, "Make believe you have a key in your left (nonpreferred) hand, and without saying anything show me how you would use it." Other tests of idiokinetic praxis include: "Make believe you have a comb in your left hand and, without saying anything, show me how you would use it." "Imagine you have a coin in your left hand and, without saying anything, show me how you would flip it." "Make believe you have a hammer in your left hand and, without saying anything, show me how you would use it." The patient should be able to mime these actions well. Common errors include awkwardly performing actions; miming only with proximal movements, while distal movements (hand and wrist) are stiff or absent; using the hand as the object itself (e.g., extending the index finger as if it were the key, hitting the imaginary nail with the fist instead of using the hand as the bearer of the object), or being unable to perform the task without verbalizing the action (verbal overflow).

In patients with interhemispheric dysconnection, idiokinetic praxis is normal in the hand (usually the right) contralateral to the dominant (usually the left) hemisphere and abnormal in the other hand. In patients with dominant parietal lobe dysfunction, idiokinetic dyspraxia occurs with both hands.

Kinesthetic Praxis

Kinesthetic praxis is the ability to mimic hand, finger, and other limb positions presented to the patient by the examiner (354). The examiner says to the patient, "What I do with my right hand, you do with your right hand, and what I do with my left hand, you do with your left hand." He then presents a variety of hand positions to the patient and asks the patient to mimic these. If the patient cannot reproduce these hand positions, he is manifesting kinesthetic dyspraxia, reflecting malfunction in the parietal lobe contralateral to the hand being tested. If the examiner places the patient's hand and fingers into various positions outside the patient's view and asks the patient to duplicate the position with the other hand, he is testing interhemispheric transfer of kinesthetic information. Kinesthetic praxis can be tested simultaneously with echopraxia.

Constructional Praxis

Constructional ability is tested by asking the patient to copy the outline of an object (e.g., a Greek cross, a key [see Figure 5.3]) (1058). To eliminate facilitating (e.g., straight lines) or distracting (e.g., other drawings) cues, each drawing should be done on a separate blank 8-by-11–inch sheet of unlined paper. The examiner should show the object to the patient and give the instructions: "I'd like you to copy the outline or shape of this object without taking your pen (or pencil) off the paper. Your drawing should be the same size as the object I am showing you and should be in the center of the page." The object to be copied should remain in full view of the patient. If the patient lifts the pen during the task, he should be asked to repeat the drawing. If the drawing is inaccurate (overall shape is important, not

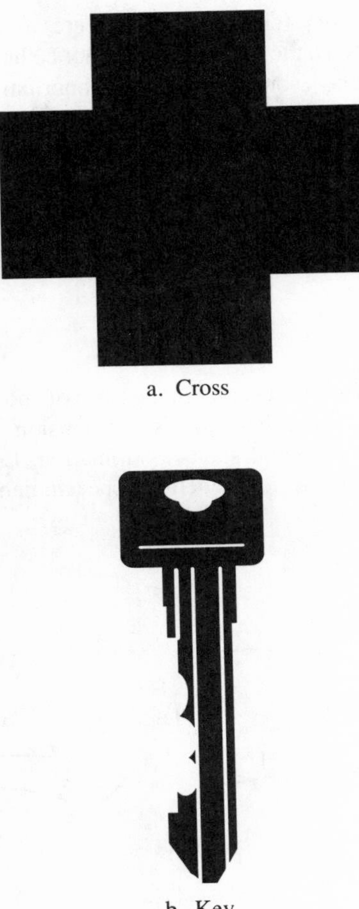

a. Cross

b. Key

Figure 5.3. Constructional Task Model Objects

details), the dysfunction is called constructional dyspraxia. The patient's inability to complete the drawing without lifting his pen in midtask may indicate that he has dyspraxia. If he draws the shape incorrectly with his preferred hand, he should repeat the drawing with the other hand. When the preferred-hand drawing is incorrect and the drawing with his nonpreferred hand is accurate, the dysfunction is likely the product of interhemispheric dysconnection (577). If both drawings are inaccurate, the dysfunction is most likely in the nondominant parietal region. The reason the patient is asked to copy only the outline of the object is to minimize the likelihood that accurate copying of the small details within the object's boundaries may require verbal reasoning (dominant hemisphere) as well as nondominant parietal lobe functioning; thus, the drawing would not be helpful in lateralizing dysfunction. Figure 5.4 displays some examples of abnormal construction.

Dressing Praxis

Dressing praxis is the ability of the patient to dress and undress himself efficiently. When a patient make errors, such as putting on clothes inside out or putting his feet in shirtsleeves, he probably has nondominant parietal dysfunction (898).

Language Functions

Language is the use of symbols, usually in the form of spoken or written words, to convey meaning. Assessment of language is an extension of the thought processes and content section of the mental status examination. Language functions (see Table 5.5) include spontaneous and repetitive speech, naming, reading and read-

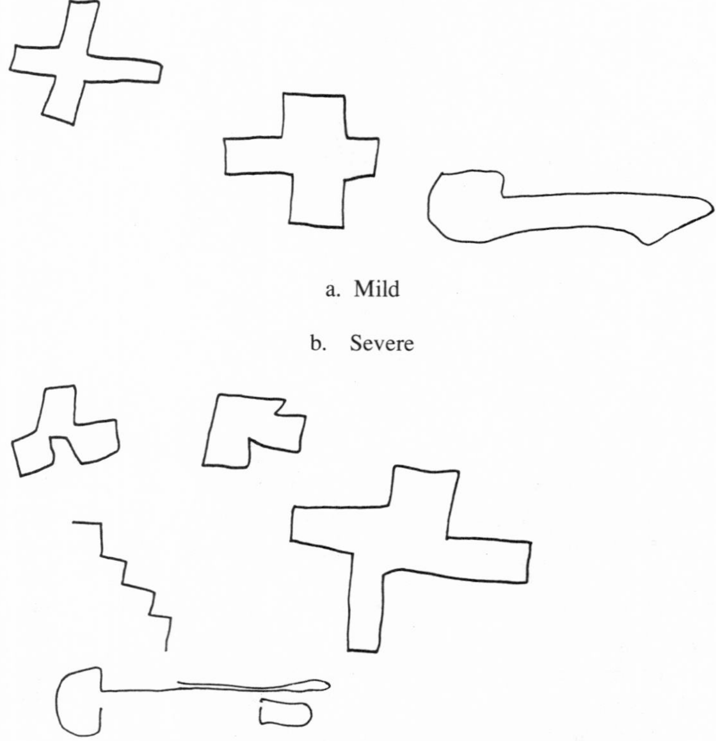

Figure 5.4. Abnormal Construction Efforts

TABLE 5.5
Language Assessment

Function	*Factors to be Assessed*
Spontaneous speech	Fluent or nonfluent Nonlabored or labored No dysarthria or dysarthria No paucity or paucity No formal thought disorder or formal thought disorder
Verbal fluency	Verbal fluency OK, verbal fluency abnormal
Naming	Naming to challenge Locating object to name
Repetition	Repeating three phrases and three sentences
Writing	Spontaneous sentence Sentences to dictation
Reading	Words Sentences Comprehending the sentences
Prosody	Spontaneous prosody and gesturing Expressive prosody Receptive prosody: tone of voice, facial expression

ing comprehension, writing, and auditory comprehension. Language functions, by definition, are primarily subserved by the dominant hemisphere, but the "affective components" of language (i.e., prosody) are subserved by the nondominant hemisphere (847, 848, 1049).

Speech

The function of speech localizes primarily to the parasylvian areas of the frontal, temporal, and parietal lobes of the dominant hemisphere for words and word usage and the nondominant hemisphere for the "affectivity" of speech. These areas in the dominant hemisphere include Broca's area, the frontal cortex deep to Broca's area, the supplementary motor cortex, the arcuate fasciculus connecting Broca's area to Wernicke's area, Wernicke's area and adjacent temporal lobe structures, and the supramarginal gyrus of the parietal lobe (92, 135). Disturbances of speech rate and rhythm are discussed in Chapter 4.

The clinician's initial assessment of the patient's speech is to determine whether it is fluent or nonfluent, labored or nonlabored. Fluency of speech is a function of Broca's area, the frontal cortex deep to it, and the supplementary motor cortex. Speech fluency can be grossly estimated simply by listening to the extent, continuity, and fluidity of the patient's utterances. A standardized, sensitive test of general verbal fluency also may be administered by asking the patient to name as many words he can think of in one minute that begin with a particular letter (A or S are usual). The patient should be instructed not to repeat words, not to include proper names, such as "Alice" or "Saturday," and not to repeat portions of words, such as "everyone. . . . everytime. . . . everyplace." The examiner should record the number of responses and the number of repetitions. Each correct word is scored as 1 point. Repeated and restricted words are not counted. People over 65 years of age should be given a 3-point bonus, and people with less than a high school education should be given a 4-point bonus. A score of 13 points or less is abnormal.

Abnormalities of speech fluency include Broca's aphasia and transcortical motor aphasia (91, 135). Patients with coarse frontal lobe disease and schizophrenia also have difficulties with word fluency tasks.

NONFLUENT APHASIAS

Broca's aphasia results from damage to the postero inferior region of the left frontal lobe area (inferior frontal gyrus, adjacent areas of the operculum and insula). Patients with Broca's aphasia often understand spoken language but are unable to express themselves fluently and, occasionally, are totally mute. Although most can speak, they must struggle to "get the words out." Even when they are able to verbalize, their sentences are often missing words, most commonly small words, such as "the," "to," or "a." Speech without these small words resembles the language of telegrams (e.g., "Don't write, send money."); hence, it is called "telegraphic." Broca's aphasia patients are often dysarthric, with labored words or mispronounced syllables (e.g., "Messodist Epistopal" for "Methodist Episcopal").

Sometimes a mild Broca's aphasia is not immediately recognizable. It can be tested by having the patient repeat sentences or phrases containing small words (e.g., "The Polish Pope now lives in the Vatican," or "No ifs, ands, or buts") or phrases difficult to pronounce (e.g., "Methodist Episcopal," "Massachusetts Avenue"). Repetitive language also involves decoding and phonemic expression, so dysfunction in posterior language areas must be ruled out if a patient has difficulty in repeating sentences.

Because of the extent of brain tissue damage associated with most diseases producing Broca's aphasia, problems not directly related to spoken language often accompany the aphasia (92, 135). These abnormalities include (1) idiokinetic dyspraxia of the ipsilateral hand, (2) buccolingual dyspraxia (the patient may have trouble puffing out his cheeks, whistling, or blowing out a match), (3) weakness or paralysis of the contralateral extremities, and (4) dysgraphia of the ipsilateral (and sometimes the contralateral) hand. In general, patients with aphasia of any type cannot compensate for the aphasia by writing. Figure 5.5 illustrates some of the intra- and interhemispheric connections that explain the nonlanguage features sometimes accompanying Broca's aphasia. Because of the typical extent of lesions leading to the aphasia, information needed to direct the left hand (LH in the figure) is disconnected in the left premotor area (PM), thus preventing the transfer of information to the right premotor and motor cortex and the left hand from properly carrying out the examiner's requests. Learned facial motor skills (e.g., whistling) are also impaired.

Transcortical motor aphasia results from damage to the frontal lobe operculum deep to Broca's area, in the supplementary motor cortex of the dominant hemisphere, or in the region between these sites. In this type of aphasia, the patient manifests a paucity of spontaneous speech. Speech is labored, as with Broca's aphasia; however, it is not telegraphic. Auditory comprehension is usually preserved, as is the ability to repeat phrases, because posterior language structures are intact.

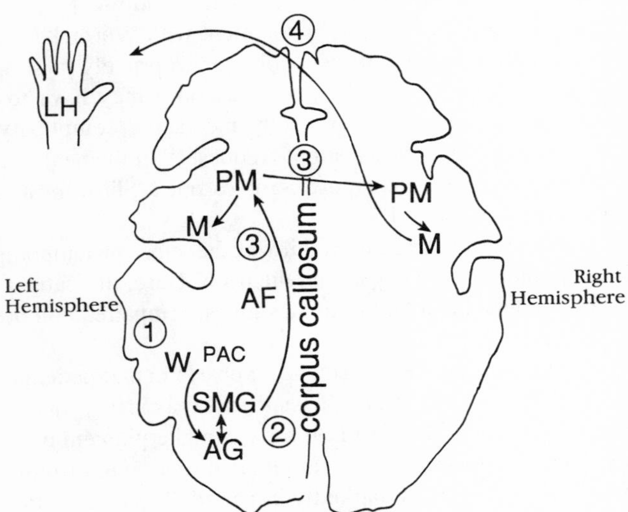

Figure 5.5 Intrahemispheric and Interhemispheric Connections

KEY: LH, left hand; W-PAC, Wernicke's area—primary auditory cortex; SMG, supramarginal gyrus; AG, angular gyrus; AF, arcuate fasciculus; PM, premotor area; M, motor area; 1, patient decodes information: "With your left hand, show me how you would use a hammer"; 2, control of idiokinetic praxis; 3, transmission of idiokinetic information from dominant parietal area to dominant frontal area and then across corpus callosum to nondominant frontal area; 4, transmission of motor sequencing (i.e., hammering) along pyramidal tract to spinal cord and then to left upper extremity.

Global aphasia is an uncommon syndrome characterized by problems in all language functions: poor verbal output, comprehension, naming, writing, and reading. It usually results from middle cerebral artery occlusion but may occur without hemiparesis.

FLUENT APHASIAS

If the patient's speech is fluent, the examiner next must decide whether (1) the speech is understandable, (2) words are appropriately used, and (3) comprehension is good. Fluent, nonunderstandable speech with poor comprehension suggests Wernicke's aphasia.

Wernicke's aphasia is the product of a lesion in or around Wernicke's area, the posterior third of the superior temporal gyrus. This language disorder is characterized by fluent, jargon-filled speech and impaired comprehension of the speech of others (355). Repetition of speech is poor. As is the case in Broca's aphasia, writing is usually aphasic. A synonym for jargon speech is driveling. In driveling speech, the rhythm, volume, modulation, and syntax are normal, but the content is meaningless. The following is an example of driveling: "You can't give them away, but if they plot for too many of them, usually handling it."

The poor comprehension of speech by a patient with Wernicke's aphasia may be immediately apparent in his not responding appropriately to simple requests (e.g., "Would you sit down, please?"), or a response may have to be elicited. Aphasiologists present requests of gradually increasing complexity. A patient sometimes can respond properly to a simple request ("Show me the picture of the baby") but is unable to respond to a more complex one ("Show me all the pictures that contain white or black or red").

Occasionally, a lesion of the middle third of the superior temporal gyrus produces a solitary defect of auditory comprehension. Here, the patient's speech is fluent, clear, and understandable, but he has grossly impaired comprehension of the speech of others.

Conduction aphasia resembles Wernicke's aphasia in that patients have repetition problems. Although conduction aphasics have reasonably intact comprehension, they have difficulty with word finding and make phonemic paraphasic errors. Reading aloud is impaired, as are naming and writing to dictation. Speech is fluent, but verbatim repetition is markedly impaired. The arcuate fasciculus near the dominant parietal lobe is usually involved (241).

Transcortical sensory aphasia is similar to Wernicke's aphasia, but repetition is preserved. Patients can repeat complex sentences but cannot understand them. Spontaneous speech is empty, circumlocutory, and paraphasic. Reading and auditory comprehension are impaired. The angular gyrus in the dominant parietal lobe is usually involved (92).

Thalamic aphasia is associated with dominant thalamic lesions (231). Patients are fluent and have good repetition. Comprehension may be variably impaired. Reading aloud, writing, and naming are impaired, and utterances can be paraphasic. The syndrome is often transient and is associated with attentional problems, avolition, and perseverative behavior. The similar patterns of thalamic aphasics and blunted schizophrenics with formal thought disorder may be of theoretical interest in understanding the neurology of schizophrenic speech. Left basal ganglia lesions (particularly the head of the caudate) can also produce a fluent aphasia. Speech is dysarthric and paraphasic, comprehension is poor, and repetition ability is variable.

The patient with dysnomia or *anomic aphasia* has difficulty naming objects but no problems with repetition. The examiner tests the patient by asking him to name a series of objects. The test should take two forms: (1) asking the patient to name objects presented to him (i.e., naming to confrontation (hold up a pen and ask, "What is this?") and (2) asking the patient to point to an object named by the examiner (e.g., "Show me a collar."). The choice of items used in testing should be commensurate with the patient's level of education. For example, following a stroke, a physician had little problem naming mundane objects; however, he was unable to name medical instruments whose function he could still describe. Dysnomia can be the product of a dominant temporal or dominant parietal lesion; it has no clearer localizing significance (92). Anomic aphasias can be mild (the above example of the physician who had trouble only with medical terms) or severe. In the severe form, the patient exhibits spontaneous but empty speech filled with circumlocutions, vague phrases, and indefinite references. Pronouns, rather than nouns, make up the content. Fluency of speech can be interrupted with multiple pauses that result in a stumbling verbal output. Repetition and comprehension are usually intact, but reading and writing disturbances can occur. Anomic aphasia is often a residual syndrome following improvement from other aphasic states.

Repetition of speech: Normal repetition ability associated with either impaired spontaneous or jargon speech suggests a conduction aphasia (see the previous subsection). Repetition is poor in Broca's and Wernicke's aphasias.

To test for repetition problems, the examiner should ask the patient to repeat phrases, such as "peanut butter," "Pennsylvania Avenue," "Methodist Episcopal," and sentences, such as "One would have been good enough." "He asked where he was when we were there." "No ifs, ands, or buts."

Reading and writing: Reading aloud and reading comprehension may need to be tested. Impaired reading ability is termed *dyslexia*. When the disability is severe, it is termed *alexia*. Reading is tested by asking the patient to read a clearly printed, standardized list of words and sentences. Figures 5.6 and 5.7 display words and sentences selected for their sensitivity to reading difficulty. Explaining the meaning of the sentences tests basic reading comprehension. Occasionally, silent reading and reading comprehension are intact, but the patient is unable to

MAMA
TIP-TOP
FIFTY-FIFTY
THANKS
HUCKLEBERRY
BASEBALL PLAYER
CATERPILLAR

Figure 5.6 Reading Tasks: Words
SOURCE: From *Principles of Behavioral Neurology* by M. M. Mesulam, 1985, Philadelphia: F. A. Davis Company. Reprinted with permission.

read aloud. This suggests a lesion in the arcuate fasciculus disconnecting Wernicke's and Broca's areas. If a patient can write but cannot read, the disconnecting lesion is between the occipital lobes and Wernicke's area.

The examiner also needs to evaluate the patient's ability to construct letters and

Limes are sour.
The spy fled to Greece.
The barn swallow captured a plump worm.
The lawyer's closing argument convinced him.
The phantom soared across the foggy heath.

Figure 5.7. Reading Tasks: Sentences
SOURCE: From *The Assessment of Aphasia and Related Disorders* by H. Goodglass and E. Kaplan, 1972, Lea & Febiger. Reprinted with permission.

words and to write a sentence that incorporates reasonable syntax and word usage. The patient should be asked (1) to write a sentence describing the weather for that day, and (2) to write sentences read by the examiner, such as "She cannot see them." "If he is not careful, the stool will fall."

Prosody and Emotional Gesturing: Language-Related Functions of the Nondominant Hemisphere

Studies of regional blood flow during spontaneous speech have revealed changes in the parasylvian regions of the nondominant hemisphere. During speech, activity in these regions "mirrors" changes in homologous regions of the dominant hemisphere and serves the functions of prosody and emotional gesturing (the "affective components" of language). Patients with normal dominant hemispheric functioning and lesions in the nondominant hemisphere have normal spontaneity, clarity, and comprehension of speech, but they have impairments of range, modulation, and melody of voice; of gesturing with speech, or of comprehension of the emotional tone of the speech of others. These abnormalities are analogous to aphasic disturbances that are due to dominant hemispheric dysfunction. For example, in an anterior (frontal) prosodic disturbance, the patient has impaired spontaneous emotionality and gesturing with speech; in posterior (temporal) prosodic disturbance, the patient has impaired comprehension of the prosody and gesturing of others (847–849, 1049). Three observations should be made in assessing prosody:

1. *Spontaneous prosody and gesturing:* As the patient speaks spontaneously, does he manifest normal range, modulation, and melody of voice? Is the tone of voice appropriate to what he is saying? Does the patient gesture sufficiently to convey the feeling associated with what he is saying? The examiner must look and listen carefully when emotionally important subjects are being discussed. This is akin to the evaluation of spontaneity and fluency of speech and part of the evaluation of emotional blunting (loss of expression).
2. *Expressive prosody:* The examiner tests expressive prosody by asking the patient to repeat an emotionally neutral sentence (e.g., "The boy went to the grocery store.") while sounding and looking sad and then angry. Tone of voice and facial expression can be rated separately. Assessing expressive prosody is analogous to assessing motor language.
3. *Receptive prosody:* The examiner tests receptive prosody by standing behind the patient (so only tone of voice can be interpreted) and asking him to determine the emotion as the examiner says the emotionally neutral sentence in voices that are sad, happy, angry, and emotionally neutral. The examiner next stands in front of the patient and mimes these emotions. Assessing receptive prosody is analogous to assessing receptive language.

Thinking

Thinking is not a monolithic function, and no single test spans the various cognitive processes subsumed under that rubric. Although proverb interpretation is still a widely used mental status strategy for assessing thinking, responses to proverbs do not correlate well with deficits in abstract thinking (42, 805, 807), and fewer than 22% of non–brain-damaged normal adults fully understand proverbs (635). A clinical assessment of "thinking," however, can be obtained by specifically assessing a patient's judgment, problem-solving ability, comprehension, concept formation, and reasoning. The extent of this assessment is determined by the individual clinical situation.

PROBLEM SOLVING AND JUDGMENT

A patient's judgment regarding situations in his life is an indirect but clinically useful global measure of thinking. Judgment should not be tested by asking hypothetical questions: "What would you do if you found a stamped, sealed, addressed envelope lying on the street?" "How would you find your way out of a forest?" This is because the typical answers are stereotyped ("I'd mail the letter") and not usually the products of problem solving and reflection. A better measure of judgment is to ask the patient to comment on specific problems or opportunities regarding such topics as family relationships, employment, and plans for the future.

More structured testing of problem-solving ability involves mathematical word problems, such as:

> "If I had three apples and you had four more than I, how many apples would you have?"
>
> "If you had 18 books and had to put them on two shelves so that one shelf had twice as many books as the other, how many books would you put on each shelf?"

Calculating ability should be tested before asking mathematically based problems. It is assessed by asking the patient to solve in his head simple math problems (e.g., 23 − 8 = ?). A poor performance on such tasks is termed *dyscalculia* or *acalculia* and is associated with dominant hemisphere (often parietal) dysfunction.

COMPREHENSION AND CONCEPT FORMATION

Some of the nonproverb items from the comprehension subtest of the Wechsler Adult Intelligence Scale (WAIS) (595, 635), such as "Why do we wash clothes?" "Why does a train have an engine?" and "Why does land in the city cost more than land in the country?" can be used to assess a patient's comprehension.

Verbal concept formation can be tested by asking the patient to state how two items are similar. For example: "In what way are an airplane and a bicycle similar?" "In what way are paint and concrete the same?" Although there are many possible "abstract" responses to such questions, correct answers are those that reveal the most important, usually functional, characteristics of the items. For example, the answer, "The plane and the bicycle are both means of transportation" is better than "Both have wheels."

REASONING

Verbal reasoning (items modified from the Stanford-Binet Intelligence Scale, [931]) can be tested by asking the patient to listen to a statement and then tell the examiner what is foolish about the statement. Such statements include:

A man had pneumonia twice. The first time it killed him, but the second time he quickly got well.

In the year 1991, many more women than men got married in Canada.

Most train accidents involve the first and last cars. To reduce the number of accidents, we should remove the first and last cars.

Visual reasoning can also be tested by asking the patient to look at a picture depicting a logical absurdity (see Figures 5.8, 5.9, and 5.10) and then tell the examiner what is foolish about the picture.

Figure 5.8.

SOURCE: From *Principles of Behavioral Neurology* by M. M. Mesulam, 1985, Philadelphia: F. A. Davis Company.

Figure 5.9.
SOURCE: From *Principles of Behavioral Neurology* by M. M. Mesulam, 1985, Philadelphia, F. A. Davis Company.

Figure 5.10.
SOURCE: From *Principles of Behavioral Neurology* by M. M. Mesulam, 1985, Philadelphia: F. A. Davis Company.

Memory

Memory can be divided into five stages (933, 934). In Stage 1, sensations immediately received (without requiring any focused attention) by the primary sensory cortex are initially stored in the sensory memory "store" (ultra–short-term store, echoic/iconic memory). If not attended to within 1 or 2 seconds, these sensations are not remembered. Stage 2 involves these sensations being immediately organized into patterns by the secondary sensory cortex and attention being paid to them. Stages 1 and 2 are not formally testable.

In Stage 3, five to seven items can be "held" or "retained" if the patient concentrates or makes an effort. This information, said to be in the short-term store (working memory), is lost within 20 seconds if not processed further. This stage of memory can be tested by slowly reading a series of five to seven numbers to the patient and asking him immediately to repeat the series. This task is termed *digit span*. Some examiners also use digit span forward and backward to test concentration and attention.

In Stage 4, what is being remembered then becomes consolidated in the transfer system if some effort is made at rehearsal (by way of repetition or use of other mnemonic devices). This function takes place within 30 seconds to 30 minutes. This stage of memory has verbal and visual components, and both are tested (see Figures 5.11 and 5.12). The examiner tells the patient that he is going to show him some words and objects. The patient is not informed that memory is being tested.

Figure 5.11. Visual Memory Forms

SOURCE: From *Principles of Behavioral Neurology* by M. M. Mesulam, 1985, Philadelphia: F. A. Davis Company.

TRAIN	STATION	WAGON
HOLLOW	FILL	FINANCE
SWALLOW	EMPTY	MONEY

Figure 5.12. Verbal Memory Word List
SOURCE: From *Principles of Behavioral Neurology* by M. M. Mesulam, 1985, Philadelphia: F. A. Davis Company.

The examiner then asks the patient to copy the 10 shapes and to make them about the same sizes as they appear in the model (this task also can be used to assess construction ability). The model shapes are removed from the patient's sight, and he is immediately asked to reproduce them. The patient must be able to reproduce successfully at least 5 shapes to proceed. If he cannot, the copying and immediate recall task should be repeated at least twice. If still unsuccessful (less than 5 shapes reproduced), this aspect of memory testing is terminated. If successful, the task is repeated but this time with words rather than shapes. After 20 minutes, during which the patient is performing other tasks, the examiner asks the patient to reproduce as many of the shapes and words as possible. As with all memory functions, these tasks are dependent on adequate attention and concentration.

Stage 5 is referred to as long-term memory, in which information is remembered beyond 30 minutes and, sometimes (depending on many factors), for years or a lifetime. This information is probably stored in secondary and tertiary cortical areas throughout the brain. A gross but reasonable assessment of long-term memory is the patient's ability to recall events and details of his life (*autobiographical memory*). This can be assessed as the examiner obtains information about the patient's personal history, childhood, and present life. In addition to the usual questions about school and jobs, the examiner should also ask about public events and celebrities during various periods in the patient's life: names of favorite television shows, movies, or athletes. Abnormal responses range from failing to recognize names of people, shows, and events and being vague, without providing details, to being unable to give any meaningful information.

Visual Spatial and Higher Perceptual Function

The abilities to recognize nonverbal (e.g., visual, auditory) patterns, to be aware of oneself in three-dimensional space, to recognize spatial relationships, and to coordinate nonverbal spatial information with motor function are some aspects of visual spatial and higher perceptual function. Copying geometric figures and other shapes is one expression of visual spatial and higher perceptual function. Facial recognition is another expression of this function; it can be tested by determining whether the patient recognizes familiar people in the examination setting or friends or relatives who accompanied the patient. This determination can be accomplished when the examination seemingly is over and the examiner and patient leave the examination room. The inability to recognize familiar faces is termed prosopagnosia (97, 659). It sometimes results in a patient accusing one or more people of being impostors. The delusion that a family member or other familiar person is an impostor is termed *Capgras' syndrome,* and often patients with Capgras' syndrome have posterior nondominant hemisphere dysfunction (2, 34). Some recent evidence suggests that prosopagnosia extends to the nonrecognition of other, nonfacial, visual phenomena and that these lesions are often bilateral (544, Chapter 17).

A related phenomenon is termed *Fregoli's syndrome* (184). Here the patient, observing another person not well known to the patient, mistakenly thinks that the other person is someone very familiar (e.g., friend, relative, or famous person) despite the fact that there is no resemblance. For example, a hospitalized patient was convinced that Charlton Heston and Marilyn Monroe had been admitted to his psychiatric unit.

Another related phenomenon is reduplicative paramnesia, in which a patient, usually with posterior nondominant hemisphere dysfunction, manifests a delusion that a duplicate of a person or place exists elsewhere (Doppelganger phenomenon) (184). For example, a Euro-American woman on a psychiatric service had the delusion that she had a twin sister and that the twin sister was an African-American woman. This patient also had Capgras' syndrome; she thought that her husband was an impostor sent to spy on her.

Three additional aspects of visual spatial and higher perceptual function are:

1. *Topographic orientation:* This is tested by first determining whether the patient has trouble finding his way about familiar streets or large buildings. The patient is then asked to point to the east, if north were directly behind him. This task requires an understanding of cardinal directions, plus being able mentally to rotate the relationship established by the examiner to fit that understanding of direction (i.e, looking down at a map, east is to the right, but in this task east is to the left).
2. *Awareness of illness:* Psychiatric textbooks often mention the patient's "insight" into his own behaviors, motivation, and symptoms. Another form of "insight" important to the neuropsychiatrist is the patient's awareness that he has an illness. Nonrecognition of a serious medical disability is termed anosognosia. For example, in Babinski's agnosia, a patient with hemiparalysis may attempt to get out of bed and walk (and be prone to an accident), despite evidence of paralysis from repeated failures to walk and despite instructions from staff and visitors not to walk. In Anton's syndrome a blind patient believes he is able to see. It is also

possible that other phenomena routinely described as "denial" are actually the product of nondominant hemisphere dysfunction and that some conversion disorders also are the product of transient nondominant hemisphere neglect (672, pp. 140–150; 1047).

3. *Spatial recognition* (544, Chapter 24): Some patients with intact left-right orientation pay no attention to the left side of their bodies or to objects in their left visual field. This left spatial nonrecognition (a product of nondominant hemisphere dysfunction) may reveal itself in a number of ways, including not shaving the left side of one's face, bumping into objects on the left, reading only the right side of printed materials, and writing only on the right side of the page (229). Patients with left frontal lobe lesions may have the same kinds of neglect for the right side of space. In addition to the above behaviors indicative of spatial neglect, any of the paper-and-pencil tests described in this chapter can be used to assess the patient's awareness of left or right space (i.e., they fail to use that part of the paper). Other tests are (1) asking the patient to draw the face of a clock with the time at 10 minutes past 11 and assessing the drawing for distortion suggestive of spatial neglect and (2) asking the patient to cross all the line segments he sees on a page where the segments are scattered across the page (29) (see Figure 5.13).

Integrating Functions

When working properly, the brain obviously functions in an integrated way. For example, to do well in a task that is testing visual memory (e.g., being able to reproduce geometric shapes from memory after a 20-minute delay), the patient also must be able to attend to the task (i.e., maintain attention and concentration) and have good constructional ability in order to reproduce what is recalled. Seeing a written sentence, reading it aloud, and comprehending its meaning require functioning connections between the visual and language systems, between receptive and motor language processors, and between memory and language systems. If a patient performs well on the above tasks, it is reasonable to assume that connections between various brain processing systems are functioning adequately. If there is some decrement in performance, however, further testing may be needed to determine if the problem is within or between cognitive systems. Figure 5.5 displays some of the more important intersystem connections that influence cognitive test performance. Constructional, kinesthetic, and ideomotor tasks comparing preferred and nonpreferred hand performance specifically test these connections. Having a patient perform a bimanual task without watching his hands (such as lacing a shoe placed in front of him) tests the corpus callosum, which must be intact if the two hands (without visual input) are to "know" what each is doing in the task. (Lacing one's own shoes is overlearned; such bimanual tasks relate to dominant frontal lobe, not corpus callosum function.)

Other specific tests of integrated function are graphesthesia and stereognosis.

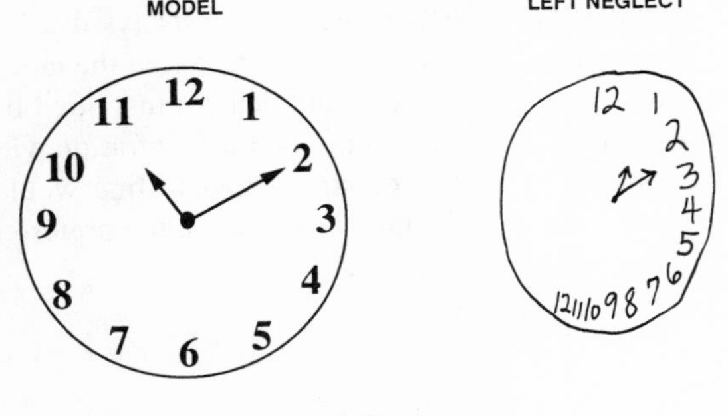

a. Clock

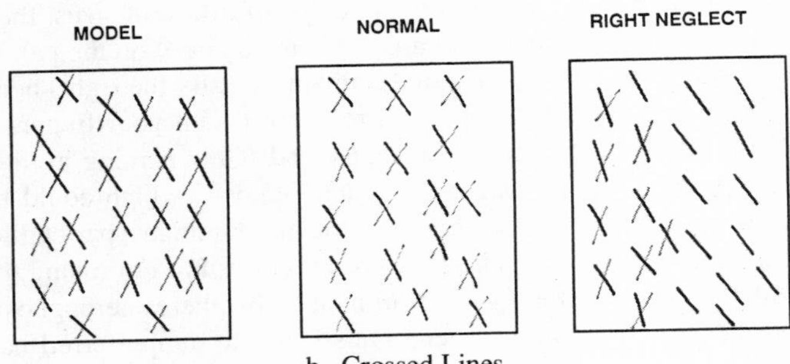

b. Crossed Lines

Figure 5.13. Spatial Neglect Tasks

Just as in the assessment of kinesthetic praxis, the evaluation of graphesthesia and stereognosis tests (1) the parietal lobe contralateral to the hand being tested and (2) the connections between the two hemispheres.

Graphesthesia

The examiner tells the patient that he is going to print some letters, one at a time, on the palms of the patient's hands by using an implement (e.g., the cap of a ballpoint pen) that leaves no ink or graphite on the patient's hand. He then asks the patient to supinate his hands and close his eyes. Then one at a time, he prints several letters on the palm (usually the left) ipsilateral to the side of his dominant (usually the left) hemisphere. After each letter, the examiner asks the patient to name it. If the patient experiences difficulty, the examiner should then test for letter gnosis by drawing the letters on the patient's palm with the patient's eyes open. If letter gnosis recognition is intact, the error is called graphesthesia. Following the test of graphesthesia on the hand ipsilateral to the patient's dominant hemisphere, graphesthesia should be tested in the preferred hand.

Graphesthesia in only the nonpreferred hand suggests dysfunction in the contralateral parietal lobe or in the corpus callosum. A lesion in the latter prevents adequate information from the nonpreferred hand being transmitted from the contralateral to the ipsilateral (dominant) parietal lobe for integration with the language system and thus the name of the letter shape. Other testing would be needed to determine which possibility is likely. Graphesthesia in the preferred hand usually reflects dysfunction in the dominant parietal lobe.

Stereognosis

The examiner tells the patient that he is going to place several objects, one at a time, in the palms of the patient's hands; he does not specify the objects. He then asks the patient to supinate his hands and close his eyes. The examiner places, one at a time, several items (e.g., a key, several coins of different sizes, the cap of a ballpoint pen—all items that make no noise when palpated) on the palm (usually the left) ipsilateral to the side of the nondominant (usually the right) hemisphere. After each placement, the patient is asked to "feel it with your fingers and then name it." If the patient experiences difficulty and if his naming ability as previously tested is intact, he is manifesting astereognosis, which could be due to dysfunction of the contralateral (in this case, the nondominant) parietal lobe or of interhemispheric connections, such as the corpus callosum. Following the test on the hand ipsilateral to the patient's nondominant hemisphere, stereognosis should be tested on the preferred hand. Astereognosis on the nonpreferred hand only, indicates that the abnormality is in the contralateral parietal lobe or corpus callosum. Astereognosis on the preferred hand only, indicates that the abnormality is in the contralateral parietal lobe.

Synthesis of Cognitive Performance Information

The third phase of cognitive assessment is the synthesis of information gathered from the examination. Once testing is complete, the examiner should review the results of each test and decide whether that test's result is normal or abnormal. An easy system for this process is to have a score card for each test and simply check the result. On any given test, when the examiner is in doubt for any reason, he checks questionable. Figures 5.14 through 5.18 (see pp. 94–118) display examples of score cards.

From the clinical interview, the mental status examination, and the Mini-Mental State, the examiner can determine whether the patient has significant and diffuse cognitive impairment. The information gathered from the detailed testing described above is used to determine if the patient has mild diffuse impairment or some localizable impairment. Although the experienced examiner can get an impression of whether this impairment is localizable to a particular brain region (e.g., frontal lobe, parietal lobe), the information gathered from the clinical cognitive examination is most valid when interpretation is limited to decisions of dominant versus nondominant (most likely left versus right) and anterior versus posterior. Figures 5.14 through 5.18 display the patterns of impairment consistent with these gross regional localizations.

To understand the thinking that leads to these decisions of gross localization, the examiner may find helpful a review of the general concepts about how the brain appears to be organized structurally and functionally in the processing of higher cognitive function. By convention, the term *dominant hemisphere* refers to the cerebral hemisphere that is organized functionally to express language. As described earlier in this chapter, the correlation between language organization and handedness is only moderate, but when a patient is purely right-handed, the clinician can reasonably assume that the patient's left hemisphere is organized for language. As the degree of right-handedness decreases, so does the confidence in lateralization of function.

A considerable body of evidence indicates that the two hemispheres process information differently and have different functional specializations. The dominant hemisphere appears to process information in a sequential, analytic, linear fashion and is particularly efficient at processing high-frequency information: language and other symbolic and detailed information. The nondominant hemisphere, the right, appears to process information in a gestaltic, holistic, parallel fashion and is particularly efficient at processing low-frequency, visual spatial information (591, 592, 611).

The corpus callosum and other subcortical structures are responsible for communicating and integrating information between the two hemispheres. Although sensory and motor long tracts do not pass through the interhemispheric structures, messages from one secondary or tertiary cortical region to another secondary or tertiary region in the opposite hemisphere do pass through these structures. For example, in a left-brain–dominant patient, the instruction, "With your left hand, show me how you would hit a nail with a hammer" is processed by the tertiary cortex for auditory comprehension in the left hemisphere and by the tertiary cortices of the left parietal and frontal lobes, and a "message" is then transmitted to the right hemisphere to initiate the motor response in the left hand. The pathway from right frontal lobe motor areas to the spinal cord and left upper extremities does not pass through the corpus callosum (354) (see Figure 5.5).

Thus, the left or right localization of lesions or dysfunction based on performance during the clinical and formal cognitive assessment can be grossly determined by dividing tests into those which are predominantly verbal and those which are predominantly nonverbal. A decrement in performance primarily limited to predominantly verbal tests suggests that the dysfunction is in the dominant

TABLE 5.6

Regional Associations of Cognitive Tasks

Left	*Bilateral*	*Right*
	Anterior	
Ideomotor praxis, nonpreferred hand only Speech fluency Articulation Verbal fluency Verbal reasoning Thinking Verbal immediate memory	Letter cancellation Serial sevens/ world backwards Frontal and basal ganglia features (unless unilateral) Spontaneous prosody Judgment Awareness of illness	Expressive prosody Visual reasoning Visual immediate memory
	Posterior	
Ideomotor praxis, both hands Constructional praxis, preferred hand only Formal thought disorder Speech repetition Naming, writing, reading aloud Reading and auditory comprehension Verbal thinking Digit span Verbal delayed memory (temporal lobe)	Cerebellar features (unless unilateral) Kinesthetic praxis (unless unilateral) Autobiographic memory Stereognosia and graphesthesia (unless unilateral)	Constructional praxis, both hands Receptive prosody Nonverbal thinking Visual delayed memory (temporal lobe) Facial recognition Topographic orientation Spatial recognition

(most likely left) hemisphere, whereas a decrement in performance primarily limited to predominantly nonverbal tests suggests that the dysfunction is in the nondominant (most likely right) hemisphere. Figure 5.14 shows the typical performance pattern of a patient with dominant hemispheric dysfunction; Figure 5.15 shows the typical performance pattern of a patient with nondominant hemispheric dysfunction.

Further localization, at times, can be accomplished by roughly dividing tests into those with a predominant motor component and those requiring minimal higher-motor functioning. A predominant motor component reflects anterior regional functioning (frontal lobe). Thinking and attention also correlate with anterior regional function. Other tests relate to functions of posterior (temporo/parieto/occipital) regions. The anatomic dividing line for these anterior/posterior regions is roughly the central sulcus of Rolando and the sylvan fissure. Table 5.4 separates the cognitive tasks along the lines of anterior/posterior and dominant/nondominant, and also indicates more specific relationships whenever possible. Figure 5.16 shows the typical performance pattern of a patient with an anterior lesion or dysfunction; Figure 5.17, the typical performance pattern of a patient with a posterior lesion or dysfunction; and Figure 5.18, the typical performance pattern of a demented patient early in the course of his illness.

Item	Normal	Questionable	Abnormal	NA
		SCORING		
Attention & Concentration				
1. Letter cancellation ("A Test")	X			
2. Serial 7's/World Backwards		X		
Motor Function				
3. Frontal lobe features		X		
4. Basal ganglia features	X			
5. Cerebellar features	X			
6. Ideomotor praxis				
a. Both hands			X	
b. Preferred hand only				X
c. Nonpreferred hand only				X
7. Kinesthetic praxis				
Both hands				X
Preferred hand only				X
Nonpreferred hand only		X		

Figure 5.14. Cognitive Assessment Score Card: Dominant Hemisphere Dysfunction Pattern

Item	Normal	Questionable	Abnormal	NA
	SCORING			
Language				
8. Speech fluency	X			
9. Articulation	X			
10. Verbal fluency		X		
11. Formal thought disorder		X		
12. Speech repetition	X			
13. Naming			X	
14. Writing		X		
15. Reading aloud			X	
16. Reading comprehension			X	
17. Auditory comprehension		X		
Prosody				
18. Spontaneous	X			
19. Expressive	X			
20. Receptive	X			

Figure 5.14. *(continued)*

Item	SCORING Normal	Questionable	Abnormal	NA
Thinking				
21. Judgment		X		
22. Problem solving			X	
23. Comprehension			X	
24. Concept formation			X	
25. Verbal reasoning			X	
26. Visual reasoning	X			
Memory				
27. Digit span		X		
28. Verbal immediate and delayed recall			X	
29. Visual immediate and delayed recall	X			
30. Autobiographical		X		

Figure 5.14. *(continued)*

Item	Normal	Questionable	Abnormal	NA
	SCORING			
Visuospatial and Perceptual				
31. Constructional ability (Gestaltic task)				
a. Both Hands	X			
b. Preferred hands only				X
c. Nonpreferred hand only				X
32. Facial recognition	X			
33. Topographic orientation	X			
34. Awareness of illness		X		
35. Spatial recognition	X			
36. Dressing ability	X			
Integrative Functions				
37. Construction, nonpreferred hand only				X
38. Ideomotor praxis, nonpreferred hand only				X
39. Bimanual task (blind)		X		

Figure 5.14. *(continued)*

		SCORING		
Item	**Normal**	**Questionable**	**Abnormal**	**NA**
40. Stereognosia				
a. Both hands				X
b. Preferred hand only		X		
c. Nonpreferred hand only				X
41. Graphesthesia				
a. Both hands				X
b. Preferred hand only		X		
c. Nonpreferred hand only				X

Figure 5.14. (*continued*)

Item	SCORING Normal	Questionable	Abnormal	NA
Attention & Concentration				
1. Letter cancellation ("A Test")	X			
2. Serial 7's/World Backwards		X		
Motor Function				
3. Frontal lobe features		X		
4. Basal ganglia features	X			
5. Cerebellar features	X			
6. Ideomotor praxis				
a. Both hands	X			
b. Preferred hand only				X
c. Nonpreferred hand only				X
7. Kinesthetic praxis				
a. Both hands		X		
b. Preferred hand only				X
c. Nonpreferred hand only				X

Figure 5.15. Cognitive Assessment Score Card: Nondominant Hemisphere Dysfunction Pattern

Item	SCORING			
	Normal	Questionable	Abnormal	NA
Language				
8. Speech fluency	X			
9. Articulation	X			
10. Verbal fluency	X			
11. Formal thought disorder	X			
12. Speech repetition	X			
13. Naming	X			
14. Writing	X			
15. Reading aloud	X			
16. Reading comprehension		X		
17. Auditory comprehension	X			
Prosody				
18. Spontaneous			X	
19. Expressive			X	
20. Receptive			X	

Figure 5.15. *(continued)*

Item	Normal	Questionable	Abnormal	NA
Thinking				
21. Judgment		X		
22. Problem solving		X		
23. Comprehension	X			
24. Concept formation	X			
25. Verbal reasoning	X			
26. Visual reasoning			X	
Memory				
27. Digit span		X		
28. Verbal immediate and delayed recall	X			
29. Visual immediate and delayed recall			X	
30. Autobiographical			X	

Figure 5.15. *(continued)*

Item	Normal	Questionable	Abnormal	NA
Visuospatial and Perceptual				
31. Constructional Ability (Gestaltic task)				
a. Both hands			X	
b. Preferred hand only				X
c. Nonpreferred hand only				X
32. Facial recognition		X		
33. Topographic orientation			X	
34. Awareness of illness			X	
35. Spatial recognition			X	
36. Dressing ability		X		
Integrative Functions				
37. Construction nonpreferred hand only				X
38. Ideomotor praxis nonpreferred hand only				X
39. Bimanual task (blind)	X			

Figure 5.15. *(continued)*

		SCORING		
Item	**Normal**	**Questionable**	**Abnormal**	**NA**
40. Stereognosia				
a. Both hands		X		
b. Preferred hand only				X
c. Nonpreferred hand only			X	
41. Graphesthesia				
a. Both hands		X		
b. Preferred hand only				X
c. Nonpreferred hand only				X

Figure 5.15. *(continued)*

Item	Normal	Questionable	Abnormal	NA
	SCORING			
Attention & Concentration				
1. Letter cancellation ("A Test")		X		
2. Serial 7's/World Backwards			X	
Motor Function				
3. Frontal lobe features			X	
4. Basal ganglia features		X		
5. Cerebellar features	X			
6. Ideomotor praxis				
a. Both hands		X		
b. Preferred hand only				X
c. Nonpreferred hand only				X
7. Kinesthetic praxis				
a. Both hands	X			
b. Preferred hand only				X
c. Nonpreferred hand only				X

Figure 5.16. Cognitive Assessment Score Card: Anterior Hemispheric Dysfunction Pattern

Item	Normal	Questionable	Abnormal	NA
		SCORING		
Language				
8. Speech fluency			X	
9. Articulation		X		
10. Verbal fluency			X	
11. Formal thought disorder	X			
12. Speech repetition		X		
13. Naming	X			
14. Writing	X			
15. Reading aloud	X			
16. Reading comprehension		X		
17. Auditory comprehension	X			
Prosody				
18. Spontaneous			X	
19. Expressive			X	
20. Receptive		X		

Figure 5.16. (*continued*)

Item	Normal	Questionable	Abnormal	NA
		SCORING		
Thinking				
21. Judgment			X	
22. Problem solving			X	
23. Comprehension			X	
24. Concept formation			X	
25. Verbal reasoning			X	
26. Visual reasoning			X	
Memory				
27. Digit span		X		
28. Verbal immediate and delayed recall		X		
29. Visual immediate and delayed recall		X		
30. Autobiographical	X			

Figure 5.16. (*continued*)

Item	Normal	Questionable	Abnormal	NA
	SCORING			
Visuospatial and Perceptual				
31. Constructional Ability (Gestaltic task)				
a. Both hands		X		
b. Preferred hand only				X
c. Nonpreferred hand only				X
32. Facial recognition	X			
33. Topographic orientation			X	
34. Awareness of illness		X		
35. Spatial recognition	X			
36. Dressing ability	X			
Integrative Functions				
37. Construction, nonpreferred hand only				X
38. Ideomotor praxis, nonpreferred hand only				X
39. Bimanual task (blind)		X		

Figure 5.16. (*continued*)

Item	SCORING Normal	Questionable	Abnormal	NA
40. Stereognosia				
a. Both hands	X			
b. Preferred hand only				X
c. Nonpreferred hand only				X
41. Graphesthesia				
a. Both hands	X			
b. Preferred hand only				X
c. Nonpreferred hand only				X

Figure 5.16. (*continued*)

Item	Normal	Questionable	Abnormal	NA
		SCORING		
Attention & Concentration				
1. Letter cancellation ("A Test")	X			
2. Serial 7's/World Backwards		X		
Motor Function				
3. Frontal lobe features	X			
4. Basal ganglia features	X			
5. Cerebellar features		X		
6. Ideomotor praxis				
a. Both hands			X	
b. Preferred hand only				X
c. Nonpreferred hand only				X
7. Kinesthetic praxis				
a. Both hands			X	
b. Preferred hand only				X
c. Nonpreferred hand only				X

Figure 5.17. Cognitive Assessment Score Card: Posterior Hemispheric Dysfunction Pattern

Item	Normal	Questionable	Abnormal	NA
	SCORING			
Language				
8. Speech fluency	X			
9. Articulation	X			
10. Verbal fluency	X			
11. Formal thought disorder		X		
12. Speech repetition		X		
13. Naming			X	
14. Writing			X	
15. Reading aloud			X	
16. Reading comprehension			X	
17. Auditory comprehension		X		
Prosody				
18. Spontaneous	X			
19. Expressive	X			
20. Receptive		X		

Figure 5.17. (*continued*)

Item	Normal	Questionable	Abnormal	NA
		SCORING		
Thinking				
21. Judgment	X			
22. Problem solving		X		
23. Comprehension	X			
24. Concept formation	X			
25. Verbal reasoning		X		
26. Visual reasoning		X		
Memory				
27. Digit span		X		
28. Verbal immediate and delayed recall			X	
29. Visual immediate and delayed recall			X	
30. Autobiographical		X		

Figure 5.17. *(continued)*

Item	Normal	Questionable	Abnormal	NA
		SCORING		
Visuospatial and Perceptual				
31. Constructional Ability (Gestaltic task)				
a. Both hands			X	
b. Preferred hand only				X
c. Nonpreferred hand only				X
32. Facial recognition		X		
33. Topographic orientation		X		
34. Awareness of illness		X		
35. Spatial recognition			X	
36. Dressing ability		X		
Integrative Functions				
37. Construction, nonpreferred hand only				X
38. Ideomotor praxis, nonpreferred hand only				X
39. Bimanual task (blind)		X		

Figure 5.17. *(continued)*

Item	Normal	Questionable	Abnormal	NA
		SCORING		
40. Stereognosia				
a. Both hands			X	
b. Preferred hand only				X
c. Nonpreferred hand only				X
41. Graphesthesia				
a. Both hands			X	
b. Preferred hand only				X
c. Nonpreferred hand only				X

Figure 5.17. *(continued)*

Item	Normal	Questionable	Abnormal	NA
	SCORING			
Attention & Concentration				
1. Letter cancellation ("A Test")		X		
2. Serial 7's/World Backwards		X		
Motor Function				
3. Frontal lobe features		X		
4. Basal ganglia features	X			
5. Cerebellar features	X			
6. Ideomotor praxis				
a. Both hands		X		
b. Preferred hand				X
c. Nonpreferred hand				X
7. Kinesthetic praxis				
a. Both hands		X		
b. Preferred hand only				X
c. Nonpreferred hand only				X

Figure 5.18. Cognitive Assessment Score Card: Early Dementia Pattern

Item	Normal	Questionable	Abnormal	NA
		SCORING		
Language				
8. Speech fluency	X			
9. Articulation	X			
10. Verbal fluency			X	
11. Formal thought disorder	X			
12. Speech repetition	X			
13. Naming		X		
14. Writing		X		
15. Reading aloud	X			
16. Reading comprehension	X			
17. Auditory comprehension		X		
Prosody				
18. Spontaneous	X			
19. Expressive	X			
20. Receptive		X		

Figure 5.18. *(continued)*

Item	Normal	SCORING Questionable	Abnormal	NA
Thinking				
21. Judgment		X		
22. Problem solving			X	
23. Comprehension		X		
24. Concept formation			X	
25. Verbal reasoning		X		
26. Visual reasoning			X	
Memory				
27. Digit span			X	
28. Verbal immediate and delayed recall			X	
29. Visual immediate and delayed recall		X		
30. Autobiographical	X			

Figure 5.18. (*continued*)

Item	Normal	Questionable	Abnormal	NA
		SCORING		
Visuospatial and Perceptual				
31. Constructional Ability (Gestaltic task)				
a. Both hands			X	
b. Preferred hand only				X
c. Nonpreferred hand only				X
32. Facial recognition	X			
33. Topographic orientation			X	
34. Awareness of illness		X		
35. Spatial recognition		X		
36. Dressing ability	X			
Integrative Functions				
37. Construction, nonpreferred hand only				X
38. Ideomotor praxis, nonpreferred hand only				X
39. Bimanual task (blind)		X		

Figure 5.18. *(continued)*

Item	Normal	Questionable	Abnormal	NA
40. Stereognosia				
a. Both hands		X		
b. Preferred hand only				X
c. Nonpreferred hand only				X
41. Graphesthesia				
a. Both hands		X		
b. Preferred hand only				X
c. Nonpreferred hand only				X

Figure 5.18. *(continued)*

Chapter 6

Laboratory Studies

There is no such thing as a routine laboratory test. Laboratory studies cost money, take time and effort, and can be discomforting to the patient. Ideally, tests should be ordered to assist either in diagnosis or in management. Within limits, however, it is also reasonable to order tests if the results will educate the clinician. As there is some validity to the aphorism, "under every patient's bed there is a lawyer," some tests are ordered to protect against successful suit. Whatever the purpose, the clinician should be consciously aware of the reason for the test and its technical and clinical limitations. The clinician also should have some idea of the most likely results for a given patient. Tests should reflect the working differential diagnostic list, with each test related to confirming or rejecting one or more of the possibilities remaining on the list.

One of the anachronisms of psychiatry is the automatic ordering of a Venereal Disease Research Laboratory (VDRL) test for central nervous system syphilis. When nearly 50% of chronic mental patients suffered from general paresis of the insane (GPI), the assumption that any given patient might be syphilitic was reasonable. Today, when so few patients have CNS syphilis, most patients admitted to a psychiatric unit do not need to have blood drawn for a VDRL. In 25 years of caring for and teaching about seriously ill psychiatric patients, I have seen only three cases of psychosis secondary to CNS syphilis; in all three, the diagnosis was made prior to obtaining the results of a VDRL.

On the other hand, few patients ever receive an EEG, although about 50% of schizophrenics and 25% of manic-depressives have abnormal EEGs and 10 to 15% of hospitalized psychiatric patients have coarse brain disease, which requires an EEG for assessment.

A number of years ago, E. Fuller Torry wrote *The Death of Psychiatry* (996), in which he concluded that if psychiatry did not firmly establish itself as a medical specialty it would be absorbed by other specialties and disappear. Torry's conclusions were based on the sad fact that as the etiology of each behavioral disorder has been identified (e.g., GPI, epilepsy), psychiatry has abandoned those patients to neurology. What is left among the axis I and II disorders are conditions for which the etiology is unknown. Explicit in this circumstance is the fact that there are no specific laboratory tests to diagnose these conditions. Thus, laboratory tests must be used diagnostically to exclude systemic disorders and CNS disease with known etiology or pathophysiology. There is no EEG finding characteristic of schizophrenia; no lesion of mania is apparent on magnetic resonance imaging (MRI). Thus, a *pattern* of combined historical, examination, and laboratory findings is needed to determine a psychiatric diagnosis. This is pattern recognition at its most basic.

Three guidelines, however, can facilitate the diagnostic process. First, the more atypical the syndrome course or presentation, the greater are the probabilities of systemic or coarse brain disease and the need for intensive laboratory study. Second, any clearly focal or circumscribed findings on tests of CNS structure or function substantially increase the probability of the behavioral disorder being due to coarse brain disease, thus justifying further testing to reach a specific diagnosis. Third, any specifically abnormal laboratory test of systemic function substantially increases the probability of the behavioral disorder being due to systemic disease and also justifies further testing. In a nutshell, "Sutton's law" can be stated: "If it's atypical or specifically abnormal, look for a secondary syndrome, *that's where the 'money' is*."* Table 6.1 displays some of the evaluation findings which require extensive or specific laboratory studies.

Modern neuropsychiatry is becoming increasingly loaded with high technology: MRI, CT, position-emission tomography (PET), topographic computerized EEG. Many clinicians are disproportionately influenced by the glitter. The fact remains that the most sensitive measure of brain function is behavior, and a thorough history and examination are still superior to high-tech assessments in discriminating patients. A noninfusion CT scan cannot discriminate the dead from the living, a PET scan cannot discriminate a schizophrenic from a manic, and an EEG cannot distinguish between a happy mood and a sad mood. Clinicians can do all three and more.

Indeed, high-tech laboratory equipment only confirms the laboratory findings previously correlated to establish clinical syndromes. For example, all well-accepted EEG patterns of seizure disorders were determined by clinicians who identified a certain patient with this or that syndrome, hooked the patient to an EEG machine, and concluded post hoc that this or that electrical output pattern related to this or that syndrome. The laboratory is helpful, but it is never a substitute for sound clinical practice.

*Captured famous U.S. bank robber Willy Sutton was asked by a television interviewer, "Willy, how come you rob banks?" Astonished, Willy replied, "Cause that's where the money is."

TABLE 6.1

Findings Suggestive of Secondary or Symptomatic Psychiatric Illness and Commonly Associated Behavioral Syndromes

Finding	*Syndrome*
Historical or Examination Evidence of Systemic Illness	
Liver disease	Delirium
Hypothyroidism	Dementia, atypical psychosis
Hyperthyroidism	Delirium, anxiety disorder
Renal stones (parathyroid disease?)	Atypical depression
Other endocrinopathies	Depression, mania
Lupus	Affective disorders
Metabolic disorders	Delirium, dementia, atypical affective states, pseudointoxication (hypoglycemia)
Overhydration and hyponatremia	Atypical psychosis, delirium
Significant dysplastic body build or features of congenital anomaly	Psychosis with developmental disorder
Cardiovascular disease	Dementia, various syndromes, secondary to stroke, anxiety disorder (secondary to hypertension)
Chronic pulmonary disease	Various syndromes, personality changes
Historical or Examination Evidence of Central Nervous System (CNS) Illness	
Head trauma (associated with focal signs, > 30 min of unconsciousness, personality change, skull fracture, blood from nose/ears	Various syndromes, most commonly frontal and temporal lobe; various psychoses; personality changes
Stroke	Various syndromes, most commonly depression
Seizure disorder	Atypical psychosis, schizophrenia-like psychosis, personality change
CNS infections/inflammation/prolonged high fever	Dementia, delirium
Gestational/labor and delivery difficulties	Various syndromes, most commonly schizophrenialike psychosis
Delayed developmental landmarks	Atypical psychoses, schizophrenia-like psychosis

(*continued*)

TABLE 6.1 (*Cont.*)

Findings Suggestive of Secondary or Symptomatic Psychiatric Illness and Commonly Associated Behavioral Syndromes

Finding	*Syndrome*
Cluster or migraine headaches	Affective disorders
Multiple sclerosis	Affective disorders, particularly depression, anxiety disorder
Basal ganglia disease (Parkinson's disease, Huntington's disease, stroke)	Depression, obsessive compulsive disorder, tic syndromes, atypical mania, catatonia
Historical or Examination Evidence of Drug Use, Toxin Exposure	
Alcoholism	Intoxication, delirium, withdrawal atypical psychosis, dementia, Wernicke's and Korsakoff's syndromes
Lysergic acid diethylamide (LSD)	Atypical psychosis, schizophrenia-like psychosis
Phencyclidine (PCP), mescaline	Affective psychosis, delirium with excitement state
Toxins, inhalants	Atypical psychosis
Stimulants	Delirium with excitement state, hypervigilant delusional psychosis
Anticholinergic drugs, including psychotropic	Delirium
Propranolol	Atypical depression, dementia (in the elderly)
Behavioral	
Altered consciousness	Delirium, ictal or postictal state, intoxication
Atypical course (e.g., late onset anxiety disorder, chronic affective disorder)	CNS or metabolic disorders listed above
Atypical symptom cluster (e.g., depressive syndrome with apathy, not sadness, hallucinosis without other psychopathology, mania with psychomotor features or stereotypy)	CNS disorders listed above
Amnesia	Various CNS syndromes
Many behavioral neurologic signs	Varous CNS focal syndromes, disconnections, delirium, dementia
Psychomotor features	Epilepsy

Because laboratory tests are confirmatory, their results should not be a surprise. Every test must have a rationale; most commonly, that rationale should be to confirm or exclude a differential diagnostic possibility. Thus, the differential diagnosis must be specific. Tests should not be ordered to "rule out" coarse brain disease or even dementia. The differential diagnostic list, made prior to laboratory testing and based on the history and examination, should be precise. If a patient possibly has a dementing syndrome, the clinician should have a specific dementing process in mind and the laboratory tests should reflect this notion. Thus, when ordering an EEG or imaging study, the clinician should inform the laboratory of the condition or conditions that he is considering. Such information helps the electroencephalographer to choose the best montage and EEG conditions or the neuroradiologist to determine what axes to scan and whether infusion is necessary. Again, every laboratory test should be linked to a specific possibility on the working differential diagnostic list. Because no specific tests are available for the so-called functional disorders, laboratory testing is done primarily to assess for intrinsic identifiable CNS illness or for illness in another organ system (for simplicity, referred to here as "systemic illness").

Conditions of Clear or Altered Consciousness

There is a logical approach to identifying the probabilities among all possibilities leading to coarse disease. This approach essentially relates to three diagnostically discriminating questions about the patient: (1) Is the patient's sensorium clear or altered? (2) If clear, is the cognitive impairment diffuse or focal? (3) If diffuse, is the onset of the disorder before age 40, between 41 and 65 years, or 66 years or older? Although the structure is oversimplified and exceptions must be allowed, a reasonable correlation exists between this approach and the logical choices. Therefore, the clinician has a useful method for reducing the possibilities on the working differential diagnosis list.

The clinician must first consider whether the patient's consciousness is clear or altered. Table 6.2 displays some of the more common possibilities associated with a behavioral syndrome characterized by altered consciousness and the laboratory studies helpful in identification. These possibilities can be significantly reduced by a careful history and examination. Although several drug-specific syndromes are listed under intoxications (see Chapter 17), these possibilities generally can be confirmed with blood and urine drug screens. Delirium is not a difficult syndrome to recognize (see Chapter 12). Among medical and surgical patients, however, subacute forms may be present in as many as 10 to 15% of patients and masked by the more glaring features of their medical or surgical disorder. Delirious patients almost always have diffusely abnormal EEGs characterized by high-voltage slow

TABLE 6.2

Commonly Encountered Coarse Brain Disease Conditions Associated with Altered Consciousness and Laboratory Studies Helpful in Identification

Altered Consciousness Disorder	*Laboratory Study*
	Intoxications
Alcoholism	Blood and urine screens
Illegal drugs	
Prescription drugs	
Over-the-counter drugs	
	Deliria
Drug withdrawal states	EEG
Metabolic disorder	EEG, Sma 6/60 and 12/60, urinalysis
Wernicke's encephalopathy	EEG, MRI
Viral or bacterial encephalitis	EEG, spinal tap, viral antibody titers
	Stupor
Paraictal state	EEG
Catatonia secondary to frontal lobe, basal ganglia, or brain stem lesion	MRI, amytal interview
Encephalitis	EEG, spinal tap, viral antibody titers
	Miscellaneous
Acute stroke	MRI, spinal tap
Acute head injury	MRI
Encephalitis	As above
Paraictal state	As above
Chronic obstructive pulmonary disease	Pulmonary studies and blood gases
Acute myocardial infarction	Cardiac function studies and blood gases

KEY: EEG, electroencephalogram; SMA, Sequential Multiple Analyzer; MRI, magnetic resonance imaging.

waves (delirium tremens is one exception in which low-voltage fast activity predominates [521]), and cognitive testing reveals a diffuse performance deficit. Metabolic disorders are usually associated with their own characteristic clinical features, as is Wernicke's encephalopathy, which is almost always associated with nystagmus and often with ophthalmoplegias and peripheral neuropathy. Herpes-related encephalitis is commonly associated with psychiatric disorder, in part due to the affinity of the virus for the temporal lobes. Bitemporal sharp-wave EEG findings are typical. Among the stuporous states and miscellaneous conditions listed, characteristic clinical features identified during the history and examination make diagnosis straightforward. The key here is to know that these conditions can result in coarse brain disorder and secondary psychiatric morbidity.

The clinician should suspect coarse brain disorder with clear consciousness when a patient's present illness, course, or past response to treatment is atypical. The more atypical the clinical picture, the more likely the patient has a psychiatric disorder secondary to coarse brain disease. The presence of any of the major antecedents of psychiatric disorder, unusual physical examination findings, or some deficit in performance on the Mini-Mental State or behavioral neurologic examinations should also alert the clinician to the possibility of coarse brain disease. These possibilities can relate to either a diffuse or a focal process. If diffuse, the process can be progressive or static, severe or mild. The diffuse possibilities are greatly affected by age of onset and present age. Focal processes can be acute or chronic. Table 6.3 displays some of the more common possibilities (i.e., some of the probabilities) in this schema. For most of these possibilities, historical and physical examination information is clear and laboratory tests simply confirm gross structural or functional brain changes and indicate the extent of the cognitive impairment. If the historical and physical examination information is ambiguous, the clinician must clearly specify to laboratory personnel what possibilities he is trying to identify.

In Chapters 9 to 19, the extensive laboratory abnormalities observed in many psychiatric patients are discussed. The extent of these abnormalities demonstrates that the mere presence of MRI-observed structural changes or neuropsychologic impairment does not mean that the patient has coarse disease. The probability of coarse disease increases, however, when the abnormalities or impairments are focal, rather than diffuse; when a specific identifying lesion is observed (e.g., bilateral lenticular atrophy in Huntington's disease); or when a specific laboratory test is abnormal (e.g., EEG bursts of spikes and slow waves).

Frequently Used Laboratory Tests in Neuropsychiatry

Electroencephalogram

The clinical EEG (1009) measures electrical activity (in microvolts) on the scalp. This activity is generated from electrical potentials deep within brain structures. The clinical EEG, therefore, is an indirect measure of brain function. Electrodes are attached in a standard pattern (the 10–20 international system) to the surface of the scalp by an electrically conductive paste, and measurements are recorded on

TABLE 6.3

Commonly Encountered Coarse Brain Disease Conditions Associated with Clear Consciousness and Laboratory Studies Helpful in Identification

Clear Consciousness Disorder	*Laboratory Study*
Diffuse Impairment (Dementia)	
Onset over age 66:	
Alzheimer's disease	MRI, SPECT, neuropsychological testing
Parkinson's disease	MRI, SPECT, neuropsychological testing
Multifocal infarct	As above, cardiovascular function studies
Chronic obstructive pulmonary disease (COPD)	As above, pulmonary function, blood gases
Chronic cardiovascular disease (CVD)	As above, cardiovascular function, blood gases
Diabetes	As above, diabetes workup
Onset between ages 40 and 65:	
Alcohol-related syndromes	MRI, neuropsychological testing, blood and urine screens, liver studies
Illegal-drug-related syndromes	As above
COPD	As above
CVD	As above
Diabetes	As above
Onset before age 40:	
Head injury	MRI, neuropsychological testing
Illegal-drug-related syndromes	As above
Alcohol-related syndromes	As above
White matter disorders	As above, evoked potential, and other special studies
Seizure disorder	As above, EEG
Focal Impairment	
Head injury	MRI, neuropsychological testing
Tumor	As above
Stroke	As above
Developmental disorder (e.g., arteriovenous malformation, agenesis)	As above
Seizure focus	As above, EEG

KEY: MRI, magnetic resonance imaging; SPECT, single-photon emission computed tomography; EEG, electroencephalogram.

a polygraph machine using from 16 to 21 leads (channels). The pattern of relationships among the leads (the montage) can be changed to maximize measurements from various areas of the scalp. Reference electrodes for psychiatric patients should be positioned on the ears. If a patient has tardive dyskinesia, the usual reference placement on the jaws results in many muscle artifacts. Recordings can be made by ink on paper or directly into a computer.

Electrical activity has two characteristics: amplitude (voltage, usually between 50–70 microvolts) and frequency (cycles per second). As the EEG is measured across the scalp, waveforms can vary and the EEG develops a pattern. During the recording, frequency and pattern vary over time as the state of the brain changes (e.g., from alert to drowsy). Whether scalp electrical activity is interpreted directly by an electroencephalographer "reading" the recorded tracing or by a computerized system (topographic EEG) providing colorized pictorial representations, the features being measured and interpreted are the same: amplitude, frequency, and pattern over time and scalp area.

The frequencies of the scalp-recorded EEG thought to reflect deep brain activity range from 0.5 cycles per second (cps) or hertz (Hz) to about 35 cps. Some researchers are interested in frequencies above 35 Hz, but clinically these frequencies often represent muscle activity. By convention, frequencies have been separated into delta 0.5–3.5 Hz, theta 4–7 Hz, alpha 7.5–12 Hz, and beta 12.5 and above. A normal, alert individual in a resting state (with eyes closed) should have a symmetric EEG pattern with little delta or theta activity, minimal beta activity, and predominantly alpha activity observed best as measured by electrodes attached to the posterior half of the head. When a normal, alert person is asked to concentrate on something, alpha activity diminishes and beta predominates. When a normal, alert person becomes sleepy, alpha activity diminishes and delta and theta activity increases.

EEG abnormalities generally fall into six categories: (1) amplitude, (2) frequency, (3) pattern of amplitude and frequency, (4) waveform, (5) some combination of the first four, and (6) EEG activity over time (usually related to sleep stage disturbances). Amplitude deviation can be high (as in delirium or epilepsy) or low (as in some dementias). Frequency can be slow (as in any lesion resulting in cell loss or diminished function) or fast (as in hyperarousal states and delirium tremens). Waveform can be abnormal, as in epilepsy (e.g., spikes and sharp waves, paroxysms of slow waves, three per second sharp- and slow-wave complexes). Amplitude and frequency can be abnormally distributed (e.g., resting alpha diminished or high-amplitude slow waves each circumscribed to a particular scalp region). Waveforms also can be abnormally affected by stimulation, such as flashes of bright light leading to spike activity.

When an EEG is ordered, the above limitations and relationships must be considered, particularly as the requested assessment should be related to a particular diagnostic possibility. The diagnostic possibility of concern can determine the procedures (e.g., flashing light, nasopharyngeal leads for deep temporal lobe foci) and montages that are used. For seizures, which are usually transient events, several assessments may be needed. Sleep deprivation prior to EEG or sedation is also helpful as it permits a patient to fall asleep while being recorded. Epileptic foci are occasionally revealed during this drowsy state. Table 6.4 displays the typical EEG findings associated with some of the disorders frequently encountered by the neuropsychiatrist.

Many medications influence the EEG. Table 6.5 lists some of the more common medications used in neuropsychiatry and their effects on the EEG (306, 307). If possible, the EEG should be performed when the patient is unmedicated.

Topographic EEG is becoming increasingly popular. Its primary advantage over traditional EEG procedures is the computer enhancement of information that is derived from the traditional assessment. The computer does this by interpolating what the voltages and frequencies are likely to be between electrodes. Rather than providing only 16 or 21 points (channels) of information, the computer creates many additional points to generate an electrical voltage map within each frequency band across the scalp. The computer also counts numbers faster than a human. All of these points (real and created) can be determined for each half Hz from 0.5–35 Hz for each second (or millisecond) of recording. The information can be color coded (i.e., the higher the voltage, now termed "power" as filters transform it, the redder the color) so that a colored map of electrical activity is created. In addition to making combinations of frequency, amplitude, and waveform deviations more recognizable as patterns, topographic EEG also permits the pictures for each time period to be cartooned. Thus, it can create a dynamic moving picture of electrical activity that occasionally reveals relationships (e.g., dipoles) otherwise obscured because the events occurred at different times and locations.

The biggest problem in EEG is artifacts (i.e., electrical activity resulting from sources other than the brain). Common artifact sources include scalp and jaw muscle activity, eye and eyelid movement, and faulty electrodes and electrode contact with the scalp. A second problem in interpretation is that the normative pattern is based on an unmedicated individual who is alert, eyes closed, thinking of nothing but not falling asleep. Psychiatric patients tend not to adhere to this standard. Their mental activity, as well as their muscle movements, can falsely distort the EEG.

One way to minimize these problems is to standardize the EEG examination by asking for EEGs with all patients sedated, receiving a standard dose of a drug, or doing a standard, verifiable mental task (e.g., mental math). When these techniques are not practical, an alternative method of assessment is evoked potential.

Evoked Potential

An evoked potential assessment involves the examiner stimulating the patient to evoke brain electrical activity (i.e., potentials). Each potential is the electrical response of brain cells to the stimulus, and each potential is time-locked to the stim-

TABLE 6.4

Typical EEG Findings in Some Common Neuropsychiatric Disorders

Disorder	*EEG Findings*
Schizophrenia	50% normal; 50% diffuse, mild slowing, choppy waveforms
Affective disorder	Two thirds or more normal; about one third diffuse, mild slowing, choppy waveforms, right posterior predominance of findings
Complex partial epilepsy	Unilateral or bilateral discharges of spike and slow waves; diffuse or focal, usually in temporal or frontotemporal areas; multiple examinations may be needed to demonstrate abnormalities
Generalized epilepsy (tonic/clonic)	Rapid rhythmic onset with decreasing frequency and increasing amplitude, slow and spike waves in clonic phase
Tumors	Focal delta and theta, regional decrease in amplitude and loss of organization of normal frequencies and background activity (alpha or beta), focal sharp or spike waves
Stroke	Local but nonspecific increase in slow activity, decreased fast activity, loss or reduction in amplitude of normal background rhythms; occasional epileptiform patterns (sharp or spike waves); if deep stroke, no EEG findings; if associated with depression, EEG changes may be in left frontal areas
Metabolic and toxic encephalopathies	Nonfocal, slowing of alpha, increased theta; polymorphic delta or rhythmic frontal delta, if severe; in chronic state, decreased voltage and slow activity; in addition, more specific sharp or spike waves in renal failure; triphasic high-voltage slow waves in hepatic encephalopathy, anoxia, uremia, hypercalcemia
Acute encephalitis	Slow activity, frontal high-voltage delta in coma; epileptiform activity

(*continued*)

TABLE 6.4 (*Cont.*)

Typical EEG Findings in Some Common Neuropsychiatric Disorders

Disorder	*EEG Findings*
Slow virus encephalitis (subacute panencephalitis, Creutzfeldt-Jakob disease)	Periodic bursts of 1–2 sec high-voltage sharp and slow waves every 5–15 sec, associated random bursts of theta and delta
Herpes simplex encephalitis	Focal sharp and slow discharges bitemporally
AIDS (and other leukoencephalopathies)	Focal or diffuse background slowing, some increased delta and theta
Alzheimer's disease	Initially normal, progresses through decreasing voltage and alpha with increasing theta and then delta; some sharp activity, asymmetries, and sleep spindles and K-complexes may diminish
Huntington's chorea	Initially normal, progresses to low-voltage and no organized rhythms
Parkinson's disease	In patients with dementia; mild background changes similar to Alzheimer's disease
Multiple sclerosis	50% normal; 50% have nonspecific, focal or generalized slowing
Normal-Pressure hydrocephalus	Initially normal; may progress to mild, nonspecific slowing
Head injury	Ranges from normal to severely abnormal, from mild increased theta to focal slow activity or bursts of slow and sharp waves
Migraine headaches	Usually normal; in complex migraine can demonstrate mild slowing focal or generalized, or unilateral high-voltage polymorphic slowing

ulus (i.e., it occurs at a specific time following the stimulus). These potentials are too small to be seen on the typical EEG. The typical EEG, however, represents a series of randomly occurring, approximately equal positive and negative waveforms that, when averaged, equal zero. After this is done, the remaining electrical activity consists of the time-locked (nonrandom) potentials evoked by the stimu-

TABLE 6.5

Medications Commonly Used or Encountered in a Neuropsychiatry Practice and Their EEG Effects

Substance	*EEG Finding*
Neuroleptics	Increased background theta and delta, slowing of alpha (to its lower range)
Benzodiazepines	Increased beta, speeding of alpha (to its higher range), increased amplitude
Barbiturates	Increased beta, speeding of alpha (to its higher range, increased amplitude)
Lithium	Increased theta, sharp waves
Tricyclic antidepressants	Increased background theta and delta, increased beta, some decrease in amplitude
Monamine oxidase inhibitors	Decreased alpha, some increased beta and decrease in amplitude
Anticonvulsants (diphenamine, carbamazepine, valproic acid)	In therapeutic doses: suppression of spike activity, increased normal voltages; at high or toxic doses: increased background slowing, high amplitude, diffuse delta
Anticholinergics	Same as tricyclic antidepressants
Opiates (in analgesic doses)	Increased alpha
Hallucinogens (lysergic acid diethylamide [LSD], mescaline, psilocybine)	Increased beta, decreased amplitude
Stimulants (amphetamine, cocaine, methylphenidate)	Increased beta, decreased amplitude

lus. Many of these potentials are then averaged to enhance them, and the electrical waveform that is produced represents the brain's electrical response to the stimuli. From many studies, the anatomic sources of the various components of this evoked, averaged waveform have been roughly determined. Thus, the examiner can follow the brain's response to the stimuli from the brain stem to the cortex. Topographic evoked potential permits the response to be followed across the cortex and even across the corpus callosum. Stimuli can be auditory (tones), visual (flashes of light, patterns, or words), or somatosensory (electrical).

Evoked potentials have been extensively used to study the way the normal brain and the brains of psychiatric patients process information. Evoked potentials are also clinically helpful to the neuropsychiatrist. Visual and auditory evoked potentials are important for the diagnosis of multiple sclerosis (delayed wave formation and abnormal waveforms resulting from demyelinating axonal conduction problems). In contrast, evoked potentials are normal in patients who are malingering or hysterical. Brain tumors can compress surrounding axons and thus produce prolonged interwave periods; gliomas, acoustic neuromas, and chiasmic lesions can be identified by such localized or lateralized evoked potential abnormalities. Postconcussion syndrome also produces prolonged interwave periods, whereas ischemic lesions lead to waves of lower amplitude without changes in when they occur. In addition, dementias can result in abnormal evoked potentials with delays in wave onset (Parkinson's dementia) or decreased wave amplitude (Huntington's and Alzheimer's diseases). Brain stem evoked potentials help to determine the degree of coma and whether brain death has occurred. Finally, many neurosurgical procedures are performed under evoked potential monitoring to guard against cranial nerve compression and stretching (177).

Neuropsychological Testing

Experimental neuropsychology, one of the disciplines conceptually underlying neuropsychiatry, focuses on the relationships between brain structure and information processing and cognition (544, 595). Clinical neuropsychology uses the concepts and data provided by experimental neuropsychology to develop strategies and measuring instruments for assessing the information processing and cognitive function of patients with brain damage or disease. Many of the more popular test batteries (e.g., Halstead-Reitan, Luria-Nebraska) and even the Wechlser Adult Intelligence Scale (WAIS), used as an measure of intelligence, were developed to discriminate brain damaged patients from the healthy.

If the neuropsychiatric clinician follows the diagnostic procedures and logic outlined in previous chapters and judiciously utilizes the cognitive and behavioral neurologic examination described in Chapter 5, further neuropsychological testing for diagnostic purposes is rarely needed. When additional diagnostic testing is needed, it is generally used to assess specific functions in greater detail in order to confirm or eliminate a diagnostic possibility (e.g., circumscribed right hemisphere or frontal lobe lesion).

Neuropsychological testing is also useful in vocational and social planning for the patient. After a patient recovers from an acute episode, neuropsychological assessment of the patient's cognitive strengths and weaknesses provides important information for the design of an appropriate rehabilitation program. This assessment also furnishes information about a patient's thinking ability. Along with personality testing, it is useful in designing psychological interventions.

Neuroimaging

Computed tomography (CT) is an imaging technology that measures the attenuation of an x-ray beam as it passes through the brain. The computer divides the brain into serial "slices." Each slice is further divided into tiny cubes, or voxels. The greater number of voxels per area, the higher is the resolution of the image. The degree of attenuation of the x-ray beam is measured through each voxel, and each measurement is coded on a scale of shading from white through gray to black. The shading pattern forms the picture of the structures being scanned. The x-ray beam is least affected as it passes through cerebrospinal fluid, which appears darkest in the picture. White matter attenuates the x-ray beam the most, and it appears lightest. Scanning is limited to the transverse or transaxial plane. CT is used clinically and for research. Many psychiatric patient groups have been found to have some abnormalities on CT. None of these is pathognomonic (48, 49) (see specific disorders in Chapters 9 through 19 for details).

Magnetic resonance imaging (MRI) has four advantages over CT: (1) images are of much greater resolution; (2) images can be obtained in all planes; (3) a relatively safe magnetic field and radio waves, rather than x-rays, are used to generate images; and (4) bone artifacts are not a problem with MRI.

MRI works by placing the patient in a magnetic field, which slightly realigns hydrogen protons. The patient is then bombarded with a radio frequency signal that "jiggles" the protons. The computer can measure the original changes in realignment through changes in the magnetic field and, following the radio frequency signal bombardment, the relaxation of the protons in various dimensional planes (T1 and T2 relaxation times). Patients whose bodies contain metal objects (e.g., aneurysm clips, skull plates, pacemakers), which can shift in the magnetic field, cannot be evaluated by MRI. Patients are placed in a tubular structure; claustrophobia is a problem for about 10% of them. This can be minimized by adequate preparation and, if needed, the wearing of a sleep mask.

MRI is generally preferable to CT. Coronal images permit visualization of structures of particular interest to the neuropsychiatric clinician: basal ganglia, amygdala, and hippocampus. T1-weighted scans are best for visualizing these structures. Posterior fossa structures are also best visualized with MRI, and bony artifact is avoided. T2-weighted scans are particularly good for visualizing tumors, multiple sclerotic plaques, and microinfarcts. The indications for CT and MRI are similar (see Table 6.2) (48, 49).

Single-photon emission computed tomography (SPECT) (722) is available at most medical centers. SPECT uses xenon 133 or iodine 123 isotopes, which emit single photons. Each is stable, with a relatively long half-life; thus, SPECT is practical in the clinical setting. Xenon and iodine are not normally present in humans and have low affinity to naturally occurring compounds. The risk for introducing these agents is unclear. As they have low affinity, they are basically suitable for measuring blood flow. Xenon is quickly cleared (about 30 minutes), so it can be used for repeated assessments of the same patient over a short period of time. Images can be made only in the transaxial plane. Compared with MRI, unfortunately, resolution is low.

The principle underlying the value of cerebral blood flow measurement is that blood flow reflects brain cell activity. Blood is diverted to brain regions that are actively working (i.e., processing information). Patients can be measured while at rest or while performing various cognitive tasks related to different cognitive/anatomic systems. Their SPECT patterns then can be compared to those observed in normal subjects under the same conditions.

Clinically, SPECT is potentially helpful in further clarifying lesions that affect blood flow or produce a specific pattern of neuronal damage or dysfunction resulting in more or less neuronal activity and, thus, more or less blood flow to that region. Imaging time varies from 10 to 45 minutes for most studies.

As SPECT does not have the resolution of either CT or MRI, it is not as helpful in identifying and characterizing static structural lesions. SPECT can be helpful, however, in documenting clinically ambiguous strokes. Some patients with acquired immunodeficiency syndrome (AIDS) demonstrate patchy areas of decreased perfusion in the early stages of CNS involvement. Caffeine and nicotine produce generalized decreases in cerebral perfusion, whereas anxiety states are associated with a generalized increase. Excitatory lesions (i.e., seizure foci) produce a localized increase in perfusion only during ictus and reduced or normal perfusion interictally.

SPECT also can be helpful in discriminating elderly patients with depression and pseudodementia from those with early Alzheimer's disease (with or without depressive features). Nearly 80% of Alzheimer patients have a decrease in blood flow in the posterior temporoparietal regions. Depressed patients with pseudodementia have either normal perfusion or a generalized or anterior (left greater than right) decrease in perfusion.

Positron emission tomography (PET) (759), although superior in image resolution to SPECT, remains an impractical technology for most medical centers. Cyclotron-produced positively charged electrons (positrons) of short half-life (2–30 minutes) are often used. Because they attach to metabolically active molecules in the brain, PET can be used to study cell activity directly, as well as indirectly through blood flow. Imaging time is somewhat longer than that of SPECT.

Fluorodeoxyglucose (FDG) is a commonly used tracer. As FDG is not fully metabolized, it becomes embedded in the glucose utilization pathway of a cell. The amount embedded during the 30 or so minutes of scanning time reflects the activity of the cell in that time period. Usually, axial images are reconstructed from the distribution of FDG. Three-dimensional images also can be created. ^{11}C-deoxyglucose and $^{15}0_2$ are other isotopes used for measuring glucose and oxygen metabolism, respectively. Image resolution depends on the scanner.

PET is primarily a research tool; PET findings related to specific syndromes are presented in Part II. No finding, however, is pathognomic, and some are conflicting. Common PET patterns reported are reduced frontal metabolism ("hypofrontality") and abnormal cortical and subcortical metabolic relationships in schizophrenics and manics, mild frontal hypofrontality and abnormal basal ganglia metabolism in some depressives, and increased parahippocampal and septohippocampal or basal ganglia metabolism among some patients with anxiety disorder (399, 405, 536).

Cerebral Blood Flow Imaging

Although PET can be used to measure cerebral blood flow (CBF) as well as cellular metabolism, CBF imaging is a less expensive and more practical technology. CBF imaging is based on the scintillation detection of the rates in which inert freely diffusible radioisotopes (e.g., krypton 85, ^{133}xenon) are cleared from the brain following intracarotid injection or inhalation. Analysis of clearance curves are transposed into two- and three-dimensional images of the brain that represent gray and white matter perfusions.

CBF studies in schizophrenic, manic, and depressive patients have produced findings similar to those with PET. CBF imaging also has been used to study Alzheimer's patients (decreased posterior flow), Pick's patients (decreased frontotemporal flow), patients with multi-infarct dementia (patchy areas of reduced flow), patients with Huntington's disease (high frontal and low parietal flow), chronic alcoholics and alcoholics in withdrawal (diffuse reduced flow in both groups), and drug abusers (decreased flow in smokers and caffeine and barbiturate users, increased flow with stimulants) (366, 637).

PART II

Syndromes

Chapter
7

History and Classification

Karl Kahlbaum was first to organize mental disorders systematically on the empirical basis of symptom clusters and course (493). He described five nosologic categories: (1) idiopathic, progressively deteriorating disorders affecting all aspects of psychic life (akin to Kraepelin's later concept of dementia praecox); (2) idiopathic, postpubescent disorders with circumscribed symptoms (including what today are termed mood disorder and delusional disorder); (3) syndromes with known etiology and mixed symptomatology that affect all aspects of psychic life (akin to the old organic mental syndrome category and the new "secondary" classification system); (4) disorders acquired before, during, or shortly after birth that are characterized by symptoms lacking in psychological content (akin to today's dementias and psychoses of perinatal origin); and (5) disturbances associated with stages of transition of biologic processes (e.g., adolescence, menopause).

Kahlbaum's 1874 (494) monograph on catatonia (or "tension insanity") was also a milestone in the evolution of psychiatric nosology. With his pupil Ewald Hecker, who characterized hebephrenia (430), Kahlbaum was the first to apply Sydenham's principles for establishing the diagnostic validity of disorders without known etiology to mental illness (827). Kahlbaum considered catatonia's distinctive clinical features and course, as well as the variety of neuropathology he observed during the autopsies of many of his patients, to confirm his contention that catatonia was a distinct disease entity.

Influenced by Griesinger's (389) concept of unitary psychosis, in which insanity passed through stages of melancholia, mania, amentia, and finally dementia, Kahlbaum carefully detailed the sequential emergence of each stage of catatonia. He described an initial, short-lasting episode of motor symptoms characterized by immobility, posturing, and waxy flexibility that ended in a hyperkinetic state; a second stage of melancholia often with stupor; a third stage of "exaltation and rapid and pressured speech" ("a certain pathos-filled 'ecstasy,' this entrains a compulsion to talk in oratorical style"); and, finally, after recurrent exacerbations and remissions of states of passivity and exaltation, an end stage of dementia. Patients could recover from one or another of the earlier stages and not progress to a demented state. Kahlbaum was convinced that catatonia was an expression of a pathologic brain process.

Although he was never awarded a major teaching post and was ignored by major publishers, Kahlbaum's work influenced Kraepelin's development of the concept of dementia praecox (553, 554). Eugen Bleuler (116) changed the dementia praecox terminology to schizophrenia and elaborated on Kraepelin's disease concept. Bleuler fully endorsed much of Kraepelin's notions, however, and both men accepted Kahlbaum's basic nosology.

Kraepelin's contribution to Kahlbaum's classification system and disease concept consisted of the algorithms (i.e., the logical structure) he devised to separate dementia praecox from affective disorder (see Chapter 9). The Kahlbaum/Kraepelin system was the template for DSM-I and II.

DSM-III was a major departure from its predecessors in that more detailed criteria replaced general pattern descriptions, the neurosis category was abandoned (although syndromes were retained), and the personality disorder category was revised, including shifting cyclothymia from the personality disorders into the affective states (Kahlbaum's original idea). DSM-III-R is a minor modification of DSM-III, whereas the proposed DSM-IV may have some fundamental changes that will include discarding the organic mental syndrome label for "secondary" or "symptomatic" terminology.

The chapters that follow essentially adhere to the specific syndrome labels of the DSM system. The broader category labels, however, differ from that of the DSM system, as they follow the conceptual guidelines described in Chapter 8. The four categories are (1) idiopathic morbid states (generally incorporating the psychoses and some DSM-III-R personality disorders that appear to be mild morbid states of illness, rather than extremes of trait, i.e., personality disorders); (2) secondary or symptomatic morbid states (analogous to the DSM-III-R organic mental disorder section and the proposed DSM-IV secondary strategy); (3) extremes of traits (incorporating the rest of the DSM personality category); and (4) state disorders of extremes of trait (incorporating the old DSM-II neuroses plus adjustment, somatization, and appetitive disorders) (see Table 7.1). Future research will determine the validity of this system, which is used here because it provides a conceptual framework (DSM-III-R is atheoretical) for understanding the relationships between disorders and seems well suited to the practice of neuropsychiatry.

TABLE 7.1

Idiopathic Morbid States

I. Mood Disorders:

Major

- Melancholia/pseudodementia
- Mania/bipolar mood disorder: mixed mood states, lethal catatonia
- Cyclothymia, bipolar spectrum and borderline disorder
- Schizoaffective disorders: unipolar, bipolar types
- Puerperal psychoses and premenstrual syndromes
- Brief reactive psychosis

Minor

- Dysthymia ("reactive" subgroup)
- Nonmelancholic depressions
- Atypical depressions

II. Delusional/hallucinatory states:

Schizophrenia: various subtyping schemata (paranoid versus nonparanoid, positive versus negative symptom)
Schizoidia: schizotypal and schizoid disorders
Delusional disorders: simple delusional disorders, paranoid personality, schizophreniform psychosis, induced psychotic disorder, atypical psychotic disorder

Secondary or Symptomatic Morbid States

I. Dementia

II. Delirium

III. Specific brain syndromes:

A. Epilepsy and epileptic psychosis
B. Frontal lobe syndromes: orbitomedial, convexity
C. Parietal and temporal lobe syndromes
D. Right-hemisphere syndromes
E. Other secondary psychotic syndromes
F. Amnestic syndromes
G. Head trauma: postconcussion syndrome, post-traumatic dementia, thalamic syndrome
H. Dissociative states
I. Sleep disorders
J. Headache

Extremes of Trait

I. Dramatic or erratic behavior disorders:

A. Antisocial
B. Histrionic
C. Narcissistic

II. Anxiety and fearfulness behavior disorders:

A. Avoidant
B. Obsessive compulsive
C. Passive-aggressive
D. Dependent
E. Cognitive and somatic trait anxiety syndromes

State Disorders of Trait Extremes

I. Anxiety disorders:

A. Panic disorder
B. Agoraphobia
C. Social phobia
D. Simple phobia
E. Generalized anxiety disorder
F. Post-traumatic stress disorder
G. Adjustment disorders

II. Obsessional syndromes:

A. Obsessive compulsive disorder
B. Gilles de la Tourette's syndrome
C. Anorexia nervosa and bulimia
D. Post-traumatic stress disorder
E. Trichotillomania
F. Hypochondriasis

III. Somatoform disorders:

A. Somatization disorder (Briquet's syndrome)
B. Conversion symptoms
C. Somatoform pain disorders
D. Hypochondriasis
E. Other somatoform disorders

IV. Substance abuse (alcoholism and drug abuse)

V. Sexual dysfunctions

Chapter 8

Concepts of Illness and Personality

The array of psychiatric syndromes often appears forbidding to inexperienced clinicians: DSM-III-R lists more than 150 adult conditions and syndromes organized into 18 broad categories. A perspective from which to view these syndromes can help in understanding why some co-occur, why others appear to share a common liability, and why various treatments work for some syndromes and not for others.

One of the first basic decisions a clinician makes about a patient is whether or not the patient has an illness (i.e., whether the deviant behavior or the patient's concerns result from a pathologic process). This decision is particularly important in psychiatry, as boundaries between normality and abnormality are not always clear. For example, in their studies of bereavement, Clayton (188) observed that a large proportion of recent widows met research criteria for major depression, although neither the widows nor the investigators believed this represented illness. In addition, some forms of hallucinations (e.g., pseudo, hypnogogic) can occur in people who have no illness or diagnosable condition. Finally, everyone has experienced anxiety. Nevertheless, the basic question of whether or not the patient has an illness can guide the organizing of psychiatric nosology into a more understandable whole. This organization divides adult psychiatric disorders into three broad categories: (1) definite morbid states (conditions with identifiable, although not always specific, pathology, the etiology of which is often not known, e.g., Alzheimer's disease, schizophrenia); (2) definite deviations from the perceived norm (i.e., some abnormal personalities), some of which (such as schizotypal disorder) will turn out to be illnesses (i.e., due to pathology), and others of which (such as passive dependent personality) will turn out to be extremes of human trait behavior resulting from nonpathologic processes; and (3) states of disorder (such as some anxiety disorders) that tend to occur under certain circumstances in individuals with deviant traits. Each of these categories is discussed in the chapters of

Part II that follow. To understand their relationships, however, one must understand the concept of illness.

The Concept of Illness

When measured by virtually any yardstick, human behaviors fall along a continuum in a normal distribution: the famous bell-shaped curve. On almost all dimensions, the largest proportion of individuals are always measured to be somewhere in the middle of the curve. By social convention, the behaviors (their form, content, intensity) exhibited within this middle part of the distribution are considered "normal." The farther away from the middle a behavior (or the person exhibiting that behavior), the more abnormal it is. Figure 8.1 displays such a distribution for a group of hypothetical behaviors, termed *A*, with extremes to the right and to the left of the norm. Individuals with extremes of *A* in either direction are, by statistical definition, far from the norm and, therefore, are "abnormal." As they deviate significantly from the norm, they are also literally deviant. In this sense, deviant and abnormal mean the same thing. However, neither implies that the deviant (abnormal) *A* behavior results from pathology (i.e., a morbid process). Further, although often the case, this deviance or abnormality does not imply "bad". For example, having a high intelligence quotient (IQ) is considered by society to be good. The "high" of the high IQ, however, means deviation from the norm, and a person with an IQ of 150 is abnormal.

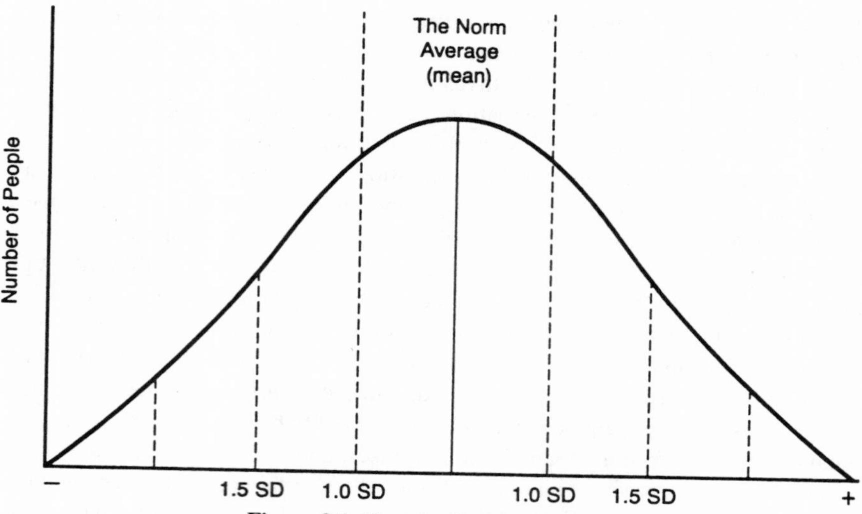

Figure 8.1 Hypothetical Behaviors *A*

KEY: SD, standard deviation.

Height is another example of the above concept. In the United States today, the average (norm) height for an adult male is about 5 feet, 10 inches. Some individuals are much taller: 6 feet 5 inches and above; in Figure 8.1, they would be found in the far right of the distribution. All of these tall individuals are deviant or abnormal. Some of them play professional basketball and, although abnormal, have wonderfully coordinated bodies and central nervous systems. Their abnormality of height is clearly not the result of pathology. On the other hand, there are other individuals, equally tall and, therefore, deviant, whose abnormal height results from pituitary tumors. The abnormality of height in these individuals results from pathology. All very tall people are abnormal, but only some are pathologically tall.

Nevertheless, tall people (pathologically so or not) often have a difficult time in a society designed by and for the majority, or the people in the middle of the distribution. The very tall person often needs specially made clothes and an extra-long bed; he must be careful in buildings with low door frames and ceilings. All of these things, and many more, are usually constructed for the person of average height. Because of the body mechanics involved, very tall people also must be careful to avoid back injury when bending or stooping to pick up heavy objects. Some of them, despite their precautions and attempts to obtain especially designed items, have problems because of their deviance: neck and lower back pain. Their abnormal height is not the result of pathology, but it can result in pathology.

The above applies to psychiatric disorder, and these analogous relationships are illustrated in Table 8.1. Specific evidence for associated pathology in each disorder in this illustration is discussed in the following chapters; various forms of treatment are described in Part III. A study of Table 8.1 should suggest, however, that specific treatment approaches for certain disorders are likely to be more effective than others. For example, in personality disorders without pathology, biologic intervention (e.g., medication) is unlikely to be of benefit. One would not prescribe a medication to shrink (pun intended) a basketball player. Trying to shrink some personality deviations with medication is likely to be equally unsuccessful. On the other hand, the very tall individual may have difficulties in adjusting to a world designed for much shorter people. Counseling, education, and persuasion may help that person and, indeed, may prevent the secondary conditions (e.g., back pain) for which the very tall "unadjusted" person is at risk. A metaphorical psychotherapy vignette may be helpful here:

> A very tall person loves little red sports cars and insists on buying them. Continued cramming of his body into these cars has taken its toll and the very tall person now suffers from bruised knees, a sore back, and headaches. Shrinking the very tall person is unfeasible. Through the use of persuasion, counseling, and education, however, some therapists (depending on their personalities) might convince this very tall person that alternatives to little red sports cars will be satisfying, will not lead to aches and pains, and will allow the present aches and pains an opportunity to heal.

TABLE 8.1

Deviation and Pathology: An Analogy

Height Metaphor	*Psychiatric Disorder*
Average height ± 1.5 standard deviation (the "normal range")	No diagnosis
Deviation with no pathology (the very tall)	Most personality disorders
Conditions secondary to deviation with no known primary pathology (the very tall with bad backs)	Anxiety disorders, somatization disorders
Deviation with pathology (the very tall who may have endocrinopathy or other aberrations, e.g., xyy)	Borderline personality, schizoid, schizotypal, paranoid personality
Deviation with pathology (the very tall acromegalic)	Psychoses, coarse brain syndromes

The treatment strategy highlighted in this vignette is often employed by the neuropsychiatric clinician in his care of patients. Although interpersonal, rather than biologic, this treatment strategy is based on the recognition of the biology of the disorders that patients suffer. This strategy also implies that the clinician concerned with the treatment of patients with psychiatric disorder must be prepared to treat more than just the pathologic process. Behavioral deviation of any kind, and for whatever reason (pathologic or not), may require intervention. When a deviation adversely affects an individual's function or adaptation, causes pain or increases his risk for morbidity or mortality, or leads to the subjective sense of discontent or ill ease, that deviation becomes proper concern for the neuropsychiatric clinician.

Personality

Historical Development

Many of the DSM-III-R categories relate to personality deviation (with and without pathology). Personality is established early in life and remains fairly constant over time and across settings. Such constancy is referred to as trait phenomena, as opposed to state conditions that appear to have specific beginnings and endings (e.g., an episode of depression). Personality refers to characteristic, habitual behaviors that have developed from a complicated (and little understood) interaction between genes and environment (biologic, interpersonal, and cultural). Specifically, personality has affective (temperament and arousal) and cognitive (speed, manner of information processing) components.

Much of the history of personality theory relates to the ancient humoral theory of disease: four bodily fluids have to be in balance for health. From this theory derive such words as sanguine (optimistic, from too much blood), phlegmatic (apathetic, from too much phlegm), and choleric (irritable or irascible from too much "yellow" bile). An excess of the fourth humor, "black" bile, was believed to cause melancholia.

In the early nineteenth century, Gall developed the notion of phrenology (skull configuration and bumps reflecting underlying brain structure) and made the first organized connection between brain and behavior. Nineteenth-century writers (Pritchard, Koch, Kraepelin) developed the idea that deviant personality either resulted from brain pathology or was a maladaptive extreme of the normal (226). Kretschmer (560), and later Sheldon (892, 893), related personality type to body type (see Table 8.2). Schneider (879) and Slater (917) considered some personality deviations to represent a "neurotic constitution" predisposing individuals to such states as anxiety disorder and obsessive compulsive disorder. They referred to these disorders as "personality illness."

Modern Systems of Personality Theory

The study of personality and personality disorder has become more scientific during the past 20 years. Thousands of normal and abnormal individuals have been assessed in various ways to uncover the determinants of personality and its deviations. Two approaches are discussed here.

TABLE 8.2

Sheldon's Body Type and Behavior Schema

Endomorphic	*Mesomorphic*	*Ectomorphic*	*Dysplastic*
Cyclothymic Extroverted Hysterical traits	Psychopathy Assertiveness Low anxiety	Schizoid personality Introversion Depressive traits Anxious traits Obsessiveness Overly restrained Self-conscious	Developmental, congenital, and chromosomal disorders

One approach is that espoused by Tellegen (985, 986) and Cloninger (193, 195), who have developed overlapping views of normal personality and its assessment. From studying families, twins, and adoptees, Tellegen and others have determined that several traits (characteristic, habitual patterns of behavior) are normally distributed in the general population and that these traits have high heritability (i.e., about 40% of their variability can be attributed to genes). These traits are *positive emotionality* (akin to extroversion), *negative emotionality* (akin to neuroticism), and *constraint* (related to conformity). The traits are further broken down into 11 personality dimensions with specific behavioral descriptions for high and low scorers on each dimension. Table 8.3 describes Tellegen's personality dimensions.

Cloninger has expanded Tellegen's approach by incorporating neurochemical and psychophysiologic dimensions into his personality schema. As they interact, these processes result in three personality dimensions of high heritability: *novelty seeking*, *harm avoidance*, and *reward dependence*. Novelty seeking is the tendency toward frequent exploratory behavior and intense and pleasurable responses to novel stimuli. Harm avoidance is the tendency to respond intensely to aversive stimuli, and to avoid punishment, novelty, and nonreward. Reward dependence is the tendency to respond intensely to reward and succor and to maintain rewarded behavior. Table 8.4 shows Cloninger's personality dimensions. Cloninger also proposes that these dimensions can be used to understand personality deviation without pathology, as well as the normal range of personality. For example, the combination of low harm avoidance and reward dependence plus high novelty seeking delineates an antisocial personality, whereas the opposite defines passive-dependent and avoidance personalities. Table 8.5 displays the relationships between the personality traits defined by Cloninger and the personality extremes delineated in the DSM classification. Cloninger further relates his three personality dimensions to neurotransmitter systems. Novelty seeking is associated with low basal dopaminergic activity, harm avoidance with high basal serotonergic activity, and reward dependence with low basal noradrenergic activity. Data from studies of humans and nonhumans tend to support this concept (193). The Tellegen and Cloninger systems probably measure similar biologic dimensions. Each uses a self-rating personality questionnaire. These questionnaires provide the neuropsychiatric clinician with more reliable and valid information than what is usually obtained from projective psychological tests (e.g., Rorschach), and other widely used assessment instruments (e.g., MMPI).

Whereas Tellegen and Cloninger focus on personality dimensions normally distributed in the general population, Tyrer's approach focuses on the extremes of these dimensions (the abnormal) and their relationship to state conditions (the personality illnesses of the mid–twentieth-century writers). In a series of studies, Tyrer and associates (1011–1013) demonstrated that personality disorders, as de-

TABLE 8.3

Tellegen's Personality Dimensions

	High Scorer	*Low Scorer*
	Positive Emotionality	
Well-being	Happy and cheerful disposition; feels good about self; optimistic; lives an exciting, active live	Reports few experiences of joy and excitement, is seldom really happy
Social potency	Is forceful and decisive, is persuasive and likes to influence others, enjoys leadership roles, takes charge of and likes to be noticed at social events	Prefers others to take charge and make decisions, does not like to persuade others, does not aspire to leadership, does not enjoy being the center of attention
Achievement	Works hard, likes long hours, enjoys demanding projects, persists where others give up, puts work and accomplishment before many other things, is a perfectionist	Does not like to work harder than necessary, avoids demanding projects, does not persist when success is unlikely, is not ambitious or a perfectionist
Social closeness	Sociable and likes people; takes pleasure in, and values, close interpersonal ties; is warm and affectionate; turns to others for comfort and help	Likes being alone, does not mind pulling up roots, is aloof and distant, prefers to work problems out on his own
	Negative Emotionality	
Stress reaction	Nervous, feels vulnerable and is sensitive, worrier, easily upset and irritable, has changing moods, can feel miserable without reason, is troubled by guilt feelings	Can put fears and worries out of mind, quickly gets over upsetting experiences, is not troubled by emotional guilt or guilt feelings
Alienation	Thinks of self as victim of bad luck, feels mistreated, is a target of false rumors, believes others wish him harm, feels betrayed and used by "friends"	Does not see self as victim, feels treated fairly, does not feel taken advantage of

(*continued*)

TABLE 8.3 (*Cont.*)

Tellegen's Personality Dimensions

	High Scorer	*Low Scorer*
Aggression	Will hurt others for own advantage, is physically aggressive, is vindictive, likes to frighten and discomfit others, likes violent scenes	Will not take advantage of others, is not violent, would rather turn the other cheek than seek revenge, does not enjoy others' misfortunes, does not like to witness physical aggression
	Constraint	
Control	Reflective, cautious, careful, and plodding; is rational and sensible; likes to anticipate events; likes to plan his activities	Impulsive and spontaneous, can be reckless and careless, prefers to "play things by ear"
Harm avoidance	Does not enjoy the excitement of adventure and danger; prefers safer activities even if they are tedious or aggravating	Enjoys risky stunts and adventures, may enjoy the excitement of a dangerous emergency or disaster, might expose self to possible attack or injury
Traditionalism	Endorses high moral standards, supports religious values and institutions, condemns selfish disregard of others, deplores permissiveness, endorses strict child-rearing practices, values propriety and a good reputation	Does not belabor the importance of high morals, considers traditional religion outdated, questions established authority, sees merit in selfishness, values rebelliousness and freedom of expression, does not believe in punitive discipline, is not very prudish
Absorption	Is emotionally responsive to engaging sights and sounds, is readily captured by entrancing stimuli, thinks in images and has synesthetic and other "cross-modal" experiences, can summon and become absorbed in vivid and compelling recollections and imaginings, experiences episodes of expanded (extrasensory, mystical) awareness and other altered states (high scorers consistent with low constraint)	Is not easily caught up in sensory and imaginative experiences, does not readily relinquish a realistic frame of reference (low scorers consistent with high constraint)

SOURCE: After Tellegen.

TABLE 8.4

Cloninger's System of Personality

Dimension	*High Scorer*	*Low Scorer*
Novelty seeking (behavioral activation, dopaminergic activity)	Low basal dopaminergic activity: curious, exploratory, fickle, easily bored, impulsive, impressionistic, disorderly, unconventional, quick-tempered, excitable, evasive, deceptive	High basal dopaminergic activity: content, quiet, rigid, patient, methodical, reflective, frugal, orderly, reserved, stoical, regimented, forthright
Harm avoidance (behavioral inhibition; serotonergic activity)	High basal serotoninergic activity: cautious, worrying, apprehensive, pessimistic, restrained, fearful, shy, fatigable, asthenic, inhibited	Low basal serotoninergic activity: carefree, risk-taking, bold, vigorous, outgoing, fearless, confident, optimistic, energetic
Reward dependence (behavioral maintenance, noradrenergic activity)	Low basal noradrenergic activity: sentimental, socially sensitive, vulnerable, narcissistic, helpful, persistent, heroic, tender-hearted, dedicated	High basal noradrenergic activity: practical, insensitive, self-disciplined, tough-minded, emotionally cool, detached, irresolute, cold-blooded

SOURCE: After Cloninger.

TABLE 8.5

Cloninger's Personality Dimensions and DSM Personality Extremes

Personality Extreme	*Novelty Seeking*	*Harm Avoidance*	*Reward Dependence*
Antisocial	High	Low	Low
Histrionic/ narcissistic	High	Low	High
Passive-aggressive	High	High	High
Dependent/ avoidant	Low	High	High
Obsessional	Low	High	Low

fined by the DSM and ICD systems, are at the extreme end of a multidimensional continuum (similar conceptually to Cloninger's and Tellegen's systems) and that certain of these extremes are associated with state disorders. Table 8.6 displays Tyrer's findings. Five trait patterns (i.e., personality extremes) were identified by Tyrer, three of which relate to state phenomena. The fact that schizoid and dysthymic traits do not relate to what used to be called "the neuroses" is consistent with evidence (see Chapters 10 and 11, respectively) that they are, in fact, low-grade chronic forms of illness: i.e., deviations with pathology. Of equal interest to the clinician is the fact that whereas the DSM system for antisocial (or sociopathic) personality relies solely on historical, social class–related diagnostic criteria (e.g., truancy, drug abuse, criminality), the Tyrer system provides some cross-sectional behaviors that can be directly observed by the examiner (e.g., irritability, callousness).

Combining the Tellegen-Cloninger focus on normal personality traits and Tyrer's focus on personality extremes and their associated state conditions provides a practical framework for assessing personality and making clinical predictions from that assessment.

The DSM system is somewhat different from those suggested by Tellegen, Cloninger, and Tyrer. Given the above discussion of personality, deviation, and illness, however, the DSM system can be more clearly organized, as demonstrated in Table 8.7. In assessing for deviation, the clinician has two options. First, he can ask the patient to complete one of the self-rating instruments for assessing personality. These questionnaires can be easily scored and, along with the questionnaire descriptors, provide the clinician with a detailed pattern of the patient's trait behaviors. Second, as part of his evaluation, the clinician can focus on the patient's

TABLE 8.6

Tyrer's Classification of Personality Deviation and Related States

Personality Extreme	*Associated States*
Sociopathy: aggressive, irritable, impulsive, callous, emotionally labile, irresponsible	Violence Criminality
Passive-dependent: vulnerable, submissive, sensitive, dependent, resourceless, childish, asthenic, histrionic, irresponsible, anxious, emotionally labile	Phobias Anxiety
Anancastic: rigid, conscientious, nonimpulsive, hypochondriacal, anxious	Phobias Obsessiveness
Dysthymic: anxious, introspective, sensitive, pessimistic	—
Schizoid: emotionally aloof, suspicious, eccentric, nonlabile, avoidant	—

interpersonal and social history to obtain information that would characterize the patient's trait behaviors. In this latter effort, the clinician should ask questions that pertain to the group headings in the first column of Table 8.4. For example, the assessment of the patient's social and personal history should reveal if his hobbies and interests suggest high or low novelty seeking (soldier of fortune and world travel versus mild-mannered bank teller for 20 years), harm avoidance (hang gliding versus crossword puzzles), and reward dependence (lover of romance novels

TABLE 8.7

Modified DSM System of Personality Disorders

Group	*Types*
Disorders of odd, eccentric behavior (mild forms of illness)	Paranoid, schizoid, schizotypal
Disorders of dramatic, emotional or erratic behavior	Histrionic, narcissistic, antisocial (sociopathy), borderline*
Disorders of anxiety and fearfulness	Avoidant, compulsive, passive-aggressive, dependnet

*Most likely, this is also a mild form of illness (mood disorder).

versus exclusive reader of nonfiction and business magazines). More specific assessment can incorporate the detailed descriptors for high and low traits into question forms, such as: "Are you the kind of person who usually. . . ? Would you say you are . . . ? Do people think of you as a person who . . . ? Are you easily . . . ? Are you overly . . . ?" Specific personality extremes are discussed in Chapters 14 and 15.

Chapter

9

Idiopathic Morbid States

I. Schizophrenia

History

Early Development

In the fifth edition of his *Textbook of Psychiatry*, Kraepelin (551) detailed his classification of mental illness, in which dementia praecox and manic-depressive insanity were differentiated. That book undoubtedly has had a more profound effect on twentieth-century descriptive psychiatry than any other single written work. Modern psychiatric classification throughout the world is but a variation of Kraepelin's work. The two principal forces behind his synthesis of mental illness were the ideas of Karl Kahlbaum (494) and Ewald Hecker (430) and Kraepelin's own training in experimental psychology (545).

Nineteenth-century psychological theory divided the mind into the Platonic notion of three regions of function: (1) thinking, (2) volition or will, and (3) feelings or emotions (278, 433). Kraepelin's concepts of psychological disease were rooted in this notion of a tripartite mind (no longer considered valid), and his cross-sectional criteria for dementia praecox included deficits in all three spheres. In contrast, he believed that manic-depressive insanity involved a disturbance in feeling but spared the other two mind spheres. Kraepelin also delineated the two disorders by their courses: dementia praecox began in early adulthood (ages 15 to 25) and deteriorated into dementia; manic-depressive insanity began a decade later and was an episodic, remitting illness.

Another important influence on Kraepelin's thinking was Kahlbaum and Hecker's delineation of what they believed to be discrete illnesses: catatonia and hebephrenia. Kraepelin was thoroughly versed in their writings and considered the clinical criteria and course of illness established by Hecker for hebephrenia especially applicable to Kahlbaum's notions about catatonia. As both disorders had an early onset, could result in chronic personality deterioration, and affected all three regions of the tripartite mind, Kraepelin felt justified in considering the two syndromes as variants of a single disease process. In later writings (554) he incorporated dementia paranoides and other dementias, along with catatonia and hebephrenia, under Morel's (687) term *dementia praecox*.

Contrary to the present notion that Bleuler dramatically altered Kraepelin's concept of dementia praecox, Bleuler actually reinforced many of Kraepelin's ideas (116). Bleuler believed, however, that the term *dementia praecox* was too specific and did not always fit the clinical course, which he believed more variable than originally described. He also felt that hallucinations and delusions were secondary features. He considered the core, or primary, features of schizophrenia to be affective blunting, autism, ambivalence, associational loosening, and passivity. The first four of these have become his "four A's." Nevertheless, Bleuler fully agreed with Kraepelin that dementia praecox or, as he termed it, schizophrenia (split mind, i.e., mental functions affected to different degrees) affected the three regions of the tripartite mind (his "four A's" are a reworking of this concept); was "one or very few diseases, a single disease accounting for the vast majority of cases"; and always resulted in some residual deficit. This remains our present-day notion of the nature of schizophrenia. The modern diagnostic criteria—Feighner (299), RDC (927), DSM-III (60)—encompass all of the basic characteristics delineated by Kraepelin and Bleuler. Table 9.1 displays Kraepelin's, Bleuler's, and DSM criteria for schizophrenia within the tripartite mind concept.

Twentieth-Century Misconceptions

Among laypeople, schizophrenia has become synonymous with psychosis. In large part, this misconception derives from past deficiencies in psychiatric diagnostic reliability and research methodology (925), which permitted an extraordinary overdiagnosis of schizophrenia (776, 976). A concurrent lack of adherence to basic Kraepelinian concepts of the syndrome also led to a broadening of the requirements for diagnosis (59) and resulted in a clinical description that would have been unrecognizable to Kraepelin and Bleuler.

To put the degree of past overdiagnosis in perspective, federal and state statistics, prior to the mid-1970s (1015, 1090), indicated that the national range of the psychiatric admission prevalence of schizophrenia then was 24 to 40%, that 30% of all first admissions to psychiatric hospitals were labeled schizophrenic, that 60% of all mental hospital beds were occupied by such individuals, and that, because of the relatively large number of state mental hospital beds compared with

TABLE 9.1

Diagnostic Criteria for Schizophrenia within the Tripartite Mind Concept

	Emotion	*Will/Volition*	*Thinking*
Kraepelin	Dullness, indifference, apathy, no sense of shame	Catatonia, stubbornness, stupor	Denial of illness, noncompliance with treatment
Bleuler	Affective flattening	Ambivalence, passivity	Autistic thinking, associational loosening, formal thought disorder
DSM-III-R	Flat or grossly inappropriate affect, residual-phase features (marked social isolation and withdrawal, blunted and inappropriate affect)	Catatonia, residual-phase features (markedly decreased initiative, interests, energy, marked impairment in personal hygiene and grooming)	Incoherence or marked loosening of associations; residual beliefs or magical thinking; digressive, vague speech; poverty of speech

total beds of other specialties, 25% of *all* U.S. hospital beds, regardless of specialty, were occupied by individuals labeled schizophrenic. These figures are fallacious.

During the 1960s, the United States and the United Kingdom collaborated in a study of diagnostic patterns in the two countries (558). This international pilot study of schizophrenia (219, 865) demonstrated that U.S. psychiatrists overdiagnosed schizophrenia and underdiagnosed mood disorder and personality deviation. Mood disorder was actually diagnosed 20 times more frequently in England and Wales than in the United States. Project diagnosticians, using specific diagnostic criteria, were in general agreement with U.K. psychiatrists, who diagnosed one half of the schizophrenia, three times as much depression, and nine times as much mania in the same patient sample as did the U.S. psychiatrists. Other studies (889) comparing international patterns of diagnosis supported the U.S.–U.K. observation of the American psychiatrists' propensity to overdiagnose schizophrenia at the expense of mood disorder and personality disorders. Numerous additional studies (688, 968, 969) also demonstrated that patients clinically labeled as acute, good-prognosis, paranoid, catatonic, and schizoaffective schizophrenia rarely satisfied research criteria for schizophrenia and most frequently satisfied research criteria for mood disorder.

Among many studies of the 1970s, in which modern diagnostic criteria were applied to samples of consecutive psychiatric admissions, the average prevalence of schizophrenia was less than 4%, whereas between 25 and 33% of most samples satisfied criteria for affective disorder. Pope and Lipinski (776) estimated that at least 40% of patients previously diagnosed as schizophrenic actually suffered from mood disorders. These figures represent a more than tenfold decrease in the observed hospital prevalence of schizophrenia. Population studies and family risk studies (12, 1004) also consistently found figures for schizophrenia lower than previously reported with old diagnostic methods. These studies suggest that chronic schizophrenia is now a rare disorder, affecting between 0.3 to 0.6% of the population. All of these statistics would come as no surprise to Kraepelin (550), the father of the schizophrenia disease concept, who made the diagnosis of schizophrenia in only 5% of patients admitted to his Munich Clinic in 1893.

The low figures for schizophrenia are a function of rigorous criteria and not a change in its true prevalence. This is demonstrated in one study (949), in which the application of broad criteria led to a hospital admission prevalence for schizophrenia of 20 to 25%, whereas the application of research criteria to the same sample identified from 1.5–3.3% of the patients as schizophrenic. Data from several studies (72, 512, 562) demonstrate that failure to use rigorous criteria allows cultural sensitivity, theoretical bias, and availability of new treatments to influence unduly the frequency of diagnosis.

Another factor leading to the overdiagnosis of schizophrenia, particularly at the expense of mood disorder, was the misconception that certain psychopathologic features, specifically Schneider's first-rank symptoms, are pathognomonic of schizophrenia. Although these phenomena occur in a substantial proportion of schizophrenics (50 to 75%), they also occur in mood states. Their presence in mania or depression does not predict a poor treatment response or increased familial risk for schizophrenia (11, 162).

Catatonic behaviors also have been mistakenly considered pathognomonic of schizophrenia. Research (969) demonstrates, however, that catatonia is a syndrome associated with a variety of disease processes and that, whereas few catatonic patients (about 10%) satisfy research criteria for schizophrenia, many (30 to 50%) satisfy research criteria for mood disorder, respond well to treatment, and have a high risk for mood disorder among their first-degree relatives.

"Bizarre behavior" is frequently invoked to support a diagnosis of schizophrenia. However, manic patients also display a wide variety of exotic behaviors (159, 555, 601, 972, 975). For example, in a group of patients, each of whom met DSM-III-R inclusion criteria for mania, responded to lithium, and had family members with mood disorder, the following bizarre behaviors occurred:

> A woman put a pile of ashes on her head and wore these about town to prevent radio waves from affecting her thoughts.
>
> A man dressed in a black leather suit raced down Main Street and attacked tall buildings with long kitchen knives, as if he were Don Quixote.
>
> A woman placed furniture strategically throughout her house so she could hop from one piece to another without touching the floor, because she thought to do so would endanger her children.

Misdiagnosis also results from the false notion that incomprehensible speech is synonymous with schizophrenia. Formal thought disorder (see Chapter 4) is observed in more than 40% of hospitalized schizophrenic patients (982). Incomprehensible speech in the form of flight of ideas and clang associations, however, is observed in 70% of manics (159, 601, 972). These utterances are often imprecisely labeled as schizophrenic thought disorder, thereby satisfying one criterion for schizophrenia in several sets of diagnostic criteria and increasing the probability of a false-positive diagnosis. Understanding the nonspecificity of first-rank symptoms, catatonic features, bizarre behavior, and differentiating thought disorders is critical for the accurate diagnosis of the major psychoses.

Description

Behavior

The description by nineteenth- and early twentieth-century psychiatrists of behavior characteristic of what today we call schizophrenia cannot be surpassed. The works of Bleuler (116), Hammon (418), Haslam (423), Kahlbaum (493), Kraepelin (551, 553, 554), Peterson (755), and Spitzka (930), are essential reading for anyone truly interested in psychopathology.

Although the physical impression of schizophrenia today is often confounded by chronic exposure to neuroleptics, early workers in the predrug era described schizophrenics as physically awkward, gangly in appearance, and dyskinetic in movement. Fine hand movements were particularly jerky in nature; poor sequential finger movement was characteristic; and a tendency to grasp objects with an ulnar (primitive, using the palm), rather than radial (maturated, using index finger and thumb), dominance was, and still is, often observed (116, 172, 970).

Schizophrenics also demonstrate poor motor regulation, varying from perseverative behavior (repetitive movements and actions) and motor inertia (difficulty starting motor actions and stopping them once started) to motor overflow (adventitious movements) and motor impersistence (inability to maintain a single motor task despite adequate motor and sensory function).

Emotional blunting has been considered a core feature of schizophrenia since the earliest descriptions of the syndrome. Studies (7, 45) have demonstrated that emotional blunting can be assessed reliably (see Chapter 3). Globally, patients with emotional blunting appear withdrawn and indifferent to their surroundings. They lack emotional spontaneity, and their moods are shallow. They are often apathetic or lazy; lack warmth and empathy; are vocally and facially expressionless; are indifferent to their families and friends; have little concern for their present situation; and have no plans, ambitions, desires, or drive. Classically, this profound deficit in affect begins in the late teens or early 20s and rapidly progresses to a stage in which the sufferer is unable to maintain employment, has no friends, remains unmarried or separated from his spouse, has no sexual drive and may never have had sexual intercourse, and prefers to spend his time alone at home and dependent on others. These patients often end their days at the fringes of society—dirty and disheveled, living in the streets, hoarding garbage in rooming houses, or aimlessly wandering the grounds of state hospitals.

Thought disorder is the second core feature of the schizophrenic syndrome, but it is a misnomer. Nineteenth- and early twentieth-century writers used the term to characterize abnormalities of language production (e.g., paraphasic speech, speech without content, neologisms), rather than to define aberrant concept formation and abstraction (e.g., unable to recognize the basic category of such objects as apples and pears), which also are observed in schizophrenics. Thus, schizophrenic language, phenomenologically, is not schizophrenic thought, although disturbances in the former often have been asserted to result from the latter. Formal thought disorder, by convention, refers to schizophrenic language production.

It long has been asserted (171, 533) that the language of schizophrenics shares phenomenologic similarities with aphasic speech (see Chapter 4). The data from several studies (292, 569) suggest that, although aphasics (particularly those with fluent language disorder) and schizophrenics do share similar errors of speech, the language productions of schizophrenics do not fit classic aphasic patterns associated with vascular disorders. These differences primarily reflect the schizophrenic's ability to use polysyllabic words (e.g., territorial imperative), whereas fluent aphasics have difficulty with such complex words and also have a significant deficit in auditory comprehension that results in frequent nonsequitive utterances. Both fluent aphasics and schizophrenics have fluent speech with reduced meaning and content words (e.g., nouns).

Approximately 40% of schizophrenics exhibit formal thought disorder. This language production is characterized by the use of words or phrases without precise meaning (word approximations), the use of nonsense words (neologisms) or real words with private meanings (out-of-class semantic paraphasias), driveling speech in which the syntax appears intact but the meaning (content) of the speech is lost, and responses that are nonsequitive or vague and beside the point (tangential). Schizophrenics frequently speak in a stilted, manneristic fashion, and the fluency of their speech may be intermittently disturbed, with paucity of speech, verbigeration (associations repeated in a stereotyped manner, palilalia in the aphasia literature), or perseveration (words or phrases repetitively inserted in the flow of speech).

Schizophrenics often experience hallucinations and delusions. To be classified schizophrenic, a patient must have one or the other phenomenon. The most dramatic of these are the first-rank symptoms of Schneider. Among schizophrenics, approximately 50 to 75% exhibit first-rank symptoms; 30 to 40%, delusional ideas; and 40 to 60%, hallucinations of one form or another (972, 975).

The essential common features of most schizophrenics is progressive and permanent deterioration in volition and affect, beginning in late adolescence or young adult life. This is the classic Kraepelinian concept of dementia praecox first described systematically by John Haslam, a British psychiatrist, in 1809 (423). Table 9.2 summarizes the typical behaviors associated with schizophrenia. From a neuropsychiatric viewpoint, the pattern for schizophrenia is an illness that develops in a young adult without known CNS coarse disease, and is characterized by motor and receptive aprosodia; frontal lobe and cerebellar motor dysregulation; perceptual disturbances; and fluent, paraphasic speech with intact repetition.

Subtyping

Theorists have perceived the dementia praecox/schizophrenia notion, almost from its conception, to represent some heterogeneity. As clinicians moved further away from the Kraepelinian concept and broadened the behavioral limits required for the diagnosis, heterogeneity was perceived to increase. This process led to numerous attempts to subtype schizophrenia into more clinically homogeneous variants. Two basic subtyping schemata have emerged.

The first relates to the recognition that some patients diagnosed as schizophrenic, in contrast to the classic syndrome, had a notable number of features of depression or mania and a benign course. This recognition led to descriptions of putative schizophrenialike syndromes, none of which, with the exception of schizoaffective disorder (498), has survived the test of time. These schizophrenialike syndromes were conceptualized as either variants of schizophrenia or as separate diseases; they included reactive psychosis (476), schizophreniform psychosis (572), cycloid psychosis (581), and remitting schizophrenia (1017).

Although there is a voluminous literature describing various clinical and biologic characteristics of schizoaffective disorders (334, 968), concordance is weak among definitions and concepts of this clinical notion (133) and a number of investigators have rejected its validity (4, 777). Those who maintain that such a syn-

TABLE 9.2

Characteristic Behaviors of Schizophrenia

Feature	*Behaviors*
Appearance	Ectomorphic or dysplastic, disheveled and unkempt, nicotine-stained fingers, dirty
Global behaviors	Collecting garbage; talking to self in public; hoarding food; in hospital, lies on floor, sits in twisted position, rubs head or twists hair
Motor	Poor coordination, dysynergy, stereotypies, perseverations, mannerisms, odd procedural movements, stimulus bound
Soft neurologic symptoms	Motor overflow, poor fine sequential hand movements, motor inertia, inability to maintain motor tasks
Affect	Absent shallow mood; lacks warmth or empathy; expressionless; indifferent to and withdrawn from surroundings (inaccessible); indifferent to family and friends; unconcerned for present situation; has no plan, ambition, desires, or drive
Speech and thought	Manneristic or stilted, scanning or explosive, vague and digressive, overelaborate or metaphorical, circumlocutory, aphasic
Psychosis	First-rank symptoms, other nonaffect-laden hallucinations and delusions, dysmegalopsia and other perceptual abnormalities

drome exists have concluded that it represents pathophysiologic heterogeneity (623). Among these adherents, however, there is additional disagreement: some consider most patients to be schizophrenic (1067) and some consider most to be affectively ill (777). Still others consider the schizoaffective/unipolar subtype to be linked to schizophrenia and the schizoaffective/bipolar subtype to be linked to affective disorder (52, 189).

Although DSM-III-R provides criteria for diagnosing schizoaffective disorder, clinicians tend to utilize this choice only when the patient does not fit either of the two classic psychotic patterns, schizophrenia and affective disorder (i.e., the patient has mixed symptomatology or other clinical ambiguities, such as course or family illness patterns). Schizoaffective disorder and its management are further discussed in Chapter 11.

The second subtyping schema for schizophrenia incorporates a dichotomy based on the presence of emotional blunting (the absence of emotional expression and loss of volition) and other so-called negative features (i.e., deficits of thought, speech, activity). The earlier literature used paranoid versus nonparanoid (e.g., hebephrenia) (1003) to characterize this dichotomy, whereas the modern literature often refers to it as positive-symptom versus negative-symptom schizophrenia (51). The validity of these subcategories is unclear. However, patients characterized as nonparanoid often have persecutory delusions (i.e., they are "paranoid") and patients with negative symptoms often also have positive symptoms (i.e., hallucinations and delusions). In addition, although no evidence exists that positive features or persecutory delusions have good predictive validity (i.e., are helpful in predicting prognosis, treatment response, biological markers), there is evidence that the degree of emotional blunting and affective features do predict these factors. A general clinical rule can be applied: Once a patient is believed to be psychotic (by convention, has hallucinations or delusions), the more negative features and the fewer affective features the patient has, the worse is the prognosis. The reverse is also generally true. Patients who satisfy diagnostic criteria for schizophrenia usually are those with no, or minimal, affective features. Further dividing schizophrenics into patients with and without significant negative features is probably more useful than the present DSM subtyping system.

Course

Numerous studies have been done of the long-term outcome of schizophrenia. Despite the application of different diagnostic systems to this question (from DSM-I and DSM-II general descriptions to the more specific criterion-oriented RDC and Feighner systems), results of these studies are fairly consistent. Psychotic patients with few affective symptoms and many negative features do not do well and, over a 40-year period, do significantly worse than do patients with mood disorder. "Not doing well" and being "worse" affect all outcome measures: the proportion of time that the patient is symptomatic, months spent in the hospital, and job and interpersonal functioning. The long-term outcome for schizoaffective disorder is somewhere between that of schizophrenia and mood disorder (66, 139, 240, 472, 1003).

More specifically, illness onset is usually insidious with an accretion of odd behaviors and progressive isolation that eventually culminate in a psychotic episode. Illness onset is usually (80% of patients) in the late teens or early 20s and rarely develops after age 40. Males become ill earlier than females (average onset age about 21 and 27, respectively); however, the gender ratio is about even for all patients with the diagnosis. Males predominate among chronic patients (60 to 70%). Deterioration is most marked following the first or second episodes and then gradually levels off. Over the years, positive symptoms tend to become less intense and patients respond less dramatically to treatment (758). Between 60 to 80% of patients become chronically ill, although virtually all patients suffer some degree of functional loss (1005). Because of their interpersonal and occupational decline, schizophrenics tend to be concentrated in lower socioeconomic groups. This downward drift results from their dysfunction; the socioeconomic distribution of parents of schizophrenics reflects that of the general population (275).

Laboratory Findings

There are no laboratory findings pathognomonic of schizophrenia, although schizophrenics show abnormalities on several laboratory tests. Some evidence indicates, however, that laboratory abnormalities occur more frequently in chronic, emotionally blunted patients. These abnormalities can be observed fairly early in the illness course, but remain stable thereafter (1069). It is also unclear how many schizophrenics have abnormalities, as some studies do not find them (422). In those that do, most of the findings reflect mean differences between a group of schizophrenics and a comparison group. For example, although 30 to 50% of schizophrenics have CT-scan brain changes relative to comparison groups, a radiologist would feel that very few schizophrenics have a clinically significant abnormality (i.e., one that would affect treatment choice or require further testing). Finally, these abnormal laboratory findings are not specific to schizophrenia; many of them are also observed in other psychiatric patient groups. Table 9.3 displays the abnormal laboratory findings observed in schizophrenia.

Diagnosis

By convention, a diagnosis of schizophrenic requires that a patient be psychotic (experiencing a delusion or hallucination); have few affective features, and have no historical, examination, or laboratory evidence of specific coarse brain disease. The number and combination of psychopathologic features needed to satisfy different sets of criteria is arbitrary. Table 9.4 displays the core features of the syndrome. If present, these features identify patients who can satisfy virtually any DSM version and all sets of diagnostic research criteria. Patients who meet the core criteria are likely to have an early illness onset and chronic course, as well as some of the laboratory findings outlined in Table 9.3.

TABLE 9.3

Laboratory Profile of Schizophrenia

Measurement	*Findings*	*Reference*
Resting Electroencephalogram (EEG)	50% abnormal nonspecific, left frontotemporal asymmetry	8, 1028
Power spectral EEG	Decreased variability on left, increased beta power and alpha power on left, less suppression during verbal tasks	314, 335
Evoked potential	Increased amplitudes (auditory and visual), variability, and low topographic late waves on the left	314, 692
Computed tomography/ magnetic resonance imaging	30–50% lateral ventricular enlargement; some cortical atrophy, particularly frontotemporal; 20% vermal atrophy	49, 50, 186, 201, 953
Positron emission tomography/cerebral blood flow	Decreased flow and uptake in left frontal areas; increased flow in left posterior areas	140
Cognitive neuropsychiological (NP) test batteries	75% marked impairment; bilateral impairment, worse on the left or frontal; deficit in discursive thinking; poor motor-perceptual coordination; right-left disorientation; reading/writing/language comprehension deficits; difficulty performing simple motor tasks (ideomotor dyspraxia); difficulty in recognizing body parts (agnosia)	978, 979

Management

The vast majority of patients satisfying modern criteria for schizophrenia require periodic hospitalization. Many eventually require long-term institutionalization or placement in a structured community setting, such as a halfway house or hostel. Day treatment centers and day hospitals also can be beneficial in the continuing care of schizophrenics, although the cost-effectiveness of these facilities has not been established.

TABLE 9.4

Required Core Critiera for Schizophrenia

1. Psychosis
   Manifested by any hallucinations, delusion, or formal thought disorder, each of sufficient intensity, frequency, or duration to affect functioning
2. Emotional blunting
   At least some degree of avolition and loss of emotional expression
3. No past or present affective episodes or prominent affective features, other than irritability
4. Clear consciousness
5. Illness not due to coarse brain disease, systemic illness, or drug or alcohol abuse

The primary goal of hospitalization of a schizophrenic is to provide a structured setting for proper diagnostic evaluation and treatment. As schizophrenia may be a syndrome representing several pathophysiologic processes, treatment must be individualized. Neuroleptic administration, however, remains the primary treatment modality. Treatment goals should be the reduction of the symptoms that led to hospitalization and the commencement of social and vocational rehabilitation. Although 50 to 60% of patients, who have been ill less than three years and who receive medications have a social recovery (73), it is the rare patient who has a complete remission. The degree of outcome is extremely variable at first, with most patients having a deteriorating course with permanent social and job impairment.

Neuroleptics

Pre-1970 studies of the efficacy of neuroleptics in the treatment of schizophrenia concluded that daily doses below 400 mg of chlorpromazine or its equivalent were not effective. These studies were undoubtedly contaminated by inclusion of a significant number of manic patients in varying states of excitement, thus suggesting that for rigorously diagnosed schizophrenics, who are rarely excited, doses can be considerably less. Reports from England in the 1950s and 1960s that recommended lower doses in schizophrenia than those used in the United States probably reflected the narrow British concept of the disorder and the elimination of many manic patients from drug trials. Chlorpromazine, or its equivalent (200–600 mg daily) should suffice for controlling symptoms in the majority of schizophrenics who satisfy modern diagnostic criteria. In university centers in the United States, haloperidol appears to be the most commonly used neuroleptic for psychosis, with daily doses for schizophrenia usually between 20–40 mg. Some patients can be treated with lower doses without loss of efficacy.

Unfortunately, recent advances in developing plasma assays for neuroleptic blood levels have not led to clinically meaningful monitoring. Studies suggest, however, that low plasma levels and treatment failure are likely due to noncompliance or drug interactions affecting enzyme induction. The therapeutic value of very high neuroleptic plasma levels has not been established (1021).

For neuroleptic treatment-resistant schizophrenics (those unable to be discharged after 4 weeks of steady-state, maximum-dose neuroleptic treatment), ECT should be considered, particularly if the patient is not emotionally blunted (183, 967). The addition of lithium to the neuroleptic also benefits a small percentage of schizophrenics despite the absence of affective features. The use of anticonvulsants and other compounds has not been found to benefit such patients (183). Clozapine, an atypical neuroleptic, has received widespread notoriety and may also benefit some treatment-resistant patients. The degree of benefit weighed against the increased risks for agranulocytosis with clozapine, however makes it the treatment of last resort (861).

After the patient is discharged, the dose should be maintained for a minimum of 8 months. Discontinuation prior to that time results in relapse in 50 to 75% of patients. As the risk for tardive dyskinesia in these patients is great, neuroleptics should be tapered and discontinued, if possible, after 1 year and the need for further neuroleptic treatment evaluated. It is unclear how many patients require further treatment.

Haloperidol (50 mg/mL) and fluphenazine (25 mg/mL) are also available in long-acting (depot), intramuscular (IM) form. This form can be administered every 2 to 3 weeks to provide adequate doses for noncompliant patients who previously have been successfully treated with oral neuroleptic. The administration of the long-acting IM form should overlap with oral administration, which is then tapered and discontinued. The patient remains on the maintenance dose (0.5–1 mL of haloperidol or 1–2 mL of fluphenazine). Many patients develop significant extrapyramidal side effects unless doses for the long-acting forms are increased gradually. The automatic use of antiparkinson agents with depot neuroleptics is not a satisfactory alternative to measured dosage increases. As the risk for tardive dyskinesia can be significant for patients receiving prolonged treatment with long-acting preparations (495), they should not be used until all other methods have failed for increasing compliance (e.g., using single, bedtime doses; having family members monitor compliance or administer medication; using behavior modification techniques to reward compliance). Further, long-acting preparations provide no therapeutic flexibility and are inappropriate for the treatment of acute episodes.

The automatic use of additional medications during the acute phase of illness is also not justified. Antiparkinson drug use carries risks and should be withheld until sufficient extrapyramidal symptoms develop to warrant treatment. Once employed and an effective dosage schedule established, antiparkinson drugs should be continued for 3 to 4 months, at which time they should be gradually stopped, as only one third of patients require further treatment with these compounds (534, 726).

Behavioral Approaches

Most schizophrenics have significant cognitive impairment, which in severity and number of functions affected is similar to that observed in some demented patients (978). Elaborate psychotherapeutic interventions demanding high-level abstraction and comprehension, therefore, are not helpful for these patients. The intense interpersonal nature and inherent ambiguity of psychotherapeutic interactions tend to exacerbate the schizophrenic's already significant confusion and anxiety. Direct, reality-oriented, concrete comments are most helpful. A calm, reassuring, caring manner is also helpful in reducing anxiety and in gaining the patient's cooperation for needed tests and compliance with medication and rehabilitation.

A structured inpatient setting, with formalized reinforcers of positive social behaviors (e.g., off-unit privileges, special foods) also can reduce the frequency of objectionable "management problem" behaviors. The interpersonally intense therapeutic community setting or an emotionally intense family setting do not benefit these patients and may make them worse. Efforts to reduce levels of interpersonally expressed emotion may reduce relapse rates (294, 578, 579, 1070). The long-term residential psychoanalytic institute is anachronistic for schizophrenics (642, 915).

Management Problems

Because of their deficits in volition and emotional spontaneity, most schizophrenics usually are easily managed in a hospital setting. Most do nothing and bother no one.

On the other hand, most of the management problems they do present also result from their lack of drive and loss of social graces. These problems include not keeping clean and properly dressed, lying on the floor in hallways, constantly smoking in the rooms (often burning bedding and furniture), not taking medication, and doing nothing on a unit in which the nursing staff takes pride in its structured activities program. These problems usually can be avoided or controlled by (1) the appropriate pharmacotherapeutic and interpersonal strategies described above, (2) the education of staff concerning the nature of the patient's illness, and (3) a formal structured reinforcement program for rewarding positive social behaviors. An essential component to this program is a set of clear, easily understood, unambiguously enforced unit rules and regulations that include precise privileges and rewards for adhering to unit rules and behaving acceptably.

Less commonly, schizophrenics are irritable, agitated, socially disruptive, or uncooperative (refusing to follow unit rules, to take medication, or to cooperate with diagnostic tests). Violence, however, is uncommon and usually stereotyped (e.g., automatically striking out at someone without provocation). When a schizophrenic becomes violent, it usually is against a background of emotional blunting. Thus, violent behavior from these patients is difficult to predict. Occasionally, a schizophrenic is menacing, stares hostilely at the staff, speaks threateningly, or exhibits aggressive behaviors, such as punching walls or angrily shouting. These behaviors should be treated as an emergency (see Chapter 23).

Discharge Planning

Appropriate discharge planning must consider (1) the degree to which the symptoms leading to hospitalization have been ameliorated, (2) the degree to which the patient's family or guardian has accepted the treatment plan, and (3) available community resources for bed, board, and job training and placement.

Educating and counseling the patient's family and gaining its understanding and support are critical for the success of the discharge plan. This is true whether the patient returns home or is placed in a community care program. The family educational process should begin early in hospitalization and involve the family in discussions about placement or aftercare programs.

Any retraining, placement, or behavioral intervention aftercare programming also must consider the cognitive strengths and weaknesses and residual psychopathology of the individual patient. Neuropsychological assessment of higher cortical functions and vocational assessment of job skills are helpful aids in any meaningful discharge plan. For example, a patient who has significant fine motor dysregulation most probably will fail if given training involving the use of machinery, whereas the same patient might do well in a job requiring only heavy lifting (primarily involving axial muscles) and other unskilled movement.

Theory of Etiology

Most investigators believe that schizophrenia develops from complex interactions between a premorbid vulnerability and a process that damages the central nervous system. No scientist takes seriously the notion of the psychologically schizophrenogenic mother or that an imbalance of intrapsychic forces can result in schizophrenia. The intensity and emotionality of interpersonal interactions, however, can influence the course of schizophrenia (high intensity and emotionality being detrimental), and life stress in some nonspecific way (as in almost every other disease) can make management more difficult and lead to hospitalization.

The processes most often considered as potential triggers of the syndrome are: CNS viral infection (660), gestational and perinatal adversity affecting neural development (613, 658, 701), head injury (1062), the use of street drugs (54), and seizure disorder (998). The vulnerability most often considered is a genetic liability that either requires a trigger to express itself or is of sufficient strength in some individuals that it is expressed regardless of the person's experience. Thus, the commonly held theoretical model of schizophrenia is of a group of processes leading to phenotypes (the expression of genes) and phenocopies (the mimicking of genetic expression) sharing similar signs and symptoms. In this model, some patients are schizophrenic because of their genetic liability, some because of what happens to their nervous systems, and others because of some combination of genes and experience. To complicate matters, the model permits (and predicts) that there may be several genotypes, each with its own expression and vulnerability. Thus, one genotype might be sensitive to the adverse consequences of gestational problems, whereas another might be neutral to these problems but sensitive to certain viruses.

As schizophrenia tends to express itself early in life and as a high proportion of children born to mothers diagnosed as schizophrenic exhibit neuromotor and other abnormalities of CNS integration (114), another commonly held idea is that whatever the determinants of schizophrenia, they are activated early in development (1045).

The prototypical model for the disorder, then, is of some gene (or genes), alone or in combination with a CNS biologic stressor, or a powerful biological stressor alone that adversely affects fetal neural cell generation or migration or affects fetal and neonatal cell pruning (the most fundamental processes of early brain development). The abnormality of cell generation, migration, or pruning results in a "lesion" or "lesions," and the associated dysfunction becomes increasingly profound as the brain areas involved are progressively required for normal activity during further development.

To present all the data supporting the above concept is beyond the scope of this book. Because family history can be helpful information for diagnosis (affecting the probabilities) and much of the above concept is based on a genetic hypothesis, however, the data from family twin and adoption studies in schizophrenia is briefly summarized. Much of this literature before 1980 is methodologically limited: inadequate diagnostic criteria and patient selection procedures, poor clinical assessment, and the diagnosis of relatives whose familial and diagnostic relationships to the patients are known (12, 377). Nevertheless, these older studies are consistent with newer ones indicating that, by most diagnostic criteria, schizophrenia is familial (513, 1002). That is, although the population prevalence is 0.6% or less, the age-corrected prevalence (morbid risk) in first-degree relatives (i.e., parents, siblings, children) is about 4%. This familialness is consistent across generations. It is also supported by twin studies that indicate a greater degree of like diagnoses (concordance) in monozygotic than in dizygotic twins (about 40% versus 10%). Patients with emotional blunting are most likely to have ill relatives (723, 1003). Adoption studies also tend to find that the biologic parents of adopted-away offspring, who also happen to have schizophrenia, have greater risks for schizophrenia than do biologic parents of control adoptees (377, 513). Despite an enormous amount of data, none clearly fits a genetic model of transmission, and gene mapping studies have yet to identify the schizophrenic genotypes (522, 897).

Chapter 10

Idiopathic Morbid States

II. Schizoidia and Delusional Disorders

Schizoidia

History

Since Bleuler's description of latent schizophrenia (116), the idea has persisted that there is a nonpsychotic spectrum of traits and disorders somehow related to schizophrenia. By latent, Bleuler meant a deviation of behavior that either was a mild form of the illness or represented predisposing traits to illness. Bleuler perceived these deviant behaviors to cluster about the themes of eccentricity and a decrement in emotional expression and volition. He adopted the term *schizoid* (115) to define them. Essen-Moller (289) introduced the term *schizoidia* (used here), and Meehl (662) introduced the term *schizotypy* to characterize these behaviors.

In 1925, Kretschmer (560) provided the first systematic description of schizoid patients and concluded that they represented three behavioral themes: (1) eccentricity, (2) emotional coldness, and (3) insensitivity and oversensitivity. Heston (443) reviewed the literature of "schizoid disease" and suggested, as did others before him, that it had a genetic relationship to schizophrenia. This appeared to be confirmed by the Danish adoption study (526), Kety and Spitzer's impressions of this spectrum (926) and Millon's (676) studies of personality led to the DSM-III concept of two disorders: schizoid and schizotypal.

Although DSM-III and DSM-III-R classify schizoid and schizotypal as personality disorders, most clinicians and investigators consider these syndromes to be expressions of some morbid process. It is unclear whether that process is a mild form of one of the underlying processes of schizophrenia or represents a separate pathophysiology. There is evidence (see the section on laboratory findings), however, for considering these disorders as idiopathic morbid states (398, 663, 908, 995).

Behavior and Course

One of the reasons why schizoid and schizotypal disorders are presently categorized as personality deviations is because they are clusters of apparent trait behaviors (i.e., characteristic continuous patterns of behavior), rather than series of episodic state phenomena (e.g., as observed in the psychoses). Schizoid and schizotypal behaviors are present by adolescence, but precise onset is unclear. Some behaviors may have been observable since infancy (e.g., overly quiet baby, uninterested in being held or in receiving affection). Males and females appear equally affected, although the population prevalence is unclear. As some investigators have observed schizoidia to be about three times as common as schizophrenia in first-degree relatives of schizophrenics and the population prevalence of DSM-III–defined schizophrenia is about 0.6%, the population prevalence of schizoidia may be about 2% (652).

Although DSM-III-R lists seven criteria choices for schizoid personality, all of them are expressions of either a loss of emotional expression or avolition. Schizoid personality is essentially mild, chronic emotional blunting without psychotic features or clear-cut episodes of markedly deviant behaviors. The emotional blunting scale (see Chapter 3) or other instruments for measuring negative features can prove helpful in assessing such patients, who generally obtain a moderate score on these instruments (i.e., about halfway between normal and schizophrenic).

Schizotypal disorder is more complicated than schizoid disorder because it has at least two dimensions: (1) loss of emotional expression and avolition, and (2) eccentric behavior. The first dimension is identical to that of schizoid disorder. The second includes behaviors that, in fact, may be mild forms of positive symptoms: perceptual abnormalities, thought disorder, and delusions. These forms are manifested by recurrent illusions; odd manneristic speech; suspiciousness; and preoccupation of thought, usually of culturally deviant topics (e.g., satanism, magic, ghosts). Although there is some overlap in symptomatology, most studies indicate no relationship between schizoid and schizotypal disorders, and avoidant and dependent personality disorders (999). Tables 10.1 and 10.2 list schizoid and schizotypal behaviors, respectively, and some interview questions or comments for eliciting information about these behaviors.

The course of schizoidia is also unclear. Anecdotal observations suggest that

TABLE 10.1

Schizoid Behaviors and Related Interview Questions and Comments

*Behavior**	*Interview Questions or Comments***
Unable to express anger	Do you lose your temper from time to time . . . can you have arguments with people and then make up . . . can you remember a time when you were very angry?
Emotional coldness and aloofness	Tell me about the people you are closest to; how often do you see these people; what is your fondest memory of that person?
Lack of close friendships	Do you have many close friends, people you can confide in; tell me a little about them so I can get an impression of what they are like.
Indifference to feelings of others	Does it bother you when someone else feels sad or troubled . . . do you cheer up when others around you feel happy?
Indifference to praise or criticism	Does it make you happy when someone praises you or tells you that you have done something well . . . does it bother you when you are criticized?
Indecisive in actions	Are you the kind of person who has trouble making everyday decisions . . . do you have trouble deciding how to handle your free time?
Self-absorbed	Do you tend to enjoy yourself the most when you are alone . . . do you like to include family members and friends in your plans and activities?
Absentmindedness	Do you frequently find yourself misplacing or forgetting things . . . are you the kind of person who forgets appointments, important dates, etc. . . . are you absentminded . . . do people tell you that you're absentminded?
Excessive daydreaming	Do you daydream when you should be doing other things . . . how frequently do you do this?
Detached from environment (depersonalization)	Have you ever felt detached, as if you were outside your own body, watching yourself . . . do people tell you that you're in a fog?

*Behaviors are based on DSM critiera.

**Additional questions to assess schizoid personality are discussed in the section on blunting (see Chapter 3).

TABLE 10.2

Schizotypal Behaviors and Related Interview Questions or Comments

*Behavior**	*Interview Questions or Comments***
Illusions	Do you often see the shape of people or faces in shadows . . . do you often see faces and figures in patterns (as in wallpaper) . . . do you often mistake noises for voices . . . do you often mistake sudden sounds for something dangerous?
Depersonalization/ derealization	Have you ever felt you were outside your own body, detached, watching yourself . . . have you ever had the experience where you were awake but felt as if you were in a dream and things around you were not real?
Ideas of reference	Have you frequently felt as if people (even apparent strangers) were watching you or paying special attention to you . . . have you frequently experienced hearing a remark between people you apparently did not know, but you felt the remark still referred to you?
Suspiciousness	Do you think that people are criticizing you . . . talking about you behind your back?
Persecution	Are people somehow trying to make life difficult for you . . . trying to hurt you . . . follow or spy on you?
Magical thinking	Do you think you can read people's minds . . . foretell the future . . . have a sixth sense . . . can ward off evil?

*Behaviors are based on DSM critiera.

**Additional questions to assess schizotypal disorder are discussed in the sections on emotional blunting and thought disorder (see Chapters 3 and 4). Schizoid behaviors in Table 10.1 also overlap with schizotypal behaviors.

these patients do not deteriorate and few become psychotic. The specific relationship of schizoidia to schizophrenia is unresolved. For example, although some studies indicate an increased risk for schizoidia in first-degree relatives of schizophrenics, an increased risk for schizophrenia in the relatives of patients with schizoidia has not been established (517, 518, 994, 995). There also may be an increase of schizoidia in the relatives of patients with affective disorder.

Laboratory Findings

No clear biologic correlates of schizoidia are known. Certainly, no laboratory findings are helpful to the clinician. The few published studies, however, suggest that findings will be either normal or similar to those in non-ill children of schizophrenic parents. For example, studies of schizoid and schizotypal individuals suggest the following mild cognitive disturbances: (1) problems in attention and conceptualization, (2) problems during the early stages of information processing, (3) perseveration responses during reaction time tests (667, 843, 924). There is also some evidence that schizoidia traits are associated with decreased electrodermal responses (795) and smaller late waves (reflecting cortical activity) on auditory evoked potential (563). Other studies (908) indicate schizotypal traits are also associated with low-platelet monoamine oxidase (MAO) activity, abnormal smooth eye pursuit, decreased speed in information processing, and mild cerebral atrophy. These deviations are also observed in schizophrenics and in their well relatives.

Management

The management of patients with schizoidia is difficult. Some evidence indicates that low-dose neuroleptic treatment may be of benefit to patients with schizotypal personality (462). Support and a commonsense interpersonal approach with these patients also may help to ameliorate their discomfort. Education in how to minimize annoying or upsetting others with their odd behavior is also helpful.

Delusional Disorder

History

The currently used term *delusional disorder* represents the latest development in the conceptualization of paranoia. Originally a lay term for insanity, paranoia (beside one's self) was first conceived by Heinroth (433) as delusional ideas secondary to affective disturbances. Kahlbaum (493) next defined paranoia as a distinct disease entity, similar in many respects to Esquirol's monomania (288), that denoted a disorder characterized by a single overwhelming delusional idea but without personality or intellectual deterioration. Kraepelin (554, 555), who ultimately incorporated paranoia into his concept of dementia praecox, initially used the term to describe a chronic disorder of unshakable delusional ideas with an insidious onset and little deterioration of personality. Kraepelin later coined the term *paraphrenia* to denote milder delusional syndromes, distinct from dementia praecox, that developed in middle and late life (dementia praecox having an early onset) with little subsequent deterioration. Roth's (851) late paraphrenia and the paranoid reactive psychoses of Scandinavian psychiatry (termed paranoid states in the United States) (644) are variations of Kraepelin's paraphrenia concept. *Paranoid personality*, characterized by hypersensitivity, rigidity, suspiciousness, feelings of envy and jealousy, excessive self-importance, and a tendency to blame others, has been proposed as the trait underlying paranoid states (439, 506). The validity of this notion is unknown (1043), although there is some evidence that paranoid personality disorder is more common in the biological relatives of schizophrenic adoptees than in those of control adoptees (516).

The term delusional disorder was suggested by Winokur (1072) to avoid the confusion resulting from the diverse concepts of paranoia and the ambiguity of that term, which has been used to denote insanity, suspiciousness, persecutory or grandiose delusions, schizophrenia, and a specific disease entity distinct from other psychoses.

Behavior and Course

Delusional disorder (or simple delusional disorder if hallucinations are absent) as currently defined phenomenologically, is characterized by systematized delusional ideas; no prominent affective features; no first-rank symptoms or formal thought disorder; and little, if any, emotional blunting or personality deterioration. No predisposing personality has been established as an antecedent of this disorder. More than half of these patients are male, and more than half are married at the time of onset, which is in the fourth or early fifth decade. It is a rare condition affecting less than .03% of the population. The disorder occurs particularly among immigrants (514, 1072).

Follow-up data suggest that few of these patients develop schizophrenia and that about 25 to 40% become chronically ill (compared with as many as 80% of schizophrenics) (724, 816, 1072). Family studies (519, 1043, 1072) indicate little increased risk for schizophrenia or affective disorder and a low risk for delusional disorder. Etiology is unknown, and treatment remains symptomatic. It appears to be a psychosis distinct from schizophrenia and affective disorder.

The following vignette illustrates the condition:

A 34-year-old, unmarried Euro-American woman sought hospitalization because she wished to prove that she did not have a brain disease and that her conviction that her employer was trying to kill her was fact, not fancy. She requested an EEG, a CT scan, and neuropsychiatric and neurologic evaluations. Although she recognized the possibility that she might be mentally ill, she thought this "unlikely" and systematically provided details to support her contention of a plot against her.

Approximately 2 years earlier, she had become convinced that her employer at that time was covering up a scandal about nuclear material. She also believed that the employer had begun spying on her and ultimately had tried to kill her when she found out about the scandal and tried to make it public. She was fired from that job.

On learning of the firing, her mother, whom the woman had not seen for 6 months, traveled to see her. Her mother described her as cool and distant (no longer hugging and kissing her as she had when they were last together). The mother stated that other than this lack of warmth and full emotional spontaneity, her daughter was the same as always. She had been a good student in high school, had a year of business training following school, and had been a popular person and a "good" daughter. She never had a serious illness or a head injury, never used street drugs, and used alcohol only in appropriate social circumstances, never to excess. There was no family history of psychiatric illness.

On examination, the patient was precisely groomed and well-spoken. She appeared extremely efficient—a no-nonsense, cool, unemotional individual. She dispassionately related her beliefs about her past employer and stated that her present employers also had been trying to kill her since she had had learned of their unethical business practices. She provided elaborate details about events, the people involved in the plot, and their motivations. Some of the details proved false and others exaggerated. Most of her interpretations were clearly arbitrary, such as "I am sure the person who moved in across the street is a spy, because that house has been unoccupied for almost a year and suddenly he moved in!" She exhibited no other psychopathology.

All laboratory results and psychological tests were within normal limits. Nevertheless, she agreed to treatment. Full consecutive courses of lithium, carbamazepine, haloperidol, ECT, and monoamine oxidase inhibitors were tried without success. Following discharge, she quickly obtained employment as a bookkeeper with another firm.

Management

The above case illustrates the relative unresponsivity of these patients to standard treatment. Treatment response studies (816, 818) are unhelpful because they are anecdotal or lack adequate scientific design. A supportive, pragmatic, interpersonal approach is a reasonable management plan. Simple delusional disorder has some of the characteristics of obsessive compulsive disorder (OCD) (repetitive, intrusive, disturbing, and often unwanted thoughts). It may be clinically helpful, although speculative, to think of simple delusional disorder (without other psychotic features and with intact affect) to be a severe variant of pure obsessional disorder and to treat these patients as if they had that condition. Management for OCD is discussed in Chapter 16.

Other Delusional Conditions

The DSM nosology includes several other diagnostic categories of nonaffective psychosis: schizophreniform disorder, induced psychotic disorder, and psychotic disorder not otherwise specified (NOS). Brief reactive psychosis is also included in this category, but the little data that exist regarding this condition suggest a mood disorder (see Chapter 11).

The term *schizophreniform psychosis* was first used by Langfeldt (572) to describe schizophreniclike patients with acute onset illness and intact affect. These patients tend to have good premorbid personalities and relatively good outcomes. The DSM version of schizophreniform bears no resemblance to the Langfeldt concept. Instead, it incorporates the basic criteria for DSM schizophrenia, with the exception that duration of the episode is less than 6 months. The validity of this distinction is unclear.

Induced psychotic disorder (folie à deux) refers to a delusional condition that develops in a patient who has a close relationship with another person, when that person already has the same delusional ideas. The validity of the condition is unknown.

Psychotic disorder not otherwise specified (atypical psychosis) is a category for nonaffective psychotic disorders that do not fit into any other category. If a mood disorder (see Chapter 11) or behavioral neurologic syndrome (see Chapter 13) can be demonstrated, the patient should be treated for that condition. Neuroleptics are the likely primary treatment for the remaining patients in this clinically heterogeneous category. Their degree of emotional blunting probably will predict response.

Management

The management of schizophreniform psychosis, as presently defined by DSM, should be carried out as if the patient has schizophrenia. Patients with psychosis NOS require further diagnostic subtyping based on treatment choices (see the logical tree Figure 10.1).

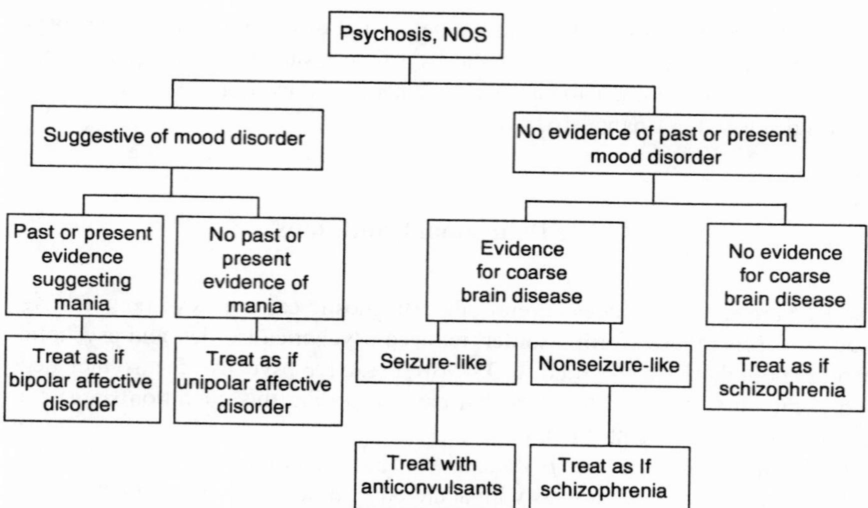

Figure 10.1. Treatment-Based Subtyping of Psychosis Not Otherwise Specified

Chapter

11

Idiopathic Morbid States

III. Mood Disorders

History

Pathologic disturbances in mood have been recognized and recorded since classical antiquity. At least since the twelfth century, the term melancholia has been used to identify depressive illness. In the Middle Ages, melancholia was also used to identify what today would be considered dysthymia, "minor" depressions, and hypochondriasis. Since the seventeenth century, the term melancholia has been used in a stricter, modern meaning. In contrast, until the nineteenth century, mania was a general term for madness (maniac), although it was recognized that episodes of melancholia and elation could occur in the same individual. The first organized medical description of patients with mood disorders was provided by John Haslam in *Observations on Madness and Melancholy* (423), which he compiled while at the Royal Bethlam Hospital in London (also know as "Bedlam"). In the midnineteenth century (594), the Falrets (the father in 1854 and the son in 1879) and Baillarger in 1854 independently delineated folie circulaire as an uncommon hereditary disorder characterized by recurring attacks of melancholia, excitement, and mixed mood states in the same patient. In 1882, Karl Kahlbaum described cyclothymia as mild form of circular illness.

In 1883, William Hammond (418), at what was to become Bellevue Hospital in New York City, provided what is still an extraordinarily accurate picture of mood disorder. His classification included simple melancholia (an illness of recurrent depressions consistent with today's unipolar category), melancholic stupor, hypochondriacal depressions, and circular psychosis (consistent with today's bipolar disorder). His descriptions of the demographics, clinical features, co-occurring conditions (e.g., alcoholism), and course of these disorders humble the modern researcher with their accuracy. Edward Spitzka (930), a neurologist at the New York City Ward's Island Hospital for the pauper insane, further detailed bipolar and unipolar variations of mood states and associated the former with Kahlbaum's newly described catatonia.

Kraepelin (551) incorporated all of the above concepts and descriptions into his manic-depressive illness category. He considered manic-depressive illness an hereditary disorder that affected only the emotional aspect of the tripartite mind and was episodic with full recovery between episodes. Karl Leonhard suggested that Kraepelin's manic-depressive illness be divided into two separate illness categories: (1) unipolar disorder characterized by only recurrent melancholia and (2) bipolar disorder characterized by recurrent mania, mixed states, or episodes of melancholia and mania. Other variations of these disorders and a variety of other mood states, the validity of which are unclear, have been suggested. Table 11.1 displays the various mood disorder terms currently in use. Although divided into four subcategories, bipolar, unipolar, schizoaffective, and spectrum, the validity of these distinctions is unclear (see discussion below). For the clinician, six important concerns are:

1. Is the patient suffering from a mood disorder?
2. If so, is this mood disorder depression?
3. If depression, is it melancholia or one of the other forms of depression?
4. If depression, is it associated with psychosis, significant risk of suicide, stupor, catatonia, pregnancy, old age, or high risk of medical complication?
5. If a mood disorder, is it maniclike in cross section or longitudinally (i.e., is it bipolar)?
6. If bipolar, is it associated with psychosis, significant excitement, catatonia, or alcoholism?

In addition to their obvious diagnostic importance, these questions are important for proper patient management. Table 11.2 displays the relationships between answers to the above questions and choice of biologic treatment. The rationale for these choices is discussed below.

Syndromes

Melancholia

Melancholia, a syndrome probably affecting 2% or more of the general population (413), is found in both genders, all social classes, all ethnic groups that have been studied, and Western and non-Western societies. Affected individuals rarely become ill for the first time before puberty or after age 60 (376, Chapters 6 and 7). About 15 to 20% of private psychiatric hospital patients and about 10% of public psychiatric hospital patients are admitted for melancholia (450, 819).

TABLE 11.1

Mood Disorders—Affective Disorders and Manic-Depressive Illness

Term	*Essential Characteristics*
Bipolar disorder	One or more manic or hypomanic episodes
Unipolar mania	Manic episodes only
Circular	Manic and depressive episodes
Seasonal	Episodes occurring at specific times of the year, usually depression in fall/winter and mania in spring/summer
Mixed	Episode combining manic and depressive features
Cyclothymia	Numerous mild episodes of depression and hypomania
Hypomania	Mild manic episode
Mania	Severe manic episode
Bipolar II	One or more hypomanias *and* one or more major depressions
Unipolar disorder	One or more depressions *and* no mania or hypomania
Major depression	Clinically significant depression
Melancholia (endogenous depression)	Profound depression with vegetative features
Dysthymia (neurotic, reactive, or atypical depression)	Chronic low-grade nonmelancholic depression
Schizoaffective disorder	Mixed episode with both affective and schizophrenic-like features; can be subdivided into unipolar, bipolar types
Affective spectrum disorders	Co-occurring or co-morbid conditions
Winokur (877, 1073)	Depression-alcoholism-sociopathy
Akiskal (27)	Temperament disorders (affective [bipolarlike]; characterological [dysphoria/substance/abuse/ sociopathy]; hysteroid dysphoria; borderline personality)

TABLE 11.2

Mood Syndromes and Typical Biologic Treatments

Syndrome	*Treatments (in Order of Preference)*
Bipolar disorder	
Acute manic phase	1. Lithium 2. Anticonvulsants 3. ECT 4. Neuroleptic 5. Anticonvulsant and lithium
With excitement	1. Neuroleptic 2. ECT or anticonvulsant 3. Lithium and neuroleptic 4. Anticonvulsant 5. Anticonvulsant and lithium
With catatonia	1. ECT 2. Benzodiazepines 3. Anticonvulsants 4. Lithium and anticonvulsant
Depressed phase	1. Lithium 2. ECT 3. Anticonvulsant 4. Lithium and anticonvulsant
Mixed state	Same as for acute manic phase
Cyclothymia	1. Lithium 2. Anticonvulsant
Hypomania	1. Lithium 2. Anticonvulsant
Bipolar II	1. Lithium 2. Anticonvulsant 3. ECT
Schizoaffective bipolar	
Manic phase	Same as for acute manic phase
Depressive phase	Same as for acute depressed phase

TABLE 11.2 (*Cont.*)

Mood Syndromes and Typical Biologic Treatments

Syndrome	*Treatments (in Order of Preference)*
Unipolar disorder	
Mild melancholia	1. Cyclic antidepressant (with or without thyroid enhancement 2. MAOI 3. Lithium 4. ECT 5. Anticonvulsant 6. Combination of 1, 2, or 3
With psychosis	1. ECT 2. Anticonvulsant 3. Lithium 4. Lithium and anticonvulsant 5. Cyclic antidepressant and neuroleptic
With suicide risk	Same as for melancholia with psychosis
With stupor	Same as for melancholia with psychosis
With catatonia	Same as acute manic phase with catatonia
With pregnancy, old age	1. ECT 2. Medications as described in Chapters 20 and 22
Nonmelancholic depression	
Dysthymia (reactive, neurotic, atypical)	1. Cyclic antidepressants 2. MAOI 3. Cyclic antidepressant and MAOI
Affective spectrum	Same as for dysthymia

KEY: ECT, electroconvulsive therapy; MAOI, monoamine oxidase inhibitor.

The cardinal feature of melancholia is an unremitting, often profound feeling of unnatural sadness, apprehension, or despair that pervades all mental activity and colors all mental content. When associated with irritability, this mood combination is termed dysphoria (105). The melancholic mood veils all activity and is autonomous from environmental stimuli. It will not "lift" under cheery or lively circumstances, although it may have a rhythmicity of its own (less intense in the late afternoon or early evening and worse in the early morning). Melancholics are anhedonic, and appear worried, apathetic, or over-

TABLE 11.3

Characteristic Features of Melancholia

Sad, Apprehensive, or Dysphoric Mood
Distinct quality, different from "normal" feelings of sadness
Not reactive or responsive to environment (autonomous)
Relentless; patient does not experience any "good" days
Diurnal variation; worse in morning
Anhedonia; total loss of enjoyment in usual activities, friends, even family

Motor
Retardation, may progress to stupor
Agitation
Omega sign (fixed, furrowed brow)
Veraguth's folds (fixed, distant, or hollow stare)
May have catatonic features
Perseverations

Thought Content
Guilt, self-reproach, self-blame
Worthlessness, low self-esteem
Hopelessness
Suicide, fatal attempts typical (15% of melancholics)
Loss of insight into abnormal nature of experiences

Physiology
Insomnia, with early-morning wakening (difficulty staying asleep)
Anorexia; must be strongly encouraged to eat
Weight loss (usually > 5 lb in 2–3 weeks)
Loss of libido
Decreased salivation, decreased intestinal secretions and motility; constipation
Inability to cry, no tears
Oligomenorrhea, amenorrhea
Morning sweats
Altered temperature and cortical circadian rhythms

Psychosis
Delusions or hallucinations of guilt, sin, poverty, ill health, death
Other perceptual experiences (illusions, dysmegalopsia)

Cognition
Impaired attention and concentration
Imapired memory
Slowed, inefficient thinking and problem solving; delayed verbal responses
Bifrontal, nondominant hemisphere impairment pattern

whelmed and mentally confused. Table 11.3 displays the clinical features of melancholia (71; 376, Chapter 2).

Many of the symptoms of melancholia are "vegetative," presumably reflecting dysfunction in the autonomic and neuroendocrine systems controlled by the hypothalamus. Thus, alterations in circadian (diurnal) rhythms occur that affect the sleep-wake cycle, body temperature, menstrual cycle, and libido. Appetite is decreased, and gastrointestinal secretions and motility are impaired. Measurable alterations occur in heart rate and sweating. These symptoms are lacking in nonmelancholic dysthymias, which are predominantly distinguished by characterological abnormalities and a variety of anxiety-related symptoms.

All sets of diagnostic criteria for melancholia include: (1) an autonomous altered mood, (2) some combination of symptoms (insomnia with early waking; diurnal mood swing that is worse in the morning; anorexia with a 5-pound or more weight loss in 3 weeks or less; motor retardation or agitation; suicidal thoughts or behavior; feelings of hopelessness, worthlessness, or guilt); and (3) exclusion of other psychiatric and neurologic conditions. Table 11.4 displays one set of criteria for melancholia.

Melancholic patients have been roughly divided into those who have predominant psychomotor retardation and those who are agitated. Many melancholics are concurrently retarded and agitated, however, and there is no evidence that melancholics with extreme retardation (stupor) differ in any other way from melancholics with extreme agitation. Melancholics often can be identified by observation alone. Retarded melancholics sit alone and rarely speak to people or participate in activities going on about them. They move slowly, almost painfully. They have sad facial expressions (with omega sign and Veraguth's folds) and appear preoccupied, worried, or perplexed. Agitated melancholics may rock their bodies and

TABLE 11.4

Required Diagnostic Criteria for Melancholia

1. Profound, unremitting, autonomous mood change characterized by unnatural sadness, apprehension, or dysphoria
2. Three of the following:
   A. Anorexia with a > 5-lb weight loss in 3 weeks
   B. Insomnia with early-morning wakening
   C. Suicidal thoughts or behavior
   D. Diurnal mood swing; worse in morning
   E. Psychomotor retardation or agitation
   F. Feelings of guilt, hopelessness, or worthlessness
3. No evidence of coarse brain disease, or episode due to drug or alcohol use.

rub their hands and faces perseveratively; they abrade their skin and leave open sores. They give the pictorial impression of the phrase, "Woe is me, what's to become of me?" They hauntingly pace hallways and, occasionally, scream out at "inner demons." Rushing up to a nurse or doctor, they rock, wring their hands, and plead for relief in a whining tone of voice. Dysphoric melancholics remain aloof; when approached, they turn away, are sarcastic, or refuse to cooperate with even the simplest requests.

Psychotic Depression

About 20% of melancholic episodes are associated with delusions or hallucinations. DSM-III-R makes further distinction between delusions that are mood congruent (depressive in content) and those that are mood incongruent (persecutory in content or in the form of a first-rank symptom). Mood-congruent delusions are consistent with mood disorders, and mood-incongruent delusions are believed by some clinicians to be more characteristic of schizophrenia. Although the presence of these psychotic phenomena in a depression increases the likelihood that the patient has had or will have a bipolar course, they have no other clear diagnostic implications. For example, in a study of melancholics, Abrams and Taylor (13) found that melancholics with mood-incongruent delusions were younger at age of illness onset and their first-degree relatives had higher risk for affective disorder than melancholics without delusions, but otherwise the two groups were similar. Recently, Kendler (515) reviewed the literature regarding the diagnostic implications of mood-incongruent delusions. He concluded that these delusions do not define a subgroup of schizophrenia or indicate a schizoaffective condition, but rather that they might reflect a subtype of affective illness. Kendler further noted that the literature indicates these patients respond well to ECT (about 80% have a good response and more than 50% are fully recovered at discharge from the hospital). Psychotic depression is most likely just a severe form of melancholia.

Of particular importance are studies that indicating that psychotic depressives do not respond well to antidepressant medication. Two schools of thought regarding treatment have developed in response to these studies. One prefers the combination of antidepressants plus neuroleptics; and this combination is effective in about 70% of patients (705). The other school of thought, endorsed here, takes the position that neuroleptics should be avoided, if possible, as the risks for tardive dyskinesia and neuroleptic malignant syndrome may be greatest in affectively ill patients. For these patients, the preferred treatment is ECT, which gives the lowest frequency of side effects and the highest response rate (80% or better). If pharmacotherapy is used, the preferred choices are (1) lithium alone or (2) lithium in combination with carbamazepine, valproic acid, or a monoamine oxidase inhibitor (MAOI).

Depressive Pseudodementia

Melancholia in older patients may initially occur as a dementing disorder with diffuse decrements in cognitive functioning, particularly attention, concentration, and registration (315, 316). Often, these patients are incorrectly diagnosed as having dementia of the Alzheimer's type by physicians who have failed to note, or have discounted, the presence of insomnia, weight loss, retardation, and other features of melancholia. Sadness or despondency may be absent, and the patient may simply appear perplexed, bewildered, or frightened. Scores on the Mini-Mental State average around 20 points (range 15–25) and, thus, may be in the demented range. These individuals often live alone. In their confusion, they might neglect to feed and clothe themselves properly and present a misleading picture of profound deterioration. As mentioned in Chapter 6, SPECT studies can be helpful in distinguishing these patients from other dementia syndromes. The distinction is important, as patients with pseudodementia respond well to treatment, particularly ECT.

Dysthymia

DSM criteria for dysthymia are similar to those for major depression, with two exceptions: (1) dysthymia is a chronic disorder, and (2) the more severe symptoms associated with major depression (e.g., hallucinations, delusions) are absent. The dysthymia category, however, represents a heterogeneous group of patients, some of whom have a mild form of melancholia (unipolar or bipolar) and others have depressive syndromes previously termed "neurotic," "reactive," or "characterological" (23, 168). The heterogeneity of the dysthymia category arises, in part, from the DSM decision to dichotomize depression into major (including melancholic and nonmelancholic) forms versus minor (dysthymic) forms, rather than by the older endogenous (melancholia) versus reactive (neurotic) dichotomy.

The endogenous/reactive dichotomy originally implied that there were two types of depressions, one characterized by a mood reactive to the environment (the patient has anticipatory anhedonia but can enjoy pleasurable circumstances once involved) and the other unaffected by environmental stimuli (the patient is always sad). Although not without challenge, the validity of the endogenous/reactive dichotomy derives from several sources. A number of investigators have applied sophisticated statistical analyses to clinical information of depressed patients, and related their symptom clusters to responses to ECT or tricyclic antidepressants (3, 620–622). In most instances, the clinical features of the endogenous type of depression correlated best with a favorable response to treatment, particularly to ECT, whereas failure to respond was associated with features of the reactive type of depression. Two laboratory measures, the sedation threshold test (748, 884) and the dexamethasone suppression test (163), also have been used to discriminate the two types of depression. In the sedation threshold test, endogenous depressives are relatively sensitive to the central effects of IV barbiturates; the reverse is true for reactive depressives. In the dexamethasone suppression test, almost all depressives with a positive test have the endogenous syndrome, and almost none of the reactive depressives show a positive test (163).

Overlapping to a large extent with the endogenous/reactive dichotomy is the division of depressed patients into psychotic and neurotic groups. As the terms are generally used, neurotic depression approximates reactive depression and, to a lesser extent, dysthymia. Psychotic depressions, defined by the presence of hallucinations or delusions, are usually found in the endogenous depressive, or melancholic, group of patients.

The terms endogenous and reactive have no etiologic implications. Both syndromes are equally likely to have been preceded by an identifiable environmental stress or precipitating event (321). The two terms merely identify symptom clusters, or syndromes, and might just as well be called Type I and Type II depression. Melancholia, as described above, is preferable to the phrase "endogenous depression" because it avoids any suggestion of etiology. Table 11.5 displays the clinical features of the reactive/neurotic segment of the dysthymia category.

Atypical Syndromes or Depressions Not Otherwise Specified

The DSM category of NOS provides a nosologic alternative for syndromes that do not fully meet criteria for specific conditions. It also provides a nosologic home for atypical conditions. The NOS category represents pathophysiologic heterogeneity. In some studies (1075), nearly 30% of depressives fall into the NOS category. However, when alternative, more research-oriented diagnostic criteria are applied to these patients, about half can be reclassified as having major depressions, some of which are melancholic in form. In addition, over half the NOS depressives have a sufficient number and severity of depressive symptoms to warrant biologic treatment. The following is a reasonable treatment guideline for the clinician: If the NOS depressive has primarily symptoms of neurotic depression and few or no melancholic features, treat for neurotic depression; if the NOS depressive has vegetative features of melancholia, treat for melancholia, regardless of the number or intensity of neurotic features.

Bereavement

Recently bereaved persons may experience many symptoms of depression, including some symptoms of melancholia (e.g., decreased appetite, insomnia). However, a person in mourning does not feel "ill" and usually does not seek psychiatric care (188). Generally, the intense mourning period lasts about 3 to 4 months, with lingering feelings for up to a year. Intense mourning beyond 6 months is deviant and may require treatment. The symptoms of typical bereave-

TABLE 11.5

Characteristic Features of Reactive Segment of Dysthymia Category

Mood
Quality similar to "normal mood swings" of sadness
Reactive to environment
Fluctuating; patient has some "good" days; no diurnal swing
Anticipatory anhedonia and preservation of consummatory pleasure, responds to suggestion and persuasion
Anxiety, lability, irritability, and dysphoria also may be present
Weeps easily; lachrymose

Behavior
Mild or absent psychomotor retardation; no hallucinations or delusions

Thought Content
Tendency to blame others or outside circumstances for troubles
Self-pity
Helplessness
Suicide; nonfatal attempts typical
Full insight into abnormal nature of experiences
Hypochondriacal

Physiology
No vegetative signs
Insomnia with difficulty falling asleep, followed by tendency to oversleep
Anorexia, but eats "because I know I have to" (may overeat)
Weight loss, < 5 lb in 2–3 weeks (may gain weight)
Fatigue
Anxiety symptoms

ment are best resolved within the family, however, and not by removal of the bereaved person to the unfamiliar environment of a hospital. If the bereaved person has no family or friends, a brief period of counseling or a support group can help.

Suicide

Suicide is common. In the United States, the population rate is 12.1/100,000, resulting in almost 30,000 deaths annually. In Austria, West Germany, Hungary, Japan, Denmark, Finland, Sweden, and Switzerland, the rate exceeds 25/100,000 per year (323). In some cases, suicide results from inadequate diagnosis or treatment. For example, many patients who commit suicide have had prior successful treatment with ECT for major depressive episodes (79, 826), but they or their doctors choose not to repeat this treatment during the depression leading to the suicide. Some patients are given inadequate doses of cyclic antidepressants. Other patients receive unncessary barbiturates because of sleep problems, or neuroleptics (79) as a result of the misdiagnosis of schizophrenia. Another suicide prevention consideration is the lethality of large overdoses of cyclic antidepressants, barbiturates, neuroleptics, and lithium. In over 50% of suicides by overdose, the substance taken is supplied during a recent visit to a physician (695). In one study (79), about 65% of patients who committed suicide had visited the family doctor during the preceding month and 40% had done so within the prior week. More than 50% had received care for psychiatric illness in the year preceding suicide, and about 35% had such care during the final month (826). The following specific factors are associated with suicide risk:

High Risk

I. Suicidal ideation and intent

II. Diagnoses, including the following:

   A. Melancholia

   B. Alcoholism

   C. Serious systemic illness (particularly when chronic or painful), including renal failure and emphysema

III. Middle-aged or elderly patient

IV. Male gender

V. Mental status phenomena (hopelessness, sustained sadness, severe agitation or motor retardation, psychosis)

VI. Single, widowed, divorced, or separated patient

VII. Euro-American or Native American

VIII. Protestant

IX. Prior suicide attempt

X. Family history of suicide

Low Risk

I. No suicidal ideation

II. Mood improvement as interview progresses and patient becomes reactive to environmental stimuli

III. Good general health

IV. Child

V. Pregnancy

Probably the most important factors are the presence of suicidal intent, coupled with a diagnosis associated with high suicide risk, especially melancholia. One 18-year follow-up of a large sample of depressed patients found that long-term prediction of suicide was correlated best with severe dysphoria, past alcoholism, and chronic systemic illness (274).

The majority of patients communicate suicidal intent to others. Because of the tendency of suicidal patients to convey these thoughts, the clinician should always ask a patient if he is contemplating suicide. The following questions are helpful:

Would you like to go away and never come back?
Would you like to go to sleep and never wake up?
Would you like to end it all?
Would you be better off dead?
Do you want to die?
Are you thinking of harming yourself, of suicide?
When you feel this way, do you consider killing yourself?

When the patient answers yes to any of these questions, the clinician should follow up with questions about suicidal intent:

Have you actually planned how you would do it?
How would you go about killing yourself?
Do you feel you need to be in a locked room or under close supervision to prevent you from doing this?

These questions are often reassuring to the suicidal patient because they reveal the clinician's awareness of the patient's desperation and his concern for preservation of the patient's life. Although data are mostly anecdotal (607), there is no evidence that such questions stimulate suicidal patients to commit suicide.

Major depression is most highly associated with death by suicide; indeed, about 15% of melancholic patients eventually commit suicide. Many (about 60%) do so during the year following the depressive episode, thus mandating careful maintenance treatment (407). The degree to which dysthymic disorder is associated with suicide is not clear, although it is somewhat higher than that of the general population.

Alcoholism is also highly correlated with suicide, although the evidence is certainly not striking that alcoholism per se (alcoholism unaccompanied by mood change or psychosis) is an immediate and direct cause of suicide. One would not hospitalize a patient as a suicide risk simply because he is alcoholic. The suicide rate is also higher in schizophrenics (1065) and drug abusers (126) than in the general population.

The frequency of suicide is also greater for Native Americans than for Euro-Americans. The Euro-American/African American suicide ratio in the United States is approximately 2:1. Because suicide is as common for African Americans in adolescence and early adulthood as it is for Euro-Americans in middle age and old age, the differences in racial suicide rates are accounted for by the differences among the middle-aged and elderly. The reasons for these racial and ethnic differences are not known. There is no evidence that ethnic differences in suicide are related to income.

The frequency of suicide among Protestants is higher than among Catholics. Suicide rates in predominantly Catholic countries are lower, in general, than in predominantly Protestant countries, but exceptions occur. For example, Austria and Hungary, both predominantly Catholic, have high suicide rates. Suicide rates also increase during times of economic hardship. The United States had the highest rate in its history during the Great Depression. The highest suicide rates by occupation are among police officers, dentists, musicians, lawyers, and women professionals (770).

Mania

Mania or hypomania must be present to diagnose bipolar affective disorder. The risk for mania in the general population is about 0.5 to 1%, and manics constitute up to 25% of acute public psychiatric hospital admissions (450). Not surprisingly, one population prevalence study found no manics in a door-to-door survey of New Haven (1052). Most are far too ill to remain at home.

There is no mania equivalent of the endogenous/reactive dichotomy, although secondary mania (471) may occur in relation to such exogenous causes as viral infections, toxic states, head trauma, and cerebral hemorrhage. Kraepelin classified mania along a continuum of severity ranging from irritable personalities and hypomania to delirious mania (555).

The classic triad of euphoria, overactivity, and pressured speech are the core manic features. Other, frequently observed features are grandiosity and flight of ideas. Mood is not always elevated, however, and irritability and lability are most common. Table 11.6 lists a number of the characteristic features of mania. It is striking how many of these are consistent with frontal lobe dysfunction. Impaired attention and concentration, distractibility, the stimulus-bound attitude, perseveration, loss of social inhibitions, and Witzelsucht are all seen in syndromes of the frontal lobe, particularly after damage to the orbitomedial areas (94). In mania, however, these phenomena are state related and remit with successful treatment.

Variations on the Manic Theme

MIXED STATES

Mixed states of manic and depressive symptoms are not uncommon (about 20% of cases) (555). This syndrome is not simply the frequently reported occurrence of brief depressive symptoms or emotional lability in manic patients; it is a true com-

TABLE 11.6
Phenomenology of Mania

Affect
Intense
Broad
Labile
Related

Mood
Euphoric (64%), elated, expanisve
Irritable (78%), hostile
Transient depression (36%)

Thought and Speech
Rapid, pressurized, flight of idas (72%), circumstantial
Racing thoughts
Clang associations, rhyming, punning, joking, Witzelsucht, grandiosity

Dominant Themes (often grandiose)
Religion
Sex
Business/financial
Persecution
New theories/inventions

Cognitive
Distractibility
Stimulus-bound
Short attention span
Impaired concentration
Bifrontal, nondominant hemisphere pattern

Behavior
Hyperactive, hypergraphic, restless, agitated
Intrusive, importunate, demanding, impulsive
Loud, vulgar, obscene, verbally abusive
Aggressive/assaultive, threatening/menacing (40%)
Sexually provocative/seductive (7%)
Nudity, sexual exposure
Incontinence of urine/feces
Fecal smearing

(*continued*)

TABLE 11.6 (*Cont.*)
Phenomenology of Mania

Self-decoration, head decoration ("Mohawk" haircut, outlandish hats, wigs)
Laughing, singing, dancing, gesticulating, saluting, military and sporting gestures, poses, postures
Psychotic features: catatonia (13%), first-rank symptoms (15%), persecutory delusions (33%), hallucinations (auditory, 19%; olfactory, 15%; visual, 25%), grandiose delusions (42%)

Social Behavior
Extravagance
Bad checks
Big bills
Sudden trips
Gifts
Gambling

Vegetative Signs
Insomnia (feels less need for sleep) (43%)
Increased libido
Increased appetitie

bination of states that may have stability over time and is more difficult to treat than either state alone. Such mixed states also occur during the "switch" process (142) from depression into mania and in bipolar patients with prominent diurnal variation, who may be depressed in the morning and pass through a mixed state, even becoming hypomanic, by evening.

PSYCHOSENSORY FEATURES

A number of investigators (see the section below on the theory of etiology) have reported that some patients with psychotic mood disorders, particularly bipolar patients, experience a significant number of psychosensory symptoms. These may include déjà vu and jamais vu (the intense experience of familiarity or unfamiliarity, respectively), sudden transient emotional changes, gustatory/olfactory/tactile hallucinations, and altered perceptions of auditory (sounds seeming too loud or too soft) and visual stimuli (dysmegalopsia). These patients have no clinical or EEG evidence of seizure disorder. The proportion of patients with mood disorder who exhibit two or more of these features is unclear, but it is possibly as high as 10 to 20%. Also uncertain is whether the presence of several of these features predicts response to anticonvulsants (427, 911) or other clinical factors (e.g., family history, polarity, laboratory variables).

Lethal Catatonia

In 1934, Karl Stauder coined the term fatal catatonia (later changed to lethal catatonia) to describe a condition characterized by the sudden onset of intense excitement (a mixed state of mania and delirium), development of catatonic features, and high fever in a patient apparently previously in good health. Without treatment, death resulted in about 50% of patients. When a specific etiology can be ruled out (most often infectious), ECT can be lifesaving and often leads to remission. Lethal catatonia is often indistinguishable in appearance from neuroleptic malignant syndrome (160, 328, 585). One review (625, 626) of 292 cases of lethal catatonia, however, concluded that the condition can be distinguished from neuroleptic malignant syndrome in three fourths of patients primarily on the timing of hypothermia. Well-documented extreme hyperthermia occurs during the precatatonic excitement phase of lethal catatonia, whereas hyperthermia emerges later in the neuroleptic malignant syndrome with the onset of stupor. It is also uncommon for the patient with neuroleptic malignant syndrome to exhibit echophenomena, ambitendency, bizarre postures, or automatic obedience.

Other Features Associated With Mania

Manics are the most outlandish and changeable patients. Although not generally included as psychopathologic phenomena, the following behaviors of manic patients typify clinical experience: greeting the clinician at the entry to the inpatient unit, saluting the staff, commenting on the clinician's clothes or hair, throwing objects out of windows, using makeup or profanity out of keeping with their socioeconomic backgrounds, making disturbances at airports, and upsetting traffic at busy intersections. The likelihood of psychotic patients being manic increases with the more noise they make, the more questions they ask, the more jokes they tell, the more words they utter, the more often they are observed on the inpatient unit, and the more makeup and fewer clothes female patients wear. Table 11.7 displays one set of diagnostic criteria for mania. DSM criteria also include other manic features, but there is no evidence that these additional requirements improve discrimination (1091). Jampala et al. (472, 474), however, have demonstrated that manics with avolition or formal thought disorder (about 5 to 10% of patients) do not respond well to treatment and may be pathophysiologically different from manics without these features. Also, Double (272) has demonstrated that manic patients may cluster into four categories: (1) a mildly ill group, (2) a severely ill group characterized by elation and rapid and pressured speech, (3) another severely ill group characterized by irritability, and (4) a group with thought disorder that may be pathophysiologically different from the other groups.

TABLE 11.7

Diagnostic Criteria for Mania

1. An altered mood characterized by sustained euphoria or irritability, or characterized by lability with periods of euphoria and irritability
2. No avolition or loss of emotional expression
3. Hyperactivity
4. Rapid or pressured speech
5. No evidence of coarse brain disease, substance or alcohol abuse, or systemic illness

Soft Bipolar Spectrum

The term *cyclothymia,* or cyclothymic personality, traditionally described a person who was endomorphic (pyknic), extroverted, outgoing, cheerful, and optimistic, but who was also impulsive and subject to sudden unexplained fits of moodiness, during which he would be depressed, irritable, or short-tempered (26). Cyclothymia is analogous to dysthymia in that it represents a mild prolonged form of a mood (in this case, bipolar) disorder.

In addition, Akiskal and colleagues (24, 27, 167) have suggested a partial return to the Kraepelinian unitary notion of manic-depressive illness. They based this suggestion on evidence indicating that other apparent trait patterns are, in fact, mild forms of mood disorder. In addition to cyclothymia, they also included as mild illness forms the following three temperaments: (1) *hyperthymic* temperament, overtalkative, extroverted, uninhibited, vigorous, short sleeper, bombastic, cheerful, irritable, and, at times, mildly hypomanic; (2) a form of *dysthymic* temperament, hypersomnolent, brooding, and anhedonic; and (3) *irritable* temperament, brooding, hypercritical and complaining, dysphoric and restless, ill-humoredly joking, irritable, and choleric. All of these "personalities" are grouped as a soft bipolar spectrum.

Borderline Personality Disorder

Until the 1970s, borderline personality was not systematically studied. Since then, research suggests what clinicians have long suspected—the category represents clinical heterogeneity (333). Further, within this heterogeneity, a significant proportion of borderline patients, although not all (650, 651), appear to have a form of mood disorder, particularly the bipolar form (25, 28, 397). This relationship between borderline and mood disorders has face validity, as DSM-III-R diagnostic criteria for borderline are consistent with a mild form of bipolar affective disorder. Among the eight criteria, five are clearly mood related: (1) impulsiveness in at least two areas that are potentially self-damaging (e.g., spending, sex, substance abuse, shoplifting, reckless driving, binge eating . . . ; (2) affective instability: marked shifts from baseline mood to depression, irritability, or anxiety usually lasting a few hours and only rarely more than a few days . . . ; (3) inappropriate, intense anger or lack of control of anger . . . ; (4) recurrent suicidal threats, gestures, or behavior or self-mutilating behavior . . . ; and (5) chronic feelings of emptiness or boredom.

As descriptors, these criteria are reminiscent of Kraepelin's (552) characterization of the manic-depressive temperament. Additional indications that borderline personality represents a mild morbid mood state rather than a pattern of deviant nonpathologic traits are: (1) a large proportion of borderline patients (25 to 50%) meet criteria for bipolar II (discussed below) or cyclothymia, and bipolar disorder and borderline disorder co-occur in the same individuals (21); (2) the relatives of borderline patients have an increased risk for mood disorder (21, 344, 775) and alcoholism (609); (3) a large proportion of borderline patients (about 50 to 60%) fail to suppress to dexamethasone (87); (4) some borderline patients (25 to 30%) have mildly abnormal EEGs (224, 921), evoked potentials (563, 564), and neurologic soft signs (338), although CT findings are normal (610); and (5) some borderline patients respond to lithium, MAOIs, and carbamazepine (223).

Brief Reactive Psychosis

The DSM syndrome of brief reactive psychosis (also see Chapter 23) is consistent with the European tradition of reactive psychosis first delineated by Jaspers (476). The five basic criteria are: (1) a precipitating stressful event, (2) a rapid-onset psychosis developing in temporal relationship to the stressful event, (3) significant affective lability and mood intensity, (4) symptom content congruent with the stress event, and (5) rapid resolution once the stressful circumstances are ameliorated. Some predisposing vulnerability is implied but never has been established. The validity of this disorder is also unclear. McCabe (644), however, demonstrated a relationship between reactive psychosis and mood disorder, with the former occurring early in the course and in younger relatives and the latter occurring later in the course and in older relatives. Treating reactive psychotics as if they had mood disorder may provide them with the best short-term and long-term recovery.

Bipolar and Unipolar Disorder

The unipolar/bipolar dichotomy was introduced by Leonhard, who reported different familial transmission in depressed patients with and without a prior diagnosis of mania. Perris confirmed this (749) by showing more bipolar illness in first-degree relatives of bipolar patients and the analogous finding for relatives of unipolar patients. Although this classification is widely used and part of the DSM system,incr i t v 2 n shavefailedtofindanysignificantdifferenceinthefamilyriskfor

unipolar and bipolar affective disorders in the first-degree relatives of unipolar and bipolar probands (977, 981), thus suggesting that Kraepelin's original description of a single disorder may have been correct. This relationship may be particularly true when the unipolar disorder is restricted to episodes of melancholia and to patients with early-illness onset and trait patterns suggestive of irritability or hyperthymia.

Another dichotomy is *bipolar I/II* (276), introduced to differentiate depressed patients with a clear history of treated mania (bipolar I) from those with a history of manic symptoms mild enough to go untreated (bipolar II). No significant biologic, familial, or treatment-responsive differences between bipolar I and II patients have been conclusively demonstrated, and the dichotomy is of no clinical help. Finally, a number of investigators have suggested that bipolar patients with four or more episodes per year or with specific forms of episodes during certain seasons of the year may physiologically differ from each other and from other bipolar patients. To date, no convincing evidence exists that these *rapid cyclers* or *seasonal affectives* represent unique pathophysiologies, although rapid cycling is more likely to occur later in the course of illness (376, Chapters 4 and 6).

Thus, a number of researchers consider bipolar and unipolar disorders to be on a continuum of severity, with bipolar being the more severe form. There are some clinical differences between these forms, however, as displayed in Table 11.8 (376, Chapter 2).

Schizoaffective Disorder

Most investigators are aware that the DSM boundaries defining psychoses are somewhat arbitrary and that schizophrenia and mood disorder ultimately will be delineated, in part, by conclusions about the existence and nature of schizoaffective states (950). The boundaries between schizophrenia and affective disorder, however, are unclear. Many investigators believe that these disorders are discrete diseases (198, 377, 513, 690), whereas others argue that there is no sound empiric basis for this dichotomous view of psychosis and that, in fact, schizophrenia and mood disorder are poles of a continuum, with schizoaffective states being intermediary forms (232, 233, 351, 971).

Patients with the schizoaffective diagnosis, whatever its nature, comprise between 10 to 30% of psychotics who have no evidence of coarse brain disease. Recent validity studies primarily focus on family history. Unfortunately, most family studies of schizophrenia do not assess for intermediary forms of psychosis

TABLE 11.8

Clinical Features of Bipolar and Unipolar Variants of Major Affective Disorder

Feature	*Bipolar*	*Unipolar**
Typical onset age (years)	20–30	35–50
Female (%)	60	70–80
Chronic (%)	30	5–15
All major affective cases (%)	20	80
Population risk (%) (estimated)	0.5	2.5
Family illness risks		
For bipolar (%)	5–10	1–3
For unipolar (%)	10–20	10
With positive family history (%)	30	10–15

*Melancholia.

(i.e., schizoaffective disorder) in first-degree relatives. Several studies that have done so, however, find the risk for schizoaffective disorder in relatives of schizophrenics to be elevated (about 2%) (220, 513, 971). Other studies have demonstrated an elevated risk for schizoaffective disorder (about 2 to 3%) in first-degree relatives of mood disorder patients (56, 220, 352). Among the family studies of patients with schizoaffective disorder (see reviews: 4, 350, 968), the mean risks in relatives for schizophrenia, schizoaffective disorder, and mood disorder are about 4, 5, and 15%, respectively.

The most practical approach for the clinician is not to worry about the pathophysiology or nosologic nature of schizoaffective states. The clinician needs to be aware that, virtually by definition, such labels imply some diagnostic uncertainty and atypicality. Treatment issues are clearer: if it does not hurt the patient, treat him for the diagnostic probability with the best prognosis. Thus, schizoaffective states should be managed as if they were severe forms of mood disorder.

Postpartum Psychoses

Women are at their greatest lifetime risk for psychiatric illness during the first several weeks after childbirth. Although the risk for psychosis is about tenfold greater for women during the postpartum period than at other times, during their lives, postpartum psychoses occur in only about 1/1,000 births. The incidence of other psychiatric disorders does not increase during parturition (718). The majority of postpartum psychoses begin within the first 7 to 10 days following childbirth. A second, much smaller peak occurs 6 to 8 weeks later and appears to be associated with the first postpartum menses (253, 537, 789). The onset frequency curve mirrors falling serum progesterone levels, and the massive hormonal changes occurring after childbirth have been implicated in the pathophysiology of postpartum states (984). Although the risk for psychopathology among women is lowest during pregnancy, women who develop postpartum psychoses usually exhibit some symptoms late in pregnancy (253). The presence of psychopathology, however mild, during the third trimester increases the likelihood of a postpartum psychosis. Unfortunately, except for a prior episode of postpartum psychosis, there are no long-term predictors of the condition (502, 718). Two thirds of patients develop the condition following their first pregnancy (789). No clear association is evident between postpartum psychosis and premenstrual syndromes (132).

Prior to modern advances in obstetric care, the majority of postpartum states were toxic in character, were associated with fever and disorientation, and were often fatal. Today, mood disorder is the most frequently observed postpartum syndrome and depression the most frequent postpartum affective state. Mania also occurs, however, and accounts for 10 to 15% of cases (132, 253, 789).

Postpartum psychosis is not a distinct disease. Phenomenologic, genetic, and treatment response data (132, 253, 502, 718, 789) suggest that puerperal states are heterogeneous and that the type of postpartum syndrome observed is essentially the same illness as its nonpuerperal counterpart. Nevertheless, postpartum psychotics are younger than nonpuerperal control subjects. Also, in comparison with patients who have nonpuerperal mood states, postpartum manics are more often disoriented, are unable to concentrate, and complain that "things are going too fast," whereas postpartum depressives are more likely to be delusional and to experience hallucinations. In addition, the data suggest that postpartum psychoses are extremely responsive to treatment, particularly ECT (253, 718, 789). As postpartum manics often have cognitive impairment that may worsen with neuroleptic or lithium treatment, and postpartum depressives are often delusional and thus less likely to respond to antidepressant drugs (245, 360), ECT is the treatment of choice for this disorder. In general, significant psychiatric illness during pregnancy also should be considered a clinical indication for ECT (63, 967). Follow-up studies indicate that, with appropriate initial treatment, long-term outcome is good (243, 244).

Premenstrual Syndrome

Premenstrual syndrome (PMS) is most prevalent in women during their mid-30s. Although symptom patterns vary significantly among patients, PMS is characterized by: (1) *water retention* (breast pain or swelling, weight gain, puffiness and edema, reduced urinary output), (2) *general discomfort* (headaches, backaches, joint or muscle pain, abdominal discomfort), (3) *impulsivity* (irritability, aggressive or violent outbursts), (4) *depression* (usually dysthymic in symptom pattern), and (5) *impaired social functioning* (staying home from work, concentration difficulties, poor judgment, family problems).

In PMS patients with moderate or severe depression, the syndrome appears associated with mood disorder. Women with PMS have a greater lifetime prevalence of major (usually nonmelancholic) depression than do women without PMS. Women with PMS who report previous phobias, obsessive compulsive disorder, and dysthymia, however, do not have an increased lifetime prevalence for major depression. Women with major depression are also more likely to report PMS. As with the postpartum period, the premenstrual period is most likely a nonspecific biologic stress that pushes some women over a threshold of a specific vulnerability. The specific vulnerability then determines the form of the illness. Although uncomplicated PMS has been successfully treated with diuretics and prostaglandin agents, the associated depressive disorder or other co-occurring conditions require specific treatment (e.g., antidepressants) (285, 409, 1040).

In addition to the more traditional psychiatric syndromes, epileptic seizures also may occur during the premenstrual period. If the seizure is of the complex type, it can be confused with mood disorders or schizophrenia. When psychotic episodes begin during the premenstrual period, are atypical in episode characteristics or illness course, and are associated with a notable number of psychosensory features, the presence of a seizure disorder should be determined (785).

Diagnosis

Classic, nonpsychotic melancholia and mania are not difficult disorders to diagnose. Diagnosis becomes more challenging when a patient (1) does not exhibit all of the symptoms necessary to meet diagnostic criteria, (2) has mixed symptomatology, (3) has many psychotic features traditionally associated with schizophrenia (e.g., persecutory delusions, auditory hallucinations), (4) has an atypical pattern of symptoms (e.g., avolition or thought disorder with mania or apathy with depression), or (5) has a depression associated with diffuse cognitive impairment.

Where there is no certainty, probability rules. In the case of a patient with an ambiguous mood state, the possibility of successful diagnosis increases in proportion to the number of affective features. If coarse brain disease can be ruled out, or, if it is identified, no contraindication to biologic treatment is evident, the patient should be diagnosed as having a mood disorder. Other than being somewhat helpful in deciding which treatment for affective disorder is best for each patient nonaffective psychotic features (e.g., delusional versus nondelusional melancholia), should be ignored in the diagnostic process.

Co-Occurrence of Mood Disorders, Alcoholism, and Drug Abuse

Between 30 and 50% of patients with a mood disorder (bipolar more so than unipolar) abuse alcohol, and 20 to 40% (bipolar more so than unipolar) abuse street drugs. About 50% of those who abuse these substances are also dependent on them. Among primary alcoholics, about 25% also have a mood disorder. About 20% of drug abusers (particularly cocaine and opiates) meet criteria for a mood disorder. It is unclear, however, whether these co-occurring mood states in drug abusers represent bipolar and melancholic unipolar conditions or other forms of mood disorder.

Alcoholism and mood disorder are each familial. The risk for alcoholism in the first-degree relatives of patients with mood disorders also appears to be greater than that of the general population. Figures are extremely variable across studies, however, and it is unclear which forms of mood disorder and alcoholism co-occur in the same families. Also undetermined is whether familial co-occurrence represents the same pathophysiology, the mood disorder patient self-medicating with alcohol, or some other unknown relationship. There appears to be no significant familial relationship between substance abuse and mood disorder (Chapter 17; 376, pp. 210–226). Anecdotally, patients who develop a late-onset bipolar illness (after age 40) may have a previous history of alcohol abuse. Despite this difference in course, these patients are treated similarly to other bipolar patients.

Clinically, the issue is clearer. Mood disorder patients with co-occurring alcoholism or drug abuse (referred to as "dual diagnosis" patients) are difficult to treat. Programs designed to treat patients with mood disorders are rarely equipped to handle the alcohol- or drug-dependent patient. Alcohol and drug rehabilitation programs usually adopt an antimedical and antimedicine model, thus denying participation to many patients whose mood disorders are controlled by maintenance medication. These patients are also likely to suffer from secondary alcohol- or drug-related systemic or coarse brain disease problems that further complicate management.

Course

The population risk for mood disorders is unclear. This is due, in part, to differences among epidemiologists as to what to include in the category. For example, should melancholia and dysthymia or melancholia and nonmelancholic major depression be counted as the same or as different mood disorders? Should bipolar and unipolar disorder be counted as one, two, or more conditions? Should schizoaffective disorder be counted as a mood disorder? The lack of clarity regarding population risk is compounded by the fact that many modern epidemiologic surveys of mental illness use structured clinical instruments of only modest reliability and rely on lay interviewers, who sometimes include as cases people unlikely to be included by trained professionals (57).

What is known, however, is that women are at greater risk than men for all forms of mood disorder; for bipolar disorder and unipolar melancholia combined, the ratio is about 7:3. The population risk for these two conditions combined is about 3%. An additional 5 to 6% of the population is at risk for the other forms of mood disorder. The age at onset for some depressions appears to be getting younger (termed a cohort effect), and the risk for these depressions also appears to be elevated in people born in more recent decades (termed a period effect). It is unclear whether these effects include melancholia, and they may be, in part, artifacts of counting procedures, diagnostic criteria, and the training of interviewers.

Illness onset in mania is usually acute, with the first episode generally appearing in the late teens or early 20s. In one study, the typical age at onset for 50 consecutive patients was 18 years (972). Depression is not commonly the first episode of bipolar disease; only 5 to 10% of first-episode depressed patients, usually those with an early onset, go on to develop a manic episode later in the course (1073). About one third of manic patients never have a depressive episode, but these "unipolar manics" do not differ in any important way from those with both manic and depressive episodes (9). Melancholia as a first episode, beginning in the late 20s or 30s, usually evolves over a period of several months. Overall, the age of risk for bipolar and unipolar disorders ranges between 15 and 60 years.

The course of bipolar disorder and unipolar melancholia is variable, and the notion of a cyclic illness occurring at set intervals during particular times of the year (melancholia in the fall or winter, mania in the spring or summer) reflects the course of only a small portion of these patients. The more typical pattern is one of scattered, isolated episodes interspersed with paroxysms, in which multiple episodes are bunched together. This is particularly true for bipolar disorder; over the years, it tends to result in more prolonged episodes with shorter intervals of relative health. Bipolar disorder is not a benign condition. Because of the combined effect of recurrent episodes of illness on social and interpersonal life and employment, as well as the toll of these episodes on brain function, about 30% of bipolar patients become chronically impaired (376, Chapter 6; 721; 1054). Post has suggested a sensitization process to explain this pattern, where early episodes, triggered by environmental stress, adversely and permanently affect brain function, thus leading to more frequent, prolonged, and severe future episodes that can occur without stress. This vicious circle continues to chronicity (see the later section on the theory of etiology).

The above pattern suggests that, to reduce chronicity, the treatment of early episodes should be aggressive and rapid and followed by equally aggressive, multidimensional maintenance strategies. Further, the clinician faced with a patient in the midst of multiple, closely spaced episodes should not become pessimistic, as these episodes may reflect a paroxysm that, if aggressively treated, could lead to a period of relative quiescence (sometimes years or decades).

Laboratory Findings

Many of the laboratory findings in the mood disorders mimic those for schizophrenia. Differences tend to be quantitative, rather than qualitative. Although, based on laboratory results, the clinician often can distinguish patients with bipolar disorder or unipolar melancholia from normal subjects, it is usually impossible for him to differentiate these patients from other psychotic patients through such studies. One reason is that current nosology is not perfect; some patients presenting with clinical syndromes that appear to differ, actually have the same underlying pathophysiology. A second reason for the similarities in laboratory findings among psychotic patients relates to what is being measured. Usually, this is either an epiphenomenon (e.g., dexamethasone nonsuppression) not directly reflecting the etiologic process or some final common pathway that may result from different determinants (e.g., in schizophrenics, ventricular enlargement perhaps is caused by cell loss, whereas the same finding in some depressives may be reversible because it results from high cortisol levels and water loss).

From a diagnostic viewpoint, therefore, laboratory studies in the mood disorders are mostly unhelpful. As with schizophrenia, the presence of a focal or circumscribed finding on any test suggests coarse brain disease and, consequently, a possible secondary mood state. Table 11.9 displays the laboratory findings in patients with mood disorders. Two of these, imaging and neuroendocrine findings, are of particular interest because of their clinical implications.

Structural brain abnormalities have been observed in patients with mood disorder. For example, numerous CT studies of manics have found a significant proportion of them to have enlarged lateral ventricles (266, 700, 876), frontotemporal sulcal widening, and cerebellar atrophy (603, 700). As with schizophrenia (48, 49, 201), a few studies do not find these abnormalities (700). Clinical correlates (e.g., treatment response, pattern of symptoms) have not yet been established. Depressed patients, particularly those with psychotic features (270, 961), increased cortisol levels (510), severity, and poor outcome (876) also show ventricular enlargement and frontotemporal sulcal widening.

MRI abnormal T1 values have also been reported in bipolar patients (796, 845), with some resolution following lithium treatment. Ventricular enlargement in some depressives also has been reported to resolve with clinical improvement (510), as is the case in some patients with cerebral atrophy secondary to therapeutically or pathologically related hypercortisolism (98). In addition, MRI studies have demonstrated decreased frontal lobe size in bipolar patients and elderly depressed patients (48, 49, 201). MRI has also demonstrated abnormally small temporal lobe volumes in bipolar patients (425) and reduced caudate volumes in depressed patients (647). This pattern is particularly similar to T1 findings on MRI in schizophrenics (108).

TABLE 11.9

Laboratory Profile of Mood Disorders

Measurement	*Findings*	*References*
Resting EEG	25–30% of patients have mild, diffuse, slowing, or a choppy EEG with transient small sharp waves; bipolar patients have some asymmetry to right posterior regions.	8, 750
Evoked potential	In delusional melancholics, variable amplitude changes; augmentation of amplitude to repeated stimuli seen in mania.	268, 327, 885
CT/MRI	Some bipolars and delusional melancholics show ventricular enlargement and cortical atrophy with frontotemporal accentuation; on MRI also greater T1 relaxation time in frontotemporal areas (indicating more water or cell loss?) and white matter hyperintensities; diminished caudate volumes in some depressives.	201, 277, 485, 647, 700, 876
Cerebral blood flow	CBF is reduced in some depressives. Perhaps greater activation is in left anterior and right posterior regions during cognitive tasks.	399, 400, 636, 860, 912
PET	Diffuse low metabolic rate is most marked in frontal regions, bipolar more so than unipolar melancholics; also, left dorsal anterolateral prefrontal pattern in melancholics; low caudate metabolism.	82, 140, 141, 208, 399
Neuropsychological measures (test batteries and other modalities)	Significant proportion of patients have mild to moderate impairment and other findings reflecting bifrontal nondominant hemisphere dysfunction.	137, 138, 979

KEY: EEG, electroencephalogram; CT, computed tomography; MRI, magnetic resonance imaging; CBF, cerebral blood flow; PET, positron emission tomography.

The proportion of mood-disordered patients with the above structural abnormalities is unclear. Of importance to the clinician, however, is the fact that these structural abnormalities, combined with the cognitive impairment often seen in these patients, particularly the elderly and depressed, can influence the clinician to diagnose the patients as demented. Previous episodes of mania or depression or a family history of affective disorder can help in discriminating these patients. If all else fails, the clinician can reasonably rely on the clinical rule: When possible, diagnose the condition with the best prognosis. If treatment is employed carefully, little harm is likely to be done even if the patient is suffering from a dementing illness, the depressions of which can also respond to treatment.

Neuroendocrine findings in patients with mood disorders also have clinical implications. These abnormalities are believed to be epiphenomenal to the pathophysiology of mood states and not of etiologic significance. Nevertheless, such tests as the dexamethasone suppression test (DST) and thyrotropin-releasing hormone (TRH) test have been suggested as diagnostically helpful, particularly for discriminating mild melancholia from other depressions.

The DST (163) is performed by administering 1–2 mg of dexamethasone at 11:30 P.M. and obtaining plasma cortisol levels at 8:00 A.M., 4:00 P.M., and 11:00 P.M. the next day. At any of these times, a cortisol level greater than 5 mcg/dL is considered abnormal. About 50 to 60% of melancholics are nonsuppressors, whereas nonsuppression in other types of depression is uncommon (about 10%). False-positive tests can result from pregnancy, Cushing's disease, malnutrition with 25% total body weight loss, recent exposure to barbiturates and other enzyme inducers, and major systemic illness. Abnormal tests tend to return toward normal with successful treatment. The TRH test requires an overnight fast. A baseline sample of blood is then obtained for thyroid-stimulating hormone (TSH), and a 500-mg IV bolus of TRH is administered. Blood samples are obtained at 15, 30, 60, and 90 minutes. A peak value of less than 6 mcU/mL of TSH is considered abnormal. The TRH test is less frequently used than the DST, but there is some evidence that combining the two tests increases the discriminating ability of either test alone.

Although strongly associated with mood disorder, particularly melancholia, the DST may be less specific than previously thought. For example, an extensive analysis of data from the literature (1026) found that 26% of schizophrenics were nonsuppressors, a figure significantly higher than that of 5% in normal controls. Further, 39% of unmedicated RDC/DSM-III schizophrenics were found to be nonsuppressors (957), related to negative but not to depressive symptoms. In addition, of 54 DSM-III schizophrenics divided into subtypes for positive and negative symptoms, 40% were found to be nonsuppressors, with 62% of the negative-symptom subtype being nonsuppressors (39).

Thus, diagnostically, the DST and probably the TRH test, as well, have limited usefulness. Both tests measure hypothalamic-pituitary function, however, and can be used as laboratory adjuncts for treatment monitoring. For example, if a melancholic has an abnormal DST prior to treatment and the test reverts to normal following treatment, this suggests that treatment has modified the pathophysiology of that depression. In depressives who have an abnormal baseline DST that reverts to normal following treatment and then becomes abnormal again, relapse may be expected and extra clinical precautions taken (e.g., review of maintenance pharmacotherapy adequacy, more frequent office visits or telephone check-ins, patient and family alerted to be watchful for early [particularly vegetative] features and to seek immediate consultation if these appear).

The neuroendocrinology of mania has not been as extensively studied as that of melancholia. Nevertheless, abnormalities have been reported in unmedicated manics. They include increased blood levels of cortisol, nonsuppression of cortisol in the DST, blunting of TSH response to TRH, and increased release of melatonin (218). The clinical implications of these findings are unclear.

Management

Melancholia

Melancholics often require hospitalization because of serious suicidal ruminations or attempts or other severe symptoms, such as profound anorexia and weight loss, retardation or stupor, or psychosis. Seriously depressed patients should be treated in a locked unit under close observation. Even in the absence of specific suicidal thoughts or behavior, melancholics have a markedly increased suicidal risk (407), particularly if they are older, have recently lost a spouse, or are in poor general health. They should not be engaged in intense interpersonal exchanges or forced into unit activities, as their inability to participate only makes them feel worse. All forms of exploratory and interpretive psychotherapy should also be postponed. These patients often feel guilty and worthless; these feelings may intensify with such interactions. They should be informed, however, that their illness has a biologic basis and is not under their voluntary control and that they are likely to make a speedy and full recovery. This message may need frequent repeating because patients' self-doubts and guilty ruminations quickly erase the modest effects of reassurance. Once recovered, however, many patients describe the gratitude they felt but could not express for such support.

The role of nursing and other professional staff is to provide support and reassurance, to encourage patients' acceptance of and compliance with the primary treatment, to observe and record patients' behavior, and to prevent patients from committing suicide. Acutely suicidal patients may require continuous one-to-one observation, as a determined patient can kill himself while hospitalized (e.g., by running at full speed and ramming his head against the wall).

Patients should be weighed daily and their sleep charted to document alterations in these vegetative features and to provide a baseline for assessing improvement. Severely depressed patients do better with short, rather than prolonged, visits by family members until significant improvement has occurred. Many melancholics are unable to feel any emotion, even for their loved ones, and seeing them may increase guilt and self-reproach. Nighttime sedation should be administered liberally for insomnia.

ECT, cyclic antidepressants, and lithium are the primary treatments for melancholia. If a patient is depressed enough to require inpatient care, ECT is likely to be the treatment of choice (see Chapter 21). This is particularly true for patients who have failed a course of antidepressant treatment prior to admission. Those who refuse ECT may be treated with a cyclic antidepressant alone or combined with an MAOI, or, if bipolar, with lithium alone or combined with an anticonvulsant or an MAOI. Drug treatment takes longer and may not provide as thorough a result as ECT (713).

If ECT is successfully used the patient should be given a 3 to 6-month course of maintenance drug treatment to reduce relapse rates (10%, rather than 30 to 60%). Either a cyclic antidepressant or lithium is appropriate; each has been shown to reduce significantly the relapse rate (751). Cyclic antidepressant dosages for post-ECT maintenance are the same as those used in treating acutely ill depressives (e.g., imipramine or amitriptyline, 200–250 mg/day); if plasma levels are monitored, they should be kept in the standard therapeutic range. The dose of lithium also should be adjusted to maintain a serum level close to 1.0 mEq/L. These drugs are equally effective in preventing short-term relapse in unipolar and bipolar depressives; however, about 10% of patients relapse despite maintenance drug treatment. Such patients are candidates for maintenance with anticonvulsants or ECT. When the maintenance phase of treatment is completed, cyclic antidepressant doses should be gradually tapered and then discontinued to minimize cholinergic rebound symptoms (anorexia, nausea, vomiting, diarrhea, abdominal and muscle pain, chills, headaches, dizziness, nightmares, increased salivation, diaphoresis).

If cyclic antidepressants are used as a first-line treatment (also see Chapter 20), a single, bedtime dose is preferable. Improvement in sleep and reduction of apprehension are often the first signs of recovery; they usually are observed within 7 to 10 days, but significant therapeutic effects may not occur for 2 to 3 weeks (486).

Some melancholic women patients benefit from adjunct triiodothyronine (T_3) treatment (25–50 mg/d) for 3 to 6 weeks. Baseline thyroid studies should be done prior to this treatment. Thyroid enhancement of antidepressant treatment can be used to accelerate the onset of response or, more commonly, to provide additional antidepressant effect in patients who are somewhat resistant to combined lithium–cyclic antidepressant therapy (487). Table 11.10 displays the treatment steps for melancholia.

TABLE 11.10

Treatment Steps for Melancholia

Unipolar Melancholia

1. Begin with ECT or cyclic antidepressant (see Chapters 20 and 21 for specific guidelines).
2. If cyclic antidepressant is begun first and there is < 50% improvement in 4 weeks or no signs of improvement by 10 days, offer ECT.
3. If ECT is refused and a cyclic antidepressant is not fully effective, add an MAOI.*
4. If a cyclic antidepressant–MAOI combination is unsuccessful, taper combination, introduce carbamazepine, and then discontinue all other drugs. Lithium also may be used to enhance antidepressant.
5. If patient is psychotic or catatonic, ECT is treatment of choice; if ECT is refused, begin with carbamazepine.

Bipolar Melancholia

1. Begin with ECT or lithium (see Chapters 20 and 21 for specific guidelines).
2. If lithium is begun first and there is < 50% improvement in 3 weeks or no signs of improvement in 1 week, offer ECT.
3. If ECT is refused and lithium is not fully effective, add a cyclic antidepressant.
4. If lithium–cyclic antidepressant combination is not fully effective, add an MAOI or, if patient is female, either MAOI or T3.
5. If none of the above drug combinations is fully effective and if ECT is still refused, taper all drugs, introduce carbamazepine or valproic acid, and then discontinue all other drugs.

KEY: ECT, electroconvulsive therapy; MAOI, monoamine oxidase inhibitor; T3, triiodothyronine

*For some women patients, thyroid enhancement may be effective.

Nonmelancholic Depressions

Patients with a nonmelancholic dysthymia or an atypical depression usually do not require hospitalization. Primary treatment is accomplished with a cyclic antidepressant or MAOI (see Chapter 20). Cognitive or "interpersonal" psychotherapy also has been recommended for these patients. There is some evidence that a combination of pharmacotherapy and psychotherapy in nonmelancholic depressives may be more effective than either treatment alone and that such a combination has no negative interactions (853, 1050). It is unclear, however, whether the enhanced therapeutic effect of combined treatment reflects the specific theoretical content and related strategies of the psychotherapy (e.g., in cognitive therapy, identifying negative distortions of reality and then developing techniques to counter the distortions) (1084), or whether it is due to the close attention paid to the interpersonal and social context in which the depressive episode occurs (e.g., positive and negative life situations) and how the patient's habitual ways of dealing with these contextual issues can be altered to reduce stress. Depressives likely to respond best to cognitive therapy are those who (1) have mild pretreatment depressive features, (2) are married, and (3) have few or mild dysfunctional attitudes (e.g., perfectionistic standards, concern about approval from others, degree of feeling inadequate) about themselves and their life situations (475). Stereotactic cingulotomy also has been reported to benefit some patients with intractable depression, particularly the nonmelancholic type. Side effects are modest and similar to those of any neurosurgical procedure. This treatment is best limited to patients with intact personalities (129).

Mania

Acute Mania

Acute mania always requires urgent treatment and often constitutes a medical emergency. Excitement, overactivity, and elation rapidly may be replaced with irritability, argumentativeness, and aggressive and assaultive behavior. Intrusive, importunate, and demanding patients may become extremely angry at only slight provocation. When persecutory delusional ideas are present, the risk of violent attack is sharply increased. Potentially assaultive and extremely uncooperative patients should not be interviewed alone in a closed office. Neuroleptic administration and, when necessary, seclusion are the safest and most rapidly effective measures. They should be instituted without delay if the diagnostic probability of mania is high and after CNS and systemic illnesses, for which there are specific treatments, have been are ruled out. The use of oral medication under such circumstances, regardless of dosage, is a mistake; the delay in drug action can lead to an uncontrollable patient who injures himself or others.

For the acute manic who is or may become assaultive, the drug of choice is haloperidol (20–30 mg), given deep in the gluteal muscle. The large volume of solution (4–6 mL) may require that two injections be given, one in each buttock, and the nursing staff should prepare the necessary syringes and paraphernalia well in advance. Lower dosages (e.g., 5–10 mg haloperidol) administered at hourly intervals until the desired effect is achieved only delays the process and increases the risk of injury to patients and staff. A 20–30 mg injection of haloperidol is much more rapidly effective than several 10-mg injections at hourly intervals. There are no serious side effects from the higher doses (866).

The typical order is "20 mg haloperidol IM, stat. and b.i.d." It is continued for at least 48 hours, even if the the patient has a dramatic response to the first injection, because too hasty a switch from parenteral to oral administration frequently results in a rapid relapse. The vast majority of acutely ill manics respond well to such a regimen, although an occasional patient may require 20 mg IM three times a day or 30 mg IM twice a day. It is poor practice simply to give a "stat." dose of a neuroleptic and prescribe subsequent injections on a "p.r.n." basis. Such a method increases the likelihood that patients will again develop acute symptoms between doses. Once the decision to treat has been made, it should be carried out systematically for continuous relief.

When the change to oral medication occurs, a brief period of overlap with parenteral treatment is needed to smooth out the transition. For most patients, a single nighttime oral dose of a neuroleptic can be instituted at a dosage 50% greater than the parenteral one. This dose (e.g., 60 mg oral haloperidol for a patient receiving 40 mg parenterally) should be given for two or three nights before discontinuing the parenteral dosage. The increase in dosage counters the reduced efficacy of the oral versus the parenteral route of administration. Some clinicians recommend IV haloperidol for treating the agitated manic, particularly if response to IM medication is delayed or incomplete (see Chapter 20).

By the end of the first week of neuroleptic treatment, most manic patients are fully stabilized and lithium treatment can be instituted. Combined treatment with lithium and a neuroleptic is routine. When the patient reaches a steady state of lithium in about 2 to 3 weeks, the neuroleptic dose should be tapered and then discontinued.

About 10% of acute manic patients do not respond to even the most intense drug treatments and may progress to a toxic, dehydrated, and febrile state. If 5 days of parenteral, high-dose neuroleptic treatment has not ended the acute phase of the illness, medications should be discontinued and ECT given without further delay. Two bilateral ECTs daily for the first 2 to 3 days may be needed to bring the episode to a halt. When this has been accomplished, usually by the second or third session, the remainder of the course is given at the usual frequency. Manics require more ECTs than depressives, the usual course being 8 to 12 treatments. Even if the patient recovers by the 5th or 6th treatment, it is best to continue to at least 8 treatments in order to avoid rapid relapse.

Mild Mania and Hypomania

When the patient is not extremely excited, overactive, or assaultive and is willing to accept oral medication, lithium treatment should be started. As there is a lag of 5 to 7 days before the onset of significant antimanic activity with lithium, the staff and the other patients must be able to tolerate the frequently annoying and occasionally disruptive behaviors typical of manic patients. In a healthy individual who has no clinical evidence of renal, thyroid, or cardiac disease, lithium can be started as soon as blood is drawn for the initial laboratory tests without waiting for the results. A dose of 1,200–1,800 mg/day usually produces a blood level within the therapeutic range (1–1.5 mEq/L) by the end of 7 to 10 days. Serum lithium levels should be obtained twice weekly until a stable therapeutic level is achieved. If a therapeutic level is not achieved within a reasonable time at a dose of 1,800 mg/day, three possibilities should be considered: (1) the patient is not swallowing all of the medication, (2) polyuria with excessive lithium loss is occurring, or (3) the dose is too low. Manic patients with grandiose or persecutory delusions frequently prefer not to take medications and find lithium tablets or capsules easy to sequester in the cheek or under the tongue for subsequent disposal. Such patients are readily identified as the ones who rush to the water fountain or bathroom as soon as they have "swallowed" their pills. Using liquid preparations and having the patient sit in or near the nursing station for 20 minutes after each dose resolves this problem.

The anti-diuretic hormone (ADH) effect of lithium causes some patients to excrete a large volume of dilute urine, carrying with it a considerable amount of lithium, and makes it difficult or impossible to achieve a therapeutic level. Chlorothiazide (500–1,000 mg/day) may be prescribed to block the ADH effect, thereby reducing urinary output and increasing serum lithium levels (617). Patients should be closely observed for signs of lithium toxicity during this maneuver and serum lithium levels should be more frequently monitored.

When the first two potential causes of lithium treatment failure have been ruled out, there remains a small group of patients who simply require more than 1,800 mg/day of lithium to achieve a therapeutic level. Such patients typically exhibit no side effects at 1,800 mg/day, and a stepwise increase in dosage is indicated until therapeutic levels are obtained.

Lithium Failure, Anticonvulsants, and Drug Combinations

The strategy for treating most acute manics is straightforward. Table 11.11 outlines the steps to consider, depending on the degree of severity of the manic episode. If the patient is hypomanic or a manic under reasonable control (20% of cases), lithium alone should be tried first. Using one of the steady-state prediction systems (see Chapter 20) may shorten the therapeutic trial. Patients who ultimately respond well show clinical changes rather quickly, usually within 4 days of an adequate lithium dose. The initial changes are subtle; they include increased sleep time, a dusky skin color and loss of skin luster in Euro-Americans (in contrast to rosy cheeks and shiny skin during mania), a moderate slowing of speech and a decrease in activity level, and a thickening of saliva. Three weeks of steady-state treatment should be sufficient to stabilize the patient and to resolve most, if not all, psychopathology. If the patient shows less than 75% improvement at the end of 3 weeks, the clinician should consider ECT or the addition of an anticonvulsant to the lithium regimen.

As described above, if the patient is manic and assaultive or otherwise uncontrollable, a neuroleptic is the treatment of choice. IM haloperidol followed by overlapping oral haloperidol or, in rare instances, IV haloperidol followed by the

TABLE 11.11

Treatment Steps for Acute Mania

Hypomanic/Controllable Manic

1. Use lithium alone for 3–4 weeks.
2. If less than 75% improvement in controllable manic, offer ECT.
3. If patient refuses ECT or is a hypomanic with less than a 75% improvement on lithium alone, add carbamazepine or valproic acid to lithium.
4. If patient continues to be resistant to 3 weeks of anticonvulsant-lithium combination, offer ECT again; if patient refuses, taper original anticonvulsant and introduce the other anticonvulsant, then discontinue the original.
5. If patient continues to be resistant, the only options are ECT or experimental pharmacotherapy (e.g., methylene blue, verapamil)

Agitated, Aggressive Manic

1. Control behavior with anticonvulsant.
2. If anticonvulsant cannot control patient or patient is too severely agitated, treat initially with neuroleptic.
3. If neuroleptic (including IM and IV administration) does not control behavior within 1 week, offer ECT.
4. Once controlled, treat with lithium or combined pharmacotherapy as outlined in treatment steps for controllable manic (above).

KEY: ECT, electroconvulsive therapy; IM, intramuscular; IV, intravenous.

oral form usually works. When the patient is on the oral neuroleptic, lithium can be administered and the neuroleptic tapered.

Some mildly agitated manics can be initially controlled with carbamazepine or valproic acid, rather than with a neuroleptic. Carbamazepine and valproic acid are the drugs of choice for manic patients who also suffer from Parkinson's disease, as lithium can exacerbate this condition by decreasing dopamine synthesis (624). Systemic conditions that can aggravate mania (e.g., thyroid disease, low estrogen levels) should be controlled as quickly as possible because these conditions can cause pseudoresistance to antimanic drugs.

Maintenance

The goal of maintenance treatment is to prevent or ameliorate future episodes of illness (721). Post's hypothesis of sensitization (see the subsection on kindling and sensitization under etiology below) suggests that another goal of maintenance treatment is to reduce interepisode chronicity and improve interepisode functioning. The tactics for achieving these goals vary with the form of the acute episode and the previous illness course (see Table 11.12).

TABLE 11.12

Maintenance Tactics for Mood Disorders

Condition	*Tactics*
First episode of melancholia	1. Pharmacotherapy for 1 year (cyclic antidepressant or lithium), then discontinue gradually unless symptoms re-emerge 2. Baseline, postepisode assessment of cognitive strengths and weaknesses for present or future need for vocational or rehabilitative training 3. Baseline, postepisode personality assessment to facilitate stress reduction training 4. Stress-reduction training and advice on life situations to reduce stress
First period/episode of dysthymia	1. Pharmacotherapy for 1 year (cyclic antidepressant or MAOI), then discontinue gradually unless symptoms re-emerge 2. Same as above for items 2–4 3. Possible further behavioral change with cognitive/behavior therapy
First episode of mania	1. Lithium or anticonvulsant for one year, then discontinue 2. Same as for melancholia, items 2–4
First period/episode of hypomania or cyclothymia	1. Same as for first episode of mania
Recurrent episode of bipolar disorder	1. Indefinite pharmacotherapy (lithium, anticonvulsant, or combination) for episodes less than 2–3 years apart; same as for first episode of mania if episodes more than 5 years apart; if more than three episodes (even if spaced 5 or more years apart), indefinite pharmacotherapy 2. Same as for melancholia, items 2–4 3. For particularly frequent episodes, maintenance ECT
Recurrent episode of unipolar disorder	1. Indefinite pharmacotherapy with lithium, anticonvulsant, or combination, or maintenance ECT for episodes less than 2–3 years apart 2. Same as for melancholia, items 2–4

KEY: MAOI, monoamine oxidase inhibitor; ECT, electroconvulsive therapy.

Biologic maintenance treatment is generally uncomplicated if initial treatment has stabilized the acute condition. Periodic drug blood levels, renal or liver function monitoring, thyroid studies, and other testing in a high-functioning, physiologically and behaviorally stable patient are needed primarily for perceived medico-legal, rather than patient care, purposes. Change in behavior usually presages any problem. Special circumstances, such as co-occurring systemic or other CNS illness, the patient who is older than age 65, or a drastic diet change, however, require more frequent and specific testing. Blood drug levels every 2 to 4 months and laboratory monitoring of other organ systems likely to be affected by the maintenance medications every 12 months is usually sufficient. There is some evidence that patients who are rapid cyclers respond best to maintenance treatment with lithium and an anticonvulsant, rather than either drug alone (267).

Theory of Etiology

Genetics

Most investigators agree that mood disorders, regardless of the pathophysiology, are familial and probably due to genetic liability (376, Chapter 15; 1001). For example, twin studies find the monozygotic and dizygotic twin concordance rates to be about 60% and 20%, respectively. Concordance is somewhat higher for bipolar than for unipolar disease. Adoption studies also demonstrate higher rates of mood disorder among the biologic relatives of adopted-away offspring who develop mood disorder than among control parents or the adopting parents. In the twin studies, however, about 20% of concordant pairs have different illness forms (one bipolar and the other unipolar). Thus, to find a significant difference between biologic and control parents for the prevalence of mood disorder, unipolar and bipolar forms must be counted as a single condition.

Family studies are consistent with both familiality for mood disorders and some overlap between bipolar and unipolar disorders. For example, the risks for unipolar and bipolar disorders in the first-degree relatives of bipolar patients are about 12% and 6%, respectively, whereas these risks in the first-degree relatives of unipolar patients are about 10% and 3%, respectively. Some studies report much higher risks, but almost all find the same pattern: first-degree relatives of bipolar patients have more unipolar than bipolar disorder, and relatives of unipolar patients have more unipolar and bipolar disorder than do controls. In addition, the relatives of unipolar and bipolar patients have greater risks (2% and 3%, respectively) than do controls (about 0.3%) for schizoaffective disorder. No study has been able to provide a satisfactory unifying genetic explanation for these data; linkage studies to the X chromosome (blood groups and color blindness), chromosome 11, and studies of human leukocyte antigens have not been confirmed. The genetics of mood disorders is further complicated by the fact that (1) patients with anorexia nervosa have first-degree relatives with risks for unipolar and bipolar disorder similar to those in relatives of bipolar patients; and (2) although the risk for alcoholism in bipolar patients and their relatives is higher than in controls, this increased risk may not reflect shared liability. Thus, significant genetic heterogeneity and complex etiologic overlapping of some syndromes (e.g., unipolar and bipolar disorders) may exist.

Models

Various animal models have been proposed for depression (e.g., primate neonate separation from the mother, learned helplessness), but none explains bipolar disorder (657, 815). Stimulant drug effects on dopamine systems have been suggested for mania, but the hyperactive state induced by these compounds is not typically similar to mania; also, the switch process from mania to depression is not explained. A fluctuation between activated dopaminergic function (mania) and reduced serotonergic function (depression) has been proposed to explain the cycles, but drug models for this process do not produce a clear bipolar pattern or typical syndromes. None of these models explains the data, and none is clinically useful (376, Chapter 17).

Biochemical Hypotheses

Various biochemical hypotheses have been proposed as underlying mechanisms in mood disorder. The earliest of these was the catecholamine hypothesis suggesting that depression and mania resulted from a deficiency and an excess, respectively, of catecholamine. A serotonin hypothesis required deficits in both states. Other neurotransmitters (e.g., gamma-aminobutyric acid [GABA], acetylcholine), biogenic amines (phenylethylamine); neurotransmitter-related enzymes (monoamine oxidase, catechol-o-methyltransferase) have also been theoretically implicated. Evidence for all of these hypotheses has been sought from studies of metabolites, uptake and receptor activity and density measurement, postmortem results, and interactions between drugs and neurotransmitter systems. No theory is theoretically satisfying, and none has direct clinical application (376, Chapter 17).

Kindling and Sensitization

More recently, sensitization and kindling have been proposed as potential analogues to the pathophysiology of mood disorder. Post and colleagues (779–782) first suggested electrophysiologic kindling as a model and, more recently, behavioral sensitization.

Electrophysiologic kindling refers to the propensity of some neurons to become sensitized to repeated low-level electrical stimulation to the extent that eventually a previously subconvulsive stimulus induces an electrical seizure. If subconvulsvie stimuli continue to be administered, spontaneous seizures (without stimulation) eventually occur. The hippocampus and amygdala are particularly prone to kindling. This provides a useful model for mood disorders because (1) MRI and CT abnormalities have been observed in the frontotemporal regions of mood disorder patients, (2) secondary mood disorder syndromes have been clinicopathologically associated with frontolimbic disease, (3) some patients with mood disorder exhibit psychosensory features (e.g., déjà vu, dysmegalopsia), (4) the course of mood disorders with increasing episode frequency over time is a kindlinglike pattern, and (5) treatment modalities (ECT, anticonvulsants) that raise the seizure threshold and modify kindling are efficacious in mood disorder.

Behavioral sensitization is similar to kindling. In this model, neurons become increasingly responsive, as measured by behavioral activity, to repeated administrations of the same dose of a stimulant drug (e.g., cocaine). Behaviors become more severe, onset more rapid, and changes more prolonged; behaviors are more likely to be triggered by stress without inducement by the offending drug. The propensity of neurons to be sensitized (and to kindle) involves a significant genetic component and raises the possibility that the proposed genetic liability in mood disorders is related to such a process. Further, in nonhuman studies, younger animals are more vulnerable, which is akin to the early-onset pattern of bipolar disorder.

If valid, these models have serious clinical implications and offer four suggestions to minimize chronicity: (1) Early episodes, in particular, should be shortened to reduce the kindling/sensitization process; (2) prevention of future episodes is important beyond the immediacy of this or next year's episodes; (3) biologic treatments that have direct effects on such processes may be most efficacious in the long run; and (4) stress reduction and the development of adaptive behaviors to stress (by psychologic intervention following recovery) may help to reduce the frequency of episodes later in the course of illness.

Chapter

12

Secondary or Symptomatic Morbid States

I. Delirium and Dementia

Delirium and dementia are behavioral syndromes characterized by diffuse cognitive impairment. Delirium is always associated with some alteration in consciousness (for assessment, see Chapter 5) and is almost always an acute state. Dementia is usually associated with a clear sensorium and is usually chronic.

Delirium

The prevalence of delirium is unclear; from 10 to 15% of acute medical/surgical patients and 30% of elderly inpatients may suffer from it (58, 100, 154). Further, only 1% of patients receive a diagnosis of delirium, which indicates widespread missed diagnosis. Delirium is most likely to occur in patients with (1) multiple medical problems (particularly those associated with hypoxia, hypoglycemia, infection, or fever); (2) compromised renal function; (3) conditions associated with an elevated white blood count; (4) use of drugs with significant anticholinergic properties; and (5) use of such drugs as propranolol, scopolamine, or flurazepam. Intoxications and severe drug withdrawal states are forms of delirium (see Chapter 17).

Behavior

The classic delirious patient is perplexed, disoriented, anxious, and agitated. Tremulousness, tachycardia, sweating, and vasoconstriction resulting in cold, clammy skin and circumoral pallor are common. These patients are "fitful," cannot understand events taking place around them, fear staff members and other patients, and may become irritable and assaultive. The last occurs particularly at night (the "sundown" syndrome), when reduced lighting and fewer staff interactions exacerbate already impaired information processing.

Delirious patients often have perceptual dysfunction. Affect-laden illusions and visual hallucinations are common. A delusional mood and delusional ideas, usually with persecutory content, can occur. Random fragments of nongoal-directed associations are typical (rambling speech). Cognitive impairment, although diffuse, characteristically is most striking in the areas of memory (immediate recall, recent memory, and long-term memory each may be affected), orientation, and concentration. Motor coordination also is often impaired (18, 100, 590). Onset may be gradual or acute, but most deliria resolve with good treatment.

Laboratory

Most commonly, the clinical presentation of delirium is nonspecific, and the determination of etiology requires specific historical and laboratory investigation. The latter may include determinations of blood glucose; urea nitrogen and electrolytes; liver function; arterial PO_2 and PCO_2 and drug levels; urine glucose, acetone, and cells; and an electrocardiogram (ECG). EEG shows diffuse slowing (788). Specific symptom patterns include drug-induced anticholinergic delirium, Wernicke's encephalopathy, and alcohol withdrawal states. (These disorders are discussed in Chapter 17.) Other common causes of delirium are epilepsy, head trauma, central nervous system infection, drug overdoses, urinary tract disease, pulmonary and cardiovascular dysfunction, and systemic infection.

Diagnosis

Severe delirium is rarely misdiagnosed. Mild or subacute delirious processes, however, often are unrecognized, particularly on acute medical/surgical services. Subacute delirium should be suspected in patients whose systemic condition and treatments cannot alone account for their behavior. These patients are unexpectedly lethargic and easily fatigued. They have difficulty feeding, washing, or dressing themselves and are unable to understand simple and clear self-care instructions. They appear uncertain, hesitant, or perplexed when faced with simple hospital tasks expected of many patients (e.g., going to the bathroom, finding one's way from the visitor's room to bed).

DSM-III-R criteria for delirium require the addition of significant operational details to be clinically helpful. These criteria and the studies cited at the beginning of this section suggest the cardinal features of delirium: (1) diffuse cognitive impairment, (2) altered sensorium, (3) fluctuating behavior, (4) increased motor activity (restlessness or severe agitation), and (5) altered sleep-wake cycle with insomnia or daytime lethargy. Table 12.1 lists operational definitions for these

TABLE 12.1

Operational Definitions of the Cardinal Features of Delirium

Feature	*Operational Definition*
Diffuse cognitive impairment	Mini-Mental State score of < 22
Altered sensorium	Abnormal letter cancellation test, or missing the time of day by more than 2 hours
Fluctuating behavior	A rating of 2 or more on the following scale for increasing fluctuation: 0 None 1 Questionable 2 Definite (mild, at least one discrepancy in global behavior during nursing shifts or change in performance on cognitive tests) 3 Definite (several—2 or more discrepancies or changes)
Increased motor activity	A rating of 2 or more on the following scale for increased motor activity: 0 None 1 Questionable 2 Restless (fidgets in bed, plays with bedclothes) 3 Agitated (needs siderails and restraints)
Altered sleep-wake cycle with insomnia or daytime drowsiness	Less than 5 hours of sleep at night or more than 3 hours of sleep during the day

features. In addition, any patient suspected of being delirious should have an EEG. A normal tracing (without evidence of slowing) with minimal muscle artifact is strong evidence *against* delirium (286). Delirium tremens is the exception to the rule; its EEG pattern is increased fast activity (521).

Delirium is a syndromal label. Once the patient is diagnosed as delirious, the clinician must try to reach an etiologic diagnosis so that specific management can be prescribed. For medical or surgical patients, the most likely cause of delirium is recent medication or a metabolic process secondary to the treatment or to the disease that led to hospitalization. In most cases, an examination of laboratory findings and treatments ordered reveals the likely etiology. Common causes of delirium in psychiatric patients are recent medications, intoxications, withdrawal from substances of abuse, seizure disorder, and mania.

Management

The first steps in the management of the delirious patient are behavioral control and identification of the specific etiology. Treatment should be directed toward resolving the primary disease process. If the cause of the delirium is not known, initial treatment should concentrate on potential life-threatening conditions or conditions that, if left untreated, can lead to permanent brain damage. Hypoglycemia, hyperthermia, and hypoxia are the most common situations requiring rapid intervention. All patients with deliria of unknown etiology should be tested for blood glucose levels with a meter that reads glucose levels from a finger-stick sample of blood (747). The validity of these readings depends on hematocrit levels; if there is any question regarding glucose levels all patients should receive intravenous dextrose (50 mL of a 50% solution) and be immediately examined for hyperthermia, hypotension, myocardial infarction and cardiac arrhythmia (frequently resulting in deliria in the elderly), pulmonary disease, and anemia.

The delirious patient is best managed in a quiet, calm, structured setting. A softly lighted hospital room and constant observation by familiar people and staff who clearly identify themselves and what they are doing help to reduce the patient's anxiety and agitation. The proper environment often makes pharmacotherapy unnecessary. When sedation is required, anxiolytics are the drugs of choice.

Theory of Etiology

A number of theoretical mechanisms have been proposed to explain delirium. Each assumes the syndrome to be an expression of pathophysiology in some final common pathway, as so many different conditions can result in delirium. Three of these hypotheses are (1) derangement in cerebral oxidative metabolism, (2) damage to the blood-brain barrier, and (3) derangement in enzyme systems or other metabolic pathways. None of these theories has any present clinical usefulness (602, 1020).

Dementia

Dementia can occur at any age. Particularly common among the elderly, it affects 5% of people over age 65 and 20% or more of those over age 80. There is some evidence that African Americans are at significantly greater risk for dementia (specifically the multi-infarct type) than are Euro-Americans (445). Dementia, however, is not a normal variant of the aging process. It is a syndrome characterized by diffuse cognitive impairment, usually of slow onset. Particularly in the early stages, sensorium is usually clear. Although some dementing processes can resolve (e.g., those secondary to normal-pressure hydrocephalus, myxedema, depression in the aged), most terminate in a chronic defect state. As theoretically defined, delirium implies a physiologic or biochemical dysfunctional state, whereas dementia implies loss of nervous tissue. In clinical practice, neither implication is absolute (93, 237).

Behaviorally, the classic demented patient is deteriorated in personality, often disoriented to time and place, amnestic, and occasionally psychotic. These patients may develop a coarsening of personality and become tactless, cruel, ill-mannered, and ill-groomed. Their speech is perseverative, cliche-ridden, and stereotyped. They are often restless (rubbing, tapping, and folding hand movements are common) and occasionally severely agitated. Patients may display emotional lability, Witzelsucht (a shallow, silly, fatuous mood), emotional blunting, or emotional incontinence (sudden and unexpected brief outbursts of laughter or crying often unassociated with the corresponding mood). They may have multiple soft neurologic signs, changes in muscle tone (often weakness and rigidity without cogwheeling), a puppetlike gait, nystagmus, the Klüver-Bucy syndrome (oral ingestive behavior, lack of sexual inhibition, placidity, visual agnosia), urinary incontinence, and pupillary changes. Frontal, temporal, and parietal lobe cognitive syndromes can be present. In the late stages of many dementing processes seizures of all types can occur.

Profound memory deficit, disorientation, and readily observed nonbehavioral neurologic features facilitate diagnosis during the later stages of a dementing process. In the early stages of dementia, however, signs and symptoms are frequently ambiguous and behavioral changes may be most prominent. Patients are often misdiagnosed as suffering from major depression, dysthymia, or schizophrenia. Neurologic, behavioral neurologic, and mental status examinations are essential in early identification of these patients, so that those with resolvable disorders can receive appropriate care without exposure to unnecessary psychiatric treatments.

During the early stages of dementias with insidious onset (e.g., Alzheimer's type) frequent complaints include fatigue, mild sadness, headache, poor concentration, and loss of efficiency. Patients often show decline in their general activities and lose interest in sports and hobbies. They may report a vague difficulty in using words (particularly the expression of polysyllabic words) and word finding. They may become lost in familiar places and lose efficiency in previously learned skills (e.g., cooking meals, typing, driving in heavy traffic). Denial of illness is frequently observed, and patients may offer outlandish excuses for poor performance of simple cognitive tasks. A general lack of spontaneity and mild recent memory problems are also common. As women are at greater risk than men for most non–alcohol-related and noncardiovascular dementias, and as many dementing processes begin in the sixth decade or later, the early stages of dementia are most often confused with major depression. Such patients even may have a mild or transient improvement with antidepressant medication or ECT.

Diagnosis

Dementia, as delirium, is a syndromal label. Table 12.2 presents the cardinal features of the syndrome and their operational definitions. Once the decision is made that a patient's most probable diagnosis is dementia, the clinician must try to reach a specific diagnostic conclusion because some dementias can be successfully treated. Table 6.2 in Chapter 6 divides dementias by onset age and lists the most probable specific diagnoses within each onset age group. These relationships should be taken as guideposts only.

Table 12.3 lists some of the more common dementing disorders encountered on a psychiatric service and typical characteristics of each condition. In addition to a history, and systemic, neurologic, behavioral neurologic, and mental status examinations, diagnostic evaluation for dementia may include specific laboratory studies (brain imaging and other x-rays, hemogram, serum B_{12} and folic acid levels, VDRL, serum protein studies, blood urea nitrogen [BUN], serum glucose, thyroid studies, serum enzymes, serum calcium, serum copper and ceruloplasmin, serum electrolytes, urinalysis and urinary protein, copper and porphobilinogen, blood gas studies, serum and urine screens for toxic substances), skeletal x-ray studies, spinal fluid studies for protein and VDRL, EEG and CT evaluations, and neuropsychological testing. Angiography and blood and spinal fluid flow studies also may be required. The clinician should have in mind (from the working diagnostic list) which tests to order and why and which tests to omit.

The differential diagnosis between dementia with a secondary depression and pseudodementia is particularly important, as the latter can respond fully to treatment. Secondary depressions may be identified clinically; patients appear more apathetic than profoundly sad, and several soft neurologic signs may be present. Pseudodementia patients also tend to complain more of cognitive loss and other

TABLE 12.2

Operational Definitions of the Cardinal Features of Dementia

Feature	*Operational Definition*
Diffuse cognitive impairment	Mini-Mental State score < 22 in early stages, or < 20 in later stages
Clear sensorium	Normal letter cancellation test, or, if abnormal, restricted to errors of commission (suggesting distractibility)
Impairment in memory	(See memory testing, Chapter 5)
Impairment in thinking	(See tests of thinking, Chapter 5)

TABLE 12.3

Dementing Disorders Commonly Seen Among Psychiatric Patients

Irreversible Conditions	*Typical Clinical Features*	*Treatment*	*Comments*
Alzheimer's/senile dementia	More common in women Gross disorientation early Neurologic signs and abnormal EEG late features Two onset peaks in 50s and 70s, respectively	Symptomatic	Familial Identical neuropathology Early stages may be confused with depression Nucleus basalis (in basal forebrain) may be involved in Alzheimer's Associated with Down's syndrome and leukemia
Multi-infarct dementia	More common in men Gross disorientation late Seizures Rarely develops before age 65 Sudden onset and focal neurologic signs common	Symptomatic; prevention of progression by treating primary cause	Other evidence of cardiovascular disease must be established to confirm diagnosis
Huntington's chorea	Prominent frontal lobe cognitive features Dysarthria, gait disturbances, motor overflow features Multiple onset peaks, typically ages 35–45 "butterfly" ventricular CT scan pattern diagnostic Psychosis can be first expression of the illness	Symptomatic (haloperidol may have specific GABA effect reducing choreiform movements)	Autosomal dominant gene transmission Possible GABA deficit

Parkinson's disease	More common in women Prominent frontal lobe cognitive features Extrapyramidal signs prominent Onset, ages 50–60	L-Dopa of little benefit for behavioral and cognitive features Symptomatic behavioral treatment	Occurs in 20–40% of parkinsonian patients May see similar pattern in patients with tardive dyskinesia
Korsakoff's syndrome	More common in males Gross disorientation Gross memory impairment Ophthalmoplegias, peripheral neuropathies, cerebellar ataxia Typical onset in late 50s	Thiamine Multivitamins Symptomatic behavioral treatment	Confabulation need not be present 90% of cases are alcoholics Possible genetic predisposition to low thiamine levels
Pick's disease	More common in males Lobar syndromes predominate: frontal convexity, dominant temporal, and parietal lobes Early (age 40) and late (age 50) onset peaks EEG, CT scan abnormal but nonspecific Spinal fluid may show increased globulins	Symptomatic	Early onset cases confused with schizophrenia

(*continued*)

TABLE 12.3 (*Cont.*)

Dementing Disorders Commonly Seen Among Psychiatric Patients

Reversible Conditions	*Typical Clinical Features*	*Treatment*	*Comments*
Normal-pressure hydrocephalus	Prominent frontal lobe features Ataxia Urinary incontinence CT scan diagnostic	Ventricular shunting works best in patients with alteration of consciousness or early ataxic signs	10% are alcoholics
Wilson's disease	Prominent frontal lobe cognitive features Prominent motor features (facial bradykinesia, tremors, limb rigidity, dysarthria, "wing-beating," choreoathetosis) Seizures Hepatolentricular degeneration Onset peak, ages 15–25	D-Penicillamine	Kayser-Fleischer rings not always present
Drug-induced dementia	More common in the elderly Sudden onset Gross disorientation EEG usually abnormal but nonspecific, often reversible	Stop all medications not essential to life	Common offending agents include digitalis, propranolol, phenacetin, bromides, anticholinergic medications, barbiturates, psychotropics

Dementias caused by metabolic disorder	Lethargy and disorientation most common Onset slow	Correction of metabolic imbalance	Thyroid dysfunction (hypo- and hyper-) most common etiology; also hypo- and hyperparathyroidism, hypercalcemia, liver disease, Cushing's disease, uremia, hypernatremia, dehydration, and carcinoma
Dementias caused by deficiency states	Lethargy and confusion common Onset slow Symptoms of depression may be reversible	Replacement treatment Symptomatic	Vitamin B_{12}, folate, general malnutrition
Dementias caused by other systemic conditions	Lethargy and confusion Onset slow May be reversible	Symptomatic Correction of systemic disorder	Common conditions include myocardial infarction, dysrhythmias, bilateral carotid artery disease, lupus, pickwickian syndrome

KEY: CT, computed tomogarphy; GABA, gamma-aminobutyric acid; EEG, electroencephalogram.

distress and have more psychomotor retardation. Secondary depressives tend to have no prior history of depressive illness and no family history of psychiatric disorder. EEG and brain imaging studies at this stage may reveal few, if any, abnormalities. Dexamethasone challenge is unhelpful, as a significant proportion of demented patients without depressive features are nonsuppressors (923). Neuropsychological testing, can be helpful, however, as a sensitive measure of coarse disease (312), in addition to SPECT studies (see Chapter 6). There is also some evidence (260) that evoked potential studies are beneficial in this discrimination. Specifically, when patients are asked to perform a memory scanning task, the amplitude of the positive waveform occurring about 300 milliseconds after the stimulus (the "P300") is reduced in Alzheimer's patients but not in age-matched controls.

Specific Dementias

Many conditions can lead to dementia (217, 237, 745). Some of them are briefly discussed below.

Alzheimer's Disease

Dementia of the Alzheimer's type (DAT) usually begins after age 50 and typically after age 70. It usually leads to death from secondary infection within a decade of illness onset. The most common dementia, DAT accounts for at least half of all cases. Prevalence increases with age from 5% of the population at age 65 to 20% by age 90. Women are slightly more at risk than men.

DAT is familial; close to half of first-degree relatives are affected by their mid-80s. Also, a familial relationship to Down's syndrome and to some leukemias leads to the notion that the common denominator in these disorders involves deranged aging in specific cell lines. Some molecular genetic studies suggest a deviant genotype on chromosome 21 that may be expressed in the accretion of amyloid in blood vessels and neurons (504, 697, 855).

Some investigators distinguish between Alzheimer's disease and simple senile dementia, which is a sporadic, rather than familial, disorder. Some evidence indicates that the two clinically similar conditions can be distinguished neuropathologically, with Alzheimer's disease but not simple senile dementia, being characterized by neuronal loss in the basal nucleus of Meynert (956).

Clinically, DAT progresses through three overlapping stages. In *Stage 1*, speech becomes progressively empty and ideas restricted. Anomia, mild dysgraphia, poor verbal fluency, mild memory impairment, and deficits on visual spatial tasks are commonly observed. Laboratory measures are usually normal. An associated depression, usually characterized by apathy and loss of interest, rather than profound sadness, is most commonly observed in this stage (30 to 50% of patients).

In *Stage 2*, cognitive and behavioral deterioration increases, and fluent aphasia may occur. Memory impairment becomes a dominant cognitive theme. Periods of agitation, loss of some skills in grooming and hygiene, and a coarsening of the personality can also occur. In *Stage 3*, severe deterioration develops, incontinence is common, and constant custodial care is often necessary.

The DAT pattern consists of (1) dementia occurring after age 65, (2) a uniformly diffuse cognitive decline highlighted by memory loss, and (3) no serious problems with hypertension or heart disease.

Pick's Disease

Pick's disease accounts for about 5% of dementias, and males are somewhat more at risk than females. Onset age is usually between ages 40 and 60. Although Pick's and Alzheimer's diseases have many overlapping features, patients with Pick's disease tend to have less gross cognitive impairment and more personality changes (coarsening). There is some evidence that Pick's begins in anterior brain regions and progresses posteriorly. As frontotemporal areas (perhaps more on the left than the right) are usually most severely involved in the early stages of Pick's disease, this stage is similar to the frontal lobe convexity syndrome. This pattern, combined with the higher risk for males and the relatively early onset, occasionally results in the misdiagnosis of these patients as late-onset schizophrenics. EEG and imaging findings circumscribed to the frontotemporal areas help to differentiate between Pick's disease and schizophrenia. Loss of volition but with some sparing of emotional expression and onset over age 40 in Pick's disease also are distinguishing features.

In both Pick's disease and DAT, bilateral hippocampal degeneration can result in the Klüver-Bucy syndrome. This can be an early feature in Pick's disease but occurs late (stage 3) in DAT.

The Pick's disease pattern consists of (1) dementia occurring before age 65, (2) a frontotemporal emphasis in behavioral change and cognitive decline, (3) personality and behavioral changes overshadowing cognitive changes, and (4) no serious problems with hypertension or heart disease (444).

Multi-Infarct Dementia

Multi-infarct dementia (MID), the second most common dementia, accounts for 10% of cases. Onset usually occurs during the 50s or 60s; men are at higher risk than women.

MID usually results from sustained hypertension that leads to necrosis and occlusion of cerebral arterioles, with an erratic but progressive disruption of cognitive function. Atherosclerosis of large blood vessels, vascular inflammatory conditions, and hematologic disorders are other causes. Most commonly affected areas are the thalamus, basal ganglia, internal capsule (lacunar state), and hemispheric white matter (Binswanger's disease). Behavioral and cognitive pattern changes vary from patchy to diffuse. Secondary and tertiary preventive treatments of the underlying condition may help to stem progression of the disorder. Anticoagulants and aspirin also may be beneficial in preventing thrombus formation. The MID pattern consists of (1) dementia occurring between ages 50 to 70, (2) erratic progression without clear deficit pattern, and (3) significant vascular disease.

Dementia Associated with Basal Ganglia Disease

Parkinson's disease, Huntington's disease, and Wilson's disease form the majority of extrapyramidal disorders that can lead to dementia. Cummings and Benson (238) have proposed that the dementia associated with these disorders differs in pattern from those dementias primarily associated with cerebral cortical disease. They refer to this pattern as *subcortical dementia*. Although there is significant symptom overlap between this and other dementias, the subcortical pattern, when clear, can be helpful in the differential diagnosis of dementia. The subcortical pattern consists of (1) psychomotor retardation (bradykinesia), (2) memory impairment, (3) diffuse cognitive impairment, (4) mood disturbances (most commonly depression), (5) speech and motor abnormalities (typical of the underlying condition), and (6) the absence of cognitive features associated with cortical damage (aphasia, agnosia, apraxia).

Dementia Associated with White Matter Disease

Several morbid processes affecting white matter can result in dementia. *Binswanger's disease*, mentioned above, is one of these. Others are progressive multifocal leukoencephalopathy, multiple sclerosis, metachromatic leukodystrophy, adrenoleukodystrophy, AIDS, vitamin B_{12} deficiency, traumatic brain injury (diffuse axonal injury), and neurotoxicity (e.g., secondary to toluene, alcohol). Most patients with these conditions do not develop dementia; however, if the white matter involvement is extensive, diffuse cognitive impairment in clear consciousness (i.e., dementia) can result. For example, somewhere between 50 and 75% of AIDS patients develop significant cognitive impairment. The prevalence and severity of the impairment, however, appears to increase with the severity of the illness (381); thus dementia develops only in later stages of AIDS.

The pattern of white matter dementia consists of (1) a dementia usually developing before age 50, (2) mild progression of cognitive impairment, (3) sparing of personality, and (4) a subcortical dementia pattern. Table 12.4 displays some of the factors that the clinician should consider in the differential diagnosis of these disorders.

TABLE 12.4

Differential Diagnostic Factors of White Matter Dementia

Condition	*Diagnostic Factors*
Progressive multifocal leukoencephalopathy	Almost always seen in patients with chronic, lymphoproliferative or myeloproliferative, or granulomatosis disease A slowly progressive papovirus infection Multiple demyelinating lesions and abnormal glial cells
Multiple sclerosis	Periventricular cerebral lucencies on CT Will have eye movement disturbances
Metachromatic leukodystrophy	Rare autosomal recessive Dementia and peripheral neuropathy
Binswanger's disease	Multi-infarcts in hemisphere white matter Dementia and hypertension
Acquired immunodeficiency syndrome (AIDS)	HIV-positive Overt AIDS and related syndromes Discrete parenchymal or focal lesions on MRI
Vitamin B_{12} deficiency	Behavioral and cognitive changes can occur before megaloblastic anemia develops Patchy demyelination in hemispheres and posterior and lateral columns of spinal cord

KEY: CT, computed tomography; HIV, human immunodeficiency virus; MRI, magnetic resonance imaging.

Management

The treatment of dementia is rarely specific. Specific treatments include D-penicillamine for Wilson's disease, vitamin and hormonal replacement for nutritional and endocrine disorders, ventricular shunting for normal-pressure hydrocephalus, penicillin for CNS syphilis, and surgery for vascular malformations and subdural hematoma (93, 814, 852). Selegiline (10 mg daily), an irreversible MAOI that is specific for the MAO-B isoenzyme, has been reported to benefit some patients with DAT through improvement in cognition; reduction in psychotic features, activity disturbances and anxiety; and alleviation of caregiver stress (364).

TABLE 12.5

Guidelines for Psychosocial and Behavioral Care of the Demented Patient

Area of Concern	*What to Do*
Living quarters	1. Keep quarters uncluttered, tidy, well lit, unchanging, and familiar. 2. Use nightlights and reflecting tape to reduce nighttime confusion. 3. Develop a system of clearly displayed, simply written instructions, reminders, or directions.
Activities	1. Establish a daily routine for meals, medication, exercise, recreation, and hobbies. 2. Match activities to patient's cognitive abilities. 3. Include special activities with central pleasurable sensory theme (food, pets, music, visits to park or botanic garden).
Self-care	1. Simplify and routinize all self-care tasks (bathing, dressing, cleaning living quarters). 2. Rely on less complex utensils and clothes (velcro straps instead of laces or buttons, clip-on ties).
Caretaker's behavior	1. Pace interactions to match patient's response time. 2. Expect, and be, calm during overly emotional reactions to failure or confusion. 3. Expect denial and be firm but nonconfrontational in maintaining injury prevention procedures. 4. Use distraction rather than confrontation to control irritable or socially inappropriate behavior. 5. Pitch voice to lower, easier-to-hear register (also less stressed sounding). 6. Use short, simple sentences. 7. Explain all interactions and activities and, as much as possible, include patient in decision-making process. 8. Always make eye contact, and use gestures. 9. Avoid distractions and more than one person speaking at a time.

Nonspecific pharmacologic treatment includes low-dose, high-potency neuroleptics for psychosis and anticonvulsants for seizures. The type of seizures determines the choice of anticonvulsant. Haloperidol for psychosis is usually the first-line neuroleptic because of its high potency, relatively mild anticholinergic and hypotensive side effects, and availability in IM and IV forms. ECT for psychoses secondary to dementia also can be effective, particularly when depressive or manic features predominate.

Hospital management must be structured. Demented patients often are negligent about their self-care and food intake. Careful attention is required in maintaining their hygiene and providing them with an adequate diet. Continued physical activity in structured exercise, sports, and socialization programs can delay deterioration and significantly enrich a patient's life. Anecdotally, participation in frequent "special events" (picnics; visits to museums, botanic gardens, zoos) seems to delay cognitive decline. Family members and friends should be encouraged to visit often and participate in these activities. Physicians and ward staff often underestimate the capabilities of demented patients. The cognitive, behavioral, and physical abilities of patients should be quickly assessed, and they should be expected and encouraged to participate in activities to the level of these abilities. Elderly and demented patients should not be treated as children. The use of first names, "we" instead of "you," and such childish terms as "tummy" are inappropriate. The mere fact that a patient is disoriented does not mean he likes to play with mud pies, and the content of any activity program should be interesting to adults. Table 12.5 displays some of the psychosocial and behavioral guidelines helpful in the management of dementia patients (616).

Chapter 13

Secondary or Symptomatic Morbid States

II. Epilepsy, and Localized Coarse Brain and Other Syndromes

Neuropsychiatry draws heavily on brain and behavior relationships clarified by the work of behavioral neurologists and neuropsychologists. It also provides its own insights into the neurology of psychopathology. Because all behavior, normal and abnormal, in its final common path reflects brain function, all behavioral syndromes (e.g., phobias, anxiety states, psychoses, personality deviations) can be considered neuropsychiatric conditions. This chapter, however, focuses on those conditions in which the neuropathology is more firmly established and the evidence is clear that brain pathologic processes underlie the observable behavioral phenomena. Also, discussion is limited to conditions that are likely to be encountered in the practice of neuropsychiatry.

Epilepsy

The association between seizure disorders and abnormal behavior has been known since the earliest Greek medical writers. Modern surveys (774, 998) suggest that 75% of epileptics develop behavioral difficulties or intellectual deficits in association with their seizure disorders and that nearly 50% have interictal psychiatric symptoms affecting social functioning and ability to work. Epileptics comprise approximately 10% of psychiatric admissions. Clinicians must be prepared to recognize and manage these patients, whose behaviors can make them difficult to treat on most neurologic services.

The prevalence of seizure disorders is about 6 in 1,000 in the general population. The etiology in most cases is unknown, although mesial temporal sclerosis is the most common cause of complex seizures. No differences are reported among social classes (143). Follow-up studies (729) indicate the course in many patients is poor, and the prognosis is worse with early onset. Seizure disorders are classified into three types:

1. *Generalized:* The initial electrical discharge is generalized and originates from all or most centrencephalic structures.
2. *Localized:* The initial electrical discharge is focal, local, or partial; cortical or subcortical; and may or may not become generalized.
3. *Mixed* forms.

Generalized seizures can be idiopathic or symptomatic of a recognized acquired morbid process. They include petit mal, myoclonic, infantile spasms, clonic, tonic, tonic-clonic (grand mal), atonic, and akinetic seizures. Localized, or *partial epilepsy,* includes seizures which are: *simple* (attacks without significant impairment of consciousness accompanied by motor and sensory symptoms) or *complex* (attacks with significant impairment of consciousness accompanied by behavioral, cognitive, and affective phenomena) (95, 998).

Behavior

Behavioral changes associated with epilepsy can relate directly to the seizure (the ictal state), the prodromal (hours to weeks preceding the seizure), the postictal period (hours to days subsequent to the seizure), or to the interictal period. Because the seizure rarely lasts more than 15 minutes and most often less than 1 minute, the behaviors that lead to psychiatric hospitalization or treatment are typically nonictal.

Prodromal symptoms usually develop a few hours or days prior to the seizure. Irritability and dysphoria are most common, although psychosis can occur. Prodromal syndromes usually improve following the seizure. Observation of this relationship contributed to the development of induced seizures for the treatment of psychiatric disorders (661).

Ictal phenomena requiring psychiatric treatment are most commonly seen in patients with partial seizures. Another term used to identify these syndromes is psychosensory. The term psychomotor epilepsy, although still used, is no longer officially in vogue. Temporal lobe epilepsy (TLE) is the most common type of psychosensory epilepsy. Epilepsy in other cortical areas, particularly the frontal lobes, also can produce psychosensory phenomena. In addition, Petit mal status can produce a confusional psychosis that can last for days or weeks, but any chronic, generalized seizure disorder eventually can result in psychosis (84, 246, 998).

Psychosensory, complex partial seizure syndromes are associated with some alteration in consciousness. The alteration can be extremely subtle, and the patient may appear only slightly hesitant or somewhat distracted in his responses. Also, perplexity; oneiroid (dreamlike) states; syndromes characterized by disorientation and agitation; and complex behavior patterns, during which the patient is unresponsive to all but the most intense stimulation (e.g., shouting, physical restraints), can occur. Absence phenomena are also observed, but these tend to be longer and less frequent than those of petit mal and more gradual in onset and termination. Psychosensory episodes generally are short in duration, frequent, and, for a given patient, similar in form and content from one episode to another (998).

Every type of psychopathology has been reported during psychosensory states. The classic psychosensory ictal presentation is that of temporal lobe epilepsy; it is characterized by automatic, repetitive behaviors termed automatisms, which can take the form of complicated acts. Some reported automatisms are laughing, weeping, sobbing, raging, screaming, assuming odd postures, dressing and undressing, continual repetition of the same phrases, getting something to eat or drink, fugue states, and violent behavior. Other repetitive ictal behaviors are coughing, sneezing, yawning, hiccupping, gagging, vomiting, and belching.

During a seizure, the patient may appear unblinking, wide-eyed, and expressionless and stare ahead or to one side. Partial or complete loss of posture may occur, as well as pupillary dilation, pallor or flushing, perioral cyanosis, salivation, sweating, tachycardia, hypertension, gastrointestinal motility changes, incontinence of urine (rarely of feces), respiratory rate changes, and gasping or even apnea.

Associated experiences include sudden and intense alterations in mood; emotional incontinence; forced thinking (similar to experiences of control and alienation); feeling of impending doom and anxiety; déjà vu and jamais vu; depersonalization and derealization; oneiroid states; visual distortions (macropsia, micropsia), hallucinations (pleasant and unpleasant) in any sensory modality, particularly visual, olfactory, and gustatory; autoscopic phenomena (hallucinating oneself); autonomic nervous system paroxysms (palpitations, sudden intense feeling of cold or heat); and abdominal pains or a feeling of abdominal emptiness (hollowness) that "rushes" up into the subcostal area and, sometimes, through the chest and into the head. These episodes are usually short in duration and are always followed by some degree of amnesia for the event and some postictal fatigue, sleepiness, confusion, or depression (95, 540, 998).

Many attempts have been made to relate psychosensory phenomena to particular lesion sites: cortical versus subcortical, dominant versus nondominant, or a specific cortical region. None of these attempts has been completely successful, especially in lateralizing and localizing cortical foci. Nevertheless, certain patterns have emerged from clinicopathologic and stimulation studies. Table 13.1

TABLE 13.1

Localizing Patterns of Psychosensory Phenomena

*Subcortical**	*Cortical*
Rising epigastric sensations and alimentary automatisms	Ictal aphasia and thought disorder***
Autonomic signs**	Postictal dysphasia***
Aura of fear or panic	Prolonged auditory hallucinations***
Olfactory or gustatory hallucinations	Disorientation***
Oral automatisms**	Auditory and visual hallucinations
Sexual behaviors	Illusions, dysmegalopsia
Aggression and violence	
Learning and memory problems**	
Déjà vu**	
Absence and dreamy states**	
Indescribable sensory experiences	
Derealization and depersonalization	

*Particularly amygdala, parahippocampus, hippocampus, hippothalamus, and septum.
**Nondominant hemispheric association.
***Dominant hemispheric association.

displays several of these relationships, which should be used only as clinical guidelines (998). Additional evidence suggests that sudden, transient, shallow expressions of sadness or tearfulness are associated with nondominant hemispheric lesions, whereas sudden, transient, shallow expressions of euphoria or laughter are associated with dominant hemispheric lesions (20, 336, 858).

Other ictal syndromes are:

1. *Parietal lobe syndrome:* characterized by feelings that body parts are unusually heavy, dead, as if made of metal; painful tingling similar to electrical shocks; unpleasant coldness or burning feelings; feelings that an arm or leg is moving on its own; experiences of body parts in new locations (e.g., a hand in one's abdomen); and altered attitude toward pain (painful stimuli become pleasant so that self-inflicted painful injuries may result, "pain asymboli"). These experiences may lead to secondary delusional ideas of being possessed, being controlled by an outside force, or being dead (229).
2. *Frontal lobe syndrome:* characterized by speech arrest, periods of shallow euphoria and depression, irritable outbursts, dysphoria, posturing, diminished wakefulness, hyperactivity, disorientation, uncontrollable confabulations, and lack of self-control (429).

Postictal Behaviors

Postictal behaviors usually last only a few minutes but can extend to several hours or days. Most commonly, neuropsychiatric intervention occurs as a result of postictal behaviors. These behaviors are more variable and complex than most ictal phenomena. They include confusion (of all types), orienting behaviors (looking about, walking around, "absentminded" talking, straightening up one's clothes), sleepiness, irritability (including violent rage), sexual arousal, sexual behaviors that are usually socially inappropriate, and undressing. Confusional or delirious states, usually occurring after grand mal seizures, can last hours or days. Hallucinations and delusions can also occur. These postictal psychoses characteristically fluctuate daily or hourly in severity. They are occasionally mistaken for schizophrenic psychoses, but a history of seizurelike phenomena or episodes, an alteration in consciousness, and a fluctuation in symptom severity should alert the clinician. The postictal period EEG in these patients is usually abnormal and characterized by diffuse slow activity.

Patients with petit mal epilepsy may also experience a prolonged subacute delirious state with altered consciousness, termed petit mal status. Such episodes, lasting from hours to several weeks, are characterized by disorientation or perplexity, hallucinations, vague delusional ideas, rambling speech, and agitation. The EEG characteristically shows a spike and wave pattern (284, 836).

Interictal Behaviors

Interictal behavioral changes are varied and experienced by 40 to 60% of epileptics (83, 303, 998). The behaviors do not predict location of the lesion or type of seizure disorder. Many nonepileptic psychiatric patients also exhibit these behaviors (694). Excluding behaviors associated with mental retardation or developmental abnormalities, the most common behavioral changes are those of personality. Personality changes associated with chronic epilepsy usually take a decade or more to develop. Several types have been described; the most common is termed "adhesive" or "viscous" (94).

Patients with an adhesive personality are verbose, circumstantial, and perseverative. They are slow in thinking and speak in a pedantic manner. They lose sight of basic concepts and themes and focus on minutiae. Nothing is trivial; every detail must be considered ad nauseam, mulled over, and digested in a humorless fashion. These patients lack spontaneity and use common expressions of speech and trite sayings almost to the exclusion of original word sequencing.

A second interictal personality is characterized by a profound deepening of the patient's emotional responses. These patients tend to overrespond to provocative stimuli. They have explosive rages followed by hearty good-naturedness. They are emotionally labile, rash, suggestible, and excitable. They may develop a heightened sense of justice, morality, or religious conviction. Mundane, petty events assume cosmic significance. These patients often keep detailed, perseverative, and trite written records; they fill page after page of notebooks and scraps of paper with "universal truths." On occasion, they become suspicious and develop vague delusional ideas. An interictal personality syndrome has been specifically described in temporal lobe epileptics (83). These behaviors (hypergraphia, hyposexuality, circumstantiality, and pseudoprofundity) are diagnostically nonspecific (694), although they probably reflect temperolimbic dysfunction. Other interictal syndromes, in decreasing prevalence, are anxiety states, depression, and neurasthenia. Deviant sexual behavior also can occur; all late-onset (> 35 years of age), major changes in sexual behavior (e.g., transvestism, fetishism, homosexuality) should be suspect as manifestations of a seizure disorder (95, 246, 303, 540).

Epilepsy in some patients is associated with intellectual deterioration. Although progressive dementia can result from long-term phenytoin or primidone treatment, intellectual decline in some epileptics was reported before the drug era. An epileptic whose seizure disorder begins early in life, lasts a long time, is associated with frequent seizures (particularly a combination of focal and generalized), results from identifiable brain pathology (e.g., brain damage, tuberous sclerosis), and resists treatment is more likely to suffer intellectual decline than a patient with idiopathic or familial epilepsy (395, Chapter 5).

Psychosis

The association between epilepsy and psychosis has been known for centuries. It is unclear whether psychoses are consequences of the seizures or late-onset manifestations of the pathophysiologic process that caused the seizures. In either case, epileptics usually develop psychoses 10 to 15 years after the first clinical seizure (84, 95, 246, 540).

Psychoses in epileptics probably are most prevalent in patients with other behavioral changes (e.g., interictal personality changes). Studies also suggest that once psychotic episodes begin, their frequency is inversely related to the number of observable clinical seizures (i.e., the more psychotic episodes, the fewer seizures). Although the prevalence of psychoses in epileptics varies across studies (1 to 10%), the figures are particularly dramatic when epileptics are segregated into those with temporal lobe foci and those with other foci, with about 20% of temporal lobe epileptics developing psychoses. Nevertheless, these psychoses can occur with any type of seizure disorder.

"Schizophrenialike" conditions have been most commonly described in epileptics, particularly those with temporal lobe foci. The degree of interest in schizophrenia and epilepsy results in part, however, from the misconception that persecutory and grandiose delusions, auditory hallucinations, and catatonic behavior (all observed in the psychoses associated with epilepsy) are specific for schizophrenia, rather than clinical phenomena observable in any psychosis. Nevertheless, epileptics, particularly those with left-sided or bilateral frontotemporal discharges, can present with nonaffective psychoses consistent with modern criteria for schizophrenia (998). These conditions, referred to as symptomatic or secondary schizophrenias, may differ from the idiopathic variety in four ways: (1) preservation of affect with the ability to maintain good rapport and express warm feelings, (2) lack of significant personality deterioration despite years of illness, (3) frequent presence of psychosensory phenomena, and (4) greater likelihood of being married and having a productive school and employment record. Psychotic features commonly observed include delusional ideas, auditory and visual hallucinations, catatonic features (particularly stereotypies and posturing of the hands about the head and face), and formal thought disorder.

Affectivelike syndromes also are found in epileptics. Because they are typically episodic, are associated with reasonable interepisode functioning, and may occur with typical depressive or manic features, differentiation from primary affective disorder is often difficult and requires an especially thorough behavioral neurologic evaluation. Devinsky and Bear (263), in their review of depressive syndromes associated with epilepsy, found that rapidity of mood change, dysphoria, and fear, as opposed to just sadness, were particularly characteristic of these epilepsy-related depressions.

Atypical psychoses also may be associated with epilepsy. A safe clinical rule is to consider seriously coarse brain disease in any patient whose presentation, course, or demographic characteristics are unusual. Four examples are (1) the patient with insomnia, appetite disturbance, psychomotor retardation, and loss of interest but no significant sadness; (2) the patient with complete auditory hallucinations (or any first-rank symptom of Schneider) and virtually no other psychopathology; (3) the patient who develops a schizophrenic syndrome after age 40; and (4) the patient with a mood disorder that is chronic rather than episodic.

Several factors have been identified (998) as increasing the likelihood that an epileptic will develop a psychosis. (see Table 13.2). Family studies find no specific relationship between a family history of psychosis and the risk for psychosis in an epileptic patient. Further, although a relationship appears to exist between left-side foci and schizophrenialike psychoses, the obverse has not been observed. There is no clear laterality of foci with affective psychoses.

The following clinical vignette illustrates psychosis associated with epilepsy:

> A 54-year-old man was hospitalized because of assaultive behavior. The admitting physician found him to be hyperactive, irritable, and expansive in mood, with rapid and pressured speech and flight of ideas. He was not delusional and had no first-rank symptoms of Schneider or perceptual dysfunction. During the month prior to admission, he was sleeping less and involving himself in numerous projects, none of which he completed. He

TABLE 13.2

Factors That Increase an Epileptic's Risk for Psychosis

Sinistrality
Female
Onset age of epilepsy shortly after puberty
More than one lifetime seizure
Complex partial seizures that secondarily generalize
Complex partial seizures
Seizures with associated automatisms, aura of fear, déjà vu phenomena, or epigastric auras
Left-sided foci (particularly for schizophrenialike and delusional psychoses)
Temporal lobe foci (particularly mediobasal)
Bilateral spike and wave activity

was becoming a neighborhood nuisance because of intrusive behavior that included arguing and fighting with passersby. He had a 20-year history of similar episodes interspersed with depressions.

The patient had been a successful animation cartoonist during his late 20s and early 30s. Following a head injury, he began having grand mal and partial complex seizures, and his ability to work deteriorated. His partial complex seizures were characterized by brief but frequent episodes of staring, perceptual distortion in several sensory modalities, and paresis of the left arm.

After 10 years, during which his seizures were only moderately controlled, he began experiencing depressions and then alternating depressions and manias. Interepisode functioning decreased somewhat, and he developed interictal behavioral changes, including hyposexuality, adhesiveness of personality, circumstantiality, and hypergraphia (notably drawings). His seizures decreased in frequency as his psychoses became more frequent, although he experienced more complex "fitlike" episodes, which his physicians felt were "hysterical." The patient responded moderately well to a combination of carbamazepine and lithium.

Pseudoseizures

Pseudoseizures are clinical seizurelike behaviors without concomitant paroxysmal electrical discharges. They occur most frequently in epileptics (20 to 30% of patients). The ability to identify pseudoseizures is important in order to monitor properly the control of seizures in epileptics and to treat adequately nonepileptic patients who exhibit these phenomena (895).

The nonepileptic with pseudoseizures most likely has a preexisting psychiatric diagnosis (most commonly somatization disorder, hypochondriasis, histrionic personality, conversion disorder, antisocial personality, or factitious syndrome). Seizurelike episodes tend to follow a precipitating stress event and to occur where the episode can have the greatest impact on observers. Onset is usually variable, rather than stereotyped as in true seizures. These episodes may vary widely in form and content. Little, if any, alteration in consciousness is reported or observed during an episode, and communication with the patient may be possible.

Pseudoseizures are characterized by little or no memory loss. Corneal reflexes are intact, and plantar reflexes are flexor. There is no associated incontinence, postepisode drowsiness, or depression of either stretch reflexes or the oculovestibular (caloric) response during grand mal–like episodes. The tongue is rarely bitten, the patient is generally not injured, and the EEG is normal (821).

The individual exhibiting true epileptic seizures most likely has a normal premorbid personality, interictal personality changes, and episodes that are more random in occurrence and influenced primarily by diurnal and sleep patterns, sleep deprivation, menses, strong visceral stimuli (e.g., eating a large meal, coitus), or, occasionally, specific sensory stimulation, such as flashing lights or music. True epileptic seizures tend to be stereotyped and repetitive within the same patient. Episodes are associated with alterations in consciousness, some memory loss, and unresponsiveness to all but the strongest stimuli. In grand mal–like attacks, tongue biting and injury, absent corneal reflexes and extensor plantar reflexes, incontinence, postictal drowsiness, and depression of stretch reflexes or oculovestibular (caloric) response are observed. The EEG, particularly if properly and serially performed and utilizing the highest yielding montages, nasopharyngeal leads, hyperventilation, strobe light stimulation, and sleep tracing, is usually abnormal (821). Studies (212) suggest that prolactin levels rise significantly after true seizures but not after pseudoseizures. Obtaining a serum prolactin level during a nonseizure period and again 15 to 20 minutes after an episode may prove diagnostically helpful. In patients who have been drug free for 72 hours or more, a postepisode prolactin level of 50 ng/mL or more strongly suggests a true seizure disorder (212). Other investigators suggest using IV saline plus suggestion (e.g., "This medication may induce some of your symptoms.") as a provocative test for pseudoseizures while recording the EEG. In one study of 57 patients, 48 had pseudoattacks in response to this provocation (206). The investigators also observed that 37% of patients had abnormal EEGs, but only 12% had spike or spike and wave discharges. There is also some evidence that temporal lobe epileptics, unlike nonepileptics with pseudoseizures, have temporal lobe perfusion abnormalities on SPECT (559).

Treatment

Treatment of the behavioral changes associated with epilepsy depends on the management of seizures. Seizure control is based on (1) reliable and valid recording of seizure frequency, (2) accurate record keeping of anticonvulsant drug consumption, (3) periodic monitoring of anticonvulsant drug levels, and (4) regular follow-up clinical assessments. Prolonged pharmacotherapy, however, should not be instituted unless the patient has a history of two or three grand mal seizures without an obvious provocative cause or a history of frequent partial seizures that interfere with social function and ability to work (998).

Once the decision to treat is made, the drug of choice should be selected and initially administered in the lowest possible therapeutic dose to minimize adverse side effects (see Table 13.3). Serum steady-state levels should be reached before the dose is increased. Increases should be gradual and monitored by serum drug levels. If side effects become unacceptable before seizure control is achieved, a gradual change to another drug should be made by tapering off the first drug while slowly introducing the second drug. If the alternate drug also has limited benefits, specific combinations of two drugs (134, 998) may be tried. Routine polypharmacy (e.g., two or more drugs, each in low doses) usually leads to increased adverse reactions without offering any additive antiepileptic effect. Most patients respond best to one drug (134). The clinician also must be sensitive to the fact that adverse behavioral change is a side effect of anticonvulsants. Should the patient begin to have novel psychopathology during treatment, decreasing rather than increasing the dose may be required. Indeed, in one study (901), the reduction to a single anticonvulsant (successful in 72% of 40 chronic patients) not only resulted in improvement in alertness, concentration, mood, behavior, and sociability but also improved seizure control in 55% of the sample.

When pharmacotherapy is successful, it should be maintained until the patient is free from attacks for a period of 2 to 4 years. The medication then can be gradually discontinued over a period of 6 to 12 months. A long history of seizures prior to control, the presence of structural brain damage, the occurrence of partial complex seizures, and seizures of more than one type are poor prognostic signs and suggest that a relapse is more likely if medication is stopped (729, 998).

The effectiveness of psychotropic medications is limited in severe prodromal syndromes, prolonged postictal phenomena, and psychoses associated with epilepsy. Carbamazepine is probably the drug of choice for these conditions, but ECT may be the treatment of choice. Its effect is rapid, and significant improvement often occurs after a single induced seizure. Should ECT be prescribed, a patient receiving a neuroleptic can be rapidly withdrawn from the drug; however, a patient receiving an anticonvulsant needs a longer withdrawal period to avoid a spontaneous, uncontrolled seizure. Unfortunately, there is no known effective

TABLE 13.3

Profile of Commonly Used Anticonvulsants in Adult Epileptics with Psychiatric Syndromes

Characteristic	*Phenytoin*	*Carbamazepine*	*Sodium Valproate*	*Phenobarbitone*
Starting dose (mg)	100 b.i.d.	100 b.i.d.	200 b.i.d.	30 at night
Daily dose range (mg)	150–600	400–1800	600–3000	30–240
Minimal daily frequency	Once	Twice	Once	Once
Time to peak serum level (hours)	4–12	4–24	1–4	1–6
Percentage bound to plasma	90	75	92	45
Half-life (hours)	9–140	10–30	8–20	50–160
Time from start to steady state (days)	7–21	10	4	Up to 30
Therapeutic serum level (ng/ml)	10–20 20–30 (severe cases only)	5–12	25–80 80–160 (severe cases)	20–25 25–40 (severe cases)
Group	Hydantoin	Tricyclic	2-chain fatty acid	Barbiturate
Dose/serum relationship (free and bound)	Linear	Linear	Nonlinear	Linear
Primary indication(s) (in order of preference)	Tonic-clonic seizures Simple partial seizures Complex partial seizures	Simple partial seizures Complex partial seizures Tonic-clonic seizures	Tonic-clonic seizures Petit mal absences Myoclonic seizures Akinetic seizures Simple partial seizures Complex partial seizures	Tonic-clonic seizures

treatment for interictal behavior changes. Pseudoseizures are managed by confronting the patient with the nonepileptic nature of the attacks (including, if possible, videotapes of the pseudoseizures, along with EEG evidence). Hypnotherapy, counseling, and family therapy also have been found helpful (895).

Localized Coarse Brain Syndromes

The neuropsychiatrist can expect frequent encounters with atypical patients who do not have the profound diffuse cognitive impairment of dementia or the episodic paroxysmal behaviors of epilepsy, but whose symptoms appear to be "organic" in some vague, indescribable manner. Phenomenologically, these patients may have well-formed delusions and hallucinations, as well as language difficulties. Their behavior often seems to be odd. Although soft neurologic features are common, focal nonbehavioral neurologic features are rare in these patients. They account for about 10% of acute psychiatric admissions.

Biologic treatment for such patients is nonspecific. Nevertheless, discrimination of syndrome subgroups can be helpful in deciding whether to treat them or to permit spontaneous recovery, in planning rehabilitation and discharge, and simply in reducing the ambiguity of practice. It is likely, however, that each syndrome results from multiple causes and lesions involving different brain regions. Head trauma, viral infections (e.g., influenza, mononucleosis), gestational-obstetric problems, and illicit drug use are frequent premorbid events that are causally related. Vascular accidents and malformations and slow-growing tumors also can produce these syndromes. For many patients, no likely etiologic event can be discerned (431, 544).

Frontal Lobe Syndromes

Two principal frontal lobe syndromes have been described in association with significant frontal lobe injury: the convexity syndrome and the orbitomedial syndrome (429; 544, Chapter 19; 611; 952). The *convexity syndrome*, related to lesions within or near the lateral surface of the frontal lobes, is characterized by "negative symptoms." Patients are apathetic, indifferent to their surroundings, and emotionally unresponsive. They appear to have lost all drive and ambition. Loss of social graces is common, and they frequently appear disheveled and dirty. Their movements are slow and reduced in frequency (motor inertia). Occasionally, they may remain in positions for prolonged periods (catalepsy) and may posture. A slight flexion at the waist, knees, and elbows is a typical body position of these patients. They sometimes move with a floppy, shuffling gait and then progressively pick up steam, only to slow down gradually to a stop (glissando/deglissando gait). Unlike patients with Parkinson's disease, muscle tone is decreased and "pill rolling" is not present. These patients have difficulty attending to tasks but do respond to irrelevant, particularly intense stimuli (distractibility). They tend to walk next to walls (just touching them), rather than in the middle of the hallway, and may even follow architectural contours instead of taking a direct route across open space.

If the convexity syndrome is due to dominant hemisphere pathology, it is often associated with deficits in language and in verbal reasoning. Impoverished thinking (vague and without detail) is almost always present; verbal fluency is significantly impaired; speech is often stereotyped with perseverative and verbigerated utterances; and Broca's or transcortical motor aphasia may be present. Many frontal lobe cognitive and soft neurologic signs can be observed in these patients, who also may be dyspraxic (gait, buccolinguofacial, ideomotor) and incontinent of urine. Patients with a frontal lobe convexity syndrome often appear to be motorically disconnected from complex sensory input. Thus, despite receiving instructions that appear to be understood and can be repeated, such patients are unable to perform correctly a required task. They cannot learn new motor procedures and appear distractible and often perseverate.

The *orbitomedial syndrome* is associated with dysfunction in the orbitomedial areas of the frontal lobes. Some patients may be asthenic and easily fatigued, bland, akinetic, aphonic, withdrawn, and fearful. They may have diminished wakefulness and be in an oneiroid, or even stuporous, state. Other patients may have an intense affect and express euphoria, irritability, or extreme lability of affect with rapid mood shifts or mixed and cycling mood states. These affectively intense patients are hyperactive and overresponsive to stimuli. They rapidly terminate one incomplete goal-directed behavior and start another; they may appear frenetic as they run about from one activity to another but never complete a task. These patients lose their inhibitions and become reckless. They are impulsive and may engage in buying sprees or other high-risk behaviors; lack foresight; cannot make decisions; are unable to persevere; have uncontrollable associations. They are strongly stimulus bound, distractible, intrusive, and importunate. These patients interrupt conversations and mimic the examiner's movements and comments; despite repeated injunctions, they may continually enter a room in which a group of people are in conference, pull fire alarms simply because they see them, or constantly change television channels. They may have uncontrollable, often fantastic confabulations and, when prevented from doing as they please, may have violent outbursts. When not irritable, these patients often exhibit an inane jocularity (Witzelsucht). They may be hyperactive, have sexual preoccupations and engage in inappropriate (coarse) sexual behavior (although sexual aggression is rare), and appear hypomanic.

The obvious similarity of behaviors in patients with the frontal lobe orbitomedial syndrome and patients with bipolar affective disorder requires particularly careful diagnostic evaluation. Localized CT-scan and EEG abnormalities, neurologic (particularly soft) signs, the shallowness of affect (little true humor, noninfectious humor, lack of warmth), a prolonged and insidious onset, a chronic nonepisodic course, and a negative family history for affective disorder suggest coarse disease.

To avoid the controversy regarding the degree to which the syndromes specifically relate to frontal lobe lesions, Tucker (personal communication) has proposed that they be termed *apathetic syndrome* and *disinhibited syndrome*. Table 13.4 displays some characteristics of these syndromes.

Parietal Lobe Syndromes

Coarse lesions of the parietal lobes can be associated with significant psychopathology (e.g., delusional ideas, experiences of alienation) (229; 544; 611, Chapter 17). Two patterns of symptoms have been observed in patients with parietal lobe lesions. Lesions of the dominant parietal lobe usually are associated with disorders of language (dyslexia, word-finding problems, conduction aphasia), problems with calculation, dyspraxias (ideomotor, kinesthetic), difficulties in abstraction, and contralateral sensory (graphesthesia, astereognosis) and motor (hypotonia, posturing, paucity of movement) deficits. The best-known dominant parietal lobe syndrome is the controversial Gerstmann's syndrome (dysgraphia, dyscalculia, right-left disorientation, finger agnosia), putatively involving a lesion in the posteroinferior aspect (angular gyrus) of the dominant parietal lobe. Although its validity has been questioned by some authors, Gerstmann's syndrome has been reported (110) in more than 20% of chronic psychiatric patients.

Lesions of the nondominant parietal lobe are associated with profound (occa-

TABLE 13.4

Frontal Lobe Syndromes

Apathetic Syndrome	*Disinhibited Syndrome*
Indifference	Impulsivity
Diminished activity	Witzelsucht
Motor and cognitive perseverations	Poor modulation of affect and mood (emotional lability and inapprorpiate intensity)
Motor inertia	Poor judgment
Poor sustained attention	Anosognosia
	Easily distractible
	Loss of previous social behaviors

sionally delusional) denial of illness (anosognosia), left-sided spatial neglect, constructional difficulties, problems dressing, and contralateral sensory and motor deficits. Capgras' syndrome (delusional ideas that close friends or relatives are impostors) and the first-rank symptom of experience of alienation (body parts or thoughts not belonging to one) have been described in patients with nondominant parietal lesions. They may complain that their bodies are somehow different—an arm or leg feels heavy or bigger than usual, or they are not always sure of the location of an arm or leg. These patients also may have difficulties in orienting themselves to the environment. They complain that "things look confused" or "jumbled." They say they cannot find their way along previously familiar routes and that they can no longer drive a car because they lose track of the other vehicles around them. This visual disorientation, termed *Balint's syndrome,* is usually associated with lesions that include the visual association cortices.

Temporal Lobe Syndromes

Some patients can have temporal lobe lesions in the absence of temporal lobe epilepsy. Patients with stroke, head injury, viral disease (particularly herpes), vascular malformations, and degenerative disease involving the temporal lobes may present with delusions, hallucinations (particularly auditory and visual), and mood disturbances. Patients with fluent (temporoparietal) aphasia and patients with formal thought disorder share many of the same elements of language dysfunction. There is a strong association between temporal lobe dysfunction and psychopathology, and the absence of a classic epileptic picture and course is not sufficient to eliminate a temporal lobe etiology from the differential diagnosis of a psychotic patient.

Disturbances in language and memory are most commonly observed in psychiatric patients suffering from temporal lobe dysfunction. When the dysfunction is in the dominant temporal lobe, the psychopathology is likely to include euphoria, auditory hallucinations (often "complete" voices), formal thought disorder, and primary delusional ideas. These clinical phenomena are associated with such cognitive deficits as decreased learning and retention of verbal material (read or heard), poor speech comprehension, and poor reading comprehension. When the dysfunction is in the nondominant temporal lobe, the psychopathology more likely consists of dysphoria, irritability, depression, and difficulty in interpreting the emotional expressions of others (receptive aprosodia). These phenomena are associated with such cognitive deficits as decreased recognition and recall of visual and auditory nonverbal material, amusia (loss of ability to repeat musical sounds), poor visual memory, decreased auditory discrimination and comprehension of tonal patterns, and decreased ability to learn and recognize nonsense figures and geometric shapes. Bilateral temporal lobe involvement is usually associated with dementia.

Right Hemisphere Syndromes

Large lesions of the posterior right hemisphere often result in behavioral abnormalities. Typically, these include (1) varying severities of anosognosia, denial, and neglect and (2) aprosodia. A commonly observed pattern consists of motor impersistence, denial, dressing apraxia, neglect, and difficulties with facial recognition. Visual-perceptual and spatial cognitive impairment is also common (observed on tests of construction, visual memory, and figure and design matching tasks). Although these patients can see, the meaning of their perceptions is altered or lost. Agnosias are common and may lead to poor performance on cognitive tests of language because of this disturbed recognition. One clue to this right-hemisphere language "problem" occurs in naming tasks. The patient with agnosia (rather than true anomia) either says, "I don't know," or gives the correct category (e.g., flower, animal) but cannot be specific (e.g., rose, cat).

Patients with right hemisphere lesions may also exhibit psychopathology that can overshadow the typical features described above and lead to psychiatric hospitalization and treatment. This psychopathology includes agitation, inattention, perseveration of thought and motor behavior, irritability, anxiety, disinhibited social behavior (inappropriate sexual behavior, loss of social graces) delusions and hallucinations, and manic and depressive syndromes. These affective syndromes are characterized by sudden onsets and atypical patterns (e.g., depression without sadness, mania with avolition) (446, 784).

Treatment of Symptomatic or Localized Coarse Brain Syndromes

Treatment of localized coarse brain syndromes is essentially symptomatic and focuses on the specific neurologic condition underlying the psychopathology. The psychopathology often resolves at the same rate and to the same degree as the cognitive impairment and any neurologic signs. In many cases where there is spontaneous remission, no somatic treatment is necessary. When psychopathology is severe, it can be managed best by trying to fit the patient's clinical features to a standard psychopathologic syndrome (e.g., mania, depression, schizophrenia, or dysthymic disorder) and then apply specific treatment. Thus, manic-like syndromes can respond to neuroleptics, lithium, anticonvulsants, or ECT; depressive syndromes can respond to ECT and, occasionally, to lithium or cyclic antidepressants; schizophrenialike syndromes may respond to neuroleptics; and dysthymic disorders may respond to MAOIs or cyclic antidepressants. Neuroleptic doses tend to be lower than those required for patients without coarse disease, whereas doses for other drugs are similar to those required for the idiopathic syndrome.

Psychological treatment, rehabilitation, and disposition must take into account the specific cognitive impairment of each patient. Thus, it would be inappropriate to expect a patient with dominant temporal lobe dysfunction to do well in a psychotherapeutic setting where good language and reasoning skills are required, to send a patient with significant nondominant parietal lobe dysfunction for training in a job requiring good motor perceptual coordination, or to expect a patient with a frontal lobe convexity syndrome to live alone and fully care for himself. Neuropsychological assessment can help to establish each patient's cognitive strengths and weaknesses and provide guidelines for ongoing care.

Other Syndromes

Syndromes of Specific DSM Categories Secondary to Coarse Brain Disease

All the major DSM syndrome categories include an exclusion criterion requiring the clinician to rule out coarse brain disease or systemic illness as the cause of the syndrome. Although syndromes resulting from coarse brain disease (secondary psychoses and other mood disorders, anxiety states, and personality disorders) can appear identical in most ways to idiopathic varieties, these secondary syndromes tend to have three common characteristics: (1) atypical course (e.g., unusual onset age or pattern of episodes); (2) with the exception of affective states (351), no family history of psychiatric illness; and (3) atypical episode pattern (e.g., depression without sadness, schizophrenia without emotional blunting).

Secondary syndromes occur for all DSM diagnostic categories, but secondary depression is the one most frequently seen. Some common causes of secondary depression are stroke (835), basal ganglia disease (643, 867, 902), epilepsy (262), head trauma (913), aging (312), lupus erythematosus (357), and multiple sclerosis (677).

Treatment for secondary depressions, as with other secondary syndromes, is symptomatic. When possible, treatment should focus on the primary condition. If successful treatment for the primary condition does not resolve the secondary psychiatric syndrome, a practical treatment rule is: "What works for the idiopathic form is also likely to work for the secondary form." Thus, secondary depressions can be successfully managed with antidepressant medication or ECT and delusional and hallucinatory states with neuroleptics.

Syndromes of Memory Disturbances

Complaints of memory disturbances (745, Chapter 12; 934) are commonly expressed by psychiatric patients. Most often, these complaints refer to disturbances in concentration or being easily distracted. The causes of such problems usually can be established through careful history taking and cognitive testing. Complaints of concentration difficulties or distractibility are commonly associated with (1) acute depression or mania, (2) anxiety disorders, (3) acute alcohol and drug states, (4) adjustment disorders, or (5) normal people in abnormal circumstances. If the primary condition is adequately treated, the memory complaints invariably resolve.

More serious are complaints of forgetfulness and inability to remember. The former involves forgetting to remember to do something; it can be an early sign of dementia. It is also characteristic of subcortical dementias. The complaint of inability to remember new information can reflect acute (transient) or chronic (insidious) problems. When associated with deficits in concentration, acute memory problems suggest acute alcohol or drug states, seizure disorder, toxic-metabolic confusional states, or migraine or cluster headache; when concentration is intact, they suggest transient global amnesia, post-traumatic anterograde amnesia, or personality disorder with malingering. Chronic memory problems suggest dementia, residual secondary morbid states, or residual psychotic states. Confabulation, typically associated with perseverative behavior, impaired self-monitoring, and a failure to inhibit incorrect responses, is most commonly caused by frontal lobe lesions (887).

Head Trauma Syndromes

Head trauma and its behavioral consequences represent a major neuropsychiatric problem. In the United States, about one-half million people incur brain injury each year; about 20% of victims are left with significant disability. Head injuries received in war are usually the penetrating type and lead to focal syndromes. In nonwar circumstances, closed head injuries are most common, and 90% of patients survive. The most frequent causes of head injury are automobile and sporting accidents and falls. Injury results from acceleration-deceleration forces and can affect cortex and subcortical and brain stem structures. Closed head injuries can lead to mild changes (postconcussion syndrome or mild frontal lobe personality changes) or to more dramatic regional brain syndromes, dementia, or seizure disorder (395, Chapter 1). Several of these syndromes are described above. Postconcussion syndrome, post-traumatic dementia, and post-traumatic thalamic syndrome are discussed below.

Post-concussion Syndrome

A significant but unknown number of patients have persistent symptoms following mild head injury despite little, if any, clinical evidence of neuronal damage. The injury sustained usually results in a brief or mild disturbance in consciousness, followed by headache, dizziness, hypersensitivity to sound or light, fatigue, poor concentration, and, rarely, irritability. Mild depressive features and physiologic signs of anxiety are commonly observed. Most postconcussion syndromes resolve within a few days or weeks of injury, but some persist and result in significant deficits in social function and ability to work (33; 395, Chapter 5; 670; 916). Several studies (596, 963) have demonstrated that the majority of these patients are not malingering and had no preexisting neurotic traits. Patients may exhibit abnormal caloric testing (421), and many also demonstrate unequivocal vestibular dysfunction on electronystagmography and abnormal brain stem auditory evoked potentials (854). In one study (854), only 21% of patients were normal on both measures. Gronwall and Wrightson (392), reporting the clinical course of such patients who were monitored with serial psychological testing, concluded that persistent cognitive dysfunction was the main factor in the syndrome. Patients with prolonged postconcussion syndromes should receive careful neuropsychological evaluation. Those with mild cognitive impairment (often nondominant hemisphere and frontal in pattern) may respond to amphetamines or MAOIs or amantadine (396), in standard doses. Patients who are irritable and become assaultive, particularly during the initial phase of the syndrome, may respond to propranolol in doses as high as 320 mg daily.

Patients may develop a "postconcussionlike" syndrome following a viral infection. Mononucleosis, viral hepatitis, and influenza, the most common viral syndromes observed, can be followed by prolonged behavioral changes without recognizable encephalitis, although direct brain involvement appears to be the most likely etiology. These patients also may respond to stimulants or MAOIs.

Post-Traumatic Dementia

In severe closed head injury, mechanical forces at the moment of impact can produce a shearing effect that leads to diffuse axonal (i.e., white matter) injury. Whether it occurs independently or in conjunction with the more circumscribed effects of acceleration-deceleration lesions, this injury often results in a complex classic picture of a subcortical dementia plus a regional cortical syndrome. Management is symptomatic (118).

Post-Traumatic Thalamic Syndrome

Relatively circumscribed injury to the thalamus can occur after a closed head injury. This syndrome is characterized by a variable initial period of generalized analgesia, followed by lateralized (contralateral to a unilateral lesion) or generalized spontaneous pain or pain as a response to a stimulus not usually considered pain inducing. Constant or paroxysmal symptoms can be associated with frontal lobe cognitive and language problems; thalamiclike aphasic responses; and odd sensations, such as formication (tactile hallucinations of itching or crawling insects under the skin) or other paresthesias and gnawing, crushing, or freezing sensations. Odd behaviors, including verbal or physical abuse, use of obscenities, and intolerance to unfamiliar faces, also may occur (587). The syndrome can be mistaken for hysteria or an atypical psychosis. Diagnosis requires particularly careful evaluation, including brain imaging studies. Carbamazepine (also used for trigeminal neuralgia) has been recommended for treating patients with this syndrome, as have other tricyclics (e.g., amitriptyline) (720). Other recommendations are clonidine and beta-blockers (395, Chapter 1).

Dissociative States

The psychiatric literature is replete with case reports of patients who have experienced episodes during which they exhibited complex behaviors, often different in character from their usual behavior pattern, but for which they have no or little recollection. Little systematic research has been done to illuminate the nature of these conditions. When malingering can be ruled out, coarse brain disorder is the most likely cause of such states. Etiological factors include epilepsy, intoxications and metabolic disorders, migraine, transient global amnesia (usually from transient ischemic attacks), postconcussion anterograde amnesia, encephalitis, and somnambulism. Management of dissociative states is directed at the underlying condition.

Of specific focus in the psychiatric literature are such states as fugue, multiple personality, Ganser's syndrome, and depersonalization. *Fugue states*, sudden episodes of travel away from one's home, can last for hours or even months. When not associated with coarse brain disease (almost always the briefer episodes), it appears to be associated with personality disorder (histrionic, antisocial) and outright malingering. The same can be said for *multiple personality* and *Ganser's syndrome*. The validity of the former remains in question, but case reports suggest a strong association with temporal lobe epilepsy and the syndrome representing an extreme dissociative state (96, 874). Ganser's syndrome, also termed "hysterical pseudodementia," is classically reported in prisoners who suddenly become confused and respond to questions with answers that are silly but suggest that the question is understood.

These responses are termed answers beyond the point and are characterized by such exchanges as:

Q. How many legs does a three-legged stool have?

A. Four.

Q. What was the color of George Washington's white house?

A. Brown.

A recent study of 15 patients (909) concluded that coarse brain disease (particularly head injury) or antisocial and histrionic personality disorders accounted for most cases.

The experience of demonic or supernatural possession, as with multiple personality, also is most likely associated with chronic limbic epilepsy. Unfortunately, even when seizure disorders are documented by EEG, these patients are often resistant to anticonvulsant treatment (671).

Depersonalization (see Chapter 4), when not the result of coarse brain disease (particularly related to temporal or parietal lobe lesions), is associated with anxiety states and mood disorders.

Sleep Disorder Syndromes

Sleep disorders include (1) syndromes related to excessive daytime sleepiness (narcolepsy, sleep apnea), (2) the insomnias, and (3) the parasomnias (somnambulism, night terrors).

Excessive daytime sleepiness is common in the elderly (41). When onset occurs in younger people, the disorder may result from environmental difficulties that lead to poor or little nighttime sleep, the abuse of drugs or alcohol, or CNS or respiratory system dysfunction.

Narcolepsy is characterized by unwanted sleep episodes, cataplexy, sleep paralysis, and hypnagogic or hypnopompic hallucinations. It affects 0.5% of the general population (most often males), usually begins after puberty and rarely after age 50, is probably heritable (736, 817), and may be associated with histocompatibility complex antigen HLA-DR2, linking it, in some cases, to the short arm of chromosome 6 (570). Because of their excessive and inopportune napping, narcoleptics may experience reduced work performance and memory problems and are prone to accidents. Narcolepsy is related to a disturbance in rapid eye movement (REM) sleep, characterized by extremely short latencies between sleep and REM onsets. Unwanted sleep episodes (15 to 60 minutes in duration) occur several times daily; they are the only feature in about 25% of cases. Cataplexy (sudden loss of muscle tone) can be mild or serious enough to result in falls. It can be triggered by strong mood states. Cataplexy may be the ambulatory equivalent of sleep paralysis, which is associated with a REM sleep episode partially intruding into wakefulness and may last for several minutes. Although frightening, it is benign. Cataplexy and sleep paralysis appear to represent the inhibition of muscle activity during REM that normally occurs during sleep but intrudes into wakefulness in narcolepsy. Hypnagogic and hypnopompic hallucinations and automatisms, also experienced by narcoleptics, are disturbing, but they do not require neuroleptic treatment. They resolve with specific treatment for narcolepsy that consists of antidepressants and stimulants in doses used for anxiety disorders and dysthymias (680).

Sleep apnea is common in the elderly (50% of men and 30% of women over age 65) (41) and may affect 1 to 2% of the general population. It usually results from upper airway collapse and obstruction, which can lead to hypoxemia. Snoring results from the effort to force air past a partially obstructed oropharynx. Less common is the cessation of all respiratory effort (10 seconds or more). This may occur in conditions that cause accumulated blood CO_2, such as heart disease, some frontal lobe lesions, and chronic hyperventilation syndrome (including anxiety disorder) or at high altitudes with low ambient oxygen. Obesity and alcohol use increase the risks for prolonged sleep apnea. Chronic brain hypoxia during sleep can result in hypertension and heart disease, respiratory infection, cognitive impairments, reduced libido and impotence in men, and irritability. In the elderly, these daytime consequences of prolonged sleep apnea can be mistaken for pseudodementia. Treatment for sleep apnea includes (1) abstinence from alcohol and sedative drug use, (2) use of nasal continuous positive airway pressure, and (3) in rare instances, anatomic repair of oropharyngeal abnormalities (e.g., enlarged tonsils) (531).

Insomnia is a symptom. Most often, it results from environmental factors (stress, work shift changes, unfamiliar sleep setting), depression, anxiety disorder, or drug withdrawal. Insomnia also can result from *restless leg syndrome* (nocturnal myoclonus), characterized by bilateral leg movements, occasionally violent, during the lighter stages of sleep. Patients with this condition may benefit from bedtime administration of bromocriptine (2.5–50 mg), clonazepam (0.5–1.5 mg) or L-dopa with benserazide (50–100 mg) (199). Insomnia is best managed by treating the underlying condition, rather than only prescribing sedative/hypnotics as if the insomnia were the condition.

Parasomnias are actions during sleep that behaviorally, but not physiologically, resemble those occurring during wakefulness. Parasomnias usually start in childhood or adolescence and are often distressing to patients and their families.

Somnambulism (sleepwalking) occurs during the first few hours of deep sleep in children and in other non-REM sleep stages in adults; 15 to 30% of children and 1% of adults sleepwalk. Episodes may last for several minutes and are limited to clumsy walking. The sleepwalker can avoid some, but not all, obstacles and usually returns to bed, with no memory of the event. Sleepwalking is familial. An adult who sleepwalks after years of remission should be assessed for drug use (iatrogenic and illicit), which can alter sleep cycles (505).

Pavor nocturnus (night terror) and sleepwalking can co-occur in the same individuals. Both forms of parasomnia take place during non-REM, usually deep-sleep stages, and are familial. They are associated with bursts of high-voltage slow waves on sleep EEG. Night terrors occur in 6% of children and 1% of adults. In a child, pavor nocturnus is characterized by the child suddenly sitting up in bed, looking frightened, screaming, and, occasionally, running from the room. The episode ends in minutes, and the child returns to sleep.

Somnambulism and night terrors are treated by (1) protection of the sleeper to avoid injury (e.g., removing harmful objects, locking doors and windows), (2) benzodiazepine nighttime sedation for 6 months, followed by a drug-free trial period, and (3) education of the patient and family (311).

Headache

Most patients complaining of headache do not have coarse brain disease. Headaches that are dull, described as "a pressure feeling," generalized, and constant for several consecutive days rarely are associated with brain disease. Headaches that have sudden onset, awaken a patient from sleep, or are unilateral are usually associated with pathology. Cervical osteoarthritis, eye pathology or visual acuity problems, dental pathology, sinusitis, temporomandibular joint problems (including the temporomandibular syndrome of unilateral, deep-seated pain in the side of the face caused by jaw muscle spasms), and hypertension should all be considered in any diagnostic evaluation of headache (1078).

Headaches caused by brain tumors result from increased intracranial pressure and, rarely, from traction of the tumor on pain-sensitive intracranial structures. Headaches from brain tumors have no characteristic pattern, may be similar to tension headaches, and may be mild, dull, bilateral, and fluctuating in severity. Their only distinguishing feature is their onset, which is usually within a few weeks of seeking medical attention.

Migraine headaches are throbbing and severe. They last for several hours, are associated with nausea and vomiting, and are exhausting or even prostrating. Migraines are usually but not always unilateral. They are usually preceded by ischemic symptoms from cerebral vasoconstriction, such as flashing lights, scintillating scotomata, or sensory or motor symptoms. The headache is produced by distension of the external carotid arteries and surrounding sterile inflammation. The initial vasodilation is believed to result from the release of vasoactive neurotransmitters from a site of disordered microcirculation in the brain stem (744). Patients with migraine tend to be young females with a family history of migraine. Onset is rarely after age 30. Ergot-containing preparations and propranolol are usually effective if begun during the early phases of an attack. Lithium may also benefit patients with cyclic migraine.

Infrequent "tension" headaches respond to analgesics, but analgesics, anxiolytics, and sedatives are usually ineffective in the treatment of headaches for which a neurologic basis cannot be established. When the condition is chronic, cyclic antidepressants are often effective. When the headache is associated with significant features of depression, cyclic antidepressants, MAOIs, lithium (particularly good for cluster headaches), and ECT have been reported to be beneficial (873).

Chapter 14

Extremes of Trait

I. Dramatic and Erratic Personality Disorders and Their Related State Syndromes

Among the DSM-III-R personality disorders, histrionic, narcissistic, and antisocial personalities share the common feature of erratic behavior related to affective instability. DSM-III-R includes borderline personality among this group, but data suggest (see Chapter 11) that, although some borderline patients may have extremes of trait, many patients appear to have a morbid process related to mood disorder.

Applying Cloninger's model of personality and his dichotomous view of anxiety (see Chapters 8 and 15), histrionic, narcissistic, and antisocial personality disorders also should share a common liability (e.g., similar familial illness patterns suggesting similar genotype), similar associated states (e.g., somatoform disorders), and similar treatment responsivity. As histrionic and narcissistic personalities are mostly observed in women and antisocial personality mostly in men, the differences between these deviations may reflect the effects of gender related factors (e.g., developmental and endocrine influences) on the common pathophysiology. Consistent with the apparent relationship among these personality extremes is their similar co-occurring states: somatoform and related disorders, drug and alcohol abuse, and, to a lesser extent, criminality.

Antisocial Personality Disorder

Antisocial personality is characterized by chronic and recurrent antisocial and erratic behavior. In Cloninger's system, individuals with this type of personality have patterns of behavior consistent with high novelty seeking (impulsive, unconventional, quick-tempered, excitable), low harm avoidance (carefree, risk-taking, bold, vigorous, outgoing, fearless, energetic), and low reward dependence (cold-blooded, insensitive, practical, evasive, deceptive). From Tyrer's work and clinical anecdotes, these patients appear either cold and callous, irritable and aggressive, or glib and superficially charming and open. Table 14.1 displays the clinical features characteristic of antisocial personality.

The overall prevalence of antisocial personality disorder (sociopathy) is not known. Cloninger (192) estimates its population prevalence to be about 4%, and recent epidemiologic data suggest about 3% of men and 1% of women in the general population are antisocial (810). In one outpatient series, 15% of men and 3% of women psychiatric outpatients had this disorder (1082). It is more frequent among men than among women (9:1), in cities than in rural areas, and among people of low socioeconomic status. Its prevalence is greater for African Americans (9%) than for Euro-Americans (3%), but as Cloninger (192) writes, "The difference is not 'racial' in a genetic sense; when populations are matched for socioeconomic status, the racial difference disappears." The majority of patients with antisocial personality come from families in which parents were separated or divorced or in which one or both parents died when the patient was a child, deserted the family, or was alcoholic or criminal. Twin studies of criminals (the majority of whom have antisocial personality) suggest indirectly that there is a genetic causal component to the disorder (182). Adoption studies of criminals also suggest a genetic causal component, as well as nongenetic causes (149, 234). In families of antisocial persons, there is an increased frequency of antisocial personality, somatization disorders, alcoholism, and drug dependence (197, 408). People with antisocial personality tend to marry individuals with these conditions (406).

The natural history of the disorder includes significant behavioral problems before age 15, such as enuresis, fire setting, cruelty to animals, running away from home, drug or alcohol abuse, truancy, fighting at school, suspension or expulsion from school, habitual lying, arrests, early age of sexual intercourse, promiscuity, prostitution, and minimal brain dysfunction/hyperactivity syndrome (89, 90, 151, 828). Conversion disorders and venereal disease are also more common in these patients than in the general population.

For some patients, there is a slight improvement in behavior during middle age. The life expectancy of patients with antisocial personality is diminished, with an increased frequency of deaths by homicide, accidents, or complications of drug or alcohol dependence (440, 831).

In the absence of superimposed illness, the mental status examination is normal for the most part, but certain findings, predominantly in the areas of appearance and affectivity, are associated. These include a motorcycle gang style of dress, tattoos, needle tracks, and swaggering gait. The patient is often glib and may convey a shallow warmth or may also appear cold and callous (1011). An initial compliance and superficial friendliness, if present, readily give way to irritability

TABLE 14.1

Clinical Features Associated with Antisocial Personality (Sociopathy)

Affective instability
Physical fights (often using a weapon)
Child and spouse abuse
Cruelty
Deliberate destruction of property
Irritability
Rape
Impulsivity
Truancy
Running away from home
Vagrancy
Wanderlust
Impulsive, not making plans
Erratic work history: absences, firings
Other
Fire setting
Lying, use of alias
Criminality
Recklessness
Prostitution (heterosexual and homosexual)
Promiscuity
Early sexual activity and marriage
Infidelity and divorce
Venereal disease
Homosexuality
Alcoholism
Drug abuse
Low normal or borderline IQ
Increased prevalence of conversion symptoms, somatization disorder
School failure
Childhood hyperactivity
High novelty seeking
Low harm avoidance
Low reward dependence
High somatic anxiety
High reactive dysphoria

when the patient's requests are not met, more so than for the average medical or psychiatric patient. Many patients take the position that recent and past wrongs against them justify their antisocial behaviors, and many convey a sense of entitlement (192). An increased frequency of nonspecific abnormalities is demonstrated on the EEG (64, 378, 447).

Antisocial personality itself is not responsive to any treatment (1083). Biological treatments are of value only for superimposed disorders. Lest an unrealistic expectation of therapeutic success be created, some patients must be told that they have a style of behavior (or a "personality disorder") that is not amenable to treatment; that they are responsible for their actions; and that as they get older they may develop more self-control and maturity. If the subject of having children arises, these patients can be told that their children would be at somewhat greater risk of developing a similar behavior pattern.

Histrionic Personality Disorder

Histrionic personality disorder is a new term that replaces hysteria and hysterical personality. Despite evidence that many patients who meet DSM-III-R criteria for histrionic personality also meet criteria for somatization disorder, DSM-III-R continues to separate these categories. The two core features of histrionic personality disorder are (1) overly dramatic and intensely emotional behavior and (2) disturbances in interpersonal relationships. The latter is probably secondary to the former. Table 14.2 displays the clinical features associated with these extremes of trait. Individuals with histrionic personality traits are also likely to have behaviors associated with high novelty seeking and reward dependence and low harm avoidance. Consistent with this pattern of personality traits is the strong relationship between histrionic and antisocial personality disorders that is suggestive of a common etiology expressed differently in men (antisocial) and women (histrionic) (599).

Narcissistic Personality Disorder

The validity of narcissistic personality disorder is unclear. Some patients with narcissistic personality also meet criteria for histrionic personality; perhaps narcissistic personality is a variant of histrionic personality. Narcissistic personality could be considered histrionic personality with extreme egocentricity and feelings of self-worth. Consistent with their overlapping behavior patterns, narcissistic and histrionic personalities are characterized by heightened emotional responsivity.

TABLE 14.2

Clinical Features Associated with Histrionic Personality

Excessive or erratic emotionality
Inappropriate, angry outbursts or tantrums
Emotionally overreactive to minor events
Exaggerated expression of emotion
Rapid shifting and shallow expressions of mood
Craving for activity and excitement
Overly dramatic
Style of speech impressionistic and theatrical
Overly concerned with physical attractiveness
Inappropriately, sexually seductive in appearance or behavior
Disturbances in interpersonal relationships
Incessant drawing of attention to oneself
Inconsiderate, vain, demanding, egocentric
Superficially dependent, helpless
Constant seeking for reassurance
Prone to manipulative suicide threats
Other
High novelty seeking
Low harm avoidance
High reward dependence
Histeroid dysphoria (atypical depression with intense, dramatic affectivity)
Conversion symptoms

Of the nine DSM-III-R criteria for narcissistic personality, three are related to intense emotion, whereas the others refer to egocentric behavior. Table 14.3 displays the clinical features associated with narcissistic personality. Individuals with narcissistic personality traits are also likely to have behaviors consistent with high novelty seeking and reward dependence and low harm avoidance.

The prevalences of histrionic and narcissistic personality disorders are unclear. Histrionic personality can be estimated from studies of hysteria and somatization disorder (Briquet's syndrome), as some evidence suggests these co-occur in the same individuals. This estimate is just under 1% of the general population (1052). The prevalence of narcissistic personality disorder is unknown. Considering its overlap with histrionic personality, however, estimates of 1% for both histrionic and narcissistic personality disorders and 4% for antisocial personality disorder are probably reasonable.

Many of the behaviors associated with these trait deviations can be observed in

TABLE 14.3

Clinical Features Associated with Narcissistic Personality

Emotional behaviors
Reactions to criticism (even mild) with rage, shame, or humiliation
Preoccupation with feelings of envy
Grandiose sense of self-importance
Egocentric features
Interpersonal exploitation: takes advantage of others
Belief that own problems are unique
Preoccupation with grandiose fantasies
Sense of entitlement and unreasonable expectation of favorable treatment
Requirement for constant attention and admiration
Lack of empathy
Exhibitionism
Alternation between extremes of overidealization and devaluation
Extreme self-centeredness and self-absorption
Other features
Histrionic behaviors
Antisocial behaviors
Nonmelancholic depressions

childhood, and the disorders are fully expressed by early adolescence. Although there are behavioral fluctuations in intensity over time, the traits appear permanent. Laboratory studies searching for their biologic pathophysiology have not be fruitful, with the exceptions of studies of violence and the related state syndromes.

Related State Syndromes

Somatoform Disorders

Under this category, DSM-III-R includes somatization (encompassing the concepts of hysteria and Briquet's syndrome), conversion, hypochondriasis, somatoform pain disorder, body dysmorphic disorder, undifferentiated somatoform disorder, and somatoform disorder not otherwise specified.

Somatization disorder is characterized by multiple, medically unexplained symptoms in multiple organ systems. Onset is usually in the early teens, or even in childhood, and virtually never begins after age 30. Ninety percent of patients are female. Symptoms fluctuate in intensity and content, but the syndrome appears permanent. Frequent hospitalizations, surgery, and polypharmacy are complications. The patient with a classic somatization disorder is a woman with a long history of medically unexplained complaints and multiple hospitalizations. She reports that her physicians rarely offer a diagnosis and dismiss her complaints with such statements as, "It's all in your head." She answers questions dramatically and is suggestible, answering "yes" to questions about myriad medical symptoms. In the absence of superimposed disorders, the initial physical examination and laboratory tests reveal no clear abnormalities. DSM requires at least 10 unexplained symptoms from a choice of 35.

For a symptom to be counted as present, the individual must report that the symptom caused her to take medicine (other than aspirin), alter her life pattern, or see a physician. The symptoms, in the judgment of the clinician, are not adequately explained by observable disorder or injury and are not side effects of medication, illicit drugs, or alcohol. The clinician need not be convinced that the symptom was actually present (e.g., that the individual vomited throughout her entire pregnancy); report of the symptom by the individual is sufficient. Symptoms fall under the following seven categories:

1. *Sickly.* A belief that one has been sickly during most of lifetime.
2. *Conversion or pseudoneurologic symptoms.* Difficulty in swallowing, loss of voice, deafness, double vision, blurred vision, blindness, fainting or loss of consciousness, memory loss, seizures or convulsions, trouble with walking, paralysis or muscle weakness, urinary retention or difficulty in urinating
3. *Gastrointestinal symptoms.* Abdominal pain, nausea, vomiting spells (other than during pregnancy), bloating (gassy), intolerance (e.g., gets sick) of a variety of foods, diarrhea
4. *Female reproductive symptoms.* Judged by the individual as occurring more frequently or severely than in most women: painful menstruation, menstrual irregularity, excessive bleeding, severe vomiting throughout pregnancy or causing hospitalization during pregnancy
5. *Psychosexual symptoms.* For the major part of the individual's life: sexual indifference, lack of pleasure during intercourse, pain during intercourse, impotence, burning sensations in or around genitals
6. *Pain.* Pain in back, joints, extremities, genital area (other than during intercourse); pain on urination; other pain (other than headaches)
7. *Cardiopulmonary symptoms.* Shortness of breath, palpitations, chest pain, dizziness

Screening questions for somatization should focus on seven symptoms: (1) vomiting (other than during pregnancy), (2) amnesia, (3) difficulty in swallowing, (4) painful menstruation, (5) burning sensations in genitals, (6) shortness of breath without exertion, and (7) extremity pain. Two or more symptoms in men and three or more symptoms in women are suggestive of the disorder.

The prevalence of somatization is unclear. In one urban community, .04% of interviewees satisfied diagnostic criteria (1052). The disorder occurs in 1 to 2% of women and is relatively rare in men (920, 1081); however, it is more common among men seeking or receiving disability compensation (904, 905) and may also be somewhat more common among homosexual men. Somatization disorder runs in families and occurs in about 20% of first-degree relatives of patients with the disorder. An increased prevalence of antisocial personality and alcoholism is evident among male relatives of patients with somatization, as well as an increased prevalence of somatization among female relatives of patients with antisocial personality or alcoholism (920). Individuals with somatization disorder are more likely than others to marry people with antisocial personality, alcoholics, or drug abusers (920). Adoption studies also indicate that adoptees have a greater than expected frequency of somatization if their biologic parents have antisocial personality (149, 1037).

People with somatization disorder (as well as those with antisocial personality) have an increased prevalence of conversion disorders and increased rates of hospitalization and unnecessary surgical procedures (920). Somatization is common among female felons, 41% of whom meet the criteria of Feighner et al. (299) for Briquet's syndrome (406). Of these female criminals, the majority have a concurrent diagnosis of antisocial personality (406). Patients with somatization disorder also have an increased frequency of suicidal thoughts and suicidal attempts, but completed suicide is rare (689, 920).

If a diagnosis of somatization is made in an emergency room or consultation service, the patient rarely needs to be admitted to a psychiatric unit. Occasionally, however, the diagnosis is overlooked, and the patient may be admitted because of a depressed mood or suicide attempt. When the diagnosis is established, this should be explained to the patient. Some patients are grateful for what is probably the first cohesive explanation of their recurrent symptoms that they have ever received, but the degree of genuine acceptance of the diagnosis is highly variable.

Despite the temptation to recommend seemingly reasonable "prescriptions" (696) for the management of patients with somatization disorder, there is no known effective treatment. These patients, as those with antisocial personality, should be told that there is nothing that medical science can do to alter the overall course of the condition. When a patient has been referred by another clinician, the consultant should personally inform the referring clinician of the diagnosis and provide him a detailed explanation about somatization disorder if he does not have a working knowledge of the syndrome.

Conversion Disorder

The classic concept of conversion is that of a pseudoneurologic condition, with signs and symptoms that incompletely resemble those of neurologic disorders. Such conditions include paralysis, aphasia, seizures, coordination disturbances, akinesia, dyskinesia, blindness, tunnel vision, anosmia, anesthesia, and paresthesia. The classic concept also includes the requirement that unless the pseudoneurologic condition (e.g., conversion anesthesia) is superimposed upon a clear-cut neurologic disorder (e.g., multiple sclerosis), the signs that are present (e.g., hemianesthesia to the midline only) do not fit what is currently known about nervous system structure and function (e.g., that dermatomes cross the midline). To extend this statement: unless the conversion symptom is superimposed, laboratory studies reveal no classic abnormalities, such as spiking on the EEG or infarction on CT scan. Most commonly, conversion symptoms involve the organs of special sense (e.g., eyes, ears) or voluntary musculature.

DSM-III and DSM-III-R have a broader characterization of conversion, including any alteration in "physical functioning" suggesting a "physical disorder" *if* "psychological factors are judged to be etiologically related to the symptom," a temporal relationship between a psychosocial stressor that is apparently related to a psychological conflict or need, and the emergence or exacerbation of the symptom. DSM-III-R also requires that the patient not be conscious of intentionally producing the symptom and that the symptom not be a culturally sanctioned response pattern. Further, the symptom cannot be limited to pain or disturbed sexual functioning. An example of this is pseudocyesis (false pregnancy), which would be the conversion of a wish for and a fear of pregnancy (the psychological conflict) into the physical symptoms (e.g., amenorrhea, lactation) of a false pregnancy.

This hypothesis, that the conversion symptoms result from a conflict between an unconscious wish (e.g., to strike somebody) and an unconscious counterwish (e.g., it is wrong to strike somebody), that is resolved by a process of "somatization," with the sign or symptom (e.g., paralysis of the "striking" extremity) symbolizing the wish and the counterwish (32), is accepted in DSM. This hypothesis, however, presents three significant problems: (1) unconscious conflicts are inaccessible to observation; (2) medical illnesses are often preceded by stressful events (453), and stressful events do not distinguish conversion symptoms from initially undiagnosed medical disorders (799, 1042); and (3) regardless of the type of illness, the sick role is associated with avoidance of activities that might exacerbate the illness (738).

The intermingling of theory and observation in the DSM conversion criteria is potentially harmful to patients, as the presence of a conversion symptom (particularly in the absence of antisocial, histrionic personality disorders or Briquet's syndrome) suggests possible coarse brain or systemic disease. For example, Slater and Glithero (918) followed 85 hospitalized patients with a diagnosis of conversion disorder. During the 10-year follow-up period, 12 patients died, which represented a higher mortality rate than would be expected. Of the 73 living patients, 19 had a diagnosis of conversion disorder, coupled with another medical diagnosis; 22 had a medical illness, which was present but undetected when the conversion disorder diagnosis was made; 11 had a psychotic disorder; and only 21 had "no demonstrable organic pathology." Other follow-up studies (345) found similarly high co-occurrence of illness.

Further, the combination of galactorrhea and amenorrhea, which typify pseudocyesis, is associated with hyperprolactinemia in 50 to 70% of patients and with prolactinomas in 35 to 60% (681). Whitlock (1059) found that more than 60% of patients with symptoms of conversion disorder had significant coexisting or preceding coarse brain disorder, in contrast to about 6% of control subjects. Stefansson et al. (939) diagnosed "organic illness" in 56% of conversion disorder patients seen on a consultation service and also noted that, among patients in a large county case register with an antemortem diagnosis of conversion disorder, 20 (28%) died within a year of the date of the conversion diagnosis. These and other studies (656) demonstrate that 30 to 50% of conversion disorder patients, in fact, have diseases explaining their symptoms, and that an additional 25 to 33% have another primary psychiatric disorder (1093). Watson and Buranen (1042), in whose study 25% of conversion disorder patients had systemic illness or coarse brain disease, wrote, "The results appear to confirm the hypothesis that conversion reaction diagnoses often represent misdiagnosed physical disease. . . . The conditions most often mislabeled as hysteria appear to be those involving degenerative conditions affecting skeletal, muscular and connective tissues, the spinal cord and peripheral nerves." Included among these are dystonia musculorum deformans, transverse myelopathy, thoracic outlet syndrome, cerebrovascular accident, brain tumor, multiple sclerosis, and phenothiazine reaction (799). Epilepsy, particularly of the psychosensory type (712, 939), and multiple sclerosis are the neurologic diagnoses most prominently mentioned (799).

Gould et al. (379) further point out that women, homosexual men, the psychiatrically ill, and patients with plausible psychogenic explanations for their condition are at greatest risk to be misdiagnosed and that movement disorders and paralysis are most often misdiagnosed as hysterical conversion.

In addition to the high prevalence of concurrent illness in patients with conversion symptoms that raises doubts about its validity, a related unanswered question is: What do the "pseudoneurologic" or other conversion symptoms represent? Since the signs of conversion symptoms are usually, if not always, identical to those seen in malingerers, one possibility is that the patient is malingering. Although any patient diagnosed as having a conversion symptom could be a malingerer (particularly one with antisocial personality), there is no evidence that malingering routinely explains conversion symptoms. The high prevalence of diagnosable medical illness in patients with conversion symptoms supports the conclusion that large numbers of conversion symptoms are not those of malingering.

Another view (943) refers to the conversion symptom as a type of anosognosia, whereby a patient is unaware that part of his body is or is not functioning normally. A hemiparalyzed patient might try to walk because he does not know he is paralyzed (Babinski's agnosia), or another patient might not try to move his left upper and lower extremities because he is unaware that they function normally. Thus, what appears to be a motor dysfunction could be a gnostic dysfunction. This is consistent with the physical findings in patients with conversion symptoms. The evidence for this view is modest. Several studies (19, 669, 943) have shown that a significant majority of conversion signs occur on the left side of the body, which is consistent with the association of anosognosia with right-hemispheric dysfunction (943). A notion stating that the left side of the body is more often affected because it is more "convenient" for the patient has been refuted, because the left side of the body is also more frequently affected in left-handers (669). Although it has been shown that indifference to the affected part of the body ("la belle indifference") is not nearly as common in conversion symptoms as was previously believed (799), it occurs and is consistent with the phenomenon of anosognosia. Finally, Flor-Henry et al. (313) found a greater than expected frequency of lateralized EEG abnormalities in patients with somatization disorder, a condition with a higher than expected risk of conversion symptoms.

Given the uncertain validity of the conversion disorder diagnosis and the high frequency of concurrent systemic or psychiatric illness, the patient with conversion symptoms should be diagnosed and treated like any other patient with a psychiatric or medical disorder. There should be a vigorous search for a coexistent medical or psychiatric illness; if present, it determines the prognosis (918). EEG, CT or MRI scans of brain or spinal cord; lumbar puncture; electromyography; and auditory, visual, and somatosensory evoked potentials (384, 410) are often valuable. Evoked potentials and MRI are the best means of diagnosing multiple sclerosis and reveal abnormalities in the majority of patients with multiple sclerosis (384).

The treatment of a patient with conversion symptoms should be that of the concurrent medical or psychiatric illness, if one can be identified. If a diagnosis cannot be made, the patient should be told this Also, he should be seen for follow-up examinations whether or not the conversion symptoms spontaneously disappear.

Although the frequency of conversion symptoms appears to have decreased during this century, as many as 20% of patients admitted to general medical hospitals and clinics experience such symptoms during their lifetimes (920). Women are more commonly affected than men, and conversion is more often observed in patients from rural areas or with low socioeconomic backgrounds.

Somatoform Pain Disorder

The DSM-III-R criteria for somatoform pain disorder are similar to those of conversion, and problems with the validity of the diagnosis are similar in both disorders. One study (809) demonstrated that 98% of chronic pain patients had a DSM-

III axis I psychiatric diagnosis, and 37% had an axis II disorder. Further, Hendler et al. (437) employed thermography in 224 consecutive patients, who had no radiologic, neurologic, orthopedic, or laboratory abnormalities but had been diagnosed as having somatoform pain, and found the diagnosis to be reflex sympathetic dystrophy, nerve root irritation, or thoracic outlet syndrome in 19% of these patients. Sympathetic nervous system dysfunction can be easily misdiagnosed as somatoform pain unless thermography is employed. As is the case with conversion symptoms, management includes a vigorous search for a "coexisting" psychiatric or systemic disorder, which itself determines the treatment and the prognosis. For patients with intractable chronic pain, in whom no concurrent psychiatric or systemic illness, including depression, can be identified, physical rehabilitation and behavior modification programs offer the best, but by no means fully satisfying, management. Medication should be avoided because these patients are at high risk for addiction.

Hypochondriasis

DSM-III-R defines hypochondriasis as "an unrealistic interpretation of physical signs or sensations as abnormal, leading to preoccupation with the fear or belief of having a serious disease." As in conversion and somatoform pain disorders, the validity of the diagnosis as a discrete entity remains to be established. Kenyon (524, 525), in a literature review and a controlled study of 512 psychiatric patients with hypochondriasis, found that hypochondriasis was always secondary to another syndrome, usually depression. Another association is with OCD.

An unexplained fact is this statement by Kenyon (525): "Generally speaking, hypochondriacal symptoms as part of another syndrome seem to make the prognosis worse, as for example in depression." The treatment of hypochondriacal symptoms is that of the underlying illness.

Malingering and Factitious Illness

Malingering is the simulation or fraudulent exaggeration of symptoms, or the deliberate production (e.g., heating a thermometer to produce "fever") of physical signs with fraud in mind. *Factitious illness* is the deliberate production of physical signs, whether or not fraud is involved. Most factitious illnesses constitute malingering, but some do not; for example, some melancholics excoriate their skin when they are agitated.

Malingering is not rare. It occurs primarily among persons with psychopathology, most commonly antisocial personality (904). In one series of patients thought to be malingerers, 90% had co-occurring psychiatric diagnoses, including antisocial personality, drug dependence, and alcoholism (837, 904).

Malingering is more frequent among people who are in extremely unpleasant circumstances, such as prison or combat; who are homeless; or who have an opportunity (such as an accident) to claim compensation. People who have been identified as malingerers in the past are more apt to malinger again. Among people with factitious illnesses, there is a disproportionately large number of medical and paramedical personnel.

Most patients faking psychiatric disorders claim to be hallucinating or suicidal. Occasionally, patients falsely claim to be anxious or to have post-traumatic stress disorder, or they feign mutism. Some signals of psychiatric malingering include odd combinations of symptoms; endorsement of "symptoms" created by the suspicious examiner ("Most people who have the problems you have experience periodic itching of their feet and palms of their hands; how about you?"); coexisting antisocial personality, alcoholism, or drug abuse; and recent problems with the criminal justice system, with parents (if the patient is a teenager), or with a sexual partner.

Most malingering, however, involves feigning systemic illness. Methods typically used are thermometer heating, injection or ingestion of symptom-producing substances (e.g., ingesting thyroid hormone), exacerbation of wounds, genitourinary tract manipulation, self-inflicted injuries, phlebotomy, and falsification of a medical history (811). Fraud usually can be identified. For example, in auscultation of the respiratory tree in factitious asthma, wheezing is usually loudest over the larynx. Also, the inhalation of methacholine does not reduce forced expiratory volume. In factitious dermatitis, the lesions are typically on accessible skin surfaces, such as the left forearm in a right-hander. In factitious "fever of unknown origin," the pulse rate may be much lower than expected from the temperature reading, and the fever pattern may not show typical diurnal variation. Strategies for diagnosing factitious fever include taking simultaneous oral and rectal temperatures, checking thermometer serial numbers, and taking the temperature of fresh urine specimens (699). The evaluation of fever of unknown origin should also include a thorough inspection of the skin for needle puncture wounds.

Excluding epileptics who also fake seizures, the EEGs of people feigning epilepsy show no spiking or other paroxysmal features, and prolactin levels do not rise. A more effective tool (if available) is continuous EEG telemetry with simultaneous videotaping of the patient's activities. For other types of malingered neurologic abnormalities in unsophisticated patients, findings may include hemianesthesia to the midline, stocking or glove anesthesia, and absence of pathologic reflexes, atrophy, or clonus. One maneuver in hemiparalysis is for the examiner to place one hand beneath the heel of the paralyzed foot, with the patient lying in the supine position, and the other hand above the ankle for the functioning foot. He then asks the patient to elevate the "good leg" against the resistance of the examiner's hand atop the ankle. As the patient attempts this, if the "bad" extremity is not paralyzed, pressure is automatically exerted against the examiner's hand beneath the heel of the "bad" foot.

Ophthalmologists have many tests for malingered blindness. Most involve the patient's unwittingly having to see with his "blind" eye to produce a response that could have occurred only if the patient could see with that eye (557). For example, a tongue depressor is placed vertically in the midline 6 or 7 inches in front of a patient, who is instructed to keep both eyes open and read printed material placed 10 to 14 inches in front of him. A person with good vision in one eye and blindness in the other must move his head to read the printed material. A malingerer may not appreciate this and continue to read without head movement. Another strategy is to ask the patient to touch the tips of his index fingers together. A bilaterally or unilaterally blind person with normal position sense, spatial orientation, cerebellar functioning, and interhemispheric connection does this with ease; a malingerer with these functions intact may hesitate (557). In the evaluation of deafness, the use of auditory evoked potentials or pure tone–delayed auditory feedback (834) can be helpful. In factitious thyrotoxicosis induced by ingestion of thyroid hormone, serum thyroglobulin levels are low or absent, iodine 131 (^{131}I) uptake is suppressed, TSH levels are decreased, and no ectopic thyroid tissue is found on ^{131}I body scan (630, 841).

Unless the malingered act is observed (e.g., the patient is seen to be heating a thermometer) or there is strong circumstantial evidence (e.g., secreted syringes or medications in the patient's clothes cabinet), the patient should not be told outright that he is faking; he will only try to save face. If he believes he is being wronged, he may retaliate by complaining, suing, or otherwise expressing his anger. One malingerer murdered several orthopedic surgeons who claimed that he was feigning back pain in a compensation case (735). If the patient is to be confronted, it should be done tactfully. The patient should be permitted to save face so that he will comply with management recommendations for alternative methods of dealing with the circumstances that led to the malingering or accept the physician's recommendation for discharge.

Other Disorders

DSM-III-R also includes *body dysmorphic disorder*, in which the patient is preoccupied with a specific body part or organ; *undifferentiated somatoform disorder;* and *somatoform disorder not otherwise specified*. Body dysmorphic disorder may be a variant of OCD, but the latter two are "wastebasket" categories of no demonstrated validity or usefulness.

Chapter

15

Extremes of Trait

II. Anxious and Fearful Personality Disorders and Their Related State Syndromes

Anxious and Fearful Personality Disorders

Anxious and fearful personality extremes include avoidant, dependent, passive-aggressive, and obsessive compulsive personality disorders. These trait extremes share a number of common features. Within Cloninger's system, most are low in novelty seeking (passive-aggressive people are high), high in harm avoidance, and either high (passive-aggressive, dependent, and avoidant) or low (obsessional) in reward dependence.

Common behavior patterns of patients who are low in novelty seeking can be subclassified as:

Pattern A: rigid, methodical, frugal, orderly, regimented

Pattern B: content, quiet, patient, reflective, reserved

For patients who are high in harm avoidance, these behavior patterns include:

Pattern A: restrained, shy, inhibited, fatigable, asthenic

Pattern B: apprehensive, fearful, worrying, cautious, pessimistic

Avoidant Personality Disorder

Avoidant personality disorder conceptually developed from combining some of the socially aloof behaviors associated with schizoid personality and the social and occupational failure patterns of what used to be termed inadequate personality. In Cloninger's system, avoidant personality is particularly associated with pattern B behaviors in low novelty seeking and with Pattern A behaviors in high harm avoidance, as subclassified above. These patients also have the high reward dependent characteristics of social sensitivity and interpersonal vulnerability. They are introverted, anxious, self-conscious, socially awkward, shy, and mistrustful of others and have low self-esteem.

Passive-Aggressive and Dependent Personality Disorders

It is unclear whether dependent trait extremes can be meaningfully separated from passive-aggressive trait extremes. Nevertheless, dependent personality is characterized by submissiveness, difficulties in making even mundane decisions, and a willingness to let others make important decisions (e.g., where to live, what job to take). Individuals with dependent personalities are also said to have difficulty in initiating projects. They feel uncomfortable or helpless when alone and avoid being alone. They are preoccupied with fears of being abandoned, are easily hurt by criticism or disapproval, and agree with people so as to avoid rejection. In Cloninger's system, dependent people are particularly associated with Pattern A behaviors in low novelty seeking and Pattern B behaviors in high harm avoidance. They also tend to have the high reward dependence behaviors of social oversensitivity, helpfulness, and overdedication.

Passive-aggressive personality is characterized by indirect resistance to authority, demands of others, obligations, and responsibilities. Passive-aggressive individuals are procrastinators. They dawdle, are purposefully slow, and may do poorly on tasks they do not want to do, and avoid obligations by "forgetting." They are resentful of suggestions for improvement; obstructionistic; unreasonably critical of people in authority; and, often, irritable, sulky, argumentative, discontented, disgruntled, and whiny. They are high in all three of Cloninger's personality traits. Tyrer associates passive-dependent traits with phobias and other anxiety disorders.

Obsessive Compulsive Personality Disorder

Obsessive compulsive trait extremes are consistent with Cloninger's low novelty seeking and reward dependence and, to a lesser extent, Pattern A behaviors in high harm avoidance. DSM-III-R characterizes obsessive compulsive personality disorder as a "pervasive pattern of perfectionism and inflexibility" that interferes with daily functioning. Such individuals are preoccupied with details, rules, lists, and order, thus losing the point of an activity. Tasks go uncompleted because self-imposed standards cannot be met. These individuals are often unreasonable in insisting that others submit to their methods of doing things and are also reluctant to permit others to do things because of the conviction they will not do them correctly. People with obsessive personalities are further described as excessively devoted to work to the exclusion of leisure activity; indecisive because of ruminations about how best to do things; overconscientious, scrupulous, and inflexible on matters of morality and values (all is black and white); restricted in affect (cold); lacking generosity; and having a tendency to hoard.

Tyrer et al. (1012), using the term *anancastic personality*, characterized these patients as rigid, overly conscientious, nonimpulsive, hypochondriacal, and anxious. Tyrer found an association between these traits and phobias and obsessiveness. Not all obsessive persons, however, develop obsessive compulsive disorder, and not all patients with obsessive compulsive disorder have premorbid obsessive personalities. The relationship is thus unclear.

Relationship of Extremes of Trait to Anxiety and Other State Disorders

There are no known biologic treatments for the avoidant, dependent, passive-aggressive, and obsessive personality disorders, and the efficacy of behavioral interventions for these extremes of trait is unclear. For these reasons, the relevance of these disorders to the neuropsychiatrist is limited. The neuropsychiatrist can identify the pattern of deviation for the patient and educate the patient about the condition. Supportive counseling and practical suggestions regarding problems of living related to the traits also can be provided. By identifying the trait extreme, the neuropsychiatrist may offer potential benefit through early detection of developing state problems; however, the degree to which these extremes of trait relate to abnormal states has not been established.

What does seem established, is the high frequency of some preexisting personality disorders among certain patients with state disorders. The precise frequency of the preexisting traits and the specific trait-state relationships are unclear. For example, in studies examining the frequency of personality disorder in anxiety disorder patients, rates range from 27 to 58% (329, 541, 808). Most investigators report the excess to be among the DSM-III-R "C disorders" (avoidant et al.) (385, 640, 808), but other trait disorders also have been implicated (329).

Recently, Klass et al. (532) and Alnaes and Torgersen (38) have looked at these relationships. Each study found avoidant and dependent personality disorders to be particularly associated with anxiety disorders and with anxiety disorders complicated by nonmelancholic depressions. In the study by Klass et al., almost 70% of patients had preexisting DSM-III-R "C" cluster trait disorders; in the Alnaes and Torgersen study, 40% had preexisting "C" cluster diagnoses.

Although one can reasonably assume that the preexisting trait extremes and their co-occurring states are pathophysiologically related, it is unclear whether trait extremes predispose to a state or whether the traits and their states are expressions of a common process, with the traits simply being expressed before the states occur. The latter relationship implies that these traits (as with schizoidia) may be, in fact, mild morbid states, whereas the former relationship makes no presumption of trait morbidity. In either case, the possibility exists that controlling the extreme trait behaviors might prevent or ameliorate the state process. Cloninger's approach to personality is based on variability in neurotransmitter systems, so that potential medications affecting that variability early in personality development might reduce deviation. This, however, is speculative. Present day treatments are limited to education, counseling, stress reduction, and the unclear benefits of behavioral and cognitive therapies.

Cognitive and Somatic Anxiety

A large number of studies (193), using sophisticated statistical analyses (factor and cluster analysis) and information from the clinical rating of patients and nonpatients, have consistently delineated two groups of relatively constant (i.e., trait) features that tend to occur together in the general population and in some psychiatric patients. These trait features have been labeled *cognitive* and *somatic* anxiety. Table 15.1 displays the features of the two forms of trait anxiety.

Cognitive anxiety is characterized by anticipatory apprehension, ruminative worry, feelings of insecurity, social awkwardness, muscle tenseness, and poor recuperative ability following stress or illness. Somatic anxiety is characterized by diverse aches, pains, and signs of autonomic nervous system disturbance; distractibility; and a general feeling of unease.

Cognitive anxiety relates to low novelty seeking, high harm avoidance, and low reward dependence. It incorporates many of the behavioral traits associated with anxious and fearful personality extremes. An association also appears to exist between cognitive anxiety and the anxiety disorders.

In contrast, somatic anxiety relates to high novelty seeking, low harm avoidance, and high reward dependence. It incorporates many of the behavioral traits associated with dramatic and erratic personality extremes. Studies also have found that these two forms of trait anxiety differ in information processing style and other physiologic measurements. It is possible that cognitive anxiety represents a low-grade, chronic form of anxiety disorder (analogous to the relationship be-

TABLE 15.1

Cognitive Versus Somatic Anxiety

Feature	*Syndrome*	
	Cognitive	*Somatic*
Personality Traits		
Novelty seeking	Low	High
Harm avoidance	High	Low
Reward dependence	Low	High
Extroversion	No	Yes
Introversion	Yes	No
Sociability	Low	High
Impulsivity	Low	High
Cognition/Information Processing		
Anticipatory	Frequent	Infrequent
Ruminations	Yes	No
Distractibility	Low	High
Vigilance	Hyper	Hypo
Sensitivity to stimuli	High	Low
Attention to detail	High	Low
Speed and accuracy	High	Low
Integration/organization	Good	Poor
Decision making	Analytic	Intuitive
Intelligence quotient	High	Low/normal
Physiology		
Sedation threshold	High	Low
Pain sensitivity	Low	High
Muscle relaxability	Slow	Rapid
Fatigability	Rapid	Slow
Tolerance for stress	Low	High
Tolerance for stimulants	Low	High
Evoked potentials	Reducing	Augmenting
Galvanic skin response habituation	Poor	Poor
Deviant Behaviors		
Passive-dependent	Yes	No
Obsessional	Yes	No
Histrionic	No	Yes
Antisocial	No	Yes
Familial criminality	No	Yes
Anxiety disorders	High	Low
Neurotic depression	High	Low
Aches and pains	No	Yes
Recuperation from minor illness	Slow	Fast

tween cyclothymia and bipolar affective disorder) and that somatic anxiety represents a mild form of the personality traits consistent with somatoform disorders. If true, this interpretation of the two clusters suggests that patients with the cognitive anxiety cluster may respond to the treatments effective for anxiety disorders, whereas those patients with the somatic anxiety cluster are less likely to do so. Table 15.2 summarizes these anxious and fearful state and trait relationships.

Anxiety Disorders

History

William Cullen, an eighteenth-century Scotsman, coined the term neurosis to identify a group of conditions that included disorders with palpitations (today's anxiety disorders), hysteria, hypochondriasis, a form of melancholia, and several fibrile disorders associated with disturbed mood. He assumed some CNS dysfunction as the underlying cause. Charcot and Janet, in the late 19th century, also proposed CNS degenerative hypotheses as a cause for these states. In 1893, Hecker (of hebephrenia fame) grouped the different states of anxiety and proposed them as a separate diagnostic category (1095).

Perhaps the best early descriptions of anxiety disorders are provided by Alfred Stille, an American Civil War surgeon, who in 1863 described "soldier's heart," and Jacob Da Costa, who in 1871 reported 300 cases in the Union army. Da Costa

TABLE 15.2

Relationship of Anxious and Fearful Traits and States

Cognitive Anxiety	*Somatic Anxiety*
Traits	
Low novelty seeking	High novelty seeking
High harm avoidance	Low harm avoidance
Low reward dependence	High reward dependence
Anxious and fearful personality extremes	Dramatic and erratic personality extremes
States	
Anxiety disorders	Somatoform disorders
Some dysthymias	

also concluded that anxiety syndromes were familial. Neurasthenia, neurocirculatory asthenia, and phobic-anxiety-depersonalization syndrome are other terms used to identify these patients.

Undoubtedly, the two seminal points in the conceptual development of anxiety states were Freud's introduction of his psychogenic theory of neuroses in the late nineteenth and early twentieth centuries and Pitts and McClure's (769) report that panic attacks could be induced in patients, but not in control subjects, by IV infusions of sodium lactate. Freud put the neuroses on the map; Pitts and McClure put them in the laboratory.

One of the major changes incorporated into DSM-III and DSM-III-R was the dropping of the term "neurosis," with reorganization of the anxiety disorder category to include (1) panic disorder (with and without agoraphobia), (2) agoraphobia, (3) social phobia, (4) simple phobia, (5) generalized anxiety disorder, (6) posttraumatic stress disorder (PTSD), and (7) obsessive compulsive disorder. (The last is discussed in Chapter 16.) The evidence for the DSM classification system is weak. For example, there is no clear distinction between panic disorder with agoraphobia and pure agoraphobia, as almost all agoraphobics have panic attacks. The relationship between obsessive compulsive disorder (OCD) and the other anxiety disorders is unknown, whereas a relationship appears to exist between OCD and Gilles de la Tourette's syndrome (see Chapter 16), which is not included in the anxiety disorder category. Further, PTSD appears to be a heterogeneous category, with some patients having anxiety disorder and others with personality disorder or substance abuse as the co-occurring diagnosis. For the clinician, a reasonable sorting out of the above confusion is to separate these disorders into five groups, each with different treatment and prognosis implications, as well as some laboratory distinctions. These groups are (1) simple phobia; (2) agoraphobia, incorporating agoraphobia, panic attacks with agoraphobia, generalized anxiety disorder, and social phobia; (3) simple panic disorder, incorporating panic disorder without agoraphobia; (4) PTSD; and (5) OCD (see Chapter 16).

Basic Panic Syndrome—Anxiety Attack

Table 15.3 lists the behaviors observed in a panic (anxiety) attack. As anxiety is a component of the normal physiologic response to potential or real threat, many features of a panic attack are potentially adaptive. These are included under flight-or-fight phenomena. For example, some degree of pupillary dilation and exophthalmus, respectively, lets more light into the eyeball and increases the range of eyeball movement, thus aiding visual scanning. Vascular shunting reduces blood flow to the periphery (reducing the potential for blood loss should injury occur) and to splanchnic vessels (digestion is not a priority during flight or fight), while increasing flow to the musculature (in preparation for exertion). The changes ob-

TABLE 15.3
Panic Attack

Mood
Apprehension, fear

Cognition
Notion of impending doom, fear of dying or of going crazy, inability to concentrate, depersonalization

Flight/fight phenomena
Dilated pupils, exophthalmos, piloerection, increased muscle tone, tachycardia, sweating, vascular shunting

Nonadaptive features
Tremors, dry mouth, blurred vision, chest pain/discomfort, palpitations, air hunger, dyspnea, hyperventilation, paresthesias, flushes or chills, weakness, fatigue, easy fatigability, inner shakiness, lump in throat, vascular throbbing, increased bowel motility, nausea or abdominal distress, dizziness or syncopy

served in a panic attack are essentially no different than those observed in flight-or-fight situations, except that (1) there is no real threat and (2) the symptoms evolve beyond adaptation (769, 955).

Simple Panic Disorder

Panic disorder is characterized by recurrent episodes of rapidly developing, severe, and, at least to some extent, incapacitating anxiety without an obvious threat. For a DSM-III-R diagnosis, at least four attacks must have occurred within a 4-month period or one attack must have been followed by a period of at least 1 month of persistent fear of another attack. An attack must unfold within a 10-minute onset. The usual attack lasts about 30 minutes and is followed by a variable period of fatigue and occasional mild apprehension. Most clinicians, however, modify these arbitrary requirements and treat patients with less frequent and slower-onset attacks. Tyrer (1010) has argued that few patients with simple panic disorder evolve into agoraphobics.

Agoraphobia

Although listed separately, agoraphobia may be the severe form of the same morbid process accounting for many panic disorders. Thus, if the first panic attack happens to occur suddenly while the patient is away from home, he may subsequently become disinclined ever again to travel alone for fear that another such attack might render him helpless and without succor. For unknown reasons, such agoraphobics are frequently women ("housebound housewives") who become utterly dependent on their family or friends for even the shortest trips away from home. In other instances, anxiety symptoms gradually insinuate themselves into a previously normal existence until their accumulated weight over the years results in a socially and occupationally crippling disability.

Individual clinical features may predominate in any one patient and give a characteristic stamp and title to the syndrome. Thus, hyperventilation syndrome (tachypnea, light-headedness, facial pallor, paresthesias), neurocirculatory asthenia (palpitations, chest pain, fatigue, exercise intolerance), panic disorder (sensation of impending doom, depersonalization, muscular weakness), and agoraphobia may be manifestations of the same underlying disorder, may be observed at various times in the same patient, and respond to the same treatment.

DSM-III-R characterizes *generalized anxiety disorder* (GAD) as persistent features of anxiety without any of the more specific features associated with panic or phobic disorders. There is no evidence for this distinction; patients with GAD have panic attacks and often are socially restricted and isolated by their symptoms. In its pure form, GAD may be simply a low-grade, chronic form of panic or agoraphobia, perhaps analogous to dysthymia being a chronic, low-grade form of depression. Social phobia seems identical to GAD, except that the patient experiences more specific anxiety-inducing social situations.

Simple Phobia

A phobia is an irrational fear of specific objects, places, situations, or activities. The fear and physiologic response are disproportionately greater than any actual danger (e.g., some snakes are dangerous, but a patient phobic to snakes panics in the proximity of all snakes, sometimes even those caged). Simple phobias are circumscribed; that is, the patient is anxious only in proximity to or in anticipation of nearness to the phobic object or situation. Simple phobic fear does not transfer from object to object or situation to situation and tends not to generalize to nonphobic situations (so-called "free-floating" anxiety). It is therefore stimulus-locked, and most people with simple phobias are fearful of only one thing. If they can avoid the phobia, they feel well. The usual content of simple phobias, in decreasing frequency, is: (1) animal (e.g., snakes, spiders), (2) situational (e.g., flying, height, public speaking, thunderstorms, speaking on the phone), and (3) blood and injury.

Post-Traumatic Stress Disorder

Anyone who has been involved in a life-threatening situation (e.g., automobile accident, rape, environmental catastrophe, war) is aware of the stress that results. This stress can lead to symptoms; their content relates to the stressful situation, and their form resembles certain anxiety disorders, OCD, and some types of depression. In recognition of this diversity, DSM-III and DSM-III-R provide diagnostic criteria for patients whose poststress response is deviant in severity and duration. About 1 to 2% of the general population meet these criteria. The onset of symptoms is usually within hours or days of the event. Notions that the response can be delayed for years are unproved.

The Department of Veterans Affairs (VA) has been particularly concerned with PTSD. Many VA hospitals have inpatient and outpatient programs for veterans who have symptoms of the disorder. The old terms for this syndrome were "shell shock" (World War I) and "combat neurosis" (World War II). The amount of federal funds devoted to the care of veterans with PTSD is enormous. Many programs provide a therapeutic community treatment approach based purely on a psychological understanding of symptoms. These programs, as well as pharmacotherapy programs, tend to assume clinical homogeneity. Clinical homogeneity is unlikely, however, and studies further show that 80% or more of PTSD veterans have co-occurring conditions.The most common of these are alcoholism, drug abuse, antisocial personality, somatization disorder, OCD, anxiety disorder, and depression (436, 905, 906). Studies of PTSD veterans also demonstrate that many exhibited the behaviors leading to diagnosis during or before military service.

Thus, the validity of the PTSD syndrome is unclear. It is clear, however, that co-occurrence with other conditions is significant and many of the co-occurring disorders (anxiety disorder, OCD, substance abuse, depression) can be successfully treated with regimens of known efficacy and safety. The clinical rule of making the diagnosis that has the best prognosis, when possible, may best serve these patients by giving them the primary diagnosis of the co-occurring disorder and its appropriate treatment.

Adjustment Disorders

DSM-III introduced the term adjustment disorder (the concept goes back beyond the "transient situational personality disorder" of DSM-I). It characterizes a group of heterogeneous conditions, in which symptoms develop rapidly in response to a stress and resolve within 6 months. DSM-III-R requires the exclusion of virtually all other disorders. Eight subtypes of adjustment disorder are defined by the predominant feature (e.g., depressed, anxious, conduct disturbance). These conditions tend to occur in adolescents and young adults in response to events that few others would consider overwhelming (53). Those patients who do not recover within the 6-month limit tend to evolve into other, more serious disorders (e.g., psychosis, antisocial personality, drug abuse). Perhaps 5% of the population is at risk.

Course

The course of simple phobic disorder differs from the courses of simple panic disorder and agoraphobia, which are similar to each other. Simple phobic disorder usually begins in childhood; school phobia is the most common. The younger the age at onset of simple phobia, the better the prognosis. Half of individuals who have childhood-onset simple phobias are symptom-free within 5 years of expression, and virtually all patients improve somewhat. In adolescent- and adult-onset simple phobias, smaller proportions of patients are symptom-free after 5 years, with only 5% of adult-onset phobics being asymptomatic at follow-up. Total lifetime prevalence of simple phobia is about 25%. Women are at greater risk than are men (3:2) (829, 1051).

In contrast, agoraphobia and simple panic disorder begin in the early and middle 20s, respectively. Onset almost never occurs before puberty or after age 35 (about 80% of patients have onsets before age 30). Once panic disorder is developed, the pattern of waxing and waning symptoms and the overall functioning of patients usually remain constant, whereas agoraphobics tend to become progressively isolated and suffer social and employment deterioration. GAD also begins in the early 20s, with 25% of patients developing panic attacks and an unknown number of phobias. GAD patients can become housebound but are not as limited as patients with agoraphobia.

Epidemiologic studies find that about 2% of women and 1% of men develop panic disorder, 3% of women and 1 to 2% of men develop agoraphobia; and 6% of the population (men somewhat more than women) develop GAD. Although these figures may be somewhat inflated, anxiety disorders are fairly common; the majority of patients seen in a general medical practice may present with such disorders (77).

Laboratory Findings

No readily available laboratory diagnostic tests are particularly helpful in identifying idiopathic anxiety disorders. For example, panic patients have been tested with MRI, CT, and EEG, but results from the studies are unclear. Fontaine et al. (318), using MRI, found 40% of panic patients had abnormal scans versus 10% of control subjects. Atrophy was particularly observed in the right temporal lobe horn. Kellner and Uhde (511) found mild to moderate atrophy on CT scans in over one half of a small sample of patients but also reported (1014) that these abnormalities were related to the amount of benzodiazepine used. Lepola et al. (582) found 20% of panic patients to have "incidental abnormalities." Although a proportion of panic patients do show atrophy on MRI or CT, the findings are mild and nonspecific and may result from drug use.

EEG findings in anxiety patients are also inconclusive. Stein and Uhde (940) reported nonspecific, nonepileptic EEG abnormalities in a small proportion of patients, whereas Beauclaire and Fontaine (85) reported that 10 to 27% of their anxiety patients had epileptic abnormalities. Both atypical panic and panic associated with instability increase the likelihood of this type of EEG, and these patients should be treated for seizure disorder (280, 1036). The vast majority of panic patients, however, have normal EEGs (582).

Diagnosis

Other than the overly restrictive criteria requirements regarding frequency of panic attacks, DSM-III-R criteria for the anxiety disorders are clinically useful. In practice, it is usually not difficult to determine whether a patient has a panic or phobic disorder or agoraphobia. More challenging is the decision as to whether the anxiety syndrome is primary, part of another psychiatric disorder, or secondary to coarse neurologic disease or systemic illness.

Conditions that can result in anxiety disorder are legion. Table 15.4 lists those

TABLE 15.4

Conditions Commonly Implicated in Anxiety Disorder Syndromes

Neurologic
Temporal lobe epilepsy (mimics panic disorder)
Parkinson's disease
Postconcussion syndrome
Multiple sclerosis

Systemic
Endocrine disorders (particularly hyperthyroidism, Cushing's disease)
Cardiovascular disease
  Hypertension
  Mitral valve prolapse
Pulmonary embolus
Cardiac arrhythmias, myopathies, and artery disease
Asthma
Pheochromocytoma
Hypoglycemia
Irritable bowel syndrome

Other
Withdrawal states (alcohol, benzodiazepines)
Caffeinism
Stimulant drug abuse

most commonly implicated. A review of systems and physical examination should alert the clinician to most of these possibilities. Five additional signals are (1) anxiety disorder onset after age 35, (2) male gender, (3) motor disturbances other than tremor, (4) panic attacks of prolonged onset or associated with irritability, and (5) panic attacks associated with any alteration in sensorium. Laboratory tests should be structured to confirm diagnostic suspicions of a neurologic or systemic cause and not be used as screening devices. Further, several conditions tend to co-occur with anxiety disorder; they include some forms of depression, PTSD, and OCD (discussed in Chapter 16), some forms of drug abuse, mitral valve prolapse, and irritable bowel syndrome.

Irritable bowel syndrome may affect more than 10% of the general population, and up to 70% of these patients may have psychiatric symptoms, most commonly anxiety and depression. When irritable bowel co-occurs with anxiety disorder, treatment with cyclic antidepressants may successfully resolve both conditions. It is unclear, however, whether this co-occurrence represents common etiology and pathophysiology (i.e., co-morbidity) and which syndrome is primary (501).

Anxiety disorders and mitral valve prolapse also co-occur. Mitral valve prolapse has a symptom pattern similar to that of GAD: anxiety, palpitations, chest discomfort, and fatigue. In some studies, 50% of anxiety patients had such prolapse, whereas only 10% of the general population has this cardiac deviation. The clinical significance of this relationship is unclear, but co-morbidity seems unlikely.

The most common disorder co-occurring with anxiety disorder is depression (612, 634). About 50% of patients with panic disorder have a major depression during their lifetimes; most patients with anxiety disorder (of any type) have occasional, often atypical depressions; and 3 to 4% of the general population have both anxiety disorder and mood disorder during their lifetimes. Further, although relatives of patients with pure anxiety states do not have an increased risk for depression, relatives of patients with co-occurring anxiety and depression do. This individual and familial co-occurrence most likely results from clinical heterogeneity, particularly of depression. For example, nonmelancholic depressives, whose illnesses begin with panic disorder, have depressions that appear to be either states of demoralization or depressivelike states that are variants of the primary panic disorder (583). There is no increased risk for mood disorder in their first-degree relatives. Akiskal and colleagues (714) refer to the condition as *panic-depressive disorder*. Studies support this view; they also suggest that the relationship between anxiety disorder and mood disorder is limited to the nonmelancholic-dysthymic unipolar part of the mood disorder spectrum and that common denominators may be the cognitive anxiety construct and anxious-fearful premorbid personality traits (22, 169, 1022). For treatment purposes, the clinician can clarify the issue somewhat by determining whether or not the depression is melancholic and whether the patient or his family has evidence of bipolar disorder. If either case is likely, the patient should be treated for manic-depressive illness. Treatment would include the use of lithium, anticonvulsants, or ECT. If the patient or his family has no evidence of bipolar disorder or if the co-occurring depression is not melancholia, the patient should be treated for anxiety disorder. This diagnosis would likely preclude the above treatments and perhaps call for the use of cyclic antidepressants and MAOIs.

Other co-occurrences seem related, in part, to misdiagnosis. For example, a patient with dysthymia and significant anxiety, and a melancholic with apprehension may receive double diagnoses, even though the features of anxiety are expressions of the depressive process. A patient with complex partial seizures also may have depressive and anxiety symptoms that are separately labeled, with the seizure disorder going unrecognized. Further, self-medication with stimulant drugs by a depressive may lead to the drug-related symptoms being misdiagnosed as anxiety.

Laboratory Induced Panic

Pitts and McClure's (769) report of a systematic, double-blind study, in which infused sodium lactate induced typical panic attacks in anxiety patients but in few control subjects, opened the modern era in the study of anxiety disorders. Although their hypothesis (chelation of interstitial calcium leading to neuronal membrane depolarization) has not resisted the test of time, lactate repeatedly has been shown to induce anxiety in predictably susceptible individuals. Other substances also have been demonstrated to induce panic; these include carbon dioxide biocarbonate, yohimbine, and isoproterenol. Laboratory-induced panic is dramatic and controllable. It provides an excellent paradigm for studying the physiologic processes of anxiety, individuals with different degrees of risk for anxiety disorder, and novel treatments of anxiety disorder.

Management

Most anxiety disorder patients receive outpatient treatment. Each patient needs education about his illness that corrects misconceptions (e.g., the condition results from masturbation), resolves secondary fears (e.g., of going crazy or having a dangerous medical problem, such as heart disease), provides a reasonable explanation for the condition (e.g., symptoms are real and reflect physiologic hypersensitivity in the brain that results in an abnormal flight-or-fight response), and offers a detailed discussion of the treatments to be used and the likely course of the illness. Although technical jargon must be avoided, the more a patient knows about his condition and its treatment, the more likely he is to comply with treatment. Specific treatments of known efficacy for anxiety disorder include pharmacologic, behavioral, and cognitive interventions. They are not mutually exclusive and are frequently combined to provide optimal benefit (501). Psychosurgery also may help some chronic patients who are resistant to these interventions.

Psychopharmacology

Pharmacologic treatments of anxiety disorders include cyclic antidepressants, MAOIs, and high-potency benzodiazepines. Beta-blockers and anticonvulsants are also used.

Cyclic Antidepressants

Cyclic antidepressants (109, 639) could be equally referred to as cyclic antianxiety agents. They work best in patients with panic disorder, GAD, and agoraphobia. Impramine is the best-studied cyclic antidepressant for panic disorder, although other cyclic agents are effective. Fluoxetine is increasingly being used to treat anxiety disorder patients. Initial doses of these compounds should be low and increased gradually because anxiety disorder patients may be particularly sensitive to them. Starting doses for such drugs as impramine should be as low as 25 mg daily, with a gradual buildup of 25 mg every 3 days until the therapeutic dose is reached (about the same as that for depression, 150–300 mg daily). A small number of patients may poorly tolerate even the initial 25-mg daily dose (too excitatory or side effects are too severe), and the dose may need to be reduced even further (10 mg daily). This gradual buildup applies to all classes of drugs used to treat patients with anxiety disorder. Between 50 to 75% of patients have a marked response to these drugs. Once remission is achieved, the patient should be maintained on the same dose for 1 year to prevent relapse. After 1 year, the dose should be gradually tapered and, if possible, discontinued over a period of about 3 months. About 60% of patients do not require immediate buildup of the dosage. Some, however, require indefinite treatment. For certain patients, beta-adrenergic blocking agents (propranolol) may be added to or substituted for the cyclic antidepressant. Doses range from 30–130 mg daily in divided doses. Patients should be instructed to refrain from consuming food and drink that contain caffeine.

Monoamine Oxidase Inhibitors

Phenelzine is the MAOI most widely used to treat anxiety disorders (109). Its efficacy in GAD and agoraphobia is equivalent to that of cyclic antidepressants. The class of drug chosen should depend on decisions regarding side effects, rather than therapeutic effect. For panic disorder, cyclic antidepressants are generally tried first. If they are not fully successful, the patient is either switched to phenelzine or phenelzine is added to the cyclic antidepressant (fluoxetine is an exception to this rule: see Chapter 20). Phenelzine also should be introduced slowly, beginning with 15 mg daily and increasing by 15 mg in 2 to 3 days and then by 15 mg each week. Therapeutic dosages range from 45–120 mg daily. In addition to a tyramine- and caffeine-restricted diet, the concomitant administration (begun before starting the MAOI) of amitriptyline (25 mg orally at bedtime) may decrease MAOI-induced insomnia and reduce the risk of a hypertensive tyramine reaction in patients whose dietary reliability is of concern (734). Stimulants, including those in over-the-counter cold preparations, should be avoided. Although MAOIs may be added to cyclic antidepressants, the reverse is not advisable because an adrenergic crisis (delirium, seizures) may result. If one MAOI is substituted for another, there should be a 14-day MAOI-free interval between drugs. Some clinicians recommend that the patient always carry several 10-mg tablets of nifedipine for sublingual use should a hypertensive reaction begin (sudden throbbing headache, sweating and flushing, nausea and vomiting, photophobia) (187).

As with cyclic antidepressants, patients successfully treated with an MAOI should be maintained on the therapeutic dose for about 1 year. The drug should then be tapered (1 tablet weekly). If relapse occurs, the MAOI should be reintroduced (a lower dose may suffice in the second course of treatment) and maintained for another year, when a second attempt at withdrawal should be made. Some patients, however, require indefinite MAOI treatment.

Benzodiazepines

Benzodiazepines are the drugs of choice for acute panic attacks (109). One or two oral or IV doses are sufficient to abolish almost all of the acute symptoms (see Chapter 23). The long-term use of these compounds for the treatment of anxiety disorder continues. As they are addictive and very difficult to discontinue once begun, however, they should be used only if cyclic antidepressants and MAOIs (alone and in combination) plus other therapies have not worked or if the patient cannot tolerate the side effects of other compounds.

Alprazolam, a high-potency compound, is the most commonly used benzodiazepine for panic disorder (3–10 mg daily). It may be as effective as cyclic antidepressants and phenelzine (75). Clonazepam (1.5–5 mg daily) and lorazepam (6–20 mg daily) are also used. Alprazolam and lorazepam are short acting, and three or four daily doses are required. Clonazepam is an intermediate-acting benzodiazepine and can be given b.i.d. The antianxiety effect of benzodiazepines is attributed to their potentiation of GABA.

Cognitive Behavior Therapy

Although cognitive behavior therapy can be mastered by psychopharmacologically oriented physicians (1053), it is generally administered by psychologists. It can be used in conjunction with pharmacotherapy or alone. Behavior therapy is the treatment of choice for simple phobias. For other anxiety disorders, cognitive behavior therapy can be used in combination with medication, or it can be substituted for medication in patients who cannot tolerate drug side effects or who are pregnant or wish to become pregnant and in situations where the risks of pharmacotherapy outweigh its benefits.

Most cognitive behavioral approaches include education of the patient regarding the illness and treatment and training in relaxation techniques. In those approaches that stress cognition, focus is on the identification and modification of panic-related negative thoughts, whereas those approaches that stress behavioral techniques expose the patient to panic-provoking stimuli by using both internal (imagery) and external (in vivo) cues (particularly useful for phobias, including agoraphobia) (390, 797).

There is some evidence (632) that behavioral and pharmacologic treatments act on similar brain receptors. Cyclic antidepressants decrease beta-adrenergic postsynaptic receptors (174), and repeated in vivo exposure to stress in rodents also leads to a decrease in these receptors (947).

Rather rapid exposure is usually recommended for patients with agoraphobia who have few associated panic attacks or who have social or specific phobias. Anxiety levels should not be permitted to become extreme, but they do not need to be very low for successful treatment. Family members or friends can help by participating in the in vivo aspect of this treatment. For agoraphobics with frequent panic attacks and patients with panic disorder, biologic treatments of the panic should be conducted first, followed by exposure therapy, if needed (55, 348). About 75% of patients have a 50% or more reduction in symptoms with exposure techniques (727).

Psychosurgery

Several psychosurgical procedures (e.g., limbic leukotomy, subcaudate tractotomy) are claimed to be effective in treating chronic anxiety disorders, with reported results in uncontrolled trials of about 50 to 60% of patients much improved or recovered. Although a definitive statement on the value of psychosurgery in anxiety states requires the results of randomized, controlled studies, some patients fail a multitude of other biologic therapies expertly administered and then experience marked improvement after psychosurgery. In patients who remain unresponsive to the standard approaches and whose anxiety symptoms seriously impair daily functioning, psychosurgery may be of benefit. The best results are obtained in patients who have supportive families, who do not abuse drugs or alcohol, and who have not exhibited any personality deterioration. As patients undergoing this procedure are usually in good general health, surgical side effects are minimal and typical of any neurosurgical procedure. These include bleeding, infection, and seizures (365, 679).

Theory of Etiology

Theories trying to explain the pathophysiology of anxiety disorders must address the fact that simple and social phobias do not run in families, whereas other anxiety disorders are familial. For example, about 25% of first-degree relatives of agoraphobics also have anxiety disorders, which may include simple panic and generalized anxiety disorder, as well as agoraphobia. Alcoholism and nonmelancholic forms of depression are also more common in these families than in the general population. A large proportion of patients with panic disorder (about 25%) also have relatives with anxiety disorder, and the risk in these relatives is three to four times that of the general population. The same appears true for generalized anxiety disorder. Although few relatives of panic disorder patients have agoraphobia, a considerable number of relatives of agoraphobics have panic disorder. Twin studies find the concordance rates for anxiety disorder (all types combined) for monozygotic and dizygotic twins to be about 30% and 5%, respectively (235, 419, 576, 719, 993).

Most theories of anxiety disorder tend to separate simple phobias from the other anxiety states. Concepts focusing on simple phobias relate the pathophysiology to learning theory, in which the response of anxiety has been conditioned to the phobic stimulus. Tyrer's work on personality deviation and state-related conditions suggests that some deviant traits may predispose individuals to develop phobias. Although this idea has not been adequately studied, it is consistent with a generalized cognitive model of anxiety (868). This model posits that a deviant trait characteristic of increased concern for threat (high harm avoidance) leads to increased baseline physiologic arousal and, thus, a predisposition to being conditioned. Life experience would then determine whether such conditioning would occur.

Most etiologic theories of other anxiety states relate pathophysiology to aberrations in one or another neurotransmitter system: noradrenergic (too much of it), GABAergic (too little of it), or serotonergic (biphasic abnormalities). These theories are based on three observations: (1) anxiety disorders are familial, (2) biologic treatments affecting these neurotransmitter systems are effective in anxiety disorder, and (3) substances, such as sodium lactate and bicarbonate, can induce attacks of panic in most anxiety patients but in few normal control subjects.

Septohippocampal Theory

An intriguing theory of anxiety has been proposed by Gray (383) that implicates the hippocampus and its afferent and efferent connections. This septohippocampal (SH) system is putatively responsible for integrating and responding to novel stimuli, particularly those that suggest punishment or nonreward. The SH system uses memory to predict the next set of stimuli, checks the accuracy of the prediction, and initiates responses to the actual and predicted stimuli. These responses involve motor inhibition and increased arousal and attention. The prefrontal cortex is only secondarily involved in this process, which, if aberrant, could lead to flight-or-fight phenomena without cognitive control. The SH process is driven by noradrenergic and serotonergic systems.

Some support for Gray's theory comes from neuroanatomic and physiologic studies (566); electrical stimulation studies of the amygdala, hippocampus, and parahippocampus (363); PET studies indicating increased uptake in parahippocampal structures (right greater than left) following induction of anxiety with sodium lactate infusion (813); and MRI studies that implicate the temporal lobe in panic disorder. Certain PET data also suggest abnormalities in basal ganglia and in occipital regions in patients with GAD (1085).

Locus Ceruleus Theory

The *locus ceruleus* (LC) is a cluster of about 400 noradrenergic neurons in the pons. It contains nearly half of the brain's noradrenergic neurons and produces more than 70% of total brain noradrenaline. The LC is part of the central control mechanism of the autonomic neuronal system. Its activation leads to fear, alarm, and flight-or-fight behaviors via its influence on the limbic system. Anxiety disorder has been linked to LC dysfunction in anatomic stimulation studies and in clinical physiologic studies of anxiety patients at rest and when stimulated cognitively or by sodium lactate or other anxiety-inducing substances (501).

Gamma-Aminobutyric Acid–Benzodiazepine Theory

GABA is an inhibitory neurotransmitter. It acts by increasing chloride ion permeability of neurons via chloride channels. Increased permeability leads to hyperpolarization and decreased excitability. GABA also may have a direct inhibitory effect on the LC. In addition, GABA is associated with a system of widely scattered receptors that have an affinity for benzodiazepines. One theory of anxiety disorder posits some combination of decreased GABA or benzodiazepine receptors as an underlying mechanism for anxiety symptoms. Psychopharmacologic studies are cited to support this theory (74, 500).

Chapter

16

Obsessional Syndromes

On close scrutiny, several seemingly disparate syndromes can be seen to share the common feature of recurrent, intrusive thoughts or actions (480). The syndromes include obsessive compulsive disorder (OCD); Gilles de la Tourette's syndrome (GTS); anorexia nervosa, and perhaps bulimia, post-traumatic stress disorder (PTSD) (in some patients); and trichotillomania. Some extreme forms of hypochondriasis, particularly when limited to one or a few recurrent health concerns, also can be considered obsessional syndromes, as can some sexual disorders (e.g., exhibitionism) (see Chapter 18).

History

Obsessional traits and their social consequences have been recognized for centuries. Afflicted individuals were once referred to as "irresolute" and plagued by "scruples" or "religious melancholy" (460, 686, 965). OCD was first described as a clearly medical syndrome by Esquirol (288). A German neurologist, Westphal, coined the term "obsessional neurosis" and associated this syndrome with phobias. Kraepelin adopted the term "obsessional neurosis," as did Freud, whose description and theories of the syndrome included compulsions. DSM-III changed the term to obsessive compulsive disorder and incorporated it into the anxiety disorder category.

Although cases of GTS were reported in Great Britain as early as 1663 and the eighteenth-century literary figure, Dr. Samuel Johnson, was described as having ticlike behaviors, the first clear medical description was provided by Itard in 1825. Georges Albert Edouard Brutus Gilles de la Tourette, for whom the syndrome is named, described nine cases in 1885, and highlighted the now well-known triad of multiple tics, coprolalia, and echolalia. Gilles de la Tourette associated the syndrome with multiple phobias and agoraphobia. Studies of GTS during the first half of the twentieth century were dominated by psychoanalytical thought. With the introduction of haloperidol in 1961 as a successful biologic treatment for GTS, research into the biology of the syndrome began (824).

Obsessive Compulsive Disorder

Obsessions are defined as recurrent, unwanted thoughts or impulses recognized (at least initially) by the sufferer as senseless and unpleasant but irresistible. Compulsions are repetitive, ritualistic acts, often but not always driven by obsessive thoughts. The sufferer is virtually never satisfied nor is anxiety significantly reduced following completion of the compulsive behavior.

OCD subtypes have been proposed, although sufferers often have mixed obsessions and compulsions. In decreasing frequency these subtypes are: handwashers (75%); checkers (40%); orderers (9%); repeaters (8%); and pure obsessionals (7%), who experience thoughts and impulses but do not engage in ritualistic behavior. Anxiety in OCD is usually related to a fear of contamination, failing to do something important that might lead to harm, or doing something that might harm others. OCD affects 2 to 3% of the general population, men and women equally. Onset is usually in the late teens or early 20s and virtually never after age 35. Onset can be acute or insidious, and the course can be unremitting (about one half of cases), episodic (about one third of cases), or mixed (773). Nonmelancholic depression, generalized anxiety disorder, and phobic disorder commonly co-occur with OCD (1098).

The relationship between OCD and obsessive compulsive personality disorder (see Chapter 15) is unclear, although Tyrer did find an association between anancastic personality and OCD. Rosenberg (844) found 53% of OCD patients to have preexisting obsessive compulsive personality, and Rasmussen and Tsuang (800, 801) also reported that over one half of OCD patients had obsessive compulsive personality. In contrast, other investigators have found that most patients with OCD have abnormal personalities, but these are often passive-aggressive, avoidant, or dependent (488, 641) and that the distribution in personality types may not differ from that of anxiety disorders. This relationship is supported by epidemiologic data from a large sample in the Baltimore, Maryland, area. The data indicated that the prevalence of obsessive compulsive personality in the general population is 1.7% and that the disorder may be associated familially to other anxiety disorders (708).

OCD appears to be familial. Although the risk for OCD is high in the families of OCD patients, so are the risks for other disorders, especially other anxiety disorders and GTS (213, 455, 1008). In family studies, about 10% of first-degree relatives of OCD patients also have OCD and an additional 10% have obsessional traits. Studies of twins report the concordance rate for OCD to be 30 to 60% for monozygotic twins and 10 to 30% for dizygotic twins. Evidence that patients with OCD have a significantly higher prevalence of type A and a significantly lower prevalence of type B blood groups suggests that the familialness of OCD is of genetic origin.

There is also growing evidence that OCD represents a morbid process (125, 1008, 1094). Frontal lobe, basal ganglia, and limbic system dysfunctions have been proposed as anatomic sites, and secondary OCD has been reported following temporal lobe epilepsy, Parkinson's disease, Huntington's disease, and basal ganglia lesions secondary to carbon monoxide poisoning. OCD patients also have more soft neurologic soft signs than normal subjects (711). Further, PET studies show OCD patients to have increased levels of glucose metabolism in anterior cortical areas, cingulate gyrus, and caudate nuclei (81, 716). Ventricular enlargement and small caudate nuclei volumes have been reported in CT scans of some, but not all, OCD patients. Also, MRI scans have revealed prolonged T1 values in right frontal white matter and T1 asymmetries (right greater than left) in orbital frontal cortex that positively correlate with symptom severity. Bifrontal stereotactic tractotomy of the orbital cortex significantly reduces symptoms in about 50% of OCD patients who are refractory to other treatments.

Electrophysiologic abnormalities also have been recorded in OCD patients. Scalp-recorded EEG studies reveal decreased alpha and increased beta activity, and evoked potential studies find shorter latencies during discrimination tasks. These findings suggest that OCD patients may be in a hyperarousal state. Two recent, remarkably consistent studies of cognitive function in OCD patients (125, 1094) revealed deficits in their visual spatial recall, recognition, and sequencing (particularly in patients with a family history of OCD). The findings were not due to co-occurring anxiety or depression. Both groups of investigators concluded that their data demonstrated cognitive deficits consistent with nondominant hemisphere and basal ganglia dysfunction in OCD patients. These findings are compatible with anatomic brain imaging and metabolic findings in OCD.

Some abnormality in serotonergic systems has been suggested as a biochemical basis for OCD. Serotonin has been implicated as a mediator for repetitive behaviors, impulsivity, and aggression; serotonin reuptake blockers (clomipramine, fluoxetine, fluvoxamine, zimeldine) are effective in ameliorating OCD symptoms. Symptom reduction also has been correlated with a reduction in platelet serotonin and serotonin metabolites in cerebrospinal fluid (798, 1008, 1099).

Gilles de la Tourette's Syndrome

The prevalence of GTS is unknown, but the currently accepted figure of 0.5/1000 population is considered an underestimation. GTS is found in all cultures and racial groups but is rare among African Americans. It is found in all social classes and occurs three to four times more often in males than in females.

Onset is usually before age 15 and, typically, begins around age 7. Although there have been no systematic long-term follow-up studies of GTS, case reports suggest that it is a lifelong illness with phases of exacerbation and relative quiescence. Although acute stress can exacerbate symptoms, no evidence indicates its etiologic importance. Symptoms are also exacerbated by psychostimulant drugs. Contrary to previous thought, tics do not disappear during sleep. There is mixed evidence that birth complications may play an etiologic role in some patients (about 33%) (202, 824).

Tics are the core feature of GTS; tics involving the eyes are the most frequent initial feature (about one half of cases). Vocalizations, most frequently repeated throat clearing, constitute the initial symptom in one third of cases. Coprolalia (uncontrollable paroxysms of profanity), a late feature, is eventually observed in about 60% of patients. GTS patients demonstrate a variety of complex repetitive movements other than tics, such as touching, hitting or striking, jumping or stamping of feet, smelling of hands or objects, retracing steps, twirling, deep-knee bending, or squatting. Echolalia and echopraxia are seen in about one third of patients. Vocalizations also include grunting, coughing, barking, snorting, screaming, hissing, clicking, and inarticulate bursts of sounds.

GTS patients with hyperactivity and attention deficit syndromes and learning disabilities also have been observed. Self-injury has been reported in 10 to 30% of patients, as have antisocial behaviors, such as inappropriate sexual activity and aggressivity, including injury to people and the killing of animals. Sleep disturbances, including insomnia, talking during sleep, nightmares and night terrors, somnambulism, and bruxism, have been observed. As many as one third of patients may have been enuretic, and one fifth have phobias (265, 824).

GTS appears to be familial when the concept of the syndrome is broadened to incorporate pure and chronic tic disorders; however, few systematic family and twin studies are available. One adoption study (886) is uninformative.

Among the family studies, Nee et al. (704) reported one third of GTS probands to have a positive family history for GTS and an additional one third to have a positive family history of tics. Kidd et al. (527) and Pauls et al. (741) also reported a familial relationship between GTS and tics and concluded the latter to be the less severe form of the disorder. Males were found to be more at risk than were females. Comings et al. (215) and Devor (264) also found this familial relationship and suggested that the data were consistent with a single dominant gene whose penetrance varied by gender. Comings and Comings (214) also found that, in addition to tics, first-degree relatives of patients with GTS are also at greater risk for mood disorders. Data from studies of twins are consistent with some genetic liability for GTS; the concordance rates for GTS are about 60% for monozygotic twins and about 10% for dizygotic twins. When GTS and chronic tics are combined, concordance rates increase to about 75 and 25%, respectively (265).

The neurobiology of GTS, although suggestive of a morbid state, is not clear (239). For example, some EEG studies report that about two thirds of patients have nonspecific abnormalities (824), but some do not (709). Evoked potential studies also have been inconsistent; when abnormalities are observed, they appear to result from deficits in attention. One study (991) evaluated the effect of a conditioning stimulus on the blink reflex and reported a response pattern consistent with increased brain stem interneuron excitability.

CT studies in GTS most often have found no abnormalities, although some studies report mild ventricular dilatation and some cortical atrophy (156). In Robertson's summary (824) of this literature, only 10% of CT scans of GTS patients were abnormal. PET findings in GTS patients indicate that some patients have hypometabolism in frontal cingulate and insular cortices and in the corpus striatum (175, 176). Recent neuropsychologic data (127) indicate that patients with GTS have mild deficits in motor and sensory perceptual performance. The last is similar to problems noted in OCD.

Relationship Between OCD and GTS

There is growing evidence that OCD and GTS share a common liability. For example, many of the symptoms of GTS can be interpreted as forms of compulsions, and studies have found that from one third to three fourths of GTS patients have typical OCD symptoms (824, 1008). About 20% of OCD patients have tics (480), and about 70% have either a personal or family history of tics (386). The course of the two syndromes is also similar: early age of onset, lifelong course with waxing and waning of symptoms, involuntary intrusive unwanted behaviors, worsening with depression and anxiety, and co-occurrence of nonmelancholic depression and anxiety disorders (239). In addition, investigators (1087) have suggested that GTS, as OCD, may be a hyposerotonergic condition; however, drugs acting on the serotonergic system apparently do not relieve tics (1023). Frankel et al. (325, 326) have suggested that evidence points to both disorders being related to dysfunction in the basal ganglia or limbic system.

Family studies also demonstrate that the prevalence of OCD is elevated in the first- and second-degree relatives of GTS patients (213, 684, 742). Pitman et al. (765) found more tics in GTS patients with a family history of OCD. Pauls et al. (742) suggested that the family evidence is consistent with a single major gene accounting for tics in some patients and OCD in others, with penetrance weighted toward tics in males and OCD in females.

Other evidence suggestive of a relationship between GTS and OCD includes a positive response to treatment with clonidine (202, 538, 598) and behavior therapy (67, 69, 942); the occurrence of coprolalia (765) and self-mutilation (787, 1087) in OCD and GTS (886, 1035), glucose metabolism abnormalities in frontal lobes and basal ganglia (175, 176, 824, 1008), and similar neuropsychologic deficits on measures of visual-spatial functioning (125, 127, 368, 463, 1008, 1094).

Eating Disorders

Anorexia Nervosa

In this uncommon but serious condition, the patient, typically a teenage girl, develops a gross misperception or overvalued idea that she is significantly overweight and must diet or use other means (e.g., self-induced vomiting, exercise programs, use of diuretics or laxatives) to lose large amounts of weight. She consequently experiences massive weight loss and associated physiologic changes (most, but not all, of which are the product of starvation). She has a 9% chance of dying during the illness from starvation or other causes. Despite the weight loss, which renders her cachectic, she does not perceive herself as gaunt, continues to fear gaining weight, and, until she suffers profound effects of starvation, remains physically active or even overactive. Despite the use of the term anorexia, the patient usually maintains a good appetite and may be preoccupied with food, collect recipes, read cookbooks, and be an enthusiastic cook for others. At times, she may gorge herself with food (bulimia) and avoid weight gain by immediately inducing vomiting.

The diagnosis of anorexia nervosa requires (1) a refusal to maintain body weight within 15% or less of an age and height norm; (2) intense fear of gaining weight or becoming fat, although underweight; and (3) a disturbed body image in which the person "feels" fat. In females, the absence of at least three consecutive expected menstrual cycles is also required. Amenorrhea is extremely common among anorexics; in some patients, the amenorrhea precedes significant weight loss (331). Usually, but not always, menses return when weight is restored. Pregnancy is a rare explanation of some of the symptoms, although conception has been reported (989) during periods of prolonged amenorrhea. Libido is considerably decreased.

Constipation is very frequent, as is diarrhea in patients who abuse laxatives. In addition to gauntness, findings sometimes include narrowing of the shoulders and hips, bradycardia, reduced basal body temperature, dry skin, and loss of scalp hair with retention of pubic and axillary hair. Lanugo hairs (blond, short, "downy" hairs) are often seen on cheeks, neck, forearms, and thighs. Repeated vomiting can lead to dental problems because gastric acidity dissolves tooth enamel. Other observations are parotid gland enlargement (from repeated bouts of emesis and hypochloremic alkalosis); edema; acrocyanosis (a circulatory problem in which the hands or feet are persistently cold, blue, and sweaty); Raynaud's phenomenon (a circulatory problem in which the fingers or toes become pale and painful when exposed to cold temperatures); orange pigmentation of palms and soles (probably due to dietary faddism with overingestion of carotene-containing foods); moderate anemia with associated pallor or petechiae (because of reduced numbers of platelets); and, in rare cases, beriberi, pellagra, vitamin K deficiency, or Korsakoff's encephalopathy (416).

Vomiting and laxative abuse may lead to electrolyte abnormalities and consequent weakness, cardiac arrhythmias, tetany, or convulsions. An unusual complication is duodenal compression by the superior mesenteric artery, which may occur in patients with weight loss from any cause and should be suspected in patients with postprandial abdominal pain or intractable vomiting. The probable mechanism is the dissolution of the fat pad lying between the duodenum and the superior mesenteric artery, which crosses it, as well as the bogginess and lack of coordinated contraction of the duodenum during starvation (146).

Additional behavioral problems include insomnia, diminished concentration, sad mood, suicidal ideation, suicide attempts, and denial of serious illness and the danger of dying. Delirium may occur in advanced cases. The depressions that have been reported, although not well characterized (228, 414), are typically nonmelancholic in form.

Although an uncommon disorder, anorexia nervosa is thought to be increasing in incidence, which is 0.37–1.6/100,000 population/year. Regardless of the population surveyed, about 95% of anorexia nervosa patients are women. Male anorexics are often homosexual (441, 442). Anorexia nervosa is usually described as more common among people of middle and upper socioeconomic status and less common among African Americans. Eighty-five percent of patients develop the illness between the ages of 13 and 20. Onset is rare below age 10 or over age 30.

The course of anorexia nervosa is not benign, and there is serious risk of death (9% in patients who have the illness for 10 years). In one series, 82% of deaths were the product of starvation and its complications and 18% the result of suicide. The complications of starvation included bronchopneumonia or other infections; renal failure; cardiac failure; electrolyte abnormalities resulting from vomiting and the use of purgatives; and complications of invasive medical treatments, such as gastric dilatation from feeding too rapidly, aspiration of tube feedings, and electrolyte imbalance from IV fluids. The first two treatment complications can be avoided by IV hyperalimentation.

Prognosis is mixed, with over 40% of patients fully remitted and 30% considerably improved at follow-up. At least 20% remain unimproved or seriously impaired, however, and 9% die as a result of the illness. The prognosis is worse if age of onset is over 20 or if the patient has (1) failed to respond to previous treatment, (2) has bulimia, or (3) had significant behavior problems prior to the onset of anorexia nervosa (340, 941).

Many laboratory abnormalities have been noted in patients with anorexia nervosa; none of these occurs in all patients or is pathognomonic, and most are products of starvation and disappear when weight becomes normal (654). They include hypokalemia (a serious complication of vomiting or diuretic abuse), hyponatremia, hypochloremic alkalosis, hypercholesterolemia, hypercarotenemia, anemia, thrombocytopenia, leukopenia, hypofibrinogenemia, increased blood urea nitrogen, diminished glomerular filtration rate, decreased basal metabolic rate, decreased erythrocyte sedimentation rate, EEG and electrocardiographic abnormalities, reversible atrophy on CT brain scan, and delayed gastric emptying.

Family studies of anorexics report an increased prevalence of "neuroses" in their first-degree relatives, but anorexia per se is less common except in female relatives, of whom about 10% are affected (499, 608). In addition, parents of anorexia patients (16% of mothers, 23% of fathers) had "weight phobias" or significantly reduced adolescent weight (1071). An increased prevalence of alcoholism, substance abuse, and nonmelancholic depressions also has been noted (40, 503). Also, evidence indicates that bipolar mood disorder is the most prevalent psychiatric illness among the relatives of some anorexic patients (353). Twin studies find monozygotic and dizygotic anorexia nervosa concordance rates to be about 50% and 10%, respectively (451, 914, 951).

Bulimia

Bulimia, meaning binge eating, is a feature of anorexia nervosa and certain neuroendocrine disorders (e.g., Kleine-Levin syndrome) and a fad behavior among some college students. DSM-III-R defines *bulimia nervosa* as a syndrome characterized by (1) episodes of uncontrollable binge eating; (2) episodes of self-induced vomiting, dieting, and fasting and of extreme exercise, all to prevent weight gain; and (3) overvalued ideas regarding body shape and weight. DSM requires at least two binge-eating episodes a week for at least 3 months; however, in practice, this number should be a guideline, rather than a requirement for diagnosis and treatment.

Bulimics typically alternate between binge eating and weight-loss activities, both of which are compulsive in form. Thought content is focused on their eating habits and body weight and shape; in form, it resembles obsession, except that the bulimic, unlike the obsessive in early stages, does not consider preoccupation with food and weight to be undesirable.

Bulimics are often overweight and may have co-occurring depression (unclear in form), alcohol or substance abuse, or kleptomania. Systemic complications include hypokalemic acidosis (from vomiting and increased renal excretion of potassium), dental problems, parotid gland enlargement and esophageal tears (also from vomiting), and metabolic acidosis (particularly from laxative abuse). During weight-loss phases, bulimics may be dehydrated, weak, and lethargic and develop cardiac arrhythmias.

Bulimia nervosa begins in the decade following puberty or, rarely, after age 30. Its demography and epidemiology are similar to that of anorexia nervosa. Bulimia nervosa is a chronic disorder with high rates of relapse (40 to 60%), and many patients experience continuous mild symptomatology. In addition to an association with OCD, evidence indicates that bulimia nervosa is associated with some mood disorders and about 50% of bulimics have one or more depressive episodes. Further, bulimics have increased co-occurrence of drug and alcohol abuse (25 to 30%), anxiety disorders (30 to 50%), and personality disorder (30% with anxious and fearful premorbid personalities) (424, 441, 470).

The etiology of bulimia nervosa is unknown, but it may be familial. Family studies indicate a small increased risk for bulimia in relatives of bulimic patients compared with relatives of control subjects (about 4% versus 2%). Twin studies suggest monozygotic and dizygotic concordance rates of about 25% and 10%, respectively (441, 520).

Laboratory studies in bulimics are difficult to interpret because of the effects of chronic bingeing and purging on many neurotransmitter systems and organ structures. Nevertheless, serotonin neuronal systems modulate appetitive behaviors. Further, serotonin agonists or agonistlike treatments tend to produce satiety, whereas serotonin antagonists or antagonistlike compounds increase food consumption and weight gain. Thus, it has been hypothesized that bulimia nervosa patients suffer from a hyposerotonergic state. Other neurotransmitters (norepinephrine), some neuropeptides (e.g., pancreatic peptide YY), and certain endogenous opioids, however, also play roles in eating behavior (441). The serotonin hypothesis of bulimia nervosa is particularly interesting, as a similar hypothesis has been proposed (214) for OCD and GTS. In this OCD-GTS hypothesis, a major gene (or genes) is theorized to result in low CNS serotonin levels, leading to limbic system and frontal lobe disinhibition and a spectrum of impulsive, compulsive, addictive, sleep, attentional, mood, memory, and anxiety disorders.

Bulimic Epilepsy

A small number of bulimics binge eat as a feature of limbic epilepsy. These patients often report odd abdominal sensations, flashes of light, unusual smells, or increasing anxiety immediately prior to binge eating. They describe their binges as unpredictable and out of their control. Some episodes occur during a depersonalized state. Following the binge eating, the patients have postictal symptoms, such as prolonged sleep, altered consciousness, disorientation, and headaches. Irritability and violent outbursts can occur, as well as episodes of dizziness, paresthesias, déjà vu, and dysmegalopsia. These patients have abnormal EEGs; their bulimic episodes decrease with anticonvulsant treatments (387, 802, 803).

Relationship Between Anorexia and OCD

Anorexia nervosa, as other eating disorders, has been traditionally viewed as a form of obsessive or compulsive behavior (273, 732). Patients with anorexia nervosa often develop a pervasive, obsessive interest in exercise and engage in ritualistic eating behaviors. Several studies have demonstrated that patients with anorexia nervosa have many obsessive and compulsive behaviors and that some obsessional patients have a history of anorexia nervosa. For example, Kasvikis et al. (500), studying 280 OCD patients, found that 10% of the women had had anorexia nervosa. These patients had an earlier age of onset of OCD than those without co-occurring anorexia. None of the male OCD patients or agoraphobics had a history of anorexia. Recently, Pigott et al. (762) also observed significant eating disorder behaviors in OCD patients. In this study, however, both male and female OCD patients exhibited these features. There is also some evidence that patients with anorexia nervosa have preexisting obsessional personality traits (342).

Indirect evidence for an association between OCD and anorexia nervosa comes from studies of nonhumans. Although biologic studies of anorexic patients have focused on the role of the hypothalamus in the disorder, studies in rodents indicate that lesions in the striatum result in prolonged aphagia and weight loss in females but not in males (254, 255). This finding is consistent with studies implicating basal ganglia lesions in OCD (176).

Other Obsessive Syndromes

Post-traumatic stress disorder (PTSD) is characterized by recurrent, intrusive thoughts suggestive of obsessional thinking. Epidemiologic studies indicate that many PTSD patients meet diagnostic criteria for OCD (see Chapter 15). Trichotillomania, or compulsive hair pulling, although classified as an impulse control disorder, also may be related to OCD, as are certain forms of hypochondriasis.

Management

The most effective treatment for OCD and related disorders is psychopharmacologic or behavioral. Combined therapy is also useful.

Pharmacotherapy

Drugs that effectively reduce OCD symptoms block serotonin reuptake, although not all serotonin uptake blockers (e.g., sertraline) are effective in treating OCD. The drug of choice remains clomipramine, a chlorinated tricyclic antidepressant. Successful treatment (about half of patients have a moderate to marked response) requires maximum doses (about 300 mg daily) for at least 12 weeks (191). A newer serotonin reuptake blocker, fluvoxamine (also about 300 mg daily), and fluoxetine (at 80 mg daily) are also effective. Buspirone, a piperazinelike sedative compound with serotonergic action, has been used with fluoxetine or fluvoxamine in the treatment of OCD (740). Daily doses range from 15 to 60 mg.

Successful treatment requires maintaining the therapeutic dose for at least 1 year to prevent relapse. After 1 year, medication should be tapered (over a 3-month period) and then discontinued. Medication should be reinstituted when relapse occurs and maintained for an additional year, at which time a second withdrawal attempt should be considered. Some patients need to be on medication indefinitely, although combining pharmacotherapy with cognitive behavior therapy may reduce this number. OCD patients resistant to serotonin reuptake blockade and who also have tics may benefit from the addition of neuroleptics, haloperidol (6–16 mg daily) or pimozide (2–12 mg) (464, 481, 483, 648). Although haloperidol remains the standard pharmacologic agent for the treatment of patients with GTS, fluoxetine (20–40 mg daily) also may benefit these patients (216).

Anorexics and bulimics may require hospitalization. In addition to cyclic antidepressants, anorexics also may respond to antihistamines (e.g., cyproheptadine). Bulimics respond to cyclic antidepressants, phenelzine, and perhaps carbamazepine (415, 441, 457, 507). Recent evidence indicates that some bulimics can benefit from cognitive behavior therapy and interpersonal therapy; treatment manuals for both of these approaches exist (441).

Behavioral Therapy

Behavioral therapy appears to work best for OCD patients with well-defined compulsive rituals. Treatment centers on in vivo systematic stepwise exposure (habituation) to the obsessional fear, coupled with prevention from carrying out the associated compulsive behavior. Relaxation techniques are used to facilitate exposure and restraint, as are thought-stopping techniques (the therapist interrupting the obsessions by shouting "stop") and paradoxical intention and mass practice (the patient is instructed to think continuously of the obsession to the point of fatigue). Seventy-five percent of patients may benefit from these procedures; long-term benefit correlates best with longer (6 weeks) treatment schedules (55, 631, 727).

Psychosurgery

Stereotactic cingulotomy has been used for more than 25 years to treat OCD patients who fail to respond to all other treatments (including modern pharmacotherapy). As patients who undergo this procedure for OCD are generally systemically healthy and have no coarse brain disease, side effects from neurosurgery (bleeding, infection, seizures) are infrequent and, when they occur, remediable. Patients whose personalities and family support structure remain intact are the best candidates; about one third experience substantial improvement (482).

Chapter 17

Substance Abuse

Alcohol-Related Syndromes

History

The official acceptance of alcoholism as a disease state was relatively recent in history. No hospital for the treatment of alcoholism existed anywhere in the world before 1857, when the first one was established in the United States. The first medical group for the study of alcoholism was founded in 1870, also in the United States (674). Much of the reluctance of society, in general, and the medical profession, in particular, to endorse the disease model of alcoholism stemmed from indecision as to whether drinking was fully under the control of the alcoholic. Attitudinal advances of the early twentieth century were severely blunted by the prohibition movement in the United States. Physicians were forced to accept the societal view that alcohol and other addictions were moral and legal, but not medical, problems. The study of alcohol and drug addiction was removed from medical school curricula, and research of addictions was dramatically curtailed.

Alcoholics Anonymous (AA) was founded in 1840. This organization played an important role in supporting the disease concept of alcoholism. Its heavy reliance on spiritual exercises derived from the writings of St. Ignatius, founder of the Jesuit order of priests (AA's 12 steps), and its opposition to medical treatment for alcoholism (including psychopharmacology for alcoholics with co-occurring mood disorder), however, limit its therapeutic effectiveness and help to maintain the nondisease aura surrounding addictions.

Jellinek's monograph, *The Disease Concept of Alcoholism* (478), published during the decade when biologic psychiatry began to reassert itself, reestablished the legitimacy of the disease concept of alcoholism. His classification of alcoholism and his concepts of the relationships among tolerance, dependence, and addiction are still reflected in present day nosology. For example, DSM-I and DSM-II, include alcoholism among the personality disorders. DSM-III and DSM-III-R, however, place alcoholism under substance use disorders and as a distinct condition of abuse or dependence. Nevertheless, a relationship appears to exist between some forms of alcoholism and some personality traits (194).

Definition

An alcoholic is an individual whose alcohol use results in medical, social, occupational, or legal problems. Alcoholics are often overtly intoxicated (greater than twice monthly), and many suffer a progressive deteriorating course despite periods of abstinence (478). Alcoholism is best defined by its consequences, rather than the amount of alcohol consumed, although there is a rough correlation between duration and degree of alcohol consumption and its adverse results. Thus, a heavy drinker—an individual who drinks 2 to 3 drinks daily, and is occasionally intoxicated—is not, by definition, a problem drinker. Probably, 10 to 20% of the U.S. population are heavy drinkers (10 to 15% of men, 3 to 5% of women) and 3 to 5% of men and 1% of women are alcoholics (1016). In the United States, heavy drinking is concentrated in high-income groups and in Euro-Americans. Expectancy rates in other countries are similar. Alcoholism (as opposed to just heavy drinking) is more prevalent in the United States among males, non-Baptists, African Americans, urbanites, people with antisocial personality or mood disorders, waiters, bartenders, longshoremen, musicians, and writers (257, 619, 830). The onset for men occurs during their late teens or 20s, whereas the onset is more variable for women. It is a misconception to think of an alcoholic only as someone who has cirrhosis, withdrawal episodes, and gin for breakfast. These are features of chronic drinking. In the early stages of the disorder, the alcoholic is more likely to experience family objections to his "drinking too much," the loss of friends because of drinking, and periods of self-doubt about drinking too much. Continued drinking usually leads to trouble at work or loss of a job, arrests for drunk driving or disturbing the peace, fights when drinking, and unsuccessful attempts at abstinence prior to the time when the alcoholic begins drinking before breakfast, experiences loss of memory when drinking, or suffers from physical deterioration caused by alcohol (373).

DSM distinguishes alcohol abuse from alcohol dependence. Abuse is characterized by persistent use that can lead to the adverse consequences described above. Dependence is characterized by evidence of (1) physiologic and psychological tolerance (the need to increase markedly the amount of alcohol, withdrawal syndrome when it is discontinued), (2) characteristic withdrawal symptoms, (3) more frequent use and intoxication, and (4) more frequent or severe adverse consequences. There is no evidence that abusers and dependent drinkers differ demographically or clinically other than in severity. Some investigators (466) further classify alcoholics into two types. One type is distinguished by early onset (in the teens), antisocial personality traits, male gender, positive family history for alcoholism, and poor response to treatment. A second type is distinguished by later onset (late 20s or 30s), more gradual increase in consumption, anxious personality traits, no family history of alcoholism, no gender distinction, and a better prognosis. About 75% of alcoholics fit into this second category.

Also suggestive of alcohol abuse or dependence are the following 11 features:

1. Acne rosacea
2. Palmer erythema
3. Full head of white hair in a middle-aged male
4. Barrel chest and potbelly in an individual with thin musculature of the limbs
5. Chest bruises from repeated falls
6. Cigarette burns between index and middle fingers
7. Enlarged painless liver
8. Food intolerance with upper abdominal tenderness radiating to the back
9. Reduced strength and sensation in lower limbs
10. Impotence in males
11. Abnormal laboratory studies indicating liver dysfunction or high levels of blood gamma-glutamyltransferase (elevated in more than 50% of alcohol abusers [997]).

Approximately 10% of admissions to short-term psychiatric treatment units in general hospitals are alcohol related (819). Alcoholics who are acutely intoxicated, withdrawing from alcohol, or suffering from Wernicke-Korsakoff syndrome, generally should not be admitted to such units. When these patients are admitted, it is usually because of antisocial trait behavior or odd or suicidal behavior associated with mood disorder. No effective treatment is known for antisocial personality, and the efficacy of treatments for primary alcoholism remains unclear. The best strategy in dealing with the heavy-drinking patient with antisocial personality is to prevent him from disrupting the care of others by immediate discharge from the general psychiatric unit. If the patient is motivated, referral to AA, an alcohol rehabilitation program, or a disulfiram maintenance program may be beneficial (373, 374).

Becuase 25 to 30% of manic-depressives are problem drinkers (see Chapter 11), a large number of patients with concomitant mood disorder and alcoholism are hospitalized. The majority of these patients are bipolar. They are also difficult to treat. In several double-blind studies (296, 535, 668), lithium was found superior to placebo in patients who suffered from both alcoholism and affective disorder; however, as the dropout rate in these studies was high, the number of patients likely to respond to lithium was unclear. Maintenance treatment is also complicated by the likelihood of relapse of one or the other condition and the sometimes dogmatic opposition of AA to support patients receiving any medication. ECT for the acute affective episode, followed by maintenance ECT to prevent future manic or depressive episodes, is a practical and efficacious alternative treatment plan. Disulfiram, which interferes with the metabolism of alcohol by blocking the action of acetaldehyde dehydrogenase, thus resulting in a buildup of acetaldehyde, also is helpful for some alcoholics (373, 374).

Behavior

Alcohol Intoxication

Acute alcohol intoxication is characterized by facial flushing, slurred speech, ataxia, nystagmus, mild diffuse cognitive impairment, loquacity, circumstantial and rambling speech, euphoria (initially), irritability, sadness, and emotional lability. Intoxication is directly related to the blood alcohol level, which is dependent on the amount and rate of alcohol consumed, the individual's body weight, and degree of pharmacologic tolerance (see Table 17.1) (173). Psychiatric intervention is usually sought because of combative or suicidal behavior.

Management focuses on controlling self-destructive or dangerous behavior. A calm, firm, and reassuring manner is sufficient to manage the majority of patients. Restraints and benzodiazepine sedation occasionally may be required (little potentiation occurs; doses as high as 50–100 mg chlordiazepoxide have been given successfully). Vital signs should be monitored, blood alcohol levels obtained, and the patient observed to prevent aspiration from vomiting. If blood levels are above 300 mg% (usually producing stupor or coma), high doses of IV fructose can significantly lower them. Alcohol is metabolized at a rate of about 1 ounce per hour; the acutely intoxicated, but otherwise healthy, individual recovers spontaneously in a short period of time (597).

TABLE 17.1

Alcohol Intoxication*

*Consumption***	*Blood Level*	*Behavior*
One or two drinks***	75 mg%	Decreased inhibitions Slightly delayed reaction time
Three drinks	75–100 mg%	Delayed reaction time Slight dysarthria and fine motor ataxia
Four drinks	100–150 mg%	Intoxication
Five drinks	>150 mg%	Sleepiness, truncal ataxia

*For nonaddicted individuals who weigh 140–175 lb.

**Rate of one drink/30 min.

***One drink = 1 oz. 100-proof alcohol; 4 oz. of wine; 12 oz. beer.

Death from acute alcohol intoxication usually follows the concomitant ingestation of sedatives or CNS depressants (373). A general screening for drugs should always be obtained. Diabetic acidosis or hypoglycemia (best treated with IV glucose) or alcohol-disulfiram reactions (flushing, tachycardia, hypotension, headache and dizziness, nausea and vomiting—best treated with pressor agents, ascorbic acid, and antihistamines) are life-threatening conditions that can masquerade as simple alcohol intoxication and also must be ruled out (1030).

Alcohol Withdrawal

The alcohol withdrawal syndrome is associated with a sudden and precipitous drop in the consumption of alcohol. Most commonly, however, the patient continues to drink but switches from high- to low-alcohol–containing beverages. The syndrome is characterized by coarse tremors of the hand, tongue, and eyelids; nausea and vomiting, general weakness and malaise; tachycardia; sweating; hypertension and orthostatic hypotension; dysphoria and irritability; and, when severe, some alteration in consciousness, diffuse cognitive impairment, insomnia, agitation, and, at times, extreme excitement. Severity of withdrawal is positively correlated with the degree and duration of alcohol consumption and inversely related to the patient's general physical health (e.g., a severe syndrome is more often observed in association with pancreatitis, infection, hepatic insufficiency, subdural hematoma, fractures, or vitamin deficiencies). In most cases, withdrawal is benign and short-lived. When withdrawal is severe (about 5% of patients develop delirium tremens), the patient exhibits an alteration in consciousness and may experience illusions and hallucinations in any sensory modality. These patients commonly have visual hallucinations, although auditory hallucinations are by no means rare (962, 1030).

Initial emergency treatment may require temporary restraints. Prolonged restraints are contraindicated; patients with alcohol withdrawal delirium may struggle against restraints until they are dangerously exhausted. Rapid sedation with anxiolytics is essential. Doses should be titrated against the patient's initial response, with mild sedation being the goal. An initial dose of 50–100 mg of chlordiazepoxide or 15–20 mg of diazepam IV should temporarily control the typical withdrawal delirium and provide an indication (based on the patient's sedative response) for a definitive withdrawal drug schedule, which may be as high as 600 mg of chlordiazepoxide daily (302). Some clinicians prefer 10–15 mL of fresh IM paraldehyde initially to control withdrawal agitation. Anxiolytics, however, have advantages over paraldehyde. IM paraldehyde is painful, whereas IV anxiolytics (particularly diazepam) have anticonvulsant properties. Also, unlike paraldehyde, they are not excreted through the lungs and so do not produce a horrendous olfactory barrier to further interactions with the patient (374). As spontaneous seizures during withdrawal are not uncommon, 100 mg of oral or IV diphenylhydantoin (poorly absorbed IM) also may be administered during emergency treatment and maintained at an oral daily dose of 400 mg during the detoxification period. Administration of anticonvulsants beyond this period is not justified. Hospitalization is always required. Additional treatment with IM thiamine, 100 mg twice daily (alcoholics often have a mild malabsorption syndrome), and multivitamins, particularly B complex and C, is important and may prevent a Wernicke-Korsakoff syndrome (1031). Magnesium sulfate (1 g/2 mL q.i.d. IM for 2 days) to prevent seizures secondary to hypomagnesemia is of questionable benefit (665). Fluid and electrolyte administration is rarely needed unless the patient's hematocrit is elevated and he exhibits other signs of dehydration. Most alcoholics are overhydrated, and seizures may be induced with unnecessary IV fluid administration. IV glucose also should be avoided; thiamine is a cofactor in carbohydrate metabolism, and a heavy carbohydrate load may further deplete thiamine stores (597).

Neuroleptics are contraindicated. They lack cross-tolerance properties with alcohol, suppress the immune system (already compromised in many alcoholics), lower the seizure threshold, tax hepatic metabolic processes, and increase morbidity and mortality rates. Barbiturates, used in some centers, are not recommended because they are mycardial irritants, and alcoholics in withdrawal often have cardiac arrhythmias.

When hallucinations persist after all signs of delirium have abated, the patient is said to have alcoholic hallucinosis (1032). The etiology of this disorder is unclear. Several studies have failed to demonstrate a relationship to schizophrenia in either outcome (90% recover by 6 months) or family history (low for schizophrenia, high for alcoholism) (882). As these patients have not responded to benzodiazepines during the acute phase of their disorder, neuroleptics or ECT may be beneficial.

Wernicke's Syndrome

This delirious state is characterized by sudden onset of ophthalmoplegia (most often abducens nerve/external rectus muscle paralysis), nystagmus (almost always present), ataxia, memory loss, altered consciousness, and diffuse cognitive impairment. Signs of peripheral neuropathy and myocarditis also may be present, and a history of Korsakoff's syndrome is typical. Wernicke's syndrome is most commonly observed in alcoholics, although any cause of profound thiamine deficiency (e.g., gastric carcinoma, pernicious anemia, hyperemesis gravidarum, malnutrition) can produce the syndrome in a genetically vulnerable individual.

The acute phase usually remits rapidly with IM thiamine and multivitamins. A residual Korsakoff's syndrome is the most common sequela. Five percent of patients die. Emergency treatment consists of restraints, when necessary; parenteral thiamine hydrochloride (50 mg); sedation with chlordiazepoxide (25-50 mg p.o. or IV) or diazepam (10–15 mg p.o. or IV); and hospitalization. As in the treatment of withdrawal syndromes, IV fluid and electrolyte replacement should not be routinely administered (1031).

Alcohol-Related Delusional Disorder

Patients with this disorder are usually male. Typically, they are chronic heavy drinkers who have had few alcohol-related difficulties until their sixth or seventh decade when they become increasingly suspicious, sullen, irritable, and finally delusional. Delusional ideas usually involve themes of a spouse's infidelity, a relative's dishonesty, a neighbor's "dirty tricks," or a municipality's illegal action. These patients become neighborhood cranks and are finally hospitalized when local authorities run out of patience from constant complaints or litigation or when family members become exasperated or fearful that the patient may hurt someone. These patients do not appear depressed or manic.

Although cortical atrophy and cognitive impairment secondary to chronic heavy alcohol use have not been fully established (158, 287), many patients with alcohol-related delusional disorder exhibit mild to moderate cortical atrophy and cognitive impairment. Occasionally, neuroleptics may be required if the delusions do not fully resolve with strict abstinence and multivitamin treatment.

Drug Abuse and Dependence

DSM-III-R requires the presence of any three of nine clinical features for the diagnosis of psychoactive substance dependence. These criteria incorporate four principles:

1. Loss of control over drug ingestion (i.e., larger amounts taken, or for a longer period of time, than intended; unsuccessful efforts to decrease or cease use; continued use despite awareness of adverse effects; a great deal of time spent in drug taking)
2. Frequent intoxication
3. Evidence of physiologic tolerance
4. Adverse consequences of use (e.g., social, occupational, health)

Drugs of abuse include sedative hypnotics and anxiolytics, opiates, stimulants, hallucinogens, arylcyclohexylamines (phencyclidine), cannabis, and inhalants. The most widely used and highly addicting drugs, however, are caffeine and nicotine, followed by alcohol. The abuse of other substances is also widespread, although the true degree of use is unclear. Some recent data suggest that, in urban areas, the lifetime prevalence for abuse or dependence is about 6%. Abuse is most common in males and urban African Americans. Drug use (as opposed to abuse) is much greater, with over 20% of Americans regularly using marijuana and 25% using cocaine. Patterns and prevalence of use fluctuate, however, as they are influenced by availability, cost, and fad. More than 50% of crimes are drug related (549, 675).

Drug abusers who are not suffering from an induced psychosis, delirium, or a coarse brain syndrome secondary to drugs should not be admitted to a general psychiatric inpatient unit. These patients are manipulative and often have marked antisocial traits. They inevitably disrupt the care of other patients and sometimes introduce street drugs into the unit.These patients are best treated in specialized detoxification and rehabilitation programs. The chronic abuser is also encountered on medical and surgical hospital services (101). Table 17.2 lists common drugs of abuse.

Sedatives-Hypnotics and Anxiolytics: Intoxication and Withdrawal

Sedatives-hypnotics, all synthetic chemicals, are general CNS depressants that produce sedation (in small doses) and sleep (in larger doses). Meprobamate and methaqualone have particularly high potential for abuse. The latter was increasingly used in the 1980s by adolescents who falsely believed it to be an aphrodisiac. People who habitually use sedatives-hypnotics tend to cluster into two groups: (1) young, often antisocial males and (2) middle-aged, often middle-class individuals who are initially prescribed a sedative-hypnotic for anxiety or sleep disorder and then continue to use the drug as physiologic tolerance and, eventually, addiction develop.

The clinical features of sedative-hypnotic intoxication are similar to those of simple alcohol intoxication. These patients, however, tend to be healthier than alcoholics. Behavioral management is similar to that for alcohol intoxication, with special attention being given to the possibility of masked hypoglycemia as the cause of the syndrome. High blood levels of a sedative-hypnotic, unlike those of alcohol, are likely to induce respiratory arrest, and patients who are markedly lethargic should be treated in medical intensive care units (449).

In mild cases of intoxication, behavioral treatment includes a safe, quiet environment where the patient's behavior, vital signs, and level of consciousness can be regularly observed. Restraints may be necessary for agitated patients. The semicomatose or comatose patient should be intubated following gastric lavage and ventilated, if necessary. Activated charcoal should be introduced into the stomach to absorb any remaining drug, and the urine should be alkalinized with sodium bicarbonate infusion (helpful primarily for phenobarbital intoxication). If meprobamate is the offending agent, a 20% IV solution of mannitol (at a rate of 50 cc/hour) should be administered. Fluid and electrolyte balance should be maintained. Aqueous or lipid hemodialysis may be helpful in removing most of the sedative-hypnotic from the blood. IV naloxone (0.4 mg) and 50% glucose (50 cc), in nonalcoholics, should be routinely given if the specific coma-causing drug is not known (250, 449).

The sedative-hypnotic withdrawal syndrome is virtually identical to that of alcohol withdrawal, with the important exceptions that coarse tremor is not always

TABLE 17.2

Common Drugs of Abuse

Sedatives-Hypnotics and Anxiolytics
Chloral hydrate
Barbiturates
a. Long acting (phenobarbital [Luminal])
b. Short acting (secobarbital [Seconal], pentobarbital [Nembutal], amobarbital [Amytal])
Methyprylon (Noludar)
Ethchlorvynol (Placidyl)
Ethinamate (Valmid)
Meprobamate (Miltown, Equanil)
Methaqualone (Quaalude)
Benzodiazepines
a. Long acting (chlordiazepoxide [Librium])
b. Short acting (clorazepam, oxazepam)
c. Intermediate acting (diazepam [Valium])

Opiates
Opium (10% morphine)
Heroin (diacetylmorphine)
Morphine
Meperidine (Demerol)
Oxymorphone (Percodan)
Codeine (methylmorphine)

Opiatelike
Talwin (pentazocine)
d-Propoxyphene (Darvon)

Sympathomimetics
Cocaine
Amphetamines
a. Amphetamines (Benzedrine)
b. Dextroamphetamine (Dexedrine)
c. Methamphetamine (Methedrine)
Amphetamine congeners
a. Methylphenidate (Ritalin)
b. Phenmetrazine (Preludin)

Hallucinogens
D-Lysergic acid diethylamide-25 (LSD)
Peyote
Mescaline (trimethoxyphenylethylamine)
Psilocybin (related to serotonin)
Corymbos (morning glory seeds [related to LSD])
Myristica (nutmeg)

Arylcyclohexylamines
Phencyclidine (PCP)

Marijuana
Cannabis (marijuana [tetrahydrocannabinol])

Inhalants
Nitrous oxide
Glues
Paints, lacquers (e.g., Toluene)
Paint thinner (e.g., turpentine)
Refrigerants (e.g., Freon)
Gasoline
Solvents (e.g., acetone)
Aerosols
Nitrites

present and grand mal seizures (also observed in alcohol withdrawal syndromes) may occur early in the withdrawal period. Symptoms begin 12 to 48 hours after the last dose but may be delayed as long as 7 to 10 days for long-acting compounds. Severity of symptoms is directly related to the daily dose and the duration of usage. With most sedatives-hypnotics, the clinician should suspect addiction if daily use at therapeutic doses or higher has occurred for more than 30 days. After 90 days of use at or above the therapeutic dosage range, addiction is virtually guaranteed. Treatment requires hospitalizing the patient (on a medical service), mildly sedating the patient with a sedative-hypnotic, and then withdrawing it over a period of 10 to 12 days (250, 449, 604).

Detoxification from barbiturates is best accomplished with pentobarbital, which should be administered initially as a 200-mg test dose by mouth and again every 2 hours until the patient exhibits mild ataxia, dysarthria, nystagmus, and lethargy. If a total of 400 mg or less produces intoxication, no further treatment is needed. If a total of 600 mg or more is needed to achieve intoxication, the patient should be placed on that daily amount in divided doses given every 6 hours. Dose reduction, beginning after 24 hours, should start with the morning and mid-day doses, with the time of dose reduction rotating so that the evening dose is retained as long as possible. Thus, for example, a patient requiring 800 mg of pentobarbital to become intoxicated would receive the following withdrawal schedule (in mg):

Day 1: 200, 200, 200, 200
Day 2: 160, 160, 200, 200
Day 3: 160, 160, 160, 160
Day 4: 120, 120, 160, 160
Day 5: 120, 120, 120, 120
Day 6: 80, 80, 120, 120
Day 7: 80, 80, 80, 80
Day 8: 80, 80, 80
Day 9: 40, 40, 80
Day 10: 40, 40
Day 11: 40
Day 12: no medication (449)

Nonbarbiturate (anxiolytic) sedative-hypnotic withdrawal is best accomplished by using the offending agent at the dose determined from a benzodiazepine challenge, milligram for milligram. If the patient is addicted to a benzodiazepine, a barbiturate challenge may result in a false-negative response. An equivalent challenge can be performed with an initial 50-mg dose of chlordiazepoxide administered by mouth and repeated every 2 hours until intoxication. Intoxication at 100 mg or less requires no further treatment. If a total of 150 mg or more is needed to induce intoxication, the patient should be placed on that amount in divided doses given every 8 hours for the first 24 hours. The dose should be reduced by 25 mg daily, following a schedule similar to that for barbiturates. Thus, a patient requiring 250 mg of chlordiazepoxide to become intoxicated would receive the following schedule (in mg):

Day 1: 75, 75, 100
Day 2: 75, 75, 75
Day 3: 50, 75, 75
Day 4: 50, 50, 75
Day 5: 50, 50, 50
Day 6: 25, 50, 50
Day 7: 25, 25, 50
Day 8: 25, 25, 25
Day 9: 25, 25
Day 10: 25
Day 11: no medication (449)

Alprozolam is particularly associated with dependence, and the withdrawal should be done slowly by about 10% of the dose level per week (664). There is some evidence that chronic use of CNS depressants can result in cognitive impairment and EEG changes that persist long beyond cessation of drug use (380, 382).

Opiate Intoxication and Withdrawal

Opiate addiction in western countries primarily involves heroin and methadone (see Table 17.2). The latter is often obtained at methadone clinics. Heroin may be sniffed ("snorting") or injected subcutaneously ("skin popping") or IV ("mainlining"). Methadone is usually taken orally. The number of addicted individuals is not known, although estimates suggest at least 500,000 in the United States. Urban African Americans and Hispanic Americans comprise the majority of opiate addicts. Physicians and nurses form the next largest group of opiate users (102, 702). Opiate use appears to be fairly constant during the past decade.

Opiate intoxication is characterized by euphoria or dysphoria followed by apathy, psychomotor retardation, slurred speech, impaired attention, concentration and memory, and then somnolence. Initially, IV administration produces flushing and a lower abdominal sensation, described as similar to orgasm ("the rush"). The second stage is a period of drowsiness ("the nod"), during which opium dreams can occur. Pupillary constriction is always initially present, but, in comatose anoxic patients, pupillary dilatation can occur. Other signs of severe intoxication are respiratory distress, apnea with cyanosis, areflexia, hypotension, and tachycardia. Pulmonary edema and grand mal seizures can occur. Needle tracks, or scarring of veins, resulting from repeated IV injection of drugs is a classic physical feature of addiction (102).

Treatment for opiate intoxication includes maintaining adequate oxygenation, preventing aspiration of vomitus, and maintaining cardiac output and blood pressure. IV naloxone (0.4 mg) is an extremely safe narcotic antagonist that should be given immediately (diluted in 10 cc of sterile normal saline) to any patient suspected of medically dangerous opiate intoxication. This dose can be repeated three or four times within the first 10 minutes of treatment if no response is seen. Intrajugular or intrafemoral vein administration is required when the usual sites of IV administration are scarred and unusable. Pupillary dilatation is often the first sign of a response. Restraints should be applied prior to naloxone injection; if it is effective, the patient awakes in severe withdrawal and is agitated, disoriented, and irritable. Severe delirium should be controlled with IV benzodiazepines. As most opiates have a longer half-life than naloxone, repeated doses may be necessary. Constant observation is essential during the next 24 hours to prevent respiratory arrest (102).

Opiate withdrawal is rarely life threatening and virtually never as dramatic as its cinematic analog. As most opiates are short acting, withdrawal signs, even if mild, begin within 8 to 12 hours after the last dose. Peak severity occurs 24 to 36 hours before withdrawal symptoms start to abate. Residual features, such as restlessness, fatigue and insomnia, last for several weeks.

The withdrawal syndrome begins with restlessness, dysphoria, lethargy, and fitful sleep, followed by tearing, nasal discharge, sweating, yawning and deep sighing respirations. These features can all be self-induced (plucking a nasal hair produces tearing and nasal discharge) or feigned, and treatment should not begin until the patient experiences piloerection. If severe addiction remains untreated, chills, muscle and joint pain, abdominal cramps, vomiting and diarrhea, tachycardia, hypertension, and fever can occur. Anorexia, insomnia, anxiety, and agitation also may be prominent (102).

Opiate abusers should not be admitted to a general psychiatric unit. These patients are frequently manipulative, disruptive, untruthful, and unpleasant. Detoxification may be required for patients occasionally admitted to medical or surgical units for drug-related conditions (e.g., hepatitis, thrombophlebitis, subcutaneous abscesses, endocarditis, pulmonary infection or emobli, osteomyelitis). These patients, however, often disrupt medical staff routine. Careful counseling and education of nursing personnel are essential if the detoxification period is to proceed without major uproar.

Detoxification from opiates is accomplished with oral methadone. If an initial test dose of 20 mg causes intoxication, no further treatment is needed. Rarely does a patient need more than 40 mg daily, divided into morning and evening doses. The following typical withdrawal schedule (in mg) reduces the dose by 5 mg each day:

Day 1: 20, 20
Day 2: 15, 20
Day 3: 15, 15
Day 4: 10, 15
Day 5: 10, 10
Day 6: 5, 10
Day 7: 5, 5
Day 8: 0, 5
Day 9: no medication

Flurazepam (30 mg p.o.) for sleep should be routinely administered throughout the withdrawal period (102). Clonidine, an alpha-adrenergic agonist, (0.1–0.3 mg t.i.d. for up to 2 weeks) also has been reported to alleviate opiate withdrawal (528).

The course of opiate addiction is probably dependent on factors other than the pharmacologic effects of opiates. For example, in one study, where most of the subjects also had a personality disorder, 98% relapsed within a 12-month period (1018), whereas among Vietnam veterans who used opium during their tour in Vietnam, less than 2% continued to use the drug during the year after their return to the United States (222). Another reason for relapse has been attributed to the return of detoxified patients to the environment in which they had used drugs, where they experience a conditioned craving (i.e., the conditioned abstinent syndrome) (179). Evidence indicates that methadone maintenance (1 to 2 years) substantially reduces the criminal activity of prior heroin addicts and that one-third of patients who remain on methadone maintenance eventually become abstinent after stopping treatment (946). A significant proportion of patients who receive methadone maintenance, however abuse cocaine or alcohol, and some sequester part of their doses for illicit street sales. Today, the most pressing problem affecting IV heroin addicts is their risk for HIV infection.

Stimulants

The two major stimulants of abuse are cocaine and the amphetamines. Cocaine is a naturally occurring CNS stimulant extracted from the leaves of the South American coca plant. It has no cross tolerance with the amphetamines. Cocaine can be physiologically addicting, but most users do not become addicted. Crack cocaine appears to be highly addictive (346). Cocaine use in the United States is of epidemic proportions and now affects all ethnic and social groups in urban and non-urban areas. Through 1985, an estimated 25 to 40 million Americans had used cocaine (703). It can be inhaled as a powder, dissolved in water and injected IV, or smoked as an ether extract ("free-basing"). Most street cocaine is adulterated ("cut") with talcum power or dry milk. Crack cocaine, free of cutting agents and salts, is highly potent and can lead to stroke and cardiac arrest (638). Because of cocaine's short but intense euphoric effect, some patients frequently readminister the drug over a period of 8 to 12 hours. Such binges cause rapid mood changes.

Cocaine produces peripheral vasoconstriction; increased body temperature and metabolic rate; excessive sweating; mydriasis, increased heart rate and blood pressure; and a sense of expansiveness, unlimited energy, and euphoria. Intoxication is also characterized by irritability, suspiciousness, fearfulness, jerky agitation, stereotypy, tactile hallucinations of insects crawling on or just under the skin ("cocaine bugs" or formication), visual hallucinations (classically of geometric shapes and patterns), and the potential for violence. Respiratory depression, hyperpyrexia, hypertension, and seizures can occur; each of these can result in sudden death (101, 102, 753).

Cocaine withdrawal is referred to as the "crash." It usually follows binge use and is characterized by anergia, anhedonia, anxiety, agitation, hypersomnolence, and dysphoria. Withdrawal begins shortly after the last dose, and symptoms peak during the next 12 to 96 hours. The best management consists of providing a controlled, calm setting and permitting the patient to sleep.

Amphetamine and dextroamphetamine are synthetic substitutes for ephedrine, which occurs naturally in a desert plant indigenous to China. Oral and IV doses of amphetamine and its congeners (methlyphenidate and phenmetrazine) have similar, although longer lasting and milder, acute effects than cocaine. Physical tolerance also develops to amphetamine. Chronic amphetamine and cocaine use can result in a delusional, hallucinatory disorder. Stereotypy is common, and emotional unresponsiveness is characteristic. These patients move in a jerky, birdlike manner and continually look about them as if scanning for some anticipated danger.They also may engage in prolonged staring at their reflections in mirrors. Withdrawal is characterized by prolonged sleep with increased REM time, fatigue, apathy, headache, sweating, muscle cramps, and increased appetite (102, 282). Desipramine, a tricyclic antidepressant, has been advocated to treat this syndrome (347).

In addition to the standard environmental and behavioral strategies generally employed in the treatment of acute drug intoxication (see above), sympathomimetic drug intoxication may require neuroleptic administration. Standard treatments for hyperpyrexia to prevent cardiovascular collapse and seizures, acidification of the urine with ammonium chloride (500–1,000 mg every 4 hours) to enhance drug excretion, and phentolamine (1–5 mg IV) for severe hypertension also may be required. The psychosis secondary to chronic administration is treated symptomatically (102, 282). Outpatient rehabilitation programs using behavioral and psychosocial techniques benefit some patients (346).

Hallucinogens

Lysergic acid diethylamide (LSD), a synthetic ergot alkaloid derivative; *peyote* and *mescaline,* extracted from a Mexican cactus; *psilocybin,* extracted from a Mexican mushroom; and *corymbos* and *myristica,* the active ingredients in morning glory seeds and nutmeg, respectively, are hallucinogenic substances primarily used by middle- and upper-class young adults. Consumption of these drugs, which in relatively low doses can induce psychosis, has decreased during the past 10 years.

Acute effects include altered perception of shape, color, and stimulus intensity; synesthesia (the perception in one sensory modality caused by a stimulus in another); paresthesias; altered consciousness; dizziness; weakness; tremors; nausea. Intense moods, lability of affect, distorted sense of time, oneiroid states, states of religious and philosophic ecstasy, hallucinations (particularly visual), delusional moods and ideas, problems with coordination, and general cognitive impairment also may occur (102, 710).

Uncomplicated and relatively mild adverse reactions rarely require hospitalization. A calm, structured, pleasant environment with moderate light and sound and a calm supportive staff are usually sufficient to resolve all symptoms. Anxiolytics and for some psychotic but nonexcited patients, a single IM dose of neuroleptic (e.g., 25 mg of chlorpromazine), may be required. Patients who are extremely agitated and excited or whose symptoms persist past 4 to 6 hours generally require hospitalization. Neuroleptics are then needed; treatment is best achieved with haloperidol. Many street drugs have anticholinergic properties, however, and neuroleptics, as potent anticholinergic agents, occasionally exacerbate drug-induced psychotic symptoms. Should this occur or if resolution of symptoms is not obtained within 3 to 5 days, ECT should be administered; it is effective and safe in the treatment of most drug-induced states (102, 967).

In some individuals, particularly those who experience "bad trips" (usually frightening psychotic states) and are thus presumably most vulnerable to the neurotropic effects of hallucinogens, a single administration of any of these drugs can result in permanent brain dysfunction. Certainly, repeated use of hallucinogens can cause cognitive impairment, recurrent psychoses, chronic hallucinosis, and a chronic avolitional state, each of which may persist long after discontinuation of the drug (236, 382, 698, 1024). Anecdotal reports are common of patients, in their late 20s, with chronic emotional blunting, formal thought disorder, and complete auditory hallucinations, who, in their late teens or early 20s used hallucinogenic drugs for a period 1 to 2 years. Despite no further drug use (confirmed by family, friends, and medical observation), these schizophreniclike symptoms persisted. None of these patients had a premorbid history suggestive of psychiatric disorder and no family history of schizophrenia.

A striking example of this syndrome was a psychiatric technician, who, according to all sources, was not previously psychiatrically ill and had never used street drugs of any kind. He was given LSD (documented) in orange juice by a psychiatric patient who was a drug abuser. The drug abuser was "celebrating" his discharge from the hospital and freely admitted spiking the juice. While playing football 30 minutes later, the technician began to experience frightening visual perceptual distortions and hallucinations. He was hospitalized and treated with a neuroleptic for 3 days. Although his acute symptoms completely abated, he lost all interest in pursuing his college education and became emotionally bland (a departure from his premorbid friendly, animated and ambitious behavior). A year later, he was encountered on a busy street corner. He was "standing around" and vacantly watching the crowds pass by. Although free of any recurrent acute symptoms during that year, he had not entered school and had stopped seeing his friends. Supported on disability insurance he spent his time doing nothing. He had no family history of psychiatric disorder.

Arylcyclohexylamines

During the early 1980s, phencyclidine (PCP) use increased to epidemic proportions, despite inconsistent reports of positive psychotropic experiences (usually an intense euphoria with feelings of unlimited power and energy) and frequent and consistent reports of adverse reactions (intense depression, psychosis, violence). Some hospitals reported detectable PCP in the urine of up to 70% of psychiatric admissions (469). Its use now appears to be on the wane. A white crystalline powder, PCP may be mistaken for cocaine and "cheap" cocaine highs are commonly reported by patients presenting with PCP intoxication. As many as 2 to 3 million Americans (most under age 25) have used PCP, which is sold as "angel dust," "hog," "crystal," and "weed," to name but a few sobriquets. PCP users commonly use other street drugs and alcohol and have a history of drug-related arrests. PCP may be snorted, smoked, or injected. There is some evidence that, once distributed in body fat, as much as 94% of a given dose remains in body tissue indefinitely. "Flashbacks" have been attributed to temporary mobilization of the molecule from fat to brain (754, 767). PCP is a dissociative anesthetic that induces catalepsy and analgesia but leaves the individual's eyes open as if awake. Because of this property, it is used as an animal tranquilizer (as often seen in nature programs on television).

Because PCP has an affinity for the vestibulocerebellar system, intoxication is usually characterized by dizziness, nystagmus, and muscular uncoordination.

Tachycardia and hypertension are also common. Pupils are normal in size or constricted. Behaviorally, a delirium with intense anxiety, suspiciousness, irritability, and violence is characteristic. Psychosis most commonly appears as a typical drug-induced psychotic state or mania (209, 754, 767). Chronic psychoses and cognitive deficits can occur (248).

Cannabis

Marijuana, a form of cannabis derived from the hemp plant, is the most widely used illicit drug. Nearly 60% of high school graduates in the United States have used the drug. Its main active ingredient is tetrahydrocannabinol. Hashish, another form of cannabis, has a high concentration of tetrahydrocannabinol. Physiologic tolerance to the drug has not been established, but psychologic dependence can occur, as well as a withdrawal syndrome characterized by anorexia, anxiety, agitation, irritability, dysphoria, tremor, and insomnia (666, 703).

Long-term usage appears to impair lung function and to suppress the immune system. Heavy cannabis smokers are at greater risk for lung cancer and fungal infections than are individuals who smoke equivalent amounts of tobacco. Reproductive and chromosomal aberrations also have been reported with chronic use (710).

Acute effects include increased heart rate and blood pressure, decreased concentration and impaired ability to acquire and store information, diminished reaction time and time sense (events appear to proceed more slowly than they actually do), and impaired coordination and judgment. Some individuals, particularly first-time users, experience acute fearfulness; confusion; dysphoria; and, occasionally, irritability, suspiciousness, delusional ideas, hallucinations, and distortions of body image. Chronic behavioral effects include an "amotivational" syndrome of apathy, loss of drive and ambition, and general mild cognitive impairment (666).

Treatment for the acute syndrome rarely requires sedation. A quiet, structured environment with a friendly and calm staff is usually sufficient to resolve the patient's symptoms. Anxiolytics are helpful in severe anxiety, but neuroleptics are virtually never required unless the acute psychosis persists for more than a few hours. There is no known effective treatment for the "amotivational" syndrome (102).

Inhalants

Inhalant use is faddish and, in the United States, is primarily observed among the young, poor, and Spanish-speaking. Chemicals producing psychoactive vapors are diverse in structure. Surveys suggest that 7 million Americans have used these solvents, which include hydrocarbons, Freon agents, ketones, esters, alcohols, and glycols. Inhalant intoxication resembles alcohol intoxication but is of shorter duration. Use of any inhalant may result in aggressive and assaultive behavior requiring restraints and sedation. Diazepam (10–30 mg p.o. or 10–15 mg IV) may be needed. Individuals who regularly use organic solvent inhalants are at great risk for brain damage. In one study, 40% of subjects scored in the severe impairment range on the Halstead-Reitan battery. Chronic use also may affect peripheral nerves and kidney and liver function. Acute intoxication is characterized by delirium; tinnitus; ataxia; tremors and fasciculations; distortions of body image; and visual hallucinations, often of colorful images and geometric shapes (210, 888). Nitrites, chemically unrelated to other inhaled substances, specifically produce a transient alteration in consciousness and are used primarily in association with sexual behavior (910).

A poetic summation of the characteristics of drug states is presented in Table 17.3.

TABLE 17.3

Poetic Description of Drug States

Barbiturates/sedatives-hypnotics, and alcohol
Labile emotions from friendships to hate;
Slurring of language, and stumbling of gait.
Heart beating faster, and reflexes down,
Vision is blurry, and acts like a clown

Opiates
Cool to the touch, unresponsive to pain,
Hunger diminished, and scars over vein.
Pupils pinpointed, and blood pressure low,
Urine diminished, and breathing is slow.

Sympathomimetics
Constantly moving, and high as a kite,
Pupils dilated, and stays up all night.
Acting suspicious, and trying to fight,
Blood pressure rising, and no appetite.

Hallucinogens
Fantastic colors and beautiful lights,
Great synesthesias, eureka insights.
Out of body, time stops for a while,
Pupils dilated, amphetamine style.

SOURCE: Reprinted with permission of The Free Press, a Division of Macmillan, Inc., from *Principles of Clinical Psychiatry* by Arnold M. Ludwig. Copyright © 1980 by The Free Press.

Theory of Etiology

Alcoholism is familial (371, 372, 760) and apparently is specifically transmitted from parent to child, whether or not the child is exposed to the alcoholic parent (150, 375). There is some evidence that alcoholism rates are higher in parents of female alcoholics than in the relatives of male alcoholics (548). Bohman et al. (123) have also shown, in an adoption study, that there is a threefold increase of alcoholism among adopted daughters with biologic mothers who were alcoholic, compared with control daughters. They also found an excess of alcohol abuse among daughters of biologic fathers who were alcoholic but no excessive rate of alcoholic daughters of fathers who were both alcoholic and criminal.

About 25% of fathers and brothers of alcoholics are alcoholic (221, 373). Twin studies have found that monozygotic twins have higher concordance rates for alcoholism than dizygotic twins. Adoption studies generally find biologic relatives of alcoholic adoptees more likely to become alcoholic than relatives of control adoptees. Cloninger and colleagues (123, 196), in several analyses of a large Swedish adoption sample, found biologic relatives of adoptees to be more at risk; however, they also identified what they believed to be two forms of familial alcoholism with distinct genetic and environmental causes and different associations with criminality and severity. The least common type, which appears to be highly heritable over the entire range of social backgrounds, is associated with severe alcohol abuse and criminality, particularly in fathers and their sons. The more common type, although heritable, is influenced more by environmental factors (prenatal and postnatal, in particular) and is associated with mild alcohol abuse in fathers and mothers but not with criminality. Molecular genetic studies of alcoholism, now in progress (715), are focusing on dopaminergic systems because acutely administered alcohol has been shown to stimulate brain reward systems through the release of dopamine. DNA samples from brains of alcoholics (the early-onset, highly heritable severe type) and nonalcoholics are being studied and a D_2 dopamine receptor gene on chromosome 11 is reported to be significantly more frequent in samples from alcoholics (70 to 80%) than in those from nonalcoholics (about 20%). Thus, alcohol abuse appears heterogeneous and to include (1) an associated behavior of some illnesses (e.g., mood disorder); (2) a sporadic late-onset disorder; and (3) an early-onset syndrome, which may represent at least two different gene-environment processes.

The specific biologic processes that would be influenced by the genes of alcohol abuse, thus leading an individual to a high level of alcohol consumption, are unknown. Theories generally revolve around the pharmacologic fact that alcohol in low doses is initially a CNS stimulant, whereas, in high doses, it is a CNS depressant that can lead to physiologic tolerance. Theories also tend to incorporate the apparent common use of alcohol by alcoholics and nonalcoholics alike in stressful social settings, particularly approach-avoidance conflict situations.

The most interesting of these theories is Cloninger's (194) neurogenetic adaptive model, in which he synthesizes genetic and neurophysiologic findings in alcoholics with his model of personality. Cloninger associates the early-onset, highly heritable form of alcoholism with the personality traits of high novelty seeking, low harm avoidance, and low reward dependence. Similar to the pattern observed in antisocial personality, his theory would explain the association between this form of alcoholism and criminality. The later-onset, sporadic form of alcoholism is associated with low novelty seeking, high harm avoidance, high reward dependence (dependent personality). Thus, in the highly heritable form of alcoholism, low basal dopaminergic activity putatively leads to behavior (novelty seeking) or drugs (dopamine agonists: cocaine, alcohol, opiates) likely to increase activity in that system. In the sporadic type, high basal serotonergic activity leads to behavioral inhibition and anxiety that are relieved by some drugs, particularly alcohol.

Support for Cloninger's view comes from neurophysiologic studies indicating that the sporadic type of alcoholic, when abstinent, is hypervigilant and apprehensive and displays a typical high-anxiety resting level EEG pattern (minimal alpha, excessive fast activity, and poor synchrony). In response to alcohol, the EEGs of these individuals show a marked increase in alpha, which is associated with a sense of calm attention and well being. Hypervigilance and avoidance behaviors are consistent with high harm avoidance and reward dependence traits. On the other hand, abstinent early-onset, high heritability alcoholics are hypovigilant with high novelty seeking traits. When studied by evoked potential and when asked to repond to stimuli, they demonstrate reduced amplitude in late component waves (P300), compared with control subjects, even though they do not make more errors than the latter. This response, also observed in nonalcoholic sons of alcoholic fathers (88), suggests a heritable deficit in ability to allocate significance to the target stimuli. Further, such alcoholics also show increasing amplitudes to stimuli of increasing intensity, rather than the more common reducing pattern.

Cloninger suggests that, as alcohol has an excitatory effect on neurons of the ventral tegmental areas (the brain's putative reward system), its use may produce a pharmacologic reward. Individuals with high novelty seeking traits, and thus high dopaminergic responsivity, would be particularly prone to the ethanol reward. The increased use of stimulant drugs in these individuals is consistent with this relationship. The alcohol- and drug-seeking behavior is thus viewed by Cloninger as a special kind of exploratory appetitive behavior. With frequent and continued use, however, tolerance develops (546) and abuse becomes addiction.

Alcohol is also anxiolytic. Individuals with high harm avoidance traits, under circumstances not understood, could begin to use alcohol to relieve anxiety. As this is a strong reinforcer, those individuals who also had high reward dependence traits would tend to continue to use the reinforcing anxiety-lowering agent. Again, frequent and continued use leads to tolerance, and abuse becomes addiction.

Substance abuse and dependence are also familial. Several studies have demonstrated that the use of alcohol, tobacco, stimulants, benzodiazepines, analgesics, caffeine, nicotine, and cannabis or other illicit drugs by parents predicts their use in children (269). Studies in twins, including those reared apart, also have suggested a significant genetic contribution to drug taking (393). In addition, one adoption study (152) suggested that the familialness of substance abuse results, in part, from genetic factors. Antisocial personality and behaviors consistent with high novelty seeking, low harm avoidance, and low reward dependence are also observed in drug abusers (1088). The above data, although scanty, suggest a similar set of relationships to that of familial alcoholism.

Chapter 18

Sexual Dysfunctions

History

Although conditions characterized by sexually deviant behavior have been recognized for centuries, the first systematic medical description of these disorders was provided by Kraft-Ebing, a Viennese psychiatrist, in 1886 (556). Kraft-Ebing believed sexual deviation to be a hereditary CNS degeneration. Freud related sexual deviation to aberrant psychosexual development and further legitimized the medical study and treatment of these disorders. More recently, sexual deviation has been interpreted as the result of mal-learning (432, 1077) or limbic system dysfunction (120).

Despite some progress in treatment and in the understanding of these disorders, the religious and social stigmata traditionally attached to them remains, thus restricting full scientific study of these conditions. Indeed, sexual behaviors considered medically normal (e.g., oral sex) remain criminal offenses in some parts of the United States. Political, as well as religious and social, pressures have also influenced the study of sexual deviation. For example, homosexuality was traditionally viewed as a sexual deviation requiring treatment; following a vote by the American Psychiatric Association membership, it was dropped as a DSM diagnostic category. A review of scientifically collected data was not part of this process. Today, homosexuality is referred to as an alternate form of sexual behavior and is not considered pathologic. Nevertheless, homosexuality is statistically deviant behavior and may be associated with certain personality traits and abilities. There is also evidence that some homosexuals have altered endocrine function (359) and smaller anterior hypothalamic nuclei (584). A neurohormonal theory of sexual orientation also has been proposed (283). This theory is based on two findings: (1) women prenatally exposed to synthetic estrogens have androgenlike effects upon brain differentiation and are more likely to be homosexual or report homosexual feelings than are unexposed control subjects, and (2) homosexual men have a femalelike luteinizing hormone response to estradiol. Although these findings are not without critics, they are supported by studies in nonhumans which suggest that mating and other gender-specific behaviors can be influenced prenatally and early postnatally by sex steroid hormones. Further, homosexual-like behavior has been observed in nonhuman species (e.g., sheep, marine birds and worms) (76, 458, 655). Of equal interest are studies showing that male homosexuality may be familial and that brothers of male homosexuals are four times more likely to be homosexual than brothers of heterosexuals (763). Twin studies are also consistent with a genetic influence on sexual orientation, with concordance rates among monozygotic twins of about 50%. Most recently, Bailey and Pillard (70) reported concordance rates of 52% for monozygotic and 22% for dizygotic twins. Gender-nonconforming behaviors were also present during childhood in the majority of the homosexual twins. Among the genetic models examined using data from the twins and their relatives, heritability ranged from 0.31–0.71 (1.0 representing 100% of the findings due to a genetic influence). An understanding of homosexual behavior would undoubtedly increase our understanding of human sexuality, but social-political forces make such study difficult. The conditions discussed below are limited to diagnostic categories in the DSM.

Behaviors

DSM-III-R delineates three categories of sexual deviation: (1) *sexual dysfunctions:* disturbances in arousal and performance; (2) *paraphilias:* inappropriate or dangerous sexual behaviors; and (3) *gender identity disorders:* classifications of childhood- and or adolescent-onset conditions.

Sexual Dysfunctions

DSM-III-R describes four categories of sexual dysfunction: disorders of desire, arousal, orgasm, and pain (see Table 18.1). Two miscellaneous categories, NOS and other, are also provided.

Hyposexuality, or decreased sexual drive, is common in neuropsychiatric disorders. It is typically observed in melancholia, schizophrenia with blunted affect, chronic psychosis, temporal lobe and other psychosensory epilepsies, hypothalamic lesions, alcohol and drug abuse, various endocrinopathies (particularly hypothyroidism, testosterone deficiency, diabetes), and most chronic systemic illnesses (e.g., heart, liver, kidneys). Psychopharmacologic agents, particularly those with anticholinergic properties, also can impair sexual function. Further,

TABLE 18.1

DSM-III-R Categories of Sexual Dysfunction

I. Sexual desire disorders
   Hypoactive or hyperactive sexual desire disorder
   Sexual aversion disorder

II. Sexual arousal disorder
   Female sexual arousal disorder
   Male erectile disorder

III. Orgasm disorders
   Inhibited female orgasm
   Inhibited male orgasm
   Premature ejaculation

IV. Sexual pain disorders
   Dyspareunia
   Vaginismus
   Sexual dysfunction not otherwise specified

hyposexuality is fairly common in individuals without psychiatric diagnosis; it occurs in more than 10% of adults of both genders (324). Some hyposexuality in normal adults is related to stressful situations, but some also results from personality trait patterns.

In neuropsychiatric clinical settings, *hypersexuality,* or increased sexual arousal and activity, is most commonly associated with mania (36). Frontal lobe orbitomedial lesions also can lead to inappropriate and increased sexual behavior. In both conditions, verbal sexual behavior is most common (sexual jokes, solicitations of sexual activity), followed by attempts to fondle people and public masturbation. Actual copulation is uncommon. Hypersexuality is also associated with seizure disorder, particularly postictally, and occurs in patients with psychosensory epilepsy with a temporal lobe focus (120, 121, 964). Other conditions associated with hypersexuality include the Kleine-Levin syndrome (hypothalamic dysfunction associated with periodic somnolence, hyperphagia, and hypersexuality) (341) and the Klüver-Bucy syndrome (bilateral temporal lobe dysfunction associated with orality, placidity, visual agnosia, and other cognitive deficits and hypersexuality) (600). Satyriasis and nymphomania are not included in DSM-III-R but most likely represent extremes of personality trait; however, when these behaviors begin abruptly in contrast to past behavior or for the first time after age 35, coarse brain disease should be suspected (369).

Sexual aversion disorder is characterized by a persistent and recurrent aversion to sexual activity and avoidance of genital contact. DSM-III-R requires that it not be due to other axis I conditions, such as OCD, phobia, or depression. If these disorders can be eliminated as possibilities and the aversion is of long duration, a personality trait disorder is the most likely diagnosis.

Disorders of sexual arousal are fairly common. At some time during their lives, 20% of all men and 30% of married women are affected. Premature ejaculation is also common and is reported in over 30% of married men. Pain during sexual intercourse (dyspareunia) and painful vaginal contractions that prevent or disrupt copulation (vaginismus) are less frequent. After elimination of systemic and coarse brain disease etiologies (e.g., endocrinopathies, peripheral vascular disease, spinal cord disease, syphilis, multiple sclerosis, chronic renal or liver disease), most of these conditions are found to be the result of personality disorders, anxiety disorders, or stressful situations. Impotence also results from systemic disease (75% of cases), most commonly diabetes, as well as anxiety disorder and substance abuse (324).

Paraphilias

DSM-III-R provides an extensive list of paraphilias, including exhibitionism, fetishism, sadism, masochism, transvestism, voyeurism, and pedophilia. These disorders are defined as recurrent, intense sexual urges or fantasies involving nonhumans, inanimate objects, children or other nonconsenting persons (rape is not included in DSM), or the suffering or humiliation of oneself or of others. The prevalence of paraphilias is unknown. Most develop during adolescence, and almost all occur in males. Most paraphilics are reported to be heterosexual.

When a paraphilia develops in adulthood, coarse brain disease should be suspected. Exhibitionism (particularly automatic disrobing), public or uncontrollable masturbation, and coital movements can occur during seizures. Temporal lobe epilepsy has been associated with ictal and interictal fetishism and transvestism (459, 1039) and, in rarer instances, voyeurism, exhibitionism, sadism, masochism, pedophilia, frotteurism (rubbing against others), genital self-mutilation, and homosexuality (543, 964). Further, postencephalic parkinsonism, frontal lobe lesions, and early Huntington's disease are associated (though rarely) with paraphilia. Abnormal EEGs, cognitive dysfunction, abnormal cerebral blood flow and structure, and endocrine abnormalities also have been observed in individuals arrested for sexually related crimes (103, 936). Rarely, Gilles de la Tourette's syndrome and OCD are associated with inappropriate sexual behavior, and some paraphilias may be variants of OCD (e.g., exhibitionism) (886). Patients with borderline personality disorder also have an increased prevalence of paraphilias and deviant sexual orientation (1100). Antisocial personality is more commonly associated with inappropriate, particularly aggressive, sexual behavior.

Gender Identity Disorders

DSM-III-R defines four gender identity disorders: (1) gender identity disorder of childhood (2) gender identity disorder of adolescent or adult onset, (3) transsexualism, and (4) gender identity disorder NOS. Little is known about these conditions. Transsexualism has received the most media coverage because of the dramatic gender-change surgery associated with this condition. Whereas transvestism involves only cross-dressing, transsexualism, entails (1) a "persistent discomfort and sense of inappropriateness" about one's apparent gender and (2) a "persistent preoccupation with removing one's primary and secondary sex characteristics and acquiring the sex characteristics of the other" gender. DSM-III-R divides transsexualists into asexual, homosexual, and heterosexual subtypes. About 70% of patients who undergo gender-change surgery are pleased with the outcome (568).

Diagnosis

The basic steps in diagnosing sexual deviations are relatively straightforward. Usually, the deviant behavior is clearly described; most often the issue is not the label but the cause. In all cases, the clinician should first make certain that the patient is not suffering from a systemic or neurologic illness that could account for the sexual deviation. If such a condition is uncovered, it should be the focus of treatment. If no systemic or neurologic disorder (particularly epilepsy) is felt to explain the sexual deviation, the clinician should search for an axis I (particularly anxiety disorder and OCD) or axis II (particularly antisocial personality) diagnosis. When the diagnosis involves as axis I disorder, it should be the focus of treatment. If a personality disorder is found to be the only co-occurring condition or if no other DSM diagnosis can be made, treatment should focus directly upon the sexual deviation. Throughout this diagnostic process, the clinician should matter-of-factly assess the form and content of the patient's sexual behavior. Embarrassment and apologies for thoroughness have no place in a medical evaluation.

Management

One approach to the understanding of sexual deviations is to consider those that are compulsive in form as variants of OCD (211); another applies an addiction model (823). Although both approaches require significant scientific validation, the clinician can find them helpful because they provide guidance for treatment (1077).

If systemic or coarse neurologic illness can be identified, it should be treated as if causally related to the deviant sexual behavior. When the behavior continues, despite successful treatment, or if no evidence of coarse neurologic or systemic illness exists, the clinician must judge whether the deviant sexual behavior best fits an OCD or addiction pattern and then treat for one or the other. In most cases, this treatment includes pharmacotherapy and behavioral therapy. If neither OCD nor an addiction seems likely, both types of therapy are still the focus of management. Behavioral approaches involve the use of relaxation exercises and systematic desensitization. Additional techniques are vaginal dilators for vaginismus and the squeeze method (squeezing the head of the penis to prevent or delay ejaculation) or local anesthetics for premature ejaculation. Treatments usually focus on couples. Outcome figures suggest substantial improvement in 70% or more of patients who complete a course of treatment.

Paraphilias, although more difficult to treat, are also managed with behavioral and cognitive techniques, as well as social skills training. Antiandrogenic libido suppressants are also used in treating these patients (104, 109, 227). Cyproterone (Androcur) is a potent compound that that blocks androgens at receptor sites, including those in the brain. Blocking reduces circulating testosterone and gonadotropin. In the motivated patient, reduced testosterone levels result in a lower sexual drive and a reduction in deviant sexual behavior. Although testosterone blood levels need to be reduced below 250 mg%, the correlation between blood level and therapeutic effect is only modest. A dose of 100 mg is usually required (100–500 mg orally/day or 100–500 mg depot/week). Side effects include reversible gynecomastia (20%) and infertility. Liver damage and thromboembolic disorders also may occur in an unknown but small percentage of patients. Medroxyprogesterone, another agent widely used in libido suppression, interferes with testosterone synthesis and target organ receptors. Depot doses are 400-600 mg /week. Side effects include hypertension, fatigue, edema, increased appetite and weight gain, and insomnia. Liver damage and thromboembolic disorders also may occur. Both compounds may decrease glucose tolerance, and treatment with either may result in depression. The nature of the depression is unclear. Reportedly, 40 to 80% of patients have significant benefits from treatment.

PART III

Patient Management

Chapter

19

Principles of Patient Management

The number of major diagnostic categories in psychiatry is small. Once the decision is reached that a patient has a disorder within a specific category (e.g., bipolar affective disorder, antisocial personality), treatment choices, also limited in number, tend to be applied in a straightforward fashion. For example, in the diagnosis of mania, pharmacologic treatment is likely to involve lithium, alone or with a neuroleptic. If the patient is atypical or unresponsive, an anticonvulsant might be used. ECT is another alternative. Treatment modalities that are most efficacious for each diagnostic category can be learned fairly quickly. Determining the combinations of treatments that are most useful requires further experience, but these pharmacologic choices also are limited. Even the use of drug combinations and combinations of treatment modalities (e.g., behavior therapy plus an MAOI for some anxiety states) can be readily learned. The difficult part of treating psychiatric patients consists of (1) sticking to the principles of treatment, (2) basing treatment choices on sound empirical evidence and clinical experience, rather than preconceived theoretical notions, and (3) using treatments appropriately in various clinical settings. For example, most clinicians recognize that it is better not to treat until a diagnosis is made, that polypharmacy is generally not as advantageous as a single drug, and that, once begun, each drug has an optimal dose range and requires a certain length of time to work. Because of the vicissitudes of clinical practice (e.g., caseload and acuity, staffing and laboratory support), however, it is difficult for some clinicians to adhere to these standards.

Clinicians are inundated with anecdotal reports of dramatically effective treatments. They may succumb to the lure of the novel treatment in spite of their awareness that most such miracles are but a flash in the pan and should not be taken too seriously. Further, some disorders, according to their location in the DSM nosology, are supposed to respond, or not, to certain treatments, but experienced clinicians know that these treatment implications may be erroneous. For example, cyclothymia, now a part of the DSM-III-R mood disorders category, is theoretically supposed to respond to treatments for mood disorder. In DSM-II, however, it was included among the personality disorders that theoretically do not respond to psychotropics. Clearly, the actual responsivity of cyclothymia has not changed with its shift from one category to another. Recognition of the somewhat arbitrary nature of psychiatric nosology and the occasional false treatment implications of the nosology present a constant clinical challenge.

Finally, clinicians are well aware that they do not practice in a vacuum. Private practice medicine is no longer private, and practice is influenced by government insurers, the limitations of health maintenance organizations, and the need to make a profit. The interpersonal, social, and ethnic dynamics of a particular clinic, mental health center, or inpatient unit also affect medical practice, with the result that one diagnosis or treatment is favored over another. Adhering to the principles of management while dealing with the realities of one's clinical setting often requires acrobatic interpersonal skills and steadfastness.

Although the treatment focus of this book is on biologic interventions to correct morbid processes, the principles of patient management apply regardless of treatment modality. Whether the primary treatment is biologic or psychological in nature, the clinician needs a framework in which to operate. Table 19.1 summarizes one such framework. Thus, whether psychotherapy or ECT is to be employed, treatment optimally should not begin until the clinician has reached the highest possible certainty regarding the patient's diagnosis. Further, in the use of either psychotherapy or pharmacotherapy, the dose and duration of treatment must to be logically considered and, when possible, based on sound empirical findings. Treatments should not be employed, started, or changed in an erratic fashion but should follow a planned course of action, with periodic monitoring of progress. Most importantly, whatever the treatment modality, the clinician is treating a pa-

TABLE 19.1

Principles of Patient Management

1. If no emergency, delay treatment until maximum diagnostic certainty is reached.
2. Begin with the treatment that offers the maximum benefit with the least side effects.
3. Once begun, administer the treatment in an adequate dose for an adequate duration.
4. Do not switch treatments erratically; use a logic tree that makes clinical sense.
5. Empiricism always supersedes theory.
6. People, not symptoms or diseases, are treated.

tient. Therefore, that patient's overall health concerns, personality, and life circumstances, as well as the specific psychiatric illness, need attention.

Principles of Psychopharmacology

Although a great deal is known about the effects of psychotropic drugs on various neurotransmitter and other neuronal processes, precisely how these agents ameliorate or resolve psychopathological symptoms is unknown. For the most part knowledge about which drug benefits which disorder is based on empirical experience, rather than on hypotheses of action or illness pathophysiology.

The principles of pharmacology are the same in neuropsychiatry as in other medical specialties. The neuropsychiatrist must consider choice of drug, dosage, preparation, route and schedule of administration, side effects, and duration of treatment. These considerations should be based on a knowledge of pharmacology, metabolism and excretion patterns, and other factors affecting the bioavailability of psychopharmacologic agents. In addition, drug prescription needs to incorporate clinical judgment regarding the patient's personality, life situation, and idiosyncrasies. For example, a person who has health concerns relating to food and chemical pollution may be reluctant to take any medication, and sophisticated persuasion and education may be needed to ensure compliance with treatment. Patients who regularly drive, drink (even modestly), or use machinery may need to compromise their daily routines to minimize adverse consequences of treatment.

Drug-Free Observation

Regardless of clinical circumstances, the understandable desire to treat should be tempered by the advantages of observing the patient in a drug-free condition. For hospitalized patients, a drug-free observation period of 2 or 3 days, or longer, offers the following advantages:

1. *It allows for spontaneous remission of psychopathology of recent, acute onset:* Some acutely excited or psychotic patients with sudden onsets of illness can fully remit without medication after 1 to 2 days of hospitalization. These include patients with reactive psychoses, certain drug-induced syndromes, and short-lived attacks of mania or hypomania. The advantages if the patient can recover without specific intervention are: (a) prognostic information concerning the natural course of illness is available; (b) the patient avoids short-term exposure to the potentially toxic effects of psychoactive medications; and (c) long-term side effects (e.g., tardive dyskinesia) are avoided because the observed clinical improvement is not attributed to any drug that was administered and the physician does not falsely conclude that long-term therapy is automatically indicated.

2. *It allows for observation of symptoms:* Except for acute emergencies requiring immediate behavioral control, it is diagnostically helpful to observe the patient's psychopathology in its unmodified state for 1 or 2 days. In a closed inpatient setting, the observation period is rarely a risk to the patient. Treatment can modify or remove symptoms before a correct diagnosis can be made and produce new symptoms that can mask or distort the correct diagnosis. For example, neuroleptics can result in motor symptoms of inhibition, rigidity, and stupor and convert an acute manic patient into a catatonic. Akathisia may mimic an agitated state, and the fixed, expressionless face of drug-induced parkinsonism may lead to an incorrect diagnosis of schizophrenia with emotional blunting. The few days devoted to observation can save weeks or years of later difficulties. For patients who require sedation because of agitation, excitement, or hyperactivity, a single dose of sodium amobarbital (250–500 mg IM) or lorazepam (2 to 5 mg, orally or IV) may be given without causing a sustained change in the clinical picture.

3. *It allows for uncontaminated laboratory investigations:* EEG and neuropsychological testing may be distorted or even rendered uninterpretable by the effects of psychoactive drugs. It is in the patient's best interest to perform such evaluations during a drug-free state. Sodium amobarbital or lorazepam also may temporarily obscure interpretation of these tests, but their effects, unlike those of neuroleptics, are gone in a few hours after administration of a single dose.

Choice of Drug

When a diagnosis has been made and a decision reached to use a psychotropic agent, the choice of drug class (e.g., neuroleptic or antidepressant) is usually straightforward. There is little evidence, to indicate that different drugs within a class (e.g., nortriptyline or fluoxetine versus amitriptyline or imipramine) vary in therapeutic effectiveness (685). Therefore, choice of drug within a class is usually determined by differences in preparation route, side effects, and other physical (e.g., color, taste) and pharmacologic (e.g., absorption and excretion) factors. In choosing a drug, the clinician also should consider the following factors when matching the characteristics of the drug with the patient's physiologic and psychological attributes: absorption, distribution, metabolism, and excretion.

Drug Dosage

Next in importance to the appropriate drug is selecting the dose. Failure to administer an adequate dose is the most frequent cause of unsuccessful drug treatment. In two surveys, for example, 60% of depressed patients referred for evaluation of treatment resistance had received inadequate trials of antidepressants (509, 872). Typically, most psychoactive drugs are more effective when administered at the upper, rather than the lower, end of the dosage range. The appropriate dose is the maximum that the patient can tolerate without undue side effects, but it is unusual to achieve a full therapeutic effect without some side effects. Although side effects are not necessary for therapeutic effect, they are often indicators of adequate delivery of a drug to the target organ. For example, dopamine blockade in the mesolimbic system may be related to the antipsychotic activity of neuroleptics, but such blockade also may be expected to occur in the nigrostriatal dopamine system and produce extrapyramidal side effects.

Preparation and Route of Administration

The choice of preparation and route of administration is determined primarily by factors affecting drug absorption and clinical needs regarding onset of drug action. For example, IM injection of a soluble salt produces a fast onset of action with neuroleptics. Anxiolytics (e.g., benzodiazepines), on the other hand, are poorly absorbed after IM injection and should be given orally (or IV, if a rapid effect is required). Cyclic antidepressants are available in the parenteral form, but the oral route is almost always used because of their slow onset of action (1 to 2 weeks). There is no parenteral preparation for lithium, so it must be given orally.

No hard and fast rules apply to all classes of psychoactive drugs. Within individual drug classes, however, certain factors may be relatively constant. For neuroleptics, IV or IM injection provides the highest blood levels in the shortest time, followed in descending order by oral concentrates, tablets, and multipellet timed-release capsules (309). The management of acute psychotic excitement states invariably requires parenteral therapy, often in very substantial dosages (866). For less severely ill patients, oral concentrates are well absorbed and have the added advantage of being difficult to sequester. As many hospitalized psychotic patients are known to "cheek" or otherwise hide their medication for later surreptitious disposal, concentrates are the oral preparation of choice on the inpatient unit.

Dosage Schedules

Dosage schedules should be primarily determined by the drug's pharmacokinetics (distribution in body tissues and excretion) and metabolism. For example, abundant evidence indicates that once-a-day dosage is safe and clinically effective for neuroleptics and cyclic antidepressants, in part because of the long half-life of these drugs. There are four advantages of a single daily dose: (1) if the dose is given at bedtime, many side effects may dissipate during sleep and the quality of sleep itself may be improved by the sedative effects of the drug; (2) nurses have to prepare and distribute medications only once a day; (3) patients at home find it easier to remember to take a single nighttime dose of medication than multiple doses throughout the day, thus missing fewer doses; and (4) taking medication at bedtime is socially acceptable and avoids the potential embarrassment of taking pills at work or in other public places.

Duration of Treatment

It is necessary for many patients to continue pharmacotherapy for a considerable period of time after improvement or remission, or they risk a relapse. Cyclic antidepressants, for example, are continued at full therapeutic plasma levels for 4 to 6 months after successful treatment of the acute episode. Lithium and anticonvulsants are maintained for years because they reduce the frequency and severity of affective episodes. Neuroleptics, on the other hand, because of the risk for tardive dyskinesia, are often discontinued at regular intervals, even in chronically ill schizophrenics, in order to assess a continued need for them. Some chronic patients can remain neuroleptic free without relapse. Many, however, need continuous treatment. No predictors of this need have been established.

Drug Combinations

There is no hard evidence of true synergism between any two psychopharmacologic agents, although additive effects occur. Fixed-dose drug combinations of a cyclic antidepressant and a neuroleptic (e.g., perphenazine and amitriptyline) should be avoided because administration of an adequate antidepressant dose invariably yields an excessive dose of the neuroleptic component (and vice versa). However, certain combinations are frequently used. These include haloperidol and lithium or carbamazepine and lithium for acute mania and cyclic antidepressants and an MAOI for some dysthymias.

Pharmacology

The pharmacology of specific drugs is discussed in Chapter 20, but some general principles are covered here and summarized in Table 19.2. The fundamental issue is bioavailability, or the extent to which the drug is available to the target organ (i.e., the brain). Once absorption processes run their course, bioavailability is primarily determined by the drug's pharmacokinetics that involve metabolism, fat solubility, protein binding, and excretion.

Drug Metabolism

Drugs are primarily metabolized in the liver, although intestinal microflora also play an important metabolic role, particularly for drugs excreted in the feces. Thus, conditions affecting liver and intestinal function affect drug metabolism.

TABLE 19.2

Clinical Situations That Affect Psychotropic Drug Blood Levels

Situation	*Drug Blood-Level Effect*	*Mechanism of Action*
	Concurrent drug use	
Barbiturate	Lowers cyclic antidepressant levels	Increases liver enzyme activity
Anticonvulsant	Decreases cyclic antidepressants and neuroleptic levels, decreases levels of other anticonvulsants	Lowers protein binding; increases renal clearance; increases liver enzyme activity
Theophylline	1. Decreases lithium levels 2. Decreases anticonvulsant levels	1. Increases renal excretion 2. Increases liver enzyme activity
Salicylate	Increases free valproic acid levels	Reduces protein binding
Anti-inflammatory drug	Increases lithium levels (variable)	Increases renal reabsorption
Antibiotic	Increases carbamazepine levels	Reduces renal clearance
Calcium channel blocker (verapamil)	Increases carbamazepine levels	Reduces renal clearance
Methylphenidate or other stimulants, including caffeine	Increases cyclic antidepressant levels	Decreases liver enzyme activity
Chlorpromazine	Increases cyclic antidepressant levels	Decreases liver enzyme activity
Progestational agent or oral contraceptive	Increases cyclic antidepressant and neuroleptic levels	Decreases liver enzyme activity
Alcohol	Decreases cyclic antidepressant and neuroleptic levels	Increases liver enzyme activity
Nicotine (tobacco)	Decreases cyclic antidepressant and neuroleptic levels	Increases liver enzyme activity

(continued)

TABLE 19.2 (*Cont.*)

Clinical Situations That Affect Psychotropic Drug Blood Levels

Situation	*Drug Blood-Level Effect*	*Mechanism of Action*
	Patient condition	
Low-salt diet	Markedly increases lithium levels	Increases renal reabsorption
Diabetes	Decreases cyclic antidepressant, neuroleptic, and anticonvulsant levels	Lowers albumin and, thus, binding
Pregnancy	1. Increases levels of cyclic antidepressants and neuroleptics 2. Lowers lithium levels	1. Decreases liver enzyme activity 2. Increases renal clearance
Elderly	1. Increases levels of cyclic antidepressants and neuroleptics 2. Increases lithium levels	1. Reduces liver enzyme activity—first-pass effect 2. Reduces renal clearance
Chronic inflammatory disease; recent trauma or surgery	Results in less available protein-free drug in cyclic antidepressants, neuroleptics, and anticonvulsants, although levels remain the same	Increases protein binding

The metabolic and excretion patterns of psychoactive compounds have practical clinical relevance. Orally administered neuroleptic and cyclic antidepressant drugs, for example, undergo modification first in the intestinal mucosa, and then in the liver via the portal circulation (251). This "first-pass" effect ensures that virtually no orally administered drug in these classes enters the systemic circulation or the brain in unmetabolized form. Although the metabolites are active, they may be less effective than an unmetabolized drug that enters the circulation directly from an IM site. This effect is reflected clinically by the repeated observation that patients who become excited or aggressive, despite substantial oral doses of a neuroleptic, often are rapidly controlled by an IM injection of the same drug at a considerably lower dose.

First-pass metabolism primarily involves microsomal enzyme systems that particularly affect lipophilic drugs (neuroleptics, tricyclic antidepressants) by oxidizing them to less active hydrophilic forms. Some of these forms enter the bloodstream, some are excreted in bile, and many are reabsorbed via the enterohepatic cycle and further metabolized. Demethylation, resulting in more active substances, also occurs during the first pass. In the second phase of metabolism, cycloplasmic enzyme systems are primarily involved and conjugation is the principal means of biotransformation. Conjugation further transforms drug metabolites into hydrophilic forms for easier excretion (bile and urine). Thus, liver metabolism of drugs is a prolonged process. Coupled with the fact that these drugs are fat soluble and extensively protein-bound, this process results in a long half-life for many drugs (neuroleptics and cyclic antidepressants), permitting a once-a-day dose regimen (73).

This multiphase hepatic metabolic process differentially affects various psychotropics. For example, most tricyclic antidepressants and neuroleptics are first-pass dependent, whereas some benzodiazepines (lorazepam) are second pass dependent. Thus, factors primarily affecting first-pass metabolism (aging, blood flow, intestinal microflora) have a greater influence on the clinical use of tricyclic antidepressants and neuroleptics, whereas factors primarily affecting second-pass metabolism (liver damage) have more influence on the use of second-pass–dependent compounds.

Drug Interactions

A number of drugs are known inhibitors or inducers of the hepatic enzyme systems for which some of the psychopharmacologic agents are substrates and thus raise or lower blood levels of those agents accordingly. Barbiturates, for example, are enzyme inducers; when given for nighttime sedation, they may lower tricyclic antidepressant blood levels. For this reason, benzodiazepines, which exhibit little or no enzyme induction, are a better choice for sedation/hypnosis in depressed patients receiving tricyclics. Methylphenidate, an enzyme-inhibiting compound, has been administered successfully to raise blood levels of tricyclic antidepressants by reducing their rate of metabolism in the liver (1057). Further, carbamazepine stimulates liver enzymes that metabolize imipramine, and phenytoin, thus reducing the effectiveness of these drugs. Chlorpromazine reduces liver metabolism of imipramine.

Further, tobacco (nicotine) and alcohol use induce liver enzymes so that larger doses of psychotropic drugs are needed to obtain usual therapeutic blood levels. Steroids, particularly progestational agents (as in oral contraceptives), inhibit drug metabolism; women using these agents or pregnant women who have high progesterone blood levels metabolize drugs less effectively than do women with normal or low progesterone blood levels. In these circumstances, more of the dose may get into the blood and lower doses may be needed to avoid toxicity. When pregnancy is over or the oral contraceptive is stopped, progesterone levels drop, liver metabolism becomes more effective, and dosage may need to be increased. In contrast, lithium is not metabolized in the liver but is excreted more rapidly by the kidney during pregnancy; thus, higher doses may be needed during this physiologic period.

Once processes related to absorption and metabolism run their course, bioavailability reflects such factors as protein binding, solubility in body fat, and excretion. Although drug blood levels can be a gross measure of bioavailability, there is enormous variability in blood levels achieved after single oral doses of medication, both among various patients and within any given patient over time. For this reason, monitoring of drug treatment by serial blood levels is needed; such procedures are routinely available for lithium, some antidepressants, and the anticonvulsants. The use and interpretation of drug levels, however, differ from one class of drugs to another. For example, the variability in serum lithium levels after single oral doses is small if the patient is in normal health and blood levels are measured at a standardized time interval following dose administration. Lithium excretion is almost entirely a function of renal plasma flow, which varies little from patient to patient. The cyclic antidepressants, on the other hand, produce extremely variable blood levels after oral doses because of individual differences in liver and intestinal metabolism, and optimal treatment requires serial plasma level determinations.

Two types of dose-response curves have been obtained for the tricyclic antidepressants. One type is a linear (or sigmoid) curve, in which increasing blood levels yield increasing therapeutic effects until a plateau is reached and beyond that, no further improvement occurs regardless of blood level. A drug of this type (e.g., imipramine) can be pushed to its upper dosage range, limited only by its toxic side effects. The second type is a nonlinear (or inverted U) dose-response curve, in which clinical improvement falls off at higher blood levels, even in the absence of disabling side effects. Thus, if a patient is unimproved on this type of drug, the dose may be either too low or too high. Proper treatment cannot be provided in the absence of blood level monitoring.

Bioavailability is also affected by the solubility of the drug or its metabolites in body fat. Drugs with high fat solubility are more psychoactive, but, if rapidly absorbed, they may be differentially stored in body fat, which makes them less available to the brain. Even after a drug has entered the brain, it is likely to be withdrawn again into body fat, thus resulting in reduced blood and brain levels and to a short activity half-life despite being in body fat for some time (long elimination half-life). Lorazepam is such a drug.

Finally, bioavailability is determined, in part, by the amount of the drug that freely circulates in the blood. Most drugs (lithium is an exception) are primarily bound to plasma albumin, with only 10 to 20% freely dissolved in the plasma water and thus pharmacologically active. Because laboratory reports of drug blood levels sum free and protein-bound drug, they can give a false impression of available active drug. For example, plasma albumin is low in liver disease and total blood levels of a given dose seem low, although the amount of free drug could be the same as that with a normal albumin level. The ability of albumin to bind a drug can vary also because of interference by other compounds (anticonvulsants lower binding) or from disease. Diabetes lowers binding, and chronic inflammatory disease, trauma, and surgery increase binding.

Evaluation of Pharmacotherapy

When to discontinue or change treatment should be decided logically. Each situation is dependent on assessing treatment results. Thus, the decision to discontinue maintenance medication after a year is based on the conclusion that the patient has achieved the maximum benefit from treatment, and treatment should stop unless symptoms return. In contrast, the decision to change treatment is based on the conclusion that the patient has not achieved maximum benefit from treatment, and additional or new treatments need to be considered. In both cases, "maximum benefit" varies among patients. Ideally, it means symptom-free and full return to premorbid function. This standard should be the goal for every patient, but the clinician must recognize that this standard is not always achieved. In practice, maximum benefit incorporates a balance between (1) no further symptom reduction and functional return over a period of time equivalent to about the typical acute treatment duration (e.g., 4 weeks for cyclic antidepressants and neuroleptics, 3 weeks for lithium, 4 to 6 weeks for ECT), and (2) physiologic and psychological tolerance to treatment side effects. Thus, if a patient has not noticeably improved further during the time frame usually considered adequate for acute treatment with a given treatment regimen and is tolerating the side effects of treatment, he has probably achieved maximum symptom reduction and functional return with that treatment (lithium prophylaxis is one exception to this rule).

If maximum benefit is considered good (definition differs for each patient), no changes in treatment need be made until that treatment's standard maintenance phase is completed. If maximum benefit is considered inadequate, the clinician must consider the reason(s) for the inadequate response. He should focus on seven possibilities (1) misdiagnosis, (2) incorrect first treatment choice, (3) incorrect dose (almost always too little), (4) incorrect duration of treatment, (5) side effects, (6) noncompliance, and (7) other physiologic factors that could have adversely influenced treatment (e.g., age, pregnancy, drug interactions, systemic illness affecting pharmacokinetics). If any of these possibilities appear causally related to the inadequate response, they should be corrected, if possible. If none of the possibilities explains the patient's inadequate response, the choice of the new treatment regimen should be based on the same factors that determined the original choice.

Principles of Inpatient Verbal Intervention and Behavioral Techniques

Interactions with Patients

In addition to medications and procedures, therapeutic assets should include the clinician's personality. For example, interpersonal and interviewing skills facilitate patient compliance. It is important for the patient to perceive that the clinician cares about him and responds intelligently to his symptoms and concerns. In addition, neuropsychiatrists who treat people are expected to care for their patients on an individual basis; to be skilled in comforting, educating, and advising them; to spend time with them; and to help them resolve situational and interpersonal problems.

Clinicians who are reasonably good interviewers in the formal examination setting often forget that *all* interactions with a patient are important to the patient. When the examiner speaks to the patient, his tone of voice, manner, and choice of words are all vital aspects of this informal contact, whether it occurs on the inpatient unit or in an outpatient setting. For example, a catatonic patient stood by the unit entrance each morning, but he was unable to say "Good morning" to any entering staff members until they had passed by him. Some staff members continued to walk on without responding, but others made a point to slow down so that when the patient did say his "Hello" they would be able to respond. After his recovery, the patient made a special point of thanking each staff member who had been sensitive to his need for an otherwise insignificant greeting. One physician never refused his patients' requests to play table tennis. The patients seemed to enjoy the interaction, and the physician said he found the games helpful in assessing their motor-perceptual coordination and concentration.

In addition, patients often focus on the words spoken to them, rather than the basic message of the statement. For example, a delusional patient, angry at being hospitalized involuntarily at his family's request, became further angered when asked why he was brought to the hospital. A rephrasing of the question to "What reasons did your family give you for their wanting you here?" ameliorated his anger, and he was then able to give a coherent history of his present illness. Nonjudgmental expressions ("How come?" rather than "Why?") and more implicitly empathic phrasings ("Do people talk about you behind your back?" rather than "Do you hear voices?") facilitate patient cooperation.

The patient's family can play a helpful role (far less frequently, a destructive one) in his treatment. This role may include persuading the patient to accept needed treatments, visiting the patient in the hospital, and monitoring the patient's treatment following discharge. Unfortunately, some clinicians keep relatives at a considerable distance during the treatment process, perhaps because of concerns that the family might contribute to the patient's stress or interfere with treatment. Although this can occur, it is important to establish a cordial relationship with one or more family members whenever possible. The majority of patients want some explanation provided to relatives. In some cases, where a relative may act maliciously or where hospitalization is extremely embarrassing to the patient, keeping the family at a distance may be necessary. On the other hand, in life-threatening situations requiring contact with a relative, the patient's confidentiality can be breached (1076).

Management of Unwanted Behaviors

In cases where spontaneous remission does not promptly occur or an underlying systemic illness cannot be identified, almost all hospitalized psychiatric inpatients require biologic treatments. In order for these treatments to produce optimal results, they must be supported by the behavioral management of patients.

As attention is a powerful reinforcer of behaviors, behavioral management relates to (1) modifying or partially extinguishing the patient's inappropriate interpersonal behaviors by ignoring them, and (2) reinforcing desirable substitute behaviors to replace the unwanted ones. Reinforcers on an inpatient service include attention and conversation, trips to the canteen, unit parties, unit movies, trips away from the hospital grounds, visits from friends, passes, television, and promotion within a progressive system of privileges. In some centers, psychologists develop formal behavior modification systems, such as token economies. These principles can be applied to many behaviors. For example, a patient may occasionally malinger or have pseudosyncopal episodes. Once morbid causes of fainting or seizures are ruled out and the patient is observed not to hurt himself when he falls, subsequent episodes should be totally ignored by the staff. Other patients are instructed to do the same. Normal behaviors are rewarded. This response is in contrast to the usual past experiences of many patients when their inappropriate behaviors rapidly mobilized large numbers of concerned staff.

Breaking and throwing things sometimes can be a precursor to violence. When that is suspected, the patient should be medicated (see Chapter 23). If a broken article belongs to the patient, the staff or relatives should be deliberately slow in replacing it and reward attempts by the patient to mend it. When the patient throws food, it should not replaced even if he is hungry. Periods of normal behavior should be rewarded.

Some patients yell, slam doors, and curse in order to receive attention or to have other needs met. If possible, staff and patients should totally ignore these behaviors, which may disappear if they are not reinforced. To maintain order and quiet on the unit when this technique is ineffectual, the patient may need to be discharged or sedated and placed in a seclusion room. When the patient has quieted down for several hours, he can be released from seclusion and reinforced for normal self-controlled behavior.

Patients frequently behave oddly, inappropriately, or annoyingly. Some examples are intruding into meetings and conversations, making importunate requests, cursing loudly, and standing too close to people when talking to them. Again, the best response to behaviors considered inappropriate is no response, that is, to ignore the behavior, to look "through" the patient at his shoulder without making eye contact, and, literally, to pretend it did not happen. A negative response (e.g., saying "No, go away" while turning away) may be reinforcing and increase such behaviors. A lack of reinforcement may reduce some patient behaviors if the staff is consistent in its approach and the behaviors to be ignored are explicitly identified. When the same patient behaves appropriately at other times, the behaviors should be reinforced immediately by means of some positive interaction with the patient.

Some behaviors cannot be ignored, however, because they adversely affect other patients. Examples are monopolizing the phone; lying on the floor in hallways and recreational areas; hoarding common supplies, unit equipment, or other patients' property; or exhibiting pseudoseizures. As most such behaviors are manifestations of illness, they resolve with appropriate treatment; simply stopping the behavior may suffice until the patient responds to treatment. Adjunctive behavioral techniques, if properly planned, can speed up the reduction in behavior frequency and thus make the patients feel better and improve the functioning of the unit (870).

For example, the patient who monopolizes the phone may get some special privilege or treat only if the number of calls or total time on the phone is below a certain level. The patient with pseudoseizures (medically evaluated, moved out of the way, and ignored during each pseudoseizure) is rewarded in some fashion if the number of episodes progressively decreases with time.

Satiation techniques may be helpful in some situations, as in the case of hoarding. Some psychiatric inpatients hoard large quantities of primarily useless items, such as pieces of paper, used paper cups, washcloths, and chalk. Obviously the condition that produces the hoarding requires treatment. In addition, the use of a satiation technique, whereby the staff actually adds items to the patient's hoard, may be effective. This is believed to work because these items often lose their reinforcing value when the individual has "had his fill" of them. Schaefer and Martin (870) cite the example of a towel hoarder. His treatment was rapid and successful when the nurses regularly placed towels in his room instead of removing them.

Some behaviors are not particularly disruptive but disturb other patients, such as chain smoking to the point where the patient's fingers are stained with nicotine and unsightly, and constantly drinking coffee or soda containing caffeine, despite the development of caffeine reactions. Most commonly, such behaviors are seen in patients who are anxious or perseverative. Although primary treatment must focus on the resolution of the patient's illness process by somatic treatment, adjunctive behavioral techniques can be of benefit. To be effective, however, behavioral techniques should include (1) specific identification of the unwanted behavior and the circumstances in which it occurs, (2) determination of the frequency of the behavior, (3) identification of specific staff responses that are considered reinforcing for that particular behavior in that patient, and (4) consistent action by all staff members.

Principles of Inpatient Unit Management

The short-term psychiatric inpatient unit is analogous to other specialized hospital units (e.g., medical/surgical, intensive care (ICU), burn, trauma) in that the physician has the ultimate professional responsibility and liability for treatment, but most patient care activities are carried out by other professionals (nurses, aides, technicians, social workers). Functioning as a cohesive group and concentrating on patient care, these individuals form the core of a well-run unit. In many psychiatric units, unfortunately, more energy is spent in maintaining the spirit of cooperation among staff members than in treating patients. Too often, many members of the professional staff are more concerned with gaining control of the "best" patients for pet treatments, winning professional rivalries, amassing personal power, and, ultimately, controlling the unit itself than with caring for patients (937). These intrastaff interactions lead to an essential social structure on the unit that must be understood and managed if patients are to receive good care. This social structure exists in all types of hospitals—public, private, teaching, nonteaching, general, and psychiatric.

The professionals on the unit quickly become a social group in which professional and personal roles, status, and leadership must be established if the unit is to function well. Impinging upon this internal structure is the relationship of the unit to the rest of the hospital. As intragroup structures crystallize and unit functioning increases in efficiency and quality, the unit develops a sense of territory, of us-versus-them, of group loyalty, which reinforces the unit's cohesiveness and simultaneously creates problems for the unit leadership in dealing with the rest of the hospital. Physicians who ignore these factors or who assume a one-dimensional authoritarian role toward the rest of the staff are not optimally effective in caring for their patients and may even harm them (170, 937).

Varying degrees of intrastaff difficulties inevitably occur on well-established units. In managing such a unit, it is important to identify the specific details of the unit's social structure; establish clear-cut professional roles based on the differing expertise of each discipline; identify and use specific strengths of individual staff members, regardless of professional identity; clearly establish a leader; and establish a daily patient care and staff program and a treatment philosophy that are understood and endorsed by all staff members.

Specifically, psychologists, social workers, psychiatrists, and nurses traditionally fight about who works harder, who is in charge, who serves patients best, whose expertise is worth more, and who is to treat each patient. Unit management must recognize this infighting and establish a primary goal of welding these individuals into a cohesive, mutually supportive group. A helpful first step is to encourage individual attributes of staff members that transcend professional expertise and are important in patient care. Thus, who has what interaction with a given patient may have more to do with the personality of a given staff member than with that staff member's professional training. Clearly, defined professional roles also are important, and the expected contributions of the respective professionals must be explicitly stated. Much bickering and jockeying for power arises from professionals who deprecate what they are traditionally trained to do best and falsely ascribe more value to what they perceive as the important treatment style. For example, social workers too often consider social service casework a necessary but demeaning obligation and derive their real satisfaction from treating patients with psychotherapy. Similarly, nurses devalue nursing care, psychologists devalue psychological assessment and behavioral techniques, and psychiatrists devalue their medical expertise. Optimal unit functioning occurs when everyone has access to interact with patients but each discipline is primarily responsible for its particular area of expertise and that expertise is valued for its utility.

Establishing clear-cut unit leadership is important. The neuropsychiatrist may not have sufficient expertise to qualify for leadership in some specialized units for behavior modification or alcohol rehabilitation. For a unit, however, that serves most other patients (e.g., patients with behavioral neurologic disease, affective disorder), the neuropsychiatrist theoretically has the best combination of skill and knowledge to assume the leadership role. Obviously, the best leader is the person who combines expertise with the qualities of personality necessary for the role. This leadership model also requires the establishment of the medical model as the specific program and treatment philosophy of the unit; that is, the unit's objective is primarily to treat patients with brain disease or dysfunction (affective disorder, schizophrenia, behavioral neurologic disease). Although there must be significant flexibility of action within this system, all staff professionals should basically endorse it.

The social structure of a unit also involves the goals and expectations of staff members and their professional role interactions with patients (170). Thus, a staff recruited for a unit with the primary goal of treatment cannot be expected to launch enthusiastically and efficiently into a research project or training program without significant preparation, discussion, and education to demonstrate that the research or training will directly or indirectly enhance patient care.

The inpatient neuropsychiatrist must handle staff problems and, consequently, devote significant time and energy to staff management. Even the private practitioner who spends relatively little time on the unit must deal with staff problems that affect the care of his patients. Because the staff forms a more cohesive social group than do the patients, intensive staff management efforts are unavoidable. In a newly established inpatient unit, much intrastaff bickering and wasted energy can be avoided if the unit's goals and treatment philosophy are clearly defined; professional roles are explicitly described; programming clearly reflects treatment philosophy, professionally compatible staff members, who endorse the unit's goals and treatment philosophy, are recruited; and the staff is directed by one individual. In the inpatient unit, which treats primarily individuals with major mental illness, medical management (diagnosis and somatic treatment) is the primary therapeutic approach. Milieu influences and psychological interventions are important adjuncts but, alone, are of minimal therapeutic benefit to such patients (391, 642, 928).

Inpatient Program Structure

A principal goal of psychiatric hospitalization is to control the patient's behavior. For some patients, particularly those who are suicidal, hospitalization may be literally lifesaving and, thus, is itself a treatment. An extension of this control is a program structure that provides patients with hourly schedules that help to shape their social behaviors. These schedules contain planned activities, each with stated objectives. Frequently, patients are unable to concentrate, plan, or successfully carry out daily tasks. A schedule with appropriate rest periods and free time provides the necessary daily structure until the patient is able to plan for himself. The schedule should be flexible, so that, as the patient improves, he can progressively assume more responsibility for his own activities. This can be accomplished by a "step system," which details the specific behaviors that determine the responsibilities and privileges of a particular patient. The system, like all unit schedules and rules, should be simply stated and prominently displayed. Step changes (up or down) are usually decided each morning with input from the entire staff. Part of the step system should be a schedule of daily activities that patients should or may attend at different steps.

Patients hospitalized in a short-term psychiatric unit differ from patients hospitalized in medical or surgical units. They are usually fully ambulatory and, when they begin to improve, need to be physically occupied. Patients also must be educated about the illness and treatments and learn to deal with social and occupational disruptions causes by the illness. Some patients need behavioral programs to alter the frequency of specific behaviors, and all need emotionally supportive interactions with various staff members. A program structure planned by unit personnel can provide for these needs. Group meetings generally should be devoted to educating patients about their illnesses and treatments and discussing the practical, interpersonal difficulties they face with family, friends, and employers. Some groups may specifically teach patients strategies for coping with the problems of living they encounter. The staff involved in the groups should meet briefly following each session to discuss patient problems or behavioral observations that should be communicated to other staff members. A biweekly unit meeting for all patients and as many of the staff as can attend is usually needed to discuss specific unit problems and activities.

A daily hourly schedule is also needed for the unit staff. What staff members are supposed to do, when they are supposed to do it, and why they do it should be explicitly stipulated. The morning report should include as much of the staff (all disciplines) as possible. The charge nurse for the day or the head nurse should present the nursing report from the night shift, briefly summarize any new admissions to the unit, and review any problems from the previous 24 hours. Potential problems for the day should be discussed and a plan of action devised for each. The day's discharges and last-minute discharge preparations also should be discussed.

The staff of most psychiatric units is divided into interdisciplinary teams, with each team responsible for the patients of that team's physicians. Team meetings should include all members and function as informational, specific problem-solving, and planning sessions. In teaching hospitals, doctors' rounds should be scheduled at the same time each weekday morning. Participants include house staff, students, and other team members (particularly a nurse and social worker). Teaching rounds should have specific training goals as the physician in charge briefly sees each new patient and reviews the progress of the other patients. In nonteaching hospitals, doctors' rounds are still important as an occasion for evaluating patients, communicating with other team members, providing mutual education, and identifying problems that require nursing and social service skills. A monthly meeting for all staff members is also helpful in resolving unit problems, reinforcing unit philosophy, and introducing future plans. Evening and night shift personnel should periodically attend staff meetings, which should be scheduled close to shift changes so that little time is lost. In order to maintain efficiency and enthusiasm, educational activities should be a regular part of the staff schedule. The unit structure also extends to individual staff-patient interactions. What is said to a patient, how it is said, and by whom relate to an important aspect of the overall treatment plan.

The ability of the staff to observe and report psychopathology in a reliable manner is necessary for overall unit efficiency. Despite previous training, most mental health professionals require additional observation and communication skills, and a system should be established for ensuring intrastaff reliability of observation. A number of clinical rating scales are available (438, 454). They are short, easily learned, and extremely helpful as adjuncts to overall patient care.

Inpatient Problems

Uncooperative Patients

Violence, although relatively infrequent, is the most serious unit problem. Discussions of violence and emergency measures in response to violence are presented in Chapter 23. More common than an actually assaultive patient, however, is a patient who is agitated and irritable and refuses to cooperate with basic unit policies, such as keeping his room and body clean and permitting a physical examination and diagnostic evaluation. In responding to such a patient, the first decision to be made is whether the patient is suffering from an illness that is causing his uncooperativeness, agitation, and irritability or whether the patient is simply manipulating the hospital system. When the latter is strongly suspected, the patient should be told he must either cooperate or be discharged immediately. If he fails to cooperate, he should then be discharged. For a patient considered ill, the lack of a physical examination and basic diagnostic tests (e.g., blood work) might be life-threatening if serious illness progresses undiscovered. The decision to be made at this point is whether the patient is competent to participate fully in decisions concerning his treatment. If he is competent, the reasons for the examination, diagnostic evaluation, personal hygiene, or other procedures or activities should be explained again. He should be told that he cannot be helped unless he cooperates and allows the staff to help him and that he has a choice of cooperating or seeking help elsewhere. If he chooses the latter, his family or friends should be notified. If they cannot persuade him to cooperate, he should be discharged.

When a patient is determined by the staff to be incompetent or dangerous to himself or others and is not already in the hospital as an involuntary patient, his family should be informed of this assessment. If the family concurs, the patient should be converted to involuntary status, restrained, and sedated, if necessary. He is then examined, and blood samples are drawn. If x-rays and other tests are needed, they can be obtained while the patient is sedated. Should the patient's family refuse to support these procedures, which can be considered emergency measures in that they are needed to prevent, identify, or treat, a potential life-threatening illness, the family can be asked to transfer the patient to another hospital. Most families are relieved to know that firm action is being taken to find out what is wrong with the patient and usually agree to the necessary procedures. Under no circumstances should a patient be hospitalized for longer than 24 hours without a physical examination and necessary laboratory work.

The agitated, uncooperative patient is on the lowest level of any step system. He may need to be sedated and possibly placed in seclusion for varying periods. When minimal knowledge has been obtained regarding the patient's condition and there is reasonable likelihood that neuroleptic treatment is not contraindicated, he should receive IM neuroleptics for 2 to 5 days until he is no longer agitated and uncooperative. Oral neuroleptics should be introduced later and overlap with IM administration. If the patient remains agitated and uncontrollable despite several days of IM medication, IV medication (i.e., haloperidol) or ECT should be administered. Uncooperativeness specifically refers to patients who are so ill that they are unmanageable. Such patients refuse to shower and clean up their personal areas. They lie on the floor, masturbate or undress in public, and generally disrupt the unit and upset the other patients. The behaviors most often reflect illness and require treatment. For the safety of these patients and those around them, such behaviors must be stopped (almost always, some degree of force is needed, from "show of force" to restraints and seclusion) and medicatation administered.

The overriding issue in the situations described above is to ensure that a patient does not harm himself or others. Also, he must be prevented from undermining his own treatments and from behaving in a manner that disrupts the functions of the unit and disturbs other patients. The obvious theme of this approach is patient control. Society continues to struggle with the issue and the degree to which individual rights can be denied to protect both the individual and society as a whole. That subject is beyond the scope of this book, but suffice it to say that once a person is identified as being ill and is hospitalized because of that illness, he has the right to treatment. The decision to abridge the patient's civil liberties in order to treat him, however, cannot be made solely by the physician. If the patient's behavior is dangerous, physicians are legally permitted to restrain and treat for a limited time. Further involuntary treatment usually requires court approval. In the case of a patient who is not dangerous but is clearly psychotic or severely ill, the physician must decide whether the patient is competent to judge his own condition and the prescribed treatments. If the patient is competent, the decision to be treated is his; if the patient is incompetent, he should be treated. Court approval, however, must be obtained before definitive nonemergency involuntary treatment can be legally administered. In most instances, consultation with the patient's family is helpful in obtaining the patient's consent to treatment and in reducing the risk of suit for treating the patient while court approval is being obtained. The vast majority of patients, when recovered, express their gratitude that they were stopped from doing "those crazy (embarrassing, dangerous) things."

The use of IM medication, restraints, and seclusion does not particularly upset or anger patients if it is clear that these methods are used as treatments, not as punishments, and that the staff truly cares about the patient's well-being. Integral to these responses to deviant behaviors are warm, caring, and concerned supportive responses to the patient's other symptoms and interpersonal needs.

Patients Requiring Restraints and Seclusion

The use of seclusion and restraints is a particularly sensitive issue. Established rules for restraining and secluding patients should be clearly understood by each staff member. Physical restraints should be used only as a therapeutic measure to protect the patient from injuring himself or others. Restraints should never be used to punish or discipline a patient or for staff convenience.

Restraints should be employed only on the written order of a physician after he has examined the patient. Orders for restraints are usually valid for up to 12 hours, at which time the patient must be formally reexamined by a physician for subsequent restraints. Nevertheless, periodic evaluation by a qualified staff member should be made every 15 to 30 minutes. In ordering restraints, the physician should specify the duration of their application and, in an accompanying progress note, indicate the events leading to the need for restraints, the purpose of restraints, and the length of the restraint period. In emergencies, orders for restraints may be given to a nurse by telephone, or the nurse or other qualified examiner may order restraints subject to prompt confirmation (within 1 hour) by a physician in writing and with appropriate documentation. While in restraints, the patient should be closely supervised and made as comfortable as possible. Special attention should be given to the patient's temperature and fluid intake to avoid dehydration and hyperthermia.

When a specific seclusion room is not available, a patient bedroom may be used, provided there is one-to-one observation by nursing personnel, with the room unlocked and free from furniture. All rules that apply to ordering and monitoring restraints also apply to the use of the seclusion room.

Suicidal Patients

Occasionally, depressed patients commit suicide while hospitalized. Placing a suicidal patient on "suicide precautions," although legally necessary, is often insufficient to prevent such deaths. Patients have killed themselves by hanging (using ceiling and shower fixtures), ramming their heads into walls, jumping off high furniture or wall molding headfirst onto the floor, and cutting their wrists with eating utensils or on broken window glass. The suicidal patient should be placed in hospital clothes and continuously observed by a specifically assigned staff member. He may require seclusion and restraints. The patient should be on the lowest level of any step system and should never be allowed off the unit unescorted. Should a patient on suicidal precautions attempt suicide on the unit, emergency ECT should be administered as a potentially lifesaving procedure.

Self-Mutilators

Patients sometimes injure themselves as part of a pattern of self-mutilation, rather than because of a desire to die. These patients usually inflict superficial cuts and burns on the arms, legs, and chest or may insert objects into the urethra. Some of them actually experience pleasure while harming themselves. Such a paradoxic response to pain (pain asymboly) should alert the clinician to the possibility of coarse brain disease, particularly a seizure disorder. Some OCD patients and patients with GTS syndrome also exhibit self-mutilating behaviors (326, 886). Self-mutilators may require restraints until a specific diagnosis can be made and treatment instituted.

Although there is no known treatment for self-mutilators who do not have behavioral neurologic disease or OCD, there is some evidence (394, 791) that such patients who have been admitted to a short-term treatment unit of a general hospital experience dramatic cessation of self-mutilitating behaviors when they are transferred to a chronic care facility. Direct behavior modification techniques have minimal effect in reducing the frequency of these behaviors.

Patients with Overt Sexual Behaviors

Most short-term inpatient units admit men and women. Although the general experience of units that have become "coed" is increased socialization and normalization of patient behavior, inappropriate sexual behavior occasionally occurs. Observing overt sexual behavior in other patients is frightening to some patients, and the sexual behavior, if not immediately stopped, may lead patients to feel that the involved patients are out of control and that the staff is unable to control them. Whereas expressions of warmth and affection can be appropriate, specific sexual behavior (e.g., passionate kissing, embracing, and fondling) must be stopped immediately and treated as any other behavior that is inappropriate in a hospital or public setting. Liaisons that occur in patients' bedrooms, although showing discretion on the part of the individuals involved, also must be prevented from recurring, because they too indicate that the participants may have lost control or that one of the participants (with diminished judgment or volition or with hypersexuality) is being taken advantage of by a patient with a less severe illness. Separation and close monitoring of these patients and a reevaluation of their diagnoses and treatments should be the minimal response. Continued attempts at sexual liaisons by a patient may require his seclusion until specific treatment (e.g., lithium, neuroleptics) becomes effective. If the patient is voluntarily hospitalized and deemed not a danger to himself, discharge from the unit may be necessary. At no time, however, should overt sexual behaviors be ignored. Calm but firm discussions with the participants and other patients on the unit are often helpful in reducing anxieties. Failing to curtail these behaviors, in addition to potentially harming patients, can lead to successful malpractice suits.

Agitated Patients

The patient who is agitated, although not assaultive, is also a management problem. Agitation is the motor expression of an intense mood. When the patient is not assaultive or irritable, the most likely cause of agitation is depression. As the profound sadness and dysphoria of the depression improve with biologic treatment, the agitation resolves. During the interim between admission of the patient and any significant improvement resulting from the primary treatment, sodium amytal or lorazepam may be beneficial. Occasionally, patients with neuroleptic-induced akathisia are mistakenly identified as agitated. The patient with akathisia, however, describes an inner restlessness and a jumpiness in his arms and legs, which become overpowering unless he moves about. Also, he may exhibit other neuroleptic side effects.

Patients with Insomnia

Most patients on a psychiatric unit have difficulty sleeping, particularly during the first few nights of hospitalization. Hypnotics are routinely ordered "p.r.n." in most hospital units. When a patient simply cannot sleep (he is not upset or agitated) and the full hypnotic dose has been administered, however, the night staff should recognize that the patient is probably not manipulating the system but simply exhibiting a symptom of his illness. Rather than make an issue of his being awake—causing the patient to feel guilty and the staff angry—the staff should allow him to sit up in a day area where he can read, watch television, or talk with a staff member. The insomnia invariably improves with resolution of the illness.

Substance Abusers

Patients who are substance abusers are particularly difficult to treat in a short-term general inpatient psychiatric unit. Patients in acute alcohol withdrawal states are at increased risk for seizures and death and may require IV fluid and electrolyte replacement. Generally, they are best treated on specialized detoxification or medical units.

Occasionally, however, patients addicted to opiates or barbiturates are admitted to a general psychiatric unit. These patients frequently have antisocial traits and can create havoc on the unit. They manipulate staff and other patients, abuse other patients, demand and often receive unwarranted medication, and may even introduce illicit drugs to the unit's ill patients. In general, all patients who are primarily substance abusers and have no psychosis or major illness, such as depression, or who have antisocial personalities should be discharged as quickly as possible.

VIPs

Patients who are physicians or mental health professionals can present a particular management problem. They often assume a stafflike manner and, actually, may be of help to other patients. Nevertheless, if they have been appropriately hospitalized (that is, if they have a major psychiatric disorder), they require the same psychological and biologic treatments as anyone else. If they are to receive the best available treatment, the staff must recognize the tendency of these patients to act the role of treater and the tendency of staff members to permit this, often at the expense of the patient's optimal care. A professional who is a patient can "help out" during the recovery phase of his illness, but his knowledge of his illness and treatments, his response to his illness and family, and his personal concerns should not be taken for granted. These patients deserve "full service."

Famous or exotic patients also can tempt staff members to respond to their reputation or status, rather than to their personal qualities and the treatment requirements of the illness. A dramatic example occurred at a municipal inner city teaching hospital. A young, attractive actress was transferred to psychiatry from the medical unit after a suicide attempt. Although not melancholic and fully recovered from the physiologic sequela of her overdose, she remained in the hospital for several more weeks "holding court." Long lines of medical students and residents from three services came to see her and "help her through her crisis." Her histrionic, dependent, and egocentric behaviors received unlimited reinforcement at the expense of any reasonable plan to help her deal with her problems of living. Although the staff was aware of the phenomenon, it was never discussed in a staff meeting and, thus, never resolved so that the patient could receive appropriate care.

Outsiders

A common problem on inpatient units is that of the staff assuming an adversary relationship to outsiders: visitors, hospital personnel from other patient care areas (e.g., medicine, emergency room), and support services personnel (e.g., x-ray, laboratory). The adversary attitude develops as the unit's cohesiveness evolves. Staff behaviors that suggest this attitude are suspiciousness and irritability toward strangers entering the unit, defensiveness and guardedness toward the families and friends of patients, expectations of "special" service from hospital support areas (e.g., obtaining all requested supplies in optimal quantities before other patient care areas receive their supplies), and expressions of unrealistically low opinions about other patient care areas (particularly similar units or units to or from which patients may be transferred). Paradoxically, these behaviors are often a sign that the unit is functioning well, but they can simultaneously result in internecine squabbling, which reduces the unit's effectiveness, as well as its needed supports from the "outsiders." Recognition and staff discussion of these behaviors and the attitudes leading to them usually suffice to prevent significant problems.

Principles of Consultation

Neuropsychiatric consultants perform individual patient evaluations to assist other physicians and, occasionally, other mental health professionals. Hospitalized patients should be seen within 24 hours for routine consultations and within minutes or hours for an emergency, depending on circumstances. Emergency hospital consultations require a conversation between the primary physician and the neuropsychiatrist. The primary physician should make the neuropsychiatrist aware of the reason for the consultation, and the neuropsychiatrist should specify when he will arrive and recommend temporary measures until then. The primary physician should tell the patient a consultant will arrive and should explain the reason for the consultation. The neuropsychiatrist should usually extend his evaluation beyond the stated reason for the consult request.

In closing the examination, the neuropsychiatrist should present the patient with conclusions and recommendations and add that implementation of recommendations is the province of the patient and the primary doctor. The neuropsychiatrist should not write orders unless requested to do so by the referring physician. The note should be especially detailed in the sections on differential diagnosis and recommendations. Recommendations should also address the following six points, as needed:

1. Additional information needed to establish a diagnosis (e.g., old records, history from family members, laboratory tests)
2. Degree to which current treatment may be contributing to, or ameliorating, the patient's behavioral dysfunction (e.g., advantages and disadvantages of medications being used or of interpersonal dealings with the patient)
3. Temporary and definitive medical treatments of the patient's condition, including the value of aspects of current management, addition of psychiatric (e.g., psychoactive medications or ECT) or general medical (e.g., vitamins, fluids, and electrolytes) treatments
4. Noninvasive interventions (e.g., encouraging visitors, supportive conversations by nurses, visit by social worker, night light, behavior modification tactics)

5. Further involvement by the consultant, if needed (e.g., follow-up visits on the ward or outpatient clinic, transfer to the psychiatry service)
6. Explicit recommendations about further psychiatric care or discharge (e.g., "no need to postpone surgery for psychiatric reasons," "do not let patient leave the hospital," "no reason to keep patient in hospital for psychiatric reasons")

The principles and techniques of interviewing and diagnosis on the consultation service are identical to those used on the psychiatric service. What differs is the frequency of the conditions observed. Common diagnoses of medical patients referred for psychiatric consultation include situational reactions, alcohol and substance abuse syndromes, coarse brain disease, and depression (899).

Common Consultation Situations

Consultations frequently involve patients with the following conditions: (1) simultaneous manifestations of systemic illness and abnormal behaviors, (2) abnormal behavior by a patient who is receiving medication known to affect the brain; (3) coarse brain disease of unknown cause; (4) symptoms of pathology where no pathology can be found; and (5) behavior affected by drug overdose. Common hospital consultations also include intensive care and surgical patients, narcotic addicts on medical and surgical services, and medical and surgical patients who refuse transfer to the psychiatry service.

For hospital consultations, the solution to the problem is often found in the laboratory data or medications sections of the chart or in the nursing notes.

Concurrent Systemic Illness or Medication

The patient with concomitant systemic illness and abnormal behavior is one of the most common types of referral. The consultant must determine if the behavior (1) is the product of the illness for which the patient was admitted, (2) results from the treatment, or (3) is due to coexisting psychiatric illness, such as mood or anxiety disorder. The consultant should consider the following four factors:

1. If the patient has an active systemic illness known to affect the brain, the abnormal behavior is caused by that illness until proved otherwise.
2. If onset of the abnormal behavior follows onset of the systemic disease or follows treatments known to affect the brain, the behavior is more likely a result of that illness or treatment than of a separate psychiatric disorder.
3. The more pronounced the cognitive dysfunction, the more likely it is that the patient has coarse brain disease.
4. If the patient has had prior psychiatric illness with similar manifestations or has a family history of psychiatric disorder (especially mood disorder), the chances increase that the behavior is due to a coexisting psychiatric syndrome unrelated to the systemic illness.

Diffuse Coarse Brain Disease of Unknown Cause

Twenty percent of medical patients have diffuse cognitive dysfunction (539), and diffuse coarse brain disease is the primary diagnosis in 15% of psychiatric consultations on medical and surgical services. When the cause is unknown, the referring clinician is grateful for a differential diagnosis and suggestions for further evaluation (see Chapter 12).

The key to management of patients with diffuse cognitive dysfunction is to identify and treat the cause. Until the cause is found and corrected, or if the illness is incurable, management should be directed at preventing exacerbation, particularly at night when the environment provides insufficient clues to orientation and support. The following 11 steps are helpful:

1. Use a night light.
2. Redirect lights if frightening shadows are cast on the walls.
3. Place a clock and calendar in view.
4. Encourage visits by family and friends.
5. Turn on the television or radio.
6. Make available familiar items, such as photographs and newspapers.
7. Prescribe, repair, or replace glasses or hearing aids.
8. Have the staff make supportive and orienting conversation.
9. Keep the patient close to or in view of the nursing station.
10. Minimize the use of physical restraints—a Posey belt is preferable to full leather restraints.
11. Avoid barbiturates and neuroleptics unless behavior is uncontrollable.

If control of the patient is necessary, haloperidol is the safest of the neuroleptics. It should be avoided, however, when delirium is caused by (1) anticholinergic toxicity (physostigmine is the proper treatment) or (2) hypnotic drug withdrawal (treatment is replacement with a hypnotic drug).

Systemic Symptoms with No Diagnosable Systemic Illness

Patients are frequently referred with medically unexplained systemic symptoms or symptoms that occurred with an intensity exceeding expectations. Similarly, pain that exceeds expected intensity or has no explanation is sometimes a reason for referral. In the differential diagnosis, the neuropsychiatrist should consider primary psychiatric conditions, especially (1) malingering, (2) depression, (3) anxiety disorders, and (4) somatization disorders.

When a psychiatric syndrome known to produce pain is ruled out and no other medical explanations are forthcoming, other measures are often tried, regardless of proven efficacy. Such measures include the use of fixed interval analgesic schedules, behavior modification, progressive relaxation, biofeedback, acupuncture, hypnosis, massages, warm packs, physical therapy, psychotherapy, cyclic antidepressants (e.g., amitryptiline, 150–300 mg daily, regardless of whether the patient is depressed), and ECT. When nothing alleviates the pain, the clinician must seek further consultation or explain to the patient that he must attempt to tolerate his pain.

Intensive Care Units

Patients in intensive care units are at high risk for developing abnormal behavior, largely because they are among the sickest in the hospital, have conditions likely to affect brain function, and often receive large amounts of potent medications. In many hospitals, the following five features of an intensive care unit may contribute to the problem: (1) alien environment with unfamiliar people; (2) sensory monotony, because much of the stimulation from monitors and other devices is impersonal and not thought-provoking; (3) physical discomfort caused by disease; (4) crowding and lack of privacy; and (5) illness and death of other patients (530).

Narcotic Addicts

Sometimes narcotic addicts are admitted to medical or surgical services for conditions (e.g., knife wound, bacterial endocarditis, lung abscess) that cannot be treated elsewhere. Although narcotic withdrawal is rarely fatal, its symptoms are uncomfortable and, if untreated, lead to noncompliance with medical and surgical care. Based on the extent of the habit, a daily oral dose of methadone (Dolophine, usually 10–20 mg b.i.d.) can be given. This dose can be maintained throughout the patient's hospital stay or gradually tapered over a period of 1 to several weeks. If the patient experiences pain (e.g., postoperative pain) unrelated to opiate withdrawal, he can be given analgesics in doses that would be appropriate were he not addicted.

Refusal of Transfer to Psychiatry Service

Patients on medical and surgical services (e.g., for an overdose), who belong on the psychiatric inpatient service, sometimes refuse transfer to the psychiatric unit while accepting medical or surgical hospitalization. The neuropsychiatrist and primary physician have the choices of involuntary hospitalization on the psychiatric service, discharge home, or continued care on the medical or surgical service. If the patient is potentially dangerous to himself or others, involuntary psychiatric hospitalization is appropriate. If the patient is very ill but not potentially dangerous, he may be allowed to sign out against medical advice or, if he consents, be permitted to remain on the medical or surgical unit for psychiatric treatment. The latter option carries some legal liability (e.g., if the patient makes a suicide attempt while on the medical service) and may be contrary to hospital policy. When hospital policy permits this option, however, and if the neuropsychiatrist and primary physician feel that better care can be provided to a relatively cooperative and noncommittable patient on a medical or surgical service than at a psychiatric hospital or outpatient clinic, such treatment can be attempted on a trial basis. This decision requires a clear justification in the patient's chart.

Surgical Patients

Several studies show that preoperative mental status often predicts postoperative morbidity and mortality from all causes. Patients with any of the following seven characteristics are prone to develop postoperative delirium (691):

1. Previous or current psychiatric illness, such as alcoholism, depression, coarse brain disease, or psychosis
2. Preoperative insomnia
3. Advanced age
4. Retirement adjustment problems
5. "Functional" gastroenterologic disturbance
6. Low socioeconomic status
7. Family history of psychiatric illness

Good preoperative psychological management, consisting largely of explanations of procedures and thoughtful responses to questions, is associated with a better postoperative course. Prior to elective surgery, therefore, consideration of the patient's psychiatric history and mental status by the primary physician or consulting neuropsychiatrist and treatment of readily managed psychiatric conditions by the neuropsychiatrist are in order. Prior to any surgery, the procedures and anticipated experiences of the patient should be discussed in whatever detail the patient wishes and is capable of understanding.

Chapter 20

Psychotropic Medications

Relatively few classes of pharmacologic agents are specific to neuropsychiatry, compared with other medical specialties. In the use of these agents, the following eight guidelines apply:

1. Know the use of a few drugs thoroughly, rather than a large number superficially.
2. Avoid prescribing more than one drug of the same class at the same time.
3. When one drug is unsuccessful, switch to a different group or class of drug, rather than to a second similar drug.
4. Do not switch to a second drug before an adequate trial (optimal dose and duration) with the first drug.
5. Limit the number of drugs simultaneously prescribed. One is best, two are reasonable, three or more are usually bad.
6. Limit the number of daily administrations.
7. Be sensitive to patients with special pharmacologic needs, including pregnant or breast-feeding women, elderly patients, and individuals with disease in other systems.
8. Be sensitive to the life situations and daily habits of patients that may affect their compliance with treatment.

Neuroleptics

Chlorpromazine, the first neuroleptic, was introduced in 1952. Since then, dozens of neuroleptics of several chemical classes have been developed; all have approximately the same therapeutic indications and efficacy (109, 227). Although all neuroleptics are sedating to some degree, they are not truly hypnotic. Unlike barbiturates, neuroleptics do not directly suppress conduction in the reticular activating system. Instead, they increase the central arousal threshold by suppressing afferent sensory transmission from the periphery (131, 529) and filter out incoming stimuli without decreasing alertness. Hence, they produce "sedation without sleep."

Neuroleptics are highly lipophilic. Once in the bloodstream, they readily bind to protein and are rapidly distributed in body tissues (half-life of about 2 hours). Because of their biphasic liver metabolism and secondary release from body fat, a second slower redistribution occurs (half-life of 20 to 30 hours). Thus, neuroleptics have both rapid and prolonged bioavailability.

The most important neuropharmacologic effect of neuroleptics is believed to be the blockade of dopaminergic (D_2) transmission in the central nervous system. This is a postsynaptic receptor blockade and occurs (at least in nonhumans) in varying degrees in each of the dopaminergic pathways: nigrostriatal, tuberoinfundibular, mesolimbic, and mesocortical. Blockade of the nigrostriatial system is responsible for the neuroleptic extrapyramidal syndrome and is causally unrelated to the antipsychotic activity of neuroleptics. Blockade in the tuberoinfundibular system produces a variety of hormonal effects, of which the most prominent are hyperprolactinemia (pseudopregnancy, gynecomastia, lactation) and inhibition of pituitary gonodotropins. There is no specific evidence of a causal relationship between these endocrine changes and antipsychotic efficacy. Blockade in the mesolimbic and mesocortical dopamine systems remains the most difficult to measure. A relationship is presumed between such blockade and inhibition of aggressive behavior in several species, including humans, but specific evidence is lacking. Nonetheless, the prevailing notion is that the antipsychotic properties of the neuroleptics reside in their ability to block dopaminergic transmission in limbic structures and related cortex.

Alpha-adrenergic blockade is seen most prominently with the aliphatic tricyclic neuroleptics (e.g., chlorpromazine) and is responsible for their frequent hypotensive effects. Neuroleptics, especially the piperidine tricyclics (e.g., thioridazine), also have anticholinergic effects, which, in the case of thioridazine, are equipotent with those of the tricyclic antidepressant amitriptyline. In addition, the neuroleptics exhibit antihistaminic and antiserotonin effects, induce hypothermia, and potentiate the CNS depressant effects of alcohol, barbiturates, and opiates.

Studies in normal humans have demonstrated significant cognitive and EEG effects of neuroleptics. Single-dose trials typically produce impaired performance on tests of speed, reaction time, and accuracy on timed tasks (678). When subjects are allowed to proceed at their own pace, however, the error rate is not different from that with placebo. The computer-analyzed resting EEG exhibits a characteristic pattern of increased theta and delta activity with a reduced mean alpha frequency (306).

Clinical Indications and Treatment Techniques

Neuroleptics are effective for a variety of syndromes regardless of etiology. Thus, psychotic excitement is an indication for neuroleptic treatment whether exhibited by manics, schizophrenics, or patients with drug-induced psychoses. Nevertheless, symptoms should not be treated in isolation from the underlying disorder that produces them. One drug is not used for excitement, a second for hallucinations, and a third for euphoria in a manic patient. Lithium, the drug of choice for manics, can resolve all manic symptoms regardless of their form or combination.

Table 20.1 presents the classification of neuroleptics. One representative drug is listed for each class or subclass. As a rule, as neuroleptic potency increases, the sedative and hypotensive effects decrease and the acute extrapyramidal side effects increase. Neuroleptic potency is also highly correlated with dopaminergic blockade.

Neuroleptics are rapidly metabolized by the liver and excreted in the feces (and, to a lesser extent, by the kidneys). Intestinal microflora can metabolize inactive metabolites back into active ones, thereby helping to prolong therapeutic half-life; therefore, maintenance of intestinal health can have clinical importance. Because neuroleptics have anticholinergic properties, their use can result in constipation. The clinician should give particular attention to the need for high-fiber foods, adequate fluid intake, fecal softeners (in the elderly), and the use of bulk laxatives. Their anticholinergic effects also lead to dry mouth, and many patients self-treat this annoying condition with chewing gum and hard candy. If these are used, they should be sugar-free to prevent oral candidal infection.

Also, drug interactions must be considered. For example, antacids decrease oral absorption and lower blood levels; antiparkinsonian agents and tricyclic antidepressants potentiate the anticholinergic effects of neuroleptics and can result in paralytic ileus in elderly patients and anticholinergic delirium in patients of all ages; anticonvulsants decrease neuroleptic blood levels by increasing clearance or by inducing metabolism (particularly with haloperidol); and ascorbic acid may enhance haloperidol effectiveness (804). Monitoring of neuroleptic blood levels is not clinically useful; the clinician must titrate dose to the degree of symptom reduction and severity of side effects. Complete familiarity with one low-potency neuroleptic and one high-potency neuroleptic should suffice for most circumstances and provide the most effective clinical practice.

Psychotic Excitement States

Neuroleptics are most effective in patients who are overactive, restless, or agitated. Physiologically, these patients have dilated pupils, rapid pulse, reduced total sleep time, and a desynchronized EEG. They have markedly impaired judgment, are unable to control their excited behavior, and most often are delusional and

TABLE 20.1

Neuroleptics

Class/Subclass	Generic name	Trade Name	Usual Antipsychotic Dose (mg)	Special Comments
Phenothiazine				
Aliphatic	Chlorpromazine	Thorazine	400–600	Sedating; postural hypotension a problem
Piperidine	Thioridazine	Mellaril	400–600	Doses above 600 mg lead to corneal opacities and vision loss; sedating; postural hypotension a problem
Piperazine	Fluphenazine	Prolixin	20–80	Comes in long-acting form
Thioxanthene				
Aliphatic	Chlorprothixene	Taractan	400–600	
Piperazine	Thiothixene	Navane	20–80	
Dibenzoxazepine	Loxapine	Loxitane	60–100	
Butyrophenone	Haloperidol	Haldol	20–80	Best all-around neuroleptic; comes in long-acting form; can also be administered IM or IV
Dihydroindolone	Molindone	Moban	200	
Diphenylbutylpiperidine	Pimozide	Orap	20–30	Effective in Gilles de la Tourette's syndrome and perhaps monomanias
Dibenzodiazepine	Clozapine	Clozaril	20–60	Agranulocytosis more common than with other neuroleptics

hallucinating. Patients may become threatening and assaultive, and all psychotic excitement states require immediate treatment. Mania is the most frequent primary syndrome in this group of patients, although coarse brain disease (e.g., drug-induced psychosis) and schizophrenia also may produce excitement states. Psychotic depression with agitation also constitutes an example of psychotic hyperarousal, but for reasons described below and in Chapters 11 and 21, neuroleptics are not the best pharmacologic alternative treatment for these patients.

Once the decision is made to give a neuroleptic to an excited patient, the drug is usually given parenterally. A neuroleptic with minimal alpha-adrenergic blocking properties, such as haloperidol, is best to avoid hypotensive cardiovascular collapse. An IM injection of 20 mg (range 10–30 mg) is administered immediately and two or three times daily for a minimum of 48 hours before switching to an oral preparation. Three rules should be followed when changing the route from parenteral to oral: (1) the oral dose should be given only once a day at bedtime, (2) the daily oral dose should be about 30 to 50% larger than the parenteral dose, and (3) parenteral administration should not be discontinued until the oral dose has taken effect. This usually requires an overlap of 48 to 72 hours from the administration of the first oral dose to that of the last parenteral one.

When an IM neuroleptic is insufficient to resolve a patient's excitement state, IV haloperidol may be used (17, 164, 304, 988). The patient should be physiologically stable and unresponsive to total daily IM doses up to 80 mg. One procedure for the administration of IV haloperidol involves three steps:

1. After discontinuing all other psychotropics, administer an IV bolus of 10 mg of haloperidol diluted into 1 cc of saline.
2. Immediately follow the haloperidol bolus with 1 mg of lorazepam (for sedation and to prevent delirium as the patient awakens) diluted into 1 cc of saline administered IV over 1 minute.
3. Monitor blood pressure and pulse every 15 minutes for 1 hour. This procedure can be repeated daily for up to 5 days at the same dose or for up to 3 days at 20 mg of haloperidol. Dramatic antipsychotic and excitement responses have been anecdotally reported with this procedure, which is then followed by the more typical administration of neuroleptics or other appropriate medication.

Other Psychotic Syndromes

Nonexcited psychotic patients (i.e., those with a delusional-hallucinatory syndrome) also respond to neuroleptics. When the psychosis is severe or the patient menacing, parenteral treatment may be required. Most patients can be managed with oral medication, however, so long as parenteral forms are immediately available. A typical regimen using haloperidol (another neuroleptic might be used) begins with 20–30 mg twice daily (taking advantage of an initial daytime sedating effect) for two to three days and changes to a single nighttime dose of 60–80 mg for the remainder of the treatment course. Some patients may require as much as 120 mg/day of haloperidol for maximum improvement, but doses exceeding this amount rarely augment the clinical response. Low-dose, high-potency neuroleptic treatment (e.g., < 10 mg of haloperidol daily) has been recommended by some clinicians (496). The results of such an approach are uncertain for the acutely ill, excited patient; for the calmer psychotic, akathisia is often an intolerable side effect with low doses.

A reduction in the patient's emotional response to the particular psychotic sign is usually the first observable clinical change. This is followed by a gradual diminution and eventual disappearance of the sign itself. Thus, a patient who is initially tormented by derogatory auditory hallucinations may, after a day or so on neuroleptics, report that he still hears the voices but that he no longer pays attention to them. As the days pass, the voices diminish in frequency and intensity and usually disappear after 1 to 2 weeks of treatment. Delusions follow a similar course: The patient initially loses the intense mood associated with the delusional idea, then claims that the delusional idea occurred only in the past, and, eventually (if treatment is fully successful), realizes that the event never occurred. Some patients are particularly prone to develop extrapyramidal side effects at this point in treatment, presumably as a result of intense dopamine receptor blockade. They may require gradual dose reduction or the administration of an antiparkinsonian agent.

The response of catatonic motor features to neuroleptic treatment is variable. When mannerisms and stereotypies occur as part of a manic state, for example, these features remit along with the other elements of the syndrome. Mutism, rigidity, catalepsy, and stupor, however, rarely respond to neuroleptics and are frequently aggravated by them. This lack of response is consistent with the clinical observation that neuroleptics can induce the syndrome of negativistic stupor in patients previously free from catatonic signs.

Emotional blunting is usually unresponsive to neuroleptics. Indeed, as neuroleptics are themselves capable of inducing some of the elements of blunting (e.g., expressionless face, monotonous voice, affective indifference), the syndrome may be intensified by their use.

Because of the potential for long-term side effects (tardive dyskinesia), conditions that are not known to be specifically responsive to neuroleptics contraindicate their use. These conditions include dysthymic and anxiety disorder, personality disorders (schizotypal may be the exception), and situational reactions. Neuroleptics should never be used solely for their hypnotic/sedative effects.

For patients with psychotic depression, the use of neuroleptics is controversial. Some authors recommend their use in combination with a cyclic antidepressant, and some evidence indicates that such treatment may be effective (705). Because of the risks for tardive dyskinesia and other neuroleptic side effects, however, it seems more prudent not to prescribe neuroleptics for depressed patients regardless of the presence of psychotic symptoms, so long as the option remains for administering ECT. This latter method is safe, rapid, and highly effective in patients with psychotic (delusional) depression. (See Chapter 11 for specific pharmacologic strategies for treatment-resistant patients with affective disorder.)

Neuroleptics, especially haloperidol and pimozide, also can benefit patients with Gilles de la Tourette's syndrome and those with nonaffective psychoses associated with coarse brain disease and alcohol and drug abuse.

Duration of Treatment

Most patients can be maintained on two thirds or less of the dose required to resolve the acute episode. The duration of neuroleptic maintenance depends on the nature and severity of the underlying disorder, the age of the patient, and the number and frequency of illness episodes. Drug discontinuation studies have demonstrated that a substantial portion (up to 60%) of patients on maintenance neuroleptics can have their treatment interrupted for many months without experiencing a return of symptoms (786). As time passes, however, a fairly constant proportion of this drug-free group experiences relapse (249). In addition to tardive dyskinesia, complications of long-term neuroleptic treatment include obesity, parkinsonism, and akathisia. Because of these potential complications, maintenance neuroleptic treatment should be stopped after 8 to 12 months in every patient who has not had a drug-free trial. Even in those who relapse and require reinstitution of neuroleptics, a drug-free trial should be attempted at least once or twice more at two-year intervals to determine if treatment is still required. Maintenance doses range from one third to the full dose that was needed to resolve the acute episode.

Neuroleptic Side Effects and Their Management

Central Nervous System

Inhibition of dopaminergic transmission in the nigrostriatal system is responsible for neuroleptic-induced acute extrapyramidal symptoms, parkinsonism, and dystonia. Table 20.2 displays the commonly used medications to treat these conditions and their effects. The parkinsonian triad of tremor, rigidity, and bradykinesia is easy to recognize and may be accompanied by greasy skin and a fixed, unblinking stare. Parkinsonism and all other extrapyramidal side effects occur most frequently with high-potency neuroleptics (e.g., piperazine phenothiazines, haloperidol) and are managed by administration of an antiparkinsonian agent. There is also a reported inverse correlation between neuroleptic dosage and the occurrence of extrapyramidal symptoms (820, 866). It is best to try one of the less toxic antiparkinsonian agents first (e.g., the dopaminergic amantadine) and reserve the more toxic anticholinergics, such as benztropine, for nonresponders to the safer

TABLE 20.2

Drugs Used to Treat Extrapyramidal Side Effects of Neuroleptics

Drug	*Usual Daily Oral Dose (mg)*	*Therapeutic Effects*	*Adverse Effects*
Amantadine (Symmetrel)	100–400	Broad spectrum for all EPS syndromes; may potentiate benefit of other compounds	Indigestion, light-headedness, decreased concentration, jitteriness; excreted in urine so renal function must be adequate
Benztropine (Cogentin)	2–6	Relieves muscle rigidity, sialorrhea, and drooling	Potent anticholinergic effects
Diphenhydramine (Benadryl)	150	Dystonia (best when used 50 mg IV)	Somnolence
Propranolol (Inderal)	30	Useful for akathisia	Problematic drug interactions, diffuse cognitive impairment in elderly
Benzodiazepines			
Diazepam (Valium)	15	Akathisia; 10 mg IV for dystonia	Drowsiness and lethargy
Lorazepam (Ativan)	4–6	Akathisia	Time-limited because of addiction potential
Piperidines			
Procyclidine (Kemadrin)	5–30	Mild broad spectrum for all EPS syndromes	Significant peripheral anticholinergic effects, confusion in elderly
Trihexyphenidyl (Artane)	5–15	Broad spectrum	Same as for procyclidine

KEY: EPS, extrapyramidal side effect.

agents. Antiparkinsonian agents may be discontinued in about 50% of patients after 3 months without a return of parkinsonian symptoms (589). Prophylactic use of these compounds is not indicated. Akathisia, a particularly troublesome symptom, presents as a relentless motor restlessness and inability to sit still, and it may masquerade as agitation. Dose reduction is the only truly satisfactory management of akathisia, although beta-blockers may be of benefit. Elderly women and patients with a high intake of caffeine are most at risk.

Acute dystonia (most common in young men) is a dramatic, early, and sometimes alarming occurrence, but it carries no permanent morbid risk and responds rapidly to benztropine (1–2 mg IV or IM) or diphenhydramine (25–50 mg IV or IM). Tardive dystonia is a rare disorder, in which more prolonged dystonic spasms occur later in treatment. It is treated with antiparkinsonian agents.

Convulsions in patients without prior seizures may occur with very large neuroleptic doses (e.g., chlorpromazine in doses over 2,000 mg/day), but they are quite rare and respond to dose reduction. Such patients should be further evaluated for a seizure disorder.

About 15% of patients receiving long-term (> 6 months) neuroleptic treatment develop tardive dyskinesia, a syndrome of involuntary choreiform movements that persist after the drug is discontinued. Among the chronically ill, the prevalence may be over 50%. The symptoms differ from those of the acute extrapyramidal triad and include periodic tongue protrusion and lip smacking, puffing and chewing movements of the mouth, athetoid hyperextension of the fingers, and a restless shifting of weight from leg to leg. A study of autopsy material from patients with tardive dyskinesia demonstrated histopathologic changes in midbrain structures (181). The biochemical alterations are believed to be either excessive dopamine accumulation in the basal ganglia or an increase in dopamine receptor sensitivity. Some patients with tardive dyskinesia also have cognitive problems in attention and thinking (1038).

The treatment of tardive dyskinesia is unsatisfactory. Antiparkinsonian agents can aggravate the syndrome (61) and should not be used. Apparently, however, they do not constitute a risk factor (339). Cerebral amine-depleting agents (reserpine), cholinergic agents (diethylaminoethanol, physostigmine, choline, lecithin), and GABA-ergic agents (sodium valproate, baclofen) all have been reported effective in scattered, small clinical trials, but no methodologically adequate studies have shown any of them to be unequivocally and substantially more effective than placebo. Reinstitution of another neuroleptic, particularly a potent dopamine-blocker such as haloperidol, may also ameliorate tardive dyskinetic symptoms.

Tardive dyskinesia has been reported to occur after only a brief (< 6 months) course of neuroleptic treatment. For this reason, these drugs should be reserved exclusively for the treatment of severely ill or psychotic patients. Their use in nonpsychotic depressed or neurotic patients is not warranted, and their use in children and pregnant women should be avoided whenever possible.

Cardiovascular System

Neuroleptics, especially chlorpromazine, thioridiazine, and chlorprothixene, produce orthostatic hypotension, which is dose related and occurs more frequently in older patients and with parenteral administration. Adaptation to this phenomenon often occurs over a period of a week or two; patients should be warned to rise slowly and in stages (e.g., lying to sitting, sitting to standing) from lying or sitting positions. Orthostatic hypotension apparently results from alpha1-adrenergic receptor blockade. In addition to careful and slow postural changes, this particularly troublesome side effect can be managed in the elderly with the use of support hose and abdominal binders. Triiodothyronine (25 mg daily), methylphenidate (5 mg daily), or salt tablets (600–1,800 mg daily) also may be useful. For high-dose parenteral neuroleptic treatment, the more potent neuroleptics (e.g., haloperidol, fluphenazine, thiothixene) are best, as they have little hypotensive effect.

Repolarization abnormalities are frequently seen on ECG with the use of neuroleptics, particularly thioridazine and mesoridazine. Flattening, notching, splitting, and inversion of T waves; prolongation of PQ and QT intervals; and ST segment depression all may occur. These ECG changes are partly related to drug-induced myocardial potassium depletion and are reversed by oral potassium replacement (e.g., bananas, apricots, commercial supplements). Neuroleptics should be used cautiously in patients with myocardial disease, as there is a possible relation between the ECG abnormalities and the rare instances of autopsy-negative sudden death in patients receiving these drugs.

Hematopoietic System

Agranulocytosis is a rare and dangerous idiosyncratic allergic response to neuroleptics. It usually occurs between the 2nd and 6th weeks of treatment at doses exceeding 150 mg/day of chlorpromazine (or the equivalent). Agranulocytosis is not related to the common but clinically unimportant relative leukopenia (10–20% drop from baseline) observed with neuroleptic treatment. Frequent white cell counts are ineffective in the early detection of agranulocytosis, as the onset can be precipitous. Painful oropharyngeal infections and fever are the usual presenting complaints; they may occur within 24 hours of a normal white cell count. The complaint of sore throat or mouth or the occurrence of fever in a patient receiving neuroleptics requires that medication be withheld until an immediate white cell count is obtained. If the white cell count is above 4,000 cells/cc, treatment may be continued; if the count is less than 3,000 cells/cc or 1,500 neutrophiles/cc the patient must be seen by a hematology consultant without delay. Once agranulocytosis occurs with a neuroleptic, it always occurs with any subsequent exposure and is also likely to occur with other neuroleptics of the same class.

Autonomic Nervous System

The anticholinergic properties of neuroleptics are responsible for their most commonly described dose-related side effects: dry mouth, stuffed nose, impaired taste, blurred vision, constipation, paralytic ileus, and urinary retention. Antiparkinsonian agents, which have their own anticholinergic effects, aggravate these symptoms. Inhibition of ejaculation occurs most frequently with thioridazine and mesoridazine. Dry mouth can be treated by instructing the patient to use sugarless gum and hard candies to stimulate salivation, or by using a cholinergic agonist (pilocarpine rinse three or four times daily, 4 drops of 4% pilocarpine in 12 drops of water). A 1% ophthalmic solution of pilocarpine (1 drop b.i.d.) helps to alleviate blurred vision. Dry mouth and visual blurring during the day can be minimized by limiting drug administration to a single bedtime dose. Constipation is best treated with bulk laxatives, high-fiber foods, and stool softeners. As a last resort before lowering the neuroleptic dose, bethanechol (25 mg p.o., t.i.d.) may alleviate these anticholinergic side effects. However, this cholinergic agent can produce abdominal cramps and diarrhea, rhinorrhea and tearing, and tremor; it is risky for patients with conditions adversely affected by cholinergic stimulation (asthma, peptic ulcer). Neostigmine (7.5–15.0 mg), taken 30 minutes before sexual intercourse, may enhance libido and reverse delayed ejaculation. The above tactics are also effective for managing the anticholinergic side effects of cyclic antidepressants (772).

Skin and Eyes

The greatest amount of a neuroleptic found in body tissue is in skin. Photosensitivity is reported by patients receiving neuroleptics, and painful sunburn may result from only brief exposure. Patients should be warned of this possibility and advised to use a strong sun block. Ocular photosensitivity, which can be prevented with sunglasses, and a maculopapular erythematous eruption also may occur with the use of neuroleptics.

Long-term effects of phenothiazine neuroleptics include a characteristic blue-gray pigmentation of the skin that results from formation of a neuroleptic-melanin complex and the development of stellate lenticular and corneal opacities visible only on slit-lamp examination. These ocular changes have no known clinical sequelae but seem to be permanent. They are a function of the total lifetime dose of medication received and have been reported most often after chlorpromazine therapy.

Pigmentary retinopathy leading to blindness has occurred in patients who received more than 800 mg/day of thioridazine. No more than 600 mg/day of this drug should be given. If high-dose neuroleptic treatment is anticipated, thioridazine is a poor initial choice.

Liver

Benign intrahepatic cholestatic jaundice occurred during the early years of chlorpromazine use but is now a rare complication of neuroleptic treatment. Patients receiving neuroleptics often have mildly abnormal liver function tests, but their significance is obscure. No untoward results occur if treatment is continued.

Hormonal Changes

Impaired glucose tolerance with elevated fasting blood sugars, observed more often in women than in men, may result from the use of neuroleptics. It has no known clinical significance, and no treatment is recommended. A temporary pseudopregnancy syndrome (due, in part, to increased prolactin secretion), with amenorrhea, lactation, breast swelling, and false-positive pregnancy tests, may occur in women. Also, gynecomastia has been reported in men who receive neuroleptics.

Fatalities

Sudden death in patients receiving neuroleptics has various causes. Autopsy-negative deaths in psychiatric patients were reported before the introduction of neuroleptic drugs, and patients who died in febrile/dehydrated states were described as having lethal catatonia, Bell's mania, or manic exhaustion. Altered temperature regulation secondary to the anticholinergic effects of neuroleptics and commonly prescribed antiparkinsonian agents has produced hyperpyrexial deaths during hot weather. Asphyxiation by food bolus has been discovered at autopsy in some patients; patients with tardive dyskinesia are at particular risk because of esophageal muscle dysfunction. Hypotensive deaths have been reported, and some deaths have been ascribed to drug-induced cardiac arrhythmias. The neuroleptic "malignant syndrome" putatively resulting from an idiosyncratic response to neuroleptic dopamine blockade can also occur. It is characterized by fever and rigidity and resembles the malignant hyperpyrexia occasionally seen with anesthetic agents (160). Treatment relies on bromocriptine (15–60 mg daily) or ECT, both dopamine agonists. Amantadine (645) and dantrolene sodium also have been used with some success.

Contraindications

Contraindications to neuroleptics are rare. They include narrow-angle glaucoma, pronounced prostatic hypertrophy, and prior idiosyncratic reactions (e.g., agranulocytosis). These drugs should not be routinely prescribed for pregnant women because neuroleptics cross the placenta and enter the fetal brain with unknown, but presumed undesirable, consequences. They also are excreted in mother's milk.

Mood Stabilizers

Substances that stabilize mood and anxiety disorders include cyclic antidepressants, monoamine oxidase inhibitors, lithium and anticonvulsants. These compounds are also effective in treating bulimia and anorexia nervosa, migraine, certain chronic pain syndromes, and enuresis. Although specific strategies for treating these disorders are discussed in Part II, general considerations for each class of mood stabilizers are discussed below.

Cyclic Stabilizers

The cyclic group of antidepressants includes mono-, bi-, tri-, and tetracyclic compounds. Amitriptyline and imipramine, two tricyclic compounds, are the oldest cyclic mood stabilizers. The tricyclic central ring structure apparently gives these molecules their antidepressant and other therapeutic properties, whereas their side chains determine potency, sedative, and other properties. If a fourth ring is added at right angles to the original three, the molecule becomes a tetracyclic (e.g., maprotiline). Removing rings can result in bicyclic (fluoxetine) or monocyclic (bupropion) molecules.

Cyclic mood stabilizers are completely absorbed from the gut. First-pass metabolism initially converts 30 to 90% of a given dose via demethylation from a tertiary to a secondary amine that is more lipophilic and, thus, more active. Hydroxylation and then conjugation make the secondary substances more water soluble for excretion in urine. Peak plasma level from a single oral dose occurs in about 30 to 60 minutes, and 80 to 90% is protein bound. These substances are highly lipophilic and become concentrated in myocardial and cerebral tissue. Elimination half-life ranges from 20 to 36 hours; thus, a single daily dose is feasible. Many cyclic mood stabilizers are powerful anticholinergic agents. This feature, combined with their affinity for myocardial tissue, makes their use risky in elderly patients.

The mechanism of therapeutic action of cyclic mood stabilizers is unknown, although they have powerful effects on various neurotransmitter systems. Most of these compounds affect norepinephrine, dopamine, and serotonin to varying degrees. Desipramine and protriptyline are particularly strong norepinephrine reuptake blockers, and fluoxetine is a powerful enhancer of serotonin.

Table 20.3 displays some of the more commonly used cyclic mood stabilizers, doses required for adequate antidepressant effect in major depression or nonpsychotic unipolar melancholia, and particular clinical characteristics of these compounds. The efficacy of cyclic stabilizers in the treatment of melancholia is only moderate in the majority of published studies. Indeed, about one third of double-blind, placebo-controlled comparisons reveal no effect at all. It is possible that

TABLE 20.3

Cyclic Mood Stabilizers

Class/Drug	*Minimal Adequate Daily Antidepressant Dose (mg) or Blood Level (ng/ml)*	*Special Comments*
Tricyclic		
Amitriptyline (Elavil)	> 200	Potent anticholinergic; weight gain; orthostatic hypertension a significant side effect
Imipramine (Tofranil)	> 200	Potent anticholinergic; also used for anxiety disorders, enuresis, chronic pain; cardiac problems and dizziness; orthostatic hypotension a significant side effect
Nortriptyline (Aventyl or Pamelor)	> 75 or plasma level between 50–150	Few side effects; best management because of available blood levels
Protriptyline (Vivactil)	> 40	Potent, little sedation
Desipramine (Norpramin)	> 200	Few side effects
Clomipramine (Anafranil)	> 200	Mostly used to treat OCD; potent anticholinergic; available IV for 24-hour infusion for treatment-resistant OCD patients
Bicyclic		
Fluoxetine (Prozac)	> 30	Most effective when used for nonmelancholic depressions and anxiety disorders; dangerous when combined with MAOI; reported side effect of inducing suicide or homicide unfounded
Dibenzoxazepine		
Amoxapine (Asendin)	> 200	Anticholinergic

(*continued*)

TABLE 20.3 (*Cont.*)

Cyclic Mood Stabilizers

Class/Drug	*Minimal Adequate Daily Antidepressant Dose (mg) or Blood Level (ng/ml)*	*Special Comments*
Triazolopyridine		
Trazodone (Desyrel)	> 200	Weak therapeutic effect; few side effects; not recommended
Tetracyclic		
Maprotiline (Ludiomil)	> 150	Seizures may occur in daily doses higher than 225 mg; orthostatic hypertension a significant side effect; no advantage over other compounds; not recommended
Monocyclic		
Bupropion (Wellbutrin)	> 300	Seizures may occur; mild anti-cholinergic properties; cannot be given once daily; not recommended

KEY: OCD, obsessive compulsive disorder; MAOI, monoamine oxidase inhibitor.

drug dosages have been too low, however, and that plasma-level monitoring might significantly improve the usual reported rate of 65% of patients who are much improved or recovered with the use of these compounds (109, 227, 486).

Plasma-Level Monitoring

Several studies have demonstrated a modified linear relationship between plasma levels of imipramine and clinical response in depressed patients (62, 361). In general, the therapeutic effects of imipramine begin at plasma levels around 150 ng/ml, increase progressively from that point to around 225 ng/ml, and level off thereafter. One study, for example, reported that 73% of depressed patients with levels of 180 ng/ml responded after 4 weeks, whereas only 43% responded at blood levels less than 180 ng/ml (362). Enormous variability in blood level occurs among patients who receive the same drug dose; without plasma-level monitoring, there is no way to determine whether nonresponse is primary or results from inadequate dosage. Although the mean daily dose of imipramine was 225 mg in the study cited above, 40% of the patients exhibited subtherapeutic blood levels.

Nortriptyline is another cyclic antidepressant for which valid and reliable plasma-level determinations have been developed. With this drug, clinical response begins around 50 ng/ml, peaks at 90–120 ng/ml, and falls off at levels exceeding 170 ng/ml. In order to achieve maximum therapeutic benefit, some nonresponders require dose reduction and others an increase in dosage.

Side Effects

The tricyclic antidepressants share many side effects of the tricyclic neuroleptic parent drugs but have more pronounced anticholinergic properties. Thus, postural hypotension, ECG changes, dry mouth, blurred vision, heartburn, constipation, adynamic ileus, and urinary hesitancy and retention occur. Tetracyclics are reported to induce fewer anticholinergic side effects than tricyclics, but the data are unimpressive. Single nighttime dosing can minimize some of these problems (blurring of vision, dry mouth), as can the use of sugarless gum and candy (dry mouth), and bulk laxatives (ileus). Decreased libido and impaired ejaculation also may occur; they can be treated with dose reduction or a peripheral cholinesterase inhibitor (neostigmine, 7.5–15 mg at 30 to 60 minutes prior to intercourse). Extrapyramidal syndromes are rare, and tardive dyskinesia has not been demonstrated. A troublesome, persistent fine tremor, similar to that in thyrotoxicosis, may occur. This tremor is resistant to antiparkinsonian agents and does not diminish over time. Dose reduction may be required; when this is not advisable, a beta-adrenergic blocking agent (e.g., propranolol, 10–30 mg/day) may be used concurrently with some success. Some patients have an idiosyncratic response to cyclic antidepressants that are potent serotonin uptake blockers (e.g., fluoxetine) and develop a syndrome characterized by restlessness, hyperreflexia, myoclonus, insomnia, diaphoresis, nausea, diarrhea, and abdominal cramps. If severe, this "serotonin syndrome" can be treated with dose reduction or with cyproheptadine (4–8 mg daily), a serotonin antagonist.

Some patients with anxiety disorder experience an increase in autonomic symptoms and anxiety during the first few days of treatment with tricyclic antidepressants. The prevalence and severity of this "early tricyclic syndrome" can be minimized by using small initial doses and gradually increase dosage. This reaction has not been reported with MAOIs.

ECG alterations are more frequent with the cyclic antidepressants (109, 839) than with their parent neuroleptic compounds. Early reports of increased mortality from cardiac complications, however, are now thought to be exaggerated (111). Nevertheless, at therapeutic doses, tricyclics frequently prolong PR and QRS intervals. Rarely, atrioventricular block occurs. In patients with heart disease, cyclic antidepressants may produce quinidinelike arrhythmias; if these arrhythmias develop, they should be treated as one would treat a quinidine overdose. When significant tricyclic cardiovascular side effects are likely (a patient with heart disease) or when they occur, ECT becomes the treatment of choice for a patient with melancholia.

Hematologic abnormalities also occur with cyclic antidepressants. Management is the same as for agranulocytosis, noted above in the section on neuroleptic side effects. Intrahepatic cholestatic jaundice is also reported as a rare idiosyncratic response to amitriptyline and requires termination of the drug. Profuse night sweating along the superior cervical ganglia distribution (head, neck, arms) occurs in about 25% of patients receiving tricyclics, particularly imipramine. This phenomenon is not observed with neuroleptics.

The cyclic antidepressants may induce mania in bipolar depressed patients (about 10%), a response also observed with ECT. It is unclear whether this response occurs with greater frequency in treated patients than it does in bipolar patients who are not treated with antidepressants. The occurrence of mania or hypomania following treatment for depression in a patient without prior history of such disorders suggests that he suffers from bipolar disorder.

Overdosage with cyclic antidepressants can induce a toxic psychosis. This anticholinergic delirium is characterized by disorientation, clouding of consciousness, dilated pupils, dry skin, and a history of cyclic antidepressant drug ingestion. It responds to the central cholinesterase inhibitor, physostigmine (2 mg IV); the dosage may be repeated in 20 minutes and again in 30 minutes (145). Narrow-angle glaucoma and severe prostatic hypertrophy are contraindications to tricyclic antidepressants.

Monoamine Oxidase Inhibitors

MAOIs were initially introduced for the treatment of melancholia, although they are rarely effective alone in this treatment. Instead, studies show that MAOIs are effective in the treatment of anxiety disorders, dysthymia, and atypical depression; in combination with cyclic antidepressants in the treatment of melancholia; and, with lithium, in the treatment of bipolar affective disorder (109, 227, 490, 833). The most clinically important MAOIs (e.g., phenelzine) are hydrazine derivatives and are inactivated by acetylation in the liver. Tranylcypromine is a nonhydrazine, amphetaminelike compound with weaker MAOI activity. By inhibiting mitochondrial enzymes that oxidize monoamines (serotonin, noradrenaline, dopamine), these drugs increase the bioavailability of the monoamines; presumably, this effect is the basis for their therapeutic action. As they also inhibit the oxidation of tyramine, the MAOIs can cause a tyramine hypertensive crisis in patients who eat foods high in tyramine during treatment. Phenelzine inhibits MAO-A, which oxidizes serotonin and noradrenaline, and it is used to treat psychiatric syndromes.

Selegiline inhibits MAO-B, which oxidizes dopamine, and it is used to treat parkinsonism. These drugs also inactivate liver enzymes that metabolize barbiturates, antiparkinsonian agents, cyclic antidepressants, and phenytoin and thus increase the bioavailability of these drugs. In addition, MAOIs inactivate the oxidizers of naturally occurring GABA.

MAOIs are rapidly absorbed and are metabolized in the liver. Phenelzine is metabolized by acetylation. About 50% of Europeans and southern and central Africans and 10 to 15% of Asians are slow acetylators (a mendelian recessive). This delayed metabolism can result in greater than expected initial blood levels from a given oral dose, and a more gradual dose increase may be needed to minimize intense side effects in these individuals.

Phenelzine, the most widely used MAOI, should be given in a starting dose of 15 mg/day and be increased slowly by 15 mg to a total of 90–120 mg/day. Twice daily dosages are satisfactory; the second dose should be given before 6 P.M. so as not to cause insomnia. Some patients eventually adapt to a dose closer to bedtime, and it may be more convenient for them to take the second dose then. Other patients are able to tolerate a single daily dose in the morning. As more experience has accumulated with phenelzine, there is little reason to prescribe other available MAOIs, especially as there is no evidence of therapeutic benefits greater than those of phenelzine. Antidepressant and anxiolytic effects occur at similar dosages.

Side Effects

The most important side effect of MAOIs (about 1% of patients) is the hypertensive crisis that may occur in patients who eat foods with a high tyramine content. This reaction may range from a sudden, throbbing headache to a paroxysmal hypertensive crisis with subarachnoid hemorrhage and, rarely, death. It results from failure of the body to metabolize the ingested pressor amine tyramine because of inhibition of monoamine oxidase, for which tyramine is a substrate. Treatment of the hypertensive crisis requires an alpha-adrenergic blocking agent; parenteral phentolamine (5 mg IV, followed by 0.25–0.50 mg IV every 4–6 hours) is the standard. Many physicians provide their patients on MAOIs with one or two 10-mg tablets of the calcium channel antagonist, nifedipine, and instruct them to take one sublingually for its alpha-adrenergic antagonistic effects immediately upon noticing any signs of acute hypertension. Foods of concern to patients who take MAOIs are listed in Table 20.4. Data show, however, that even if the dietary proscriptions are occasionally transgressed, serious or fatal reactions are quite rare (322). Patients also must not take any medications with adrenergic properties, including amphetamines and related compounds, or cocaine. Central nervous system depressants are potentiated by MAOIs; opiates (particularly meperidine) and barbiturates should be avoided. Patients should be instructed to consult with their

TABLE 20.4

Foods of Concern to Patients Taking Monoamine Oxidase Inhibitors

Absolutely Unsafe	*Safe*
Red wine, particularly vermouth, Chianti	Chocolate
Unpasteurized, strong, or aromatic cheese	Figs
Smoked or pickled fish	Raisins
Liver, especially chicken liver	Yeast breads
Dry sausage and pâté	Caffeine-containing beverages
Fava or broad beans	Distilled spirits
Brewer's yeast	
Yeast extracts (Bovril, Marmite)	
Unsafe in Large Quantities	
Ales and beer	
Ripe avocado	
Ripe banana	
Sour cream	
Fresh cottage or cream cheese	
Yogurt	
Soy sauce	
Foods with monosodium glutamate	
White wine and champagne	
Artificial sweeteners (aspartame)	

physician before taking any over-the-counter medications. Many of these medications contain pressor amines for their decongestant action. Phenylephedrine and ephedrine, contained in many preparations of nose drops, should be avoided. For dental procedures, local anesthetics without epinephrine should be employed.

It was asserted for many years that tricyclic antidepressants and MAOIs should never be combined because fatal reactions had ensued from such treatment. A detailed review (881) of such cases, however, failed to demonstrate convincingly a negative drug interaction, and there is now little doubt of the safety of TCA–MAOI combined treatment. Indeed, one study demonstrated a protective effect of imipramine against tyramine-induced hypertension in patients on MAOIs (734). Best results are achieved when the tricyclic is begun first and raised to therapeutic levels, and then the MAOI is gradually added. Among patients resistant to treatment with tricyclic antidepressants, about 75% benefit from the addition of an MAOI (376, p. 638).

Autonomic side effects of MAOIs are similar to, but milder than, those of the cyclic antidepressants. They include postural and orthostatic hypotension at rest, blurred vision, dry mouth, constipation, paralytic ileus, and urinary retention. Increasing salt intake in cardiovascularly healthy patients (one or two 0.5-g salt tablets daily) and use of an abdominal binder may alleviate hypotension in some patients. Triiodothyronine (25 μg daily) or a salt-retaining steroid, fludrocortisone (0.1 mg, once or twice daily), also may help. When all else fails, low doses of 9-alpha-fluorhydrocortisone (0.025–0.05 mg b.i.d.) have been reported to alleviate MAOI-induced hypotension and that caused by other antidepressants. The side effects of this compound include edema, cardiac hypertrophy, and hypokalemia; it should be prescribed with caution (772).

Increased libido is also experienced by some patients taking MAOIs, and transient impotence or delayed ejaculation also has occurred. These and other (anorgasmia) sexual dysfunctions may occur in 20% of patients; reduction of the MAOI dosage or the use of cyproheptadine may alleviate them. Complaints of numbness and tingling in the fingers early in treatment should alert the clinician to the possible development of a pyridoxine deficiency-induced carpal tunnel syndrome. This can be successfully treated with vitamin supplements, which will not affect the MAOI dosage. Weight gain and skin rash, myoclonus, and hypomania (207) also may be problems for some patients. Well-controlled diet and exercise can minimize the former, whereas the drug may need to be discontinued if the rash is severe (111). Some patients with personality disorders abuse tranylcypromine because of its amphetaminelike properties. An amphetaminelike psychosis can result. This toxic psychosis occurs in a clear consciousness, unlike the delirium of cyclic drug overdosage, and responds to neuroleptic drugs or ECT.

Lithium

Lithium (489) is the only psychopharmacologic agent that is not an organic (i.e., a carbon-containing cyclical) compound. It is an alkali metal and precedes sodium in the periodic table of elements. It is widely distributed in the earth's crust, where it leaches into the drinking water and is daily ingested in minute amounts by millions of people.

Lithium is rapidly and almost completely absorbed from the gastrointestinal tract. Peak serum lithium concentrations are reached about 2 to 3 hours after an oral dose. The half-life of a single dose (about 36 hours) is significantly longer in manic patients than in matched normal subjects, which suggests an illness-related lithium retention in the former group (37). The differential retention of a lithium loading dose by manics is also reflected in an increased red blood cell (RBC)/plasma lithium concentration ratio in manic-depressives compared with control subjects (614).

More than 95% of ingested lithium is excreted in urine and the remainder in the sweat and feces. Lithium diffuses freely into all body compartments, as well as the glomerular filtrate, and has a renal clearance of about 80 ml/minute, substantially less than the glomerular filtration rate of 120 ml/minute. About 50% of a given dose is cleared in 5 to 8 hours. Active reabsorption of lithium takes place in the proximal tubule and utilizes the same transport system as sodium, with which it competes. Thus, in the presence of a reduced renal sodium load (e.g., as with a low-salt diet), more lithium is reabsorbed, possibly leading to toxicity. This is the likely mechanism for most of the deaths reported when lithium was marketed as a salt substitute in the 1940s (489, pp. 73–78).

Lithium diffuses passively across all cell membranes and is actively extruded against a gradient by a variety of mechanisms (733). It is not significantly stored anywhere in the body; the amount circulating in blood reflects a balance between oral dose and urinary excretion. During the first week or so of lithium treatment, there is a sodium diuresis, with polyuria, as lithium replaces a portion of intracellular sodium. This is followed by several days of lithium diuresis around the time of clinical improvement. Following lithium diuresis, a "steady state" is achieved in which lithium and sodium (as well as water and potassium) reach a stable balance and maintain equilibrium for the remainder of the treatment course.

In comparison with neuroleptics and antidepressants, very little is known of the neuropharmacology of lithium and its mechanism of action. It is an inhibitor of adenosine 3′:5′-cyclic phosphate (cyclic AMP), a substance that, among other things, acts as a second messenger (the first being a neurotransmitter) and mediates the transfer of regulatory influences from the external milieu of a cell to its internal metabolic machinery. The reported increased cellular norepinephrine reuptake induced by lithium in nonhumans may be related to its effect on cAMP, as this substance is involved in the regulation of tyrosine hydroxylase, the rate-limiting step in norepinephrine synthesis (320).

Behavioral pharmacology of lithium has not been extensively studied. In general, few behavioral effects are observed at nontoxic doses. Nonhumans given lithium exhibit modest decrements in spontaneous motor behavior, and normal human subjects exhibit a modest reduction in "mental efficiency," manifested by impairment on timed cognitive tasks at blood levels around 1.0 mEq/l (492). At doses close to the toxic range, lithium induces EEG slowing (489, pp. 240–245).

Clinical Indications and Treatment Techniques

The primary indication for lithium administration is in the treatment and prevention of bipolar and unipolar mood disorders.

ACUTE MANIA

Most manic patients (about 80%) are too excited or irritable to be managed initially with lithium alone. Even when willing to cooperate with oral treatment, the 5 to 7-day lag in onset of lithium's antimanic effects often proves too great a burden for other patients and the staff. After several days of neuroleptic treatment, however, it is usual to start lithium with the aim of tapering and discontinuing the neuroleptic when steady-state lithium levels are achieved. For manic patients initially treated with lithium alone, the rate of marked improvement/recovery is about 80%. Attempts to define the specific variables responsible for nonresponsiveness to lithium generally have been unsuccessful (489, pp. 57–59; 561; 973, 974). Rapid cycling (four or more episodes per year prior to initiation of lithium) and paranoid-destructive attitudes have not been confirmed as predictors of lithium failure, nor have reduced RBC/plasma lithium ratios or a family history negative for affective disorder. Regardless of the cause, however, lithium nonresponders (20 to 30% of bipolar patients), who then receive additional or alternate treatments (e.g., neuroleptics, anticonvulsants, ECT), ultimately show as much improvement as those who do not, although at the cost of a significantly longer hospital stay (561).

The same 80% efficacy rate holds initially for preventive (prophylactic) lithium treatment in mania, and the effectiveness of such treatment increases with each passing year. Thus, relapse and hospital readmission during a patient's first year on lithium prophylaxis do not constitute a reason to terminate the treatment (relapse rate drops from two thirds to one fourth of patients after the first year). Continued lithium prophylaxis significantly decreases the likelihood of such relapse the following year and even more so the year after (489, pp. 38–40; 856).

ACUTE DEPRESSION

Most double-blind, placebo-controlled studies demonstrate lithium to have an acute antidepressant effect (489, pp. 35–38). This effect may be most pronounced for bipolar patients who are depressed and for depressed patients who have not responded to cyclic antidepressants. About 75% of bipolar melancholics and 65% of unipolar melancholics (the same percentages of patients treated with cyclic antidepressants) have a significant response. When melancholics do not fully respond to cyclic antidepressants, the addition of lithium (900–1,200 mg daily) is a significant benefit to about 70% of these patients (856). Lithium also enhances the therapeutic effects of carbamazepine and MAOIs in some depressed patients. With both cyclic and MAOI antidepressant augmentation, lithium's effect usually begins within the first 10 days of its administration.

OTHER USES FOR LITHIUM

Lithium has been used in the treatment of anorexia nervosa and bulimia, alcohol and drug abuse, cluster and migraine headaches, episodic dyscontrol syndromes and aggression, periodic hypersomnia, premenstrual syndrome, and OCD and other anxiety disorders. It has also been used to stimulate the production of granulocytes in patients receiving medication (e.g., antineoplastic agents) that may result in significant leukopenia. At best, results in all of these conditions are mixed (477; 489, pp. 44–50). For example, some anorexic patients gain significant amounts of weight when taking lithium at serum levels of 0.9–1.4 mEq/l. The percentage of anorexics who are potential responders to lithium and the degree to which the acute response to lithium is maintained are unknown.

Based on the rationale that alcohol abuse has been linked to mood disorders, lithium is used in the treatment of alcoholics. Those with co-occurring features of depression appear to benefit from lithium at blood levels of 0.6–1.2 mEq/l, but dropout rates are very high and the number of alcoholic patients likely to benefit from lithium is small. Lithium in standard or low doses (900 mg/day) has been reported to benefit patients with cluster headaches, migraine, and cyclic migraine; any relief occurs within the first week of treatment. No prophylactic effect is reported. Reports of lithium in the treatment of OCD and anxiety disorder, particularly phobias, have been disappointing, although some OCD patients seem to benefit from lithium augmentation of cyclic antidepressant treatment. Studies (890, 891, 1007) of prisoners with histories of irritability and aggressive outbursts unassociated with other features of mood disorder suggest a therapeutic trial of lithium in such patients may be beneficial.

Monitoring of Serum Levels

Serial serum lithium determinations are used to monitor the course of lithium treatment. Blood levels are obtained in the morning, 12 hours after the last dose. They should be in the range of 1.0–1.5 mEq/l for successful treatment of acute mania. After remission of symptoms, the dose should be reduced to provide a blood level at 0.8–1.2 mEq/l. Blood levels are obtained twice weekly until a steady state has been reached, after which time weekly levels suffice for inpatients and monthly levels for outpatients.

There is some evidence (752, 954) that lithium daily steady-state dose can be predicted from blood levels 24 hours after a single test dose of 1,200 mg. In practice, these predictions generally underestimate the final dose needed. Their advantage may be in reducing initial trial and error and shortening the time needed to determine the proper dose, but most clinicians find the required calculations too complicated for everyday use.

Side Effects

During the initial week or so of treatment, patients may experience a fine tremor, mild fatigue or drowsiness, nausea, abdominal fullness, and increased thirst and polyuria (60% of patients). These symptoms do not require reduction of dosage and usually remit when stable blood levels are achieved. When tremor is prolonged (more likely in males and heavy coffee users) or if interpersonal or job factors make the tremors problematic, they may be controlled by reducing the dose and prescribing lithium once daily at bedtime with a snack or with propranolol (20–120 mg daily) or other beta-blockers with less potential for a depressing effect on mood (nadolol, 20–40 mg, or metoprolol, 25–50 mg, each twice daily). Vomiting immediately after ingestion of lithium sometimes occurs and can be avoided by taking lithium with food. Side effects usually correlate with high-peak blood levels, and most patients (80%) experience at least one. These can be avoided by giving lithium only twice daily (avoiding the cumulative late afternoon peak of t.i.d. or q.i.d. doses) or in a single moderate dose at bedtime. There is also some evidence that a dose once daily decreases the risk for renal damage (489, pp. 103–140).

Genuine toxicity rarely appears below serum lithium levels of 2.0 mEq/l. It is characterized by profuse vomiting or diarrhea, slurred speech, ataxia, coarse tremor, lethargy, myoclonus, stupor, and coma. Atypical neurologic syndromes may occur, with unilateral focal signs mimicking a stroke. Treatment of moderate lithium toxicity is supportive. The drug is stopped, fluids are forced, and adequate food (and salt) intake is encouraged. No specific antidote is available for lithium toxicity. Renal hemodialysis is the only known method for actively removing lithium from the body (489, pp. 154–158). Although the data are insufficient for a definitive statement on its efficacy, dialysis should be instituted in the presence of severe lithium toxicity (e.g., coma, inadequate renal elimination of lithium, serum lithium level > 4 mEq/l). In addition, standard supportive procedures are instituted (parenteral fluids, prophylactic antibiotics, frequent turning in bed, airway maintenance).

Lithium should be used with extreme caution in patients who have impaired renal function. These patients require low doses (e.g., 150 mg b.i.d. or t.i.d.) and frequent serum lithium determinations. Caution also should be observed in cardiac patients; ECG repolarization abnormalities are seen during treatment with lithium. This drug should not be prescribed for cardiac patients receiving diuretics or a low-sodium diet, as severe lithium poisoning may rapidly occur in salt-depleted patients. (An exception is the use of chlorothiazide; see below.) Lithium excretion also can be affected by nonsteroidal anti-inflammatory drugs (e.g., aspirin, indomethacin, ibuprofen). Concomitant use of these agents with lithium may lead to higher than expected lithium serum levels (ranging from clinically insignificant changes for aspirin to increases of 100% for indomethacin). When such drugs are being prescribed with lithium, lower lithium doses may be necessary (489, pp. 183–186). Osmotic diuretics, caffeine, and theophylline administration can lower lithium blood levels by increasing excretion.

As an inhibitor of cAMP/adenyl cyclase, lithium impairs the function of two major types of hormones mediated by this system: antidiuretic hormone (ADH) and the thyroid hormones, triiodothyronine (T_3) and thyroxine (T_4) (320). The effect on ADH is to prevent its action on the kidney, thus producing secondary nephrogenic diabetes insipidus (which is ADH-resistant) manifested by a large output of dilute urine and hypernatremia with normal blood sugar levels (this may occur in up to 20% of patients). Because of the large urine volume (> 3 l/day), adequate serum lithium levels are difficult to maintain, and the therapeutic results may suffer. In such cases, chlorothiazide is indicated to reduce urine volume and increase serum lithium levels (593). The mechansim for this paradoxic response is unknown. Long-term effects may be related to this syndrome, as well. Several reports indicate that patients with the syndrome may develop glomerular changes observable on renal biopsy. These patients often have a prior history of severe lithium toxicity. Despite these biopsy findings, follow-up studies have not shown significant long-term impairment in renal function in patients maintained on lithium, and no case of end-state renal disease in a patient on maintenance lithium has been reported (717, 1027). It would be prudent, however, to reduce or discontinue lithium in patients who develop secondary diabetes, if possible.

Because of the antithyroid effect of lithium, about 3% of patients receiving long-term maintenance lithium treatment develop nontoxic goiters that shrink with discontinuation of lithium or the addition of small doses of thyroid. Onset is usually between 5 and 24 months of treatment. The patients are usually clinically euthyroid, but signs of hypothyroidism and the myxedema syndrome (though rare) may occur. The T_3/T_4 levels are often reduced, and there is an increased uptake of radioactive iodine (30% of patients). Women are more frequently affected than men.

The safe use of lithium in pregnant women is not established, but sporadic reports have indicated possible teratogenic effects, particularly cardiovascular (1048). Lithium is excreted in mother's milk (880), and mothers on lithium treatment should bottle-feed their babies. Excessive weight gain and acneiform eruptions are frequent troublesome side effects of lithium that respond to dose reduction. The former phenomenon, unfortunately, is a frequent occurrence in women and is often the primary reason for their discontinuance of lithium treatment. Diet is the only known remedy for the weight gain. Some patients who are forced to stop lithium because of rash can restart treatment without recurrence. If a patient suffers hair loss while on lithium, the hair grows back following discontinuation of the drug; however, hair loss recurs with subsequent courses of treatment.

There are no specific guidelines on the duration of lithium maintenance treatment (see Chapter 14). Patients who have remained well on such a regimen for years may relapse in a week's time when lithium is discontinued. The duration of treatment depends largely on the number, rate, and severity of prior attacks of illness.

Manic episodes are frequently followed by depression in patients receiving lithium. It is unclear whether the drug increases the frequency of the pattern. If depression occurs and is mild, lithium should be continued without further intervention. Should the depression become significant, antidepressants may be needed. If they are ineffective or if the depression is severe, all drugs can be discontinued and ECT initiated.

Patient noncompliance with lithium treatment presents a clinical challenge. The most frequent reasons given are unpleasant side effects (e.g., weight gain, cognitive problems, tremor, thirst, fatigue, rash), missing of hypomanic highs or feeling less creative, and feeling well and seeing no need to continue. Patients most likely to discontinue treatment include young patients, males, patients with infrequent episodes, or patients who incompletely respond to lithium. The use of specialized lithium clinics and self-help groups reduces the rate of noncompliance (489, pp. 127–132).

Anticonvulsants as Mood Stabilizers

Although anticonvulsants are used in the treatment of seizures (see Chapter 13), they are also recognized by modern neuropsychiatry as mood-stabilizing drugs. Carbamazepine and valproic acid are most commonly used for this purpose. Anticonvulsants are easily absorbed from the gut and circulate in the blood, partly free and partly bound to plasma protein (75% for carbamazepine, 90% for valproic acid). Carbamazepine and valproic acid are rapidly metabolized by the liver and must be taken several times daily to maintain a therapeutic blood level. Because they are enzyme-inducing agents (cytochrome system), they often lower the blood levels of most psychotropic drugs. Their use also may lead to reduced steroid levels from oral contraceptives and other steroidal agents.

Carbamazepine

Structurally similar to tricyclic antidepressants, carbamazepine acquires its anticonvulsant activity through action on membrane sodium channels and peripheral-type benzodiazepine receptors. It is a GABA agonist and inhibits kindling. As a mood stabilizer (60 to 70% response rate), carbamazepine is effective in the treatment of acute mania and resistant bipolar states and in the prevention of manic and depressive episodes. Its effect as an antidepressant is modest. Carbamazepine offers some benefit in atypical panic disorder. It also is used to supplement alcohol withdrawal treatment and, in combination with lithium or beta-blockers, to control assaultive behavior. The usual starting dose is 100 mg at night or twice daily for 1 week, 100–200 mg twice daily the second week, and a usual total daily dose of 600–1,200 mg to achieve therapeutic blood levels at 0.8–1.2 µg/ml. Acute doses, however, may reach 2,400 mg daily, if necessary. Maintenance treatment aims for effective blood levels of 0.6–1.0 µg/ml. Asian and elderly patients obtain therapeutic blood levels at lower doses.

Carbamazepine is combined routinely with lithium and, to a lesser extent, with neuroleptics. The latter combination often involves haloperidol, despite the fact that carbamazepine decreases haloperidol blood levels. Carbamazepine blood levels are increased when the drug is used in conjunction with calcium channel blockers (verapamil) and with many antibiotics (due to reduced clearance). Carbamazepine blood levels are decreased when the drug is used in conjunction with other anticonvulsants, including barbiturates, or with theophylline (altered enzyme induction).

SIDE EFFECTS

Carbamazepine has side effects similar to those of cyclic antidepressants (as listed in the section on mood stabilizers above) and to other anticonvulsants (drowsiness, dizziness, ataxia, headache, nausea, chills, fever, blurred vision, diplopia). Side effects can be minimized by increasing doses slowly. If rash (10 to 15% of cases), hepatocellular or cholestatic jaundice, hyponatremia, water intoxication, dyscrasias, dystonias, or other side effects become problematic, a transient dose reduction is usually sufficient to resolve the difficulty. After several weeks of treatment, liver enzyme–increased metabolism often leads to increased drug tolerance. The most troublesome side effects, other than liver involvement and rash, are blood dyscrasias, including thrombocytopenia, agranulocytosis, and aplastic anemia. Liver and blood studies should be done prior to treatment and then weekly until steady state is achieved (8 weeks). Afterward, monthly assessments for 6 months and then semiannual testing are usually recommended. If carbamazepine is to be discontinued, gradual tapering before stopping is important, even in non-epileptics, as withdrawal seizures may occur.

Valproic Acid

Valproic acid (649) has anticonvulsant, antikindling, and GABA-agonistic actions. It is also effective in the treatment of acute mania and as a prophylaxis for both manic and depressive episodes. It can be used alone or in combination with lithium. Valproic acid is also reported to be helpful in treating some patients with panic disorder and is used in benzodiazepine withdrawal. Anecdotally, bipolar patients not responding fully to other treatments, including carbamazepine, may subsequently do well with valproic acid therapy. The usual dose schedule for treating mood disorders is to begin at 250 mg twice daily and increase slowly by 250 mg every 4 to 7 days to attain a serum level of 50–100 μg/ml. The daily dosage range is 750–3,000 mg. Several classes of drugs can affect blood levels. Most anticonvulsants increase levels by 30 to 50% through alteration in liver metabolism. In contrast, carbamazepine, by increasing valproic acid clearance, lowers its blood levels. Salicylates displace valproic acid from protein binding leading to increased levels of free drug, thus greater bioavailability can be achieved with less oral dose. Discontinuation of valproic acid treatment, as with carbamazepine treatment, should be done gradually.

SIDE EFFECTS

Common side effects of valproic acid include tremor (10%), ataxia, and increased appetite and weight gain. Hepatic transaminase elevations are also common; alone, however, they are unrelated to hepatic toxicity and have no clinical significance. Alopecia can occur, as can lethargy, sedation, dysarthria, and flushing. Side effects can be minimized by gradual dose increases. Serious side effects that can lead to termination of treatment are hepatic toxicity, with jaundice, malaise, nausea, vomiting, edema; pancreatitis; hematologic abnormalities, particularly bleeding; and allergic rash. These usually occur within the first 6 months of treatment and are less common in elderly patients. Pretreatment evaluation and serial liver function monitoring during treatment are helpful in determining early signs of toxicity, at which time valproic acid must be discontinued.

Anxiolytics

The designation "anxiolytic" no longer should be limited to the benzodiazepines and similar agents, as both cyclic antidepressants and MAOIs are first-line pharmacologic treatments for the anxiety disorders. Nevertheless, standard usage limits the term to the barbiturate and nonbarbiturate sedatives-hypnotics, of which the benzodiazepines represent the largest group. Other nonbarbiturate sedatives-hypnotics include (1) glycol or glycerol derivatives (e.g., meprobamate) and (2) diphenylmethane derivatives (e.g., diphenhydramine, hydroxyzine). Other than meprobamate, the first group is almost never used. Meprobamate, however, has significant addiction potential and is not recommended. Of the second group, diphenhydramine is useful in the treatment of dystonias and as a sedative in the elderly. If used as a sedative, however, the clinician should be sensitive to the possibility that urinary retention may occur in some elderly patients. The discussion below is limited to the benzodiazepines.

These compounds share with the barbiturates the properties of addiction/habituation, seizure suppression (and withdrawal seizures after prolonged high dosage), and inhibition of spinal interneuronal transmission (muscle relaxation). Compared with barbiturates, however, benzodiazepines have reduced activity in suppressing respiration and rapid eye movement sleep and in inducing hepatic enzymes. Thus, they have a wide margin of safety in the event of overdose.

Benzodiazepines have differential absorption rates from the gut. Diazepam and clorazepate are quickly absorbed, oxazepam and prazepam are slowly absorbed, and the rest have intemediary rates of absorption. Nevertheless, as a group, they are absorbed well; other than in emergencies when IV administration is required, oral doses are much preferred over IM administration where absorption is poor. Serum levels do not correlate well with clinical effects, and degree of lipid solubility (extensive redistribution to fatty tissues) determines their duration of action. This redistribution roughly divides this class into three subgroups. Table 20.5 displays these subgroups, some compounds in each, and the general properties of each. The drugs of choice are triazolam in the short-acting subgroup; lorazepam in the intermediate-acting subgroup; and in the long-acting subgroup, chlordiazepox-

TABLE 20.5
Benzodiazepines

Subtype	*Characteristics*
Short acting	
Triazolam (Halcion)	Used as a hypnotic; little anxiolytic and no anticonvulsant properties; in presently prescribed doses, it can result in prolonged altered consciousness without sedation.
Intermediate-acting	
Alprazolam (Xanax) Lorazepam (Ativan) Oxazepam (Serax) Temazepam (Restoril)	Alprazolam and oxazepam are generally equivalent with weak but broad-spectrum properties; lorazepam has significant anxiolytic and anticonvulsant properties; temazepam is used primarily as a hypnotic.
Long-acting	
Chlordiazepoxide (Librium) Clonazepam (Clonopin) Clorazepate (Tranxene) Diazepam (Valium) Flurazepam (Dalmane)	Chlordiazepoxide has only anxiolytic properties; clonazepam is used primarily as an anticonvulsant; clorazepate has some anxiolytic properties but little hypnotic or anticonvulsant properties; diazepam has significant anxiolytic and hypnotic properties and some anticonvulsant properties; flurazepam is used primarily as a hypnotic.

ide or diazepam for withdrawal states and diazepam for everything else. Regardless of duration of action, most benzodiazepines are biotransformed to desmethyldiazepam, an active metabolite with a very long (several days) half-life. These compounds include diazepam, chlordiazepoxide, clorazepate, and halazepam. Flurazepam has a similarly long half-life by virtue of its conversion to the slowly excreted active metabolite desalkylflurazepam. In contrast, lorazepam and oxazepam are excreted unconjugated, or as the glucuronide, and have a half-life of 12 to 18 hours.

The benzodiazepines have three main uses in psychiatry: (1) to treat acute anxiety states, (2) to provide bedtime hypnosis, and (3) to treat alcohol withdrawal. Alprazolam also has been recommended as a treatment for dysthymias; however, given the availability of other treatments, its limited half-life, and its addiction potential, the efficacy of alprazolam has been overstated. Lorazepam also has been recommended as a treatment for catatonia; other than as an alternative to barbiturates in the transient disinhibition of catalepsy, however, there is no evidence that lorazepam definitively treats catatonia. Clonazepam also has been recommended in the treatment of agoraphobia and in the prophylaxis of manic and depressive episodes. Its strong anticonvulsant properties and its GABA-agonistic effects, plus its potentiation of serotonin, make its use in these disorders theoretically interesting, but it is not a first-line treatment in either situation. Should it be used, reported effective daily doses are 2–9 mg for agoraphobia and 4–24 mg for mood disorders.

Acute Anxiety States

Benzodiazepines constitute the treatment of choice for managing acute anxiety states (panic attacks). IM administration is never used for this purpose; these compounds are poorly absorbed from IM sites. When the patient is extremely agitated, IV administration is preferable. Substantial dosages may be required to inhibit a panic attack (e.g., 15–20 mg of diazepam or 25–50 mg of chlordiazepoxide), but doses rarely have to be repeated in a single day because of the long half-life of these drugs. For most patients, therefore, 1 or 2 days of treatment suffice to abolish the panic attack and its short-term aftereffects; afterward, the drug can be abruptly discontinued. Benzodiazepines do not provide rational long-term treatment in the prevention of panic attacks or in the management of chronic anxiety. The invariable requirement for increasing the dose as tolerance develops over time eventually leads to habituation and addiction and to the undesirable and potentially dangerous side effects of ataxia and impaired cognition.

Bedtime Sedation and Hypnosis

The benzodiazepines have almost entirely replaced the older barbiturates as hypnotics. Triazolam (0.125 mg), temazepam (10 mg), and flurazepam (15–30 mg) are best for this purpose; those with a shorter half-life are preferred to prevent daytime sedation. Regular (almost daily) use for more than a few weeks is a risk for addiction. Triazolam in presently prescribed doses may lead to prolonged states of altered consciousness without sedation. Complex, seemingly normal behavior can occur during this state and last for several hours. Anterograde amnesia is almost always an associated complication. Thus, if used as a bedtime hypnotic, triazolam should be given in the lowest possible doses; the above state likely is dose related, rather than a specific pharmacologic response to triazolam.

Alcohol Withdrawal

The benzodiazepines are the treatment of choice for alcohol withdrawal. When severe, this withdrawal is characterized by tremor, restlessness, perceptual disturbances, disorientation, and clouded sensorium. One of the long half-life compounds should be chosen, and initially the IV route may be required because of the patient's inability to retain gastric contents. Chlordiazepoxide or diazepam are usually employed. A typical regimen with chlordiazepoxide is to give 100 mg IV and to repeat this dose every 4 to 6 hours during the first 24-hour period. After that time, oral medication usually can be tolerated. Four doses (50 mg each) given on the second day; this dosage is rapidly tapered off and discontinued by the fourth day of treatment.

Side Effects

The side effects of the benzodiazepines are limited to the CNS and include drowsiness, ataxia, and slurred speech. When administered in high dosage for a long time, there is a substantial risk of addiction. Seizures and delirium can occur after abrupt withdrawal. Thus, therapy with these compounds always should be brief and intermittent.

Other Drugs

A number of other classes of drugs are occasionally used by the neuropsychiatrist. They include psychostimulants, libido suppressants, antialcohol compounds, beta-blockers, and, to a lesser extent, calcium channel blockers, dopaminolytic agents, narcotic antagonists, and progestational agents. Only psychostimulants are discussed here. The other agents are briefly mentioned throughout Part II, as they relate to the management of specific syndromes.

Psychostimulants have a limited but important use in adult neuropsychiatry. Daily doses of methylphenidate (10–30 mg), dextroamphetamine (5–40 mg), or pemoline (37.5–112.5 mg) can be helpful in the management of adult patients with residual (from childhood) or secondary (to coarse brain disease) attention deficit disorder and in narcolepsy. Dextroamphetamine also may be used to ameliorate sedation during a sodium amytal interview. There is no compelling evidence that psychostimulants are helpful in depression, and their energizing effects without relief of depression may increase the risk for suicidal patients. These compounds work by promoting the synaptic release of catecholamines, blocking their reuptake, and preventing their metabolism. They also have direct noradrenergic receptor action. Common side effects include restlessness, insomnia, tremor, and anxiety. Toxicity can result in delirium, hyperreflexia, convulsions, and coma.

Chapter
21

Electroconvulsive Therapy

Electroconvulsive therapy (ECT) is widely used throughout the Western world. In the United States, about 2% of patients admitted to public hospitals, 10% to teaching hospitals, and 20% to private hospitals receive ECT (308). Despite its wide use and established efficacy, ECT remains controversial in the United States. In part, the controversy occurred because, for many years, American psychiatry and psychology rejected the medical model of mental illness and characterized all biologic forms of treatment, especially ECT, as harmful. More recently, ECT and other biologic treatments in psychiatry have been attacked by a loose coalition of quasi-religious organizations, patient self-help groups, and civil libertarians on grounds that such physical treatments infringe on patients' rights, are abused by psychiatrists who are unwilling or unable to provide alternative and more fundamental psychologic treatments, and cause brain damage. This attack has unfortunately convinced legislators in several states (most notably California) to pass laws restricting the use of ECT.

Some psychiatrists have contributed to this course of events. A small but significant number of private practitioners have abused ECT for their financial gain by administering the treatment indiscriminately or for excessively long courses. Other psychiatrists, working in public institutions, have used ECT thoughtlessly, mechanically, and in grim surroundings. They callously referred to the procedure as "shocking" or "buzzing" their patient and remained ignorant of advances in knowledge and technique that improved treatment results, reduced side effects, and rendered the method more acceptable to patients and staff. Until the early 1950s, ECT was administered without anesthesia or muscle relaxation; in many hospitals where ECT was given in full view of other patients, the unmodified convulsive seizure was undoubtedly frightening and disturbing. ECT today bears no resemblance to this primitive procedure, but portrayal of these archaic methods in such films as *The Snake Pit* and *One Flew Over the Cuckoo's Nest* continues to have an important negative effect on public opinion and legislators.

Modern ECT is a medical procedure performed under general anesthesia in a special suite with a treatment team, including a psychiatrist, anesthetist/anesthesiologist, nurse, and nursing assistant. ECG and EEG monitoring is routine; vital signs are measured and recorded at regular intervals; and, following treatment, the patient is observed by trained personnel in a separate recovery area until fully alert and ambulatory. Patient apprehension has been reduced or eliminated by premedication and fast-acting barbiturates. Muscle relaxants now modify the intensity of the contractions of the induced seizure, and improvements in equipment and technique of seizure induction permit many patients to be treated with minimal memory impairment or confusion.

A legitimate scientific question still exists concerning duration of the cognitive impairment induced by bilateral ECT. Although many patients find memory fully restored within 30 days after a course of ECT, some experience a longer-lasting but finite period of dysfunction and a few assert that the treatment permanently impaired their memory (966). Several well-controlled studies have not found evidence for permanent post-ECT memory disturbance, as measured by mean memory test scores in patients versus control groups. A recent study (153) of patients pre- and post-ECT and at 6 months found memory at 6 months post-ECT *better* than pre-ECT depression levels. Nevertheless, there is always the possibility that an individual patient, because of idiosyncratic sensitivity or unusual predisposition, might, in fact, suffer permanent memory impairment after ECT. Such an occurrence would be rare, and the impairment would be very limited in extent. When patients who claim such impairment are tested, they invariably function normally on standard memory test batteries. Indeed, many high-functioning individuals have been successfully treated during the course of their careers without any diminution in ability. A striking example of this was revealed in the obituary of Vladimir Horowitz, the famous classical pianist (452), who suffered from recurrent depressions that led to prolonged interruptions of his career. Following ECT, he returned to the concert stage and played at his highest musical level.

Because ECT is a medical procedure carried out under general anesthesia, it should never be prescribed casually or without regard for its potential undesirable side effects weighed against its benefits. The severity and potential morbidity and mortality of the illness to be treated and the efficacy of alternate treatments also should be considered.

Indications

After much deliberation, a scientific panel under the aegis of the American Psychiatric Association recently formulated guidelines for the use of ECT (63). The panel recommended criteria for the use of ECT as the primary (first-line) treatment and as a second-line treatment. Table 21.1 paraphrases these recommenda-

TABLE 21.1

APA Electroconvulsive Therapy Task Force Guidelines for the Use of ECT

As a Primary Treatment
1. The need for rapid, definitive response on psychiatric or medical grounds.
2. When the risks of other treatments outweigh the risks of ECT.
3. When past pharmacologic treatments were poor or past ECT response good.
4. Patient preference.
As a Second-Line Treatment
1. The patient has not responded to primary treatment.
2. The potential adverse effects of ECT are likely to be less severe than the actual adverse side effects of the primary treatment.
3. Despite treatment, the patient's condition continues to deteriorate.

tions. If the APA recommendations were taken at face value and implementation were based on the scientific literature, ECT most likely would qualify as the primary, first-line treatment for almost all mood disorders and psychoses, whether they are primary or secondary in etiology. ECT leads to the most rapid resolution of symptoms in most patients, and it has fewer side effects, including memory problems, than most psychotropics. Certainly, as an antidepressant, ECT is the most "rapid," "definitive," and safest treatment.

The guidelines of the APA task force are broadly sketched and not fully operationalized for clinical use. Further, specific indications relate to traditional diagnostic labels (i.e., disease A responds, disease B does not). Diagnostic labels, however, are organized into somewhat arbitrary systems that change as new data are gathered. They also can be misleading in their treatment implications, as illustrated by the shift of cyclothymia from a personality disorder, which is theoretically unresponsive to biologic treatment, to a mood disorder, which is theoretically responsive to biologic treatment. Finally, in most studies, 20 to 25% of patients are atypical and should be labeled "NOS." Some further definition is obviously needed to help clinicians make treatment decisions regarding such patients. Thus, for the clinician, the question is not "Which diagnostic label is likely to imply a good response to ECT?" but "What are the clinical characteristics of patients that predict a good response or suggest ECT as the primary, first-line treatment?" Although there is no infallible predictor, a large body of data and clinical experience indicate that predictors of response to ECT can be roughly divided into three groups: cross-sectional, contextual, and longitudinal. Table 21.2 displays the features in each group. The three groups are briefly discussed below; further details and related references can be found in several reviews (5, 63).

TABLE 21.2

Indications for ECT Responsivity

I. Cross-sectional
- A. Affective features
- B. Catatonia*
- C. Suicide*
- D. Stupor*
- E. Delusional depression*
- F. No emotional blunting

II. Contextual
- A. Hallucinogenic drug use
- B. Family history of suicide or affective disorder
- C. Drug failure
- D. Systemic illness
- E. Pregnancy/breast feeding*
- F. Age over 65

III. Longitudinal
- A. Acute episode
- B. Episodic course
- C. Illness onset after age 30
- D. Past response to ECT

*ECT is treatment of choice.

Cross-Sectional Indicators

Cross-sectional indicators refer to any characteristics of the patient's present episode that suggest the illness will respond to ECT or that indicate ECT may be the treatment of choice. For affective features virtually all clinicians who use ECT agree that depression is a primary indication for ECT. Psychomotor retardation, self-reproach, early-morning waking, delusions, and an episode of less than 1 year's duration are often cited as predictors of a good response. Reactivity of mood, hypochondriasis, significant features of anxiety, and premorbid anxious and fearful personality traits are cited as predictors of a poor response. Despite decades of study, the relationship between any one of these indicators and treatment response remains inconclusive. The more symptoms of depression a patient has, however, the better is the overall prediction of his response to ECT. Figure 21.1 displays a modified version of the Hamilton Rating Scale for depression. This widely used clinical instrument rates the severity of depression. A score of more than 15 suggests the patient has a depression that may respond to ECT. Indeed, the

Patient: ____________________	**Time of Examination:** **Pre-ECT** ___ **Post** ___
Date: ________________	**Examiner:** ____________________

1. Insomnia, early	0 1 2
2. Insomnia, middle	0 1 2
3. Insomnia, late	0 1 2
4. Anxiety, somatic	0 1 2 3 4
5. Anxiety, psychic	0 1 2 3 4
6. Somatic symptoms, general	0 1 2
7. Somatic symptoms, GI	0 1 2
8. Hopelessness	0 1 2 3 4
9. Hypochondriasis	0 1 2 3 4
10. Depressed mood	0 1 2 3 4
11. Guilt	0 1 2 3 4
12. Worthlessness	0 1 2 3 4
13. Suicide	0 1 2 3 4
14. Retardation	0 1 2 3 4
15. Agitation	0 1 2 3 4

Note: Hallucinations or delusions should be given a score of 4 under the related item (hopelessness, hypochondriasis, guilt, or worthlessness).

Global assessment of outcome:	worse	no change	a little better	much better	all better

Observations and comments:

Figure 21.1. Modified Hamilton Rating Scale for Depression

higher the Hamilton score, the merrier after ECT. Six to eight induced seizures are usually sufficient to resolve 90% of melancholic episodes. For the delusional depressive or the melancholic who is a serious suicide risk, where the choices are ECT, a cyclic antidepressant plus neuroleptic, or some combination of other drugs (e.g., lithium, carbamazepine, MAOI), ECT fully meets the APA guideline as the most rapid, definitive, and safest choice. It is therefore recommended as the treatment of choice in these situations. Mania is also extremely responsive to ECT, although more treatments are often required to induce a remission (8 to 15 bilateral treatments). Many practitioners would reserve ECT for manic patients who had failed to respond to lithium, or a short course of parenteral neuroleptics.

The catatonic syndrome of negativistic stupor, characterized by mutism, negativism, stupor, and catalepsy, is also extremely responsive to ECT. This motor syndrome is most frequently a manifestation of melancholia but can also occur in patients with coarse brain disease, mania, or schizophrenia. Although the syndrome may fully respond to only two or three induced seizures, additional treatments are needed to prevent relapse; the eventual outcome is determined by the prognosis of the underlying condition. The neuroleptic malignant syndrome and lethal catatonia, variants of the typical catatonic syndrome (see Chapters 3 and 23), also can be successfully treated with ECT.

Among the atypical psychoses or psychoses NOS, patients who have no emotional blunting (particularly no avolition prior to the present episode) are likely to respond well to biologic treatment. Although ECT would not be used as the first-line treatment for these disorders by many practitioners, the more affective features a patient has in association with no loss of premorbid volition, the better are the chances that patient's present episode will be responsive to ECT.

Contextual Indicators

Illness episodes do not occur in a vacuum. Other clinical, demographic, and social features, although not directly related to the pathophysiologic process of the present episode, may, influence that episode and the choice of treatment. For a patient with an atypical psychosis or psychosis NOS, and a decision regarding treatment choice needs to be made, the contextual factors of past or recent hallucinogenic drug use or a family history of suicide or affective disorder suggests that the illness may be responsive to ECT. Past or recent drug use suggests that the present episode is induced by brain dysfunction from that use. Such conditions often do not respond well to neuroleptics or can be made worse by neuroleptic treatment, but they are responsive to ECT. The family history of suicide may indicate that the patient has the same morbid process as his family (i.e., affective disorder). Therefore, he is likely to be responsive to treatments for affective disorder.

A patient who has not responded or who has been made worse by neuroleptic or mood-stabilizing drugs, also meets APA guidelines as a candidate for ECT. Guidelines for switching to ECT when faced with pharmacologic nonresponse are: (1) always begin pharmacotherapy with the drug or drugs that should offer the best chance for a full recovery, and (2) always prescribe clearly therapeutic doses for a reasonable period of time. If there is *no* response within 2 weeks to the therapeutic dose, or an inadequate response (50% or less reduction in symptoms) after 4 weeks of a maximum therapeutic dose, the clinician should regard the episode as resistant to the medication. Rather than beginning the often long process of switching from drug to drug or combination to combination, the clinician should now strongly consider the use of ECT. The rationale for this approach consists of two principles: (1) if the best pharmacologic choice is used first and is less than successful, second and third best are unlikely to be any better in the short run; and (2) if Post and his colleagues are correct in that early prolonged affective episodes can sensitize the system and result in more and longer episodes later on (see Chapter 11), the quicker an affective episode can be resolved, the less chance the patient has for chronicity.

The contextual factors of the patient being pregnant, breast-feeding, systemically ill, or elderly are also discussed in Chapters 11, 19, 20, and 22, respectively. The presence of any of one of these factors makes pharmacologic treatments more risky. Depending on the specific details of each factor and the social needs of the patient, ECT can be the safest and perhaps the best treatment choice.

Longitudinal Indicators

An illness episode, no matter how short, has a course during which symptoms unfold. Many patients have a long history of illness. Some of these longitudinal factors predict good response to treatment, including response to ECT. The acuteness of the present episode (less than 6 months), an episodic illness course with good interepisode functioning, and a first illness onset after age 30 suggest that the present episode is unlikely to be schizophrenia and more likely to be a mood disorder. Thus, the presence of any one of these longitudinal factors, particularly acuteness of episode and episodic course, suggests that the patient will benefit from ECT. A past good response to ECT also indicates that the patient will again respond well to ECT. In contrast, a previous "bad" response to ECT does not predict that the patient will not now respond well to ECT. This apparent paradox is explained by the experience that when a patient says he had ECT and it did not work, what he often means is that ECT resolved the episode but relapse quickly followed. Thus, the patient was an ECT responder, but maintenance treatment failed (usually because of inadequate pharmacotherapy). Sadly, it also remains true that, despite many advances in treatment technique, some ECT practitioners still do not recognize the need for adequate monitoring of seizure duration. Although long seizures are not necessary for a therapeutic response, seizures of 25 seconds or more are necessary. Without some type of monitoring system, duration cannot be determined. Failure of ECT for patients who had the treatment several decades ago may reflect poor treatment or maintenance technique, rather than nonresponsivity to ECT.

Technique

Pretreatment Evaluation

ECT is inherently a safe treatment (5, 63). As for any procedure under general anesthesia, however, medical screening information, including history, physical examination, chest x-ray, ECG, complete blood count, urinalysis, fasting blood sugar, and BUN, is required for all ECT candidates. In addition, patients with a history or symptoms of a specific systemic or neurologic condition should have all relevant tests. The purpose of these screening evaluations is not to detect conditions that contraindicate ECT, as few exist, but to uncover previously unsuspected pathology so that it may be corrected or ameliorated prior to initiating treatment.

The advice of a consultant is often needed for the high risk patient (see below), but not for the purpose of "clearing" a patient for ECT. The consultant should be asked to provide an assessment of the nature and severity of the patient's systemic condition and an opinion as to appropriate treatment. The final medical decision to administer ECT rests with the psychiatrist, who is the only person fully cognizant of the morbid and mortal risks of withholding, as well as giving, treatment.

Neither skull x-rays nor an EEG is a useful pretreatment screening test. The former are insensitive in detecting intracerebral pathology, and the latter lacks specificity for all but seizure disorders. As almost one third of melancholics exhibit pretreatment nonspecific EEG abnormalities that do not predict an unfavorable outcome (16), their presence is unhelpful in deciding whether or not to give ECT. If intracerebral lesions are suspected, a CT or MRI is the diagnostic procedure of choice.

Prior to the introduction in 1955 of succinylcholine muscle relaxation for ECT, many patients sustained spinal compression fractures during the tonic phase of the induced seizure, and pretreatment x-rays of the dorsolumbar spine were routinely obtained for medicolegal documentation. Today, pre-ECT spine films are unnecessary and produce only needless expense and radiation exposure. Also unnecessary is pre-ECT screening for a pseudocholinesterase deficiency, which predisposes the patient to prolonged post-ECT apnea resulting from impaired metabolism of succinylcholine. The available screening test, although sensitive and quite specific for this rare disorder (1:3, 000 individuals), leads to more than 90% false-positive results and provides no guide to action (337).

All medications being taken by the patient should be reviewed as part of the pre-ECT evaluation. Agents that are likely to increase morbidity or decrease the efficacy of ECT should be discontinued or decreased in dose prior to ECT. The APA Task Force lists benzodiazepines, most other sedative hypnotics, anticonvulsants, lidocaine and its analogs (all block or reduce seizure length), reserpine (which can cause fatal hypotension), lithium (which can increase succinylcholine-induced neuromuscular blockade and exacerbate cognitive side effects), and theophylline (which can lower seizure threshold). The APA Task Force also cautions against the continued use of all psychotropics but recognizes that moderate doses of neuroleptics may need to be continued during the early part of the ECT treatment course for some patients.

Consent for ECT

Many melancholics who are voluntary patients and legally fully competent are still unable to attend to the fine details of the informed consent process because of their distractibility or ruminations. They may have "gone beyond caring," be indifferent to their fate, and perfunctorily sign any document shown to them. Others, may comprehend the elements of the procedure, have no objection to it, and strongly desire relief from symptoms, but they still must be encouraged and coaxed into signing. Their indecision or psychomotor retardation may prove to be an almost insurmountable obstacle in obtaining consent. Their families are often asked, or may volunteer, to aid in this process. To obtain informed consent from such patients often strains the intent of the process.

Although varying somewhat from state to state, the law is generally clear regarding informed consent. Voluntary patients may receive ECT only after providing their written, informed consent. In some states, an exception to this rule is the patient who suddenly and unexpectedly becomes acutely suicidal and presents a clear and immediate danger of killing himself. Many psychiatrists would give emergency ECT to such a patient after converting his status to involuntary. Often (but not always), they first obtain the family's consent and that of the hospital director or service chief. In this instance, the emergency must be genuine and clearly documented in the patient's chart. Many states now also insist that informed consent for ECT be obtained from involuntary patients as well, recognizing that a psychosis does not necessarily rob a patient of the ability to understand the nature of the treatment offered and the rationality to refuse it. If the treating psychiatrist is thoroughly convinced that the potential benefits of ECT justify involuntary treatment, it behooves him to petition the court to direct that ECT be given against the patient's will. In addition to state requirements, the APA recommends that informed consent be specific, including the number of treatments, whether maintenance ECT is planned, and that consent may be withdrawn at any time.

The psychiatrist, like other clinicians, is frequently faced with this conflict between the letter and the spirit of the law, between what he believes is best for his patient and what the law says is best for society. Ultimately, each clinician decides for himself, case by case, the degree of ambiguity that he can tolerate in applying these legal doctrines within the context of responsible clinical practice.

Preanesthesia and Anesthesia

Once the decision to give ECT has been made and a starting date set, standard orders for the procedure should include treatment days and starting times, a prohibition against eating or drinking the day of treatment to avoid vomiting and aspiration, and atropine (0.6–1.0 mg IV) or glycopyrolate (0.2–0.4 mg IV) to be given immediately before treatment to minimize the risk of vagally mediated bradyrhythmias or asystole and to reduce bronchial secretions.

Dentures and eyeglasses should be removed and safely stored. Patients should urinate before the treatment, as incontinence occasionally occurs during the seizure. Hair oils, creams, and sprays should not be applied on treatment mornings. Patients with oily hair or residues from hair preparations should have a shampoo the night before. These precautions ensure good electrode-scalp contact.

The ultra-short–acting barbiturate methohexital, the anesthetic of choice, has replaced thiopental sodium with its greater risk of ECG abnormalities (768). An IV drip infusion is started with a 250-cc container of glucose and water, using a 19–21 gauge, thin-walled butterfly needle assembly (alternatively, a 50-cc syringe filled with glucose and water may be attached to the butterfly). After recording vital signs, 60–80 mg of methohexital (1 mg/kg) is rapidly given IV by bolus push into the IV tubing. The patient is asked to count aloud to 50. When he ceases counting, 40–50 mg of succinylcholine (0.5–1 mg/kg) is injected in the same manner as the methohexital. Subsequent succinylcholine dosage will be modified according to the strength of the first seizure. The patient is then closely observed for muscle fasciculations representing the first (depolarization) phase of succinylcholine activity. These start in the face, chest, and upper extremities and progress to the lower extremities over a period of 10 to 20 seconds. When the fasciculations begin to fade in the calves and small muscles of the feet, the patient is ready to be treated.

The patient should be oxygenated by using positive-pressure ventilation from the onset of anesthesia until resumption of spontaneous respirations, except during the brief period of the application of the stimulus and the subsequent muscular spasm before the actual seizure begins. Oxygenation should be with 100 oxygen at a flow rate of at least 5 liters/minute and a respiration rate of 15 to 20 breaths/minute. A flexible mouth bite should be used to protect teeth and mouth from damage, and the patient's head and neck should be slightly extended to help maintain an airway. The patient's chin should be held during the passage of the current to keep the jaws tightly closed and avoid injury.

Treatment Electrode Application

Bilateral ECT is the original method. It is administered through bifrontotemporal electrodes, one on each side of the head, placed an inch above the midpoint of an imaginary line joining the outer canthus of the eye and the external auditory meatus. Unilateral ECT, a modification introduced in 1958, is most frequently administered through electrodes placed temporoparietally over one side of the head only, the nondominant hemisphere. The lower (temporal) electrode is placed as for bilateral ECT, and the upper (parietal) electrode is placed above this, about 1 inch ipsilateral to the vertex. For patients receiving unilateral ECT, it is best to give right-sided ECT initially because the left hemisphere is dominant for speech in almost all right-handers and many left-handers. If a left-handed patient exhibits verbal memory impairment after the first treatment, he may be assumed to be right-hemisphere dominant for speech, and the treatment electrodes should be moved to the left hemisphere for subsequent treatments.

Unilateral ECT was introduced in a successful attempt to reduce the memory loss and confusion frequently observed after conventional bilateral ECT. Controversy remains over the relative therapeutic efficacy of unilateral and bilateral ECT. With the unilateral electrode placement indicated above and the use of pulse wave-current (see below), unilateral ECT and bilateral ECT are therapeutically equivalent for many patients. When there is no special urgency to achieve symptom relief, patients may be started on unilateral ECT and changed over to bilateral ECT if significant improvement is not observed after four or five treatments. If a rapid response is required, as in suicidal, psychotic, agitated, or stuporous depressives or in manics, bilateral ECT is preferable.

Treatment Current

Two types of ECT devices, which employ either sinusoidal or pulsed currents, are available. Sinusoidal (alternating) currents are characterized by a continuous flow of electricity, first in one direction and then in the other, at a frequency of 60 Hz. Such currents were used in 1938 to give the first ECT and are still employed in some machines. Some machines also have a "glissando" dial, which was introduced in the pre–succinylcholine era in an attempt to reduce the incidence of fractures by slowing the rate of application of the treatment stimulus. The "glissando" mode, however, substantially increases the electrical dosage and memory problems and is of no benefit to patients. Sinusoidal currents can be modified electronically to provide a series of brief rectangular pulses that stimulate the brain more efficiently and induce seizures with substantially less electrical energy and, therefore, less memory loss (1046). Brief pulse current is clearly preferable.

Stimulus Dosing

The APA Task Force provides guidelines and information regarding the characteristics and safety measures of various ECT devices. How the clinician goes about determining stimulus dose depends in part, on which machine is used. Most pulse wave ECT machines deliver about the same amount of energy, and settings should be based on the manufacturer's specifications. In general, the primary consideration is to deliver an adequate amount of energy to induce a grand mal seizure. In determining the actual settings for a given machine, the clinician must consider the great individual differences in seizure threshold, with generally higher thresholds (therefore, more energy is needed for a seizure) in the elderly and in men. Seizure threshold also increases over the course of treatment. Further, there is some evidence, particularly with unilateral ECT, that stimuli marginally above the seizure threshold are less therapeutic than those delivered at higher intensity but that grossly suprathreshold stimuli lead to more cognitive impairment without an equivalent increase in therapeutic effect. This inverted U-shaped dose response curve is analogous to those for imipramine and amitriptyline (825, 857).

The Seizure

Although the relative therapeutic roles of the induced cerebral seizure and the electrical stimulating current remain undefined, little doubt exists that a fully developed grand mal brain seizure is a major element in the treatment process (1046). The motor manifestation of this seizure is irrelevant. In most patients, the seizure is easily recognized, despite the effects of succinylcholine, which rarely obscures entirely the stereotyped tonic-clonic progression of the induced seizure. Missed, abortive, or partial seizures occasionally occur, most often with unilateral ECT; when this happens, the electrical stimulation should be repeated until a full seizure is obtained. Even with extreme degrees of muscle relaxation, a tonic seizure phase characterized by pronounced plantarflexion lasting for 5 to 10 seconds; usually can be observed. In the absence of such a response, it is best to repeat the electrical stimulation as quickly as possible in order to take advantage of the temporarily lowered seizure threshold from the initial stimulus. Additional evidence for the occurrence of a seizure includes piloerection (gooseflesh), pupillary dilatation, and tachycardia. An EEG monitor is of only modest assistance in this regard; the passage of the stimulating current overloads the EEG amplifiers, so that it takes at least 10 seconds for the recording pens to return to baseline. By then, the tonic phase will have passed, along with the optimal period during which a repeat stimulus of the same intensity is likely to induce a seizure. A simple and effective technique for monitoring seizure activity is to inflate a blood pressure cuff over one arm to exceed the systolic blood pressure before the succinylcholine is given. This technique prevents the succinylcholine from entering the muscles of that arm, so that they remain polarized. The unmodified seizure then can be observed in the occluded extremity.

The primary value of EEG monitoring is to ensure adequate seizure duration;

unlike the tonic phase, the clonic seizure phase may be markedly attenuated and even totally obscured by succinylcholine, except for very fine rhythmical twitching movements of the small muscles underlying the skin around the eyes and nose. If total seizure time, as measured by stopwatch or EEG, is less than 25 seconds, the electrical stimulation should be repeated at a higher intensity after waiting about 1 minute for the refractory period to pass. Almost never is additional succinylcholine needed in this event, as an adequate degree of muscle relaxation for ECT continues for several minutes after the peak effect has been reached. Also, Seizure time can be indirectly determined by measuring the duration of ECT-induced tachycardia (574).

Missed or inadequate seizures usually result from poor electrode contact, premature termination of the stimulus, or disconnected cables. Occasionally, despite adequate doses and proper equipment, a patient does not develop a seizure. Reducing the dose of anesthetic, hyperventilating prior to stimulation, or IV caffeine (100–250 mg pure; 200–500 mg sodium benzoate) over a 1-minute period, given 2 to 3 minutes prior to anesthesia, may lower the seizure threshold sufficiently to permit seizure induction.

ECT exerts its most prominent effects on the cardiovascular system, through both a direct initial Valsalva effect and a subsequent seizure-induced generalized autonomic and motor discharge. Heart rate and blood pressure, along with the EEG, should be monitored. Both increase moderately during the initial Valsalva effect, followed by further marked increases during a period of 1 to 2 minutes after the electrical stimulus. Pulse rates typically rise to 130–190/minute with accompanying systolic blood pressure levels of 250–300 mm Hg. A sharp drop in heart rate correlates with the end of the seizure (usually in less than a minute), and heart rate and blood pressure return to baseline a minute or so after the seizure ends. Cerebral blood flow increases after an initial brief reduction during the electrical stimulus; this is accompanied by doubling of cerebral oxygen consumption and glucose utilization during the induced seizure. There is no evidence, however, of cerebral anoxia during succinylcholine-modified ECT, which is probably explained by the very small amounts of oxygen used up peripherally by the paralyzed muscles.

Termination of the seizure signals the end of the treatment phase. The remaining task is to monitor the patient's emergence from anesthesia and the cognitive disruption caused by the seizure. Assisted ventilation is continued for several minutes until spontaneous respirations return, at which time the IV is removed. The patient is then turned on his side and wheeled to a nearby recovery area, where he should be observed by trained personnel until he awakens. During the recovery phase, an airway and adequate exchange of air are maintained. Suction and oxygen equipment, although rarely required, should be immediately available.

Complications and Side Effects

About 5 to 10% of patients develop a state of pronounced restlessness or agitation as they emerge from anesthesia. This is an "emergence delirium," for which patients are amnestic. No amount of calm reassurance or firm persuasion is of any avail in preventing a patient from climbing out of bed, even over raised side rails, and possibly injuring himself. The patient must be restrained and given IV sedation, preferably with diazepam (10 mg), in order to terminate the episode. Repeat episodes usually occur with each subsequent treatment and may be prevented either with diazepam, (10 mg) by direct IV injection immediately after the induced seizure terminates or with a 20% increase in the dose of succinylcholine. Untreated, emergence delirium rarely lasts longer than 15 to 20 minutes.

Prolonged apnea is a rare complication of ECT muscle relaxation that results from a relative deficiency of pseudocholinesterase, the enzyme that degrades succinylcholine. If spontaneous respirations do not return by 5 minutes after the seizure has ended, preparation should be made for intubation; if assisted respiration is still required after 10 minutes, a cuffed endotracheal tube should be inserted and inflated in order to maximize the efficiency of air exchange. Most patients with this complication breathe spontaneously within 30 minutes and the remainder within 60 to 90 minutes.

Occasionally, a seizure persists for more than 180 seconds. Because no evidence indicates that prolonged seizures are beneficial, they should be terminated by diazepam (10 mg IV).

The principal side effect of ECT consists of the temporary disorientation and memory loss seen most clearly after bilateral ECT. These phenomena are directly related to the number and frequency of treatments and may be exaggerated in patients over age 60. The memory loss consists of two parts: (1) a fully recoverable retrograde amnesia for events preceding the first treatment, with the patient exhibiting a gradient of severity more pronounced for recent than remote events; and (2) an anterograde amnesia for events occurring after the patient awakens from treatment, which is permanent because it results from failure to consolidate new memories during several postictal hours. Following the course of treatments, retrograde amnesia gradually ebbs over a period of several weeks and generally disappears entirely within 30 to 60 days after the final treatment. Because of anterograde amnesia, however, patients often complain of memory gaps for parts of the hospital stay. As depression also impairs cognitive function, memory may be incomplete for events prior to treatment when the depression was at its worst.

Memory change following unilateral ECT administered to the nondominant hemisphere is much less than after bilateral ECT (932). Immediately following a seizure, personal orientation returns more rapidly with unilateral ECT than with bilateral ECT, as does recall of items learned immediately prior to the seizure.

Both retrograde amnesia and anterograde amnesia are less, as well as the cumulative memory impairment following a course of treatment. Recent studies indicate that, with brief-pulse stimulation, long-term effects of ECT on memory are even less prominent than previously supposed (153).

Induced convulsions are characterized not only by the electrical discharge of the seizure but also by EEG changes that persist into the interseizure period. These changes take the form of slowing, increased amplitude, and increased rhythmicity. They appear all over the head, with the degree of slowing directly related to the number and frequency of seizures and the location of the treatment electrodes (15). These EEG changes typically resolve within 4 to 6 weeks.

High-Risk Patients

There are no contraindications to ECT, although several conditions increase a patient's risk for side effects and complications (35, 426). Whether of neurologic or systemic origin, many of these conditions occur in the elderly patient. Untreated, the mortality rate of the depressed elderly is increased. The risks of pharmacotherapy, however, are also greater in the elderly than in younger patients; elderly individuals are more likely to have co-occurring chronic systemic illness and are physiologically more sensitive than younger patients to the anticholinergic, cardiotoxic, and hypotensive effects of medications. If appropriate precautions are taken, the risks from ECT in these patients are significantly less than those from medications. Also, the elderly often respond better to ECT than younger patients.

Co-occurring systemic or neurologic illnesses that qualify a patient of any age as a high risk for ECT include cardiovascular conditions (arrhythmias, hypertension, recent myocardial infarction, occlusive vascular disease, aneurysms and their surgical repair, recent stroke), chronic obstructive pulmonary disease, degenerative joint disease, severe osteoporosis, dementias, brain tumor, and pheochromocytoma. Table 21.3 displays some high-risk problems and the ECT techniques to resolve them or to minimize risk to the patient.

Maintenance Treatment

Pharmacotherapy

Without maintenance treatment, the post-treatment 6-month relapse rate with ECT ranges from 30 to 60% (peaking during the first 10 days and over the first 6 weeks post-ECT). Follow-up treatment with cyclic antidepressants (particularly for uni-

TABLE 21.3

High-Risk Electroconvulsive Therapy Problems and Their Management

Problem	*Possible Consequence if Given ECT*	*Management*
Pre-ECT severe hypertension	Post-ECT hypotension and bradyarrhythmia	Pretreat with propranolol (Inderal) (0.5 mg IV) to prevent; atropine (0.25 mg IV) post-treatment to resolve.
Pre-ECT premature ventricular contractions (PVCs)	Ventricular fibrillation	Have lidocaine drip ready during ECT should PVCs increase post-ECT; pre-ECT control with propranolol or metoprolol (Lopressor).
Degenerative joint disease/ severe osteoporosis	Fractures	Increase succinulcholine dose by 40% or more.
Prosthetic heart valve	Embolus	Maintain prothrombin time at about 1.5 times; control with maintenance warfarin therapy.
Dementia	More severe and prolonged ECT-induced cognitive impairment	Use unilateral ECT and reduce treatments to two weekly or three biweekly.
Brain tumor	Increased intracranial pressure	Perform pre- and post-ECT neurologic and eye-ground examinations; trimethaphan drip (0.1% solution at 3–4 mg/min) to control hypertension; IV diazepam to control post-ECT delirium.
Pheochromocytoma	Hypertensive crisis	Same as for patient with brain tumor.
Unstable cardiac function	Heart failure, fibrillation	Stabilize, if possible, before ECT; pacemaker; severe hypertension can be controlled by sublingual nitroglycerine.
Recent stroke	Intracranial hemorrhage	Delay treatment, reduce hypertension with trimethaphan drip.
Demand pacemaker	May respond to ECT-induced muscle potentials, resulting in severe bradycardia	Convert to fixed-mode operation during seizure by placing ring magnet over the pacemaker's pulse generator.
Aortic aneurysm or surgical graft	Rupture (although no reported cases)	Increase muscle relaxation.

polar melancholia) or with lithium or an anticonvulsant (particularly for bipolar disorder) after a successful course of ECT reduces the relapse rate to about 10 to 15%. Maintenance doses are the same as those used when the acute treatment is also pharmacologic.

Maintenance ECT

For patients who relapse despite continuation treatment with cyclic antidepressant, anticonvulsants, or lithium, maintenance ECT has been used successfully, but objective data supporting this technique are minimal. With maintenance ECT, patients return at regular intervals for additional treatments, even in the absence of any recurrence of symptoms. A typical schedule for a patient who has fully recovered with a course of ECT might have the patient return for two or three additional treatments at biweekly intervals, and then monthly for a total of six to eight maintenance treatments. There is no rationale for continued maintenance ECT for prolonged periods (e.g., over 6 months), except in unusual circumstances. The continued use of maintenance ECT for years has no clinical justification and may result in continuous cognitive dysfunction.

The ECT Unit

The modern ECT unit is similar in many ways to a minor surgery suite. The treatment area must comfortably accommodate several pieces of equipment (treatment machine, pacemaker-defibrillator, oxygen tank, crash cart), the patient on a stretcher, and four to six personnel (depending on whether residents or medical students are present). About 300 square feet of space are required. The recovery room must accommodate five to six patients on stretchers, oxygen and suction equipment, and two to four personnel; it should be approximately the same size as the treatment room.

Treatment and recovery rooms should be separate but connected by a door. The ideal procedure is for patients to enter the treatment room through one door, be transferred to the recovery room through another door, and leave the recovery room through a third door.

ECT is a brief procedure requiring 8 to 10 minutes per patient. Efficiency can be maximized by following four steps to control patient flow:

1. The patient has emptied his bladder, his vital signs have been recorded, and he is lying on a stretcher outside the treatment room.
2. When the treatment team is ready, the patient is wheeled into the treatment room; the next patient is prepared and placed on a stretcher outside.

3. While an IV infusion is being started, the nursing assistant applies the ECG and EEG electrodes. As soon as a few seconds of baseline recording are obtained, anesthesia is rapidly induced and the anesthetist starts forced oxygenation immediately when the patient loses consciousness. The muscle relaxant is injected at the same time the psychiatrist applies the treatment electrodes. As soon as the fasciculations disappear in the calf muscles, the anesthetist inserts a rubber bite block, if needed, and hyperextends the neck, and the electrical stimulus is given. The anesthetist continues forced ventilation throughout the seizure until the return of spontaneous respirations, at which time the patient is placed on his side and an airway inserted. The stretcher is rolled into the recovery room.
4. The next patient is then brought into the treatment room.

For maximimum safety and efficiency, ECT should be given by an experienced team composed of (at a minimum) a psychiatrist, a nurse (trained in the procedure and responsible for maintaining the suite), an anesthetist or anesthesiologist, and a nursing assistant. The psychiatrist is the director of the ECT unit and has overall medical responsibility for the procedure, analogous to the surgeon's role in the operating suite.

Chapter 22

Management of Elderly Patients

Compared with other age groups, the elderly are increasing more rapidly in numbers, have the highest prevalence of psychiatric illness, and are the most psychiatrically underserved. Aging involves anatomic and physiologic decline, which occurs in widely varying degrees among individuals (147). For that reason, the aged are more likely than the young to have disease in multiple organ systems and are more vulnerable to iatrogenic (particularly drug-induced) illnesses. The most common syndromes of the elderly include mood disorders (especially depression) and coarse brain diseases (particularly dementia and delirium). Despite the above factors, the prognosis for recovery from some of the chief psychiatric syndromes (e.g., mania, melancholia, certain dementias, and deliria), as well as disorders treated in other branches of medicine, is excellent. Failure to distinguish illness from normal aging, however, can result in not recognizing clinical features of treatable conditions. Geriatric psychiatry (in addition to child psychiatry) is now a recognized subspecialty and has its own certification examination. Although the principles of diagnosis and treatment of the elderly are identical to those of the young, the physician must be more cautious in his medical therapeutics lest he cause or intensify illness.

Thirty million Americans (12% of the population) are over 65 years of age. By 2030, they will constitute 20% of the population (148). The number of psychiatrists interested in the care of the elderly is growing (204), but the elderly remain a psychiatrically underserved group. Also, most cognitive disorders in elderly patients are not identified by general practitioners and other specialists (317). Ouslander (730) writes: "On medical and surgical services, little time and effort is placed on meaningful mental status examinations."

In addition, the elderly underutilize psychiatric facilities (279, 945) and, when treated, often face physician bias against them (148, 894). Contributing to this bias are the correct perception that geriatric patients are more likely to have disease in multiple systems and the usually incorrect notion that the prognosis for recovery of the elderly for given psychiatric (298, 580) and systemic illnesses (812) is poorer than that for younger people. In a questionnaire mailed to psychiatrists, case studies were presented in which all details were the same except for the patient's age. When the case study described an elderly patient, the psychiatrists were more likely to regard the prognosis as poor and to treat the patient differently (319).

Biology and Pathophysiology of Aging

The exact nature of aging is unknown. There are two perspectives on the subject. First, a genotype is "programmed" into the cells so that specific disease is not required to cause cell death; it occurs after a fixed and predetermined number of cell replications. Evidence for this programming comes from work (428) demonstrating that human fibroblast cells, both in vivo and in vitro, undergo a fixed number of replications, regardless of environmental events. A variation of the above view relates to the premise that all cell death is programmed to occur by default unless suppressed by signals from other cells. Dependence on specific signals for survival would provide a simple way to eliminate developmentally misplaced cells and to regulate the total number of cells (794).

The second understanding of aging is that it is the product of such events as DNA damage, mutation, formation of free radicals, formation of cross-linkages between molecules, wear and tear, accumulation of toxic metabolites, and impaired supply of nutrients (900). Some combination of all the above factors probably determines how an individual ages.

Because of public health and other medical interventions, life expectancy has greatly increased. In the late eighteenth century, old age began during an individual's 30s and 40s. Children who lived to age 5 survived to age 38 or 39 (290). There is no evidence, however, that the aging process itself has been altered.

Aging (senescence) involves a decline in physiologic function as the years progress. The rate of organ decline varies considerably among and within individuals. For almost every test of systemic health or brain functioning, the variability is significantly greater among groups of old people than among groups of young people (1064). Thus, many individuals can function outstandingly to advanced ages (e.g., Leonardo, Titian, Durer, Michelangelo, Voltaire, Goethe, Verdi, Renoir, and Picasso). In 1982, a 65-year-old man swam the English Channel (178).

For the elderly as a group, however, there is a distinct anatomic and physiologic decline. Actual numbers of active metabolic cells and cellular functions decrease over the life span. Table 22.1 lists some of these changes (586). In addition, aging

TABLE 22.1
Deterioration with Age

Physical Characteristic	*Percentage of Deterioration From Age 30 to Age 75*
Number of taste buds	64
Power of hand grip	45
Vital capacity	44
Number of kidney glomeruli	44
Number of fibers in nerves	37
Glomerular filtration rate	31
Maximum rate of work	30
Resting cardiac output	30
Blood flow to brain	20
Total body water content	18
Basal metabolic rate	16
Body weight in men	12
Brain weight	10

may result in shortened stature, stooped posture resulting in part from inadequate dietary calcium and decalcification of bones, depigmentation and loss of hair, wrinkling of skin, decrease in muscle mass and strength, slowing of movements and halting of gait, redistribution of fat, loss of teeth, altered facial architecture, loss of high-frequency hearing, decrease of visual acuity, and increased systolic blood pressure (128, 523, 633, 850). The kidneys, lungs, and skin age more rapidly than do the heart and liver (305, 523). Nevertheless, aerobic exercise training has significant positive effects on the cardiovascular and pulmonary systems and behavior in older males and females (119).

Of particular concern to the neuropsychiatrist are normal age-related changes observed in liver and kidney function because they directly affect psychopharmacologic treatment. The liver decreases in mass, and, throughout the life span, hepatic blood flow drops 50%. Microsomal enzyme activity also decreases and, combined with blood flow changes, results in diminished first-pass biotransformation of drugs that are initially oxidized by the liver. The result is a prolonged half-life and increased bioavailability of those drugs that would otherwise undergo extensive first-pass hepatic metabolism. These changes are more marked in men than in women (349, 523).

Normal age-related changes in renal function delays elimination of active drug metabolites excreted in the kidneys, thus extending their bioavailability. Decreases include renal blood flow, glomerular filtration rate, tubular secretion, and the ability to compensate for acid-base and electrolyte abnormalities and free-water load. The capacity to conserve sodium declines with increased osmoreceptor sensitivity, with the result that more vasopressin and water retention (an inappropriate antidiuretic hormone secretion syndrome) are produced (305, 523). Table 22.2 summarizes some of the physiologic changes in aging that effect psychopharmacologic treatment.

Neuropathologic changes include a decrease in the number of dendrites, neuro-

TABLE 22.2

Physiologic Changes of Aging That Affect Psychopharmacologic Treatment

Change	*Effect*
Osteoporosis	Increased risk of hip fracture from falling secondary to orthostatic hypotension from cyclic compounds
Increased body fat	Increased concentration of plasma lithium and water-soluble drug metabolites; decreased plasma concentration of lipid-soluble drug metabolites, but increased total body distribution and prolonged elimination half-life
Liver changes	
Decrease in albumin	Increased free benzodiazepine (increased bioavailability at same total plasma levels)
Decreased enzyme activity	Decreased demethylation of tertiary amine tricyclics and benzodiazepines with active desmethyl metabolites
Decreased hepatic blood flow	Some reduction in first-pass metabolism
Kidney changes	
Decreased renal blood flow; decreased glomerular filtration rate; and decreased renal tubular secretion	Decreased lithium clearance; decreased clearance of cyclic antidepressant metabolites
Decreased intestinal motility	May delay peak blood levels; increased risk for paralytic ileus with drugs that have anticholinergic properties
Prostatic hypertrophy	Increased risk for urinary retention with drugs that have anticholinergic properties
Diminished thyroid reserves	Increased risk for hypothyroidism with lithium treatment

fibrillary degeneration, granulovascular degeneration, lipofuscin accumulation, Lewy's bodies, senile plaques, amyloid deposits, shrinkage of dendritic arbor, decrease of extracellular space, corpora amylacea, and myelin remodeling of the glia (812).

The elderly have a decrease in total sleep time (300) and in the amount of rapid eye movement sleep; stage four sleep almost disappears (761). There is EEG slowing in the alpha, delta, and beta frequencies. Cerebral blood flow is harder to maintain in the presence of drops in blood pressure, so that fainting and consequent injury are more likely (1080). In women, there is a dramatic decrease in estrogen levels and subtle changes in the levels of other hormones. There is decreased responsivity of the immune system (128). Pain and fever are less effective warning signals of disease. Thus, silent myocardial infarctions and infections without fever occur and may be missed (812).

There is probably a reduction of biogenic amine neurotransmitters in the brain and spinal cord, including a decreased supply of choline, choline acetyltransferase, and dopamine (586). The amount of monoamine oxidase increases in the brain, which probably contributes to the diminution of dopamine and other neurotransmitters (65, 832). The level of cerebrospinal fluid lactate also increases (1089). Plasma norepinephrine levels increase, both at rest and in response to stress (78).

During stressful learning tasks, the elderly have larger increases in free fatty acids, which do not peak until 45 minutes after completion of the task. By contrast, younger individuals have only a slight increase in free fatty acid levels in the early stages of learning. The difficulty in learning among the aged is associated with heightened autonomic nervous system activity secondary to increased neuroendocrine sensitivity in target organs (1064). This could contribute to the severity of the "catastrophic response" of some patients confronted with cognitive deficits (1068). Creativity involving truly inventive solutions to problems, in contrast to applying previously used strategies, declines with age (456). Memory impairment, however, is not always present (317).

The elderly are vulnerable to first occurrence and recurrence of most diseases that affect younger adults and have a higher frequency of some conditions, many of which are serious or fatal. The latter include cerebral arteriosclerosis and infarction, arteriosclerotic heart disease, certain cancers, Parkinson's disease, and primary degenerative dementia (812). Among people age 65 and older, 85% report having at least one chronic disease or disability and many have multiple-system disease (922), which can result in an additive effect. In 26% of autopsies in one sample of elderly decedents, no disease of sufficient severity in any one organ system was found that could itself account for each patient's death if each patient had been younger. The authors of that study attributed these deaths to "aging itself" (542).

Despite these many signs of decline during the aging process, diseases that are curable in younger people are usually curable in the elderly. In the field of internal medicine, cancer is an example. Excluding other causes of death, survival rates for patients with cancer are as high in the elderly as in the young. This also applies in psychiatric illnesses (e.g., mania, melancholia, and many deliria). In fact, first episodes of mania in the elderly were found to be less severe than for younger counterparts, and the recurrence rate is lower. Because of the above-mentioned physiologic differences between old and young, however, a number of precautions must be taken and greater vigilance is required, most importantly in the area of psychopharmacology.

Psychopharmacology

The elderly are more likely than the young to receive drugs, including psychotropics; to receive multiple drugs; to develop drug toxicity; and to have unfavorable drug interactions (106, Chapter 16; 739). Most elderly people report having some illness and being under a physician's care. Most take two to six drugs. Prescriptions for one sample of aged patients were 35 to 40% for anxiolytics, neuroleptics, sedatives, and combinations of these categories. The use of psychotropic drugs in the elderly is common. In a sample of patients in skilled nursing homes, 47% were receiving tranquilizers; 35%, sedatives-hypnotics; and 8.5%, antidepressants; also, 25% were taking more than one tranquilizing medication (148). About one half of depressed elderly patients are heavy users of most medications, especially psychotropics, and one third of medically ill inpatients may be receiving at least one psychotropic drug (863, 864). Further, some geriatric tonics contain alcohol, which can cause sedation.

This high frequency of medication use is important because the elderly are less able to metabolize and eliminate most medicines, which can lead to an increased risk of side effects for a given dose. For some medications (e.g., diazepam and nitrazepam), there is greater toxicity (e.g., CNS depression) at any plasma level, as well as for any dose. Such effects are in large part due to a combination of diminished hepatic metabolism and reduced plasma albumin, causing larger fractions of freely circulating drug; increased proportion of body fat, causing greater drug retention; and reduced renal clearance of drugs (388, 862). Unless the patient is taking anticholinergic drugs or has a disease affecting intestinal absorption, however, the absorption of medications from the gut occurs as readily in the elderly as in the young (573, 862).

Diminished cognitive function is among the most serious side effects; it is most prominently seen in attentional, nonverbal, and memory tasks and often manifested by delirium or dementia. The worst drug offenders are anxiolytics, sedatives, hypnotics, anticholinergics, and antihypertensives (1064), although the list of medications capable of producing behavioral changes is enormous. With the use of certain antihypertensives, such as reserpine and alpha-methyldopa, patients face a serious risk for depression.

One study (247) reported impaired cognition in 35% of patients over age 60 who were taking antidepressants. Another study (575) reported that the abnormal behavior of 16% of 236 patients receiving psychotropic drugs before admission to a geropsychiatric hospital unit was caused by side effects of the drugs. Straker (948) writes: "Clinicians in the geriatric field have all shared the experience of seeing a confused, demented older patient rapidly clear to a normal sensorium when all drug intake was stopped."

When abnormal behavior does occur as a side effect in the elderly, it is more likely to last longer once the drug is discontinued or the dose reduced because of the altered physiology of aging (707). For example, digoxin-induced delirium often lasts for several days after digoxin is discontinued. In some cases (e.g., the improper monitoring of insulin), the drug-induced psychopathology can be permanent or even the harbinger of a patient's death. Behavioral change is but one type of serious drug toxicity to which the elderly are more prone. Postural hypotension is more likely and is particularly common with the use of low-potency neuroleptics, cyclic antidepressants, and MAOIs. Concomitantly prescribed diuretics, nitrates, or low-salt diets can enhance this effect. Postural hypotension often leads to falls, which sometimes produce hip fractures or subdural hematomas.

Cyclic antidepressants can precipitate congestive heart failure (839). Cyclic antidepressants, neuroleptics, and lithium can produce cardiac arrhythmias. In the elderly, lithium-induced ECG changes are more common than in the young (840). Tardive dyskinesia is more likely to occur when neuroleptics are first prescribed for elderly persons (180), and it is far more common in elderly patients because many of them have had years of exposure to neuroleptics. Urinary and fecal incontinence, more common in the elderly to begin with, particularly in the demented elderly (the majority of incontinent patients have cognitive impairment and 45% are demented) (731), can be caused or aggravated by laxatives, which are often routinely prescribed without good indication (730).

Drug interactions are an important consideration. Cyclic antidepressants and neuroleptics can negate the antihypertensive effect of guanethidine. Indomethacin increases lithium retention, which can cause severe lithium toxicity. Theophylline enhances the renal excretion of lithium; unless these two agents are properly titrated, the lithium can be rendered ineffective (907). Antacids containing aluminum, magnesium, and calcium can decrease the absorption of benzodiazepines and neuroleptics. In one nursing home survey (883), antacids combined with phenothiazines accounted for 15% of all drug combinations. Milk of magnesia decreases the absorption and efficacy of all psychotropic drugs (112).

Psychopathology

Epidemiologic population surveys for psychopathology in the elderly suggest that about 10 to 15% of people over age 65 have recently had some depressivelike episode, although less than 1% had a melancholia (403). Between 5 and 10% suffer from progressive dementias (402), 4% suffer from anxiety disorder, and a significant number abuse alcohol. Clearly, the most common major psychiatric disorders of old age are depression (of all types) and coarse brain syndromes. Dementia and delirium are the most common and the most severe of the coarse brain disorders. Depending on the source, the rate of depression among the hospitalized elderly may be over 50%. The prevalence of depression in the elderly is even higher in people with systemic illness (113). Such figures are sufficiently high that the clinician who suspects early dementia in a patient should consider the statistical fact that the patient is twice as likely to be depressed as demented.

Mood Disorders

Criteria for the diagnosis of depression are the same for the elderly as for the young, as is the case for all psychiatric syndromes. Cognitive dysfunction secondary to depression (pseudodementia), however, is more common among the elderly (315), and rates are higher for cortisol secretion and dexamethasone nonsuppression among older melancholic patients (136). Unrealistic concerns about physical health are also more frequent among the elderly depressed (401, 864).

Depression is a common manifestation of coarse brain disease. Usually, if the underlying coarse brain disease is cured, the depression remits. Occasionally, when the underlying process remits, the depression "takes on a life of its own" and must be treated like any depression. When the coarse brain disease is incurable, the depression still can be treated successfully.

The combination of being old and depressed (especially with major depression) is highly associated with suicide. The odds are yet higher when the patient has a systemic illness. In one study, 85% of those over age 60 who committed suicide had had an active systemic illness; in 70% of those cases, the illness contributed to the suicide. A suicide attempt by an older person is much more likely to be fatal than an attempt by a younger person (402). For women, suicide rate and prevalence of depression peak and reach a plateau in middle age, and the plateau persists during the senium (271, 1052). For men, the suicide rate continues to rise with age, although the steepness of the rise varies greatly among countries.

The majority of severe depressions in the elderly are relapses, although new cases of depression or mania may occur over the age of 75. The ratio of depressed to manic episodes increases with age, with the "unipolar" elderly being much more numerous than the "bipolar" elderly (778). Attacks of mania or hypomania constitute about 5 to 10% of affective disorders in old age. In approximately one half of manic patients, this is a recurrence of a preexisting illness. In the other half, the first attack occurred in the senium. The prognosis for mania in the elderly is good if the patient is not neurologically impaired or a drug abuser. In the latter two categories, patients tend to develop chronic mania (448).

Coarse Brain Disease

Coarse brain diseases, particularly dementia and delirium, are also extremely common in the elderly (402), with rates twice as high in those over age 75 as in those age 65 to 75. For dementia, specifically, the population prevalence is under 3% for ages 65 to 69, and greater than 20% over age 80. Forty percent of elderly residents and about 65% of the elderly admitted to long-stay psychiatric facilities have a primary diagnosis of dementia. For every individual with severely disabling dementia in an institution, there are two living in the community. The rate for delirium may be as high as 30%, although many of these cases are not identified by clinicians (646).

Dementia is not always associated with progressive deterioration with no recovery; 15 to 20% of dementias are caused by remediable conditions (237). Of this figure, about one third of cases result from depressive pseudodementia, one fourth from normal-pressure hydrocephalus, one fifth from intracranial mass lesions, and one half of the rest from drug-related disorders (606). The same drugs that cause delirium can cause dementia (575). Of those patients who do not recover from dementia, about one half have primary degenerative dementia and one fourth have multi-infarct dementia. The rest have a variety of other disorders (987). Physicians often miss the diagnosis of dementia when the patient is compliant (237). Nevertheless, cognitive screening is much more likely to detect cognitive abnormalities in the elderly than in the young.

Besides the common causes listed above, other afflictions of the elderly result in dementia. Compared with an age-matched population, Parkinson's disease (common in the aged) is more likely to be associated with dementia. The frequency of dementia in Parkinson's disease is 22 to 40%. Creutzfeldt Jakob disease, a rare disorder (2–7/100,000 population), usually begins between ages 50 and 60, and the patient usually does not survive to age 65; however, the condition can have a later onset. Huntington's chorea (2–7/100,000 population) usually begins at about age 40 (106, Chapter 16; 739).

Following medication as the primary cause of delirium in the medically ill elderly, the most common precipitants are fever, dehydration, decreased cardiac output, electrolyte imbalance, and hypoxia (730). In cases where the patient already has compromised cerebral functioning, the very process of admission to the hospital (846), extensive laboratory testing (291), or placement in a single hospital room (1041) can precipitate delirium or intensify dementia. Delirium can be superimposed upon dementia; this is more likely in the elderly.

Alcohol and Drug Dependence

About 14% of elderly men and 1 to 2% of elderly women are dependent on alcohol or other substances. Twenty-five percent of all elderly individuals regularly use psychotropic drugs; among residents of nursing homes, more than 50% receive these compounds. The use of illicit drugs is uncommon. Abuse patterns, symptoms, and complications of alcohol and drug abuse in the elderly are the same as in younger adults. Treatments are also essentially the same, except that doses for withdrawal are usually one third to one half of those required for younger adults (673).

Significant numbers of young opiate addicts persist with their addictions into old age. One study identified 44 opiate abusers age 50 and older. Half were employed, had no family to support, and maintained a small habit (157).

Late Paraphrenia

Late paraphrenia, a term most prevalent in the British literature (851), usually refers to a first-episode delusional psychosis, developing after age 60, that is characterized by a broad affect; an intense mood of anxiety, suspiciousness, irritability, euphoria, or sadness; systematized delusional ideas; and few signs of cognitive dysfunction. This condition more frequently affects women than men and accounts for 8% of all women over the age of 65 who are admitted for the first time to a psychiatric hospital in Great Britain. It appears to be a functional, rather than a structural morbid, process that is unrelated to senile or atherosclerotic dementia. Late paraphrenia is extremely responsive to convulsive treatment. Because of complicating nutritional imbalance and systemic illness in people in this age group, their particular adverse sensitivity to psychotropic drugs, and their high death rate during chronic hospitalization, ECT is the most effective and safest therapeutic strategy (967) and can be lifesaving.

In the United States, these disorders continue to be referred to as late-onset schizophrenia (420). About 10% of all hospitalized patients with the diagnosis of schizophrenia have their first episode after age 60. Studies (484) suggest that this late-onset group has premorbid function, symptomatology, and course consistent with the concept of late paraphrenia.

Anxiety Disorders

Late-onset panic attacks or generalized anxiety require a careful search for systemic illness or coarse brain disease. Conditions likely to cause secondary anxiety disorder in the elderly include early dementia, transient ischemic attacks and strokes, endocrinopathies, heart disease, hypertension, pulmonary emboli and chronic lung disease, and drugs (particularly thyroid replacement, stimulants, vasodilators, and caffeine) and withdrawal states (31). In cases where the diagnosis of panic disorder, agoraphobia, or OCD is clear, treatment is the same as for younger people. For animal or situational phobias (other than agoraphobia), behavior modification is the treatment of choice. In cases of panic disorder and situational phobias, patients usually can be treated outside of the hospital. About 3% of older men and 6% of older women have anxiety disorders (806).

Sexual Dysfunction

Exhibitionism, genital play with children, and sexual assault of young people account for more than 12% of the offenses for which old people are prosecuted. Homosexual and heterosexual assaults against adults are less common. Cerebral degeneration is responsible for some of these misdemeanors; however, in the majority of cases, cognitive dysfunction is absent. Although violence is committed by the elderly less frequently than by the young, it does occur. In one sample, the most common diagnoses among hospitalized violent geriatric patients were, in order of frequency, late paraphrenia, coarse brain disease of unspecified type, bipolar illness (manic), senile dementia, and alcoholic dementia (757).

Primary Prevention of Aging Problems

Primary prevention efforts during youth and adulthood are relevant to geriatric dementia and delirium. Attention to diet; avoidance of smoking, heavy drinking, and drug abuse; regular exercise; and proper treatment of hypertension can contribute to avoiding such conditions as buccolingual, respiratory, and other cancers; arteriosclerotic dementias; cirrhosis of the liver; and alcoholic dementias.

Childhood and old age are the two periods of life during which regular physical examinations, even when the patient is apparently well, are unarguably beneficial. Elderly patients and their families are sometimes prone to attribute treatable disabilities to irreversible effects of age or to withhold information about symptoms for fear that an examination will reveal something ominous (148). Relatively simple interventions arising from regular checkups, such as the removal of cerumen from an ear canal, can have a significant effect on the patient's behavior.

Hospital Care

Evaluation

As the elderly patient has greater vulnerability to illness in all systems, a thorough history and physical examination are particularly significant. If the patient's cognitive functioning or cooperativeness is poor and the history incomplete, information from a relative, friend, landlady, or another physician who has cared for the patient may be invaluable. Old medical records should be reviewed. The fact that the patient may have been recently examined by a physician should not deter the neuropsychiatric clinician from obtaining or doing his own physical examination and referring the patient for consultation if a finding is not readily explainable.

Laboratory Testing

Scheduling laboratory tests requires planning. The objectives are to be thorough and safe, minimize delay, avoid unnecessary phlebotomies and trips to laboratories, and reduce waiting times in unfamiliar locations. All procedures should be discussed with the patient to the extent of his comprehension. When a test is scheduled in the hospital laboratory, a patient with significant cognitive dysfunction should be accompanied by a staff member.

Laboratory testing for the diagnosis of neuropsychiatric disorder in the elderly is no different in principle or helpfulness than it is in other age groups. Also, abnormal laboratory test findings in psychiatric syndromes do not differ in pattern because of the patient's age. It is more likely, however, that neuroimaging will reveal some cortical atrophy and ventricular enlargement (628) and the neuropsychological test performance will indicate some deficits in sustained attention, visual spatial function, and tasks with speed or motor parameters (30). Interpretation of both imaging and neuropsychological test findings requires comparison with findings in nonpsychiatrically ill, age-matched normal subjects. The clinician should be especially cautious in making too much of findings that are not circumscribed, asymmetric, specific in pattern, or moderate to severe in functional loss.

In addition to diagnostic testing, laboratory assessment in the elderly can be useful in determining a baseline from which to gauge the effects of drug treatment. For example, a pretreatment ECG is helpful in determining the degree of ischemia or dysrhythmia present. This information is necessary when cyclic antidepressant treatment is contemplated because these compounds can increase heart rate, thus increasing ischemia. Cyclic antidepressants also have a quinidinelike effect that delays conduction, and they can produce heart block in patients with underlying conduction abnormalities (839). Prolongation of conduction also peaks in 3 to 4 weeks of treatment, which makes serial ECGs necessary in patients with borderline conduction deficits who are placed on cyclic antidepressants. A baseline ECG is also helpful when lithium treatment is contemplated because lithium can affect sinus rhythm and result in a "sick sinus syndrome" (840). Creatinine clearance, to assess renal function, and thyroid studies (including TSH) are also important prior to lithium treatment, as lithium is eliminated in the kidneys and the diminished thyroid reserve associated with aging can result in lithium-induced hypothyroidism (869).

Inpatient Care

Some hospitals have specialized psychogeriatric units. Use of such services, compared with assignment of elderly patients to general psychiatric units, has not been studied sufficiently to determine their efficacy. In chronic care mental hospitals, frail elderly patients are prone to injury caused by other patients. A separate unit for frail geriatric patients in such settings may reduce the number of such injuries. Problems in establishing geriatric units may include staff cynicism and bias about caring for elderly patients. In general hospitals, acute care psychiatric units that integrate elderly patients with others offer them the best chance for normal socialization. Patients should not be automatically assigned to private rooms, even when they can afford them. For patients who prefer sharing a room with others or who have significant cognitive impairment, semiprivate arrangements may be preferable.

Although there should be some times each day when the patient can sit and rest, every effort should be made to reduce isolation and boredom. If the patient wears glasses or a hearing aid, he should use these in the hospital (they should be placed in the same location every night). The patient should have access to favorite newspapers, magazines, and books if he can read and concentrate sufficiently. When reading is impossible, the staff should offer to read newspaper or magazine articles. Television and radio should be available. When the patient is watching television, his chair should be located so that he has a good view of the screen. In preference to spending long periods of time alone in his room, the patient should be seated in a chair near the nurses' station or another orderly high-traffic area.

Visiting by family and close friends, who are aware of the patient's condition and are not perceived by him as a nuisance, should be encouraged. Visits by chaplains and hospital volunteers also may be helpful. The hospital staff should regularly engage the patient in conversation and encourage him to discuss subjects of interest. Staff interactions may range from asking the patient what he would be doing if he were not ill to listening while he talks about the past or about death and dying.

A daily program of activities geared to the patient's level of functioning should be established by the nursing staff and occupational and recreational therapists. An in-hospital "field trip," such as to the cafeteria or kitchen, may provide a welcome change of scenery for long-term patients. Giving the patient a regular task that he can manage with some success (even folding towels or watering plants) is often helpful.

Allowances must be made for cognitive and other disabilities. Compared with younger patients, extra nursing time is usually needed. Occasionally, elderly patients need assistance in eating, washing, dressing, and bathing. When a patient must be fed by another person, it may be useful to have the patient hold a piece of bread in one hand to give him a sense of helping with the meal. The staff member should usually sit close to the patient. If the patient has a hearing problem, the staff member should face him and speak slowly and loudly. The staff should be prepared to explain instructions or answer the same questions multiple times.

A paper bag for waste should be taped to the patient's bed. Dentures should never be placed in a tissue or napkin, as they could be lost. If restraints are ever needed, body jackets are preferable. Chest and waist straps are easier to put in place but are often physically irritating.

Although the staff must often make allowances for disabilities, patients always should be accorded the highest degree of respect. Calling a patient by his first name (unless he asks you to do so), using phrases like "good boy," or talking in a condescending manner are inappropriate.

Specific Management

As a rule, treatments indicated for a younger person are also indicated for an elderly one. In most cases, however, the starting doses of psychoactive (and almost all other) medications should be one third to two thirds of the usual adult starting doses (575). Also, dose increases usually are more gradual than for younger patients. Unless they are absolutely necessary, combinations of psychotropic drugs should not be given to elderly patients. Drugs that impair alertness also should be avoided when possible; if they are prescribed, they should be used with caution. Laxatives and antacids should not be prescribed routinely.

Melancholia

ECT is the treatment of choice for melancholia in the elderly. It is more effective and safer (343) than cyclic antidepressants or lithium for this condition. Usually, ECT alleviates pseudodementia associated with major depression in the elderly. It is the treatment of choice for suicidal patients with major depression in an ICU or cardiac care unit (CCU). It can be administered in the ICU or CCU itself (707) and can be safely given to patients with pacemakers (63). Nevertheless, certain precautions must be taken in giving ECT to an elderly patient. One should usually stop treatments when full remission of an acute episode has occurred, rather than necessarily completing a "routine course" of six treatments. Monitoring of cognitive functioning with brief screening tests may identify a newly developed cognitive dysfunction that can predict prolonged post-ECT delirium. The latter syndrome is more common in the elderly. Maintenance ECT can be given following remission of an episode of major depression, just as in younger adults.

If the patient has major depression and refuses ECT, antidepressants or lithium could be used with caution. Antidepressants that have less cardiotoxicity and fewer anticholinergic side effects are preferable (desipramine, nortriptyline, fluoxetine). Antidepressants and lithium are contraindicated in patients with active heart disease. If lithium is prescribed, serum levels should be checked regularly because renal function may be marginal.

Among the elderly, depression secondary to coarse brain disease or systemic illness is a significant possibility, and the clinician needs to be particularly sensitive to the presence of these conditions. He should be alerted if the patient has no past personal history or family history of mood disorder or if the depression is in any way atypical. Conditions most likely to underlie secondary depression in the elderly include basal ganglia disease and stroke (particularly with left-sided lesions), Alzheimer's disease, endocrinopathy, pernicious anemia, malignancy, systemic viral illness, self-administered and prescribed medication, and heart and other organ failure (31). Treatment for these secondary depressions is similar to that for primary depression in the elderly (200). ECT remains the treatment of choice.

Mania

The treatment of choice for mania is lithium, regardless of the patient's age. Following remission of a manic episode, prophylactic lithium should be given for 3 to 6 months. Continued use of lithium after that depends on the frequency or prior manic and depressive episodes. If such episodes occurred every several years or more often, continued use of lithium would be indicated.

If the patient's mania unfolds as catatonic stupor, ECT is the treatment of choice. If the patient develops severe excitement, ECT or a neuroleptic, such as haloperidol, must be used initially. ECT is the treatment of choice for an acute manic patient in an ICU or CCU and should be administered on the unit (707). ECT is preferable to lithium when a manic patient must be on a low-salt diet, take diuretics, or receive a medication (such as theophylline or indomethacin) that creates major problems when used in combination with lithium.

Dysthymia

The treatments of choice for dysthymia, cyclic antidepressants, MAOIs, and cognitive psychotherapy, are the same for the elderly as for the young. Although initial dosages of MAOIs must be lower for elderly patients, they have lower brain catecholamine levels; because of this, it even has been suggested (65, 832) that they could benefit more from MAOIs than young patients. Many patients with dysthymia can be treated outside the hospital.

Schizophrenia

For decades, schizophrenia has been overdiagnosed. Consequently, neuroleptics have been overprescribed. A consequence of these actions is a large cohort of elderly who carry the diagnosis of schizophrenia and the long-term effects of treatment with neuroleptics (e.g., tardive dyskinesia). Whether long-term neuroleptic use produces additional brain dysfunction is uncertain, but this is quite likely. Additional cortical dysfunction, in turn, could increase the likelihood of a diagnosis of schizophrenia in a patient for whom it was never the correct diagnosis.

The diagnosis of schizophrenia in any elderly patient needs to be reviewed. Regardless of diagnosis, if the patient has been taking neuroleptics for years and his situation has stabilized, an attempt should be made to withdraw the neuroleptics gradually within several weeks. When the patient has received an anticholinergic antiparkinsonian agent for extrapyramidal side effects of neuroleptics for at least several months, this drug can be discontinued abruptly with only a small risk of an extrapyramidal symptom relapse. As schizophrenia progresses, the frequency and intensity of hallucinations and delusions tend to diminish. Other than during occasional periods of irritability and poor personal hygiene, the elderly schizophrenic is likely to be quiet, interpersonally inaccessible, and aloof and may require minimal psychotropic medication.

Coarse Brain Diseases

Twenty percent of cases of dementia and many cases of delirium are curable (237, 606). These include major depression, drug toxicity, vitamin deficiency, Wernicke-Korsakoff syndrome (15 to 20% of patients fully recover), normal-pressure hydrocephalus, bacterial and viral infections, fluid and electrolyte imbalances, endocrine disorders, head injuries caused by falls, some brain tumors (148), and transient ischemic attacks resulting from carotid artery occlusion. Laboratory diagnostic tests for most of these conditions are discussed in Chapter 12; primary treatments are listed in Table 22.3.

It should be apparent from Table 22.3 that some dementias, once diagnosed, require the clinician to obtain medical or surgical consultation and possible transfer to a medical or surgical ward. When an antidote (such as physostigmine for anticholinergic toxicity) to drug toxicity is not available, as is often the case, the clinician may need to wait several days or weeks for the condition to clear fully. When the diagnosis of drug toxicity is correct and the offending drug is removed or the dosage markedly reduced, however, the clinician should expect progressive improvement in the patient's condition.

By far, the most common incurable cause of dementia is primary degenerative dementia (Alzheimer's type). Despite its incurability, evidence (814) indicates that the use of dihydroergotoxine mesylate (Hydergine), an ergot derivative, can improve cognitive functioning to some degree in certain patients. One report (252) states that IV physostigmine can do the same on a transient basis, but that finding

TABLE 22.3

Treatments for Curable Causes of Dementia

Condition	*Treatment*
Major depression with pseudo-dementia	Electroconvulsive therapy (second choice: antidepressants or lithium)
Drug toxicity	Removal of offending drug; give antidote if one exists
Vitamin deficiency	Replacement of deficient vitamin
"Megaloblastic madness" due to B_{12} or folic acid deficiency	Vitamin B_{12} or folic acid
Pellagra	Niacin
Beriberi or Wernicke-Korsakoff syndrome	Thiamine hydrochloride
Normal-pressure hydrocephalus	Surgical shunting
Bacterial infections	Antibiotics after obtaining cultures
Endocrine disorders	
Hypothyroidism	Levothyroxine (T_4)
Hyperthyroidism	Depending on cause, may include surgery, methimazole propylthiouracil, iodine 131, or other treatments
Hypoglycemia	Glucose; treat underlying cause
Diabetic ketoacidosis	Insulin; fluid and electrolyte replacement
Addison's disease	Cortisol; fluid and electrolyte management, if needed; treat underlying cause
Cushing's disease	Treat underlying cause
Hypoparathyroidism	Calcium, vitamin D
Electrolyte imbalance	Treat underlying cause; replace deficient electrolytes or hydrate as needed
Epidural and subdural hematoma	Surgical evacuation
Brain tumor	Neurosurgical removal (if operable) or irradiation
Transient ischemic attacks due to carotid occlusion	Carotid endarterectomy or aspirin

cannot be applied to clinical practice at this time. There is no solid evidence that lecithin, choline, Metrazol, hyperbaric oxygen, vasopressin, or procaine is effective in reducing cognitive dysfunction or improving the general health of patients with primary degenerative dementia (814). The general ward management of the demented patient is the same as that of the delirious patient.

Chapter
23

Neuropsychiatric Emergencies

Psychiatric emergencies occur in all clinical settings. The common feature is a patient who is in acute distress or whose behavior could result in immediate increased morbidity, death, injury to others, or destruction of property. Immediate remedial action is always required. A frequent early sign of an impending emergency is increasing anxiety on the part of the clinician or hospital staff about a patient's condition. When the clinician recognizes these feelings, he should make an immediate evaluation of the patient.

The evaluation of a patient during an emergency has the same goal as any other psychiatric examination: accurate diagnosis so that specific treatment can be instituted. In an emergency, however, elaborate laboratory testing and extensive interviewing often are not possible, and the primary treatment goal is to reduce significantly the risks of further morbidity, injury, or death.

Emergencies often can be prevented by proper diagnosis, behavioral management, and treatment. Acutely ill psychiatric patients frequently demonstrate significant cognitive impairment; their hallucinations, delusional ideas, and language dysfunction suggest that they have deficits in information processing. They are often frightened by their psychopathologic experiences, and their anxiety can further exacerbate cognitive deficits. This results in a vicious circle. Because agitated, violent, and other disruptive behaviors can be precipitated or exacerbated by anxiety, procedures to reduce the patient's anxiety frequently can prevent or ameliorate the emergent behavior. Behavioral guidelines relating to interpersonal communication and administrative structures should be employed.

All *interpersonal communication* with the patient, including "Good morning" and "Nice day today," should be deliberate and specifically fitted to the individual patient. For example, many patients prefer direct statements (e.g., "You look more upset" "You seem down in the dumps") to the automatic phrases of social convention (e.g., "How are you?"). Also, communications should be simple and directed at reinforcing reality and appropriate behavior. Firmness, clarity in communications, and reality-oriented comments (e.g., "People get upset when you do that") are better than psychologic "probing" (e.g., "I wonder why you're doing that") and help to reduce the patient's anxiety.

Administrative structures relating to inpatient regulations, activities, and meetings should be organized and in place. The purposes of each should be explained and reviewed with the patient. Too much activity can "overload" patients and result in increasing agitation and disruptive behavior. Rest periods and calm, structured activities are beneficial.

General Management

Evaluation

Frequently, the patient's signs and symptoms immediately suggest a specific syndrome (e.g., mania, catatonia, acute anxiety attack) or situation (e.g., suicide attempt, delirious patient, violent patient). The two main goals of diagnosis in an emergency are (1) to recognize the clinical presentation and (2) to identify rapidly any life-threatening cause (e.g., pulmonary embolus, myocardial infarction) or readily treatable disorder (e.g., anticholinergic delirium, panic attack). More than 40% of psychiatric patients have systemic illnesses (412) that are undiagnosed by the referring physician yet are causally related to the behaviors for which the patients are referred. Another study found a high proportion of psychiatric outpatients to have concurrent systemic illness; in 18% of those patients, the systemic illness alone was the cause of the psychiatric disorder (547). Systemic examination and laboratory assessment should be done, if possible.

Intervention

Emergency treatment includes psychological and biologic interventions, follow-up planning, and family counseling.

The content of the psychological intervention changes according to the nature of the emergency, the environmental factors directly related to the crisis, and the life circumstances of the patient. The form of the psychological intervention should be consistent and characterized by reassurance, empathy, calmness, firmness, and reality-oriented comments. Many true emergencies (e.g., some drug intoxications) and other situations requiring immediate action (e.g., acute problems of living) can be ameliorated or resolved simply by talking to the patient in a comforting manner, allowing him to express his feelings, and giving him reasonable advice (242).

Biologic treatments for specific emergencies are described in the appropriate sections below. The principles related to administration of psychotropics (e.g., route of administration, dosage, drug combinations) also pertain in emergencies.

Disposition planning for patients following outpatient emergency treatment is also critical if the initial intervention is to be ultimately successful. Emergency treatment is generally limited to a few minutes or hours. If the effects of successful treatment are to be sustained and subsequent relapse prevented, follow-up planning should take into consideration the effectiveness of the original emergency treatment, the definitive or long-term treatment that is most appropriate to the patient, and the patient's social and employment circumstances (1063). Structured intervention following emergency care reduces the risk of chronicity and the rate of relapse, and it should be encouraged whenever possible (185, 242). Appropriate intervention could be hospitalization; referral to a health care clinic, community agency, or specialized self-help organization (e.g., Alcoholics Anonymous), or referral to individual practitioners, counselors, or clergy. With proper planning, approximately 60% of patients treated in an emergency room (ER) for a psychiatric disorder comply with follow-up treatments (479).

As in all health care situations, the involvement of the family is helpful if treatment and disposition are to be of maximum benefit. When supportive family members are available, they should be educated about the patient's condition, the treatments that have been or will be given, how they can monitor subsequent treatment and symptoms, and what disposition is most appropriate for the patient. A "kind word" and empathy for their anxiety should not be overlooked amid the turmoil of the ER.

Sedation

Sedation with barbiturates is a time-honored method for controlling agitation and violent behavior. Unfortunately, their use in emergencies is frequently ignored by clinicians because of the mistaken belief that these agents are intrinsically more dangerous than neuroleptics. In fact, barbiturates can be used in a precise manner; they have a rapid onset, specific limits in duration of action, and minimal and controllable side effects; and, when administered IV, they achieve greater sedation than neuroleptics but still permit proper diagnostic evaluation of the patient. When the emergency probably will lead to hospitalization or if it occurs during hospitalization, barbiturates are often the preferred initial treatment of choice for controlling behavior. Because of its rapid action and intermediate length of action, sodium amobarbital is the barbiturate of choice (281, 896). If the patient is well known to the clinician, more definitive initial treatment (e.g., IM neuroleptics for manic excitement) is appropriate.

When used in an emergency, sodium amobarbital should be administered IV.

This can be readily accomplished even with the most violent patient; when restrained, he usually has dilated superficial veins that are easily entered. A tourniquet is often not necessary. IV sodium amobarbital can be delivered fairly rapidly (100 mg/15 seconds). Its sedation onset is limited only by the patient's circulation time and prior exposure to central sedatives. Dosage can be titrated to the patient's sedation threshold without undue concern about respiratory depression, which occurs at much higher doses (500 mg diluted in 20 cc of sterile water or saline suffices for most patients). The actual dose delivered varies, however, as administration stops only when sedation is reached (as much as 1,500 mg by this method without adverse effects). Subsequent doses (usually 250 mg) can be administered IM every 4 to 6 hours, but more than 24 hours of such treatment is rarely necessary. The risk of withdrawal seizures after cessation of treatment increases sharply after more than 1 day of treatment. In the event that sedation is required beyond 48 hours, the sedative should be tapered over a period of 2 to 4 days and then discontinued.

Management of Specific Cases

Violence

Although violent people often have associated psychiatric disorder, the frequency of violence among the mentally ill has been exaggerated. Most psychiatric patients are never violent. Even in the seriously ill, who frequently exhibit socially disruptive behavior, violence is uncommon. Nevertheless, violent people are often evaluated or treated by mental health professionals (411, Section IV). In a survey of 115 psychiatrists on a university faculty, 42% reported having been assaulted by a patient (618). In another survey of mental health professionals, 24% of 101 therapists had been attacked by at least 1 patient during that prior year (1061), whereas 82% of California psychiatrists and psychologists (1076) reported seeing at least 1 dangerous patient yearly, with a mean of 14 dangerous patients seen annually. In another survey (958), 35% of respondents saw violent patients at least once monthly. Interestingly, the youngest and least experienced among them had the greatest exposure to violent patients. Thus, a significant proportion of neuropsychiatric clinicians are confronted by violent or potentially violent patients.

Prediction of Violence

The long-term prediction of violence is primarily based on studies (938, 990) of inmates in institutions for the criminally insane, who upon discharge were evaluated largely through arrest records in nonpenal settings or in the community. Among such individuals, 14 to 35% are eventually arrested for violent acts. Most individuals predicted to be violent are not, and about 15% who are predicted not to be violent commit violent acts.

The extent to which data from institutions for the criminally insane can be extrapolated to other clinical settings is unknown. A clinician testifying at a commitment hearing should not state with certainty that a person will injure someone else. Rather, he should state that compared with the general population, the patient is statistically more likely (or not more likely) to be violent and give the basis for this conclusion. It is difficult to predict whether a given person will be violent; one reason is that in studies of violent individuals, the independent contribution toward violence of individual factors (e.g., gender, ethnic group, age, and diagnosis) is rarely determined statistically by employing matched control groups. Further, some associations are clinically meaningful but do not imply causality. Thus, violent behavior is more common among the young than the old; however, being young does not make one violent.

PAST VIOLENT OR CRIMINAL BEHAVIOR

All studies of the prediction of violent behavior show that past violence and criminality predict future violence (406, 682). In a study of murdered children, 90% of the cases indicated that the victims, their siblings, or both had been physically abused or neglected before the killings (497). Among maladjusted Vietnam combat veterans under psychiatric evaluation, those most likely to act violently had committed violent acts (e.g., torturing prisoners, attacking officers with grenades, mutilating the dead) in Vietnam (1086). A study of parolees demonstrated that violence was three times more likely if a parolee had been previously arrested for a violent offense (1055). In a large cohort of boys, age 10 to 18, chronic offenders were responsible for 70% of all violent acts committed by the African Americans in the study and for 45% of all violent acts committed by the Euro-Americans (1079). In 1984, 61% of individuals arrested for aggravated assault were Euro-American and 38% were African American (297).

NEUROPSYCHIATRIC CONDITIONS ASSOCIATED WITH VIOLENT BEHAVIOR

An individual's lifetime risk of violence is significantly increased if he has one of several conditions. The condition most closely associated with crime, and violent crime in particular, is antisocial personality (406). More than one half of violent offenders are likely to have antisocial personality disorder. The childhood triad of enuresis, fire-setting, and cruelty to nimals (435, 615) has been associated with antisocial personality and homicidal behavior (1033).

During manic episodes, nearly one half of patients are assaultive or threatening (972). Over one third of patients with temporal lobe epilepsy have pathologic aggressiveness (262, 683). Not all researchers agree, however, that there is a higher frequency of violence among epileptics (465, 944). Violence during partial complex seizures in psychosensory epileptics is rare. It is far more likely to occur at other times.

Intoxication with alcohol or drugs is extremely common at the time of violent crime. One study (571) compared murderers with matched nonviolent criminals; the principal difference between the two groups was that the murderers were far more likely (54% versus 5%) to have been intoxicated with alcohol or drugs. In 15 other studies of murderers, about 50% had been drinking at the time of the homicide (370, 615). In the military, 87.5% of a group of "fraggers" (killers of another soldier, usually an officer, by throwing a live grenade into his sleeping area) were intoxicated with alcohol or drugs at the time of the "fragging." A study of rapists indicated that 50% were intoxicated at the time of rape (793). Interestingly, in another study, 30% of male and 20% of female *victims* of homicide had one or more drugs other than alcohol in their bodies at the time of death (960).

A 1944 study (629) showed that aggressiveness and EEG abnormalities could be induced by giving IV alcohol to people with histories of alcohol-related violence followed by amnesia. This finding, however, could not be replicated in a controlled double-blind study in a similar group of patients (68), thus casting serious doubt on the concept of *pathologic intoxication*, defined as a deliriumlike aggressive psychosis induced by ingesting small amounts of alcohol and followed by sleep and amnesia for the event (1029).

Although violence is more likely in patients with antisocial personality disorder than in the general population, violence can be precipitated by illness in patients with any diagnosis, regardless of whether the frequency of violence in patients with that diagnosis exceeds that of the general population. Violence has been reported in drug-induced psychosis, drug intoxications, dementias, brain tumors (particularly frontal), intracranial hematomas, and major depression. In England, about 25% of homicides are followed by suicide of the perpetrators (1056); this suggests an association in some cases between homicide and depression.

ABNORMAL ELECTROENCEPHALOGRAM

A significant relationship exists between EEG abnormality and antisocial personality, criminality, and violence. This association, which has been summarized by Stafford-Clark, appears in Table 23.1. Williams (1066) found that for habitually aggressive criminals, more than 50% had abnormal EEGs, most typically slowing in the theta frequency in the anterior temporal and lateral frontal regions of the brain. He reported, as did Gibbs et al. (358), that, with aging, these abnormalities often diminish in degree, perhaps paralleling the decline in criminality as individuals become middle-aged. A recent review of this subject (1034), although supporting a relationship between violence and abnormalities on EEG, points out the limitations of the literature on which the association is based.

TABLE 23.1

Relationship of Personality Disorder to the Incidence of Abnormal Electroencephalograms

Category	*Incidence of Abnormal EEGs (percent)*	*Authority*
Flying personnel	5	Williams (1941) (ref. 1066)
Royal Army Medical Corps personnel	10	Williams (1941)
Mixed controls	15	Hill, Watterson (1942) (ref. 447)
Controls in prison	25	Stafford-Clark, Pond, Doust, (1951) (ref. 935)
Mixed psychoneurotics	26	Williams (1941)
Inadequate psychopaths	32	Hill, Watterson (1942)
Aggressive psychopaths	65	Hill, Watterson (1942)
Motiveless murderers	73	Stafford-Clark, Taylor (1949)
Insane murderers	83	Stafford-Clark, Pond, Doust (1951)

SOURCE: D. Stafford-Clark, The foundations of research in psychiatry, *British Medical Journal* 2: 1199 (1959). Reproduced with permission of the British Medical Association.

OTHER CORRELATES OF VIOLENCE

1. Male gender: Although the frequency of violence by women is increasing, the ratio of male to female violence is about 9:1 (144). Violent behaviors are more likely to occur in women who are violent around the time of menstruation, 49% of all crimes committed by women occur during menstruation or during the four premenstrual days.
2. *Teenager or young adult:* The Rand study found that habitual offenders committed a mean of 3.2 serious crimes per month as "juveniles," 1.5 per month as young adults, and 0.6 per month after that (756). A 1975 study showed that males between ages 15 and 20, who made up 8.5% of the American population, accounted for 35% of arrests for violent crimes (1097). In a study of assaultive suicidal patients, those under 45 were more likely to assault other patients or the staff while in the hospital (959). Eighty percent of individuals who committed single-offender assault in 1983 were in their 20s or early 30s (144).
3. *History of separation, divorce, lack of family support, or parental cruelty:* Felons are more likely than the general population to be separated or divorced (406). There is also an increased rate of divorce among alcoholics

and individuals with antisocial personality. The degree of support provided by the family of a recently discharged psychiatric patient is related to his ability to function in the community and, thus, may effect his proneness to violence (293). Felons are also more likely to have been reared away from the home of their biologic parents (e.g., reared in orphanages or foster homes or by friends), to have divorced or separated parents, to have observed (or been victims of) parental violence (367, 406, 468), or to have had parents who were criminals.

Assessment of the Patient to Predict Violence

The assessment of the patient's risk for violence should include questioning about past violent acts (e.g., "What's the most violent thing you've ever done?"), as well as inquiries about the following 17 factors:

1. Current violent thoughts
2. Current violent intentions
3. Jealous or persecutory feelings or delusions
4. Symptoms of current drug or alcohol intoxication
5. Symptoms of mania or depression
6. Symptoms of epilepsy and other coarse brain disease
7. Thoughts of suicide
8. Command hallucinations
9. History of alcoholism or drug abuse
10. History of trait behaviors consistent with antisocial personality
11. History of enuresis, fire-setting
12. History of cruelty to animals
13. Hospitalizations for psychiatric illness
14. Ownership and availability of weapons
15. Parental or other family violence
16. Divorces and separations
17. Employment status

Additional history, when available, should be obtained from hospital records, family and friends, physicians, and other informants. During systemic and mental status examinations, particular attention should be given to signs of drug or alcohol intoxication; tattoos; needle-tracks; motorcycle-gang style of dress; agitation; pacing; muscle-clenching; menacing gait, threatening gestures; anger or irritability; and rapidity or pressure of speech; revengeful, jealous, or threatening thought content; delusions of persecution (particularly of being poisoned); alterations of consciousness; automatisms; or postictal delirious behavior. Among laboratory tests for a potentially violent patient, an EEG (with nasopharyngeal leads, if possible) can be helpful to rule out the presence of a seizure disorder.

Four behaviors are specifically associated with imminent risk for violence: (1) recent assaultiveness; (2) homicidal or assaultive threats or intent; (3) pacing, muscle-clenching, or menacing gestures; (4) agitation, rage, shouting, or irritability. The occurrence of one or more of these behaviors demands a rapid therapeutic response.

Factors predictive of the long-term risk of violence (also influencing the acute situation) are:

1. Past criminality (particularly violent crime) or violent behavior
2. Diagnosis of one of the following:
   A. Antisocial personality (sociopathy)
   B. Drug dependence
   C. Alcoholism
   D. Mania
   E. Behavioral syndrome associated with head trauma
   F. Epilepsy
   G. Developmental disorder (abused child)
   H. Somatization disorder (Briquet's syndrome)
3. Abnormal EEG

Factors that decrease the risk of violence are:

1. No past crime or violent behavior
2. No psychiatric illness or extremes of trait

Management of Violence

The best management of hospital violence is its prevention. Patients who perceive that the staff is making a sincere effort to provide excellent care are less likely to retaliate against them. Defensiveness and arguing should be avoided. Missed appointments and anticipated visits by other clinicians should be discussed with the patient in advance.

Half of all episodes of violence in the hospital occur in the ER. The ER staff does not know the patient, but if there is some reason to anticipate violence, designated ER staff members should be available at a moment's notice and prepared to initiate immediately all appropriate measures. While greeting the patient, the physician should be accompanied by a staff member. Based on the physician's impression of the patient's greeting behavior, he can make a decision to lighten the vigilance, have a staff member listen at the office door every 5 minutes or to attend the interview, or to medicate the patient immediately, as described below.

Some ER offices are equipped with "panic button" buzzer systems, which notify crisis team or hospital security personnel that a staff member in a certain room is in trouble. Almost all mentally ill patients thought to be imminently violent should be hospitalized. When a previously calm individual with antisocial personality (or one who is alcoholic) but has no treatable condition becomes angry at the ER physician for not admitting him or for not giving him medication (popular requests are for narcotics, benzodiazepines, and mood-elevating substances), discharge home from the ER is usually still in order despite the anger. The hospital's security personnel should be called to escort the patient off the premises. In some instances, the police may have to be notified.

Many treatable violent patients are aware and afraid of their potential for violence and are glad, or at least willing, to admit themselves to the hospital. Frequently, however, the patient will need to be admitted involuntarily by certificate. In such cases, the patient should not be told that this is definitely going to happen until the staff is prepared to restrain him. If the patient must be told something concerning admission and the physician does not think the patient will become immediately violent or try to escape, the patient could be told, "I think you should be in the hospital and I'm going to try to arrange it." This statement is honest but not confrontational. If the physician has reason to suspect that the patient might become immediately violent and must tell him something concerning admission, he might have to lie by saying that he is not sure what will happen or even say that the patient will not be admitted.

When violence is not felt to be imminent, the decision to admit should depend on the treatability of the patient's condition and his willingness to be admitted. Despite an increased lifetime risk of violence, an individual with antisocial personality but with no immediate homicide risk or superimposed treatable condition (e.g., drug-induced psychoses, mood disorder) should be discharged. The neuropsychiatrist should explain to the patient that he does not feel capable of changing the patient's life-style and basic trait behavior and that the patient is responsible for his own actions. When an individual with antisocial personality is admitted to psychiatric units, he often disrupts unit routine: "The manipulator and impulse disorder patient soon gives up helpful participation in the therapeutic community and develops instead a rapacious subculture, preying on the relative helplessness of other patients or the psychiatric staff's tendency to 'treat' patients rather than 'punish' them" (605).

When admitting a violent patient to a psychiatric service, the physician should discuss the potential for violence with the staff. If the physician believes the violence to be imminent after observing that the prospect of admission apparently does not calm the patient and an immediate definitive treatment (e.g., a barbiturate for sedative-hypnotic withdrawal, an anticonvulsant for epilepsy, physostigmine for anticholinergic delirium) has not been identified, the patient should immediately receive either sodium amobarbital for sedation, or IM haloperidol (20 mg; dosage can be higher based on the patient's weight and general health). The dosage should be repeated at least once within 12 hours, with a minimum of four such doses given in the first 48 hours. Once urgent matters are dealt with, the primary objective is the treatment of the condition for which the patient was admitted.

As mentioned in Chapter 20, lithium in standard therapeutic doses may be of benefit to individuals with a history of irritability and aggressive outbursts unassociated with other features of mania or melancholia. Yudofsky et al. (1092) also reported successful treatment by using propanolol for rage and violent behavior in patients with diffuse coarse brain disease. Such treatment should be considered when other means are ineffectual in patients with diffuse coarse brain disease and associated violent behavior; however, experience with this potentially prophylactic treatment for violent behavior is limited.

If violence cannot be prevented, it must be controlled. Just as every hospital has a cardiac arrest team, every hosptial with a psychiatric service should have a crisis team composed of six or seven individuals, including a physician and nursing and security personnel. The team should be prepared to respond rapidly and must be specifically trained to interact with and physically restrain violent patients. Frequently, the presence of the team—a show of force—(particularly if uniformed security personnel are included) is sufficient to control an impending emergency, and it is always better to overuse than underuse the crisis team.

An ER patient who has a firearm or other lethal weapon should be isolated by immediately removing all other patients and personnel and, if possible, locking the patient into the evacuated area. The police should be called. A systematic search for weapons and dangerous objects should be part of the ER admission procedure.

A more common experience is that of an agitated or excited patient who is shouting, frightening other patients and staff, damaging hospital property, or attacking other patients or staff members. In this situation, the crisis team should be called, and patients in the area and staff not directly involved in the emergency should be quickly removed. Unless a crisis team is present and prepared to restrain the patient, all remaining staff should stay at least 10 to 15 feet away from the patient (close enough to talk but far enough away to avoid getting hurt or provoking an attack).

The physician in charge or a designated staff member should engage the patient in conversation. The topic is not as important as maintaining a continuous interaction, which can often reduce anxiety on both sides. The staff spokesperson (often a woman staff member appears least threatening) should address the patient in as calm a manner as possible under the circumstances. She should speak slowly, clearly, and quietly and should not use psychiatric jargon. The spokesperson must not patronize the patient or try to placate him by agreeing to unreasonable demands or requests, which obviously violate hospital rules. Being firm, without being argumentative, is the best approach. On rare occasions, honesty is not the best policy, and falsifications may be needed to preserve life and limb. When the patient is to be placed in a seclusion room or receive an injection and asks about such a decision, he should be told matter-of-factly what will happen and why. If he has an option that depends on his controlling himself, he should be told that, too. Verbal threats by the spokesperson are unhelpful and unprofessional, although a firm, loud, authoritarian command sometimes can be effective.

There should be little or no unnecessary movement during the interaction with the patient. Whatever movement does take place should be done slowly and deliberately. The spokesperson should tell the patient precisely what is going to be done.

Most threatening or potentially violent patients are agitated and move about the room or patient area. The threat of assault is significantly reduced if the patient can be persuaded to sit down. The spokesperson also should sit down, if possible. Occasionally, the best efforts fail. The patient may begin to approach the spokesperson (or other staff) in a threatening manner. A firm command to "stop," while raising her hand like a traffic policeman, becomes the last resort of the spokesperson before retreating to safety or helping to restrain the patient as part of the crisis team.

When the crisis team arrives, the spokesperson should, if possible, continue in her role. In most cases, the above approach, followed by constant reassurance and a show of force, is sufficient to gain control of the situation. Most patients then allow the spokesperson (accompanied by the crisis team) to lead him away to his bed or a seclusion room, where medication can be administered.

If the patient does not respond to the above approach and becomes increasingly agitated and threatening or actually attacks a team member (a rare occurrence), the team must be prepared to subdue, restrain, and seclude the patient.

The team should have a small soft, cotton mattress (available at each nursing station), with two handles sewn to each side. It can be manned by two team members at each side and used to shield the team and force the patient into a corner. This should be done as rapidly as possible. When he is pinned against a wall by the mattress, the patient can be forced to the floor with a team member restraining each limb and one member restraining his head to prevent biting. A team leader should be present to "direct traffic," and, ideally, a seventh member should be available to administer previously prepared medication. After being subdued, the patient should be restrained in padded leather restraints, medication should be administered, and the team should place him on a stretcher and take him to the seclusion room. He then should be placed face down on a mattress. The restraining procedure should not be interrupted or terminated until the patient is fully restrained. Abortive attempts usually lead to injury. Debates, negotiations, arguments, self-assessment, and the like have no place once the restraining process begins.

The patient should remain in restraints in the seclusion room until he is calm, so that he cannot injure himself. A staff member should observe the patient at least every 15 minutes during the restraint period. Once sedated or calm, the patient can be removed from restraints and kept in seclusion until the physician concludes that the patient is no longer a danger to himself or to others. The physician should evaluate the patient frequently during the first few hours of seclusion and then every 4 to 6 hours thereafter. Many patients are able to leave seclusion after an hour or two. It is extremely rare for a patient to require more than 24 hours of seclusion.

After the patient's condition has been stabilized or improved, the subject of passes and discharge arises. Discharge should be based on the patient's achieving maximum therapeutic benefit and no longer being imminently dangerous. The clinician should take measures (e.g., ask a friend or relative to dispose of any weapons, arrange for outpatient follow-up, give the patient appropriate medication, provide for treatment in the event of an emergency, give disulfiram if the patient is alcoholic) to decrease the probability of violence. All such efforts should be discussed with the patient (and usually with his family) and noted in the chart. The chart must also include a statement concerning the patient's short-term and long-term risks for violence, the measures to be taken to reduce these risks, and the extent to which they can be realistically reduced. Passes should be given almost exclusively under the same circumstances, as a means of testing the patient's capacity to function outside the hospital prior to discharge. If the patient wishes to leave prior to this time, he must be competent to sign out against medical advice, and he must be thought not to be a short-term suicide or homicide risk; If he is discharged, his relatives should be informed about the long-term risks of violence and the impossibility of holding the patient against his wishes based upon a long-term prediction.

Drug-Induced Deliria

Patients with anticholinergic drug–induced deliria are occasionally encountered in the ER or on acute medical services and may be admitted to psychiatric units if they are mistakenly diagnosed as suffering from acute psychosis. Drugs that contain sufficient belladonna alkaloids (scopolamine, atropine) or anticholinergic properties (e.g. cyclic antidepressants, antispasmodics, antihistamines, antiparkinsonians) can produce the syndrome. In addition to prescription medications, there are numerous over-the-counter preparations with clinically significant anticholinergic properties. These include cold remedies (Allerest, Coricidin, Romilar, Sine-Off, Contac, Sinutab, Dristan), analgesics (Excedrin P.M., Cope), and hypnotics and tranquilizers (Compoz, Devarex, Dormarex, Nytol, Sleep-Eze, Sominex).

Patients with anticholinergic deliria present with parasympathetic blockade. They have dry, hot, flushed skin; widely dilated pupils; dry mucous membranes; decreased bowel and bladder motility; mild hyperthermia; tachycardia; palpitations; and arrhythmias. They are severely agitated; they have a clouded sensorium, diffuse cognitive impairment, rambling speech, and perceptual disturbances (illusions and hallucinations), and may be delusional. When cyclic compounds are the offending agents, cardiac arrhythmias are common and heart block may occur. A descriptive summary of these patients is "mad as a hatter, red as a beet, dry as a bone, and blind as a bat."

A patient with amphetamine psychosis also may present with severe agitation and sympathetic signs. Unlike anticholinergic deliria, however, the sensorium in this state is clear. Continuous scanning of the environment is also common, and movements are rapid, jerky, and perseverative.

Phenothiazines and other psychotropics with anticholinergic properties are obviously contraindicated for anticholinergic delirium, as they exacerbate and prolong the syndrome. Emergency treatment may require restraints and sedation with IV anxiolytics (chlordiazapoxide, 25 mg, or diazepam, 10 mg IV). Primary treatment is physostigmine, which readily crosses the blood-brain barrier and counters peripheral and central cholinergic blockade. Related molecules, such as neostigmine, do not enter the CNS. A standard regimen is an initial 1–2-mg dose administered IV or subcutaneously, repeated in 30 minutes and again at 30 to 60 minute intervals for a total dose of 6–8 mg (434).

Drug-Induced Psychoses

Lysergic acid diethylamide (LSD), mescaline, psilocybin, dimethyltryptamine (DMT), 2,5-dimethoxy-4-methylamphetamine (STP), phencyclidine (PCP), mace and nutmeg (myristica), morning glory seeds, cannabis, amphetamine, and cocaine can each induce psychosis. Although specific psychotropic regimens have been recommended for the psychosis associated with each compound, response to a given dose of each of these agents is extremely variable and emergency intervention must be individualized. Many patients, for example, do not require pharmacologic treatment. For these individuals, a quiet rest area and a reassuring person who reinforces accurate perceptions suffice. Other patients may require additional oral anxiolytics, whereas some patients (particularly those who have ingested PCP) may require hospitalization, restraints, sedation and benzodiazepines, IM neuroleptics, and acidification of the urine (100, 899).

Definitive treatment is rarely possible in an emergency, because a comprehensive diagnostic evaluation usually is not feasible. A psychotic patient with a history of past drug use frequently tempts the practitioner to administer a neuroleptic when nonspecific sedation would control the emergency and permit subsequent diagnosis. When the clinician knows the specific agent that induced the psychosis and pharmacotherapy is required, however, the following treatment suggestions may prove helpful:

1. Maniform drug-induced psychoses can respond to lithium or neuroleptics administered in standard doses. PCP and mescaline are often associated with this type of affective syndrome (903, 919).
2. Amphetamine and STP psychoses are particularly responsive to haloperidol in oral or IM daily doses (20–60 mg). Lithium also may benefit these patients (230, 332).
3. PCP psychoses, particularly nonmaniform states, may respond to acidification of urine with ammonium chloride (4–8 g daily) to facilitate excretion of the compound. An initial dose of ammonium chloride (1–2%), along with flurosemide (40 mg IV) can increase excretion significantly. Beta-adrenergic blockade with propranolol (40 mg daily) can ameliorate the severe sympathetic symptoms, and a neuroleptic in relatively low doses (e.g., haloperidol 20 mg daily) can ameliorate the psychotic features. Oral diazapam (5–10 mg t.i.d. or b.i.d.) also has been recommended. The efficacy of this polypharmacy is not established (101, 871). PCP has a long half-life; once the acute episode is ameliorated, the patient should be closely watched for several days and followed as an outpatient to minimize relapse.

Frequently, patients with drug-induced psychoses do not adequately respond to pharmacotherapy. Symptoms may persist; agitation and assaultiveness may become unmanageable. Neuroleptic-induced cognitive deficits and anticholinergic side effects, including delirium, may complicate the situation. ECT is particularly effective for these drug-induced states. When a patient does not dramatically and rapidly respond to pharmacotherapy, ECT becomes the treatment of choice.

Other Deliria

Delirium is characterized by an acutely developing, diffuse cognitive impairment and an alteration in consciousness. Common associated phenomena are distractibility, fatigue, inability to perform simple tasks, anxiety, agitation, perceptual disturbances (hallucinations and illusions), and delusional ideas. Severe agitation, anxiety, and resulting uncooperativeness can disrupt medical care and endanger the patient and staff. Head trauma, toxic and metabolic disorders, drug- and alcohol-related states, and infectious disease are the most common causes of these severe deliria requiring emergency psychiatric intervention (602, 1025).

When confronted with a delirious patient in the ER, the review of systems, systemic examination, and laboratory screening are the likely means for determining etiology. With hospitalized patients, laboratory slips and medication sheets often provide the decisive clues (also see Chapter 12).

As in any psychiatric emergency, the primary goal is to prevent the patient from injuring himself or others. Restraints may be required, but delirious patients "fight" their restraints. Because these patients are already in a precarious physiologic state, restraining them is no substitute for ameliorating agitation. This can usually be accomplished by supportive, reality-focused conversation or sedation with anxiolytics or barbiturates. However, the latter group is specifically contraindicated when head trauma, porphyria, or severe renal or pulmonary disease is suspected (1025).

Occasionally, standard behavioral and pharmacologic interventions fail to relieve agitation, assaultiveness, or self-destructive behavior in a patient for whom the treatment of the underlying process (e.g., infection) has not begun to take effect. This is a life-threatening situation, in which death can result from cardiovascular collapse (from initial fluid and electrolyte imbalance, compounded by struggling against restraints), the thwarting of primary treatment (e.g., pulling out IVs, ripping off surgical dressings), or self-injury (e.g., jumping out the window to escape "the voices"). ECT is the intervention of choice in this situation and has been found particularly useful and safe in ameliorating the symptoms of delirium. One or two treatments, using bilateral electrode placement, can resolve the agitation and permit treatment of the underlying causal process (967).

The following case vignette illustrates the effectiveness of ECT in delirium:

> A 56-year-old alcoholic man became agitated and disoriented following abdominal surgery for pancreatitis. The patient began picking at his abdominal dressing and continually pulled out his IV needles and Foley catheter. Administration of IM chlordiazepoxide (25 mg IM, t.i.d. and then q.i.d.) had little effect. Restraints were applied, but the patient broke out of them, ripped open his abdominal wound, and partially eviscerated himself. Following closure under general anesthesia, he again became agitated and confused. An encephalopathy secondary to pancreatitis was diagnosed. Injections of chlorpromazine (25 mg IM, b.i.d. and then t.i.d.) had little effect. He again eviscerated himself, this time partially breaking a surgical anastomosis between his pancreas and jejunum. Although the wound was again closed under general anesthesia, the patient again picked at his wound (now held together by metal retention sutures). Leaking pancreatic and abdominal juices began to digest his abdominal wall; silver nitrate ointment was applied to the skin about the wound to prevent this. Chlordiazepoxide was added to the chlorpromazine without amelioration of his agitation and confusion.
>
> A psychiatric consultation was requested, and the consultant recommended ECT. All psychotropic medication was discontinued. Two bilateral ECT treatments were administered on successive days. Sufficient succinylcholine was used to prevent any motor activity during the seizures, which might have disrupted the abdominal wound.
>
> The patient's agitation resolved, although he remained mildly confused.

Further psychotropic treatment was not required. He remained in restraints for the new few days but did not struggle. Third and fourth ECTs were administered at 48-hour intervals, following which the patient made a slow but unremarkable surgical recovery.

Acute Psychoses

Brief Reactive Psychosis

The brief reactive psychosis syndrome was first methodically described by Karl Jaspers (476). Although its proper place in psychiatric nosology is unclear (see Chapter 11), reactive psychosis is characterized by an acute onset episode of hallucinosis, usually with delusional ideas, following a precipitating event. Affectivity is usually intense, and thought content relates to the precipitant. The disorder rapidly resolves when the patient is removed from the stressful situation; an underlying, unspecified vulnerability is hypothesized. As agitation can be severe, emergency treatment usually involves restraints and sedation. A brief hospitalization is usually required, and IV sodium amobarbital is the treatment of choice. Sedation for 48 to 72 hours, without the use of neuroleptics, often results in resolution of the psychosis. The following case vignette illustrates the syndrome:

> A 41-year-old single woman was brought to the ER by friends. Agitated and fearful, she had been up all night. She called her friends at 3 A.M. for help and constantly asked them for reassurance that she was a good person, not a "tramp." Earlier, she had spent a rare evening out with a man. When he escorted her into her apartment, he attempted to kiss her. She rejected his advances. He then became angry, said she had just teased him, called her a whore, and left. She became progressively upset and finally called her friends.
>
> In the ER, she was extremely agitated, tearful, and whining. She pleaded for reassurance, repeatedly asking: "Am I a whore?" At other times, she shouted that she was a bad person and that voices were calling her bad names. She began to run about the ER and knock over furniture and equipment. She was restrained, sedated with IV sodium amobarbital, and hospitalized. She received three IM doses of sodium amobarbital during the next 24 hours, after which she became fully alert and asymptomatic.

Excitement States

Patients suffering from acute psychotic excitement can be extremely dangerous to themselves and others. Restraints or a show of force with a crisis team and initial sedation with sodium amobarbital are often required. IM neuroleptics are indicated for patients who are well known to the clinician or whose diagnostic evaluation is complete. Specific pharmacotherapeutic details are discussed elsewhere in the text. Occasionally, an excited patient does not respond to even the highest doses of neuroleptic, even when administered IV. These patients, usually manics, race up and down hospital hallways and shout continuously at the staff, other patients, and imagined voices. Despite aggressive neuroleptic treatment, they continue to be hyperactive, although stiff, ataxic, and slurred in speech. Cardiovascular collapse, hyperpyrexia, and sudden death have been reported in such patients. Prior to somatic treatment, this severe form of excitement resulted in death in 20% of acutely ill hospitalized manics (259). Two bilateral ECTs administered daily for 2 or 3 consecutive days can be lifesaving for these patients and should be prescribed if neuroleptics cannot control the excitement within 3 to 5 days (967).

Lethal Catatonia and Neuroleptic Malignant Syndrome

The combination of fever and catatonia can reflect a life-threatening morbid process. The clinician must take rapid action to diagnose and treat patients with these features. After systemic illness or clear-cut CNS infection have been ruled out as direct causes, the two prime diagnostic candidates are lethal catatonia and neuroleptic malignant syndrome (NMS).

Lethal Catatonia

In 1934, Stauder coined the term lethal catatonia to characterize an acute, intense excitement state, combining features of mania and delirium, that was associated with fever (often high) and catatonic signs. Patients were previously in good health. Without treatment, more than one half of these patients died (969). Since the early 1940s, ECT has been recognized as lifesaving for this condition, and more recent work (626, 627, 728, 783) supports ECT as the treatment of choice. Although neuroleptics and sedatives can partially ameliorate the condition, they rarely resolve it, and deaths still occur (about 20% of patients). With one or two bilateral ECTs the condition is virtually resolved; no deaths have been reported in patients with lethal catatonia once ECT was initiated.

Neuroleptic Malignant Syndrome

NMS is clinically similar to lethal catatonia, (1, 130, 161), particularly as bipolar patients appear to be at a higher risk for the syndrome than are other psychotics (330, 508). After reviewing many cases, Mann et al. (626) concluded that NMS could be distinguished from lethal catatonia. In NMS, posturing is typically mundane in character and parkinsonianlike (slightly flexed at the waist and elbows).

Other drug-induced extrapyramidal features are present and often severe; late-onset hyperthermia follows the catatonia. In lethal catatonia, hyperthermia is present at the outset, other extrapyramidal features are absent if the clinician did not prematurely administer a neuroleptic, and postures often are odd and associated with echophenomena. Considered an idiosyncratic failure of compensatory responses to neuroleptic dopaminergic blockage, NMS can be fatal (10% of untreated patients). It is usually treated by discontinuing the neuroleptic and administering a dopamine agonist (bromocriptine, 25–30 mg/day) and a skeletal muscle relaxant (dantrolene or lorazepam [1.5–2 mg IV, b.i.d. or t.i.d.]). Amantadine (200–300 mg/day orally) also has been used successfully. Based on the recognition that ECT is also a dopamine agonistic treatment, it has been recently prescribed for NMS with almost 90% of patients having an immediate (one treatment) and dramatic improvement. Several investigators have concluded that ECT may be the most effective and rapid-acting treatment for this syndrome (166, 627, 746). Once NMS is resolved, neuroleptics can be reintroduced without recurrence of the syndrome (589).

If ECT is used and is effective for patients with either lethal catatonia or NMS, the clinician has the option of continuing and prescribing a full course of ECT for the treatment of the underlying psychosis.

Stupor

Stupor is a state of extreme psychomotor inhibition in which the patient hardly moves or speaks. Complete immobility and mutism can occur and are often associated with generalized analgesia. Stupor is usually a manifestation of affective disorder, particularly melancholia (6, 107, 975).

Stuporous patients are unable to eat or drink and, if untreated, can develop severe dehydration, hemoconcentration, hyperpyrexia, ketosis, and eventually cardiovascular collapse and death. These patients can be temporarily disinhibited by sodium amobarbital (250 mg IM) or an intermediate- or long-acting benzodiazepine. When prescribed 30 to 45 minutes prior to meals, the medication enables the stuporous patient to eat and drink sufficiently and to cooperate during an evaluation period; however, IV fluid and electrolyte replacement is often required. Psychotropics rarely improve the stuporous condition. A course of ECT serves as both the emergency and definitive treatment of choice (967).

Epilepsy

Aberrant behavior and psychopathology associated with seizure disorders that most often lead to neuropsychiatric intervention occur during preictal, postictal, and interictal periods, rather than during the seizure itself. Psychiatric emergencies associated with seizure disorders usually result when the patient becomes violent (95, 303, 992). As the patient is in an altered state of consciousness, psychological intervention is inappropriate; rapid restraint and sedation with diazepam (10–15 mg IV) or sodium amobarbital constitute the best treatment (998). Definitive anticonvulsant treatment then can be instituted. Repeated violent ictal-related episodes or irritable behavior and clouding of consciousness during a prodromal or preictal period are best treated by inducing a seizure. Indeed, the observation that spontaneous seizures often resulted in remission of psychosis led, in part, to the development of convulsive treatment. One or two bilateral treatments usually suffice (63).

Nonemergency Situations That Require Rapid Action

Panic Attack

Frequently, a patient suffering from an acute behavioral syndrome associated with severe anxiety is brought to the ER. Should a review of systems, a systemic examination (particularly to rule out pneumonia, hypertension, myocardial infarction, stroke, and thyroid and parathyroid diseases), and laboratory assessment (ECG, chest x-ray, blood glucose, urinalysis) rule out cardiovascular, metabolic, and coarse neurologic causes of this syndrome, sedation is the primary treatment of choice. These patients often respond rapidly to IV or oral long-acting anxiolytics, such as chlordiazepoxide or diazepam (doses of 25 mg or 10 mg, respectively) and can return home the same day. These compounds are not absorbed well if given intramuscularly. In most cases, patients become drowsy and even sleep for 15 to 20 minutes. On awakening, they are fatigued but no longer severely anxious. Occasionally, a second dose is required. Following additional reassurance and education about the syndrome, most patients can be sent home with sufficient medication for four to six additional doses and a referral to the appropriate clinic, practitioner, or community agency.

Some patients hyperventilate when acutely anxious. The resulting respiratory alkalosis from reduction of serum carbon dioxide and increased extracellular calcium binding secondary to pH changes can result in severe perioral and hand and foot paresthesias, dizziness, muscular cramping, and syncope. This syndrome may be alleviated if the patient rebreathes his carbon dioxide by breathing into a paper bag for a minute or so. When the hyperventilation syndrome has been resolved, additional anxiety symptoms can be controlled by chlordiazepoxide or diazepam in oral doses (25 mg or 10 mg, respectively).

Occasionally, a patient is brought to the ER with the label "hysterical reaction." The patient is most often a woman, and the symptoms are consistent with a panic attack, in which agitation is marked and the patient is tearful and noisy. This syndrome is a severe panic attack with agitation, tearfulness, and screaming. Treatment is identical to that described above.

Acute Alcohol Intoxication

Acute alcohol intoxication is easy to recognize. The triad of ataxia, slurred speech, and alcoholic breath are usually sufficient for a diagnosis. Nystagmus, a flushed face, red eyes, reduced concentration, poor recent memory, and rambling speech also occur. Other intoxications, diabetic acidosis or hypoglycemia, alcohol-disulfiram reactions, and stroke may masquerade as acute alcohol intoxication. A review of systems, systemic examination, and laboratory assessment (including blood alcohol and glucose levels) should resolve diagnostic uncertainty (374).

A period of excitement, during which the patient may destroy property and become assaultive, can occur from depression of cortical inhibitory centers. Initial emergency treatment may require restraints and then the administration of small amounts of IV anxiolytics (chlordiazepoxide, 10–25 mg, or diazepam, 5–10 mg). The risk of vomiting precludes the use of oral medication. This treatment usually ameliorates the excitement phase of the intoxication and does not significantly depress respiratory function. A "holding" area should be available for patients to be monitored until they can leave the hospital.

References

1. Abbott RJ, Loizou LA. Neuroleptic malignant syndrome. *Br J Psychiatry*. 1986;148:47–51.
2. Abrams R. Capgras' syndrome. *Br J Psychiatry*. 1977;131:550–551.
3. Abrams R. Clinical prediction of ECT response in depressed patients. *Psychopharmacol Bull*. 1982;2:48–50.
4. Abrams R. Genetic studies of the schizoaffective syndrome: A selective review. *Schizophr Bull*. 1984;10:26–29.
5. Abrams R. *Electroconvulsive Therapy*, 2nd ed. Oxford: Oxford University Press; 1992.
6. Abrams R, Taylor MA. Catatonia: A prospective clinical study. *Arch Gen Psychiatry*. 1976;33:579–581.
7. Abrams R, Taylor MA. A rating scale for emotional blunting. *Am J Psychiatry*. 1978;135:225–229.
8. Abrams R, Taylor MA. Differential EEG patterns in affective disorder and schizophrenia. *Arch Gen Psychiatry*. 1979;36:1355–1358.
9. Abrams R, Taylor MA. Unipolar mania revisited. *J Affective Disord*. 1979;1:59–68.
10. Abrams R, Taylor MA. Psychopathology and electroencephalogram. *Biol Psychiatry*. 1980; 15:871–878.
11. Abrams R, Taylor MA. The importance of schizophrenic symptoms in the diagnosis of mania. *Am J Psychiatry*. 1981;138:658–661.
12. Abrams R, Taylor MA. The genetics of schizophrenia: A reassessment using modern diagnostic criteria. *Am J Psychiatry*. 1983;140:171–175.
13. Abrams R, Taylor MA. The importance of mood-incongruent psychotic symptoms in melancholia. *J Affective Disord*. 1983;5:179–181.
14. Abrams R, Taylor MA, Stolurow KAC. Catatonia and mania: Patterns of cerebral dysfunction. *Biol Psychiatry*. 1979;14:111–117.
15. Abrams, R, Volavka J. Electroencephalographic effects of ECT. In: Abrams R, Essman WB, eds. *Electroconvulsive Therapy: Biological Foundations and Clinical Applications*. New York: Spectrum; 1982:157–167.
16. Abrams R, Volavka J, Dornbush R, et al. Lateralized EEG changes after unilateral and bilateral electroconvulsive therapy. *Dis Nerv Syst*. 1970;(GWAN suppl 31):28–33.

17. Adams F. Emergency intravenous sedation of the delirious, medically ill patient. *J Clin Psychiatry*. 1988;49(suppl 12):22–26.

18. Adams RD, Victor M. Delirium and other confusional states. In: Wintrobe MM, Thorn GW, Adams RD, et al, eds. *Harrison's Principles of Internal Medicine,* 8th ed. New York: McGraw-Hill, 1977:145–150.

19. Agnew DC, Merskey H. Words of chronic pain. *Pain*. 1976;2:73–81.

20. Ahern GL, Schwartz GE. Differential lateralization for positive versus negative emotion. *Neuropsychologia* 1979;17:693–698.

21. Akiskal HS. Subaffective disorders: Dysthymic, cyclothymic, and bipolar II disorders in the borderline realm. *Psychiatr Clin North Am*. 1981;4:25–46.

22. Akiskal HS. The interface of chronic depression with personality and anxiety disorders. *Psychopharmacol Bull*. 1984;20:393–398.

23. Akiskal HS, Bitar AH, Puzantian VR, et al. The nosological status of neurotic depression: A prospective three to four year follow-up examination in light of the primary-secondary and unipolar-bipolar dichotomies. *Arch Gen Psychiatry*. 1978;35:756–766.

24. Akiskal HS, Cassano GB, Musetti L, et al. Psychopathology, temperament, and past course in primary major depression. 1. Review of evidence for a bipolar spectrum. *Psychopathology*. 1989;22:268–277.

25. Akiskal HS, Chen SE, Davis GC, et al. Borderline: An adjective in search of a noun. *J Clin Psychiatry*. 1985;46:41–48.

26. Akiskal HS, Djenderedjian AH, Rosenthal RH, et al. Cyclothymic disorder: Validating criteria for inclusion in the bipolar affective group. *Am J Psychiatry*. 1977;134:1227–1233.

27. Akiskal HS, Mallya G. Criteria for the "soft" bipolar spectrum: Treatment implications. *Psychopharmacol Bull*. 1987;23:68–73.

28. Akiskal HS, Yerevanian BI, Davis GC, et al. The nosologic status of borderline personality: Clinical and polysomnographic study. *Am J Psychiatry*. 1985;142:192–198.

29. Albert ML. A simple test of visual neglect. *Neurology* 1973;23:658–664.

30. Albert MS. Neuropsychological testing. In: Sadavoy J, Lazarus LW, Jarvik LF, eds. *Comprehensive Review of Geriatric Psychiatry,* Washington, DC: American Psychiatric Press; 1991;223–244.

31. Alessi CA, Cassel CK. Medical evaluation and common medical problems. In: Sadavoy J, Lazarus LW, Jarvik LF, (eds). *Comprehensive Review of Geriatric Psychiatry,* Washington, DC: American Psychiatric Press; 1991; 171–195.

32. Alexander F. *Psychosomatic Medicine*. New York: Norton; 1950.

33. Alexander MP. Traumatic brain injury. In: Benson DF, Blumer D, eds. *Psychiatric Aspects of Neurologic Disease,* vol 2, New York: Grune & Stratton; 1982:219–248.

34. Alexander MP, Stuss DT, Benson DF. Capgras' syndrome: A reduplicative phenomenon. *Neurology*. 1979;29:334–339.

35. Alexopoulos GS, Young RC, Abrams RC. ECT in the high-risk geriatric patient. *Convul Ther*. 1989;5:75–87.

36. Allison JB, Wilson WP. Sexual behavior of manic patients. *South Med J*. 1960;53:870–874.

37. Almy GL, Taylor MA. Lithium retention in mania. *Arch Gen Psychiatry.* 1973;29:232–234.
38. Alnaes R, Torgersen S. DSM-III personality disorders among patients with major depression, anxiety disorders, and mixed conditions. *J Nerv Ment Dis.* 1990;178:693–698.
39. Altamura C, Guercetti G, Percudoni M. Dexamethasone suppression test in positive and negative schizophrenia. *Psychiatry Res.* 1989;30:69–75.
40. Altshuler KE, Weiner MF. Anorexia nervosa and depression: A dissenting view. *Am J Psychiatry.* 1985;253:328–332.
41. Ancoli-Israel S. Epidemiology of sleep disorders. *Clin Geriatr Med.* 1989;5:347–362.
42. Andreasen NC. Realiability and validity of proverb interpretation to assess mental status. *Compr Psychiatry.* 1977;18:465–472.
43. Andreasen NC. Thought, language and communication disorders: 1. Clinical assessment, definition of terms and evaluation of their reliability. *Arch Gen Psychiatry.* 1979;36:1315–1321.
44. Andreasen NC. Thought, language and communication disorders: 2. Diagnostic significance. *Arch Gen Psychiatry.* 1979;36:1325–1330.
45. Andreasen NC. Affective flattening and the criteria for schizophrenia. *Am J Psychiatry.* 1979;136:944–947.
46. Andreasen NC. *The Scale for the Assessment of Negative Symptoms (SANS).* Iowa City: The University of Iowa; 1983.
47. Andreasen NC. *The Scale for the Assessment of Positive Symptoms (SAPS).* Iowa City: The University of Iowa; 1984.
48. Andreasen NC. Brain imaging: Applications in psychiatry. *Science.* 1988;239: 1381–1388.
49. Andreasen NC. Evaluation of brain imaging techniques in mental illness. *Annu Rev Med.* 1988;39:335–345.
50. Andreasen NC, Ehrhardt JC, Swayze VW II, et al. Magnetic resonance imaging of the brain in schizophrenia: The pathophysiological significance of structural abnormalities. *Arch Gen Psychiatry.* 1990;47:35–44.
51. Andreasen NC, Flaum M, Swayze VW II, et al. Positive and negative symptoms in schizophrenia: A critical reappraisal. *Arch Gen Psychiatry.* 1990;47:615–621.
52. Andreasen NC, Rice J, Endicott J, et al. Familial risks of affective disorder. A report from the National Institute of Mental Health Collaborative Study. *Arch Gen Psychiatry.* 1987;44:461–469.
53. Andreasen NC, Wasek P. Adjustment disorders in adolescents and adults. *Arch Gen Psychiatry.* 1980;37:1166–1170.
54. Andreasson S, Engstrom A, Allebeck P, et al. Cannabis and schizophrenia: A longitudinal study of Swedish conscripts. Lancet. 1987;2:1483–1486.
55. Andrews G, Crino R. Behavioral psychotherapy of anxiety disorders. In: Roth M, ed. *Treatment and Outcome of Phobic and Related Disorders, Psychiatric Annals,* 1991;21:358–367.
56. Angst J, Frey R, Lohmeyer B, et al. Bipolar manic-depressive psychoses: Results of a genetic investigation. *Hum Genet.* 1980;55:237–254.
57. Anthony JC, Folstein M, Romanoski AJ, et al. Comparison of the lay diagnostic

interview schedule and a standard psychiatric diagnosis: Experience in eastern Baltimore. *Arch Gen Psychiatry.* 1985;42:667–675.

58. Anthony JC, LeResche L, Niaz U, et al. Limits of the Mini-Mental State as a screening test for dementia and delirium among hospitalized patients. *Psychol Med.* 1982;12:397–408.
59. APA Committee on Nomenclature. *Diagnostic and Statistical Manual of Mental Disorders.* 2nd ed. (DSM-II). Washington, DC: American Psychiatric Association; 1968.
60. APA Committee on Nomenclature and Statistics. *Diagnostic and Statistical Manual of Mental Disorders.* 3rd ed. (DSM-III). Washington, DC: American Psychiatric Association; 1980.
61. APA Task Force on Late Neurological Effects of Antipsychotic Drugs. *American Psychiatric Association Task Force Report No. 18, Tardive Dyskinesia.* Washington, DC: American Psychiatric Association; 1979.
62. APA Task Force. Tricyclic antidepressants, blood level measurement, and clinical outcome. *Am J Psychiatry.* 1985;142:155–162.
63. APA Task Force on Electroconvulsive Therapy. *The Practice of Electroconvulsive Therapy.* Washington, DC: American Psychiatric Association; 1990.
64. Arthurs R, Cahoon E. A clinical and electroencephalogathic survey of psychopathic personality. *Am J Psychiatry.* 1964;120:875–877.
65. Ashford JW, Ford CV: Use of MAO inhibitors in elderly patients. *Am J Psychiatry.* 1979;136:1466–1467.
66. Astrup C, Fossum A, Holmboe R. *Prognosis in Functional Psychoses.* Springfield, Ill: Charles C Thomas; 1972.
67. Azrin N, Peterson A. Habit reversal for the treatment of Tourette syndrome. *Behav Res Ther.* 1988;26:347–351.
68. Bach-y-Rita G, Lion J, Ervin FR. Pathological intoxication: Clinical and electroencephalographic studies. *Am J Psychiatry.* 1970;127:698–703.
69. Baer L, Minichiello W. Behavior therapy for obsessive compulsive disorder. In: Jenike M, Baer L, Minichiello W, eds. *Obsessive-Compulsive Disorders: Theory and Management.* Littleton, Mass: PSG Publishing Co, Inc; 1986:45–76.
70. Bailey JM, Pillard RC. A genetic study of male sexual orientation. *Arch Gen Psychiatry.* 1991;48:1089–1096.
71. Baker M, Dorzab J, Winokur G, et al. Depressive disease: Classification and clinical characteristics. Compr Psychiatry. 1971; 12:354–365.
72. Baldessarini RJ. Frequency of diagnosis of schizophrenia versus affective disorder from 1944 to 1968. *Am J Psychiatry.* 1970;127:759–763.
73. Baldessarini RJ. Drugs and the treatment of psychiatric disorders. In: Gillman AG, Rall TW, Nies AS, Taylor P. *Goodman & Gilman's The Pharmacological Basis of Therapeutics.* New York: Pergamon Press; 1990:383–435.
74. Ballenger JC, ed. *Clinical Aspects of Panic Disorder, Frontiers of Clinical Neuroscience,* vol. 9. New York: Wiley-Liss, 1990.
75. Ballenger JC, Burrows GD, Dupont RL Jr, et al. Alprazolam in panic disorder and agoraphobia: Results from a multicenter trial. I. Efficacy in short-term treatment. *Arch Gen Psychiatry.* 1988;45:413–422.
76. Barash D. *The Whisperings Within: Evolution and the Origin of Human Nature.* New York: Harper & Row; 1979:60–63.

77. Barlow DH. *Anxiety and Its Disorders. The Nature and Treatment of Anxiety and Panic*. New York: Guilford Press; 1988.

78. Barnes RF, Raskind M, Gumbrecht G, et al. The effects of age on the plasma catecholamine response to mental stress in man. *J Clin Endocrinol Metab*. 1982;54:64–69.

79. Barraclough B, Bunch J, Nelson B, et al. A hundred cases of suicide: Clinical aspects. *Br J Psychiatry*. 1974;125:355–373.

80. Bates B. *A Guide to Physical Examination and History Taking. 5th ed*. Philadelphia: JB Lippincott; 1991.

81. Baxter LR Jr, Phelps ME, Mazziotta JC, et al. Local cerebral glucose metabolic rates in obsessive-compulsive disorder. *Arch Gen Psychiatry*. 1987;44:211–218.

82. Baxter LR Jr, Schwartz JM, Phelps ME, et al. Reduction of prefrontal cortex glucose metabolism common to three types of depression. *Arch Gen Psychiatry*. 1989;46:243–250.

83. Bear DM, Fedio P. Quantitative analysis of interictal behavior in temporal lobe epilepsy. *Arch Neurol*. 1977;34:454–467.

84. Beard AW, Slater E. The schizophrenic-like psychoses of epilepsy. *Proc R Soc Med*. 1962;55:311–316.

85. Beauclaire L, Fontaine R. Epileptiform abnormalities in panic disorder. Presented at Society of Biological Psychiatry, 41st Annual Meeting. 1986 (No. 96):148.

86. Beaumont JG. Handedness and hemisphere function. In: Diamond S, Beaumont J, (eds.) *Hemisphere Function in the Human Brain*. New York: Halstead Press; 1974:89–120.

87. Beeber AR, Kline MD, Pies RW, et al. Dexamethasone suppression test in hospitalized depressed patients with borderline personality disorder. *J Nerv Ment Dis*. 1984;172:301–303.

88. Begleiter H, Porjesz B, Bihari B, et al. Event-related brain potentials in boys at risk for alcoholism. *Science*. 1984;225:1493–1496.

89. Behar D, Stewart MA. Aggressive conduct disorder of children. The clinical history and direct observations. *Acta Psychiatr Scand*. 1982;65:210–220.

90. Behar D, Stewart MA. Aggressive conduct disorder: The influence of social class, sex, and age on the clinical picture. *J Child Psychol Psychiatry*. 1984;25:119–124.

91. Benson DF. Disorders of verbal expression. In: Benson DF, Blumer D, eds. *Psychiatric Aspects of Neurologic Disease*. vol. 1. New York: Grune & Stratton, 1975:121–136.

92. Benson DF. *Aphasia, Alexia and Agraphia: Clinical Neurology and Neurosurgery Monographs*. Edinburgh: Churchill Livingstone; 1979.

93. Benson DF. The treatable dementias. In: Benson DF, Blumer D, eds. *Psychiatric Aspects of Neurologic Disease,* vol. 2. New York: Grune & Stratton; 1982:123–148.

94. Benson DF, Blumer D: *Psychiatric Aspects of Neurologic Disease,* vol 1. New York: Grune & Stratton; 1975:157–159.

95. Benson DF, Blumer D. Psychiatric manifestations of epilepsy. In: Benson DF, Blumer D, eds. *Psychiatric Aspects of Neurologic Disease,* vol. 2. New York: Grune & Stratton; 1982:25–47.

96. Benson F, Miller BL, Signer SF. Dual personality associated with epilepsy, multiple personality and the illusion of possession. *Arch Neurol*. 1986;43:471–474.

97. Benton A, Van Allen M. Prosopagnosia and facial discrimination. *J Neurol Sci.* 1972;15:167–172.
98. Benton JR, Reza M, Winter J, et al. Steroids and apparent cerebral atrophy on computed tomographic scans. *J Comput Assist Tomogr.* 1978;2:16–19.
99. Berenbaum S, Abrams R, Rosenberg S, et al. The nature of emotional blunting: A factor-analytic study. *Psychiatr Res.* 1987;20:57–67.
100. Berensin EV. Delirium in the elderly. *J Geriatr Psychiatry Neurol.* 1988;1:127–143.
101. Berger PA, Dunn MJ. Substance induced and substance use disorders. In: Greist JH, Jefferson JW, Spitzer FL, eds. *Treatment of Mental Disorders.* New York: Oxford University Press; 1982:78–142.
102. Berger PA, Tinklenberg JR. Medical management of the drug abuser. In: Freeman AM, Sack RL, Berger PA, eds. *Psychiatry for the Primary Care Physician.* Baltimore: Williams & Wilkins; 1979:359–380.
103. Berlin FS, Coyle GS. Sexual deviation syndromes. *Johns Hopkins Med J.* 1981;149:119–125.
104. Berlin FS, Meinecke CF. Treatment of sex offenders with antiandrogenic medication. *Am J Psychiatry.* 1981;138:601–607.
105. Berner P, Musalek M, Walter H. Psychopathological concepts of dysphoria. *Psychopathology.* 1987;20:93–100.
106. Bernstein JG. *Handbook of Drug Therapy in Psychiatry. 2nd ed.* Littleton, Mass: PSG Publishing Co Inc; 1988.
107. Berrios GE. Stupor revisited. *Compr Psychiatry.* 1981;22:466–478.
108. Besson JAO, Corrigan FM, Chevyman GR, et al. Nuclear magnetic resonance brain imaging in chronic schizophrenia. *Br J Psychiatry.* 1987;150:161–163.
109. Bezchlibnyk-Butler KZ, Jeffries JJ. *Clinical Handbook of the Psychotropic Drugs.* 3rd ed. Toronto: Hogrefe & Huber; 1991.
110. Birkett DP. Gerstmann's syndrome. *Br J Psychiatry.* 1967;113:801.
111. Blackwell B. Side effects of antidepressant drugs. In: Hales RE, Frances AJ, eds. *Psychiatry Update, American Psychiatric Association Annual Review.* vol. 6. Washington, DC: American Psychiatric Press; 1987;724–745.
112. Blaschke TF, Cohen SN, Latro DS, et al. Drug-drug interactions and aging. In: Jarvik L, Greenblatt DF, Harmon D, eds. *Clinical Pharmacology and the Aged Patient.* New York: Raven Press; 1981:11–26.
113. Blazer DG. *Depression in Late Life.* St. Louis: CV Mosby; 1982.
114. Blennow G, McNeil TF. Neurological deviations in newborns at psychiatric high risk. *Acta Psychiatr Scand.* 1991;84:170–184.
115. Bleuler E. *Textbook of Psychiatry.* New York: Macmillan; 1924.
116. Bleuler E, Zinkin J, trans. *Dementia Praecox or the Group of Schizophrenias.* New York: International Universities Press; 1950.
117. Bleuler M. Acute mental concomitants of physical diseases. In: Benson DF, Blumer D, eds. *Psychiatric Aspects of Neurologic Disease,* vol 1. New York: Grune & Stratton; 1975:37–61.
118. Blumbergs DC, Jones NR, North JB. Diffuse axonal injury in head trauma. *J Neurol Neurosurg Psychiatry.* 1989;52:838–841.
119. Blumenthal JA, Emery GF, Madden DJ, et al. Cardiovascular and behavioral effects

of aerobic exercise training in healthy older men and women. *J Gerontol.* 1989;44:147–157.

120. Blumer D. Changes of sexual behavior related to temporal lobe disorders in man. *J Sex Res.* 1970;6:173–180.

121. Blumer D. Hypersexual episodes in temporal lobe epilepsy. *Am J Psychiatry.* 1970;126:83–90.

122. Blumer D. Temporal lobe epilepsy. In: Benson DF, Blumer D, eds. *Psychiatric Aspects of Neurologic Disease,* vol. 1. New York: Grune & Stratton; 1975;171–198.

123. Bohman M, Sigvardsson S, Cloninger CR. Maternal inheritance of alcohol abuse. Cross-fostering analysis of adopted women. *Arch Gen Psychiatry.* 1981;38:965–969.

124. Boller F, Albert M, Denes F. Palilalia. *Br J Disord Commun.* 1975;10:92–97.

125. Boone KB, Ananth J, Philpott L, et al. Neuropsychological characteristics of non-depressed adults with obsessive-compulsive disorder. *Neuropsychiatry, Neuropsychology, and Behavioral Neurology.* 1991;4:96–109.

126. Borg SE, Stahl M. Prediction of suicide: A prospective study of suicides and controls among psychiatric patients. *Acta Psychiatr Scand.* 1982;65:221–232.

127. Bornstein RA, Baker GB, Bazylewich T, et al. Tourette syndrome and neuropsychological performance. *Acta Psychiatr Scand.* 1991;84:212–216.

128. Bortz WM. Disease and aging. *JAMA.* 1982;248:1203–1208.

129. Bouckoms AJ. The role of stereotactic cingulotomy in the treatment of intractable depression. In: Amsterdam JD, ed. *Advances in Neuropsychiatry and Psychopharmacology, Vol. 2, Refractory Depression.* New York: Raven Press; 1991:233–242.

130. Bousquet J. Neuroleptic malignant syndrome: A review of the literature. *J Clin Psychopharmacol.* 1986;6:257–273.

131. Bradley PB. The central action of certain drugs in relation to the reticular formation of the brain. In: Jasper HH, et al, eds. *Reticular Formation of the Brain.* Boston: Little, Brown; 1958:123–149.

132. Brockington IF, Cernik KP, Schofield EM, et al. Puerperal psychosis: Phenomena and diagnosis. *Arch Gen Psychiatry.* 1981; 38:829–833.

133. Brockington IF, Leff JP. Schizoaffective psychosis: Definitions and incidence. *Psychol Med.* 1979;9:91–99.

134. Brodie MJ. Epilepsy octet, established anticonvulsants and treatment of refractory epilepsy. *Lancet.* 1990;336:350–354.

135. Brown JW. *Aphasia, Apraxia and Agnosia: Clinical and Theoretical Aspects.* Springfield, Ill: Charles C Thomas; 1972.

136. Brown WA, Shuey I. Response to dexamethasone and subtypes of depression. *Arch Gen Psychiatry.* 1980;37:747–751.

137. Bruder GE, Quitkin FM, Stewart JW, et al. Cerebral laterality and depression. Differences in perceptual asymmetry among diagnostic subtypes. *J Abnorm Psychol.* 1989;98:177–186.

138. Bruder GE, Sutton S, Berger-Gross P, et al. Lateralized auditory processing in depression. Dichotic click detection. *Psychiatry Res.* 1981;4:253–266.

139. Buchanan RW, Kirkpatrick B, Heinrichs DW, et al. Clinical correlates of the deficit syndrome in schizophrenia. *Am J Psychiatry.* 1990;147:290–294.

140. Buchsbaum MS, De Lisi LE, Holcomb HH, et al. Anteroposterior gradients in cerebral glucose use in schizophrenia and affective disorders. *Arch Gen Psychiatry.* 1984;41:1159–1166.

141. Buchsbaum MS, Wu J, De Lisi LE, et al. Frontal cortex and basal ganglia metabolic rates assessed by positron emission tomography with [^{18}F]2-deoxyglucose in affective illness. *J Affective Disord.* 1986;10:137–152.

142. Bunney WE Jr, Goodwin FK, Murphy DI. The "switch process" in manic depressive illness: 1. A systematic study of sequential behavioral changes. *Arch Gen Psychiatry.* 1972;27:295–302.

143. Burden G. Social aspects of epilepsy. In: Reynolds EH, Trimble MR, eds. *Epilepsy and Psychiatry.* Edinburgh: Churchill Livingston; 1981:296–305.

144. Bureau of Justice Statistics. *Criminal Victimization in the United States, 1983.* Washington, DC: U.S. Department of Justice; 1985.

145. Burks JS, Walker JE, Rumack BH, et al. Tricyclic antidepressant poisoning: Reversal of coma, choreoathetosis, and myoclonus by physostigmine. *JAMA.* 1974;230:1405–1407.

146. Burrington JD, Wayne ER. Obstruction of the duodenum by the superior mesenteric artery: Does it exist in children? *J Pediatr Surg.* 1974;9:733–741.

147. Busse EW, Blazer DG. Disorders related to biological functioning. In: Busse EW, Blazer DG, eds. *Handbook of Geriatric Psychiatry.* New York: Van Nostrand Reinhold; 1980:390–414.

148. Butler R. Overview of aging. In: Usdin G, ed. *Aging: The Process and the People.* New York: Brunner/Mazel; 1978: 1–19.

149. Cardoret RJ. Psychopathology in adopted-away offspring of biological parents with antisocial behavior. *Arch Gen Psychiatry.* 1978;35:176–184.

150. Cadoret RJ, Gath A. Inheritance of alcoholism in adoptees. *Br J Psychiatry.* 1978;132:252–258.

151. Cadoret RJ, O'Gorman TW, Troughton E, Heywood E. Alcoholism and antisocial personality. *Arch Gen Psychiatry.* 1985;42:161–167.

152. Cadoret RJ, Troughton E, O'Gorman TW, Heywood E. An adoption study of genetic and environmental factors in drug abuse. *Arch Gen Psychiatry.* 1986;43:1131–1136.

153. Calev A, Nigal D, Shapira B, et al. Early and long-term effects of electroconvulsive therapy and depression on memory and other cognitive functions. *J Nerv Ment Dis.* 1991;179:526–533.

154. Cameron D, Thomas R, Mulvihill M, et al. Delirium: A test of the Diagnostic and Statistical Manual III criteria on medical inpatients. *J Am Geriatr Soc.* 1987;35:1007–1010.

155. Campbell R. The lateralization of emotion: A critical review. *Int J Psychol.* 1982;17:211–229.

156. Caparulo BK, Cohen DJ, Rothman SL, et al. Computed tomographic brain scanning in children with developmental neuropsychiatric disorders. *J Am Acad Child Psychiatry.* 1981;20:338–357.

157. Capel WC, Stewart GT. The management of drug abuse in aging populations. *J Drug Issues.* 1971;1:114–121.

158. Carlen PL, Wortzman G, Holgate RC, et al. Reversible cerebral atrophy in recently

abstinent chronic alcoholics measured by computed tomography scans. *Science*. 1978;200:1076–1078.

159. Carlson GA, Goodwin FK. The stages of mania. *Arch Gen Psychiatry*. 1973; 28:221–228.

160. Caroff SN. The neuroleptic malignant syndrome. *J Clin Psychiatry*. 1980;43:79–83.

161. Caroff SN, Mann SC. Neuroleptic malignant syndrome. *Psychopharmacol Bull*. 1988;24:25–29.

162. Carpenter WT Jr, Strauss JS, Muleh S. Are there pathognomonic symptoms in schizophrenia? *Arch Gen Psychiatry*. 1973;28:847–852.

163. Carroll BJ, Feinberg M, Greden JF, et al. A specific laboratory test for the diagnosis of melancholia: Standardization, validation and clinical utility. *Arch Gen Psychiatry*. 1981;38:15–22.

164. Carter JG. Intravenous haloperidol in the treatment of acute psychosis (letter). *Am J Psychiatry*. 1986;143:1316–1317.

165. Casanova MF, Kleinman JE. The neuropathology of schizophrenia: A critical assessment of research methodologies. *Biol Psychiatry*. 1990;27:353–362.

166. Casey DA. Electroconvulsive therapy in the neuroleptic malignant syndrome. *Convul Ther*. 1987;3:278–283.

167. Cassano GB, Akiskal HS, Musetti L, et al. Psychopathology, temperament, and past course in primary major depressions. 2. Toward a redefinition of bipolarity with a new semistructured interview for depression. *Psychopathology*. 1989;22:278–288.

168. Cassano GB, Musetti L, Perugi G, et al. A proposed new approach to the clinical subclassification of depressive illness. *Pharmacopsychiatry*. 1988;21:19–23.

169. Cassano GB, Perugi G, Musetti L, et al. The nature of depression presenting concomitantly with panic disorder. *Compr Psychiatry*. 1989;30:473–482.

170. Caudill W. *The Psychiatric Hospital as a Small Society*. Cambridge, Mass: Harvard University Press; 1958.

171. Chaika E. A linguist looks at "schizophrenic" language. *Brain and Language*. 1974;1:257–276.

172. Chapman J. The early symptoms of schizophrenia. *Br J Psychiatry*. 1966;112:225–251.

173. Charness ME, Simon RP, Greenberg DA. Ethanol and the nervous system. *N Engl J Med*. 1989;321:442–453.

174. Charney DS, Heninger GR, Sternberg DE, et al. Plasma MHPG in depression: Effects of acute and chronic administration of desipramine treatments. *Psychiatry Res*. 1981;5:217–229.

175. Chase TN, Foster NL, Fedio P, et al. Studies with the fluorine-18–labelled flurodeoxy-glucose positron emission tomographic method. *Ann Neurol*. 1984;15 (suppl):S175.

176. Chase TN, Geoffrey V, Gillespie M, et al. Structural and functional studies of Gilles de la Tourette syndrome. *Riv Neurol*. 1986;142:851–855.

177. Chiappa KH. *Evoked Potentials in Clinical Medicine,* New York: Raven Press; 1983.

178. *Chicago Sun-Times,* Sun-Times Wire Service. 65-year-old man swims English Channel. August 29, 1982:40.

179. Childress AR, McLellan AT, O'Brien CP. Abstinent opiate abusers exhibit conditioned craving, conditioned withdrawal and reductions in both through extinction. *Br J Addict.* 1986;81:655–660.

180. Chouinard G, Annable L, Ross-Chouinard A, et al. Factors related to tardive dyskinesia. *Am J Psychiatry.* 1979;136:79–82.

181. Christensen E, Moller JE, Faurbye A. A neuropathological investigation of 28 brains from patients with dyskinesia. *Acta Psychiatr Scand.* 1970;46:14–23.

182. Christiansen KO. A review of studies of criminality among twins. In: Christiansen KO, Mednick S, eds. *Biosocial Bases of Criminal Behavior.* New York: Gardner; 1977.

183. Christison GW, Kirch DG, Wyatt RJ. When symptoms persist: Choosing among alternative somatic treatments for schizophrenia. *Schizophr Bull.* 1991;17:217–245.

184. Christodoulou GN. Delusional hyper-identifications of the Fregoli type: Organic pathogenetic contributors. *Acta Psychiatr Scand.* 1976;54:305–314.

185. Claghorn JL, McBee GW, Roberts L. Trends in hospital versus community treatment of mental illness: A Texas example. *Am J Psychiatry.* 1976;133:1310–1312.

186. Claghorn JM, Zipursky RB, List SJ. Structural and functional brain imaging in schizophrenia. *J Psychiatry Neurosci.* 1991;16:53–74.

187. Clary C, Schweitzer E. Treatment of MAOI hypertensive crisis with sublingual nifedipine. *J Clin Psychiatry.* 1987;48:249–250.

188. Clayton P. Bereavement. In: Paykel ES, ed. *Handbook of Affective Disorders.* New York: Guilford Press; 1982:403–415.

189. Clayton PJ. Schizo-affective disorders. *J Nerv Ment Dis.* 1982;170:646–650.

190. Clayton PJ, Halikas JA, Maurice WL. The depression of widowhood. *Br J Psychiatry.* 1972;120:71–77.

191. Clomipramine Collaborative Study Group. Clomipramine in the treatment of patients with obsessive-compulsive disorder. Arch Gen Psychiatry. 1991;48:730–738.

192. Cloninger CR. The antisocial personality. *Hosp Pract.* 1978;13:97–106.

193. Cloninger CR. A unified biosocial theory of personality and its role in the development of anxiety states. *Psychiatr Dev.* 1986;3:167–226.

194. Cloninger CR. Neurogenetic adaptive mechanisms in alcoholism. *Science.* 1987;236:410–416.

195. Cloninger CR. Brain networks underlying personality development. In: Carroll BJ, Barrett JE, eds. *Psychopathology and the Brain.* American Psychopathological Association Series. New York: Raven Press; 1991:183–208.

196. Cloninger CR, Bohman M, Sigvardsson S. Inheritance of alcohol abuse. Cross-fostering analysis of adopted men. *Arch Gen Psychiatry.* 1981;38:861–868.

197. Cloninger CR, Guze SB. Psychiatric illness in families of female criminals: A study of 288 first degree relatives. *Br J Psychiatry.* 1973;122:697–703.

198. Cloninger CR, Martin RL, Guze SB, et al. Diagnosis and prognosis in schizophrenia. *Arch Gen Psychiatry.* 1985;42:15–25.

199. Coccagna G. Restless legs syndrome/periodic leg movements in sleep. In: Thorpy MJ, ed. *Handbook of Sleep Disorders.* New York: Marcel Dekker; 1990:475–478.

200. Coffey CE, Figiel GS, Djang WT, et al. Leukoencephalopathy in elderly depressed patients referred for ECT. *Biol Psychiatry.* 1988;24:143–161.

201. Coffman JA. Computed tomography. In: Andreasen NC, ed. *Brain Imaging: Applications in Psychiatry.* Washington, DC: American Psychiatric Press; 1989:1–65.

202. Cohen DJ, Bruun R, Leckman JF, eds. *Tourette's Syndrome and Tic Disorders,* New York: John Wiley & Sons; 1988.

203. Cohen DJ, Leckman JF. Tourette's syndrome. *JAMA.* 1991;265:1738.

204. Cohen GD. The movement toward subspecialty status for geriatric psychiatry in the United States. *International Psychogeriatrics.* 1989;1:201–205.

205. Cohen PR. The effects of instruments and informants on ascertainment. In: Dunner DL, Gershon ES, Barrett JC, eds. *Relatives at High Risk for Mental Disorders.* New York: Raven Press; 1988:31–52.

206. Cohen RJ, Suter C. Hysterical seizures: Suggestion as a provocative EEG test. *Ann Neurol.* 1982;11:391–295.

207. Cohen RM, Pickar D, Murphy DL. Myoclonus-associated hypomania during MAO-inhibitor treatment. *Am J Psychiatry.* 1980;137:105–106.

208. Cohen RM, Semple WE, Gross M, et al. Evidence for common alterations in cerebral glucose metabolism in major affective disorders and schizophrenia. *Neuropsychopharmacology.* 1989;2:241–254.

209. Cohen S. Angel dust. *Am J Psychiatry.* 1977;238:515–516.

210. Cohen S. Inhalants. In: Dupont RI, Goldstein A, O'Donnel J, eds. *Handbook on Drug Abuse.* Washington, DC: U.S. Government Printing Office; 1979:213–220 National Institute on Drug Abuse, U.S. Department of Health, Education, and Welfare, publication.

211. Coleman E. The obsessive compulsive model for describing compulsive sexual behavior. *Am J Prev Psychiatry Neurol.* 1990;2:9–14.

212. Collins WCJ, Lanigan O, Callaghan N. Plasma prolactin concentrations following epileptic and pseudoseizures. *J Neurol Neurosurg Psychiatry.* 1983;46:505–508.

213. Comings DE, Comings BG. Hereditary agoraphobia and obsessive compulsive behavior in relatives of patients with Gilles de la Tourette's syndrome. *Br J Psychiatry.* 1987;151:195–199.

214. Comings DE, Comings BG. A controlled family history study of Tourette's syndrome, III: Affective and other disorders. *J Clin Psychiatry.* 1990;51:288–291.

215. Comings DE, Comings BG, Devor EJ, et al. Detection of a major gene for Gilles de la Tourette syndrome. *Am J Hum Genet.* 1984;36:586–600.

216. Como PG, Kurlan R. An open-label trial of fluoxetine for obsessive-compulsive disorder in Gilles de la Tourette's syndrome. *Neurology.* 1991;41:872–874.

217. Consensus Conference. Differential diagnosis of dementing diseases. *JAMA.* 1987;258:23–26.

218. Cookson JC. The neuroendocrinology of mania. *J Affective Disord.* 1985;8:233–241.

219. Cooper JE, Kendell RE, Gurland BJ, et al. *Psychiatric Diagnoses in New York and London: Maudsley Monograph No. 20.* London: Oxford University Press; 1972.

220. Coryell W, Zimmerman M. The heritability of schizophrenia and schizoaffective disorder. *Arch Gen Psychiatry.* 1988;45:323–327.

221. Cotton NS. The familial incidence of alcoholism: A review. *J Stud Alcohol.* 1979;40:89–116.

222. Council on Scientific Affairs. Marijuana, its health hazards and therapeutic potentials. *JAMA*. 1981;246:1823–1827.

223. Cowdry RW, Garner DL. Pharmacotherapy of borderline personality disorder. Alprazolam, carbamazepine, trifluoperazine, and tranylcypromine. *Arch Gen Psychiatry*. 1988;45:111–119.

224. Cowdry RW, Pickar D, Davis R. Symptoms and EEG findings in the borderline syndrome. *Int J Psychiatry Med*. 1985;15:201–210.

225. Cox SM, Ludwig AM. Neurologic soft signs and psychopathology: 1. Findings in schizophrenia. *J Nerv Ment Dis*. 1979;167:161–165.

226. Craft M. *Ten Studies into Psychopathic Personality*. Bristol: John Wright & Sons; 1965.

227. Crammer J, Heine B. *The Use of Drugs in Psychiatry*. London: The Royal College of Psychiatrists/Gaskell UK Distribution; Washington, DC: American Psychiatric Press; 1991.

228. Crisp AA, Hsu LKG, Harding B, et al. Clinical features of anorexia nervosa: A study of 102 cases. *J Psychosom Res*. 1980;24:179–191.

229. Critchley M. *The Parietal Lobes*. New York: Hafner Press; 1953.

230. Cronson AJ, Flemenbaum A. Antagonism of cocaine highs by lithium. *Am J Psychiatry*. 1978;135:856–857.

231. Crosson B, Hughes CW. Role of the thalamus in language: Is it related to schizophrenic thought disorder? *Schizophr Bull*. 1987;13:605–621.

232. Crow TJ. Molecular pathology of schizophrenia: More than one disease process? *Br Med J Clin Res*. 1980;280:66–68.

233. Crow TJ. The continuum of psychosis and its genetic origins. *Br J Psychiatry*. 1990;156:788–797.

234. Crowe RR: An adoptive study of antisocial personality. *Arch Gen Psychiatry*. 1974;31:785–791.

235. Crowe RR. The genetics of panic disorder and agoraphobia. *Psychiatr Dev*. 1985;2:171–185.

236. Culver CM, King FW. Neuropsychological assessment of undergraduate marijuana and LSD users. *Arch Gen Psychiatry*. 1974;31:707–711.

237. Cummings JL, Benson DF. *Dementia: A Clinical Approach*. 2nd ed. Boston: Butterworth Publishers; 1992.

238. Cummings JL, Benson DF. Subcortical dementia: Review of an emerging concept. *Arch Neurol*. 1984;41:874–879.

239. Cummings JL, Frankel M. Gilles de la Tourette syndrome and the neurological basis of obsessions and compulsions. *Biol Psychiatry*. 1985;20:1117–1126.

240. Cutting J. Outcome in schizophrenia: Overview. In: Kerr TA, Smith RP, eds. *Contemporary Issues in Schizophrenia*. Washington, DC: American Psychiatric Press; 1986:433–440.

241. Damasio H, Damasio AR. The anatomical basis of conduction aphasia. *Brain*. 1980;103:337–350.

242. Darbonne A. Crisis: A review of theory, practice, and research. *Int J Psychiatry*. 1968;6:371–379.

243. DaSilva L, Johnstone EC: A follow-up study of severe puerperal psychiatric illness. *Br J Psychiatry*. 1981;139:346–354.

244. Davidson J, Robertson E. A follow-up study of postpartum illness, 1946–1978. *Acta Psychiatr Scand.* 1985;71:451–457.

245. Davidson JCT, McLeod MN, Kurland AA, et al. Antidepressant drug therapy in psychotic depression. Br J Psychiatry. 1977;131:493–496.

246. Davidson K, Bagley CR. Schizophrenia-like psychoses associated with organic disorders of the central nervous system: A review of the literature. In: "Current Problems in Neuropsychiatry", *Br J Psychiatry.* 1969 (special publication No. 4):113–184.

247. Davies RK, Tucker GI, Harrow M, et al. Confusional episodes and antidepressant medication. *Am J Psychiatry.* 1971;128:95.

248. Davis BL. The PCP epidemic: A critical review. *Int J Addict.* 1982;17:1137–1155.

249. Davis JM. Overview: Maintenance therapy in psychiatry: 1. Schizophrenia. *Am J Psychiatry.* 1975;132:1237–1245.

250. Davis JM, Benvenuto JA. Acute reactions from drug abuse problems. In: Resnich HLP, Ruben HL, eds. *Emergency Psychiatric Care.* Bowie, Md: Charles Press; 1975:81–101.

251. Davis JM, Erickson S, Dekirmenjian H. Plasma levels of antipsychotic drugs and clinical response. In: Lipton MA, Damasio A, Killam KF, eds. *Psychopharmacology: A Generation of Progress.* New York: Raven Press; 1978:905–915.

252. Davis KL, Mohs RC. Enhancement of memory processes in Alzheimer's disease with multiple-dose intravenous physostigmine. *Am J Psychiatry.* 1982;139:1421–1424.

253. Dean C, Kendell RE. The symptomatology of puerperal illness. *Br J Psychiatry.* 1981;139:128–133.

254. Deckel AW. Evidence for a tonic inhibition of food consumption and body weight by the striatum in female rats: Effects of castration. In: Schneider LH, Cooper SJ, Halmi KA, eds. The psychobiology of human eating disorders: preclinical and clinical perspectives. *Ann NY Acad Sci.* 1989;575:506–508.

255. Deckel AW, Moran TH, Robinson RG. Striatal DA systems regulate body weight in female rats. *Proc Abst Ann Meet East Psychol Assoc.* 1986;57:72.

256. DeGowin RL. *DeGowin & DeGowin's Bedside Diagnostic Examination.* 5th ed. New York: Macmillan; 1987.

257. DeLint J, Schmidt W. The epidemiology of alcoholism. In: *Biological Basis of Alcoholism.* Toronto: Wiley Interscience; 1971:423–442.

258. DeMyer W. *Technique of the Neurologic Examination. A Programmed Text,* 3rd ed. New York: McGraw-Hill; 1980.

259. Derby IM. Manic-depressive "exhaustion" deaths. *Psychiatr Q* 1933;7:436–449.

260. deToledo-Morrell L, Evers S, Hoerppner TJ, et al. A stress test for memory dysfunction. Electrophysiologic manifestations of early Alzheimer's disease. *Arch Neurol.* 1991;48:605–609.

261. DeVeaugh-Geiss J. Tardive dyskinesia and related involuntary movement disorders. The long-term effects of antipsychotic drugs. Boston Wright-PSG; 1982.

262. Devinsky O, Bear DM. Varieties of aggressive behavior in temporal lobe epilepsy. *Am J Psychiatry.* 1984;141:651–656.

263. Devinsky O, Bear DM. Varieties of depression in epilepsy. *Neuropsychiatry, Neuropsychology, and Behavioral Neurology.* 1991;4:49–61.

264. Devor EJ. Complex segregation analysis of Gilles de la Tourette syndrome: Further evidence for a major locus mode of transmission. *Am J Hum Genet.* 1984;36:704–709.

265. Devor EJ. Untying the Gordian knot: The genetics of Tourette's syndrome. *J Nerv Ment Dis.* 1990;178:669–679.

266. Dewan MJ, Haldipur V, Lane EE, et al. Bipolar affective disorder I. Comprehensive quantitative computed tomography. *Acta Psychiatr Scand.* 1988;77:670–676.

267. DiCostanzo E, Schifano F. Lithium alone or in combination with carbamazepine for the treatment of rapid-cycling bipolar affective disorder. *Acta Psychiatr Scand.* 1991;83:456–459.

268. Diner BC, Holcomb PJ, Dykman RA. P300 in major depressive disorder. *Psychiatry Res.* 1985;15:175–184.

269. Dinwiddie SH, Cloninger CR. Family and adoption studies in alcoholism and drug addiction. In: Miller NS, ed. The disease concept of alcoholism and drug addiction I. *Psychiatr Ann.* 1991;21:206–214.

270. Dolan RJ, Calloway SP, Thacker PF, et al. The cerebral cortical appearance in depressed subjects. *Psychol Med.* 1986;16:775–799.

271. Dorpat TL, Anderson WF, Ripley HS. The relationship of physical illness to suicide. In: Resnik H, ed. *Suicidal Behaviors.* Boston: Little, Brown; 1968:209–219.

272. Double DB. A cluster analysis of manic states. *Compr Psychiatry.* 1991;32:187–194.

273. Dubois FS. Compulsion neurosis with cachexia. *Am J Psychiatry.* 1949;106:107–115.

274. Duggan CF, Sham P, Lee AS, et al. Can future suicidal behavior in depressed patients be predicted? *J Affective Disord.* 1991;22:111–118.

275. Dunham HW. Society, culture, and mental disorder. *Arch Gen Psychiatry.* 1976:33:147–156.

276. Dunner DL, Gershon ES, Goodwin FK. Heritable factors in the severity of affective illness. *Biol Psychiatry.* 1976;11:31–42.

277. Dupont RM, Jernigan TL, Butters N, et al. Subcortical abnormalities detected in bipolar affective disorder using magnetic resonance imaging: Clinical and neuropsychological significance. *Arch Gen Psychiatry.* 1990;47:55–59.

278. Durant W. *The Story of Philosophy, the Lives and Opinions of the Greater Philosophers.* New York: Washington Square Press; 1961.

279. Eaton W, Kessler L, eds. *Epidemiologic Field Methods in Psychiatry: The NIMH Epidemiologic Catchement Area Program.* New York: Academic Press; 1985.

280. Edlund JM, Swann AC, Clothier J. Patients with panic attacks and abnormal EEG results. *Am J Psychiatry.* 1987;144:508–509.

281. Eichelman B, Estess FM, Gonda TA. Hypnotic agents in psychiatric evaluations. In: Barchas JD, Berger PA, Ciaranello RD, et al, eds. *Psychopharmacology from Theory to Practice.* New York: Oxford University Press, 1977:270–275.

282. Ellinwood EH. Amphetamines/anorectics. In: Dupont RI, Goldstein A, ODonnell J, eds. *Handbook on Drug Abuse,* Washington, DC: Government Printing Office; 1979:221–231. National Institute on Drug Abuse, U.S. Department of Health, Education, and Welfare, publication.

283. Ellis L, Ames MA. Neurohormonal functioning and sexual orientation: A theory of homosexuality-heterosexuality. *Psychol Bull.* 1987;101:233–258.

284. Ellis JM, Lee SI. Acute prolonged confusion in later life as in ictal state. *Epilepsia.* 1978;19:119–128.

285. Endicott J, Halbreich U, Schacht S, et al. Premenstrual changes and affective disorders. *Psychosom Med.* 1981;43:519–529.

286. Engel GL, Romano J. Delirium: A syndrome of chronic cerebral insufficiency. *J Chronic Dis.* 1959;9:260–277.

287. Epstein PS, Pisoni VD, Fawcett JA. Alcoholism and cerebral atrophy. *Alcoholism: Clin Exp Res.* 1977;1:61–65.

288. Esquirol E. *Des Maladies Mentales.* 1838. Three vols. in two. History of Medicine Series, New York Academy of Medicine. New York: Hafner Publishing; 1965. Facsimile of 1845 English edition with Introduction by Saussure, RDE.

289. Essen-Moller E. The concept of schizoidia. In: Kloesi J, ed. *Psychiatrie und Neurologie, Vol. 112.* Basel: Karger; 1946:258–271.

290. Estes JW. The practice of medicine in eighteenth century Massachusetts. *N Engl J Med.* 1981;305:1040–1047.

291. Etienne PE, Dastoor D, Goldapple E, et al. Adverse effects of medical and psychiatric workup in six demented geriatric patients. *Am J Psychiatry.* 1981;138:520–521.

292. Faber R, Abrams R, Taylor MA, et al. Formal thought disorder and aphasia: Comparison of schizophrenic patients with formal thought disorder and neurologically impaired patients with aphasia. *Am J Psychiatry.* 1983;140:1348–1351.

293. Fairweather G, Sanders D, Tornatzky L. *Creating Change in Mental Health Organizations.* New York: Pergamon Press, 1974.

294. Falloon IRH, Boyd JL, McGill CW, et al. Family management in the prevention of exacerbations of schizophrenia: A controlled study. *N Engl J Med.* 1982;306:1437–1440.

295. Fava, GA, Kellner, R, Murari, F, et al. The Hamilton Depression Rating Scale in normals and depressives: A cross-cultural validation. *Acta Psychiatr Scand.* 1982;66:26–32.

296. Fawcett J, Clark DC, Aagesen CA, et al. A double-blind placebo-controlled trial of lithium carbonate therapy for alcoholism. *Arch Gen Psychiatry.* 1987;44:248–256.

297. Federal Bureau of Investigation. *Crime in the United States 1984.* Washington, DC: U.S. Department of Justice; 1985.

298. Feigenbaum E. Ambulatory treatment in the elderly. In: Busse E, Pfeiffer E, eds. *Mental Illness in Later Life.* Washington, DC: American Psychiatric Association; 1973:153–166.

299. Feighner JP, Robins E, Guze SB, et al. Diagnostic criteria for use in psychiatric research. *Arch Gen Psychiatry.* 1972;26:57–63.

300. Feinberg I: Effects of age on human sleep patterns. In: Kales A, ed. *Sleep: Physiology and Pathology.* Philadelphia: JB Lippincott; 1968.

301. Feinberg M, Carroll BJ, Steiner M, et al. Misdiagnoses of endogenous depression with research diagnostic criteria. *Lancet.* 1979;267.

302. Femino J, Lewis DC. *Clinical Pharmacology and Therapeutics of the Alcohol With-*

drawal Syndrome. Rockville Md: National Institute on Alcohol Abuse and Alcoholism; 1982. Report No. 0272.

303. Fenton GW. Psychiatric disorders of epilepsy: Classification and phenomenology. In: Reynolds EH, Trimble MR, eds. *Epilepsy and Psychiatry*. Edinburgh: Churchill Livingstone; 1981:12–26.

304. Fernandez F, Holmes VF, Adams F, et al. Treatment of severe refractory agitation with a haloperidol drip. *J Clin Psychiatry*. 1988;49:239–241.

305. Finch CE, Schneider EL. *Handbook of Biology of Aging, Volume 2*. New York: Van Nostrand Reinhold; 1985.

306. Fink M. Quantitative EEG in human psychopharmacology: Drug patterns. In: Glaser GS, ed. *EEG and Behavior*. New York: Basic Books; 1963:177–197.

307. Fink M. EEG profiles and bioavailability measures of psychoactive drugs. In: Itil TM, ed. *Psychotropic Drugs and Human EEG*. Basel: Karger; 1974:76–98.

308. Fink M. Is ECT usage decreasing? *Convul Ther*. 1987;3:171–173.

309. Fink M, Abrams R. Selective drug therapies in clinical psychiatry: Neuroleptic, anxiolytic and antimanic agents. In: Freedman AM, Kaplan HI, eds. *Treating Mental Illness*. New York: Atheneum; 1972:287–309.

310. Fink M, Taylor MA. Catatonia: A separate category in DSM-IV. *Integrative Psychiatry*. 1991;7:2–5.

311. Fisher C, Kahn E, Edward A, et al. A psychophysiological study of nightmares and night terrors. 1. Physiological aspects of the stage 4 terror. *J Nerv Ment Dis*. 1973;157:75–98.

312. Fitzhugh-Bell, KB. Neuropsychological evaluation in the management of brain disorders. In: Hendrie, HC, ed. *Psychiatric Clinics of North America, Vol. 1/1, Brain Disorders: Clinical Diagnosis and Management*. Philadelphia: WB Saunders; 1978:37–50.

313. Flor-Henry P, Fromm-Auch D, Tapper M, et al: A neuropsychological study of the stable syndrome of hysteria. *Biol Psychiatry*. 1981;16:601–626.

314. Flor-Henry P, Gruzelier J, eds. *Laterality and Psychopathology, Developments in Psychiatry, Vol. 6,* Amsterdam: Elsevier Science Publishers BV; 1983.

315. Fogel BS. Depression and Aging. *Neuropsychiatry, Neuropsychology, and Behavioral Neurology*. 1991;4:24–35.

316. Folstein MF, Folstein SW, McHugh PR. "Mini-Mental State": A practical method of grading the cognitive state of patients for the clinician. *J Psychiatr Res*. 1975;12:189–198.

317. Folstein MF, Rabins P. Psychiatric evaluation of the elderly patient. *Primary Care*. 1979;6:609–620.

318. Fontaine R, Breton G, Dery R, et al. Temporal lobe abnormalities in panic disorder: An MRI study. *Biol Psychiatry*. 1990;27:304–310.

319. Ford CV, Shordone RJ. Attitudes of psychiatrists towards elderly patients. *Am J Psychiatry*. 1980;137:571–575.

320. Forn J. Lithium and cyclic AMP. In: Johnson FN, ed. *Lithium Research and Therapy*. New York: Academic Press; 1974:485–497.

321. Forrest AD, Fraser RH, Priest RG. Environmental factors in depressive illness. *Br J Psychiatry*. 1965;111:243–253.

322. Foulks DG. Monoamine oxidase inhibitors: Reappraisal of dietary considerations. *J Clin Psychopharmacol*. 1983;4:249–252.

323. Frances AJ, Hales RE. *Review of Psychiatry,* vol. 7. Washington, DC: American Psychiatric Press; 1988:Section III.

324. Frank E, Anderson C, Rubinstein D. Frequency of sexual dysfunction in "normal couples." *N Engl J Med*. 1978;229:111–115.

325. Frankel M, Cummings JL. Neuro-ophthalmic abnormalities in Tourette syndrome: Anatomic and functional implications. *Neurology*. 1984;34:359–361.

326. Frankel M, Cummings JL, Robertson MM, et al. Obsessions and compulsions in Gilles de la Tourette's syndrome. *Neurology*. 1986;36:378–382.

327. Franks RD, Adler LE, Waldo MC, et al. Neurophysiological studies of sensory gating in mania: Comparison with schizophrenia. *Biol Psychiatry*. 1983;18:989–1005.

328. Fricchione GL. Neuroleptic catatonia and its relationship to psychogenic catatonia. *Biol Psychiatry*. 1985;20:304–313.

329. Friedman CJ, Shear MK, Frances AJ. Personality disorders in panic patients. *J Pers Disord*. 1987;1:132–135.

330. Friedman JH, Davis R, Wagner RL. Neuroleptic malignant syndrome: The results of a six-month prospective study of incidence in a state psychiatric hospital. *Clin Neuropharmacol*. 1988;11:373–377.

331. Fries H. Studies on secondary amenorrhea, anorectic behavior, and body image perception: Importance for the early recognition of anorexia nervosa. In: Vigersky R, ed. *Anorexia Nervosa*. New York: Raven Press; 1977:163–176.

332. Furukawa T, Ushizima I, Ono N. Modifications by lithium of behavioral responses to methamphetamine and tetrabenazine. *Psychopharmacologica*. 1975;41:243–248.

333. Fyer MR, Frances AJ, Sullivan T, et al. Comorbidity of borderline personality disorder. *Arch Gen Psychiatry*. 1988;45:348–352.

334. Gabriel E, ed. Problems of schizo-affective psychoses. Symposium of the World Psychiatric Association Section of Clinical Psychopathology, Vienna, October 5–6, 1982. *Psychiatrica Clinica*. 1983;16:65–304.

335. Gaebel W, Ulrich G. Topographical distribution of absolute alpha-power in the EEG and psychopathology in schizophrenia outpatients. *Acta Psychiatr Scand*. 1988;77:390–397.

336. Gainotti G. Emotional behavior and hemispheric side of the lesion. *Cortex*. 1972;8:41–55.

337. Galen RS, Gambino SR. *Beyond Normality: The Predictive Value and Efficiency of Medical Diagnoses*. New York: John Wiley & Sons; 1975:17.

338. Gardner D, Lucas PB, Cowdry RW. Soft sign neurological abnormalities in borderline personality disorder and normal control subjects. *J Nerv Ment Dis*. 1987;175:177–180.

339. Gardos G, Cole JO. Tardive dyskinesia and anticholingeric drugs. *Am J Psychiatry*. 1983;140:200–202.

340. Garfinkel PE, Garner DM. *Anorexia Nervosa: A Multidimensional Perspective*. New York: Brunner/Mazel; 1982.

341. Garland H, Summer D, Fourman P. The Kleine Levin syndrome. *Neurology*. 1965;15:1161–1167.

342. Garner DM, Olmsted MP, Garfinkel PE. Does anorexia nervosa occur on a continuum? *Int J Eating Disord.* 1983;2:11–20.

343. Gaspar D, Samarsinghi LA. ECT in psychogeriatric practice: A study of risk factor, indicators and outcome. *Compr Psychiatry.* 1982;23:170–175.

344. Gasperini M, Battaglia M, Scherillo P, et al. Morbidity risk for mood disorders in the families of borderline patients. *J Affective Disord.* 1991;21:265–272.

345. Gatfield PD, Guze SB. Prognosis and differential diagnosis of conversion reactions. *Dis Nerv Syst.* 1962;23:623–631.

346. Gawin FH, Ellinwood EH Jr. Cocaine and other stimulants, actions, abuse, and treatment. *N Engl J Med.* 1988;18:1173–1182.

347. Gawin FH, Kleber HD, Byck R, et al. Desipramine facilitation of initial cocaine abstinence. *Arch Gen Psychiatry.* 1989;46:117–121.

348. Gelder MG. Psychological treatment of agoraphobia. In: Roth M, ed. *Treatment and Outcome of Phobic and Related Disorders. Psychiatr Ann.* 1991;21:354–358.

349. Geokas NL, Conteas CN, Majumdar APN. The aging gastrointestinal tract, liver, and pancreas. *Clin Geriatr Med.* 1985;1:177–206.

350. Gershon ES. Genetics. In: Goodwin FK, Jamison KR. *Manic-Depressive Illness.* New York: Oxford University Press; 1990:373–401.

351. Gershon ES, De Lisi LE, Hamovit J, et al. A controlled family study of chronic psychoses, schizophrenia, and schizoaffective disorder. *Arch Gen Psychiatry.* 1988;45:328–336.

352. Gershon ES, Hamovit J, Guroff JJ, et al. A family study of schizoaffective, bipolar I, bipolar II, unipolar, and normal control patients. *Arch Gen Psychiatry.* 1982;39:1157–1167.

353. Gershon ES, Schreiber JL, Hamovit JR, et al. Clinical findings in patients with anorexia nervosa and affective illness in their relatives. *Am J Psychiatry.* 1984;141:1419–1422.

354. Geschwind N. Disconnection syndromes in animals and man. *Brain* 1965;88:237–294, 585–644.

355. Geschwind N. *Selected Papers on Language and the Brain.* Boston: D. Reidel; 1974.

356. Geschwind N. The anatomical basis of hemisphere differentiation. In: Diamond S, Beaumont J, eds. *Hemisphere Function in the Human Brain.* New York: Halstead Press; 1977:7–24.

357. Giang DW. Systemic lupus erythematosus and depression. *Neuropsychiatry, Neuropsychology, and Behavioral Neurology.* 1991;4:78–82.

358. Gibbs FA, Bagchi BK, Bloomberg W. Electroencephalographic study of criminals. *Am J Psychiatry.* 1945;102:294–298.

359. Gladue BA, Green R, Hellman RE. Neuroendocrine response to estrogen and sexual orientation. *Science.* 1984;225:1496–1499.

360. Glassman AH, Kantor SJ, Shostak M. Depression, delusions and drug response. *Am J Psychiatry.* 1975;132:716–719.

361. Glassman AH, Perel JM. Tricyclic blood levels and clinical outcome: A review of the art. In: Lipton MA, Damasio A, Killam KF, eds. *Psychopharmacology: A Generation of Progress.* New York: Raven Press; 1978:917–922.

362. Glassman AH, Perel JM, Shostak J, et al. Clinical implications of imipramine plasma levels for depressive illness. *Arch Gen Psychiatry.* 1977;34:197–204.

363. Gloor P, Olivier A, Quesney LF, et al. The role of the limbic system in experiential phenomena of temporal lobe epilepsy. *Ann Neurol.* 1982;12:129–144.

364. Goad DL, Davis CM, Liem P, et al. The use of selegiline in Alzheimer's patients with behavioral problems. *J Clin Psychiatry.* 1991;52:342–345.

365. Goktepe EO, Young LB, Bridges PK. A further review of the results of stereotactic subcaudate tractotomy. *Br J Psychiatry.* 1975;126:270–280.

366. Goldberg TE, Berman KF, Mohr E, et al. Regional cerebral blood flow and cognitive function in Huntington's disease and schizophrenia. *Arch Neurol.* 1990; 47:418–422.

367. Goldberg WG, Tomlanovich MC. Domestic violence victims in the emergency room: New findings. *JAMA.* 1984;251:3259–3268.

368. Golden C. Psychologic and neuropsychologic aspects of Tourette's syndrome. *Neurol Clin.* 1984;21:91–102.

369. Goodman JD. Nymphomania and satyriasis. In: Mule S, ed. *Behavior in Excess,* New York: The Free Press;1981:246–263.

370. Goodwin DL. Alcohol in suicide and homicide. *Q J Stud Alcohol.* 1973;34:144–156.

371. Goodwin DW. Hereditary factors in alcoholism. *Hosp Practice.* 1978;13:121–130.

372. Goodwin DW. Alcoholism and heredity: A review of the hypothesis. *Arch Gen Psychiatry.* 1979;36:57–61.

373. Goodwin DW. *Alcoholism: The Facts.* New York: Oxford University Press; 1981.

374. Goodwin DW. Substance-induced and substance use disorders: Alcohol. In: Greist JH, Jefferson JW, Spitzer RL, eds. *Treatment of Mental Disorders.* New York: Oxford University Press; 1982:44–61.

375. Goodwin DW, Schulsinger F, Knop J, et al. Alcoholism and depression in adopted-out daughters of alcoholics. *Arch Gen Psychiatry.* 1977;34:751–755.

376. Goodwin FK, Jamison KR. *Manic-Depressive Illness.* New York: Oxford University Press; 1990.

377. Gottesman II, Shields J, Hanson DR. *Schizophrenia: The Epigenetic Puzzle.* New York: Cambridge University Press; 1982.

378. Gottlieb JS, Ashby MC, Knott JR. Primary behavior disorders and psychopathic personality. *Arch Neurol Psychiatry.* 1946;56:381–400.

379. Gould R, Miller BL, Goldberg MA, et al. The validity of hysterical signs and symptoms. *J Nerv Ment Dis.* 1986;174:593–597.

380. Grant I, Adams KM, Carlin AS, et al. Organic impairment in polydrug users: Risk factors. *Am J Psychiatry.* 1978;135:178–184.

381. Grant I, Atkinson JH. HIV disease: Brain-behavior. In: Ostrow D, ed. *Behavioral Aspects of AIDS and Other STDS.* New York: Plenum; 1990.

382. Grant I, Judd LL. Neuropsychological and EEG disturbances in polydrug users. *Am J Psychiatry.* 1976;133:1039–1042.

383. Gray JA. *The Neuropsychology of Anxiety.* Oxford: Clarendon; 1982.

384. Green JB, Walcoff MR. Evoked potentials in multiple sclerosis. *Arch Neurol.* 1982;39:696–698.

385. Green MA, Curtis GC. Personality disorders in panic patients: Response to termination of anti-panic medication. *J Pers Disord* 1988;2:303–314.

386. Green RC, Pitman RK. Tourette syndrome and obsessive compulsive disorder. In: Jenike MA, Baer L, Minichiello WD, eds. *Obsessive-Compulsive Disorders: Theory and Management*. Littleton, Mass: PSG Publishing Co; 1986:147–164.

387. Green RS, Rau JH. The use of dyphenylhydantoin in compulsive eating disorders: Further studies. In: Vigersky RA, ed. *Anorexia Nervosa*. New York: Raven Press; 1977:377–382.

388. Greenblatt DJ, Sellers EM, Shader RI. Drug disposition in old age. *N Engl J Med*. 1982;306:1081–1087.

389. Griesinger W. *Mental Pathology and Therapeutics,* English trans of original German ed, 1845. London: Sydenham Society; 1867. New York: Hafner; 1965;

390. Greist JH, Jefferson JW, Marks IM. *Anxiety and Its Treatment: Help Is Available*. Washington, DC: American Psychiatric Press; 1986.

391. Greist JH, Jefferson JW, Spitzer RL, eds. *Treatment of Mental Disorders*. New York: Oxford University Press; 1982.

392. Gronwall D, Wrightson P. Delayed recovery of intellectual function after minor head injury. *Lancet*. 1974;2:605–609.

393. Grove WM, Eckert ED, Heston L, et al. Heritability of substance abuse and antisocial behavior: A study of monozygotic twins reared apart. *Biol Psychiatry*. 1990;27:1293–1304.

394. Grunebaum HU, Klerman GL. Wrist slashing. *Am J Psychiatry*. 1967;124:527–534.

395. Gualtieri CT. *Neuropsychiatry and Behavioral Pharmacology*. New York/Berlin: Springer-Verlag, 1990.

396. Gualtieri CT, Chandler M, Coons T, et al. Amantadine: A new clinical profile for traumatic brain injury. *Clin Neuropharmacol*. 1989;12:258–270.

397. Gunderson JG, Elliott GR. The interface between borderline personality disorder and affective disorder. *Am J Psychiatry*. 1985;142:277–288.

398. Gunderson JG, Siever LJ. Relatedness of schizotypal to schizophrenic disorders. *Schizophr Bull*. 1985;11:532–537. Editors' Introduction.

399. Gur RE. Positron emission tomography in psychiatric disorders. *Psychiatr Ann*. 1985;15:268–271.

400. Gur RE, Skolnick BE, Gur RC, et al. Brain function in psychiatric disorders: II. Regional cerebral blood flow in medicated unipolar depressives. *Arch Gen Psychiatry*. 1984;41:695–699.

401. Gurland BJ. The comparative frequency of depression in various adult age groups. *J Gerontol*. 1976;31:283–292.

402. Gurland BJ. Epidemiology of psychiatric disorders. In: Sadavoy J, Lazarus LW, Jarvik LF, eds. *Comprehensive Review of Geriatric Psychiatry*. Washington, DC: American Psychiatric Press; 1991:25–40.

403. Gurland BJ, Copeland J, Kuriansky J, et al. *The Mind and Mood of Aging*. New York: Haworth Press; 1983.

404. Guy W. *ECDEU Assessment Manual for Psychopharmacology, Revised 1976*. Washington, DC: U.S. Department of Health, Education, and Welfare; 1976.

405. Guze BH, Baxter LR Jr, Schwartz JM, et al. PET offers insights into the physiology of mood disorders. *J Clin Brain Imaging*. 1990;1:13–22.

406. Guze SB. *Criminality and Psychiatric Disorders.* New York: Oxford University Press; 1976.

407. Guze SB, Robins E. Suicide and primary affective disorders. *Br J Psychiatry.* 1970;117:437–438.

408. Guze SB, Wolfgram ED, McKinney JK, et al. Psychiatric illness in the families of convicted criminals: A study of 519 first degree relatives. *Dis Nerv System.* 1967;28:651–659.

409. Halbreich U, Endicott J. Relationship of dysphoric premenstrual changes to depressive disorders. *Acta Psychiatr Scand.* 1985;71:331–338.

410. Haldeman S, Glick M, Bhatia NN, et al. Colonometry, cystometry and evoked potentials in multiple sclerosis. *Arch Neurol.* 1982;39:698–701.

411. Hales RE, Frances AJ. *Psychiatry Update, American Psychiatric Association Annual Review,* vol. 6. Washington, DC: American Psychiatric Press; 1987; Section IV.

412. Hall RCW. Medically induced psychiatric disease: An overview. In: Hall RCW, ed. *Psychiatric Presentation of Medical Illness, Somatopsychic Disorders.* New York: SP Medical and Scientific Books; 1980:3–9.

413. Hallstrom T. Point prevalence of major depressive disorder in a Swedish urban female population. *Acta Psychiatr Scand.* 1984;69:52–59.

414. Halmi KA. Anorexia nervosa: Demographic and clinical features in 94 cases. *Psychosom Med.* 1974;36:18–25.

415. Halmi KA, Eckert E, La Du T, et al: Anorexia nervosa: Treatment efficacy of cyproheptadine and amitriptyline. *Arch Gen Psychiatry.* 1986;43:177–181.

416. Halmi KA, Falk JR. Common physiological changes in anorexia nervosa. *Int J Eating Disord.* 1981;1:16–27.

417. Hamilton M, ed. *Fish's Outline of Psychiatry.* 3rd ed. Bristol: John Wright & Sons, Ltd; 1978.

418. Hammond WA. *A Treatise on Insanity in Its Medical Relations,* 1883. In series: Mental Illness and Social Policy. The American Experience. New York: Arno Press; 1973.

419. Harris EL, Noyes R, Crowe RR, et al. A family study of agoraphobia: Report of a pilot study. *Arch Gen Psychiatry.* 1983;40:1061–1064.

420. Harris MJ, Jeste DV. Late-onset schizophrenia: A review. *Schizophr Bull.* 1988;14:39–55.

421. Harrison MS. Notes on the clinical features and pathology of post-concussional vertigo with special reference to positional nystagmus. *Brain.* 1956;79:474–482.

422. Harvey I, Ron MA, Murray R, et al. MRI in schizophrenia: Basal ganglia and white matter T1 times. *Psychol Med.* 1991;21:587–598.

423. Haslam J. *Observations on Madness and Melancholy,* 1809 facsimile. New York: Arno Press; 1976.

424. Hatsukami J, Mitchell J, Eckert E, et al. Affective disorder and substance abuse in women with bulimia. *Psychol Med.* 1984;14:701–704.

425. Hauser P, Altschuler LL, Berretlini W, et al. Temporal lobe measurement in primary affective disorder by magnetic resonance imaging. *J Neuropsychiatry.* 1989;1:128–134.

426. Hay DP. Electroconvulsive therapy in the medically ill elderly. *Convul Ther.* 1989;5:8–16.

427. Hayes SG, Goldsmith BK. Psychosensory symptomatology in anticonvulsant-responsive psychiatric illness. *Ann Clin Psychiatry.* 1991;3:27–35.

428. Hayflick L, Moorhead P. The serial cultivation of human diploid cells. *Exp Cell Res.* 1961;25:585–621.

429. Hecaen H, Albert ML, Disorders of mental functioning related to frontal lobe pathology. In: Benson DF, Blumer D, eds. *Psychiatric Aspects of Neurologic Disease,* vol. 1. New York: Grune & Stratton; 1975;137–149.

430. Hecker E. Die hebephrenie. *Arch Pathol Anat Physiol Clin Med.* 1871;52:394–429.

431. Heilman KM, Valenstein E, eds. *Clinical Neuropsychology.* 2nd ed. New York: Oxford University Press; 1985.

432. Heiman JR, Lo Piccolo J. Clinical outcome of sex therapy. *Arch Gen Psychiatry.* 1983;40:443–449.

433. Heinroth JC; Schmorak J, trans (from the 1818 text). *Textbook of Disturbances of Marital Life,* vols 1 and 2. Baltimore: Johns Hopkins Press; 1975.

434. Heiser JF, Gillin JC. The reversal of anticholinergic drug-induced delirium and coma with physostigmine. *Am J Psychiatry.* 1971;127:1050–1054.

435. Hellman DS, Blackman N. Enuresis, firesetting and cruelty to animals: A triad predictive of adult crime. *Am J Psychiatry.* 1966;123:1431–1435.

436. Helzer JE, Robins LE, McEvoy L. Post-traumatic stress disorder in the general population: Findings of the epidemiologic catchment area survey. *N Engl J Med.* 1987;317:1630–1634.

437. Hendler N, Uematesu S, Long D. Thermographic validation of physical complaints in psychogenic pain patients. *Psychosom.* 1982;23:283–287.

438. Heninger GR, French NH, Slavinsky AT, et al. A short clinical rating scale for use by nursing personnel: 2. Reliability, validity and application. *Arch Gen Psychiatry.* 1970;23:241–248.

439. Herbert M, Jacobson S. Late paraphrenia. *Br J Psychiatry.* 1967;113:461–469.

440. Herjanic M, Meyer DA. Psychiatric illness in homicide victims. *Am J Psychiatry.* 1976;133:691–693.

441. Herzog DB, ed. Recent advances in bulimia nervosa. *J Clin Psychiatry.* 1991;52(suppl).

442. Herzog DB, Norman DK, Gordon C, et al. Sexual conflict in males. *Am J Psychiatry.* 1984;141:989–990.

443. Heston LL. The genetics of schizophrenia and schizoid disease. *Science.* 1970;167:249–256.

444. Heston LL, White TA, Mastri AR. Pick's disease. Clinical genetics and natural history. *Arch Gen Psychiatry.* 1987;44:409–411.

445. Heyman A, Fillenbaum G, Prosnitz B, et al. Estimated prevalence of dementia among elderly black and white community residents. *Arch Neurol.* 1991;48:594–598.

446. Hier DB, Mondlock J, Caplan LR. Behavioral abnormalities after right hemisphere stroke. *Neurology.* 1983;33:337–344.

447. Hill D, Watterson D. Electroencephalographic studies of psychopathic personalities. *J Neurol Psychiatry.* 1942;5:47–65.

448. Himmelhoch JM, Neil JF, May SJ, et al. Age, dementia, dyskinesias and lithium response. *Am J Psychiatry.* 1980;137:941–945.

449. Hofman FG. *A Handbook on Drug and Alcohol Abuse, The Biomedical Aspects.* New York: Oxford University Press; 1975:116–128.

450. Hohman LB. A review of one-hundred and forty-four cases of affective disorders: After seven years. *Am J Psychiatry.* 1937;94:303–308.

451. Holland AJ, Hall A, Murray R, et al. Anorexia nervosa study of 34 twin pairs and one set of triplets. *Br J Psychiatry.* 1984;145:414–419.

452. Holland-Bernard: Vladimir Horowitz, 86, virtuoso pianist, dies. *The New York Times 139:* November 6, 1989. Obituary.

453. Holmes T. Life situations, emotions and disease. *Psychosom.* 1978;19:747–754.

454. Honigfeld G, Gillis RD, Klett CJ. NOISE-30: A treatment sensitive ward behavior scale. *Psychol Rep.* 1966;19:180–182.

455. Hoover CF, Insel TR. Families of origin in obsessive-compulsive disorder. *J Nerv Ment Dis.* 1984;172:207–215.

456. Horn J, Cattell R. Age differences in fluid and crystallized intelligence. *Acta Psychol.* 1967;26:107–129.

457. Hughes PL, Lloyd AW, Cunningham CJ, et al. A controlled trial using desipramine for bulimia. *Arch Gen Psychiatry.* 1986;43:182–187.

458. Hunt GL, Hunt MW. Female-female pairing in Western gulls (Larus occidentalis) in southern California. *Science.* 1977;196:1466–1467.

459. Hunter R, Logue V, McMenemy WH. Temporal lobe epilepsy supervening on longstanding transvestism and fetishism. *Epilepsia.* 1963;4:160–165.

460. Hunter R, Macalpine I. *Three Hundred Years of Psychiatry 1535–1860.* London: Oxford University Press; 1963.

461. Hutchings B, Mednick S. Criminality in adoptees and their adoptive and biological parents: A pilot study. In: Mednick S, Christiansen KO, eds. *Biosocial Bases of Criminal Behavior.* New York: Gardner; 1977:127–141.

462. Hymowitz P, Frances A, Jacobsberg LB, et al. Neuroleptic treatment of schizotypal personality disorders. *Compr Psychiatry.* 1986;27:267–271.

463. Incagnoli T, Kane R. Neuropsychological functioning in Gilles de la Tourette's syndrome. *J Clin Neuropsychol.* 1981;3:165–169.

464. Insel TR, Akiskal HS. Obsessive-compulsive disorder with psychotic features: A phenomenologic analysis. *Am J Psychiatry.* 1986;143:1527–1533.

465. International Workshop on Aggression and Epilepsy. The nature of aggression during epileptic seizures. *N Engl J Med.* 1981;305:711–716.

466. Irwin M, Schuckit M, Smith TL. Clinical importance of age at onset in type I and type II primary alcoholics. *Arch Gen Psychiatry.* 1990;47:320–324.

467. Jablinsky A, Sartorius N, Gulbinat W, et al. Characteristics of depressive patients contacting psychiatric services in four cultures: A report from the WHO collaborative study on the assessment of depressive disorders. *Acta Psychiatr Scand.* 1981;63:367–383.

468. Jaffe P, Wolfe D. Wilson SK, et al. Family violence and child adjustment: A comparative analysis of girls' and boys' behavioral symptoms. *Am J Psychiatry.* 1986;143:74–77.

469. Jain NC, Budd RD, Budd BS. Growing abuse of phencyclidine: California "angel dust." *N Engl J Med.* 1977;297:673.

470. Jampala VC. Anorexia nervosa: A variant form of affective disorder? *Psychiatr Ann.* 1985;15:698–704.

471. Jampala VC, Abrams R. Mania secondary to left and right hemisphere damage. *Am J Psychiatry.* 1983;140:1197–1199.

472. Jampala VC, Abrams R, Taylor, MA. Mania with emotional blunting. Affective disorder or schizophrenia? *Am J Psychiatry.* 1985;142:608–612.

473. Jampala VC, Sierles FS, Taylor MA. The use of DSM-III in the United States: A case of not going by the book. *Compr Psychiatry.* 1988;29:39–47.

474. Jampala VC, Taylor MA, Abrams R. The diagnostic implications of formal thought disorder in mania and schizophrenia: A reassessment. *Am J Psychiatry.* 1989; 146:459–463.

475. Jarrett RB, Eaves GG, Grannemann BD, et al. Clinical, cognitive, and demographic predictors of response to cognitive therapy for depression: A preliminary report. *Psychiatry Res.* 1991;37:245–260.

476. Jaspers K, Hoenig J, Hamilton MW, trans. *General Psychopathology* (from the original 1923 edition). Chicago: University of Chicago Press; 1963.

477. Jefferson JW, Greist JH, Ackerman KL. *Lithium Encyclopedia for Clinical Practice.* Washington, DC: American Psychiatric Press; 1983:186–192.

478. Jellinek EM. *The Disease Concept of Alcoholism.* New Haven, Conn: College and University Press; 1960.

479. Jellinek EM. Referrals from a psychiatric emergency room: Relationship of compliance to demographic and interview variables. *Am J Psychiatry.* 1978;135:209–213.

480. Jenike MA. Obsessive compulsive and related disorders: A hidden epidemic. *N Engl J Med.* 1989;321:539–541.

481. Jenike MA. Drug treatment of obsessive-compulsive disorder. In: Jenike MA, Baer L, Minichiello WE, eds. *Obsessive-Compulsive Disorders: Theory and Management.* Littleton, Mass: Year Book Medical Publishers; 1990.

482. Jenike MA, Baer L, Ballentine T, et al. Cingulotomy for refractory obsessive-compulsive disorder. *Arch Gen Psychiatry.* 1991;48:548–555.

483. Jenike MA, Hyman S, Baer L, et al. A controlled trial of fluvoxamine in obsessive compulsive disorder: Implications for a serotonergic theory. *Am J Psychiatry.* 1990;147:1209–1215.

484. Jeste DV, Harris MJ, Pearlson GD, et al. Late-onset schizophrenia: Studying clinical validity. *Psychiatr Clin North Am.* 1988;11:1–14.

485. Jeste DV, Lohr JB, Goodwin FK. Neuroanatomical studies of major affective disorders: A review and suggestions for further research. *Br J Psychiatry.* 1988;153:444–459.

486. Joffe RT. The pharmacotherapy of depression. *J Psychiatry Neurosci.* 1991;16 (suppl 1):4–9.

487. Joffe RT, Singer W. Thyroid hormone potentiation of antidepressants. Abstract of paper presented at 141st Annual Meeting of the American Psychiatric Association, May 1988.

488. Joffe RT, Swinson RP, Regan JJ. Personality features of obsessive-compulsive disorder. *Am J Psychiatry.* 1988;145:1127–1129.

489. Johnson FN, ed. *Depression and Mania, Modern Lithium Therapy.* Oxford/Washington, DC: IRL Press; 1987.

490. Johnstone EC, Marsh W. Acetylator status and response to phenelzine in depressed patients. *Lancet.* 1973;1:567–570.

491. Jones IH. Observations on schizophrenic stereotypies. *Compr Psychiatry.* 1965; 6:323–335.

492. Judd LL, Hubbard B, Janowsky DS, et al. The effect of lithium carbonate on the cognitive functions of normal subjects. *Arch Gen Psychiatry.* 1977;34:355–357.

493. Kahlbaum KL: *Die Gruppierung der Psychischen Krankheiten und die Einteilung der Seelenstoerungen.* Danzig: A.W. Kafemann; 1863.

494. Kahlbaum KL. *Catatonia.* Baltimore: Johns Hopkins University Press, 1873/1973.

495. Kane JM. The use of depot neuroleptics: Clinical experience in the United States. *J Clin Psychiatry.* 1984;45:5–12.

496. Kane JM, Rifkin A, Woerner M, et al. Low dose neuroleptic treatment of outpatient schizophrenics. *Arch Gen Psychiatry.* 1983;40:893–896.

497. Kaplun D, Reich R. The murdered child and his killers. *Am J Psychiatry.* 1976; 133:809–812.

498. Kasanin J. The acute schizoaffective psychoses. *Am J Psychiatry.* 1933;13:97–126.

499. Kassett JA, Gershon ES, Maxwell ME, et al. Psychiatric disorders in the first-degree relatives of probands with bulimia nervosa. *Am J Psychiatry.* 1989;146:1468–1471.

500. Kasvikis YG, Tsakiris F, Marks IM, et al. Past history of anorexia nervosa in women with obsessive compulsive disorder. *Int J Eating Disord.* 1986;5:1069–1075.

501. Katon W. *Panic Disorder in the Medical Setting,* National Institute of Mental Health Washington, DC: Government Printing Office; 1989. U.S. Department of Health and Human Services Publication ADM 89-1629.

502. Katona CLE: Puerperal mental illness: Comparisons with nonpuerperal controls. *Br J Psychiatry.* 1982;141:447–452.

503. Katz JL. Eating disorder and affective disorder: Relatives or merely chance acquaintances? *Compr Psychiatry.* 1987;28:220–228.

504. Katzman R. Alzheimer's disease. *N Engl J Med.* 1986;314:964–973.

505. Kavey NB, Whyte J, Resor SR Jr, et al. Somnambulism in adults. *Neurology* 1990;40:745–752.

506. Kay DWK, Roth M. Environmental and hereditary factors in the schizophrenia of old age ("late paraphrenia"), and their bearing on the general problem of causation in schizophrenia. *J Ment Sci.* 1961;107:649–686.

507. Kaye W, Gwirtsman NC, eds. *The Treatment of Normal Weight Bulimia.* Washington, DC: American Psychiatric Press; 1985.

508. Keck PE, Pope HG Jr, Cohen BM, et al. Risk factors for neuroleptic malignant syndrome. *Arch Gen Psychiatry.* 1989;46:914–918.

509. Keller MB, Klerman GL, Lavori PW, et al. Treatment received by depressed patients. *JAMA.* 1982;248:1848–1855.

510. Kellner CH, Rubinow DR, Gold PW, et al. Relationship of cortisol hypersecretion to brain CT scan alterations in depressed patients. *Psychiatry Res.* 1983;8:191–197.

511. Kellner CH, Uhde TW. Ct scanning in panic disorders. Presented at the 141st an-

nual meeting of the American Psychiatric Association, Canada, May 1988. Abstract 37A.

512. Kendell RE, Cooper JE, Gourley AJ, et al. Diagnostic criteria of American and British psychiatrists. *Arch Gen Psychiatry*. 1971;25:123–130.

513. Kendler KS. The genetics of schizophrenia and related disorders: A review. In: Dunner DL, Gershon ES, Barrett JE, eds. *Relatives at Risk for Mental Disorder*. New York: Raven Press; 1988:247–266.

514. Kendler KS. The nosologic validity of paranoia (simple delusional disorder): A review. *Arch Gen Psychiatry*. 1980;37:699–706.

515. Kendler KS. Mood-incongruent psychotic affective illness. A historical and empirical review. *Arch Gen Psychiatry*. 1991;48:362–369.

516. Kendler KS, Gruenberg AM. Genetic relationship between paranoid personality disorder and the "schizophrenic spectrum" disorders. *Am J Psychiatry*. 1982; 139:1185–1186.

517. Kendler KS, Gruenberg AM, Tsuang MT. Psychiatric illness in first-degree relatives of patients with paranoid psychosis, schizophrenia, and medical illness. *Br J Psychiatry*. 1985;147:524–531.

518. Kendler KS, Gruenberg AM, Tsuang MT. Psychiatric illness in first-degree relatives of schizophrenic and surgical control patients. *Arch Gen Psychiatry*. 1985;140:827–832.

519. Kendler KS, Hays P. Paranoid psychosis (delusional disorder) and schizophrenia: A family history. *Arch Gen Psychiatry*. 1981;38:547–551.

520. Kendler KS, MacLean C, Neale N, et al. The genetic epidemiology of bulimia nervosa. *Am J Psychiatry*. 1991;148:1627–1637.

521. Kennard MA, Bueding E, Wortis WB. Some biochemical and electroencephalographic changes in delirium tremens. *Q J Stud Alcohol*. 1945;6:4–14.

522. Kennedy JL, Giuffra LA, Moises HW, et al. Evidence against linkage of schizophrenia to markers on chromosome 5 in a Northern Swedish pedigree. *Nature*. 1988;336:167–170.

523. Kenny AR. *Physiology of Aging: A synopsis*. 3rd ed. Chicago: Year Book Medical Publishers; 1989.

524. Kenyon FE. Hypochondriasis: A clinical study. *Br J Psychiatry*. 1964;110:478–488.

525. Kenyon FE. Hypochondriacal states. *Br J Psychiatry*. 1976;129:1–14.

526. Kety SS, Rosenthal D, Wender PH, et al. The types and prevalences of mental illness in the biological and adoptive families of adopted schizophrenics. In: Rosenthal D, Kety SS, eds. *The Transmission of Schizophrenia*. London: Pergamon Press; 1968:345–362.

527. Kidd KK, Prusoff BA, Cohen DJ. Familial pattern of Gilles de la Tourette syndrome. *Arch Gen Psychiatry*. 1980;37:1336–1339.

528. Kieber HD, Topazian M, Gaspari J, et al. Clonidine and naltrexone in the outpatient treatment of heroin withdrawal. *Am J Drug Alcohol Abuse*. 1987;13:1–5.

529. Killam KF, Killam EK. Drug action on pathways involving the reticular formation. In: Jasper HH, et al, eds. *Reticular Formation of the Brain,* Boston: Little, Brown; 1958:111–122.

530. Kimball CP. Psychosomatic theories and their contributions to chronic illness. In: Usdin G, ed. *Psychiatric Medicine*. New York: Brunner/Mazel; 1977.

531. Kimoff RJ, Cosio MG, McGregor M. Clinical features and treatment of obstructive sleep apnea. *Can Med Assoc J*. 1991;144:689–695.

532. Klass ET, DiNardo PA, Barlow DH. DSM-III-R personality diagnoses in anxiety disorder patients. *Compr Psychiatry*. 1989;30:251–258.

533. Kleist K. Schizophrenic symptoms and cerebral pathology. *J Ment Sci*. 1960; 106:246–255.

534. Klett CJ, Caffey E. Evaluating the long-term need for antiparkinson drugs by chronic schizophrenics. *Arch Gen Psychiatry*. 1972;26:374–379.

535. Kline NS, Wren JC, Cooper TB, et al. Evaluation of lithium therapy in chronic and periodic alcoholism. *Am J Med Sci*. 1974;268:15–22.

536. Kling AS, Metter J, Riege WH, et al. Comparison of PET measurement of local brain glucose metabolism and CAT measurement of brain atrophy in chronic schizophrenia and depression. *Am J Psychiatry*. 1986;143:175–180.

537. Klompenhouwer JL, van Hulst AM. Classification of postpartum psychosis: A study of 250 mother and baby admissions in the Netherlands. *Acta Psychiatr Scand*. 1991;84:255–261.

538. Knesevich JW. Successful treatment of obsessive-compulsive disorder with clonidine hydrochloride. *Am J Psychiatry*. 1982;139:364–365.

539. Knights EB, Folstein MF. Suspected emotional and cognitive disturbance in medical patients. *Ann Intern Med*. 1977;87:723–724.

540. Koella WP, Trimble MR, eds. Temporal lobe epilepsy, mania, and schizophrenia and the limbic system. *Advances in Biological Psychiatry*, vol 84. Basel: S. Karger; 1982.

541. Koenigsberg HW, Kaplan RD, Gilmore MM, et al. The relationship between syndrome and personality disorder in DSM-III: Experience with 2,462 patients. *Am J Psychiatry*. 1985;142:207–212.

542. Kohn RR. Causes of death in very old people. *JAMA* 1982;247:2793–2797.

543. Kolarsky A, Freund K, Marchek J, et al. Male sexual deviation. *Arch Gen Psychiatry*. 1967;17:735–743.

544. Kolb B, Whishaw IQ. *Fundamentals of Human Neuropsychology*. 3rd ed. New York: WH Freeman & Co, 1990.

545. Kolle K. *Grosse Nervenaerzte: Emil Kraepelin*, vol 1. Stuttgart: Thieme; 1956.

546. Koob GF, Bloom FE. Cellular and molecular mechanisms of drug dependence. *Science*. 1988;242:715–728.

547. Koranyi EK. Morbidity and rate of undiagnosed physical illness in psychiatric clinic population. *Arch Gen Psychiatry*. 1979;36:414–419.

548. Kosten TR, Rounsaville BJ, Kosten TA, et al. Gender differences in the specificity of alcoholism transmission among the relatives of opioid addicts. *J Nerv Ment Dis*. 1991;179:392–400.

549. Kozel NJ, Adams EH. Epidemiology of drug abuse: An overview. *Science*. 1986;234:970–974.

550. Kraepelin E. *Psychiatrie*. Leipzig: Weiner; 1893.

551. Kraepelin E. *Psychiatrie: Ein Lehrbuch fur Studierende und Arzte*. 5th ed. Leipzig: Barth; 1896.

552. Kraepelin E, Johnstone J, trans. *Lectures on Clinical Psychiatry*. London: Bailliere, Tindall & Cox; 1904.

553. Kraepelin E. *Psychiatrie,* vol. 3. 8th ed. Leipzig: Johann Ambrosius Barth; 1913.

554. Kraepelin E, Barclay RM (trans), Robertson GM (ed). *Dementia Praecox and Paraphrenia*. Huntington, NY: Robert E. Krieger; 1971. Facsimile of 1919 edition.

555. Kraepelin E, Barclay RM, trans; Robertson GM, ed. *Manic Depressive Insanity and Paranoia*. Edinburgh: E & S Livingston; 1921. Reprinted New York; Arno Press; 1976.

556. Kraft-Ebing RV, Rebman FJ, trans. *Psychopathia Sexualis*. English translation of 12th German ed. New York: Physicians and Surgeons Book Co; 1927.

557. Kramer KK, LaPiana FG, Appleton B. Ocular malingering and hysteria: Diagnosis and management. *Surv Ophthalmol*. 1979;24:89–96.

558. Kramer M. Cross-national study of diagnosis of the mental disorders: Origin of problem. *Am J Psychiatry*. 1969;125(suppl):1–11.

559. Krausz Y, Cohen D, Konstantini S, et al. Brain SPECT imaging in temporal lobe epilepsy. *Neuroradiology*. 1991;33:274–276.

560. Kretschmer E, E. Miller, trans. *Physique and Character. An Investigation of the Nature of Constitution and Theory of Temperament*. New York: Cooper Square Publishers; 1970.

561. Krishna NR, Taylor MA, Abrams R. Response to lithium carbonate. *Biol Psychiatry*. 1978;13:601–606.

562. Kurionsky JB, Gurland BJ, Spitzer RL, et al. Trends in the frequency of schizophrenia by different diagnostic criteria. *Am J Psychiatry*. 1977;134:631–636.

563. Kutcher SP, Blackwood DHR, Gaskell DF, et al. Auditory P300 does not differentiate borderline personality disorder from schizotypal personality disorder. *Biol Psychiatry*. 1989;26:766–774.

564. Kutcher SP, Blackwood DHR, St. Clair D, et al. Auditory P300 in borderline personality disorder and schizophrenia. *Arch Gen Psychiatry*. 1987;44:645–650.

565. Kutchins H, Kirk, SA. The reliability of DSM-III: A critical review. *Social Work Research and Abstracts*. 1986;22:3–12.

566. Lader M. Behavior and anxiety: Physiologic mechanisms. *J Clin Psychiatry*. 1983;44:5–10.

567. Lane RD, Glazer WM, Hansen TE, et al. Assessment of tardive dyskinesia using the Abnormal Involuntary Movement Scale. *J Nerv Ment Dis*. 1985;173:353–357.

568. Lancet Editorial: Transsexualism. *Lancet*. 1991;338:603–604.

569. Landre N, Taylor MA, Kerns K. Language functioning in schizophrenia and aphasic patients. *Neuropsychiatry, Neuropsychology, and Behavioral Neurology*. 1992;5:7–14.

570. Langdon N, Welsh KI, van Dam M, et al. Genetic markers in narcolepsy. *Lancet*. 1984;2:1178–1180.

571. Langevin R, Paitich D, Orchard B, et al. The role of alcohol, drugs, suicide attempts and situational strains in homicide committed by offenders seen for psychiatric assessment: A controlled study. *Acta Psychiatr Scand*. 1982;66:229–242.

572. Langfeldt G. *The Schizophreniform States*. Copenhagen: Munksgaard; 1939.

573. Larny PP. *Prescribing for the Elderly,* Littleton, Mass: PSG Publishing; 1980.

574. Larson G, Swartz C, Abrams R. Duration of ECT-induced tachycardia as a measure of seizure length. *Am J Psychiatry*. 1984;141:1269–1271.

575. Learoyd BM. Psychotropic drugs in the aging patient. *Med J Aust*. 1972;1:1131–1133.

576. Leckman JF, Clubb MM, Pauls DL. Comorbidity of panic disorder and major depression: A review of epidemiological and genetic data. In: Ballenger JC, ed. *Clinical Aspects of Panic Disorder, Frontiers of Clinical Neuroscience Series,* vol. 9. New York: Wiley-Liss; 1990:141–149.

577. LeDoux JE, Wilson DH, Gazzaniga MS. Block design performance following callosal sectioning: Observations on functional recovery. *Arch Nerol*. 1978;35:506–508.

578. Leff J, Kuipers L, Berkowitz R, et al. A controlled trial of social intervention in the families of schizophrenic patients. *Br J Psychiatry*. 1982;141:121–134.

579. Leff J, Kuipers L, Berkowitz R, et al. Life events, relatives expressed emotion and maintenance neuroleptics in schizophrenic relapse. *Psychol Med*. 1983;13:799–806.

580. Lehmann HE. Affective disorders in the aged. In: Jarvik L, ed. *Psychiatric Clinics of North America: Aging*. Philadelphia: WB Saunders; 1982:27–44.

581. Leonhard K, Robins E, ed; Berman R, trans. *The Classification of Endogenous Psychoses*. 5th ed, (1957). New York: Irvington Publishers; 1979.

582. Lepola U, Nousiainen U, Puranen M, et al. EEG and CT findings in patients with panic disorder. *Biol Psychiatry*. 1990;28:721–727.

583. Lesser IM, Rubin RT, Pecknold JC, et al. Secondary depression in panic disorder and agoraphobia. *Arch Gen Psychiatry*. 1988;45:437–443.

584. LeVay S. A difference in hypothalamic structure between heterosexual and homosexual men. *Science*. 1991;253:1034–1037.

585. Levenson JL. Neuroleptic malignant syndrome. *Am J Psychiatry*. 1985;142:1137–1145.

586. Leventhal EA. Biological aspects. In: Sadavoy J, Lazarus LW, Jarvik LF, eds. *Comprehensive Review of Geriatric Psychiatry*. Washington, DC: American Psychiatric Press; 1991;55–78.

587. Levin AB, Ramirez LF, Katy J. The use of stereotactic chemical hypophysectomy in the treatment of thalamic pain syndrome. *J Neurosurg*. 1983;59:1002–1006.

588. Levin N, Switzer M. *Voice and Speech Disorders: Medical Aspects*. Springfield, Ill: Charles C Thomas; 1962.

589. Levinson DF, Simpson GM. Antipsychotic drug side effects. In: Hales RE, Frances AJ, eds. *Psychiatry Update: American Psychiatric Association Annual Review,* vol 6. Washington, DC: American Psychiatric Press; 1987:704–723.

590. Kevkoff SE, Besdine R, Wetle T. Acute confusional states (delirium) in the hospitalized elderly. In: Eisdorfer C, ed. *Annual Review of Gerontology and Geriatrics,* vol 6. New York: Springer Publishing; 1986:1–26.

591. Levy J. The origin of lateral assymetry. In: Harnad S, Doty R, Goldstein L, eds. *Lateralization in the Nervous System*. New York: Academic Press; 1977:195–209.

592. Levy J. Psychological implications of bilateral assymetry. In: Diamond S, Beaumont J, eds. *Hemisphere Function in the Human Brain*. New York: Halstead Press; 1974:121–183.

593. Levy ST, Forrest JR, Heninger GR. Lithium-induced diabetes insipidus: Manic symptoms, brain and electrolyte correlates, and chlorothiazide treatment. *AM J Psychiatry.* 1973;130:1014–1018.

594. Lewis A. Melancholia: A historical review. In: Lewis AJ. *The State of Psychiatry Essays and Addresses.* New York: Science House; 1967:71–110.

595. Lezak M. *Neuropsychological Assessment.* 3rd ed. New York: Oxford University Press; 1983.

596. Lidvall HF, Linderoth B, Norlin B. Causes of the post-concussional syndrome. *Acta Neurol Scand.* 1974;50(suppl 56).

597. Lieber CS. The metabolism of alcohol. *Sci Am.* 1974;234:25–31.

598. Liebowitz MR, Fyer AJ, Gorman JM, et al. Tricyclic therapy of the DSM-III anxiety disorders: A review with implications for further research. *J Psychiatr Res.* 1988;22(suppl 1):7–31.

599. Lilienfeld SO, Van Valkenburg C, Larntz K, et al. The relationship of histrionic personality disorder to antisocial personality and somatization disorders. *Am J Psychiatry.* 1986;143:718–722.

600. Lilly R, Cummings JL, Benson DF, et al. The human Klüver-Bucy syndrome. *Neurology.* 1983;33:1141–1145.

601. Lipkin KM, Dyrud J, Meyer GG. The many faces of mania. *Arch Gen Psychiatry.* 1970;22:262–267.

602. Lipowski ZJ. *Delirium: Acute Confusional States.* New York: Oxford University Press; 1990.

603. Lippman S, Manshadi M, Baldwin H, et al. Cerebellar vermis dimensions on computerized tomographic scans of schizophrenia and bipolar patients. *Am J Psychiatry.* 1982;139:667–670.

604. Liskow B. Substance induced and substance use disorders: Barbiturates and similarly acting sedative hypnotics. In: Greist JH, Jefferson JW, Spitzer RL, eds. *Treatment of Mental Disorders.* New York: Oxford University Press; 1982:62–77.

605. Liss R, Frances A. Court-mandated treatment: Dilemmas for hospital psychiatry. *Am J Psychiatry.* 1975;132:924–927.

606. Liston EH. Delirium in the aged. In: Jarvik L, ed. *Psychiatric Clinics of North America: Aging.* Philadelphia: WB Saunders; 1982:49–66.

607. Littman RE, Farberow NL. Emergency evaluation of self-destructive potential. In: Farberow NL, Shneidman ES, eds. *Cry for Help.* New York: McGraw-Hill; 1961.

608. Logue CM, Crowe RR, Bean JA. A family study of anorexia nervosa and bulimia. *Compr Psychiatry.* 1989;30:179–188.

609. Loranger AW, Tulis EH. Family history of alcoholism in borderline personality disorder. *Arch Gen Psychiatry.* 1985;42:153–157.

610. Lucas PB, Gardner DL, Cowdry RW, et al. Cerebral structure in borderline personality. *Psychiatry Res.* 1989;27:111–115.

611. Luria AR, Hough B, trans. *The Working Brain: An Introduction to Neuropsychology.* New York: Basic Books; 1973.

612. Lydiard RB. Co-existing depression and anxiety: Special diagnostic and treatment issues. *J Clin Psychiatry.* 1991;52(suppl 6):48–54.

613. Lyon M, Barr CE, Cannon TD, et al. Fetal neural development and schizophrenia. *Schizophr Bull.* 1989;15:149–160.

614. Lyttkens L, Soderberg V, Wetterberg L. Increased lithium erythrocyte to plasma ratio in manic depressive illness. *Lancet.* 1973;1:40.

615. Macdonald JM. *The Murderer and His Victim.* Springfield, Ill: Charles C Thomas; 1961.

616. Mace NL, Rabins PV. *The 36-Hour Day: A Family Guide to Caring for Persons with Alzheimer's Disease, Related Dementing Illness, and Memory Loss in Later Life.* Baltimore: Johns Hopkins University Press; 1982.

617. MacNeil S, Jennings G, Eastwood PR, et al. Lithium and the antidiuretic hormone. *Br J Clin Pharamcol.* 1976;3:305–313.

618. Madden DJ, Lion Jr, Penna MW. Assaults on psychiatrists by patients. *Am J Psychiatry.* 1976;133:422–425.

619. Maddox GL, Williams JR. Drinking behavior of negro collegians. *Q J Stud Alcohol.* 1968;29:117–129.

620. Maes M, Cosyns P, Maes L, et al. Clinical subtypes of unipolar depression: Part I. A validation of the vital and nonvital clusters. *Psychiatry Res.* 1990;34:29–41.

621. Maes M, Maes L, Schotte C, et al. Clinical subtypes of unipolar depression: Part III. Quantitative differences in various biological markers between the cluster analytically generated nonvital and vital depression classes. *Psychiatry Res.* 1990;34:59–75.

622. Maes M, Schotte C, Maes L, et al. Clinical subtypes of unipolar depression: Part II. Quantitative and qualitative clinical differences between the vital and nonvital depressive groups. *Psychiatry Res.* 1990;34:43–57.

623. Maj M, Perris C. An approach to the diagnosis and classification of schizoaffective disorders for research purposes. *Acta Psychiatr Scand.* 1985;72:405–413.

624. Makeeva VL, Gol' davskaia IL, Pozdniakova SL. Somatic changes and side effects from use of lithium prophylaxis of affective disorders. *Sov Neurol R.* 1974;7:42–53.

625. Mann SC, Caroff SN. Lethal catatonia and neuroleptic malignant syndrome. *Am J Psychiatry.* 1987;144:1106–1107.

626. Mann SC, Caroff SN, Bleier HR, et al. Lethal catatonia. *Am J Psychiatry.* 1986;143:1374–1381.

627. Mann SC, Caroff SN, Bleier HR, et al. Electroconvulsive therapy of the lethal catatonia syndrome. *Convul Ther.* 1990;6:239–247.

628. Margolin R: Neuroimaging. In: Sadavoy J, Lazarus LW, Jarvik LF, eds. *Comprehensive Review of Geriatric Psychiatry.* Washington, DC: American Psychiatric Press; 1991:245–271.

629. Marinacci AA. Special type of temporal lobe (psychomotor) seizures following ingestion of alcohol. *Bull L A Neurol Soc.* 1963;28:241–250.

630. Mariotti S, Martino E, Cupini C, et al. Low serum thyroglobulin as a clue to the diagnosis of thyrotoxicosis factitia. *N Engl J Med.* 1982;307:410–412.

631. Marks IM. Review: Obsessive-compulsive disorders. In: Marks IM, ed. *Fears, Phobias and Rituals: Panic, Anxiety and Their Disorders.* New York: Oxford University Press; 1987:423–456.

632. Marks IM, Tobena A. What do the neurosciences tell us about anxiety disorders? *Psychol Med.* 1986;16:9–12.

633. Marsh R. Perceptual changes with aging. In: Busse EW, Blazer DG, eds. *Handbook of Geriatric Psychiatry.* New York: Van Nostrand Reinhold; 1980:147–168.

634. Maser JD, Cloninger CR, eds. *Comorbidity of Mood and Anxiety Disorders.* Washington, DC: American Psychiatric Press; 1990.

635. Matarazzo J. *Wechsler's Measurement and Appraisal of Adult Intelligence.* New York: Oxford University Press; 1972.

636. Mathew RJ: Cerebral blood flow in psychiatric disorders. *Psychiatr Ann.* 1985;15:257–261.

637. Mathew RJ, Margolin RA, Kessler RM. Cerebral function, blood flow, and metabolism: A new vista in psychatric research. *Integrative Psychiatry.* 1985;3:214–225.

638. Mathias DW. Cocaine-associated myocardial ischemia. *Am J Med.* 1986;81:675–678.

639. Mavissakalian M. Differential efficacy between tricyclic antidepressants and behavior therapy of panic disorder. In: Ballenger JC, ed. *Clinical Aspects of Panic Disorder, Frontiers of Clinical Neuroscience,* vol. 9. New York: Wiley-Liss; 1990;195–209.

640. Mavissakalian M, Hamann MS. DSM-III personality disorder in agoraphobia. *Compr Psychiatry.* 1986;27:471–479.

641. Mavissakalian M, Hamann MS, Jones B. Correlates of DSM-III personality disorder in obsessive-compulsive disorder. *Compr Psychiatry.* 1990;31:481–489.

642. May PRA. *Treatment of Schizophrenia: A Comparative Study of Five Treatment Methods.* New York: Science House; 1968.

643. Mayeaux R. Parkinson's disease: A review of cognitive and psychiatric disorders. *Neuropsychiatry, Neuropsychology, and Behavioral Neurology.* 1990;3:3–14.

644. McCabe MS. Reactive psychoses. *Acta Psychiatr Scand.* 1975;259(suppl).

645. McCarron MM, Boettger ML, Peck JJ. A case of neuroleptic malignant syndrome successfully treated with amantidine. *J Clin Psychiatry.* 1982;43:381–382.

646. McCartney JR, Palmateer LM. Assessment of cognitive deficit in geriatric patients. A study of physician behavior. *J Am Geriatr Soc.* 1985;33:467–471.

647. McDonald W, Husain MH, Doraiswamy PM, et al. *Diminished Caudate Volumes in Major Depression.* Presented at 143rd Annual Meeting of the American Psychiatric Association; New York; May 1990:20. Abstract.

648. McDougle CJ, Goodman WK, Price LH, et al. Neuroleptic addiction in fluvoxamine-refractory obsessive-compulsive disorder. *Am J Psychiatry.* 1990;147:652–654.

649. McElroy SL, Keck PE, Pope HG Jr, et al. Valproate in psychiatric disorders: Literature review and clinical guidelines. *J Clin Psychiatry.* 1989;50(suppl 3):23–29.

650. McGlashan TH. The borderline syndrome. I. Testing three diagnostic systems. *Arch Gen Psychiatry.* 1983;40:1311–1318.

651. McGlashan TH. The borderline syndrome. II. Is it a variant of schizophrenia or affective disorder? *Arch Gen Psychiatry.* 1983;40:1319–1323.

652. McGlashan TH. The schizotypal personality disorder. *Arch Gen Psychiatry.* 1986;43:329–334.

653. McHugh PR, Folstein MF. Psychiatric syndromes of Huntington's chorea. A clinical and phenomenological study. In: Benson DF, Blumer D, eds. *Psychiatric Aspects of Neurologic Disease,* vol. 1. New York: Grune & Stratton; 1975:267–286.

654. McHugh PR, Moran TH, Killilea M. The approaches to the study of human disorders in food ingestion and body weight maintenance. In: Schneider LH, Cooper SJ,

Halmi KA, eds. *The Psychobiology of Human Eating Disorders: Preclinical and Clinical Perspectives*. Ann NY Acad Sc. 1989;575:506–508.

655. McKay FE. Behavioral aspects of population dynamics in unisexual and bisexual poeciliopis. *Ecology*. 1971;52:778–790.
656. McKegney FP. The incidence and characteristics of patients with conversion reactions: 1. A general hospital consultation service sample. *Am J Psychiatry*. 1967;124:542–545.
657. McKinny WT. *Models of Mental Disorders: A New Comparative Psychiatry*. New York: Plenum Medical Book Co; 1988.
658. McNeil TF. Obstetric factors and perinatal injuries. In: Tsuang MT, Simpson JC, eds. *Handbook of Schizophrenia, Vol. 3, Nosology, Epidemiology, and Genetics*. New York: Elsevier; 1988.
659. Meadows J: The anatomic basis of prosopagnosia. *J Neurol Neurosurg Psychiatry*. 1974;37:489–501.
660. Mednick SA, Machon RA, Huttnen MD, et al. Adult schizophrenia following prenatal exposure to an influenza epidemic. *Arch Gen Psychiatry*. 1988;45:189–192.
661. Meduna LJ. General discussion of the cardiazol therapy. *Am J Psychiatry*. 1938;94(suppl):40–50.
662. Meehl PE. Schizotaxia, schizotypy, schizophrenia. *Am Psychol*. 1962;1:827–838.
663. Meehl PE. Schizotaxia revisited. *Arch Gen Psychiatry*. 1989;46:935–944.
664. Mellman TA, Uhde TW. Withdrawal syndrome with gradual tapering of alprazolam. *Am J Psychiatry*. 1986;143:1464–1469.
665. Mendelson JH. Biological concomitants of alcoholism. *N Engl J Med*. 1970; 283:24–32.
666. Mendelson JH. Marijuana. In: Meltzer HY, ed. *Psychopharmacology, The Third Generation of Progress*. New York: Raven Press; 1987:1565–1571.
667. Merritt R, Balogh D. The use of a backward masking paradigm to assess information processing among schizotypics: A reevaluation of Sternko and Woods. *J Nerv Ment Dis*. 1984;172:216–224.
668. Merry J, Reynolds CM, Bailey J, et al. Prophylactic treatment of alcoholism by lithium carbonate. *Lancet*. 1976;2:481–482.
669. Merskey H, Spear FG. *Pain: Psychological and Psychiatric Aspects*. London: Balliere, Tindall & Cassell; 1967.
670. Merskey H, Woodforde JM. Psychiatric sequelae of minor head injury. *Brain*. 1972;95:521–528.
671. Mesulam MM. Dissociative states with abnormal temporal lobe EEG, multiple personality and the illusion of possession. *Arch Neurol*. 1981;38:176–181.
672. Mesulam MM. *Principles of Behavioral Neurology*. Philadelphia: FA Davis; 1985.
673. Miller NS. Alcohol and drug dependence. In: Sadavoy J, Lazarus LW, Larvik LF, eds. *Comprehensive Review of Geriatric Psychiatry*. Washington, DC: American Psychiatric Press; 1991:387–401.
674. Miller NS, Chappel JN. History of the disease concept. In: Miller NS, ed. The disease concept of alcoholism and drug addiction I. *Psychiatr Ann*. 1991;21:196–205.
675. Millman RB. Drug abuse and drug dependence. In: Frances AJ, Hales RE, eds. *Psychiatry Update: American Psychiatric Association Annual Review*, vol 5. Washington, DC: American Psychiatric Press; 1986:120–232.

676. Millon T. *Disorders of Personality, DSM-III Axis II*. Toronto: John Wiley & Sons; 1981.

677. Minden SL, Schiffer RB. Depression and mood disorders in multiple sclerosis. *Neuropsychiatry, Neuropsychology, and Behavioral Neurology*. 1991;4:62–77.

678. Mirsky AF, Kornetsky C. On the dissimilar effects of drugs on the digit symbol substitution and continuous performance tests. *Psychopharmacologia*. 1964;5:161–177.

679. Mitchell-Heggs N, Kelly D, Richardson A. Stereotactic limbic leucotomy: A follow-up at 16 months. *Br J Psychiatry*. 1976;128:226–240.

680. Mitler MM, Hajdukovic R, Erman M, et al. Narcolepsy. *J Clin Neurophysiol*. 1990;7:93–118.

681. Molitch ME, Reichlin S. The amenorrhea, galactorrhea and hyperprolactinemia syndromes. *Adv Intern Med*. 1980;26:37–65.

682. Monahan J: *Predicting Violent Behavior: An Assessment of Clinical Techniques*. Beverly Hills, Calif: Sage; 1981.

683. Monroe RR. Episodic behavioral disorders and limbic ictus. *Compr Psychiatry*. 1985;26:466–479.

684. Montgomery MA, Clayton PJ, Friedhoff AJ. Psychiatric illness in Tourette syndrome patients and first-degree relatives. In: Friedhoff AJ, Chase TN, eds. *Gilles de la Tourette Syndrome*. New York: Raven Press; 1982:335–339.

685. Montgomery SA, Smeyatsky N, de Ruiter M, et al. Profiles of antidepressant activity with the Montgomery-Asberg Depression Rating Scale. *Acta Psychiatr Scand Suppl*. 1985;320:38–42.

686. Moore J. *Of Religious Melancholy*. London: By Her Majesty's Special Command; 1692.

687. Morel BA. *Traits des Maladies Mentales*. Paris: Victor Masson; 1860.

688. Morrison JR. Catatonia: Retarded and excited types. *Arch Gen Psychiatry*. 1973;28:39–41.

689. Morrison JR. Suicide in a case of Briquet's syndrome. *J Clin Psychiatry*. 1981;42:123.

690. Morrison J, Clancy J, Crowe R, et al. The Iowa 500: 1. Diagnostic validity in mania, depression and schizophrenia. *Arch Gen Psychiatry*. 1972;27:457–461.

691. Morse R, Litin E. Post-operative delirium: A study of etiologic factors. *Am J Psychiatry*. 1969;126:388–395.

692. Morstyn R, Duffy FH, McCarley RW. Altered P300 topography in schizophrenia. *Arch Gen Psychiatry*. 1983;40:729–734.

693. Munetz MR, Benjamin S. How to examine patients using the Abnormal Involuntary Movement Scale. *Hosp Community Psychiatry*. 1988;39:1172–1177.

694. Mungus D. Interictal behavior abnormality in temporal lobe epilepsy: A specific syndrome or nonspecific psychopathology? *Arch Gen Psychiatry*. 1982;39:108–111.

695. Murphy GE. The physician's responsibility for suicide: 1. An error of commission. *Ann Intern Med*. 1975;82:301–304.

696. Murphy GE. The clinical management of hysteria. *JAMA*. 1982;247:2559–2564.

697. Murrell J, Farlow M, Ghetti B, et al. A mutation in the amyloid precursor protein associated with hereditary Alzheimer's disease. *Science*. 1991;254:97–99.

698. Naditch MP, Fenwick S. LSD flashbacks and ego functioning. *J Abnorm Psychol.* 1977;86:352–359.

699. Naish JM. Problems of deception in medical practice. *Lancet.* 1979;1:139–142.

700. Nasrallah HA, Coffman JA, Olson SC. Structural brain imaging findings in affective disorders: An overview. *J Neuropsychiatry.* 1989;1:21–26.

701. Nasrallah HA, Schwartzkopf SB, Coffman JA, Olson SC. Perinatal brain injury and cerebellar vermal lobules I through X in schizophrenia. *Biol Psychiatry.* 1991; 29:567–574.

702. National Institute on Drug Abuse. *Client Oriented Data Acquisition Process (CODAP), Annual Data and Quarterly Reports, Statistical Series D & E,* Washington, DC: U.S. Department of Health and Human Services, Alcohol, Drug Abuse, and Mental Health Administration, 1980.

703. National Institute on Drug Abuse. *Drug Use Among American High School Students and Other Young Adults. National trends through 1985.* Washington, DC: U.S. Department of Health and Human Services; 1986.

704. Nee LE, Caine ED, Polinsky RJ, et al. Gilles de la Tourette syndrome: Clinical and family study of 50 cases. *Ann Neurol.* 1980;7:41–49.

705. Nelson JC, Bowers MB Jr. Delusional unipolar depression: Description and drug response. *Arch Gen Psychiatry.* 1978;35:1321–1328.

706. Nelson JC, Charney DS, Vingiano AW. False-positive diagnosis with primary affective disorder criteria. *Lancet.* 1978;2:1252–1253.

707. Neshkes RE, Jarvik L. Clinical psychiatry and cardiovascular disease in the aged. In Jarvik L, ed. *Psychiatric Clinics of North America: Aging.* Philadelphia: WB Saunders; 1982:171–199.

708. Nestadt G, Romanoski AJ, Brown CH, et al. DSM-III compulsive personality disorder: An epidemiological survey. *Psychol Med.* 1991;21:461–471.

709. Neufeld MY, Berger Y, Chapman J, et al. Routine and quantitative EEG analysis in Gilles de la Tourette's syndrome. *Neurology.* 1990;40:1837–1839.

710. Nicholi AM Jr. The nontherapeutic use of psychoactive drugs. *N Engl J Med.* 1983;16:925–933.

711. Nickoloff SE, Radant AD, Reichler R, et al. Smooth pursuit and saccadic eye movements and neurological soft signs in obsessive-compulsive disorder. *Psychiatry Res.* 1991;38:173–185.

712. Niedermeyer E, Blumer D, Holsher E, et al. Classical hysterical seizures facilitated by anticonvulsant toxicity. *Psychiatr Clin North Am.* 1970;3:71–84.

713. Nierenberg AA, Keck PE, Samson J, et al. Methodological considerations for the study of treatment-resistant depression. In: Amsterdam JD, ed. *Advances in Neuropsychiatry and Psychopharmacology, Vol. 2: Refractory Depression.* New York: Raven Press; 1991:1–12.

714. Nisita C, Petracca A, Akiskal HS, et al. Delimitation of generalized anxiety disorder: Clinical comparisons with panic and major depressive disorders. *Compr Psychiatry.* 1990;31:409–415.

715. Noble EP. Genetics studies in alcoholism: CNS functioning and molecular biology. In: Miller NS, ed. The disease concept of alcoholism and drug addiction I. *Psychiatr Ann.* 1991;21:215–229.

716. Nordahl TE, Benkelfat C, Semple WE, et al. Cerebral glucose metabolic rates in obsessive compulsive disorder. *Neuropsychopharmacology*. 1989;2:23–28.

717. Norton B, Whalley LJ. Mortality of a lithium treated population. *Br J Psychiatry*. 1984;145:277–282.

718. Nott PN. Psychiatric illness following childbirth: A case register study. *Psychol Med*. 1982;12:557–561.

719. Noyes R, Clarkson L, Crowe R, et al. A family study of generalized anxiety disorder. *Am J Psychiatry*. 1987;144:119–124.

720. Nuzzo JL, Warfield CA. Thalamic pain syndrome. *Hosp Pract*. 1985;32:32c–32j.

721. O'Connell RA, Mayo JA, Flatow L, et al. Outcome of bipolar disorder on long-term treatment with lithium. *Br J Psychiatry*. 1991;159:123–129.

722. O'Connell RA, Van Hecrtum RL, Billick SB, et al. Single photon emission computed tomography (SPECT) with [123I] IMP in the differential diagnosis of psychiatric disorders. *J Neuropsychiatr Clin Neurosci*. 1989;1:145–153.

723. Onstad S, Skre I, Torgersen S, Kringlen E. Subtypes of schizophrenia: Evidence from a twin family study. *Acta Psychiatr Scand*. 1991;84:203–206.

724. Opjordsmoen S. Paranoid (delusional) disorders in the light of a long-term follow-up study. *Psychopathology*. 1991;24:287–292.

725. Orley J, Wing JK. Psychiatric disorders in two African villages. *Arch Gen Psychiatry*. 1979;36:513–520.

726. Orlov P, Kasparian G, Damasio A, et al. Withdrawal of antiparkinson drugs. *Arch Gen Psychiatry*. 1971;25:410–412.

727. O'Sullivan G. Follow-up studies of behavioral treatment of phobic and obsessive compulsive neuroses. In Roth M, ed. Treatment and Outcome of Phobic and Related Disorders. *Psychiatr Ann*. 1991;21:368–373.

728. O'Toole JK, Dyck G: Report of psychogenic fever in catatonia responding to electroconvulsive therapy. *Dis Nerv Syst*. 1977;38:852–853.

729. Ounstead C, Lindsay F. The long-term outcome of temporal lobe epilepsy. In: Reynolds EH, Trimble MR, eds. *Epilepsy and Psychiatry*. Edinburgh: Churchill Livingstone; 1981:185–215.

730. Ouslander JG. Illness and psychopathology in the elderly. In: Jarvik L, ed. *Psychiatric Clinics of North America: Aging*. Philadelphia: WB Saunders; 1982:145–159.

731. Ouslander JG, Kane RL, Abrams IB. Urinary incontinence in elderly nursing home patients. *JAMA*. 1982;248:1194–1198.

732. Palmer HD, Jones MS. Anorexia nervosa as a manifestation of compulsion neurosis. *Arch Neurol Psychiatry*. 1939;41:856–858.

733. Pandey GN, Ostrow DG, Haas M, et al. Abnormal lithium and sodium transport in erythrocytes of a manic patient and some members of his family. *Proc Nat Acad Sci*. 1977;74:3607–3611.

734. Pare CMB, Kline N, Hallstrom C, et al. Will amitriptyline prevent the "cheese" reaction of monoamine oxidase inhibitors? *Lancet*. 1982;2:183–186.

735. Parker N. Malingering: A dangerous diagnosis. *Med J Aust*. 1979;1:568–569.

736. Parkes JD, Lock CB. Genetic factors in sleep disorders. *J Neurol Neurosurg Psychiatry*. 1989;52(suppl):101–108.

737. Parnell RW. *Behavior and Physique: An Introduction to Practical and Applied Somatometry*. London: Edward Arnold; 1958.

738. Parsons T: Definitions of health and illness in the light of American values and social structure. In: Jaco E, ed. *Patients, Physicians and Illness*. New York: The Free Press; 1972.

739. Pascualy M, Veith RC. Use of antidepressants in geriatric patients. In: Amsterdam JD, ed. *Pharmacotherapy of Depression, Applications for the Outpatient Practitioner*. New York: Marcel Dekker Inc; 1990:281–301.

740. Pato MT, Pigott TA, Hill JL, et al. Controlled comparison of buspirone and clomipramine in obsessive-compulsive disorder. *Am J Psychiatry*. 1991;148:127–129.

741. Pauls DL, Cohen DJ, Heimbuch R, et al. Familial pattern and transmission of Gilles de la Tourette syndrome and multiple tics. *Arch Gen Psychiatry*. 1981;38:1091–1093.

742. Pauls DL, Towbin KE, Leckman JF, et al. Gilles de la Tourette's syndrome and obsessive-compulsive disorders: Evidence supporting a genetic relationship. *Arch Gen Psychiatry*. 1986;43:1180–1182.

743. Paulson G, Gottlieb G. Development reflexes: The reappearance of fetal and neonatal reflexes in aged patients. *Brain*. 1968;91:37–52.

744. Pearce JMS. Migraine: A cerebral disorder. *Lancet*. 1984;2:86–89.

745. Pearlman AL, Collins RC, eds. *Neurobiology of Disease*. New York: Oxford University Press; 1990:Part 2.

746. Pearlman C. Neuroleptic malignant syndrome and electroconvulsive therapy. *Convul Ther*. 1990;6:251–253.

747. Peragallo-Dittko V. Buyer's guide to blood glucose meters. *Diabetes Self-Management*. May/June 1991:34–43.

748. Perez-Reyes M, Cochrane C. Differences in sodium thiopental susceptibility of depressed patients as evidenced by the galvanic skin reflex inhibition threshold. *J Psychiatr Res*. 1967;5:335–347.

749. Perris C. A study of bipolar (manic-depressive) and unipolar recurrent depressive psychoses. *Acta Psychiatr Scand*. 1966;42(suppl 194):1–188.

750. Perris C. A study of bipolar (manic-depressive) and unipolar recurrent depressive psychoses: VIII. Clinical-electroencephalographic investigation. *Acta Psychiatr Scand*. 1966;42(suppl 194):118–152.

751. Perry P, Tsuang MT. Treatment of unipolar depression following electroconvulsive therapy. *J Affective Disord*. 1979;1:123–129.

752. Perry PJ, Alexander B. Dosage and serum levels. In: Johnson FN, ed. *Depression and Mania, Modern Lithium Therapy*. Oxford: IRL Press; 1987:67–73.

753. Petersen RC, Stillman RC. *Cocaine 1977*. Washington, DC: Government Printing Office; 1977. National Institute on Drug Abuse Research Monograph No. 13, U.S. Department of Health, Education, and Welfare.

754. Petersen RC, Stillman RC. *Phencyclidine (PCP) Abuse: An Appraisal,* NIDA Washington, DC: Government Printing Office; 1978. National Institute on Drug Abuse Research Monograph No. 21, U.S. Department of Health, Education, and Welfare.

755. Peterson F. Mental Diseases. In: Church A, Peterson F. *Nervous and Mental Diseases*. 2nd ed. Philadelphia: WB Saunders; 1900:603–816.

756. Petersilia J, Greenwood P, Lavin M. *Criminal Careers of Habitual Felons*. Santa Monica, Calif: Rand Corporation; 1977.

757. Petrie WM, Lawson EC, Hollender MH. Violence in geriatric patients. *JAMA*. 1982;248:443–444.

758. Pfohl B, Winokur G. The evolution of symptoms in institutionalized hebephrenic/catatonic schizophrenics. *Br J Psychiatry*. 1982;141:567–572.

759. Phelps ME, Mazziotta JC, Schelbert HR. *Positron Emission Tomography and Audioradiography Principles and Application for the Brain and Heart*. New York: Raven Press; 1986.

760. Pickens RW, Svikis DS, McGue M, et al. Heterogeneity in the inheritance of alcoholism. *Arch Gen Psychiatry*. 1991;48:19–28.

761. Pickering CM. Sleep circadian rhythm and cardiovascular disease. *Cardiovasc Rev Rep*. 1980;1:37.

762. Pigott TA, Altemus M, Rubenstein CS, et al. Symptoms of eating disorders in patients with obsessive-compulsive disorder. *Am J Psychiatry*. 1991;148:1552–1557.

763. Pillard RC, Weinrich JD. Evidence of familial nature of male homosexuality. *Arch Gen Psychiatry*. 1986;43:808–812.

764. Pincus JH, Tucker GJ. *Behavioral Neurology*. 2nd ed. New York: Oxford University Press;1978:135–137.

765. Pitman RK, Green RC, Jenike MA, et al. Clinical comparison of Tourette's disorder and obsessive-compulsive disorder. *Am J Psychiatry*. 1987;144:1166–1171.

766. Pitman RK, Jenike M. Coprolalia in obsessive-compulsive disorder: A missing link. *J Nerv Ment Dis*. 1988;176:311–313.

767. Pittel SM, Oppedahl MC. The enigma of PCP. In: Dupont RI, Goldstein A, O'Donnell J, eds. *Handbook on Drug Abuse*. Washington, DC: Government Printing Office; 1979:249–254. National Institute on Drug Abuse, U.S. Department of Health, Education, and Welfare.

768. Pitts FN Jr. Medical physiology of ECT. In: Abrams R, Essman WB, eds. *Electroconvulsive Therapy: Biological Foundations and Clinical Applications*. New York: Spectrum; 1982:57–89.

769. Pitts FN Jr, McClure JN. Lactate metabolism in anxiety neurosis. *N Engl J Med*. 1967;277:1329–1336.

770. Pitts FN Jr, Schuller AB, Rich CL, et al. Suicide among U.S. women physicians, 1967–1972. *Am J Psychiatry*. 1979;136:694–696.

771. Plum P, Posner JB. *Diagnosis of Stupor and Coma*. 2nd ed. Philadelphia: FA Davis; 1972.

772. Pollack MH, Rosenbaum JF. Management of antidepressant-induced side-effects: A practical guide for the clinician. *J Clin Psychiatry*. 1987;48:3–8.

773. Pollitt J. Natural history of obsessional states: A study of 150 cases. *Br Med J*. 1957;1:194–198.

774. Pond D. Epidemiology of the psychiatric disorders of epilepsy. In: Reynolds EH, Trimble MR, eds. *Epilepsy and Psychiatry*. Edinburgh: Churchill Livingstone; 1981:27–32.

775. Pope HG Jr, Jonas JM, Hudson JI, Cohen BM, Gunderson JG. The validity of DSM-III borderline personality disorder. *Arch Gen Psychiatry*. 1982;139:1480–1483.

776. Pope HG Jr, Lipinski JF. Diagnosis in schizophrenia and manic-depressive illness: A reassessment of the specificity of "schizophrenic" symptoms in light of current research. *Arch Gen Psychiatry.* 1978;35:811–828.

777. Pope HG Jr, Lipinski JF, Cohen BM, et al. Schizo-affective disorder: An invalid diagnosis? A comparison of schizo-affective disorder, schizophrenia and affective disorder. *Am J PSychiatry.* 1980;137:921–927.

778. Post F. The functional psychoses. In: Isaacs A, Post F, eds. *Studies in Geriatric Psychiatry.* New York: John Wiley & Sons; 1978:77–94.

779. Post RM, Kopanda RT. Cocaine, kindling, and psychosis. *Am J Psychiatry.* 1976;133:627–634.

780. Post RM, Putman F, Contel NR, et al. Electroconvulsive seizures inhibit amygdala kindling: Implications for mechanism of action in affective illness. *Epilepsia.* 1984;25:234–239.

781. Post RM, Rubinow DR, Ballenger JC. Conditioning, sensitization, and kindling: Implications for the course of affective illness. In: Post RM, Ballenger JC, eds. *The Neurobiology of Mood Disorders.* Baltimore: Williams & Wilkins; 1984:432–466.

782. Post RM, Weiss SRB, Pert A. Cocaine-induced behavioral sensitizations and kindling: Implications for the emergence of psychopathology and seizures. *Ann NY Acad Sci.* 1988;537:292–308.

783. Powers D, Douglas TS, Waziri R. Hyperpyrexia in catatonic states. *Dis Nerv Syst.* 1976;37:359–361.

784. Price BH, Mesulam M. Psychiatric manifestations of right hemisphere infarctions. *J Nerv Ment Dis.* 1985;173:610–614.

785. Price TRP. Temporal lobe epilepsy as a premenstrual behavioral syndrome. *Biol Psychiatry.* 1980;15:957–963.

786. Prien RF, Cole JO, Belkin NJ. Relapse in chronic schizophrenics following abrupt withdrawal of tranquilizing medication. *Br J Psychiatry.* 1968;115:679–686.

787. Primeau F, Fontaine R. Obsessive disorder with self-mutilation: A subgroup responsive to pharmacotherapy. *Can J Psychiatry.* 1987;32:699–701.

788. Pro JD, Wells CE. The use of electroencephalogram in the diagnosis of delirium. *Dis Nerv Syst* 1977;38:804–808.

789. Protherol C. Puerperal psychoses: A long-term study 1927–1961. *Br J Psychiatry.* 1969;115:9–30.

790. Pryse-Phillips W, Murray TJ. *Essential Neurology.* 3rd ed. Garden City, NY: Medical Examination Publishing Co; 1986.

791. Quitkin FM, Klein DF. Follow-up of treatment failure: Psychosis and character disorder. *Am J Psychiatry.* 1967;124:499–505.

792. Quitkin FM, Rifkin A, Klein DF. Neurologic soft signs in schizophrenia and character disorders. *Arch Gen Psychiatry.* 1979;33:845–853.

793. Rada RT. Alcoholism and forcible rape. *Am J Psychiatry.* 1975;132:444–446.

794. Raff ML. Social controls on cell survival and cell death. *Nature.* 1992;356:397–400.

795. Raine A, Venables PH. Electrodermal nonresponding, antisocial behavior, and schizoid tendencies in adolescents. *Psychophysiology.* 1984;21:424–433.

796. Rangel-Guerra RA, Perez-Poyon H, Minkoff L, et al. Nuclear magnetic resonance in bipolar affective disorders. *Magn Reson Imaging.* 1982;1:229–239.

797. Rapee RM, Barlow DH. Panic disorder: Cognitive behavioral treatment. *Psychiatr Ann.* 1988;18:473–477.

798. Rapoport JL. The neurobiology of obsessive compulsive disorder. *JAMA.* 1988;260:2888–2890.

799. Raskin M, Talbott JA, Meyerson AT. Diagnosis of conversion reactions: Predictive value of psychiatric criteria. *JAMA.* 1966;197:102–150.

800. Rasmussen SA, Tsuang MT. The epidemiology of obsessive compulsive disorder. *J Clin Psychiatry.* 1984;45:450–457.

801. Rasmussen SA, Tsuang MT. Clinical characteristics and family history in DSM-III obsessive-compulsive disorder. *Am J Psychiatry.* 1986;143:317–322.

802. Rau JH, Green RS. Compulsive eating: A neuropsychological approach to certain eating disorders. *Comp Psychiatry.* 1975;16:223–231.

803. Rau JH, Green RS. Soft neurological correlates of compulsive eating. *J Nerv Ment Disord.* 1978;166:435–437.

804. Rebec GV, Bentore JM, Alloway KD. Ascorbic acid and the behavioral response to haloperidol: Implications for the action of antipsychotic drugs. *Science.* 1985; 227:438–440.

805. Reed JL. The proverbs test in schizophrenia. *Br J Psychiatry.* 1968;114:317–321.

806. Regier DA, Boyd JH, Burke JD, et al. One-month prevalence of mental disorders in the United States. *Arch Gen Psychiatry.* 1988;45:977–986.

807. Reich JH. Proverbs and the modern mental status exam. *Compr Psychiatry.* 1981;22:528–531.

808. Reich JH, Noyes JR, Troughton E. Dependent personality disorder associated with phobic avoidance in patients with panic disorder. *Am J Psychiatry.* 1987;144:323–326.

809. Reich JH, Tupin JP, Abramowicz SI. Psychiatric diagnosis of chronic pain patients. *Am J Psychiatry.* 1983;140:1495–1498.

810. Reich JH, Yates W, Nguaguba M. Prevalence of DSM-III personality disorders in the community. *Soc Psychiatry Psychiat Epidemiol* 1989;24:12–16.

811. Reich P, Gottfried LA. Factitious disorders in a teaching hospital. *Ann Intern Med.* 1983;99:240–247.

812. Reichel W, ed. *The Geriatric Patient.* New York: Hospital Practice Publishing Co; 1978.

813. Reiman EM, Raiche ME, Robins E, et al. The application of positron emission tomography to the study of panic disorder. *Am J Psychiatry.* 1986;143:469–477.

814. Reisberg B, Ferris SH, Gershon S. An overview of pharmacologic treatment of cognitive decline in the aged. *Am J Psychiatry.* 1981;138:593–600.

815. Reite MZ, Anders TF, Greil W, et al. Animal models: Group report. In: Angst J, ed. *The Origins of Depression: Current Concepts and Approaches.* Berlin: Springer-Verlag; 1983:405–423.

816. Retterstol N. Course and outcome in paranoid disorders. *Psychopathology.* 1991;24:277–286.

817. Richardson JW, Frederickson PA, Lin SC. Narcolepsy update. *Mayo Clin Proc* 1990;65:992–998.

818. Riding J, Munro A. Pimozide in the treatment of monosymptomatic hypochondriacal psychosis. *Acta Psychiatr Scand.* 1975;52:23–30.

819. Ries R, Bokan J, Schuckit MC. Modern diagnosis of schizophrenia in hospitalized psychiatric patients. *Am J Psychiatry.* 1980;137:1419–1421.

820. Rifkin A, Quitkin F, Carillo C, et al. Very high dosage fluphenazine for nonchronic treatment-refractory patients. *Arch Gen Psychiatry.* 1971;25:398–403.

821. Riley TL, Roy A, eds. *Pseudoseizures,* Baltimore: Williams & Wilkins; 1982.

822. Riskind JH, Beck AT, Berchick RT, et al. Reliability of DSM-III diagnoses for major depression and generalized anxiety disorder using the structured clinical interviews for DSM-III. *Arch Gen Psychiatry.* 1987;44:817–820.

823. Robertson J. Sex addiction as a disease: A neurobehavioral model. *Am J Prev Psychiatry Neurol.* 1990;2:15–18.

824. Robertson MM. The Gilles de la Tourette syndrome: The current status. *Br J Psychiatry.* 1989;154:147–169.

825. Robin A, de Tissera S. A double-blind controlled comparison of the therapeutic effects of low and high energy electroconvulsive therapies. *Br J Psychiatry.* 1982;141:357–366.

826. Robins E. *The Final Months.* New York: Oxford University Press; 1981.

827. Robins E, Guze SB. Establishment of diagnostic validity in psychiatric illness. Its application to schizophrenia. *Am J Psychiatry.* 1970;126:983–987.

828. Robins LN. *Deviant Children Grown Up: A Sociological and Psychiatric Study of Sociopathic Personality.* Baltimore: Williams & Wilkins; 1966.

829. Robins LN, Helzer GE, Weissman MM. Lifetime prevalence of specific psychiatric disorders in three sites. *Arch Gen Psychiatry.* 1984;41:949–958.

830. Robins LN, Murphy GE, Breckenridge MB. Drinking behavior of young negro men. *Q J Stud Alcohol.* 1968;29:657–684.

831. Robins LN, O'Neal P. Mortality, mobility and crime: Problem children thirty years later. *Am Soc Rev.* 1958;23:162–171.

832. Robinson DS. Changes in monoamine oxidase and monoamines with human development and aging. *Fed Proc.* 1975;34:103–107.

833. Robinson DS, Nies A, Ravaris CL, et al. The monoamine oxidase inhibitor, phenelzine, in the treatment of depressive-anxiety states. *Arch Gen Psychiatry.* 1973;29:407–413.

834. Robinson M, Kasden SD. Clinical application of pure tone delayed auditory feedback in pseudohypoaucusis. *EENT Monthly.* 1973;52:31–33.

835. Robinson RG, Starkstein SE. Heterogeneity in clinical presentation following stroke: Neuropathological correlates. *Neuropsychiatry, Neuropsychology, and Behavioral Neurology.* 1991;4:49–61.

836. Roger J, Lob H, Tassinari CA. Generalized status epilepticus as a confusional state (petit mal status or absence status epilepticus). In: Vinken PJ, Bruyn GW, eds. *Handbook of Clinical Neurology 15.* Amsterdam: North Holland; 1974:145–182.

837. Rogers R, ed. *Clinical Assessment of Malingering and Deception.* New York: Guilford Press; 1988.

838. Roose SP, Glassman AH. Cardiovascular effects of tricyclic antidepressants in depressed patients with and without heart disease. In: Amsterdam JD, ed. *Pharmacotherapy of Depression, Applications for the Outpatient Practitioner.* New York: Marcel Dekker Inc; 1990:267–280.

839. Roose SP, Glassman AH, Giardina EGV, et al. Tricyclic antidepressants in patients with cardiac conduction disease. *Arch Gen Psychiatry.* 1987;44:273–275.

840. Roose SP, Nurnberger J, Dunner D, et al. Cardiac sinus node dysfunction during lithium treatment. *Am J Psychiatry.* 1979;136:804–806.

841. Rose E, Sanders T, Webb JL, et al. Occult factitial thyrotoxicosis. *Ann Intern Med.* 1969;71:309–315.

842. Rosebush PI, Hildebrand AM, Furlong BG, et al. Catatonic syndrome in a general psychiatric inpatient population: Frequency, clinical presentation and response to lorazepam. *J Clin Psychiatry.* 1990;51:357–362.

843. Rosenbaum G, Shore D, Chapin K. Attention deficit in schizophrenia and schizotype: Marker versus symptom variable. *J Abnorm Psychol.* 1988;97:41–47.

844. Rosenberg CM. Personality and obsessional neurosis. *Br J Psychiatry.* 1967; 113:471–477.

845. Rosenthal J, Strauss A, Minkoff L, et al. Identifying lithium responsive bipolar depressed patients using nuclear magnetic resonance. *Am J Psychiatry.* 1986; 143:779–780.

846. Roslaniec A, Fitzpatrick JJ. Changes in mental status in older adults with four days of hospitalization. *Res Nurs Health.* 1979;2:177–187.

847. Ross ED. The aprosodias: Functional anatomic organization of the affective components of language in the right hemisphere. *Arch Neurol.* 1981;38:561–569.

848. Ross ED, Harney JH, deLacoste-Utamsing C, et al. How the brain integrates affective and propositional language into a unified behavioral function: Hypothesis based on clinico-anatomic evidence. *Arch Neurol.* 1981;38:745–748.

849. Ross ED, Mesulam MM. Dominant language functions of the right hemisphere? Prosody and emotional gesturing. *Arch Neurol.* 1979;36:144–148.

850. Rossman I. Bodily changes with aging. In: Buss EW, Blazer DG, eds. *Handbook of Geriatric Psychiatry.* New York: Van Nostrand Reinhold; 1980:125–146.

851. Roth M. The natural history of mental disorder in old age. *J Ment Sci.* 1955;101:281–301.

852. Roth M. The management of dementia. In: Hendrie HC, ed. *Psychiatric Clinics of North America, Vol. 1/1, Brain Disorders: Clinical Diagnosis and Management.* Philadelphia; WB Saunders; 1978:81–99.

853. Rounsaville BJ, Klerman GL, Weissman MM. Do psychotherapy and pharmacotherapy for depression conflict? Empirical evidence from a clinical trial. *Arch Gen Psychiatry.* 1981;38:24–29.

854. Rowe MJ, Carlson C. Brainstem auditory evoked potentials in postconcussional dizziness. *Arch Neurol.* 1980;37:679–683.

855. Rumble B, Retallack R, Hilbich C, et al. Amyloid A4 protein and its precursor in Down's syndrome and Alzheimer's disease. *N Engl J Med.* 1989;320:1446–1452.

856. Rybakowski JK. Lithium potentiation of antidepressants. In: Amsterdam JD, ed. *Pharmacotherapy of Depression, Applications for the Outpatient Practitioner.* New York: Marcel Dekker Inc; 1990:225–239.

857. Sackeim HA, Decina P, Kanzler M, et al. Effects of electrode placement on the efficacy of titrated low-dose ECT. *Am J Psychiatry.* 1987;144:1449–1455.

858. Sackeim HA, Greenberg MS, Weiman AL, et al. Hemispheric asymmetry in the expression of positive and negative emotions. *Arch Neurol.* 1982;39:210–218.

859. Sackeim HA, Gur RS, Saucy M. Emotions are expressed more intensely on the left side of the face. *Science*. 1978;202:434–436.

860. Sackeim HA, Prohovnik I, Apter S, et al. Regional cerebral blood flow in affective disorders: Relations to phenomenology and effects of treatment. In: Takahashi R, Flor-Henry P, Gruzelier J, Niwa A, eds. *Cerebral Dynamics, Laterality, and Psychopathology*. New York: Elsevier; 1987:477–492.

861. Safferman A, Lieberman JA, Kane JM, et al. Update on the clinical efficacy and side effects of clozapine. *Schizophr Bull*. 1991;17:247–261.

862. Salzman C. Key concepts in geriatric psychopharmacology. In: Jarvik L, ed. *Psychiatric Clinics of North America: Aging*. Philadelphia: WB Saunders; 1982:181–190.

863. Salzman C, Van Der Kolk BA. Psychotropic drugs and polypharmacy in a general hospital. *J Geriatr Psychiatry*. 1979;12:167–176.

864. Salzman C, Van Der Kolk BA. Psychotropic drugs and polypharmacy in elderly patients in a general hospital. *J Am Geriatr Soc*. 1980;28:18–22.

865. Sandifer MG, Hordern A, Timburg GC, et al. Similarities and differences in patient evaluation by US and UK psychiatrists. *Am J Psychiatry*. 1969;126:206–212.

866. Sangiovanni F, Taylor MA, Abrams R, et al. Rapid control of psychotic excitement states with intramuscular haloperidol. *Am J Psychiatry*. 1973;130:1155–1160.

867. Sano M. Basal ganglia diseases and depression. *Neuropsychiatry, Neuropsychology, and Behavioral Neurology*. 1991;4:24–35.

868. Sarason IG: Theories of anxiety and its clinical treatment. *J Drug Res*. 1982;7:7–15.

869. Sawin CT, Castelli WP, Hershman JM, et al. The thyroid: Thyroid deficiency in the Framingham study. *Arch Intern Med*. 1985;145:1386–1388.

870. Schaefer HH, Martin PL. *Behavior Therapy*. New York: McGraw-Hill; 1969:867.

871. Schaffer CB. Treating phencyclidine intoxication. *Am J Psychiatry*. 1978;135:388.

872. Schatzberg AF, Cole JO, Cohen BM, et al. Survey of depressed patients who have failed to respond to treatment. In: Davis JM, Maas JW, eds. *The Affective Disorders*. Washington, DC: American Psychiatric Press; 1983:73–85.

873. Scheinberg P. *Modern Practical Neurology: An Introduction to Diagnosis and Management of Common Neurological Disorders*. 2nd ed. New York: Raven Press; 1981:177–186.

874. Schenk L, Bear D. Multiple personality and related dissociative phenomena in patients with temporal lobe epilepsy. *Am J Psychiatry*. 1981;138:1311–1316.

875. Schlegel S, Kretzschmar K. Computed tomography in affective disorders, Part I. Ventricular and sulcal measurements. *Biol Psychiatry*. 1987;22:4–14.

876. Schlegel S, Maier W, Philip M, et al. Computed tomography in depression: Association between ventricular size and psychopathology. *Psychiatry Res*. 1989;29:221–230.

877. Schlesser MA, Winokur G, Sherman BM. Hypothalamic pituitary adrenal axis activity in depressive illness: Its relationship to classification. *Arch Gen Psychiatry*. 1980;37:737–743.

878. Schneider K; Hamilton MW trans. *Clinical Psychopathology*. New York: Grune & Stratton; 1959.

879. Schneider K. *Psychopathic Personalities*. London: Cassell; 1958.

880. Schou M, Amdisen A. Lithium and pregnancy: 3. Lithium ingestion by children breast-fed by women on lithium treatment. *Br Med J*. 1973;2:138.

881. Schuckit M, Robins E, Feighner J. Tricyclic antidepressants and monoamine oxidase inhibitors: Combination therapy in the treatment of depression. *Arch Gen Psychiatry*. 1971;24:509–514.

882. Schuckit MA, Winokur G. Alcoholic hallucinosis and schizophrenia: A negative study. *Br J Psychiatry*. 1971;119:549–550.

883. Shader RI, Georgotus A, Greenblatt DJ, et al. Impaired desmethyldiazepam from clorazepate by magnesium aluminum hydroxide. *Clin Pharmacol Ther*. 1978; 24:308–315.

884. Shagass CS, Naiman J, Mihalik JM. An objective test which differentiates between neurotic and psychotic depression. *Arch Neurol Psychiatry*. 1956;75:461–471.

885. Shagass CS, Roemer RA, Straumanis JJ Jr, et al. Topography of sensory evoked potentials in depressive disorders. *Biol Psychiatry*. 1980;15:183–207.

886. Shapiro AK, Shapiro ES, Young JG, et al. *Gilles de la Tourette Syndrome*. 2nd ed. New York: Raven Press; 1988.

887. Shapiro BE, Alexander MP, Gardner H, et al. Mechanisms of confabulation. *Neurology*. 1981;31:1070–1076.

888. Sharp CW, Brehm ML. *Review of Inhalants: Euphoria to Dysfunction*. Washington, DC: Government Printing Office; 1977. National Institute on Drug Abuse Research Monograph No. 15, U.S. Department of Health, Education, and Welfare.

889. Sharpe S, Gurland BJ, Fleiss JL, et al. Comparisons of American, Canadian and British psychiatrists in their diagnostic concepts. *Can Psychiatr Assoc J*. 1974;19:235–245.

890. Sheard MH. Effects of lithium on human aggression. *Nature*. 1971;230:113–114.

891. Sheard MH, Marini JL, Bridges CI, et al. The effect of lithium on impulsive aggressive behavior in man. *Am J Psychiatry*. 1976;133:1409–1413.

892. Sheldon WH, Stevens SS, Tucker WB. *The Varieties of Human Physique*. London: Harper, 1940.

893. Sheldon WH, Stevens SS, Tucker WB: *The Varieties of Temperament,* London, Harper; 1942.

894. Shem S. *The House of God*. New York: Dell; 1978:38.

895. Shen W, Bowman ES, Markand ON. Presenting the diagnosis of pseudoseizure. *Neurology*. 1990;40:756–759.

896. Shepherd M, Lader M. Rodnight R. *Clinical Psychopharmacology*. Philadelphia: Lea & Febiger; 1968:67–75, 85–125.

897. Sherrington R, Brynjolfsson J, Petursson H, et al. Localization of a susceptibility locus for schizophrenia on chromosome 5. *Nature*. 1988;336:164–167.

898. Sherwin I, Geschwind N. Neural substrates of behavior. In: Nicholi AM Jr, ed. *The Harvard Guide to Modern Psychiatry*. Cambridge, Mass: Belknap/Harvard; 1978:78.

899. Shevitz SA, Silberfarb PM, Lipowski ZJ. Psychiatric consultations in a general hospital: A report on 1000 referrals. *Dis Nerv Syst*. 1976;37:295–300.

900. Shock N. Biological theories of aging. In: Birren J, Schaie K, Warner K, eds. *Handbook of the Psychology of Aging*. New York: Van Nostrand Reinhold; 1977:103–115.

901. Shorvon SD, Reynolds EH. Reduction of polypharmacy for epilepsy. *Br Med J.* 1979;2:1023–1025.

902. Shoulson I. Huntington's disease: Cognitive and psychiatric features. *Neuropsychiatry, Neuropsychology, and Behavioral Neurology.* 1990;3:15–22.

903. Showalter CV, Thornton WE. Clinical pharmacology of phencyclidine toxicity. *Am J Psychiatry.* 1977;134:1234–1238.

904. Sierles FS. Correlates of malingering. *Behav Sci and the Law.* 1984;2:113–118.

905. Sierles FS, Chen JJ, McFarland RE, et al. Posttraumatic stress disorder and concurrent psychiatric illness: A preliminary report. *Am J Psychiatry.* 1983;140:1177–1179.

906. Sierles FS, Chen JJ, Messing ML, et al. Concurrent psychiatric illness in non-Hispanic outpatients diagnosed as having posttraumatic stress disorder. *J Nerv Ment Dis.* 1986;174:171–173.

907. Sierles FS, Ossowski MG. Concurrent use of theophylline and lithium in a patient with chronic obstructive lung disease and bipolar disorder. *Am J Psychiatry.* 1982;139:117–118.

908. Siever LJ. Biological markers in schizotypal personality disorder. *Schizophr Bull.* 1985;11:564–574.

909. Sigal M, Altmark D, Alfici S, et al. Ganser syndrome: A review of 15 cases. *Compr Psychiatry.* 1992;33:134–138.

910. Sigell LT, Kapp FT, Fusaro GA, et al. Popping and snorting volatile nitrites. A current fad for getting high. *Am J Psychiatry.* 1978;135:1216–1218.

911. Silberman EK, Post RM, Nurnberger J, et al. Transient sensory, cognitive, and affective phenomena in affective illness: A comparison with complex partial epilepsy. *Br J Psychiatry.* 1985;146:81–89.

912. Silfverskiold P, Risberg J. Regional cerebral blood flow in depression and mania. *Arch Gen Psychiatry.* 1989;46:253–259.

913. Silver JM, Yudofsky SC, Hales RE. Depression in traumatic brain injury. *Neuropsychiatry, Neuropsychology, and Behavioral Neurology.* 1991;4:12–23.

914. Simmons RC, Kessler MD. Identical twins simultaneously concordant for anorexia nervosa. *J Am Acad Child Psychiatry.* 1979;18:527–536.

915. Simpson GM, May PRA. Schizophrenic disorders. In: Greist JH, Jefferson JW, Spitzer RL, eds. *Treatment of Mental Disorders.* New York: Oxford University Press; 1982:143–183.

916. Sisler GC. Psychiatric disorder associated with head injury. In: Hendrie HC, ed. *Psychiatric Clinics of North America, Vol. 1/1, Brain Disorders: Clinical Diagnosis and Management.* Philadelphia; WB Saunders; 1978:137–152.

917. Slater E. The neurotic constitution. *J Neurol Psychiatry.* 1943;6:1–62.

918. Slater ETO, Glithero E. A follow-up of patients diagnosed as suffering from "hysteria." *J Psychosom Res.* 1965;9:9–13.

919. Slavney P, Rich G, Pearlson G, et al. Phencyclidine abuse and symptomatic mania. *Biol Psychiatry.* 1977;12:697–700.

920. Smith GR Jr. *Somatization Disorder in the Medical Setting.* Washington, DC: Government Printing Office; 1990. National Institute of Mental Health, U.S. Department of Health and Human Services, publication No. (ADM) 90-1631.

921. Snyder S, Pitts WM. Electroencephalography of DSM-III borderline personality disorders. *Acta Psychiatr Scand.* 1984;69:129–134.

922. Soldo BJ, Manton KG. Health status and service needs of the oldest old: Current patterns and future needs. *Milbank Memorial Fund Quarterly; Health and Society.* 1985;63:286–319.

923. Spar JE, Gerner R. Does the dexamethasone suppression test distinguish dementia from depression? *Am J Psychiatry.* 1982;139:238–240.

924. Spaulding W, Garbin CP, Dras SR. Cognitive abnormalities in schizophrenic patients and schizotypal college students. *J Nerv Ment Dis.* 1989;177:717–728.

925. Spitzer RL, Fleiss JL. A reanalysis of the reliability of psychiatric diagnosis. *Br J Psychiatry.* 1974;125:341–347.

926. Spitzer RL, Endicott J, Gibbon M. Crossing the border into borderline personality and borderline schizophrenia: The development of criteria. *Arch Gen Psychiatry.* 1979;36:17–24.

927. Spitzer RL, Endicott J, Robins E. *Research Diagnostic Criteria for a Selected Group of Functional Disorders (RDC).* 2nd ed. New York: Biometrics Research, New York State Psychiatric Institute; 1975.

928. Spitzer RL, Klein DF, eds. *Evaluation of Psychological Therapies, Psychotherapies, Behavior Therapies, Drug Therapies and Their Interactions.* Baltimore: Johns Hopkins University Press; 1976.

929. Spitzer RL, Williams JBW, Gibbon M, et al. *Structured Clinical Interview for DSM-III R (SCID).* Washington, DC: American Psychiatric Press; 1990.

930. Spitzka EC. *Insanity: Its Classification, Diagnosis and Treatment.* New York: Arno Press; 1973. In series: Mental Illness and Social Policy: The American Experience.

931. Spreen O, Strauss E. *A Compendium of Neuropsychological Tests, Administration, Norms, and Commentary.* New York: Oxford University Press; 1991.

932. Squire L. Neuropsychological effects of ECT. In: Abrams R, Essman WB, eds. *Electroconvulsive Therapy: Biological Foundations and Clinical Applications.* New York: Spectrum; 1982:169–185.

933. Squire LR. *Memory and Brain.* New York: Oxford University Press; 1987.

934. Squire LR, Butters N. *Neuropsychology of Memory.* New York: Guilford Press; 1984.

935. Stafford-Clark D, Pond D, Doust, JWL. The psychopath in prison: A preliminary report of a cooperative research. *Br J Delinq.* 1951;2:117–129.

936. Stafford-Clark D, Taylor FH. Clinical and electroencephalographic studies of prisoners charged with murder. *J Neurol Neurosurg Psychiatry* 1949;12:325–330.

937. Stanton AH, Schwartz MS. *The Mental Hospital.* New York: Basic Books, 1954.

938. Steadman H. A new look at recidivism among Patuxent inmates. *Bull Am Acad Psychiatry Law.* 1977;5:200–209.

939. Stefansson JG, Messina JA, Meyerowitz S. Hysterical neurosis, conversion type. Clinical and epidemiologic considerations. *Acta Psychiatr Scand.* 1976;53:119–138.

940. Stein MB, Uhde TW. Infrequent occurrence of EEG abnormalities in panic disorder. *Am J Psychiatry.* 1989;146:517–520.

941. Steinhausen H-CH, Rauss-Mason C, Seidel R. Follow-up studies of anorexia

nervosa: A review of four decades of outcome research. *Psychol Med.* 1991;21:447–454.

942. Steketee G, Foa E: Obsessive-compulsive disorder. In: Barlow D, ed. *Clinical Handbook of Psychological Disorders.* New York: Guilford Press; 1985:69–144.

943. Stern DB. Handedness and the lateral distribution of conversion reactions. *J Nerv Ment Dis.* 1978;164:122–128.

944. Stevens JR, Hermann BP. Temporal lobe epilepsy, psychopathology and violence. *Neurology.* 1981;31:1127–1132.

945. Stever J. Psychotherapy with the elderly. In: Jarvik L, ed. *Psychiatric Clinics of North America: Aging.* Philadelphia: WB Saunders; 1979:199–213.

946. Stimmel B, Goldberg J, Rothopf E, et al. Ability to remain abstinent after methadone detoxification: A six-year study. *JAMA.* 1977;237:1216–1220.

947. Stone EA. Problems with the current catecholamine hypothesis of antidepressant agents: Speculations leading to a new hypothesis. *Behav Brain Sci.* 1983; 6:535–577.

948. Straker M. Adjustment disorders and personality disorders in the aged. In: Jarvik L, ed. *Psychiatric Clinics of North America: Aging.* Philadelphia: WB Saunders; 1982:121–129.

949. Strauss JS, Gift TE. Choosing an approach for diagnosing schizophrenia. *Arch Gen Psychiatry.* 1977;34:1248–1253.

950. Strik WK, La Malfa G, Cabras P. A bidimensional model for diagnosis and classification of functional psychoses. *Compr Psychiatry.* 1989;30:313–319.

951. Strober M, Morrell W, Burroughs J, et al. A controlled family study of anorexia nervosa. *J Psychiatr Res.* 1985;19:239–246.

952. Stuss D, Benson F. *The Frontal Lobes.* New York: Raven Press; 1986.

953. Suddath RL, Casanova MF, Goldberg TE, et al. Temporal lobe pathology in schizophrenia: A quantitative magnetic resonance imaging study. *Am J Psychiatry.* 1989;146:464–472.

954. Swartz CM. Drug dose prediction with flexible test doses. *J Clin Pharmacol.* 1991;31:662–667.

955. Swinson RP, Kuch K. Clinical features of panic and related disorders. In: Ballenger JC, ed. *Clinical Aspects of Panic Disorder, Frontiers of Clinical Neuroscience,* vol. 9. New York: Wiley-Liss; 1990:13–30.

956. Tagliavini F, Pilleri G. Neuronal counts in basal nucleus of Meynert in Alzheimer disease and in simple senile dementia. *Lancet.* 1983;1:469–470.

957. Tandon R, Mazzara C, DeQuardo J, et al. Dexamethasone suppression test in schizophrenia: Relationship to symptomatology, ventricular enlargement, and outcome. *Biol Psychiatry.* 1991;29:953–964.

958. Tardiff KJ. A survey of psychiatrists in Boston and their work with violent patients. *Am J Psychiatry.* 1974;131:1008–1114.

959. Tardiff KJ. The risk of assaultive behavior in suicidal patients. *Acta Psychiatr Scand.* 1981;64:295–300.

960. Tardiff KJ, Gross EM, Messner SF. A study of homicide in Manhattan, 1981. *Am J Public Health.* 1986;76:139–143.

961. Targum SC, Rosen LN, Citren CM. Delusional symptoms associated with enlarged ventricles in depressed patients. *South Med J.* 1983;76:985–987.

962. Tavel ME, Davidson W, Batteron TD. A critical analysis of mortality associated with delirium tremens. *Am J Med Sci.* 1961;242:18–29.

963. Taylor AR. Post-concussional sequelae. *Br Med J.* 1967;3:67–71.

964. Taylor D. Sexual behavior and temporal lobe epilepsy. *Arch Neurol.* 1969;21:510–516.

965. Taylor J. *Ductor Dubitantium, or the Rule of Conscience.* London: Royston; 1660.

966. Taylor JR, Tompkins R, Demers R, et al. Electronconvulsive therapy and memory dysfunction: Is there evidence for prolonged defects? *Biol Psychiatry.* 1982; 17:1169–1193.

967. Taylor MA. Indications for electroconvulsive treatment. In: Abrams R, Essman WB, eds. *Electroconvulsive Therapy in Theory and Practice.* New York: SP Medical and Scientific Books; 1982:7–39.

968. Taylor MA. Schizoaffective and allied disorders. In: Post RM, Ballenger JC, eds. *The Neurobiology of Manic Depressive Illness.* Baltimore: Williams & Wilkins; 1984:136–156.

969. Taylor MA. Catatonia: A review of a behavioral neurologic syndrome. *Neuropsychiatry, Neuropsychology, and Behavioral Neurology.* 1990;3:48–72.

970. Taylor MA. The role of the cerebellum in the pathogenesis of schizophrenia. *Neuropsychiatry, Neuropsychology, and Behavioral Neurology.* 1991;4:251–280.

971. Taylor MA. Are schizophrenia and affective disorder related? I. A selected literature review. *Am J Psychiatry.* 1992;149:22–32.

972. Taylor MA, Abrams R. The phenomenology of mania: A new look at some old patients. *Arch Gen Psychiatry.* 1973;29:520–522.

973. Taylor MA, Abrams R. Manic-depressive illness and good prognosis schizophrenia. *Am J Psychiatry.* 1975;132:741–742.

974. Taylor MA, Abrams R. Acute mania: A clinical and genetic study of responders and nonresponders to somatic treatments. *Arch Gen Psychiatry.* 1975;32:863–865.

975. Taylor MA, Abrams R. The prevalence and importance of catatonia in the manic phase of manic-depressive illness. *Arch Gen Psychiatry.* 1977;34:1223–1225.

976. Taylor MA, Abrams R. The prevalence of schizophrenia: A reassessment using modern diagnostic criteria. *Am J Psychiatry.* 1978;135:945–948.

977. Taylor MA, Abrams R. Reassessing the bipolar-unipolar dichotomy. *J Affective Disord.* 1980;2:195–217.

978. Taylor MA, Abrams R. Cognitive impairment in schizophrenia. *Am J Psychiatry.* 1984;141:196–201.

979. Taylor MA, Abrams R. Cognitive impairment patterns in schizophrenia and affective disorder. *J Neurol Neurosurg Psychiatry.* 1987;50:895–899.

980. Taylor MA, Abrams R, Faber R, et al. Cognitive tasks in the mental status examination. *J Nerv Ment Dis.* 1980;168:167–170.

981. Taylor MA, Abrams R, Hayman MA. The classification of affective disorders: A reassessment of the bipolar-unipolar dichotomy. A clinical, laboratory, and family study. *J Affective Disord.* 1980;2:95–109.

982. Taylor MA, Greenspan B, Abrams R. Lateralized neuropsychological dysfunction in affective disorder and schizophrenia. *Am J Psychiatry*. 1979;136:1031–1034.

983. Taylor MA, Heiser JP. Phenomenology: An alternative approach to diagnosis of mental disease. *Compr Psychiatry*. 1971;12:480–486.

984. Taylor MA, Levine R. Puerperal schizophrenia: A physiological interaction between mother and fetus. *Biol Psychiatry*. 1969;1:97–101.

985. Tellegen A. *Brief Manual for the Multidimensional Personality Questionnaire*. Minneapolis, Minn: Department of Psychology, University of Minnesota; 1982.

986. Tellegen A. Structures of mood and personality and their relevance to assessing anxiety with an emphasis on self-report. In: Tuma AH, Moser J, eds. *Anxiety and the Anxiety Disorders*. Hillside, NJ: Lawrence Erlbaum Assoc; 1985:681–706.

987. Terry R. Senile dementia, and Alzheimer's disease. In: Katymen R, Terry D, eds *Alzheimer's Disease, Senile Dementia, and Related Disorders, Vol. 7, Aging*. New York: Raven Press; 1978:11–14.

988. Tesar GE, Murray GB, Cassem NH. Use of high-dose intravenous haloperidol in the treatment of agitated cardiac patients. J Clin Psychopharmacol. 1985;5:344–347.

989. Theander S. Anorexia nervosa: A psychiatric investigation of 94 female patients. *Acta Psychiatr Scand*. 1970;214(suppl):5–194.

990. Thornberry T, Jacoby J. *The Criminally Insane: A Community Follow-up of Mentally Ill Offenders*. Chicago: University of Chicago Press; 1979.

991. Tolosa ES, Montserrat L, Bayes A. Reduction of brainstem interneuron excitability during voluntary tic inhibition in Tourette's syndrome. *Neurology*. 1986;36(suppl 1):118–119.

992. Toone B. Psychoses of epilepsy. In: Reynolds EH, Trimble MR, eds. *Epilepsy and Psychiatry*. Edinburgh: Churchill Livingstone; 1981:113–137.

993. Torgersen S. Genetic factors in anxiety disorders. *Arch Gen Psychiatry*. 1983; 40:1085–1089.

994. Torgersen S. Genetic and nosological aspects of schizotypal and borderline personality disorders. *Arch Gen Psychiatry*. 1984;41:546–554.

995. Torgersen S. Relationship of schizotypal personality disorder to schizophrenia: Genetics. *Schizophr Bull*. 1985;11:554–563.

996. Torrey EF. *The Death of Psychiatry*. Radnor Penn: Chilton Book Co; 1974.

997. Trill E, Dristenson H, Fex G. Alcohol-related problems in middle age men with elevated serum gamma glutamyltransferase: A prevention medical investigation. *J Stud Alcohol* 1984;45:302–309.

998. Trimble MR. *The Psychoses of Epilepsy*. New York: Raven Press; 1991.

999. Trull TJ, Widiger TA, Frances A. Covariation of criteria sets for avoidant, schizoid, and dependent personality disorders. *Am J Psychiatry*. 1987;144:767–771.

1000. Tsai L, Tsuang MT. The "Minimental State" and computerized tomography. *Am J Psychiatry*. 1979;136:436–439.

1001. Tsuang MT, Faraone SV. *The Genetics of Mood Disorders*. Baltimore: Johns Hopkins University Press; 1990.

1002. Tsuang MT, Kendler KK, Gruenberg AM. DSM-III schizophrenia: Is there evidence for familial transmission? *Acta Psychiatr Scand*. 1985;71:77–83.

1003. Tsuang MT, Winokur G. Criteria for subtyping schizophrenia: Clinical differentiation of hebephrenia and paranoid schizophrenia. *Arch Gen Psychiatry.* 1974;31:43–47.

1004. Tsuang MT, Winokur G, Crowe RR. Morbidity risks of schizophrenia and affective disorders among first-degree relatives of patients with schizophrenia, mania, depression and surgical conditions. *Am J Psychiatry.* 1980;137:497–504.

1005. Tsuang MT, Woolson RF, Fleming JA. Long-term outcome of major psychoses I. Schizophrenia and affective disorder compared with psychiatrically symptom-free surgical controls. *Arch Gen Psychiatry.* 1979;36:1295–1306.

1006. Tucker DM. Lateral brain function, emotion, and conceptualization. *Psychol Bull.* 1981;89:19–46.

1007. Tupin JP, Smith D, Clanon TL, et al. The long-term use of lithium in agressive prisoners. *Compr Psychiatry.* 1973;14:311–317.

1008. Turner SM, Beidel DC, Nathan RS. Biological factors in obsessive-compulsive disorders. *Psychol Bull.* 1985;97:430–450.

1009. Tyner FS, Knott JR, Mayer WB Jr. *Fundamentals of EEG Technology, Vol. 2, Clinical Correlates.* New York: Raven Press; 1989.

1010. Tyrer P. Classification of anxiety disorders: A critique of DSM-III. *J Affective Disord.* 1986;11:99–104.

1011. Tyrer P, Alexander J. Classification of personality disorder. *Br J Psychiatry.* 1979;135:163–167.

1012. Tyrer P, Casey P, Gall J. Relationship between neurosis and personality disorder. *Br J Psychiatry.* 1983;142:404–408.

1013. Tyrer P, Ferguson B. Problems in the classification of personality disorder. *Psychol Med.* 1987;17:15–20. Editorial.

1014. Uhde TW, Kellner CH. Cerebral ventricular size in panic disorder. *J Affective Disord.* 1987;12:175–178.

1015. U.S. Department of Health, Education, and Welfare, National Institute of Mental Health. *Mental Health Statistical Note 138.* Washington, DC: Government Printing Office; 1977.

1016. *United States Government Public Health Reports.* 1985;101:593–598.

1017. Vaillant GE. Prospective prediction of schizophrenic remission. *Arch Gen Psychiatry.* 1964;11:509–518.

1018. Vaillant GE. A 12-year follow-up of New York narcotic addicts. *Arch Gen Psychiatry.* 1966;15:599–609.

1019. Van Allen MW, Rodnitzky RL. *Pictorial Manual of Neurologic Tests.* 3rd ed. Chicago: Year Book Medical Publishers; 1988.

1020. van der Mast RC, Fekkes D, Moleman P, et al. Is postoperative delirium related to reduced plasma tryptophan? *Lancet.* 1991;338:851–852.

1021. Van Putten T, Marder SR, Wirshing WC, et al. Neuroleptic plasma levels. *Schizophr Bull.* 1991;17:197–216.

1022. Van Valkenbierg C, Akiskal HS, Puzantian V, et al. Anxious depressions: Clinical family history and naturalistic outcome: Comparisons with panic and major depressive disorders. *J Affective Disord.* 1984;6:67–82.

1023. Van Woert MH, Rosenbaum D, Enna SJ. Overview of pharmacological therapy for Tourette syndrome. In: Friedhoff AJ, Chase TN, eds. *Gilles de la Tourette Syndrome, Advances in Neurology,* vol 35. New York: Raven Press; 1982:369–375.

1024. Vardy MM, Kay SR. LSD psychoses or LSD induced schizophrenia? A multi-method inquiry. *Arch Gen Psychiatry.* 1983;40:877–883.

1025. Varsamis J. Clinical management of delirium. In: Hendrie HC, ed. *Psychiatric Clinics of North America, Vol 1/1, Brain Disorders, Clinical Diagnosis and Management.* Philadelphia: WB Saunders; 1978:71–80.

1026. Veragoni VK. The incidence of abnormal dexamethasone in schizophrenia: A review and a meta-analytic comparison with the incidence in normal controls. *Can J Psychiatry.* 1990;35:128–132.

1027. Vestergaard P, Show M, Thomsen K. Monitoring of patients in prophylactic lithium treatment: An assessment based on recent kidney studies. *Br J Psychiatry.* 1982;140:184–187.

1028. Vianna U. The electroencephalogram in schizophrenia. In: Lader MH, ed. *Studies of Schizophrenia. Br J Psychiatry.* Kent, England: Headley Bros; 1975:54–58. Special publication, serial No. 10.

1029. Victor M. The pathophysiology of alcoholic epilepsy. In: Association for Research in Nervous and Mental Disease. *The Addictive States,* vol. XLVI. Baltimore: Williams & Wilkins; 1968:431–454.

1030. Victor M, Adams RD. The effect of alcohol on nervous system. In: Merritt HH, Hare CC, eds. *Metabolic and Toxic Diseases of the Nervous System.* Baltimore: Williams & Wilkins; 1953:526–573.

1031. Victor M, Adams RD, Collins GH. *The Wernicke-Korsakoff Syndrome.* Philadelphia: FA Davis Co; 1971.

1032. Victor M, Hope JM. The phenomenon of auditory hallucinations in chronic alcoholism: A critical evaluation of the status of alcoholic hallucinosis. *J Nerv Ment Dis.* 1958;126:451–481.

1033. Virkkunen M, Huttenen MO: Evidence for abnormal glucose tolerance test among violent offenders. *Neuropsychobiology.* 1982;8:30–34.

1034. Volavka J: Aggression, electroencephalography and evoked potentials. A critical review. *Neuropsychiatry, Neuropsychology, and Behavioral Neurology.* 1990; 3:249–259.

1035. Volkmar F, Bregman J. Stereotyped and self-injurious behavior in disorders other than Tourette's syndrome. In: Cohen DJ, Bruun R, Leckman JF, eds. *Tourette's Syndrome and Tic Disorders.* New York: John Wiley & Sons; 1988:163–178.

1036. Volkow ND, Harper A, Swann AC. Temporal lobe abnormalities and panic attacks. *Am J Psychiatry.* 1986;143:1484–1485.

1037. Von Knorring AL: *Adoption Studies of Psychiatric Illness.* Umea, Sweden: Umea University; 1983. Medical Dissertation Series No. 101,

1038. Wade JB, Taylor MA, Kasprisin A, et al. Tardive dyskinesia and cognitive impairment. *Biol Psychiatry.* 1987;22:393–395.

1039. Walinder J. Transvestism, definition and evidence in favor of occasional deviation from cerebral dysfunction. *Int J Neuropsychiatry.* 1965;1:567–573.

1040. Warner P, Bancroft J, Dixson A, et al. The relationship between perimenstrual depressive mood and depressive illness. *J Affective Disord.* 1991;23:9–23.

1041. Warshaw GA, Moore JT, Friedman W, et al. Functional disability in the hospitalized elderly. *JAMA.* 1982;248:847–850.

1042. Watson CG, Buranen C. The frequency and identification of false positive conversion reactions. *J Nerv Ment Dis.* 1979;167:243–247.

1043. Watt JAG, Hall DJ, Olley PC, et al. Paranoid states of middle life: Familial occurrence and relationship to schizophrenia. *Acta Psychiatr Scand.* 1980;61:413–426.

1044. Wegner JT, Catatano F, Gilbralter J, et al. Schizophrenics with tardive dyskinesia: Neuropsychological deficit and family psychopathology. *Arch Gen Psychiatry.* 1985;42:860–865.

1045. Weinberger DR. Implications of normal brain development for the pathogenesis of schizophrenia. *Arch Gen Psychiatry.* 1987;44:660–669.

1046. Weiner RD, Rogers HC, Welch CA Jr, et al. ECT stimulus parameters and electrode placement: Relevance to therapeutic and adverse effects. In: Lerer B, Weiner RD, Belmaker RH, eds. *ECT: Basic Mechanisms.* London: John Libbey; 1983:139–147.

1047. Weinstein EA, Kahn RL. *Denial of Illness: Symbolic and Physiological Aspects.* Springfield Ill: Charles C Thomas; 1955.

1048. Weinstein MR, Goldfield MD. Cardiovascular malformations with lithium use during pregnancy. *Am J Psychiatry.* 1975;132:529–531.

1049. Weintraub S, Mesulam MM, Kramer L. Disturbances in prosody: A right-hemisphere contribution to language. *Arch Neurol.* 1981;38:742–744.

1050. Weissman MM. The psychological treatment of depression: Evidence for the efficacy of psychotherapy alone, in comparison with, and in combination with pharmacotherapy. *Arch Gen Psychiatry.* 1979;36:1261–1269.

1051. Weissman MM. Epidemiology of panic disorder and agoraphobia. In: Ballenger JC, ed. *Clinical Aspects of Panic Disorder, Frontiers of Clinical Neuroscience,* vol. 6. New York: Wiley-Liss; 1990:57–65.

1052. Weissman MM, Myers JK. Affective disorders in a U.S. urban community. *Arch Gen Psychiatry.* 1978;35:1304–1311.

1053. Welkowitz LA, Popp LA, Cloitre M, et al. Cognitive-behavior therapy for panic disorder delivered by psychopharmacologically oriented clinicians. *J Nerv Ment Dis.* 1991;179:473–477.

1054. Welner A, Welner Z, Leonard MA. Bipolar manic-depressive disorder: A reassessment of course and outcome. *Compr Psychiatry.* 1977;18:327–332.

1055. Wenk EA, Robinson JO, Smith GW. Can violence be predicted? *Crime and Delinquency.* 1972;18:393–402.

1056. West DJ. *Murder Followed by Suicide.* London: Heinemann;1965.

1057. Wharton RN, Perel JM, Dayton PG, et al. A potential clinical use for methylphenidate with tricyclic antidepressants. *Am J Psychiatry.* 1971;127:1619–1625.

1058. Wheeler L, Reitan RM. Presence and laterality of brain damage predicted from responses to a short aphasia screening test. *Percept Mot Skills.* 1962;15:783–799.

1059. Whitlock FA. The etiology of hysteria. *Acta Psychiatr Scand.* 1967;43:144–162.

1060. Whitlock FA. *Symptomatic Affective Disorders.* New York: Academic Press; 1982.

1061. Whitman RM, Armao BB, Dent OB. Assault on the therapist. *Am J Psychiatry.* 1976;133:426–429.

1062. Wilcox JA, Nasrallah HA: Childhood head trauma and psychosis. *Psychiatry Res.* 1982;21:303–306.

1063. Wilder JF, Plutchnik R, Conte HR. Compliance with psychiatric emergency room referrals. *Arch Gen Psychiatry.* 1977;34:930–933.

1064. Wilkie FL, Eisdorfer C, Staub J. Stress and psychopathology in aged. In: Jarvik L, ed. *Psychiatric Clinics of North America: Aging.* Philadelphia: WB Saunders; 1982:131–143.

1065. Wilkinson DG. The suicide rate in schizophrenia. *Br J Psychiatry.* 1982;140:138–141.

1066. Williams D. Neural factors related to habitual aggression. *Brain.* 1969;92:503–520.

1067. Williams PV, McGlashan TH. Schizoaffective psychosis I. Comparative long-term outcome. *Arch Gen Psychiatry.* 1987;44:130–137.

1068. Williams TF (ed). *Rehabilitation in the Aged.* New York: Raven Press, 1984.

1069. Williamson P, Pelz D, Merskey H, et al: Correlation of negative symptoms in schizophrenia with frontal lobe parameters on magnetic resonance imaging. *Br J Psychiatry.* 1991;159:130–134.

1070. Wing JK. Social influences on the course of schizophrenia. In: Wynn LC, Cromwell RL, Mattysse S, eds. *The Nature of Schizophrenia: New Approaches to Research and Treatment.* New York: John Wiley & Sons; 1978.

1071. Winokur A, March V, Mendels J. Primary affective disorder in relatives of patients with anorexia nervosa. *Am J Psychiatry.* 1980;137:695–698.

1072. Winokur G. Delusional disorder (paranoia). *Compr Psychiatry.* 1977;18:511–521.

1073. Winokur G, Morrison J. The Iowa 500: Follow-up of 225 depressives. *Br J Psychiatry.* 1973;123:543–548.

1074. Winokur G, Zimmerman M, Cadoret R. 'Cause the Bible tells me so. *Arch Gen Psychiatry.* 1988;45:683–684.

1075. Winter P, Philipp Buller R, Delmo CDE, et al. Identification of minor affective disorders and implications for psychopharmacology. *J Affective Disord.* 1991;22:125–133.

1076. Wise T. Where the public peril begins: A survey of psychotherapists to determine the effects of Tarasoff. *Stanford Law Rev.* 1978;31:165–190.

1077. Wise TN. Fetishism, etiology, and treatment: A review from multiple perspectives. *Compr Psychiatry.* 1985;26:249–256.

1078. Wolff H, Dalessio DJ. *Headache and Other Head Pain.* 2nd ed. New York: Oxford University Press; 1972.

1079. Wolfgang ME. A sociocultural overview of criminal violence. In: Hays JR, Roberts TK, Solway KS, eds. *Violence and the Violent Individual.* New York: SP Medical and Scientific Books; 1981.

1080. Wollner L, McCarthy ST, Soper NDW, et al. Failure of cerebral autoregulation as a cause of brain dysfunction in the elderly. *Br Med J.* 1979;1:1117–1118.

1081. Woodruff RA Jr, Clayton PJ, Guze SB: Hysteria: Studies of diagnosis, outcome and prevalence. *JAMA* 1971;215:425–428.

1082. Woodruff RA Jr, Guze SB, Clayton PJ. The medical and psychiatric implications of antisocial personality (sociopathy). *Dis Nerv Syst* 1971;32:712–714.

1083. Woody GE, McLellan AT, Luborsky L, et al. Sociopathy and psychotherapy outcome. *Arch Gen Psychiatry.* 1985;42:1081–1086.

1084. Wright JH, Borden J. Cognitive therapy of depression and anxiety. In: MacKenzie KR, ed. *Brief Psychotherapies. Psychiatric Annals.* 1991;21:424–428.

1085. Wu JC, Buchsbaum MS, Hershey TG, et al. PET in generalized anxiety disorder. *Biol Psychiatry.* 1991;29:1181–1199.

1086. Yager J. Personal violence in infantry combat. *Arch Gen Psychiatry.* 1975;32:257–261.

1087. Yaryura-Tobias JA, Neziroglu F. *Gilles de la Tourette Syndrome Obsessive-Compulsive Disorders, Pathogenesis-Diagnosis-Treatment.* New York/Basel: Marcel Dekker, Inc; 1983.

1088. Yates WR, Fullon Al, Gabel J, et al. Personality risk factors for cocaine abuse. *Am J Public Health.* 1989;79:891–892.

1089. Yesavage J, Belger PA. Correlation of cerebrospinal fluid lactate with age. *Am J Psychiatry.* 1980;137:976–977.

1090. Yolles SF, Kramer M. Vital statistics. In: Bellack L, Loeb L, eds. *The Schizophrenia Syndrome.* New York: Grune & Stratton; 1969:66–113.

1091. Young MA, Abrams R, Taylor MA, et al. Establishing diagnostic criteria for mania. *J Nerv Ment Dis.* 1983;171:676–682.

1092. Yudofsky S, Williams D, Gorman J. Propranolol in the treatment of rage and violent behavior in patients with chronic brain syndromes. *Am J Psychiatry.* 1981;138:218–220.

1093. Ziegler GK, Paul N. On the natural history of hysteria in women (a follow-up study 20 years after hospitalization. *Dis Nerv Syst.* 1954;15:301–306.

1094. Zielinski CM, Taylor MA, Juzwin KR. Neuropsychological deficits in obsessive-compulsive disorder. *Neuropsychiatry, Neuropsychology, and Behavioral Neurology.* 1991;4:110–126.

1095. Zilboorg G. *A History of Medical Psychology.* New York: WW Norton & Co; 1941:chap 9. Norton Library, 1967.

1096. Zimmerman M. Why are we rushing to publish DSM-IV? *Arch Gen Psychiatry.* 1988;45:1135–1138.

1097. Zimring FE. Background in confronting youth crime. *Report of the Twentieth Century Fund Task Force in Sentencing Policy Toward Young Offenders.* New York: Holmes & Meier; 1978.

1098. Zitterl W, Lenz G, Mairhofer A, et al. Obsessive-compulsive disorder: Course and interaction with depression: A review of the literature. *Psychopathology.* 1990;34:73–80.

1099. Zohar J, Insel TR, Zohar-Kadouch RC, et al. Serotonergic responsivity in obsessive-compulsive disorder. *Arch Gen Psychiatry.* 1988;45:167–172.

1100. Zubenko GS, George AW, Soloff PH, et al. Sexual practices among patients with borderline personality disorder. *Am J Psychiatry.* 1987;144:748–752.

Index